Alloys

Alloys

American Sculpture and Architecture at Midcentury

Marin R. Sullivan

Princeton University Press
Princeton and Oxford

To RMF

Contents

Alloys

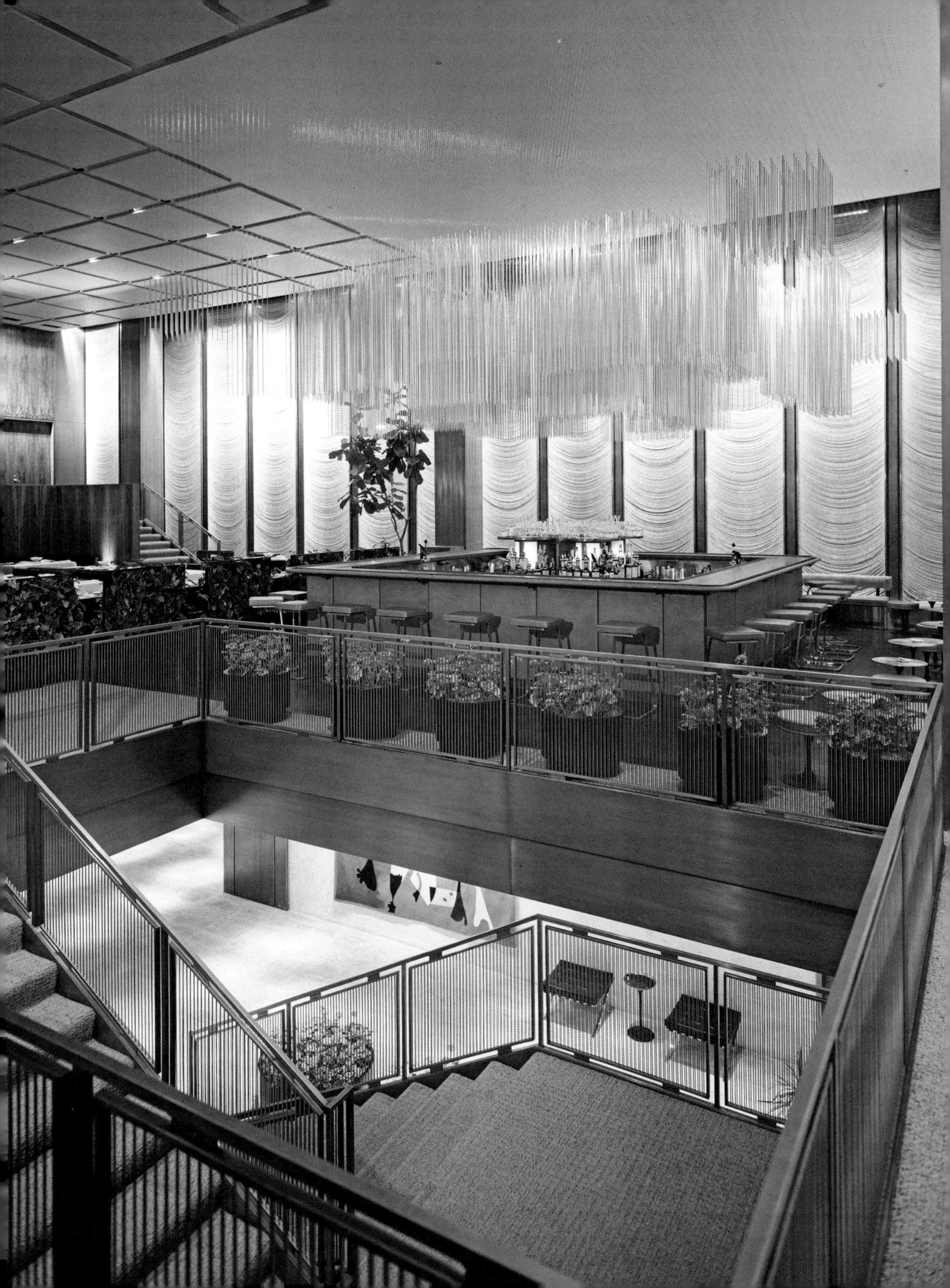

< P.1
Richard Lippold, *The Four Seasons*, 1959. Bronze and stainless steel, 11 ft. × 22 ft. × 22 ft. (no. 1); 8 ft. × 16 ft. × 8 ft (no. 2). Four Seasons Restaurant, Seagram Building, New York City. Architect: Philip Johnson.

Prologue

The Architectural Requirements of Space

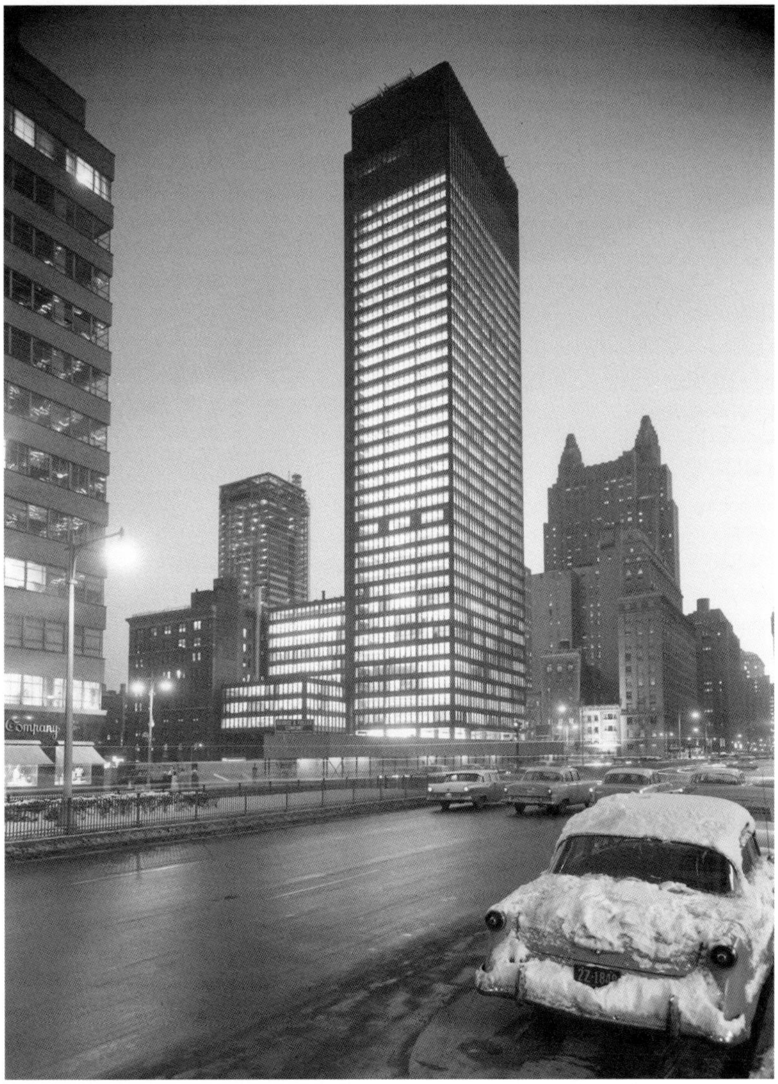

P.2
Nighttime view of the Seagram Building (1954–58), 375 Park Avenue, New York City, 1958. Architects: Ludwig Mies van der Rohe and Philip Johnson.

During the spring of 1959, the sculptor Richard Lippold installed thousands of slender vertical bronze rods, each hanging from almost imperceptible stainless-steel wires anchored to the ceiling of the Four Seasons Restaurant in New York City (figure P.1). Lippold's efforts resulted in a remarkable two-part sculpture. In one corner hung a twenty-two-square-foot configuration over the bar in the Grill Room, and in the opposite corner, a smaller rectangular cluster suspended above the mezzanine area. Lippold's work served as a sculptural exclamation point for one of the highest-profile modernist architectural projects in the United States during the approximate twenty years following the end of World War II.[1]

The new restaurant was located at the street and lobby level of the recently completed Seagram Building (1954–58) at 375 Park Avenue (figure P.2). Seagram's, the beverage company, heralded their new, namesake building as "the world's first bronze skyscraper," and as a "monumental symbol of confidence in the strength of the industrial and business future of America." While contemporary opinion was mostly positive, the significance of the Seagram Building has been steadily solidified over the past sixty years. At the end of the twentieth century, for example, *New York Times* architectural critic Herbert Muschamp declared it the most important building of the entire millennium. Phyllis Lambert, director of planning on the Seagram Building and daughter of Seagram's then-president Samuel Bronfman, described the project as the result of "unlikely convergences." She was instrumental in hiring Ludwig Mies van der Rohe to lead the project and also worked closely with Philip Johnson, who joined as the legal principal architect owing to a licensing issue between Mies van der Rohe and the State of New York.[2]

The Seagram Building stands today as an apotheosis of modernist architecture — the style prevalent during the mid-twentieth century, roughly between the 1930s and 1960s, often referred to as the International Style or International Modern. Johnson's involvement in the project, as well as the design decisions made by Mies van der Rohe himself, however, signaled something of a shift away from the "less is more" austerity that had come to dominate modern architecture by the middle of the twentieth century. As Lambert suggests, Johnson "from the outset… was interested in the Seagram Building as a Gesamtkunstwerk, a synthesis of elements that results in a work of 'total design,'" and that while the "form is Mies's… the drama belongs to Johnson." This shift toward spectacle is perhaps most visible in the Four Seasons Restaurant, which Mies van der Rohe asked Johnson to design.[3]

The Four Seasons opened in July 1959, and quickly became as iconic as the building in which it was housed. Touted as the "world's costliest restaurant," with a then-novel seasonal theme — the menu, staff uniforms, plantings, and even the ash trays changed four times a year — the press coverage marveled most at its interior design. Johnson was responsible for executing and overseeing the overall vision, but he collaborated with a wide range of creative practitioners on the project. Ada Louise Huxtable, who would become one the most important architectural critics of the second half of the twentieth century, designed a suite of tableware, as well as cheese and dessert carts with her husband, the industrial designer Garth Huxtable. The management company Restaurant Associates brought on board the interior designer William Pahlmann to assist Johnson. Pahlmann is widely credited with the idea of adding the twenty-square-foot, white Carrara marble pool that became a signature feature of the main dining room (figure P.3). Pahlmann was also responsible for the inclusion of four, seventeen-foot ficus trees placed around the pool's border, one of many elaborate plantings arranged throughout the restaurant designed by landscape architect Karl Linn. Johnson also worked with noted lighting designer Richard Kelly and the manufacturer Edison Price Lighting to implement a sophisticated, technologically advanced lighting system for the entire restaurant, which largely hid fixtures while maximizing the overall ambience and features of the interior.[4]

Johnson's design for the Four Seasons also included a full program of modern art. The walls of the restaurant featured, for example, Pablo Picasso's massive tapestry *Le Tricorne* (1919), and Jackson Pollock's painting, *Blue Poles* (1952). Neither was created specifically for the restaurant, and the latter was only a temporary addition to the private dining room until Mark Rothko completed a series of seven commissioned murals. Rothko famously reneged on his contract after the restaurant opened, when he decided that his paintings would be incompatible with the space. The artist later wrote: "By this time the place and the spirit for which they were made was functioning. Then I saw the completed destination. It was obvious that the two were not for each other." The large paintings Rothko created for the Four Seasons, now more commonly referred to as the *Seagram Murals* (1958–59) or the Seagram commission, were never shown in the space for which they were made.[5]

Various reasons have been cited for Rothko's volte-face, including his aversion to the class and politics of the restaurant's clientele, as well as the artist's own ambitions and expectations of how his work should be viewed. "Had Rothko provided us with the paintings as planned," Lambert wrote, "the upper portion of what is now the [private dining] room would have emanated a glowing, spiritual presence.... I came to understand: he was creating a series of sacred works. Eating and drinking with his paintings in the background would constitute the same inattention, the same lack of conviction and authenticity as chatting with friends while someone is playing a Bach cello concerto."[6] Lambert's sentiments concerning the failure of the Rothko commission, at least as it related to the Four Seasons, betray a widely held belief regarding art that was codified within the upper echelons of American society during the postwar period: serious modern art was not to be looked at while sipping a martini.

Rothko's failed commission for the Four Seasons' private dining room, however, serves as a particularly useful foil to understand the success and significance of Lippold's sculptures on the opposite side of the restaurant. As they had done

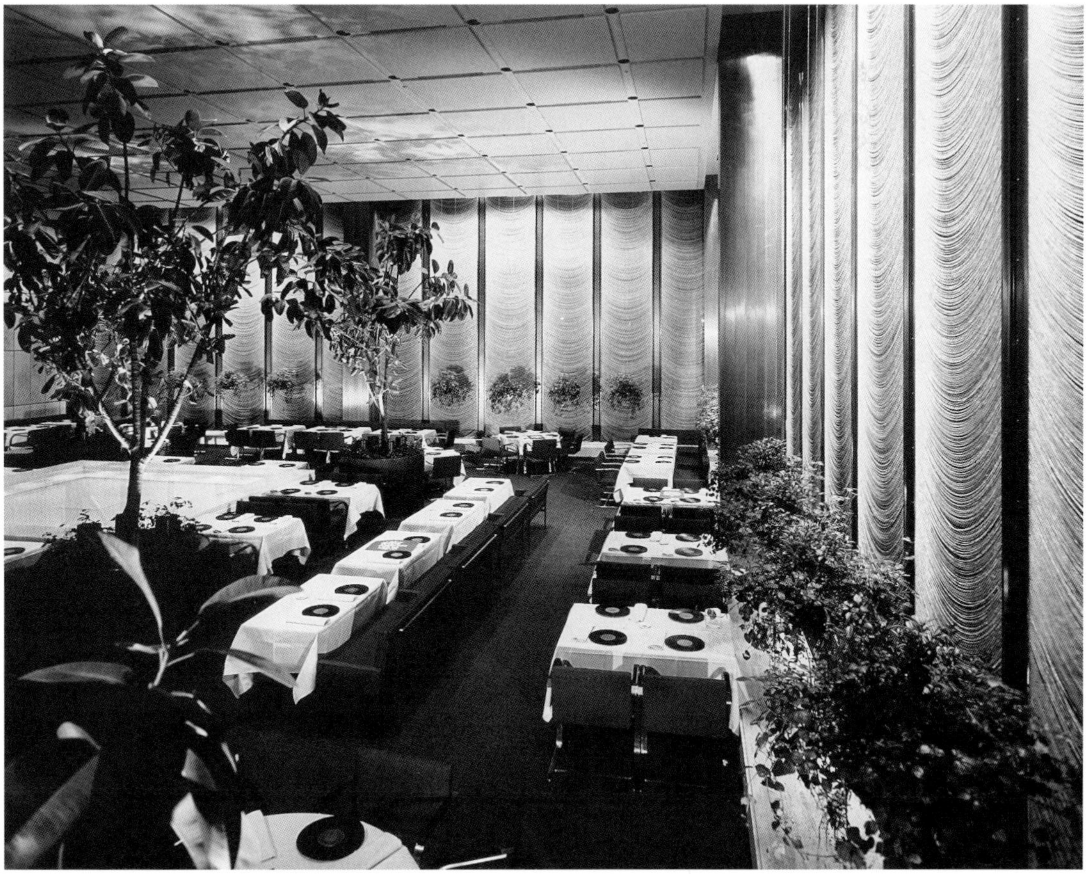

P.3
The Pool Room, Four Seasons Restaurant, Seagram Building (1954–58), New York City, 1959. Metallic curtains designed by Marie Nichols. Architect: Philip Johnson.

with Rothko, Johnson and Lambert commissioned Lippold to create a work specifically for the restaurant, though they approached him far earlier in the design process. Unlike Rothko, Lippold openly embraced associations with decorative and design-oriented projects, even if they entailed relinquishing some of his artistic ego in the process. For Lippold, a collaborative spirit was required in order to enable the commissioned work to fully inhabit its surroundings, and to orient better the "architecture toward the spectator," as he stated. The Four Seasons design team had already settled on the basic layout for the south half of the restaurant and decided on a decorative scheme built around the bronze columns and bespoke walnut paneling of the building's interior. According to Lippold, the only directive they gave was to "create a more intimate feeling over the bar than the twenty-foot-high ceiling afforded, and to create this feeling without sacrificing the elegance of the space and proportions of the room, such as a dropped ceiling might have done." They also suggested "a second sculpture in the opposite corner would be desirable to respect the room's symmetry," and serve as a visual balance (figure P.4).[7]

Lippold's solution was to create what one critic described as "extraordinary hovering objects—celestial music solidified, or possibly golden rain struck by the slanting rays of a setting sun." The sculptures provided the room both visual excitement and equilibrium, while shimmering and even at times swaying; a result of the vibrations from the subway below or as Johnson claimed, the "shock of New York." Lippold's work read as two separate yet complementary sculptural configurations of square rods organized in precise grid-like groups (figure P.5). The sculptures were distinct objects of art that simultaneously and seamlessly blended into the surrounding space while still asserting their own unique presence. The effect was not coincidental, but the consequence of Lippold's precise study of, and respect for, the Seagram Building's architecture. He used bronze rods to complement the facade and Johnson's finishes found throughout the Four Seasons, including the staircase that connected the Grill Room to the street-level restaurant entrance on 52nd Street. The verticality of Lippold's rods mimicked the interior stairwell's thin, staggered vertical rods and railings, and the building's exterior bronze mullions.[8]

The warm tone of Lippold's sculpture also played harmoniously off the Grill Room's French-walnut wall paneling, solid walnut bar top, the teak chairs designed by Hans J. Wegner and manufactured by Knoll, and the bronze piers (figure P.6). The glowing metallic sheen of the sculpture is reflected in the bronze and steel on the Johnson- and Mies van der Rohe–designed bar stools and the tops of the custom-designed Tulip tables by Eero Saarinen. The resonance between Lippold's sculpture and the custom-made aluminum curtains made by textile designer Marie Nichols further amplified the shimmering effect of the space. According to Lambert, it was actually Lippold who initially suggested using metal chains, and she was "impressed by the genius of the idea" after visiting Nichols's studio with Johnson. To create the curtains, Nichols anodized the metal and constructed each curtain panel with alternating strands of copper, yellow

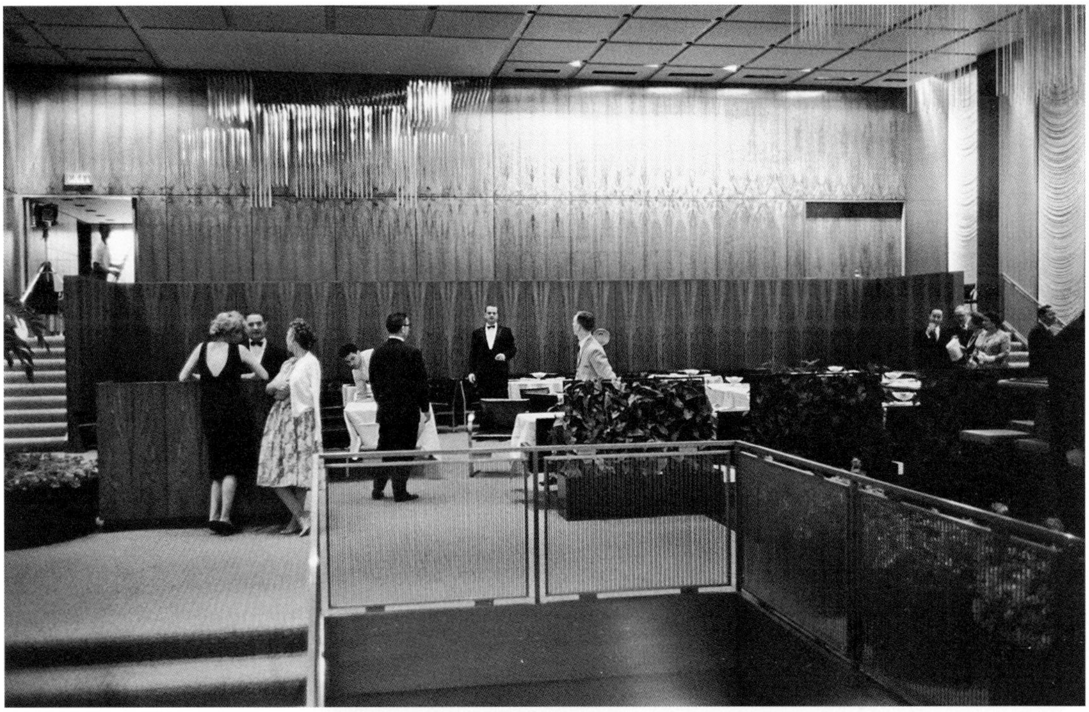

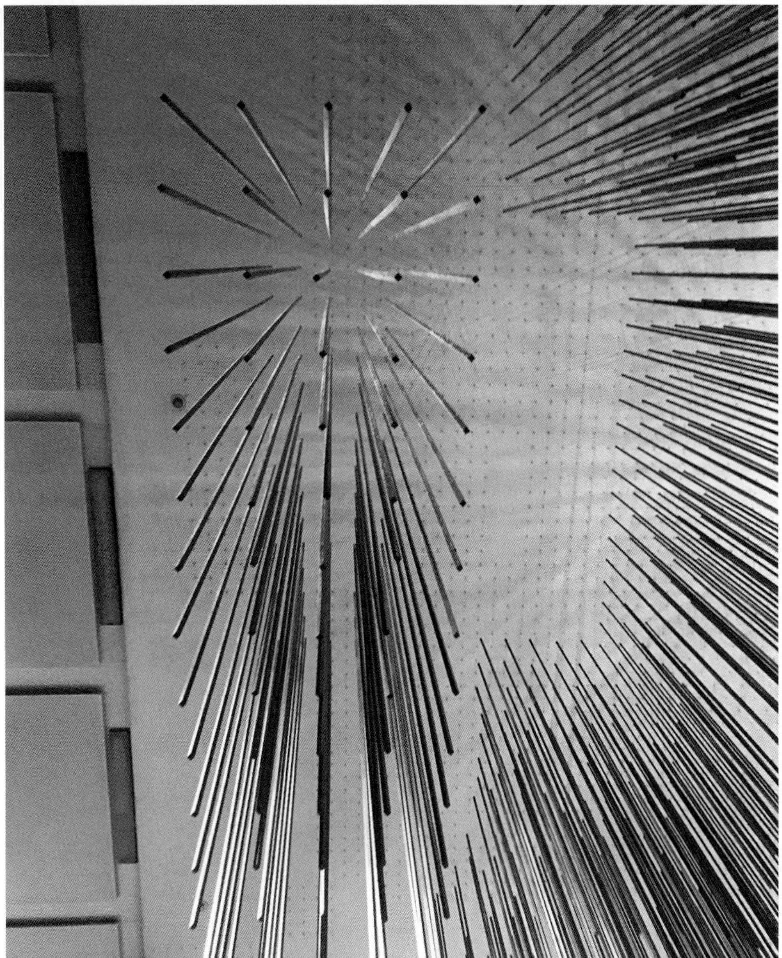

P.4
Richard Lippold, *The Four Seasons* (detail of no. 2 over the mezzanine level), 1959. Bronze and stainless steel, 8 ft. × 16 ft. × 8 ft. Four Seasons Restaurant, Seagram Building, New York City. Architect: Philip Johnson.

P.5
Richard Lippold, *The Four Seasons* (detail looking up), 1959. Four Seasons Restaurant, Seagram Building, New York City. Architect: Philip Johnson.

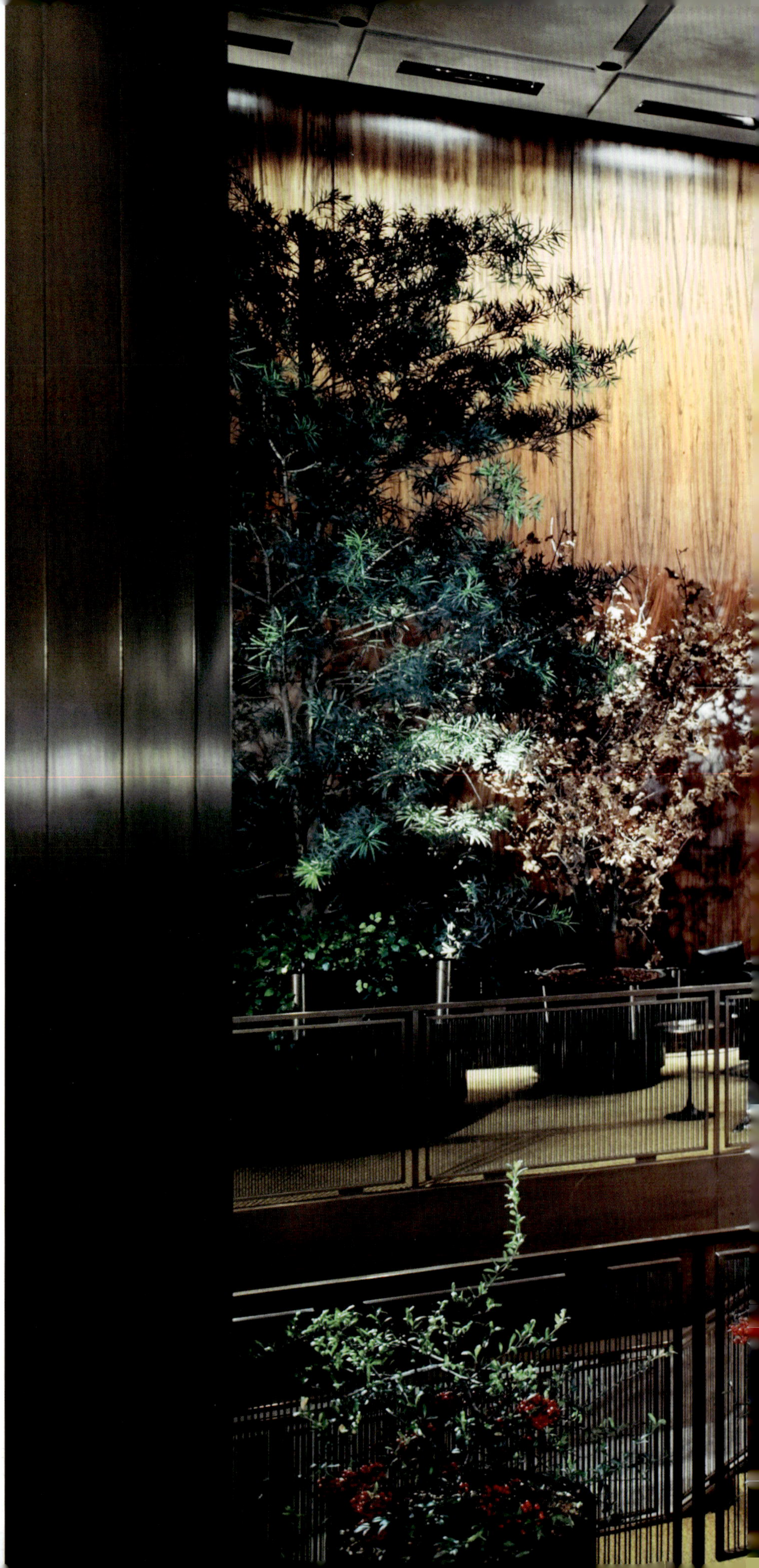

P.6
The Grill Room, Four Seasons Restaurant, Seagram Building (1954–58), New York City, 1959. Architect: Philip Johnson.

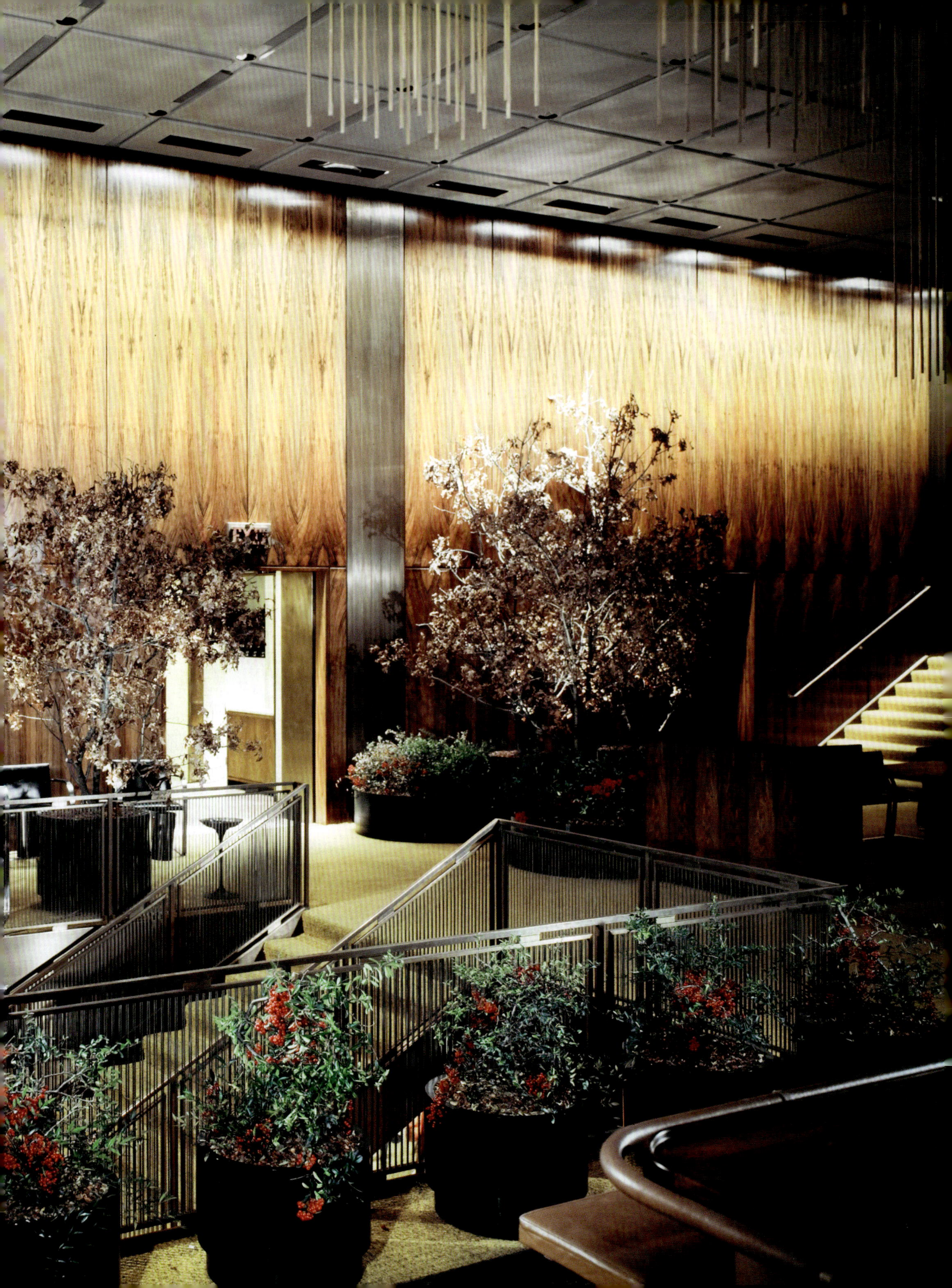

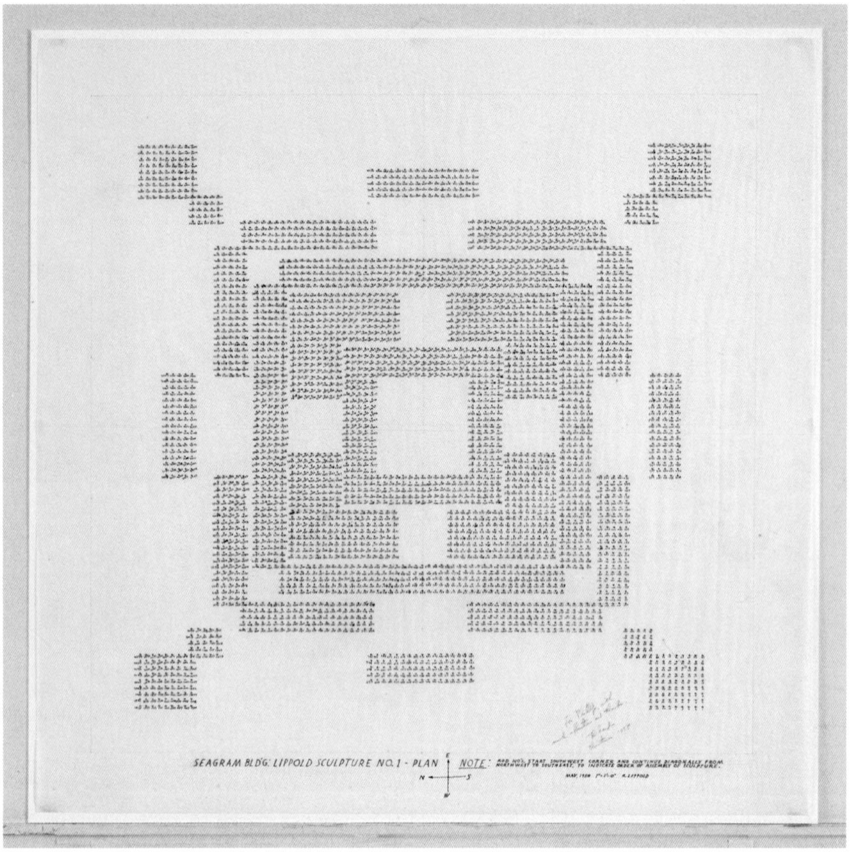

P.7
Richard Lippold, *The Four Seasons*, 1958. Pencil and ink on paper, 30 1/2 in. × 30 1/4 in. Museum of Modern Art, New York City. Gift of Philip Johnson.

gold, and dark silver. The resulting dynamic, ombré effect intensified when air convection along the windows and reverberations from the city outside caused them to sway and sparkle.[9]

The success of Lippold's commission, however, was not simply the result of thoughtful material sympathy with other elements in the Grill Room. Both his preparatory drawings and the final works reveal a precise attention to detail that structurally and spatially mirrored the architecture of the Four Seasons Restaurant and Seagram Building overall (figure P.7). As Lippold explained, he organized the individual rods in "perfect proportion to the room." The sculpture hanging over the bar "occupies one fourth of the space and half of the height," of the room making it one-eighth of its volume. Lippold arranged the rods of what he called the "echo wing" sculpture in a rectangular pattern over the Grill Room's mezzanine, one half the size of its larger counterpart or one-sixteenth of the room. "So, this creates a harmony," according to the artist, "of the large scale of the building to a detail at the interior, which is the simple, you might say, of the nature of that structure."[10] Like Johnson had done with the Four Seasons, Lippold created something uniquely his own, yet in concert with the architecture of the Seagram Building.

By all accounts, Lippold's contribution was a triumph, a crucial addition to the Four Seasons that took on, and worked through, an architectural problem. Lippold activated unused space through a striking sculptural form that hung from the ceiling. As he stated, his goal in taking on the commission was "to create a kind of heart for this building of my affections and to translate its beauties into a work of art that would enhance without distraction, repeat without redundancy the virtues of the architecture, and so make an inseparable entity of the two." Johnson echoed Lippold's assessment, stating that the sculpture at the Four Seasons was "so tied up with its space that you couldn't pull it out of there. If you did, both the sculpture and the architecture would suffer."[11]

Together, the sculpture and the architecture became more than the sum of their parts, simultaneously enhancing and being enhanced by each other. The final product was the result of a collaboration between artist and architect built around mutual respect, but also one reliant on Lippold's willingness to pursue a mode of artistic production very different from that of his contemporaries like Rothko. As Johnson remarked of the sculptor, "He is very clear about the architectural requirements of space; in other words, he does not set out to build a monument to Richard Lippold."[12] Here was serious fine art, not sequestered or depreciated, but fully enmeshed in the space of everyday life—martinis and all.

While the success of the commission certainly owed much to the cohesion and aesthetic brilliance of Lippold's sculpture with Johnson's architectural design, more was at stake with such cross-disciplinary collaboration. Modern art, when used in this way, could offer "a positive and enjoyable experience to many persons who otherwise find it meaningless," as Huxtable, in her role as critic, remarked in 1959. She continued, "At this scale, and in this kind of setting, art communicates directly with the spectator, even if its message is not literal, pictorial, or personal, and even if it does so only in a passing moment of an average day."[13] Large-scale commissioned artwork, like Lippold's sculptures at the Four Seasons, may have functioned as a decorative backdrop while people enjoyed a meal, completed a banking transaction, prayed in a house of worship, or entered a place of employment, but that also meant reaching a much larger audience.

Rothko's vision of art and the assumption that it required rarefied viewing conditions and should be sequestered from the messiness of everyday life became the more celebrated, or at least dominant, viewpoint in the annals of art history; and he remains emblematic of the prototypical modern American artist of the postwar period. While largely overlooked in comparison, Lippold provides an intriguing counterpoint, an example of what, at the time, was a prevalent alternative to artistic autonomy and individual expression. Lippold's contribution to the Four Seasons was neither an isolated event in his career, nor the only example of a commission realized by a modern artist for a midcentury modernist architectural project. Throughout the postwar period, he created numerous meticulously engineered metal sculptures for buildings across the United States, which made him one of the busiest, most in-demand artists of the time. Lippold's commission for the Four Seasons speaks to a remarkable, if short-lived, moment during the immediate postwar period that sought to reassess the reach and functionality of art, and specifically sculpture.

Introduction

Alloying Space

During the roughly twenty years following the end of World War II, a renewed relationship between art and architecture became pronounced enough to be considered a bona fide phenomenon. Modernist architects increasingly incorporated modern tapestries, textiles, murals, reliefs, and sculptures, made with a wide variety of materials, into the interiors and exteriors of their buildings. They consulted with clients to select or purchase modern paintings and sculptures, often quite large in size, and worked with designers and craft practitioners as well as firms, like Knoll or Herman Miller, to create unified, aesthetically striking, and sophisticated interiors. Fountains, plazas, and outdoor sculptures for courtyards and campuses, often realized in collaboration with landscape architects, also proliferated, though more so during the later postwar period.[1]

Among critics and practitioners alike, this disciplinary integration, or rather re-integration, became a fiercely contested topic, producing a variety of interpretations of what the concept meant and how it could be achieved. The magazine *Craft Horizons*, for example, dedicated their first issue of 1959 to the "use of arts and crafts with architecture." Ada Louise Huxtable noted in the lead feature that while there was universal support for such endeavors, there was also an equal amount of widespread disagreement over how disparate disciplines should serve one another in practice. She wrote, "The ideal of 'integration,' unfortunately, sounds far better than it is. It implies the successful fusion of architecture, the arts and the crafts into a harmonious, homogeneous whole, as we have known in the past. Its objectives are unimpeachable and its moral tone is lofty, but it is full of fallacies for our day." Huxtable's misgivings stemmed, in part, from a widespread assumption that integration equaled a kind of disciplinary consensus or conformity.[2]

What Huxtable recognized was that modern art had become increasingly "*un*-integrated" in American modern life, and thus its relationship to architecture could only achieve something closer to "apposition, not integration." "Architecturally, it means enrichment by juxtaposition, completion by contrast," she wrote. For Huxtable, the skillful selection of the most "suitable" piece of sculpture or the "correct craft," could enhance a building, making it "greater than it would have been without it." Art should not be concerned with harmony, but rather with providing a "strong counterpoint" to the austere formal simplicity of modernist architecture. Seen in this way, according to Huxtable, a sculpture or painting did not possess structural functionality, but became more than "mere elaboration or decoration."[3]

Though it was by far the most commonly deployed term at the time, integration rightfully elicited suspicion, and there is much to recommend in Huxtable's counterproposal of apposition. She, like many critics and practitioners, was admirably attempting to define and reconcile the myriad sincere, if inconsistently executed, attempts to bring together, once again, art and architecture in the midst of a rapidly changing postwar world. In actual practice, however, the use of art in architecture was never itself homogeneous. A mural, exterior frieze, or freestanding sculpture can provide, as Huxtable asserted, a "sharp, judicious, and extremely meaningful accent" to a building, but each operates within different frameworks of intent and function. Each possesses the unique limitations or specificities of its given medium. Further, an artwork commissioned for an architectural project will always carry with it a set of circumstances distinct from works selected or purchased, no matter how thoughtfully executed.[4]

While this book originated from a desire to reevaluate what was indeed a legitimate moment of cross-disciplinary exchange during the immediate postwar period, it does not seek to offer a revised, comprehensive survey of either the renewed relationship between art and architecture or the practitioners driving it. Rather, this study focuses on arguably the most high-profile manifestation to emerge from within the overall phenomenon: large-scale sculpture commissioned specifically for the highly visible and well-traversed interior spaces of architectural projects. Projects created in close consultation with architects and possessing strong material resonance with their surrounding architectural settings. This set of parameters reveals a mode of modern sculpture responsive to the imagery and effects of the space age that embraced new industrial materials and processes, and even more significantly, demonstrated the ability of art, of sculpture, to inhabit and coalesce with the lived space of architecture.

These parameters also predetermined this book's examination of sculptural projects realized by a select group of artists: Harry Bertoia, Alexander Calder, Richard Lippold, and Isamu Noguchi. These four individuals emerge from the historical record as the most active and consistently commissioned artists by modernist architects during the period. The broader, changing sociohistorical conditions of postwar America shaped the work of these artists, but their sculpture, in turn, demonstrated how art could play a more pronounced and multivalent role in contemporary society. The projects they realized for specific buildings, in collaboration with the leading architects of the period, are examples of how art can be put to use or made visible in a more public sphere, but also of how sculpture could adopt the language of architecture.

Huxtable expressed concern that the term integration carried the implication that art and architecture were fused together to create a harmonious whole. The large-scale commissioned sculptures by Bertoia, Calder, Lippold, and Noguchi examined in this book, however, present an altogether different notion of fusion, one that is not predicated on a loss but mutual gains. Contemporary theories around the principles of synergy offer a useful, alternative framework to consider the renewed relationship between sculpture and architecture. The Greek (*synergos*) and Latin (*synergia*) roots of synergy demonstrate that the concept has always maintained strong connections to the notions of process, cooperation, and working together for common benefit, but during the postwar period the term took on further, more pronounced associations with science and technology. For the polymath Buckminster Fuller, no stranger to cross-disciplinary collaboration himself, the "essence" of the modern industrial world was synergy, or the "cooperative action of discrete agencies such that the total effect is greater than the sum of two or more effects taken independently."[5]

Synergy was also visible in a new type of practitioner that Fuller referred to as "the comprehensive designer," whom he described as a "synthesis of artist, inventor, mechanic, objective economist and evolutionary strategist." Fuller also identified the underlying synergistic principles and strengthening force created in the alloying of metals like chrome, nickel, and steel. He wrote, "The strength of 'industry' as with the strength of the 'alloy' occurs through the co[n]centric enmeshment of the respective atoms." Synergy and integration are similar concepts, both centered on the act of combining. With the former, however, entities amalgamate into a new unified whole, but continue to maintain their own agency, their own material being. Copper and zinc, for example, combine to create brass, but still retain their individual properties. The same type of permutation can occur with large-scale sculpture and the architectural space for which it was commissioned. When fully realized, a new configuration of space has been inextricably fused together even while a distinct sculpture and building remain. Both are examples of alloys or alloying, a process of synergistically combining elements into an entity made stronger, better, by its respective parts.[6]

Bertoia, Calder, Lippold, and Noguchi created sculpture intended to be as permanent as the buildings they inhabited, and, as a result, their work offered something beyond just striking surface decoration or a humanizing juxtaposition to modernist architecture. Their sculptures certainly enhanced the aesthetics of the buildings they occupied, but also shared with architecture a similar mode of production, materials, size, scale, and sense of space. In the process of alloying with architecture, however, sculpture itself was forever changed as it also took on more structural, functional, and environmental qualities. The large-scale commissions realized during the immediate postwar period suggest a more expansive history of modern American sculpture, as well as an earlier origin point for some of the key concerns of contemporary sculptural practices.

Postwar Synergy

In 1946, one year, almost to the date, after the end of World War II, the Museum of Modern Art (MoMA) in New York City opened its fall season with *Fourteen Americans*. The exhibition, curated by Dorothy C. Miller, was intended to serve as a cross section of contemporary American art, and was the second in a series known as the Americans, which began with *Americans 1942: 18 Artists from 9 States* and continued into the early 1960s, with notable iterations including *15 Americans* (1952) and *Twelve Americans* (1956). *Fourteen Americans* showcased artists like Arshile Gorky, Robert Motherwell, Isamu Noguchi, Theodore Roszak, and Mark Tobey (figure I.1). The inclusion of Noguchi was a particularly significant choice at the time, given his status as a Japanese American.[7]

Miller selected modern and largely abstract works to feature in the exhibition, including Noguchi's *Monument to Heroes* (1943), *Lunar Infant* (1944), and *E=MC2* (1944). The checklist, however, reveals a more complex picture of contemporary American art, one in which artists grappled with both the residue of a

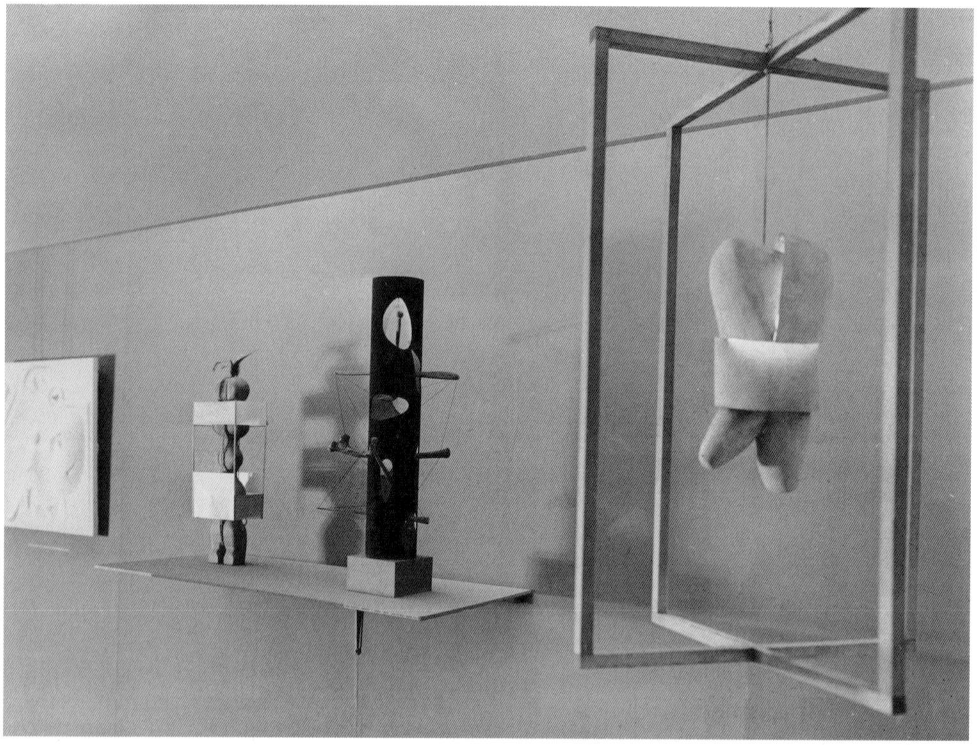

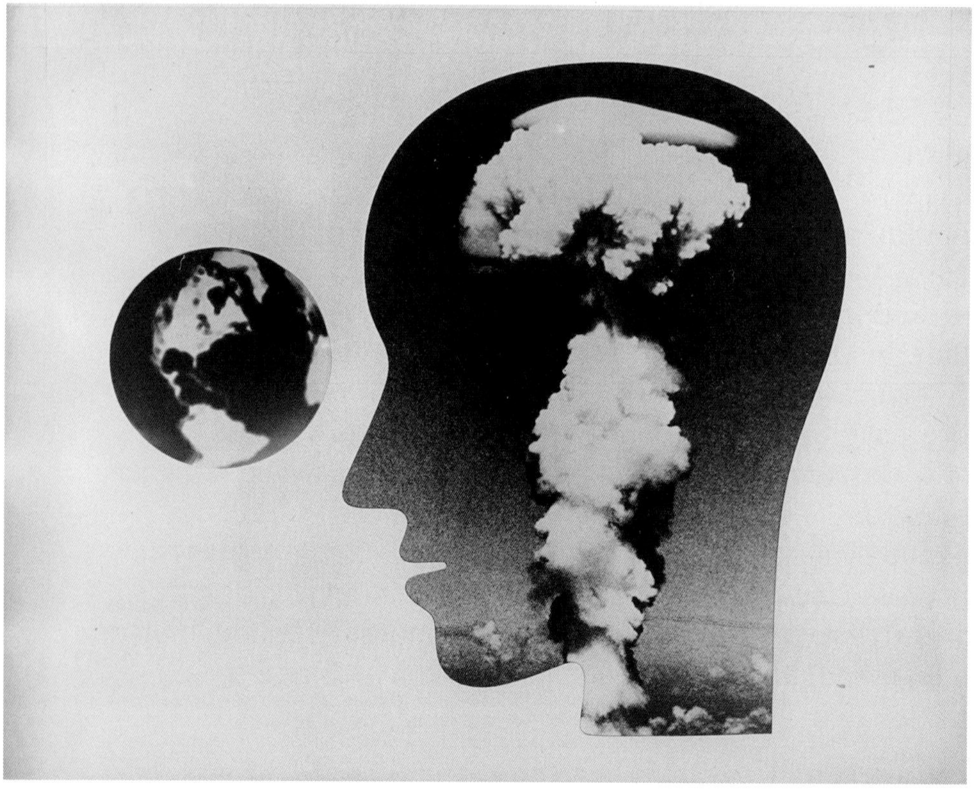

I.1
Installation view of the exhibition, *Fourteen Americans*, MoMA, New York City, September 10–December 8, 1946. Photographic Archive, Museum of Modern Art Archives, New York City, IN329.7.

I.2
Herbert Matter, *Atomic Head*, 1946. Cover for *Arts & Architecture* (December 1946). Herbert Matter papers, c. 1937–1984, Department of Special Collections, Stanford University Libraries, California.

catastrophic war and the possibilities of a new world order. As Noguchi expanded in his artist statement published in the accompanying catalogue, "The essence of sculpture is for me the perception of space, the continuum of our existence. All dimensions are but measures of it, as in relative perspective of our vision lie volume, line, point, giving shape, distance, proportion. Movement, light, and time itself are also qualities of space. Space is otherwise inconceivable. These are the essence of sculpture and as our concepts of them change, so must our sculpture change."[8] Noguchi's work from the mid-twentieth century, and his close relationships with figures like Fuller, reflected his willingness to engage with, and respond to, new conceptions of space and dimensions of reality.

While space has always been a central concept in sculptural practice, something it shares with architecture, the term carried new weight and connotations during the first two decades following the end of World War II. A building boom transformed the urban landscape of American cities, and two nuclear superpowers with competing political and economic ideologies strove for spaceflight dominance. Space was no longer just volume and mass to be shaped and contained, but evoked intergalactic exploration, molecular scientific discovery, and everything in between. The modern sculpture of Harry Bertoia, Alexander Calder, Richard Lippold, and Noguchi, as well as the clean lines of modernist architecture may, at first glance, seem detached from these broader historical contexts. Their forms, however, reflected a world forever changed by the detonation of atomic bombs, the promises of nuclear technologies, and a continued threat of global annihilation—something visually encapsulated by Herbert Matter in his design for the cover of the December 1946 issue of *Arts & Architecture* magazine (figure I.2).[9]

The response of the artists and architects examined in this book, however, seldom manifested as literal expressions of antinuclear sentiment or traumatic anguish. Rather, the sculpture and, more importantly, the commissions of Bertoia, Calder, Lippold, and Noguchi displayed a more optimistic approach, exploring the possibilities wrought by new relationships with science, technology, and industry in a postwar, atomic United States. A feature on Noguchi in *Interiors* from 1949, for example, called attention to the emerging connections between art and "contemporary scientific concepts," noting how even five years prior such a topic "would have seemed particularly strange in a magazine devoted to the subject of interior design." What had been "destroyed during the intervening years were those little mental pigeonholes that used to isolate the various arts and sciences." Or as Lippold conveyed to *Time* magazine in 1963, faith no longer resided in pyramids or cathedrals, but in "space, energy, [and] communications.... In the twentieth century we do not look at things; we look through them." In this new age, as the magazine pointed out, the "great preoccupation" was space, "not only the getting of things off the ground, but also the many ways of opening things up, from atomic fusion to psychoanalysis."[10]

An interest in cross-disciplinary exchange was not limited to sculpture, or even art and design more broadly, during the immediate postwar period, though the visual arts writ large were never as autonomous or detached from their sociohistorical context as the now-entrenched narratives of American art history might suggest. Art and design were intimately connected to, and enmeshed within, a world radically reshaped by science, technology, and an emerging military-industrial complex. The United Nations Educational, Scientific, and Cultural Organization (UNESCO) was formed in 1945 along these lines, and international events like the World's Fair resumed in the 1950s and 1960s to further international and interdisciplinary agendas. Terms like synergy, but also organicism and synthesis became common across the arts, humanities, and sciences during the postwar period. Art theorist Jack Burnham, for example, attempted to trace the combined impact of vitalist philosophy and the "effects of science and technology," declaring "for the first time in history our culture has the option of literally fusing organic activities with the linear-geometric precision of machines." He wrote that "organicism," was a "conscious concern of the designer," and "could be defined as the awareness of the interrelation between systems and their components within larger systems so that behavior of the whole ensemble can be understood and manipulated."[11]

Within academia, figures like Buckminster Fuller, György Kepes, and Norbert Wiener further promoted transdisciplinary theories of convergence, systems, and connectedness. Fuller, for example, drew from modern chemistry, geometry, psychology, philosophy, and thermodynamics to develop his theory of synergy and a "system of holistic thinking" he called synergetics (figure I.3). Alloys, Fuller further explained, were integrally synergetic and their "high cohesive strength and structural stability" were what made the jet engine possible, which in turn "changed the whole relationship of man to the Earth." All of this was "brought about by synergy," which is the "only word having its unique meaning," the "behavior of the whole systems unpredicted by the behavior of their parts taken separately." Or put more precisely: "Synergy means behavior of integral, aggregate, whole systems unpredicted by behaviors of any of their components or subassemblies of their components taken separately from the whole." As art historian Eva Díaz writes, "Ultimately, it was [Fuller's] belief in a 'synergetic,' or antispecialized, ecology of thought that he hoped to impart to his students; carving a path to the future founded in the belief in collaboration, universality, interrelatedness, and a technocratic allegiance to progress through design."[12]

Kepes similarly turned his attention to the formal and conceptual resonances between science, art, and design. He became a vocal proponent of interdisciplinary methods he referred to as "interthinking" and "interseeing," and his correspondence and numerous publications, including the six-part series he edited titled *Vision + Value*, read as a veritable who's who of artists, designers, architects, scientists, and theoreticians of the postwar period. Kepes, like Fuller, became an important midcentury interlocutor, connecting individuals across disciplines, nationalities, and geographies. He was one of the numerous European intellectuals and creative practitioners who immigrated to the United States prior to World War II.[13] More specifically, Kepes was one of the many émigrés, including Josef and Anni Albers, László Moholy-Nagy, and Ludwig Mies van der

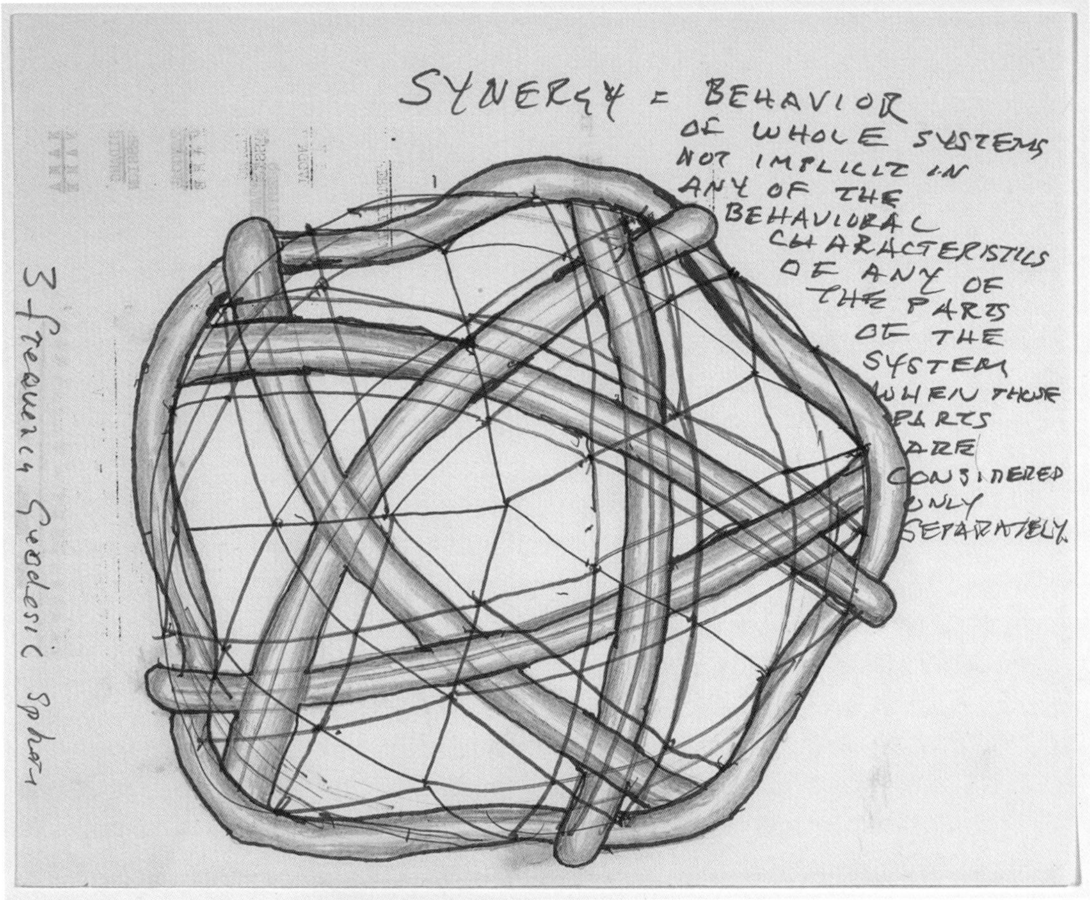

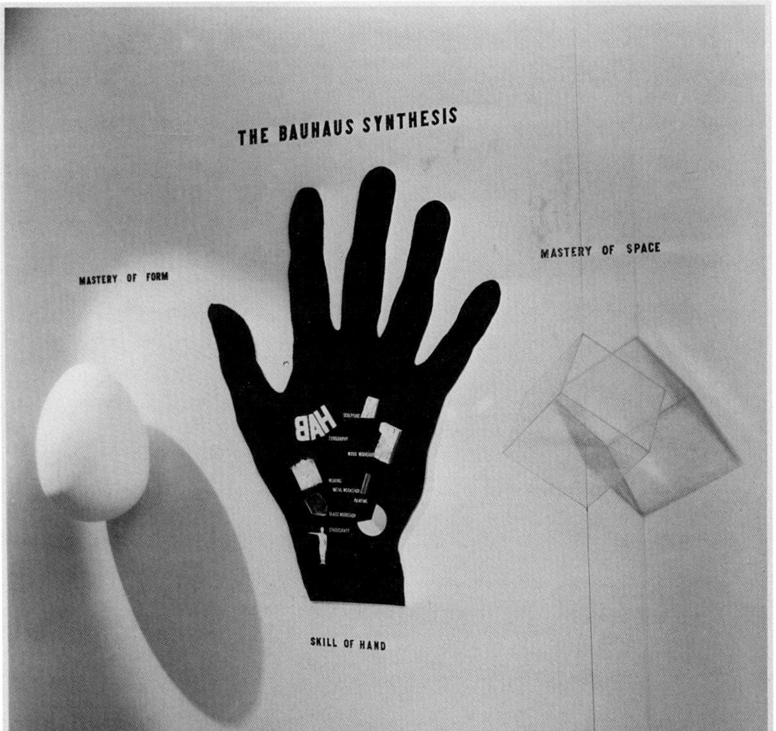

I.3
R. Buckminster Fuller, *Three Frequency Geodesic Sphere*, n.d. Graphite and felt-tip pen on paper, 8 1/2 in. × 10 1/4 in. Department of Special Collections, Stanford University Libraries, California.

I.4
Installation view of the exhibition, *Bauhaus: 1919–1928*, MoMA, New York City, December 7, 1938–January 30, 1939. Photographic Archive, Museum of Modern Art, New York City, IN82.9.

Rohe, who had previous associations with the Bauhaus, the fabled art school that operated in Germany from 1919 to 1933.

Central to the Bauhaus ideology was the reintegration of the arts, alongside craft and design, with architecture and, more broadly, modern society (figure I.4). As Walter Gropius, the school's founder, wrote in conjunction with a major exhibition about the school and its philosophy held at MoMA in 1939, "The Bauhaus strives to bring together all creative effort, to achieve, in a new architecture, the unification of all training in art and design. The ultimate, if distant, goal of the Bauhaus is the collective work of art—the Building—in which no barriers exist between the structural and the decorative arts. The guiding principle of the Bauhaus was therefore the idea of creating a new unity through the welding together of many 'arts' and movements: a unity having its basis in Man himself and significant only as a living organism."[14] The school may not have survived the rise of the Third Reich in Germany, but its spirit of connectivity and collaboration proved tremendously influential as its students and faculty dispersed during the midcentury, especially across the Atlantic.

Many émigrés, like Kepes and Josef Albers, took positions in higher education, transforming vaunted universities like Massachusetts Institute of Technology (MIT) and Harvard in Cambridge, Massachusetts, and Yale in New Haven, Connecticut, or helped to establish more specialized or experimental ones like Black Mountain College in North Carolina or the Cranbrook Academy of Art in Michigan. Gropius, for example, joined the faculty of the Harvard Graduate School of Design as the chair of the Department of Architecture in 1937. The same year, Moholy-Nagy established the New Bauhaus in Chicago, and one year later, Mies van der Rohe also settled in Chicago, becoming the head of the Department of Architecture at the Armour Institute of Technology. Both of these institutions would later merge and become the Illinois Institute of Technology. After arriving from Hungary in 1937, Kepes initially taught in Chicago at the New Bauhaus (later the IIT Institute of Design), before accepting an invitation from the MIT School of Architecture and Planning in 1947 to start a program dedicated to art and design, which eventually became the MIT Center for Advanced Visual Studies (CAVS) in 1967.[15]

The influx of Bauhaus ideology at institutions and in professional life in the United States during the mid-twentieth century impacted the pedagogy of art and architecture, but also directly reshaped the country's urban landscape. Many architectural projects, like the Four Seasons Restaurant or the Gropius-designed Harvard Graduate Center (1950), combined a multiplicity of works and aesthetic strategies to establish extensive arts programs within a single structure. In the case of the Harvard Graduate Center, Gropius and his firm, the Architects Collaborative, commissioned Lippold to create an outdoor sculpture, *World Tree* (1950) (figure I.5). He also incorporated other, mostly two-dimensional murals or reliefs by Josef Albers, Jean Arp, Herbert Bayer, and Joan Miró throughout the building's interior.

As MoMA curator Arthur Drexler stated in the catalogue for the exhibition *Buildings for Business and Government* (1957), the United States underwent a tremendous building boom that gave architects, both those who had emigrated from Europe and the younger, emerging generation of modernists they had instructed, a "new freedom." As Drexler noted, however, this growth in modern architecture was not just because of new aesthetic approaches or functional needs, but was also crucially a "new kind of patronage." He wrote, "Business and government alike are rediscovering the rewards of fine building, and the results can be seen not only in individual works of great beauty but in a generally higher standard of excellence."[16] Modernism, whether expressed via the visual arts or architecture, proved a perfect vehicle for a projection of the principles of American democracy and corporate ambition.

Modernist architecture quickly became the preferred style for high-profile public projects like embassies and civic centers during the postwar period. The private sector, however, emerged as the dominant patron and driving force of this surge in building, leading to what became referred to, often derogatorily, as corporate modernism. As art historian and editor of *Harper's* magazine Russell Lynes wrote at the time, "The corporation has, in fact, become one of the most powerful and conscientious art patrons of our day, and has established itself not only as a purveyor of tasteful objects but as an arbiter of taste as well." Whether because of "sound public relations," tax benefits, or altruistic humanism, Lynes continued, American business in the postwar period was "playing an increasingly important role in the support of cultural activities."[17]

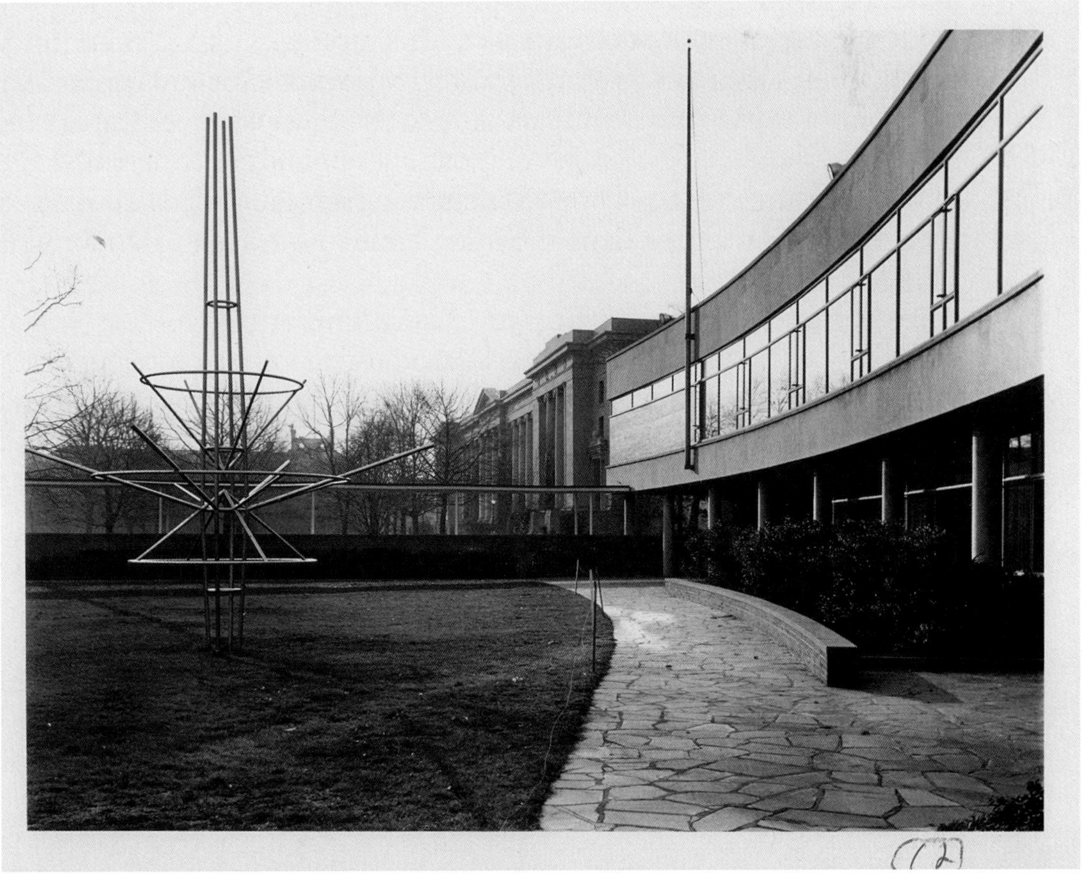

I.5
South-facing view of the Harvard Graduate Center main quadrangle with Richard Lippold's *World Tree* (1950) and partial exterior of Harkness Commons in the foreground. Historical & Special Collections, Harvard Law School Library, Cambridge, Massachusetts.

The scope of patronage, however, was also radically changing. Skyscrapers, company headquarters, and suburban campuses materialized, and with them new spaces for modern art. A significant effort, however, also went into building corporate art collections, featuring fine art in advertising and on packaging, and establishing a broad array of philanthropic sponsorship opportunities. Management at major American companies, including figures like Walter Paepcke at the Container Corporation of America, Thomas Watson at International Business Machines (IBM), and, slightly later, David Rockefeller at Chase Manhattan, not only collected artwork, but also launched significant arts initiatives. Lynes commented that while "patronage of the arts can never be more than peripheral concern of the corporation," figures like Paepcke or Arthur Houghton Jr. of Steuben Glass Works were "deeply, although sometimes it seems naively, concerned with trying to elevate the standards of what they hope is the public's inherent 'good taste.'"[18]

Numerous other individuals at companies like Abbott, CBS, Connecticut General Life Insurance, Corning Glass Works, and General Motors, devoted substantial resources to determining how art could be utilized in every facet of operations, hiring modernist architects to construct their buildings. They also contracted practitioners like Alexander Girard, Florence Knoll, George Nelson, and Eliot Noyes to formulate or reimagine their corporate images, and design every detail of workplaces, including executive suites, communal employee areas, and public-facing spaces like lobbies. As architectural historian Joan Ockman writes, "the hand of managerial capitalism became increasingly visible and munificent" during the immediate postwar years with art and architecture emerging as a central part of a much larger public relations operation.[19]

At best, the efforts of corporate architecture and image making contributed to a campaign for the principles of democratic humanism and sincere cultural reformation. At worst, they represented a savvy, manipulative strategy to heighten public prestige and propagandize American economic and political interests around the world via—"a network of networks" set against the "backdrop of multifarious international modernism," which architectural historian Reinhold Martin has called the "organizational complex." Regardless of intent, new modes of corporate patronage resulted in a profound exchange between industry, architecture, and the visual arts during the postwar period. Projects, in concept and form, further reflected an interconnected approach deeply informed by the activities and philosophies emerging across the sciences, the humanities, and the arts.[20]

Decorative Function

Large-scale commissioned sculptures from the immediate postwar period, though prevalent and widely covered by the press at the time, have received inconsistent scholarly attention. Harry Bertoia and Richard Lippold, whose careers were predominantly established through such work, have become largely forgotten figures.[21] Of the four, Alexander Calder and Isamu Noguchi were the most well known during their lifetimes, and, with the help of robust estates, maintain blue-chip standing within the art world. While they continue to generate copious amounts of scholarly and curatorial attention, however, information on their commissioned work, especially that made for interior spaces, remains scant. If addressed at all, such projects are often glossed over, mentioned as a curiosity, or dismissed as minor works. Commissioned sculptures are far more likely to appear in studies of the architectural projects for which they were made. Even in these cases, however, they are often included only as an illustration rather than a critically analyzed entity in its own right. As a result, this study relies heavily on primary or contemporaneous source material, especially architectural criticism, related to these projects.

One reason for this marginalization is that commissioned artwork inherently possesses a function and connection to decoration. A contested term since the turn of the twentieth century, the decorative occupied a simultaneously fragile and contentious place within both fine art and architectural discourse at the mid-twentieth century. There may have been a widespread interest in collapsing disciplinary boundaries during the postwar period and continuing the "egalitarian aspirations" that originated in early twentieth-century modernism, but, as curator and art historian Lowery Stokes Sims suggests of the immediate postwar years, the "lines of demarcation between 'art' and 'craft' or 'art' and 'design' in critical and theoretical circles, particularly the most advanced modernist ones, only solidified." In the subsequent decades, a pernicious narrative emerged: vanguard art should be separate from the world, invested in interrogating its own specific characteristics and the transcendent, intimate power of self-expression. Within this framework, there was little room for functional applications or public use value.[22]

The suspicion, abhorrence, or outright rejection of decoration within modern art, especially during the postwar period was largely driven by the dogma of the influential art critic Clement Greenberg, though his actual writing on the subject from the period reveals far more nuance. Although Greenberg's critical writings generally gave far less attention to sculpture than painting, in the 1950s he did see tremendous potential in the defining forms and uses of industrial materials by the best emerging sculpture. He noted in "Sculpture in Our Time," a piece for *Arts Magazine* from 1958, that the medium had taken on a language of "construction," being "built, assembled, arranged" rather than sculpted, and in the process had "acquired a new flexibility." Perhaps surprisingly given his later codification around medium specificity, in 1946 he wrote that "painting, sculpture, architecture, decoration and the crafts have under modernism converged once again in a common style." He further stated that "the new sculpture," "like architecture," was "immersed in its physical means," and beginning "to make itself felt as most *representative*, even if not the most fertile, visual art of our time," concluding without any sarcasm, "Certainly, of all arts, the new pictorial or constructivist sculpture relates best to American décor, understands it best, and would affect it most directly."[23]

As the stalwart champion of artistic autonomy and "art for art's sake," however, Greenberg would also later fret over the influence of "Good Design" in the field of the fine arts. The phrase appeared frequently in cultural criticism and media coverage of the postwar period, but became codified through the curatorial vision of architectural historian and critic Edgar J. Kaufmann Jr. and his work with MoMA beginning in 1950. *Good Design* was an ambitious collaboration between art and commerce, presented through the staging of semiannual exhibitions at the museum in New York City and at the Merchandise Mart in Chicago, which was then the nation's largest wholesale marketer (figure I.6). Between 1950 and 1954, these exhibitions highlighted modern design, including textiles, furniture, and household objects. As architect Terence Riley and architectural historian Edward Eigen wrote, "The ultimate goal of this complex strategy… was to inform consumers and manufacturers about modern design products and to ensure that these products were made widely available through retail markets." For Greenberg, such initiatives confused the boundaries between kitschy, functional interior design, and fine art, with the result that the "infiltration of Good Design into what purports to be advanced and highbrow art now depresses sculpture."[24]

Another art critic, Hilton Kramer, proffered similar concerns about functionalism and decoration. In a review of Lippold's sculpture and commissioned projects from the previous decade exhibited at the Willard Gallery, New York City in 1968, Kramer excoriated the artist, calling him "our foremost public decorator." While beginning with a pithy acknowledgement of Lippold's heightened status among "elegant" contemporary powerbrokers and tastemakers, Kramer decried the "superficialities," "pretentions to cosmic 'meaning,'" and "costume jewelry effects" of his work. Kramer saw Lippold's sculpture as a "slick and easy simulacrum" of art, and concluded his review with a curious, if not unsurprising, assurance to his readers about where they could go for the antidote. "Anyway, we can go to the museums for the real thing, can't we? And isn't that where the real thing

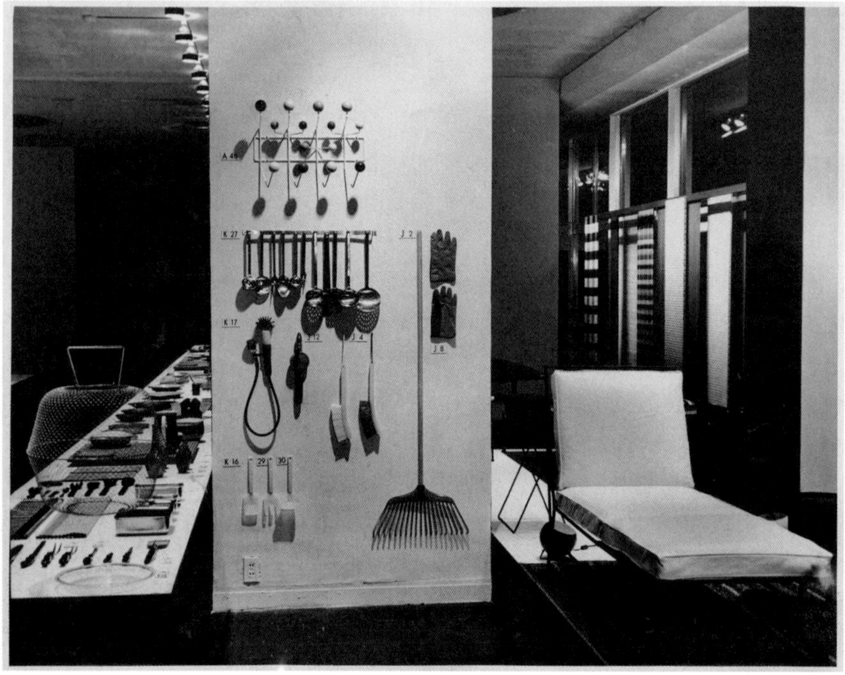

I.6
Installation view of the exhibition *Good Design*, MoMA, New York City, September 22–November 29, 1953. Photographic Archive, Museum of Modern Art, New York City, IN542.3.

belongs? It is something to think about the next time you encounter one of Mr. Lippold's glittery creations."[25]

Underlying both Kramer and Greenberg's distaste for the decorative was both an assumption that it lacked rigor and a fear that it polluted the rarefied sphere of high art with lowbrow functionalism. Work like Lippold's was not "the real thing," but a shiny, superficial bauble masquerading as art. As art historian Richard Meyer writes, "The practice of interior decoration connotes ornamental rather than structural alteration, a reworking of surfaces, textures, fabrics, and finishes, rather than a construction or substantial reshaping of space. Where the word 'design' suggests both conceptual and practical expertise ('to plan and execute [a structure, work of art, etc.]'), the term 'decorate,' conveys an almost literally superficial endeavor ('to furnish or deck with ornamental accessories')." For Kramer and Greenberg, the issue went far beyond "elegance" or functionality. Equally affronting was the artist working outside the rarified boundaries of the studio or the exhibition space of the gallery, creating artwork made not just to "decorate," but to decorate architecture.[26]

In taking on the challenges of collaborating with architects, however, artists like Bertoia, Calder, Lippold, and Noguchi presented a model of decoration that could be aesthetically ornamental while also structurally reshaping space. A well-conceived and installed tapestry or mural also has the ability to add texture and color, to activate or alter space, but its spatial orientation will almost always be flat, frontal, and bound to the surface of a wall. Large-scale sculptures like those realized by Bertoia, Calder, Lippold, and Noguchi, encroached into the space and material language of architecture itself, and, as a result, the sculptures enlivened and were enlivened by the built environment in a more physical or structural manner. These exact qualities made their work attractive to so many modernist architects at the time; however, they were also what proved detrimental to their status as fine art objects. Such transactional relationships may not have been celebrated within the formalist dogmas of Greenberg's modernism, but they were not anathema for artists like Bertoia, Calder, Lippold, and Noguchi. As the latter wrote in 1949, "It is a pity when art is to be found only in museums and in the private possession of a few individuals. After all, culture is the integration of art and life."[27] These four artists did not want their work to be autonomous—created as a closed, medium-specific circuit—but intimately and materially connected to the inhabited world.

Bertoia, Calder, Lippold, and Noguchi each developed highly unique, identifiable personal styles and approaches to artmaking, but they also shared a belief that fine art had a role to play—a function—within contemporary life. Throughout their careers, they regularly accepted commissions and created work that helped reshape the built environment of postwar America. There is little historical record of the artists developing close or sustained relationships with one another, but the worlds of art and architecture were small at the time, and the overlap between them even smaller. They all knew and knew of each other. Noguchi, for example, had first met Calder while he was in Paris on a Guggenheim

Fellowship in 1927. He wrote, "I saw a lot of Alexander Calder, often helping him with his wire circus, and then going dancing." Lippold remarked that he "knew and admired Bertoia quite a lot. Along with Noguchi, Bertoia and I were probably the first to devote a great deal of our attention to working with architecture and with sites. Bertoia had a very fine sense of architectural space."[28]

Galleries and museums frequently exhibited their smaller-scaled sculpture together, and on multiple occasions architects and corporate clients considered them for the same projects. For example, an early plan of Edward Durell Stone's American Pavilion at the Brussels World's Fair in 1958 featured a massive sculptural fountain by Lippold in the middle of the rotund space (figure I.7). The final version featured instead a selection of contemporary American sculpture, including pieces by Bertoia, Calder, and Noguchi (figure I.8). There were many instances in which more than one of them ended up contributing work to the same architectural project. Skidmore, Owings & Merrill (SOM) incorporated work by both Bertoia and Lippold in their Inland Steel Building in Chicago (1956–58), and the firm of Naramore, Bain, Brady & Johanson approached both artists to create work for their First National Bank Building (1969) in downtown Seattle. The latter project sought to "integrate the interior with the street through art," and included over two-hundred commissioned and selected works throughout the eighteen floors the bank occupied in the fifty-story building. Pauline Anglim, the consultant who helped secure the commissions, wrote to architect Perry Johanson that "since Bertoia and Lippold have known each other for a long time, and enjoy a mutual respect," they were open to working with the architects simultaneously or one at a time one the project.[29]

Bertoia, Calder, Lippold, and Noguchi also shared lifelong interests in craft, engineering, and the applied arts, and none had trained, initially, to be a fine artist. Even after they committed to their sculptural practices fulltime, each maintained strong connections to design, the performing arts, and industry. Of the four, Calder arguably had the most traditional career as a fine artist. He was born in 1898 to Nanette Calder (née Lederer), a painter, and Alexander Stirling Calder, who like his father Alexander Milne Calder before him, was a well-known American sculptor. Calder attended the Arts Students League in New York City and established his artistic career among the Parisian avant-garde in the 1930s. With his prolific oeuvre of mobile, stabile, and monumental sculptures, Calder became one of, if not the most, internationally prominent American sculptors of the twentieth century.[30]

A feature in the *Smithsonian* magazine published shortly after his death in 1976 declared him "America's own version of Matisse and/or Picasso," though notably also made a point to recount how Calder was frequently distinguished from fellow American sculptor David Smith, the former being framed as more "European" while the latter, truly "American." Real differences existed in training, geography, market, and temperament, but such a statement also points to the generalized contrasts between the two sculptors that persist today: Calder as the extroverted, commercially inclined innovator; Smith as the more introverted,

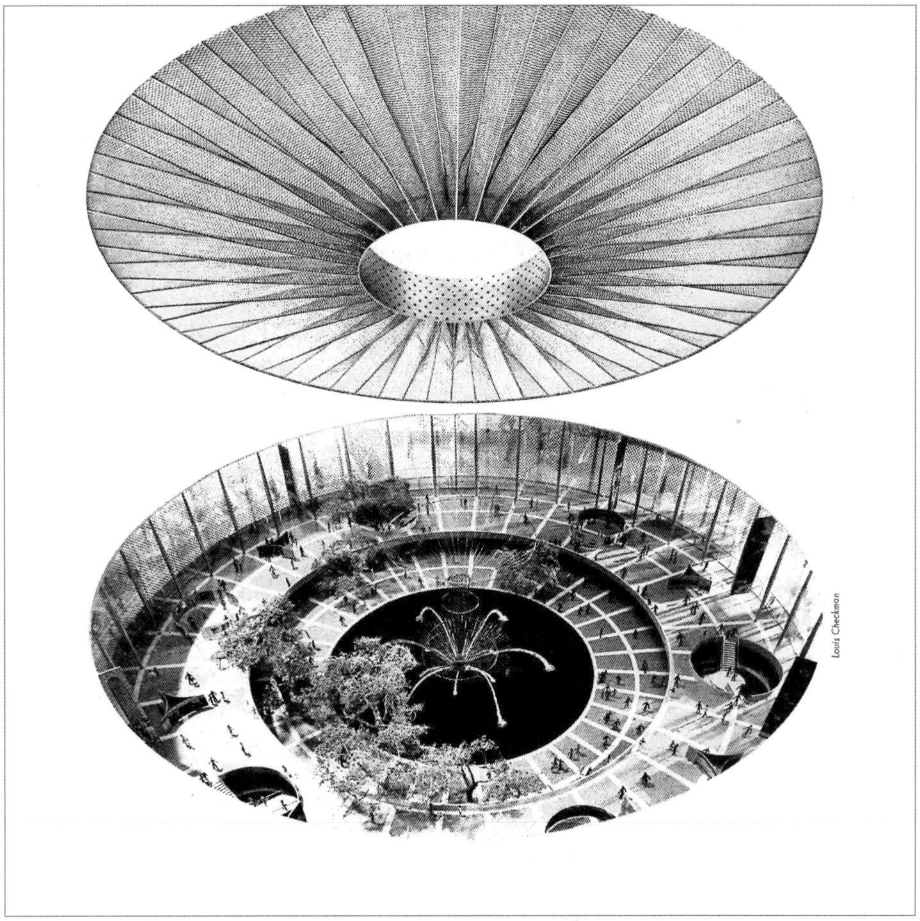

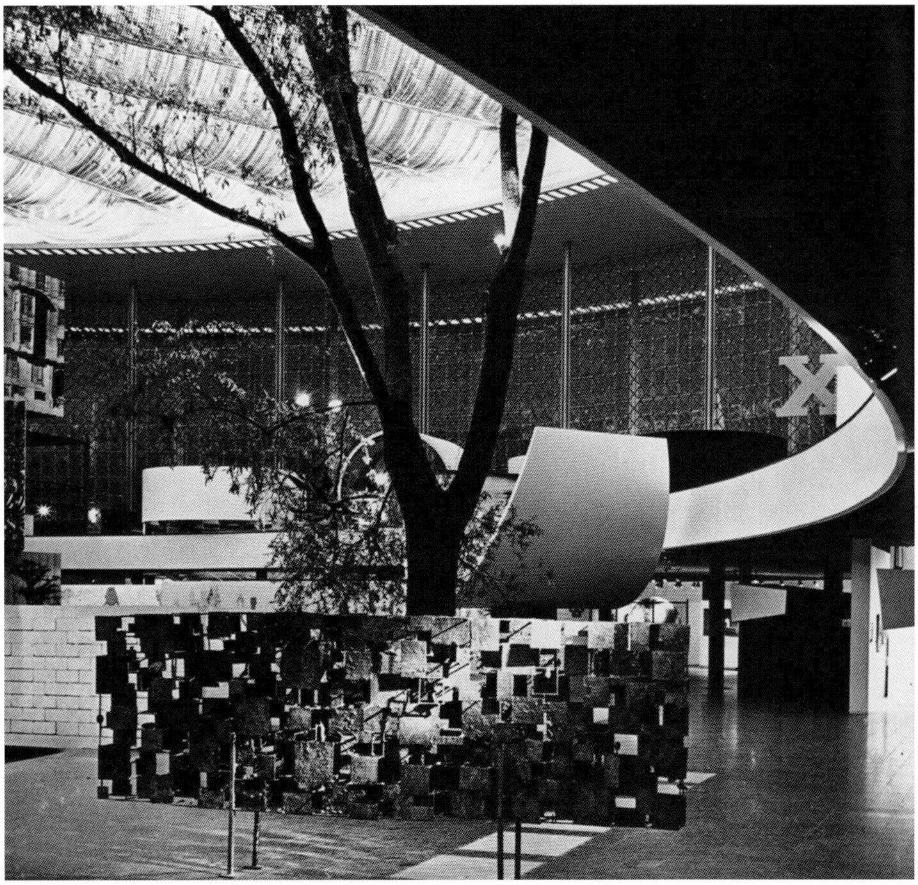

I.7
Edward Durell Stone's proposed pavilion design featuring Richard Lippold's sculptural fountain featured in "The American Pavilion, Brussels World's Fair," *Architectural Record* (July 1957).

I.8
Harry Bertoia, *Untitled*, 1958. Brass, copper, and steel, 7 2/3 ft. × 6 1/2 × 4 ft. Installed at the American Pavilion, designed by Edward Durell Stone, at Expo 58, Brussels, Belgium.

quintessential artist.[31] Calder's personality and the popularity of his work also contributed to the formation of his particular reputation, a mixture of high and low, elite and populist. This is perhaps best exemplified in his mobiles, which graced museum galleries and corporate spaces while also becoming a midcentury pop-culture phenomenon, helping dictate taste and trends in interior decoration. The dissonance also emerges through Greenberg's shifting critical stance on Calder. In the early forties, the critic spoke highly of the artist as someone making modern art "cheerful," proclaiming Calder an important figure within a new constructivist American sculpture. Greenberg praised the quality of his work alongside sculptors like Smith, but by the early 1960s, he declared Calder "overrated," and his influence never commensurate with his inflated status in American abstract art.[32]

Calder's reputation within art history has also been shaped by his willingness to engage in activities beyond the rarified sphere of avant-garde modern art. Calder received his undergraduate degree in mechanical engineering, and took jobs as a hydraulic engineer, fireman, and illustrator before committing fulltime to art. Throughout his career, he continued to produce illustrations for publications, created thousands of pieces of jewelry, and maintained connections to the performing arts, whether designing stage sets or performing the *Cirque Calder* (1926–31). There were also flashy projects for Braniff International Airlines and BMW in the 1970s, which resulted in Calder-designed paint jobs for airplanes and an automobile, respectively (figure I.9).[33]

Lippold and Bertoia, who were both born in 1915, also had training in the fields of design and engineering. Lippold moved from his native Milwaukee, Wisconsin, in the 1930s and completed a degree in industrial design at the School of the Art Institute of Chicago. He worked at the Cherry-Burrell Corporation, which manufactured equipment for the dairy industry, before establishing his own firm in Milwaukee. By 1941, he was teaching design at the University of Michigan in Ann Arbor. Lippold would later state that the "vast Midwestern prairies of his youth" influenced him as much as scientific innovation and cosmic exploration, even though he spent the majority of his life in New York and Vermont. Lippold's experience as a designer also impacted his sculptural output, as evident in the strong, meticulous, and mathematical precision of his preparatory drawings and the complex installation of his large-scale sculptures.[34]

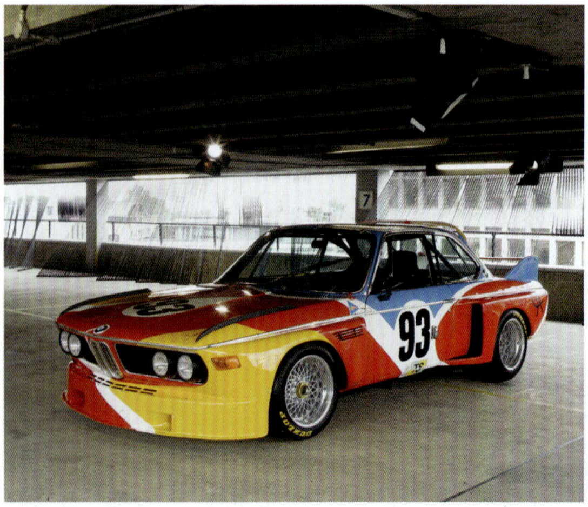

I.9 Alexander Calder, *Calder BMW Art Car*, 1974. Automotive paints on 1974 BMW 3.0 CSL, 187 in. × 80 7/10 in. × 53 in. BMW Group, Munich.

Not everyone saw these characteristics as an asset. Over a decade before he would lambast the sculptor as a "public decorator," Kramer perfectly encapsulated the criticism of Lippold's work in a review of his *Variation within a Sphere, No. 10: The Sun* (1953–56) (figure I.10). Kramer wrote, "Add to this Mr. Lippold's background as an industrial designer, the rationale of which vocation still retains its hold on his sensibility and imparts a slick elegance to the preciosity and fussiness of his visual 'ideas,' and surely such a juxtaposition of proto-industrial slickness with the authentic elegance of the handmade Oriental carpets which surround *The Sun* will suggest still another approach on the 'meaning' of the work."[35] Kramer's assessment not only debased Lippold's connections to design, but also suggested his work was neither authentically decorative like handcrafted rugs nor vanguard enough to be taken seriously as "fine art."

Lippold did, however, develop strong ties with the avant-garde art scene in New York City in the 1940s and '50s. Though critics like Kramer and Greenberg may not have celebrated it, there was a significant amount of cross-disciplinary exchange happening across visual arts, dance, and music at the time. Like Calder and Noguchi, Lippold cultivated relationships with many figures active in the performing arts. He met the dancers Merce Cunningham and Martha Graham

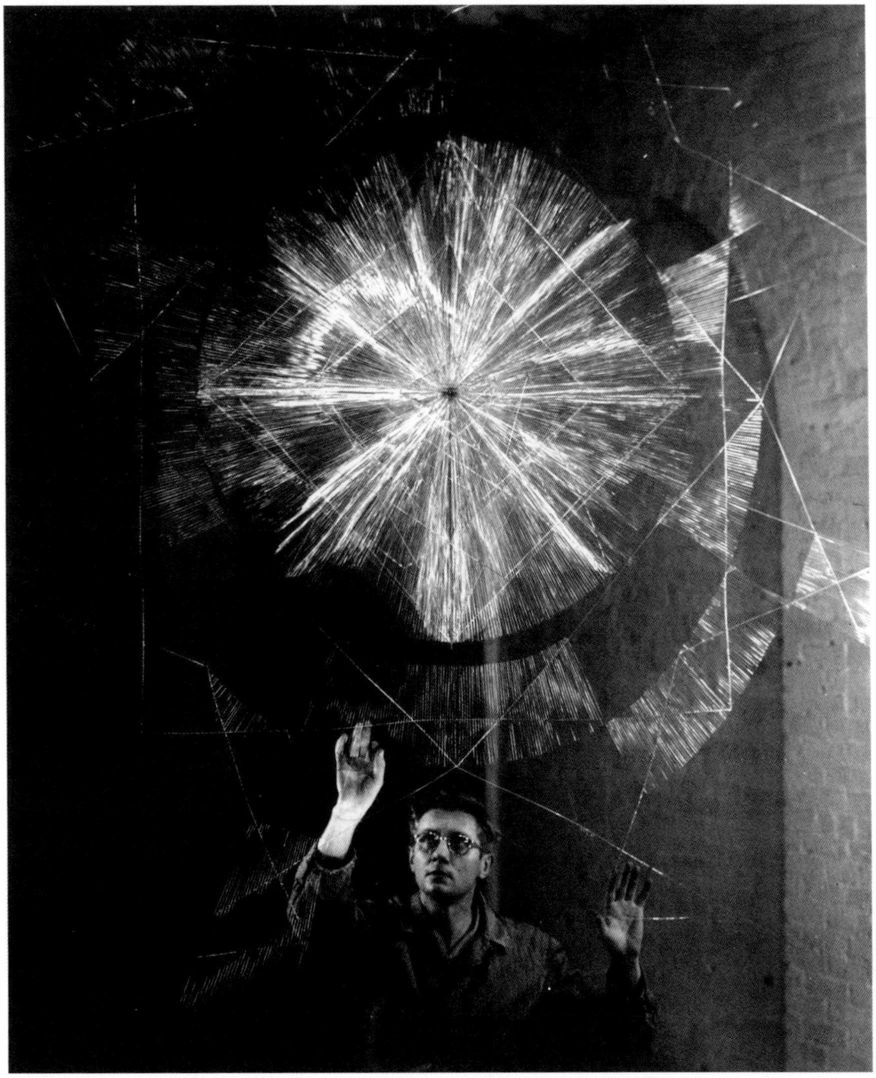

I.10 Richard Lippold with *Variation within a Sphere, Number 10: The Sun* (1953–56), by John D. Schiff, n.d. John (Hans) and Trudy Schiff Collection, Leo Baeck Institute, New York City.

through his wife, the dancer Louise Lippold (née Greuel), after the family moved to the city in 1944. His relationships with Cunningham and other figures like John Cage were strengthened when Lippold was invited in 1948 by Josef Albers, who was the school's director, to be a faculty member for the summer session at Black Mountain College. Lippold taught alongside Cunningham, Cage, Willem and Elaine de Kooning, and Buckminster Fuller, about whom he remarked was "like meeting Zoroaster speaking Islamic." Students that year also included Robert Rauschenberg and Ray Johnson. With the latter, Lippold would soon after enter a twenty-year romantic partnership.[36]

Much like Black Mountain College would prove formative for Lippold's life and career, another influential postwar institution of higher education, the Cranbrook Art Academy in Bloomfield Hills, Michigan, fundamentally shaped Bertoia's path. Following his emigration from Italy to the United States via Canada in 1930, with stints in Detroit at the Cass Technical High School and the School of the Detroit Society of the Arts and Crafts, Bertoia studied and taught at the Cranbrook Art Academy from 1937 to 1943. Like Black Mountain College, the curriculum at Cranbrook was heavily influenced by the Bauhaus and shaped by European émigrés. Finnish architect Eliel Saarinen served as president between 1932 and 1946, a period during which the school gained a reputation for being a "creative center for artists, architects and designers" that encouraged experimentation and disciplinary "cross-fertilization." The mixture of strong work ethic, open exchange, and artistic exploration during the early years of the school produced a group of alumni and staff known as the Cranbrook Circle that included Bertoia, Charles Eames, Ray Eames (née Kaiser), Eliel's son Eero Saarinen, Florence Knoll (née Schust), and Marianne Strengell, among many others (figure I.11). As critic Wolf Von Eckhardt suggested, these artists and craftspeople redefined what good

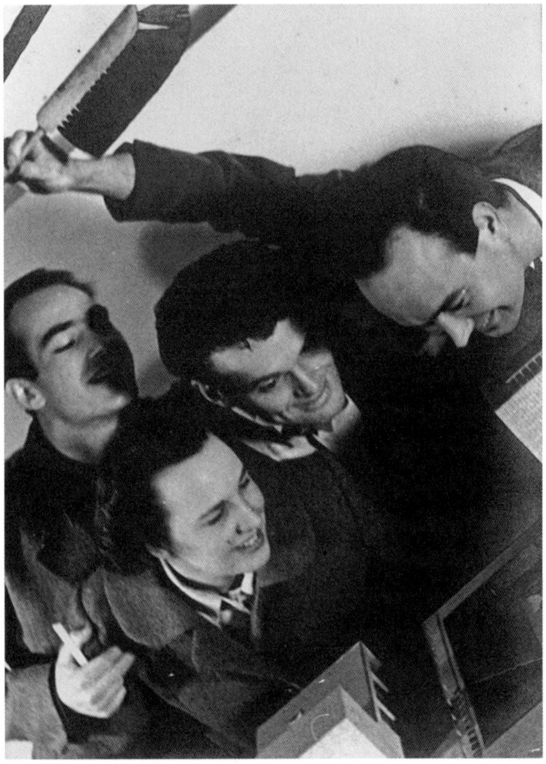

I.11 (From left to right) Harry Bertoia, Marjorie Cast, Charles Eames, and Benjamin Baldwin at the Cranbrook Academy of Art, Bloomfield Hills, Michigan, 1938.

modern design in America meant through an evolutionary approach, creating "new designs not with dogmas or preconceived notions, but by almost playful experimentation with traditional craftsmanship and styles."[37]

While at Cranbrook, Bertoia was largely involved as a student and instructor with metalwork. He made tea sets and holloware that was exhibited at MoMA and the Metropolitan Museum of Art in New York City. Bertoia's jewelry from the early 1940s, like Calder's, can be seen within the broader context of artists active in the United States in the mid-twentieth century whose work became known as modernist studio jewelry. At Cranbrook, however, no course of study was isolated. Bertoia spent much of his time in the architectural department run by Eliel Saarinen. Here, he befriended and collaborated with Eero Saarinen, who officially served as an assistant and instructor, and Charles Eames, who was an architecture student and then design faculty member. Bertoia helped construct models and prototypes, including Eero Saarinen and Eames's famous submission to MoMA's 1940 competition and 1941 exhibition *Organic Design in Home Furnishing*, and he worked at the Eames' studio in southern California during the mid-1940s. The relationships he formed while at Cranbrook would lead to numerous other collaborative projects over the succeeding years. Bertoia described his time there as "so important that I feel it was one of the basic periods of my life where things began really to change and happen."[38]

In 1950, Bertoia began working for Knoll Associates in Pennsylvania after being offered a contract by Florence and Hans Knoll. The appointment resulted in the Diamond Chair, one of the most famous pieces of midcentury modern furniture that, along with a suite of related seating by Bertoia, has been in continuous production since 1952 (figure I.12). By the mid-1950s, however, Bertoia moved away from his work with Knoll to focus fulltime on his sculptural practice,

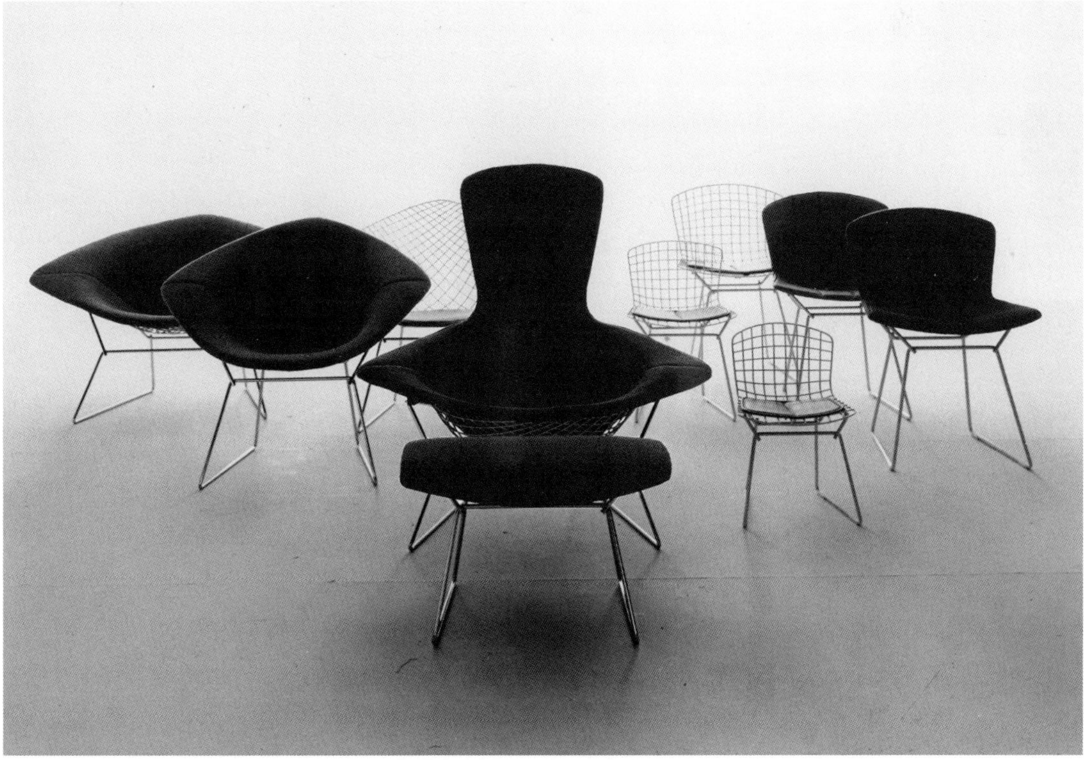

I.12 Herbert Matter, *Group Shot of Bertoia Furniture Line*, n.d. Herbert Matter papers, c. 1937–1984, Department of Special Collections and University Archives, Stanford University Libraries, California.

but on many occasions these two strands were physically reunited in the public sphere of postwar America. Knoll frequently showed and sold Bertoia's sculpture in its showrooms and helped facilitate direct sales to private clients.[39]

Knoll also collaborated with Macy's in New York City during the 1963 holiday shopping season on an exhibition of Bertoia's work. In a commercial crossover still novel for the time, Macy's ninth-floor furniture gallery featured multiple Diamond Chairs, some hanging off the wall in an abstract formation, alongside new sculptures by Bertoia. The *New York Times* reviewed the display not only as an opportunity to reach new potential customers, but also as a "contribution to consumer education," with the belief "that the show will help people see the relationship between fine art and good furniture design, which by necessity, is functional." Macy's declared: "There are few artist-designers whose work is better suited to such a display than Mr. Bertoia's. His sculptures and his furniture are both made of metal and, sharing a common material, have similar characteristics." Such a display, perhaps, demonstrates why Bertoia did not end up in the already limited canon of modern American sculptors from the immediate postwar period.[40]

The Macy's exhibition is a perfect encapsulation of what scholar and curator Elissa Auther identified as the "subordination of the decorative arts to both" a "greater interior ensemble and commercial market in which such objects circulated," that critics like Greenberg saw as the corrupting enemy of proper modern art. Bertoia was not alone in pursuing projects or work with companies like Knoll, however. Noguchi designed the Cyclone Dining and Side Tables for the company in 1954, which often featured them alongside Bertoia's furniture in advertisements and display showrooms (figure I.13). In addition to his work for Knoll, he created other pieces of furniture, both bespoke and designs for mass production, including the now iconic Noguchi Table for Herman Miller in 1947.[41]

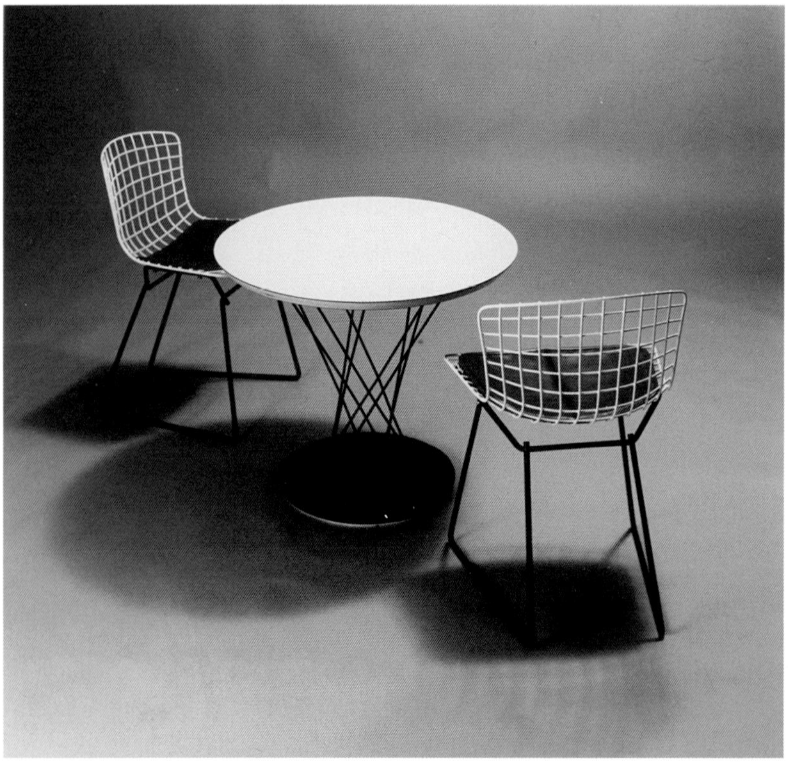

I.13 Herbert Matter, *Two Children's Chairs by Harry Bertoia with Small Noguchi Table*, n.d. Herbert Matter papers, c. 1937–1984, Department of Special Collections and University Archives, Stanford University Libraries, California.

Out of the four artists, the careers of Bertoia and Noguchi share the most parallels. Both spent considerable time during their youth outside of the United States, frequently experimented with new industrial materials, and fluidly moved across art and design throughout their careers. Each worked on significant, if niche, projects for American industry. For example, Bertoia designed a sculptural award for the R. S. Reynolds Memorial Award for Architecture in 1962, while Noguchi designed prototype Prismatic Tables for the Aluminum Company of America's Forecast Program in 1957 (figures I.14, I.15). They each created works for the Zenith Radio Corporation. Noguchi designed the *Radio Nurse*, a Bakelite baby monitor that worked in tandem with the "Guardian Ear," a separate enameled metal receiver, for Zenith in 1937 (figure I.16). Bertoia created a multipart, kinetically lit sculpture, *Sculpture Group Symbolizing World's Communication in the Atomic Age* (1959), which was the focal point of the company's Display Salon in downtown Chicago (figure I.17). Both sculptors also created numerous sculptural fountains over the course of their careers, including Noguchi's for the 1939 World's Fair in New York and Expo '70 in Osaka, Japan and Bertoia's for the Philadelphia Civic Center and the Standard Oil Building in Chicago, both of which were Durell Stone–designed projects. While Bertoia and Noguchi did not have much, if any, direct contact with

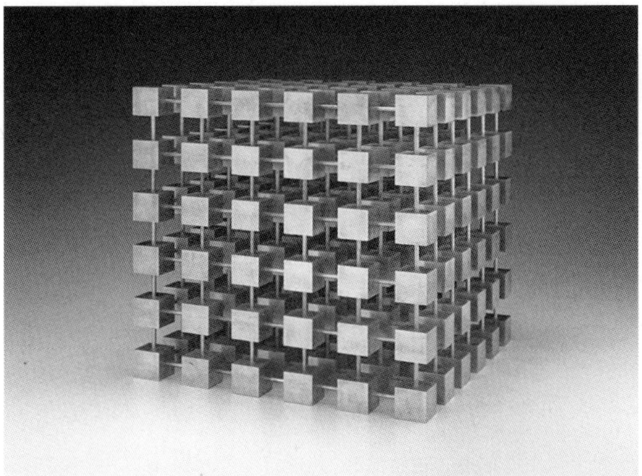

I.14
Harry Bertoia, *Cube*, 1962. Aluminum, 18 1/8 in. × 18 1/8 in. × 18 1/8 in. Virginia Museum of Fine Arts, Richmond. Gift of Reynolds Metals Company.

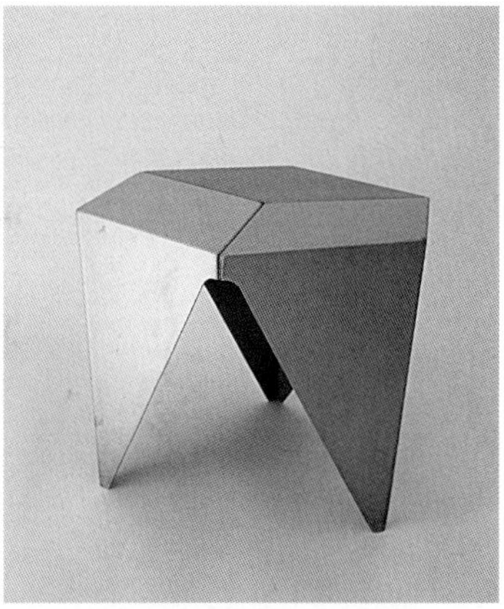

I.15
Isamu Noguchi, *Prismatic Table,* 1957. Aluminum, anodized, 14 3/4 in. × 18 1/2 in. × 16 in.

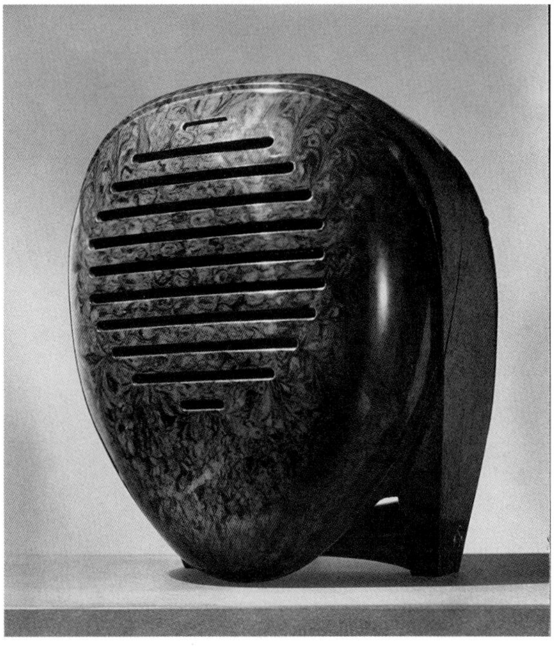

I.16
Isamu Noguchi, *Radio Nurse*, 1937. Bakelite resin, h. 8 1/4 in, diam. 6 1/2 in. Manufactured by Zenith Radio Corporation, Chicago.

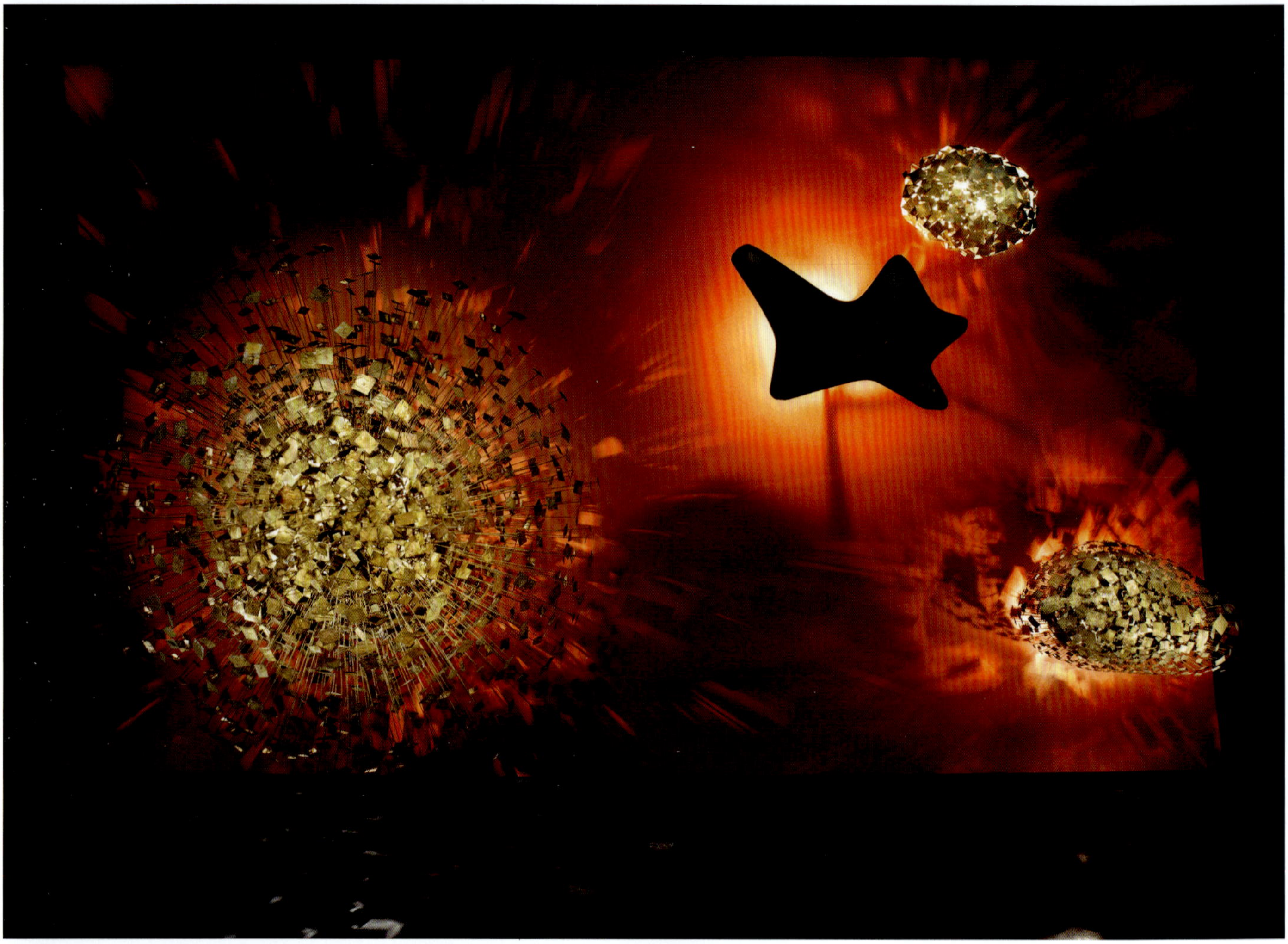

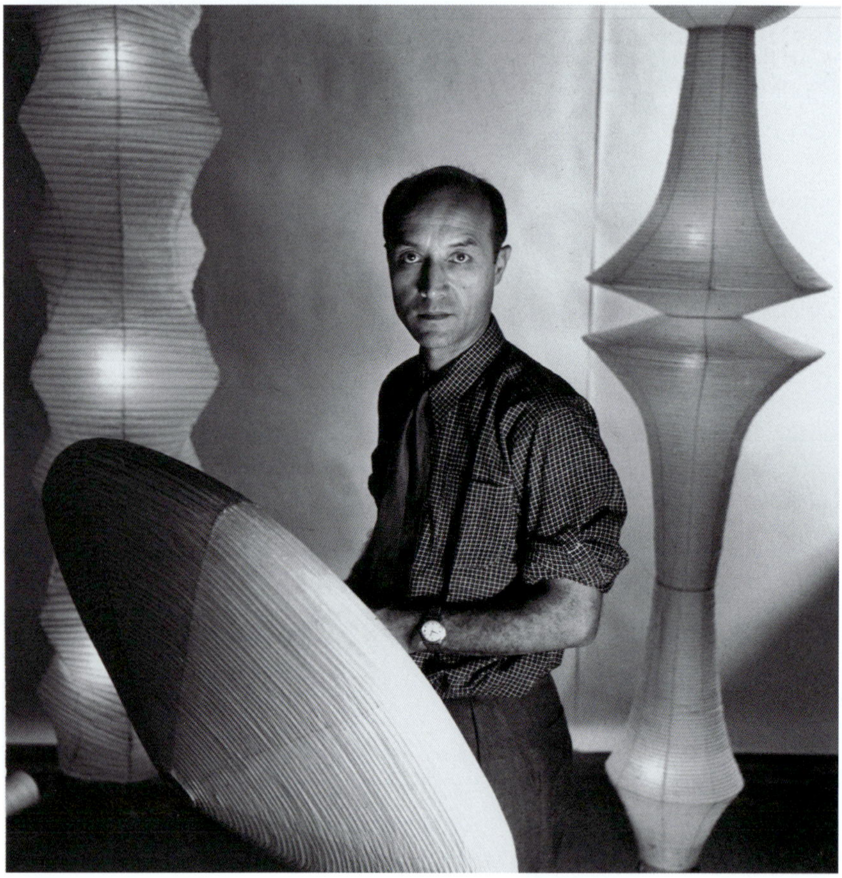

I.17
Harry Bertoia, *Sculpture Group Symbolizing World's Communication in the Atomic Age*, 1959. Brazed and welded brass and bronze, dimensions variable. Smithsonian American Art Museum, Washington, DC. Gift of the Zenith Corporation, 1979.107A-D.

I.18
Louise Dahl-Wolfe, *Isamu Noguchi, New York*, 1955. Gelatin silver print, 14 in. × 11 in. Cheekwood Estate & Gardens, Nashville, Tennessee. Gift of the Artist, 1984.24.22.

one another, they were, like all four artists, aware of each other and their work, with Noguchi for example describing Bertoia as a "talented artist."[42]

Noguchi's design activities were particularly extensive, not limited by medium or to any one decade, but closely related in form and approach to his sculptural work. He, like Calder, created stage sets, including over twenty for Martha Graham. He designed numerous gardens, landscapes, and playscape designs during the postwar period. In 1951, after a visit to the Japanese town of Gifu, Noguchi designed his first Akari Light Sculptures, lamps made of *washi* paper over now-patented metal-wire stretcher and support systems (figure I.18). As contemporary artist Josiah McElheny has written of Noguchi, he created "sculptures that look like furniture," "sculptures that function architecturally in space," and "works that suggest they can be things other than sculpture, even if that's what they are."[43]

This boundary fluidity is visible not only across Noguchi's design and commissioned projects, but also in those of Bertoia, Calder, and Lippold. While such work was only one aspect of their multifaceted practices, each strove to make sculpture that was useful and publicly visible in contemporary society. As Noguchi wrote, "For a sculptor to merely say 'I'm a sculptor and I'm making pure sculpture' (or impure, whatever it is) and that the architects can use them or not as they wish, and if they fit in, all right—that's an abandonment of a whole area which I find most interesting and important as a sculptor: that is, the relationship of sculpture and the sculptor to the world we live in and how his functioning can be a necessity. Merely to decorate, does not seem enough to me."[44]

Changes occurring in architecture further complicated the issues of individual expression, autonomy, and decoration in art. One of the defining characteristics of modernist architecture had been the removal of any extraneous ornament—though there were precedents of modern architects incorporating sculpture into their projects earlier in the twentieth century. In cases like Mies van der Rohe's installation of a Georg Kolbe's *Alba (Dawn)* (1925) in one of the water basins of his 1929 Barcelona Pavilion, however, the art selected was "premade" and mostly figural. As architectural historian Vincent Scully writes, since Mies's buildings were themselves "environmental constructivist sculpture," he was content to have architecture simply contain art.[45]

Why then was there such renewed interest in the relationship between art and architecture during the postwar period, and what did architectural decoration then mean? Not every modernist building or project included art, but those that did wrestled with the issue of how to use it. Though Philip Johnson had so successfully worked with and praised Lippold's contribution to the Four Seasons Restaurant, his solution was usually to have the architect operate more as a curator than an engaged, collaborative cocreator of space. He stated, "Pick the greatest works of art you can, put them in the best place you have, and you get the type of architecture we want in this scientific age." Outside of exceptions like Johnson, most practitioners and critics, however, concurred that simply selecting or placing a sculpture in a lobby space or in front of a building was not enough. The solution for how to decorate architecture with art ideally required involving artists early on in the process and matching individuals who approached collaboration with mutual respect and sincerity. Bertoia, Calder, Lippold, and Noguchi preferred, or at least were open to, working in this fashion. Perhaps because of the more commercial aspects of their backgrounds, they also frequently tailored their work to the design of the architect or the client's wishes without relinquishing their artistic visions. With each project, they still realized distinct sculptures that shaped and were shaped by the specificities of a given space.[46]

The most frequently touted narrative around the purpose of art as architectural decoration, however, focused on its ability to humanize and give textural richness to the cold, sterile interiors of modernist architecture. As SOM architect William Hartmann stated, "The modern architecture we identified with eliminated decoration. Basically, it was an evolution from a handicraft kind of building technology to an industrialized building technology. That was the key to it. When you gave up the handicraft part, you gave up the artisan and the craftsmen who would carve limestone and wood and these different materials that led to the expression of a building. In industrialized architecture, you were using components that were made by machine, and decoration wasn't appropriate for the machine. So, when you come to decorate an industrialized building, you decorate with an artist." The situation Hartmann described suggests art as an afterthought, a final softening touch.[47]

An additional complication of how art could be used to decorate architecture became apparent by the mid-1950s, when a younger generation of architects including Johnson, Saarinen, Stone, and Minoru Yamasaki, began to veer away from the regimented dictates of modernist architecture. Architectural historian Alice T. Friedman noted the architects' shared "broadened palette of natural materialism, the introduction of craft elements, and the use of more expressive, three-dimensional forms to convey emotion or 'humanist' themes." But with their divergent styles and approaches, these architects resisted classification as a group, despite attempts from some, including Thomas H. Creighton, editor of *Progressive Architecture*, who proposed "New Sensualism."[48]

Many critics at the time, including Robin Boyd and Vincent Scully, disparaged the move away from "the cube, the right angle, the glass wall, and the plain surface" that had come to define Mies van der Rohe–inspired modernist architecture. They derided the work of this so-called "second generation" as too decorative, too sculptural, or as Scully stated, too close to a flashy, superficial "package." He wrote, "It is no wonder, in consequence, that most American architecture of the 1950s and '60s became an affair of brightly colored bundles, gaudily bowed to catch the blearing eye." Much like that of the sculptors examined in this book whose work was similarly critiqued as superficial "decorative" baubles, the version of modernism offered by these architects reengaged with ideas of ornamentation, collapsing newfound artistic sensibility with functionalism.[49]

Architectural critic Aline B. Saarinen noted that while some architects were indeed motivated to use art for an "esthetic or formal reason," there was another, preferred motivation that transcended a mere contrast of color, texture, and pattern. In this approach, the goal was a shared mode of "expression" and "communication," drawn from an "honest use of the architectural vocabulary, rather than appliqué, or extraneous devices, or falsification, or allusions and associations." Seen in this light, the preponderance of specifically sculptural commissions, created by artists like Bertoia, Calder, Lippold, and Noguchi, becomes even less surprising. There was already a familiarity of engineering, functionality, and materials, a shared vocabulary that enabled a far more "honest use."[50] It is also perhaps not surprising, that in turn, many of these so-called decorator-architects became the most frequent and enthusiastic collaborators of the so-called decorator-sculptors during the postwar period.

Contested Collaborations

While cross-disciplinary conversations around the use of art in modernist architecture became pronounced during the immediate postwar years, they had begun earlier in the twentieth century and were never limited to the United States. The often-idealized reference point of the "long tradition of the allied arts" stretched back even further, to classical antiquity and the Middle Ages when, as one postwar critic claimed, "sculptors were in harmony with the architects and *that* all were in harmony with their time." Many of the issues underpinning a renewed relationship between modern art and modernist architecture, more specifically, originated in Europe prior to World War II. Conversations around the functionality of art in contemporary society shaped the ideology of the Bauhaus in Germany, as well as other early twentieth-century avant-gardes like Constructivism in the Soviet Union and de Stijl in the Netherlands.[51]

Le Corbusier, both as an architect and artist, wrestled with a "synthesis" of the arts, expressing a combination of optimism and skepticism. He asserted the possibility of art being utilized within architecture and stated that in the modern epoch "we no longer have the right to 'stick' something on something." Le Corbusier also argued, however, that art "ought not to be combined or merged with architecture. It should retain its own character quite separate from that of its background." Noting the immense indifference of many artists to the "contemporary architectural event," he expressed a belief that mutual respect was crucial to the equation. "When we invite to our home a guest of distinction, of dignity, of real ability, and one whom we respect, we do not surround him with noise, we listen to him and he speaks amid the silence because he has something to say. In this collaboration of the major arts and architecture, dignity is not a vain pretension."[52]

As modern architecture developed on both sides of the Atlantic, debates continued through the Congrès internationaux d'architecture moderne (CIAM, or International Congresses of Modern Architecture), which Le Corbusier along with architectural historian Sigfried Giedion helped inaugurate in 1928 in Switzerland. The writings of figures like Giedion, artist Fernand Léger, and architect Josep Lluís

Sert, as well as cross-disciplinary activities at MoMA, under the curatorial auspices of Alfred H. Barr Jr., Henry-Russell Hitchcock, and Philip Johnson also drew further attention to the issue. Discussions among modernist practitioners, curators, and critics alike focused on ideas of synthesis and a reintegration of art and architecture.[53]

Though outside the scope of this book, these international debates also resulted in a similar phenomenon in the commissioning of art, particularly large-scale sculpture, for architectural projects around the world, as Europe rebuilt its cities and modernist architecture expanded its global reach. One of the most notable, if not wholly well-received, attempts to combine art and architecture in Europe during the period, for example, was the commissioning of Jean Arp, Alexander Calder, Joan Miró, Henry Moore, Isamu Noguchi, and Pablo Picasso to create work for the new 1958 UNESCO Headquarters in Paris (figure I.19). The artists took the architecture, itself a result of a contested committee of some of the most well-known architects of the period, into varying degrees of consideration when creating their works. The majority of the resulting pieces were sited outdoors, however, and thus engaged a very different set of issues from those of primary consideration in this book, which deals predominantly with interior spaces.[54]

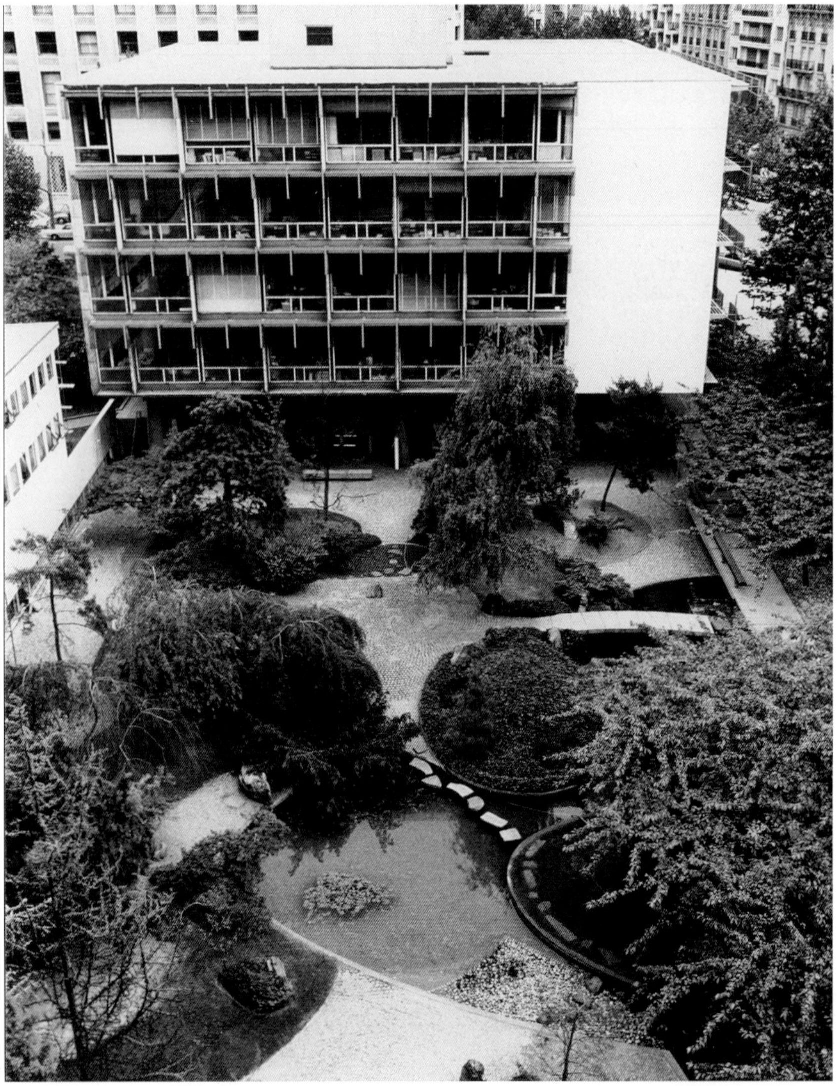

I.19
Isamu Noguchi, *Gardens for UNESCO (Garden of Peace)*, 1956–58. UNESCO Headquarters, Paris, France.

There is also further work to be done on cross-disciplinary exchange as it occurred across the Atlantic Ocean and along a Pan-American axis. In many Central and South American countries, numerous commissions were realized, and discussions around new conceptions of space echoed those occurring in Europe and North America. Figures like the Argentine-Italian artist Lucio Fontana presented his spatialist *White Manifesto* in Buenos Aires in 1946, and the Venezuelan architect Carlos Raúl Villanueva emphasized the spatial values of architecture in his writings and work. Villanueva stated that to "take possession of space is the first gesture of all living things," and "what is of value, and the only truly new element in today's architecture, is the real and conscious conditioning of space." Venezuela along with Argentina, Brazil, and Mexico saw an explosion of modernist architecture, and one of the hallmarks of modern Latin American architecture during the postwar period became the incorporation of the visual arts. Caracas, Venezuela, in particular, was transformed into a modernist world capital during the 1950s, with major projects completed there by architects Wallace K. Harrison, Richard Neutra, Oscar Niemeyer, Gio Ponti, and Villanueva, among many others. In 1958, Harry Bertoia contributed a metal screen to the facade of the US Embassy in Caracas, designed by architect Don Hatch (figure I.20). Calder also realized two

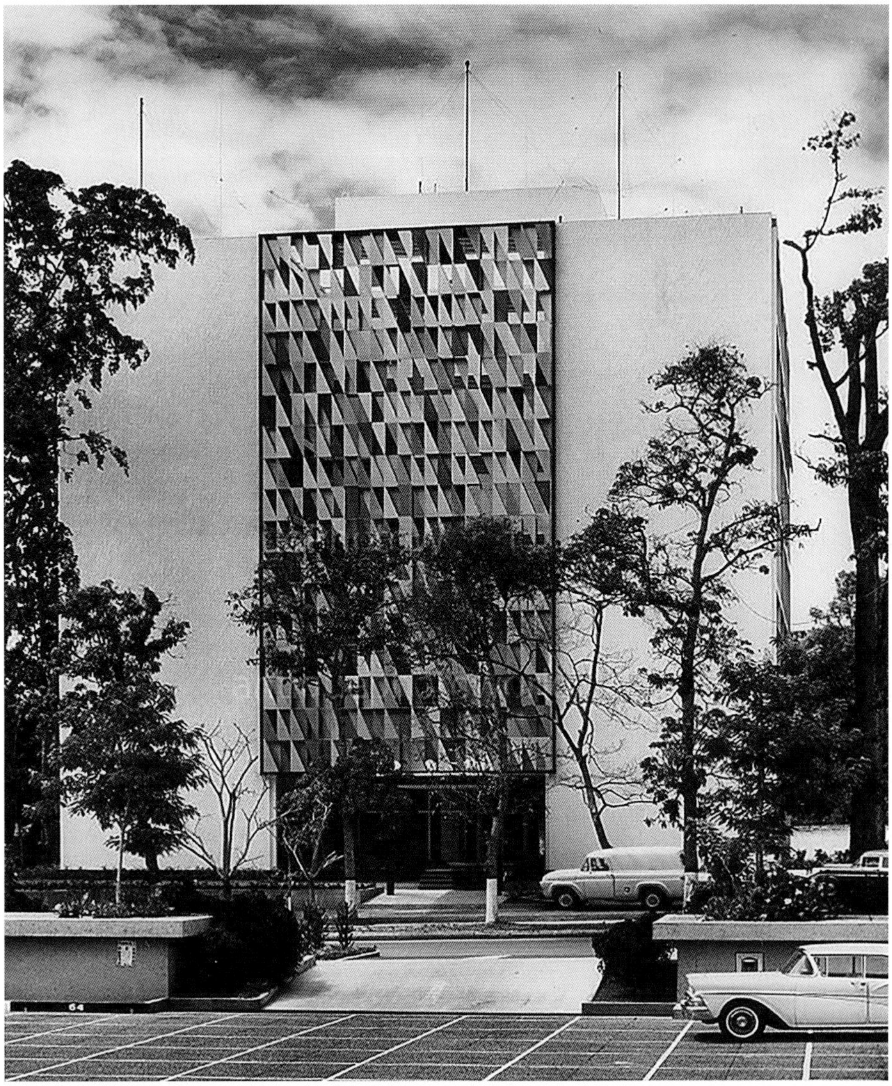

I.20
Harry Bertoia, *Untitled*, 1958. Unknown materials and dimensions. US Embassy, Caracas, Venezuela. Architect: Oficina Don Hatch.

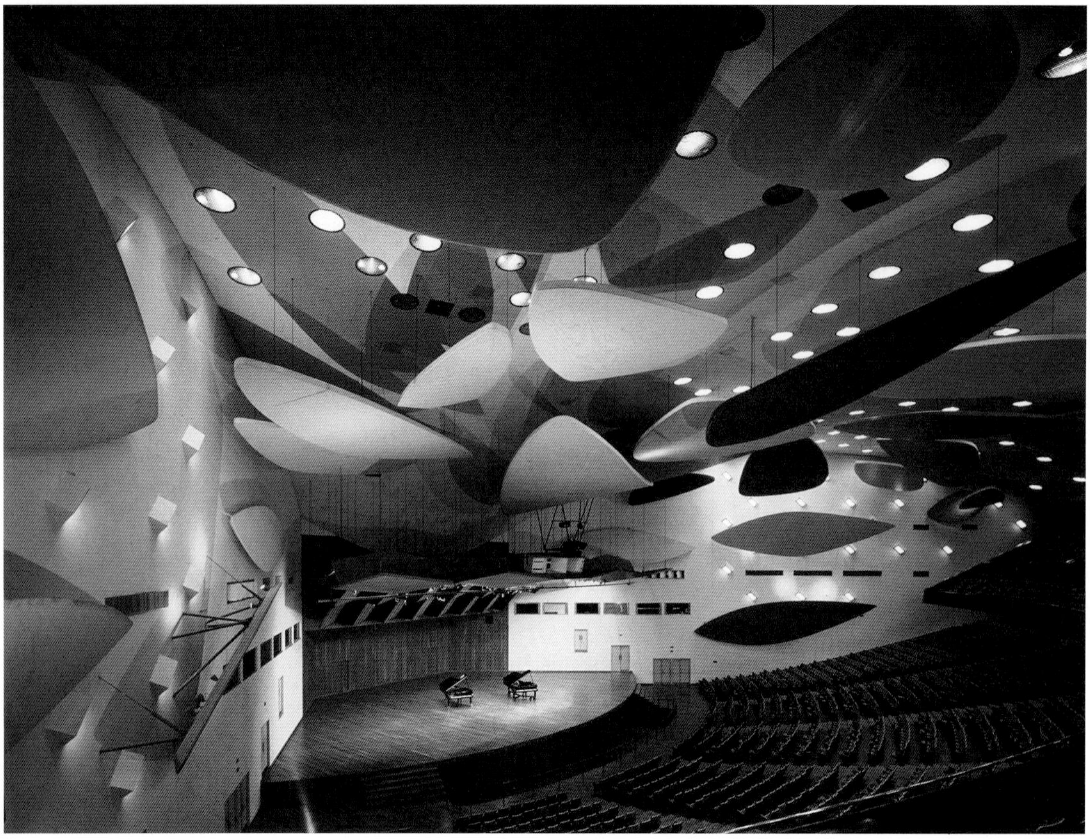

I.21
Alexander Calder, *Acoustic Ceiling*, 1954. Wood and paint, largest element: 30 ft. wide. Aula Magna, Universidad Central de Venezuela, Caracas, Venezuela. Architect: Carlos Raúl Villanueva.

large-scale projects in Caracas: a mobile for Harrison's Hotel Ávila commissioned in 1941; and his so-called floating clouds (*platillos voladores*) or *Acoustic Ceiling* for the Aula Magna theater in Villanueva's massive new Universidad Central de Venezuela campus in 1954 (figure I.21).[55]

Regardless of geography or the regional specificities of projects, however, there was a common concern among those across the globe about how true collaboration between modernist architects and modern artists could occur. Theoretical debate and a shared willingness were not enough. As the French artist Jean Gorin wrote in an open letter in 1956 referenced by Walter Gropius, "The synthesis of the arts cannot consist in putting sculpture and painting in appropriate architectural locations… because that is, when all is said and done, nothing but the program of a museum. We believe that the true synthesis of the arts is to be found in the architectural work itself and commences from the first stages of the conception." Sert was another vocal proponent for a collaborative relationship between artists and architects, which he saw not just as desirable but necessary. He wrote, "The architect, like the sculptor or painter, needs a sense of plastic values. Without them he would produce buildings, but the buildings would not be architecture."[56]

Collaboration of any sort involves a negotiation of egos and aesthetic viewpoints, but under the auspices of modernism, where individuality and autonomy reigned, both sides expressed misgivings. American sculptor Theodore Roszak, who completed a number of sculptures for the exteriors of buildings during the postwar period, was far from optimistic about the contemporary situation. He wrote, "The prospect of supplementing architecture with sculpture in a way that would permit the integration of their respective spatial orbits within a consistent community environment would be little short of miraculous."[57]

Like Roszak, fellow sculptor David Smith saw little benefit for sculptors to create functional objects or collaborate with architects. He expressed a distaste and distrust for "big architecture" that did not appropriately value, conceptually or economically, the efforts and intentions of artists. Smith noted that sculpture possessed a distinct "method of operation," which entailed the creation of an object "for visual aesthetic response, essentially executed by one man, that serves no physical function and doesn't have to be conceived with allowance for indoor plumbing." He did make the distinction between artist and designer, stating that the latter was perhaps better suited to filling the needs of architects while being paid less, working faster, and "adhering to the decor. Designers can make the compromise with something that looks like art but stays with the building." In contrast, "Good sculpture has its own form. It is based upon a different aesthetic structure." Smith concluded by reiterating that collaborations failed because architects had limited perspectives, "until the architect gives up the preconception that sculpture is merely another of his details and accepts it on its own terms, seeks it as one contemporary autonomy meeting another in a relationship of aesthetic strength and excellence, art and architecture will remain the strangers they have been for at least the last hundred years."[58]

From the other end of the disciplinary perspective, architect and critic Peter Blake decried what he saw as the unwillingness of many artists to contribute to the "total environment," or to "produce building elements or fabricate wall surfaces." He wrote, "If asked to do so, they are more likely to come up with a highly individual 'statement'—a manifesto—rather than an object that will fit, naturally, gracefully and modestly into the building organism," though he did cite exceptions from Bertoia, Herbert Bayer, and György Kepes. Architect Harris Armstrong similarly found much to recommend in the use of sculpture, writing that the medium "suggests itself to me more frequently than painting," because "architecture itself is a language of form, a thing which exists in three dimensions, rather than of color and surface pattern." Armstrong concluded, however, by acknowledging that the "rank and file of the architectural profession" were nervous to incorporate art not only for fear of an artist becoming too ambitious, but also because "it is always more trouble to work when other strong personalities are in the picture, and only the work of strong artists can make much of a contribution."[59] Many architects and artists decided that the trouble of such negotiations was not worth the effort.

Even artists and architects willing to collaborate and approach the relationship with genuine mutual respect, faced the real, logistical, and philosophical difficulties of the complex bureaucracy involved when constructing a building, and frequently fell back into well-trodden hierarchies of architecture as the "mother of all arts." Such relationships intrinsically assumed subservience of the artist to the total vision of the architect and the needs of the client. For example, Harrison, an early and ardent proponent of using art in architecture, noted that "functionalism imposes certain demands; it seems to me that the sculptor must harmonize his concepts and thinking with the new architecture."[60] After all, the resulting sculptures were the result of commercial commissions.

In the end, those who shared Smith and Roszak's skepticism may have been right, at least about the feasibility of collaboration as conceived by those like Sert or Gropius. Artists were seldom brought into the architectural process early or as equal collaborators, and consequently, failed to achieve a holistic result. For some, the issue was not about the actual practice, but the baggage of the terminology being applied. Ada Louise Huxtable, in advancing her framework of apposition rather than the moral loftiness of integration, noted that both the art and architecture of the postwar period were far different than Gothic or Baroque Europe, and that to apply the same expectations was to misdirect and doom to failure even the best endeavored attempts to combine them. She wrote, "The most effective use of art with architecture today is not based on integration, or unification or oneness, but on deliberate contrast." Huxtable was largely supportive of attempts to use art in architecture, but even in her analyses, art often remained positioned as less than architecture, as something to supplement or enhance, even if through juxtaposition, the architect's total vision. A commissioned sculpture, no matter how unselfishly conceived and masterfully executed, was seldom, if ever, considered by practitioners and users alike to be more important than the architecture that surrounded it.[61]

The perceived success of any collaboration often was, and remains, judged from the perspective of how well the artwork functioned in relation to the architecture, with far less attention given to how well the architecture served the artwork, and without any regard to the limitations or outright deficiency of the architectural design. The voices of architects and architectural critics, not those of artists, came to dominate contemporary debates, or were at least the most profuse, and as a result solidified this imbalance. Their perspective largely emphasized what art could do for architecture or how art could be used. As Aline B. Saarinen wrote, architectural decoration, "whether it is a freestanding piece of sculpture which defines space by punctuating it or whether it is a mosaic mural incorporated into a façade... must be accessory to and subordinate to the architecture in form and expression." She, like Huxtable, also consciously avoided the term "integration," but in Saarinen's case because it connoted an "equality between art and architecture which may happily arrive as a result but in which I do not believe as a goal." Architectural decoration, as Saarinen emphasized, was not about featuring "upper-case, exalted, self-sufficient expression," but art that was willing to emphasize "the dramatization, the 'vividization' of the architecture."[62]

The encounter between modern architecture and modern sculpture, in particular, occurred in a multiplicity of modes including integration, incorporation, application, addition, and confrontation. Although, as art historian Eduard Trier noted, "It is important to remember that the two partners are autonomous and meet as equals—a radically new departure in the history of their relationship for which the term 'architecture sculpture,' implying as it does the subordination of sculpture to architecture, is no longer adequate." Alloying art and architecture, or at least an attempt at a synergy between them, was rarely the result of an easy partnership of equals. Crucially, however, artists like Bertoia, Calder, Lippold, and Noguchi embraced functionality as well as the confines imposed on them in making commissioned pieces for architectural spaces during the immediate postwar period. They were careful, however, not to relinquish their creation's legibility or status as sculptural objects.[63]

Further, the relationships Bertoia, Calder, Lippold, and Noguchi fostered with noted modernist architects during the postwar period served as robust, complex rebukes to the many failed collaborations. Their large-scale sculptural commissions stand as models for how a synergy between art and architecture could be achieved; examples of successful projects, where the artist, architect, and client—and even the critic—all spoke positively about the outcome. Each of these four artists also developed close professional, and sometimes personal relationships with architects, resulting in repeated collaborations that spanned decades.

Between the early 1950s and Bertoia's death in 1978, the artist realized over fifty distinct large-scale commissioned sculptures, working with a considerable number of notable architects including Gordon Bunshaft, Victor Gruen, I. M. Pei, Kevin Roche, Eero Saarinen, Edward Durell Stone, Minoru Yamasaki, and Thomas T. K. Zung. He collaborated with most of them, especially Saarinen, Durell Stone, and Yamasaki, on multiple projects. With the latter alone, Bertoia realized six distinct commissions including *Sunlit Straw* (1964), which served as the focal point in the lobby of the downtown Minneapolis headquarters of Northwestern National Life Insurance in Minnesota (figure I.22). Marcel Breuer who had worked with Calder on a number of projects including the UNESCO Headquarters in Paris and the Stillman House in Litchfield, Connecticut, noted how the sculptor's work was "so much at home in and between our buildings—a good neighbor and interconnected part of architecture and the geometric space. Opposites to the extreme, but good friends."[64]

Skidmore, Owings & Merrill (SOM) became one of the leading architectural firms in cross-disciplinary collaborations, and their work with artists led to some of the more notable projects realized during the postwar period. A large percentage of Calder's architectural commissions, for example, including a number of his monumental outdoor stabiles and late mobiles, were done for SOM projects or facilitated with the help of their architects. Architectural historian Henry-Russell Hitchcock concluded in 1963 that, "by commissioning such things as a mobiles by Calder, screens by Bertoia and constructions by Lippold, [SOM] have certainly shown in practice a more effective devotion to the ideal of making important use of collaborating painters and sculptors than many architects who have been more vocal on the subject." In part, SOM was structurally predisposed to collaboration. Each job at the firm was run by two senior supervisors—partners responsible for the design and business interests respectively—who managed a team of architects, engineers, and designers. Following the end of World War II prominent partners at SOM, including Bunshaft, Bruce Graham, and William Hartmann, had developed sustained interest in the arts, whether personally as arts patrons or professionally as commissioners of large-scale art.[65]

I.22
Harry Bertoia, *Sunlit Straw*, 1964. Brass-coated steel rods, 14 ft. × 46 ft. × 4 ft. Northwestern National Life Insurance Company, Minneapolis, Minnesota. Architect: Minoru Yamasaki Associates.

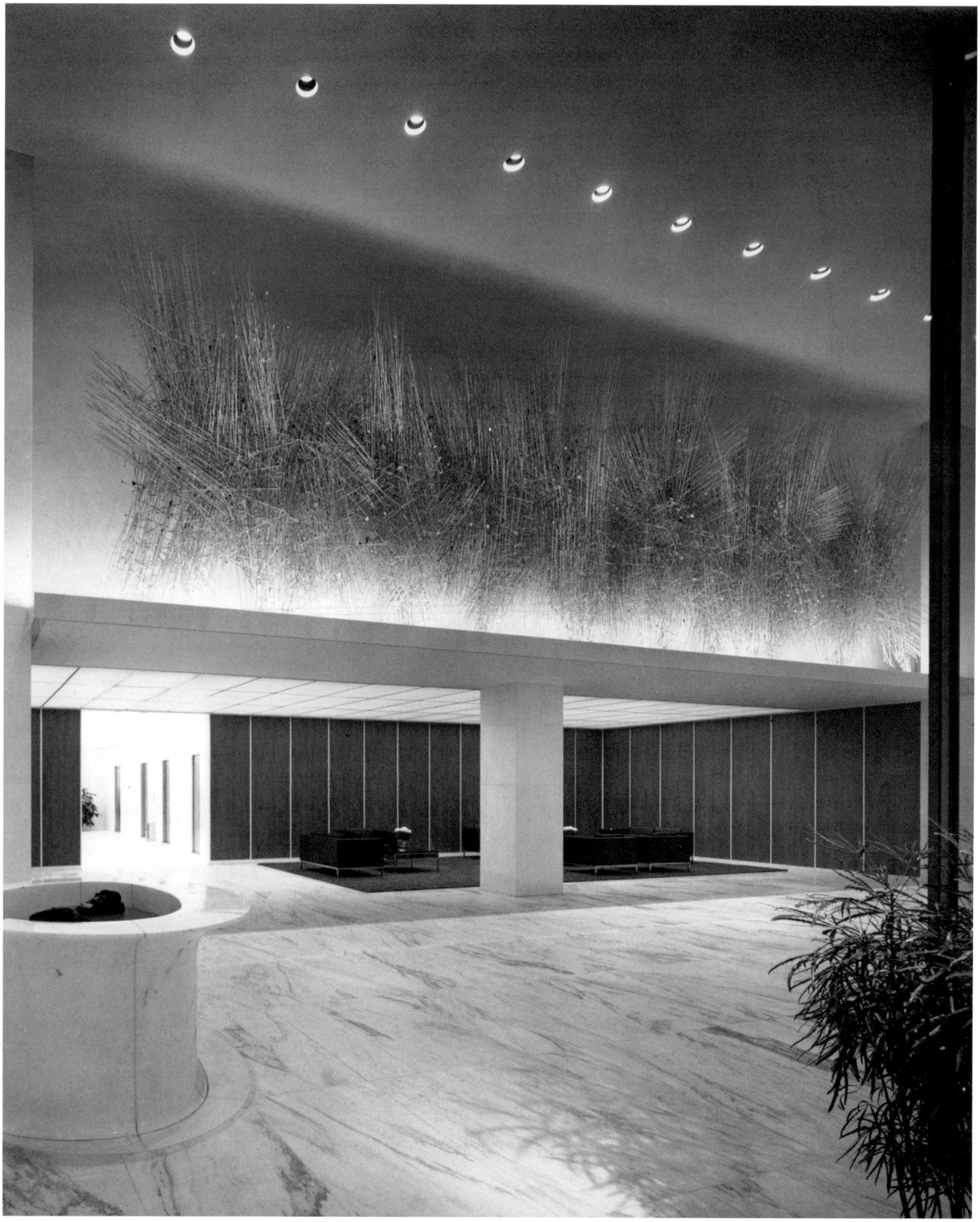

Bunshaft, perhaps more than any architect at SOM or discussed in this book, was a fervent supporter of the visual arts, especially sculpture, and often incorporated it in varying ways into his architectural projects. He became an avid art collector and supporter of modern art, becoming particularly involved as a patron and architect of the Albright-Knox Art Gallery in Buffalo, New York. As Bunshaft stated in his typically brusque manner, "Well, I've been interested in art. I've promoted a lot of art in architecture. My whole life is doing architecture, and if I have money, we buy art." He bought work by Bertoia, Calder, and Noguchi, but also collaborated with each on multiple projects while an architect at SOM.[66]

Bunshaft developed a particularly close relationship with Noguchi and held him in high regard, even if both men had very conflicted feelings over the nature and possibilities of alliances between artists and architects in general. Their work together began with a never-realized proposal for the street-level plaza of Lever House in New York City in 1952, continued with the campus for Connecticut General Life Insurance Company in Bloomfield, Connecticut (1956–57), and lasted well into the 1970s. Bunshaft's projects with Noguchi speak volumes about how and why he sought to include art so often in his architecture. Of the Lever House commission, for example, Bunshaft recalled, "We hoped to have sculpture integrated with total design, including landscape, and Noguchi was the only sculptor that I knew of in the world who had the requisite knowledge of architecture, plant material and space design.... it seemed to us wrong to have a predetermined design for a plaza and terrace and then say, 'Here, Mr. Noguchi, plunk your piece down here.'"[67]

Many outdoor sculptures created from the later 1960s on, would of course become derided for the exact quality Bunshaft hoped to avoid in engaging Noguchi's artistic services: art simply "plopped" in public spaces. The majority of Bunshaft's projects with Noguchi were outdoor commissions, objects or designs for fountains, plazas, and corporate campuses, and while there was always a concerted effort by both artist and architect to create works that thoughtfully responded to their site and surrounding architecture, such collaborations still fall outside the scope of this study. Outdoor works, whether architectural reliefs on building exteriors or freestanding sculptures engage both the surrounding architecture and the broader built environment in very different ways from the primary case studies examined in this book, which focus on large-scale sculptures structurally woven into the architecture of interior threshold spaces, like lobbies, altars, reception areas, and lounges.[68]

The particular focus on projects realized for this specific type of interior space is crucial to understanding what was at stake in the large-scale sculptural commissions realized during the immediate post-war period, and how they are distinct from public art commissions of the later twentieth century. Transitional threshold areas are usually the most visible, traversed, and publicly accessible sites in buildings. As architect Serge Chermayeff wrote, "Functionally the lobby is the building's valve, receiving, distributing, ejecting; but beyond that it is an architectural experience which on entrance and departure imprints upon the spectator's mind and eye the character and quality of the building and its organization—if it has either."[69] Artwork, commissioned for threshold spaces furthered the fortification of the public image the owner or occupant was attempting to build and project.

In recent studies, architectural historian Alice T. Friedman and art historian Amanda Douberley convincingly position commissioned art of this vein, particularly large-scale sculptures, within an expanded, more nuanced framework of public art—one that has less to do with funding sources and more with modes of public address. Friedman suggests such works function as symbols of the new "cultured corporation," while Douberley writes that these objects were deployed as "a form of public relations." The lens of patronage and corporate public relations is vital to understanding how and why industry increasingly sought out artists and their work during the postwar period. Friedman and Douberley each offer valuable, convincing analyses of such large-scale sculptural commissions. These works, however, did not just possess a different public address than their outdoor counterparts, or function as sophisticated commercial symbols, but also crucially occupied, shared, and shaped architectural space. While grounded in the broader historical context and debates that produced a renewed interest in synergy across the arts, industry, and science, this book takes as its primary focus the unique ways in which sculpture structurally and functionally alloyed with architecture.[70]

Alloys: American Sculpture and Architecture at Midcentury uses a selection of commissions created for the threshold spaces of high-profile modernist architectural projects constructed during the immediate postwar period as paradigms of cross-disciplinary collaboration. All of the analyzed case studies were created between 1946 and 1966, but this book, like the projects it examines, does not follow a clear, progressive chronology. Instead, it is organized according to how each sculpture engaged with the language of architecture, with chapters devoted to the function and typology of ceilings, walls, and the space between them. Commissions realized by artists like Bertoia, Calder, Lippold, and Noguchi never took on full structural functionality—for example, none of their sculptures proved load bearing—but each utilized materials and processes shared by architecture. These artists, like the architects who commissioned them, possessed distinct styles and arrived at distinct solutions in the face of the challenges presented by modernist architecture. Taken holistically, however, the resulting sculptures deftly engaged the tenets of modernism and charted new directions for its application beyond the rarified space of the art gallery. While each project is discussed against the historically specific context of a short-lived synergy between midcentury sculpture and architecture in the United States, the book concludes by considering how the issues with which these works engaged have attracted considerable attention in recent years, even as many have fallen victim to renovation, redevelopment, and removal.

The projects examined in this book by Bertoia, Calder, Lippold, and Noguchi offer a model, and often hard-learned lessons, of how two disciplines, two approaches to shaping the spaces of everyday life, could combine to create something new, something better. Art historian Alex Potts writes that to consider sculpture is to give prominence to materiality, to "the viewer's more embodied, potentially tactile engagement with things and environments."[71] This is particularly true with sculpture that became the environment itself. The profound, if transitory, alloying that occurred between sculpture and architecture at midcentury broke down disciplinary boundaries, creating a rupture through fusion that in its complexity proved crucial to the building of postwar America, and continues to provide valuable lessons about the purpose of art in the world today.

Chapter 1

The Space Above

In the summer of 1948, one of the first modernist hotels to be built in the postwar period opened in downtown Cincinnati, Ohio. Three years earlier, John J. Emery, then president of Thomas Emery's Sons, hired Skidmore, Owings & Merrill (SOM) to design the eighteen-story Terrace Plaza Hotel (figure 1.1). As was the case with every project at the firm, a team of architects worked collaboratively on the building. Founding partner Louis Skidmore served as the primary contact with Emery, while Bill Brown served as the project's partner-in-charge. Natalie de Blois and William Hartmann worked as the design and management supervisors, respectively. As Hartmann stated of the project, "Jack Emery was wide open for innovation and design of all the hotel, so we assembled a team of people to do interiors of all types... It was a chance to really bring modern design or new ideas about design into a major American project. I don't believe that had ever been done before."[1]

SOM ended up designing Terrace Plaza Hotel as a near "total work," from the china and glassware to the furniture and finishes, and when the $12 million hotel was completed, as one reviewer declared, Cincinnati had "something considerably more modern... than anything New York can boast." De Blois was also responsible for the hotel bedrooms and the circular, top-floor Gourmet Restaurant. The SOM team also included architects Gordon Bunshaft, after he returned from his war service in the army, and Ben Baldwin, who designed the eighth-floor Garden and Lounge. Modernist textile designer Marianne Strengell was responsible for the hotel's textiles, and designer Ward Bennett contributed some lighting features for the lounge spaces and other design elements including a wooden screen in the Gourmet Restaurant.[2]

The hotel also included an extensive program of modern art, which proved to be a defining characteristic of the project. As the president of the Cincinnati Art Museum (CAM) Board of Trustees, Emery was already interested in, or at least

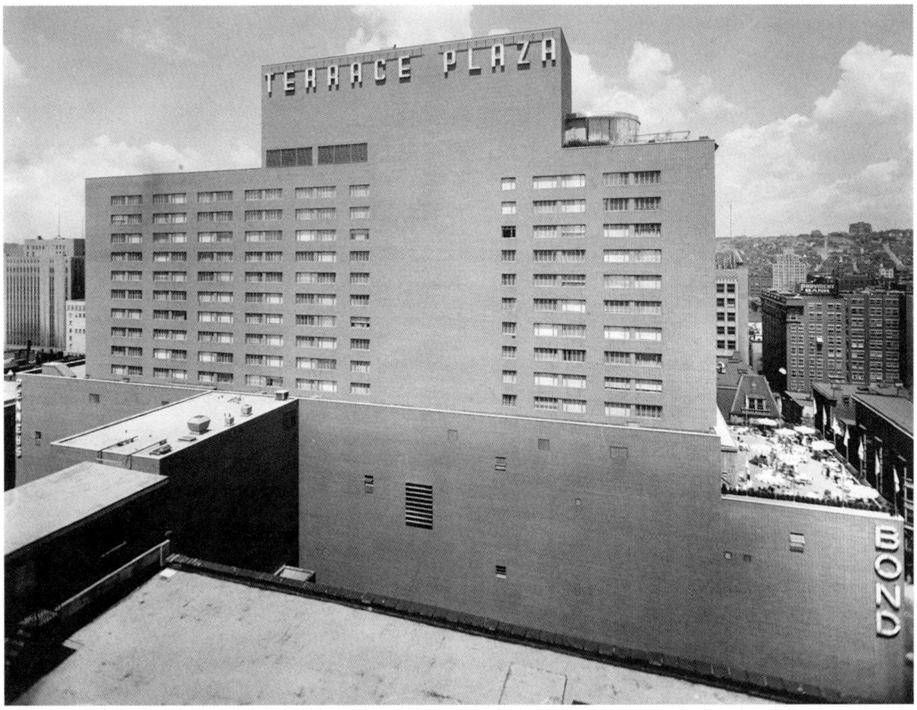

1.1 Terrace Plaza Hotel, 15 West 6th Street, Cincinnati, Ohio, 1946–48. Architect: Skidmore, Owings & Merrill (SOM).

involved with, modern art. Along with Philip R. Adams, the museum's curator, Emery and SOM commissioned multiple works for the hotel. American artist Saul Steinberg's sixteen-hundred-square-foot, multi-paneled *Mural of Cincinnati* (1947) hung in the Skyline Restaurant (figure 1.2). The work, a local favorite, depicted scenes of the city in his trademark style, usually seen in his *New Yorker* drawings. American artist James Davis contributed a group of plexiglass sculptures mounted on the wall of the Terrace Lounge. Spanish artist Joan Miró created a large mural for the hotel's Gourmet Retaurant. A large-scale mobile sculpture by Alexander Calder animated the hotel's main lobby, located on the eighth floor of the building.[3]

The copious amount of press coverage on the Terrace Plaza Hotel focused, however, predominantly on Calder's and Miró's contributions. Both artists completed their works by 1947, but owing to construction delays neither project was installed until the late spring of 1948, just in time for the hotel's opening in July. Calder and Miró were close friends and this was not the first time they had realized commissions for the same architectural project. Architect Josep Lluís Sert commissioned Calder's *Mercury Fountain* and Miró's *Le Faucheur* (*The Reaper*) for his Spanish Pavilion at the 1937 World's Fair in Paris, though Pablo Picasso's *Guernica* (1937) overshadowed their contributions. Calder's and Miró's projects for the Terrace Plaza Hotel did not stylistically deviate from their contemporaneous bodies of work, but the commissions represented a significant increase in size and scale for both artists.[4]

Calder's mobile, *Twenty Leaves and an Apple* (1946), hung from the ceiling in the middle of the hotel's main lobby above a seating area across from the elevator bank, in between the front desk and the entrance to the Terrace in between outdoor and Garden and Lounge (figure 1.3). The exact details of Calder's commission are not exhaustively documented, though Adams and the CAM certainly played a role in securing his participation. The museum previously featured a selection of Calder's work in 1942 as part of an exhibition organized in collaboration with the art dealer Pierre Matisse, who would also prove instrumental in the Miró commission for the Terrace Plaza Hotel. Matisse's wife Alexina "Teeny" Matisse-Sattler was a Cincinnati native, and maintained connections to its business and philanthropic communities. Calder claimed that Bunshaft had been the first to reach out, writing to the artist in Paris in 1946, asking him to "do an object for the Terrace Plaza Hotel."[5]

Regardless of who originally approached Calder about the project, by May 1947 he had submitted a proposal for approval. The work in this initial sketch closely resembled an earlier work he had created for a stage production of Padraic Colum's play *Balloon* at the Ogunquit Playhouse in Maine during the summer of 1946. However, Calder significantly altered the proposed design for the Terrace Plaza Hotel during the fabrication of the sculpture. For example, he changed the color scheme of the cutout sheet-metal shapes, which were originally intended to be red, yellow, blue, and white. The final work abstractly evoked the "leaves" of trees but was painted entirely black, with the exception of a single red disc.[6]

Miró's *Mural for the Terrace Plaza Hotel* (1947) contained similar geometric and organic abstract forms, but was an absolute riot of color, with black, saturated-red, yellow, green, and royal-blue shapes set against a brilliant cerulean-blue background (figure 1.4). The mural-sized canvas ran the length of a curved wall, set behind a row of banquette seating and a structural column in the intimate yet airy rooftop Gourmet Restaurant. Miró originally wanted to paint a fresco on-site and insisted on going to Cincinnati to see the space first, noting that otherwise "I would only create an easel painting in large format." He ended up, however, painting the mural on canvas in a studio in New York City that he rented from the artist Carl Holty.[7]

Though de Blois was not overly involved with the art commissions, she visited Miró at the studio in New York City to see the mural in progress shortly after she finalized the designs for the Gourmet Restaurant. The Museum of Modern Art

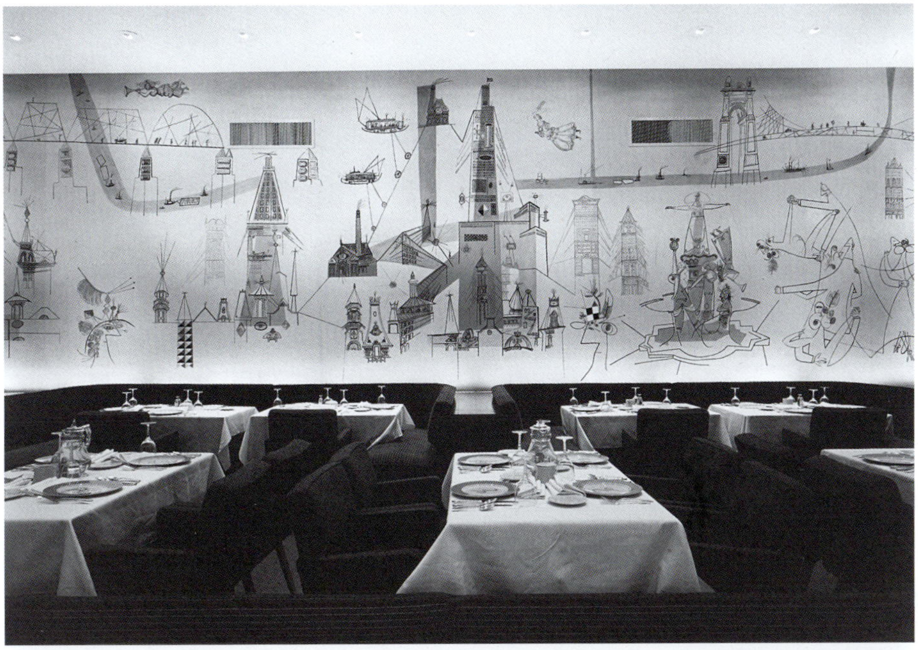

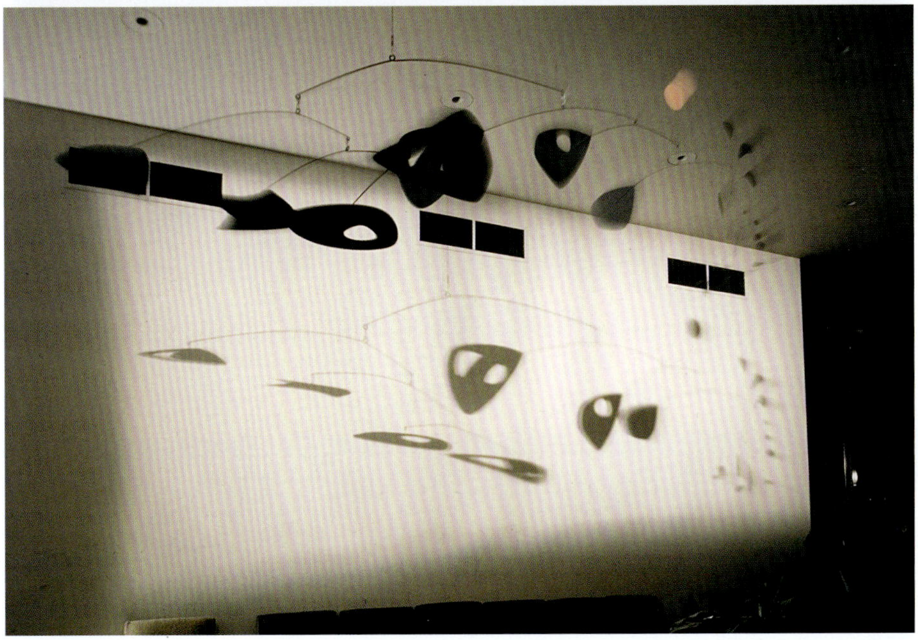

1.2
Saul Steinberg, *Mural of Cincinnati*, 1947. Oil on canvas, six panels. Terrace Plaza Hotel, Cincinnati, Ohio. Architect: Skidmore, Owings & Merrill (SOM).

1.3
Alexander Calder, *Twenty Leaves and an Apple*, 1946. Sheet metal, piano wire, and paint, 48 1/16 in. × 144 1/8 in. Terrace Plaza Hotel, Cincinnati, Ohio. Architect: Skidmore, Owings & Merrill (SOM).

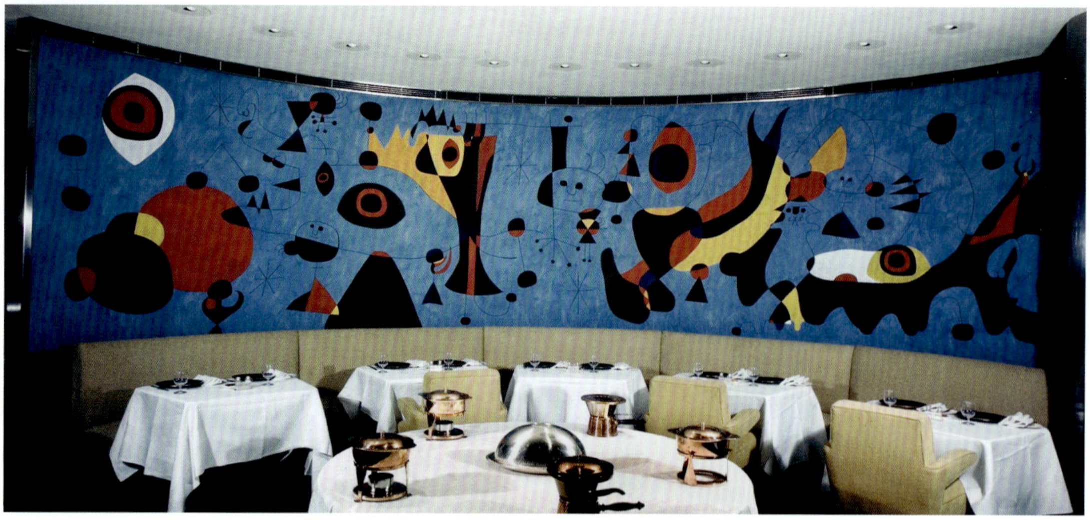

1.4
Joan Miró, *Mural for the Terrace Plaza Hotel, Cincinnati*, 1947. Oil on canvas, 102 in. × 368 1/4 in. Terrace Plaza Hotel, Cincinnati, Ohio. Architect: Skidmore, Owings & Merrill (SOM).

(MoMA) displayed the completed mural soon after, prior to its installation in Cincinnati. *Miró Mural*, a monthlong exhibition financed by Emery and intended to drum up interest in his hotel project among a sophisticated New York City audience, opened in March 1948. The museum presented the mural on a flat wall alongside architectural plans and an uncredited sketch by de Blois, which showed how the work would be installed in the dining room.[8]

The press release for the MoMA exhibition reads more like an advertisement for the progressive modern art program of the Terrace Plaza Hotel than a fine art exhibition, making particular note that works by Calder and Steinberg had also been commissioned for the project in Cincinnati. James Thrall Soby, then chairman of the museum's Department of Painting and Sculpture, echoed Miró in the press release, stating that the artist had not simply "inflated one of his easel works," but "thought out anew the special problems imposed by this panel's size and purpose." Soby, however, also called attention to the inherent functionality of the work, what he referred to as its "decoration." He wrote of the mural: "It is designed to beguile and stimulate, not to puzzle or tax; it is meant to be absorbed pleasurably rather than studied, like music heard through a summer window."[9]

New York Times architectural critic Aline B. Louchheim, who would later become Aline B. Saarinen when she married Eero Saarinen, similarly grappled with the motivations that had led to the commission. In her review of the exhibition, she remarked on both the "intrepid gesture of introducing such advanced art as this to the Cincinnati business section," and the "function and success" of the mural "deliberately as decoration." She noted that de Blois's "installation sketch" demonstrated that the "lunging rhythm of the mural is sympathetic to the circular shape of the glass and metal room," but still discussed the work as exemplary of a "growing conviction that extreme abstract painting is most suitable as a part of the modern décor." She concluded by describing Miró's mural as a "gay and diverting backdrop."[10] The subsequent coverage of the arts program at Terrace Plaza Hotel was largely positive, even enthusiastic, but there was a similar undercurrent of tension or critical unease with its method of display and use—as already expressed in Louchheim's initial assessment of Miró's mural.

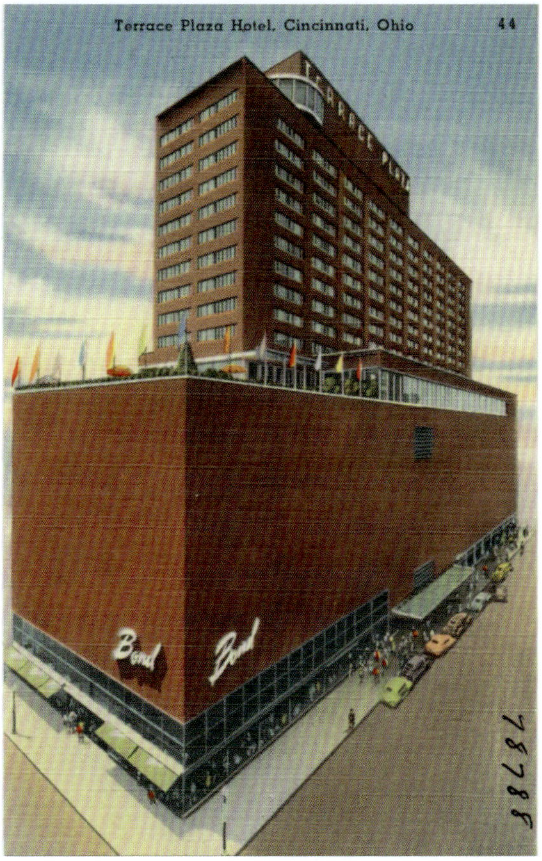

1.5
Terrace Plaza Hotel, Cincinnati, Ohio. Postcard, c. late 1940s. Tichnor Brothers Postcard Collection, Boston Public Library, Massachusetts.

While most critics seemed to celebrate the introduction of modern art in architecture through such a high-profile project, many distinguished what was visible in the Gourmet Restaurant or the hotel lobby from the kind of modernism presented in galleries and museums. One critic wrote that the commissions represented "modern art at its most frivolous (and therefore in this case most apt). For these designs are perfectly suited to their job of putting café customers in a mood of lighthearted and sophisticated gaiety." Louchheim similarly called attention to the fact that since "dining and drinking" was involved the spectator would be "in no mood for serious art," but "may happily find his eye beguiled by brilliant color or arrested by the movement of a well-conceived design, neither capricious nor pretentious."[11]

The exhibition at MoMA proved to be only one part of a widespread promotional plan to publicize the Terrace Plaza Hotel with its innovative modernist architecture and modern art (figure 1.5). In addition to regional publications, national outlets like *Fortune, Harper's, Life,* and *Time* as well as more industry-specific publications like *Art Digest*, *Hotel Monthly*, and *Architectural Forum*, among others, printed substantial features on Terrace Plaza. *Architectural Forum* alone published four feature spreads on the project between December 1946 and December 1948. Renowned architectural photographer Ezra Stoller shot many of the images used to illustrate these features, all of which touted the radical newness of the building and the holistic approach of both the client and the architects in incorporating the visual arts.[12]

The press noted the unusual location of the lobby on the eighth floor, the technologically advanced lighting and air-conditioning systems, and the modern interior design of the hotel rooms. They also, however, paid great attention to the art, to how the "surrealist stencils" and "delicate yet arresting traceries" played off against the other notable modern elements of a building project one critic referred to as a "new marriage of culture and commerce" and another "a triumphant marriage of art and economics." The costs of the commissioned artworks were justified for the "very compelling reason that good art brings prestige—helpful to all hotels, essential to new ones." Or as *Architectural Forum* remarked, "By integrating into the scheme of appropriately 'fresh' works of top-flight contemporary artists, and by making every plane, every surface and color, carry its freight of decorative expression, the architects have achieved an atmosphere at once light and refreshing." The consensus that emerged across the press revolved around not just the presence of art, but more importantly its combination with architecture and industry, which had merged to create "a prototype of the mid-century hotel" and "something entirely new."[13]

The inclusion of art at the Terrace Plaza Hotel lent the project a certain level of cultural capital and decorative glamour, both reinforcing and complicating the modernist design of the hotel. Although one of the earliest attempts to bring together art and architecture during the postwar period, the heavy reliance of wall-supported work reinforced associations with benign decoration and the application of something on a surface meant to provide visual interest. Miró's and Steinberg's murals were tremendous artistic achievements that contributed to, and even arguably defined, their respective architectural spaces, but both were still paintings hung on a wall, whether curved or long. While Miró's may have been the most remarked-on artwork commissioned for the Terrace Plaza Hotel, the sculptural contributions warrant further analysis, especially for how they activated and alloyed with the surrounding architecture.

Looking into the lobby from the outdoor Garden and Lounge on the eighth floor, both Davis's colorful plexiglass constructions and Calder's mobile were visible, the latter through a glass dividing wall between the two areas (figure 1.6). Davis's three constructions were reliefs and, like the two murals, still relied on the support of a wall, but their transparency and use of light as an integral aspect of the work extended their reach and effect beyond the physical boundaries of the sculptures. For Davis, traditional forms of media were too static and thus were becoming obsolete. He argued that contemporary artists should follow modern architects using "modern materials," and adopt the "new tools and materials which modern science and industry provide." Davis and Calder both embraced this approach, though in their own unique way. Their plastic and metal sculptures shared a material language with the architecture of the hotel as a whole. Perhaps even more crucially, though, it was through lighting that their "fitness for the space they occupy" truly became tied into the total scheme.[14]

Modern lighting techniques played a supporting, even vital, role in the realization of commissioned sculpture. Artists had to take into account how their work would “absorb, reflect, and vary the intense light of modern buildings,” as architectural historian Eleanor Bittermann stated. Two-dimensional works also had to contend with lighting designed to illuminate their surfaces within a given space. This could certainly alter the experience of the architecture, as evidenced by the dramatic moody effect cast over Steinberg’s mural at the Terrace Plaza Hotel. For sculpture, with its inherent three-dimensionality and greater volumetric occupation of space, lighting became a material extension of its form. In Davis’s case, the spotlights merged and refracted the planes of colored plexiglass, creating shadows well beyond the boundaries of the sculpture’s physical shape. *Twenty Leaves and an Apple* was also intentionally lit to cast shadows, increasing the reach of the work and creating an “ever-changing pattern” on the white walls facing the elevators. Because Calder’s sculpture was not just an open lithe object, but it also hung from the ceiling, it operated in a far more dynamic and structural manner than any

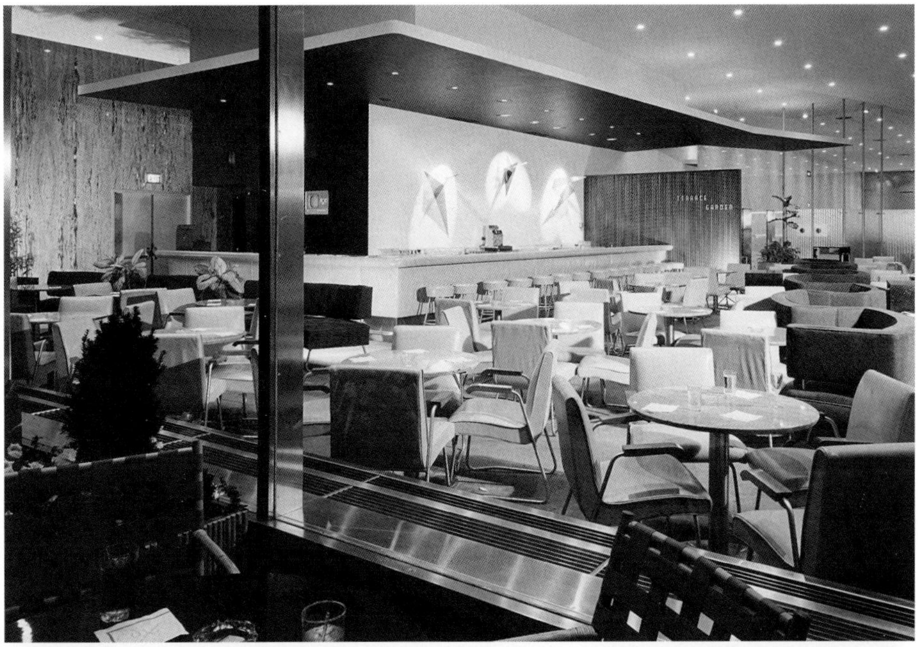

1.6
Terrace Garden, Terrace Plaza Hotel, Cincinnati, Ohio, 1959. Architect: Skidmore, Owings & Merrill (SOM).

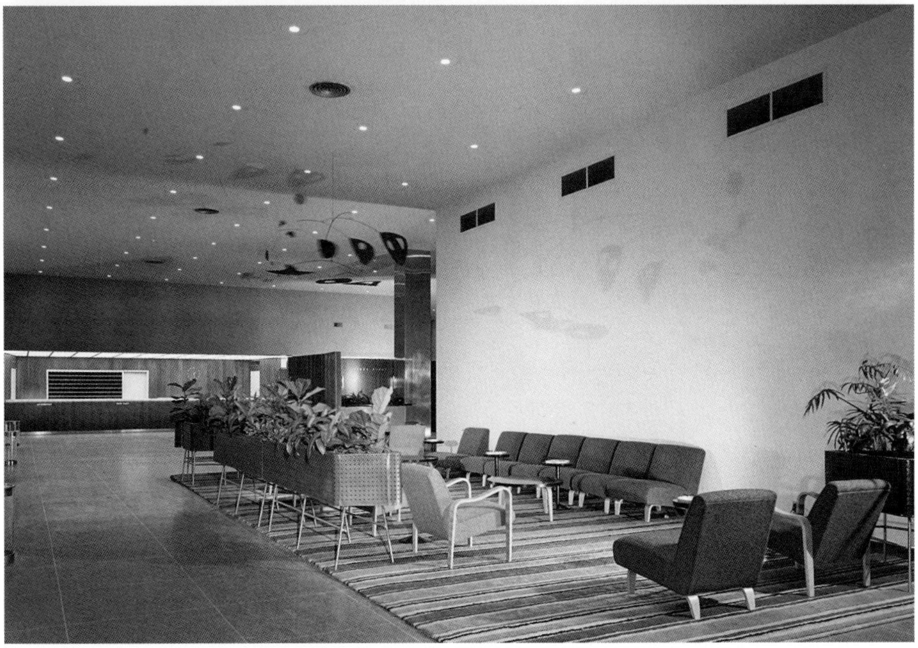

1.7
Alexander Calder, *Twenty Leaves and an Apple*, 1946. Sheet metal, piano wire, and paint, 48 1/16 in. × 144 1/8 in. Terrace Plaza Hotel, Cincinnati, Ohio. Architect: Skidmore, Owings & Merrill (SOM).

other art included in the hotel. The mobile as a form was already a marvel of midcentury artistic kineticism; but applied here, on a larger scale and commissioned for a specific space, it highlighted new ways that sculpture could operate with and within architecture. As visible in an intentionally blurred photograph by Stoller, the thin metal plates suspended on piano wire regularly swayed and swirled because the sculpture was placed near two vents of the sophisticated central air-conditioning system of the hotel (figure 1.7).[15]

On the most basic level, the lighting effects and movement of *Twenty Leaves and an Apple* created a dynamic decorative visual interest in the Terrace Plaza Hotel lobby, bringing a "gaiety into [the] ascetic surroundings" of the engineered environment, as Bitterman phrased it. The work became a place marker, an object under which people met, and because of its unique placement on the ceiling it functioned like a chandelier—an aspect that the lighting further accentuated. The emphasis on light and kineticism, however, is also what helped alloy the artwork with the architecture. The power of the sculpture did not only come from its form or functionality, but also from how well the work responded to the specifics of the lobby, which, in turn, altered the experience and flow of the space. Calder's mobile for the Terrace Plaza Hotel became something of an architectural keystone, while simultaneously existing extraneously to the space of the lobby—as a functional object and a useless sculptural thing. Removing it would not destabilize the lobby's structural integrity, but it would radically alter the design integrity of the space and function of the sculpture itself.[16]

Calder was not the only sculptor to mine the potential of ceilings during the postwar period. Isamu Noguchi took a slightly different path, creating sculptures that became actual lit ceilings, as he did in 1948 for Harris Armstrong's American Stove Company Building in St. Louis, Missouri. Richard Lippold—in his commissions for Max Abramovitz's Philharmonic Hall at Lincoln Center for Performing Arts in New York City in 1962 and the Caudill Rowlett Scott–designed Jesse H. Jones Hall in Houston, Texas in 1966—like Calder, created sculpture that hung from ceilings. All these projects directly confronted the encumbered traditions and connotations of the decorative, leading to comparisons with chandeliers and other ornamental lighting fixtures. Each sculpture, however, also adopted a more pronounced structural functionality by activating what is often dead or empty space in threshold interiors. Harry Bertoia's 1955 screen for the Dallas Public Library in Texas, the final case study examined in this chapter, also hung from a ceiling, but instead offers a complex, controversial counterpoint to similar commissions from the postwar period. The difficult circumstances of its installation demonstrated the fine balance between artist, architect, and client, as well as artwork and site, needed to achieve a synergy between sculpture and architecture.

Sculpture as Ceiling

In 1946, the new centralized administrative building for the American Stove Company opened in St. Louis, Missouri (figure 1.8). The six-story modern glass and local-brick structure included offices for accounting, sales, and executives, as well as a library, cafeteria, and boardroom, all of which occupied the top five floors. The company hired architect Harris Armstrong, who had made his name in St. Louis designing modern structures that blended the International Style with a more regional approach influenced by both Scandinavian architecture and fellow midwesterner Frank Lloyd Wright. The American Stove Company, the leading manufacturer of gas ranges in the United States at the time, dictated that the ground floor of the building feature a showroom for its popular Magic Chef appliances. Armstrong amplified the display possibilities of the space by doubling it in height and enclosing it on three sides with glass curtain walls, making it open and airy (figure 1.9). There was a curving central staircase that went up to a sales office on the mezzanine level, with additional space given to a customer lounge, main lobby, reception desk, and a two-car elevator bay.[17]

The elevator bay provided a design challenge, as the area was not immediately visible from the entrance and main space of the lobby (figure 1.10). Armstrong approached Isamu Noguchi to help solve the problem, commissioning him to create a sculptural ceiling feature that would help lead visitors to the elevator. The architect stated, "I had an idea that Isamu could create forms that would compel people around the corner to the doors."[18] Armstrong discussed the plan with the president of the American Stove Company while the building was under construction and took the architectural drawings to Noguchi. The artist then produced a one-inch-scale plaster model that would address the specific issues of the space (figure 1.11).

Armstrong's firm prepared working drawings from Noguchi's model. Blueprints dated from 1946, for example, clearly show the outline of Noguchi's ceiling sculpture (figure 1.12). Local fabricators from the Robert Campbell Plastering Company, or "union mechanics" as *Architectural Forum* described them in their extensive feature on the completed building, realized the sculpture at the

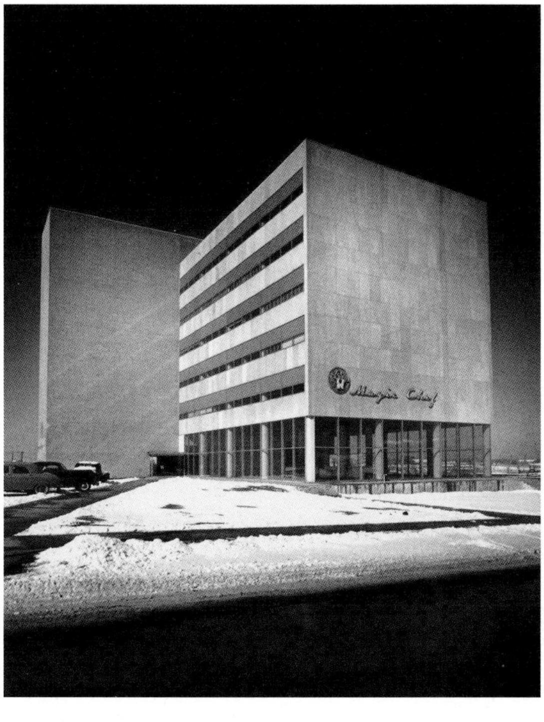

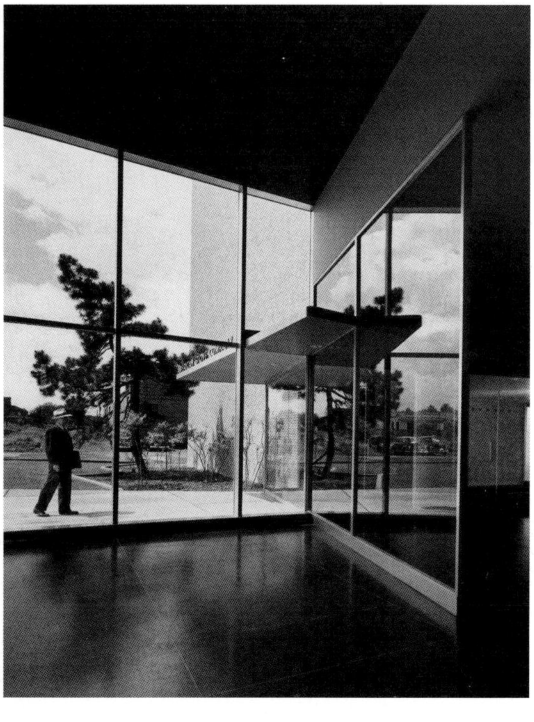

1.8
American Stove Company Building, 1641 South Kingshighway Boulevard, St. Louis, Missouri, 1946–48. Architect: Harris Armstrong.

1.9
Lobby (looking outward toward entrance) of the American Stove Company Building, St. Louis, Missouri, 1946–48. Architect: Harris Armstrong. Harris Armstrong Collection, 1924–1972. University Archives, Department of Special Collections, Washington University Libraries, St. Louis, Missouri.

1.10
Entrance of the American Stove Company Building, St. Louis, Missouri, 1946–48. Architect: Harris Armstrong. Harris Armstrong Collection, 1924–1972. University Archives, Department of Special Collections, Washington University Libraries, St. Louis, Missouri.

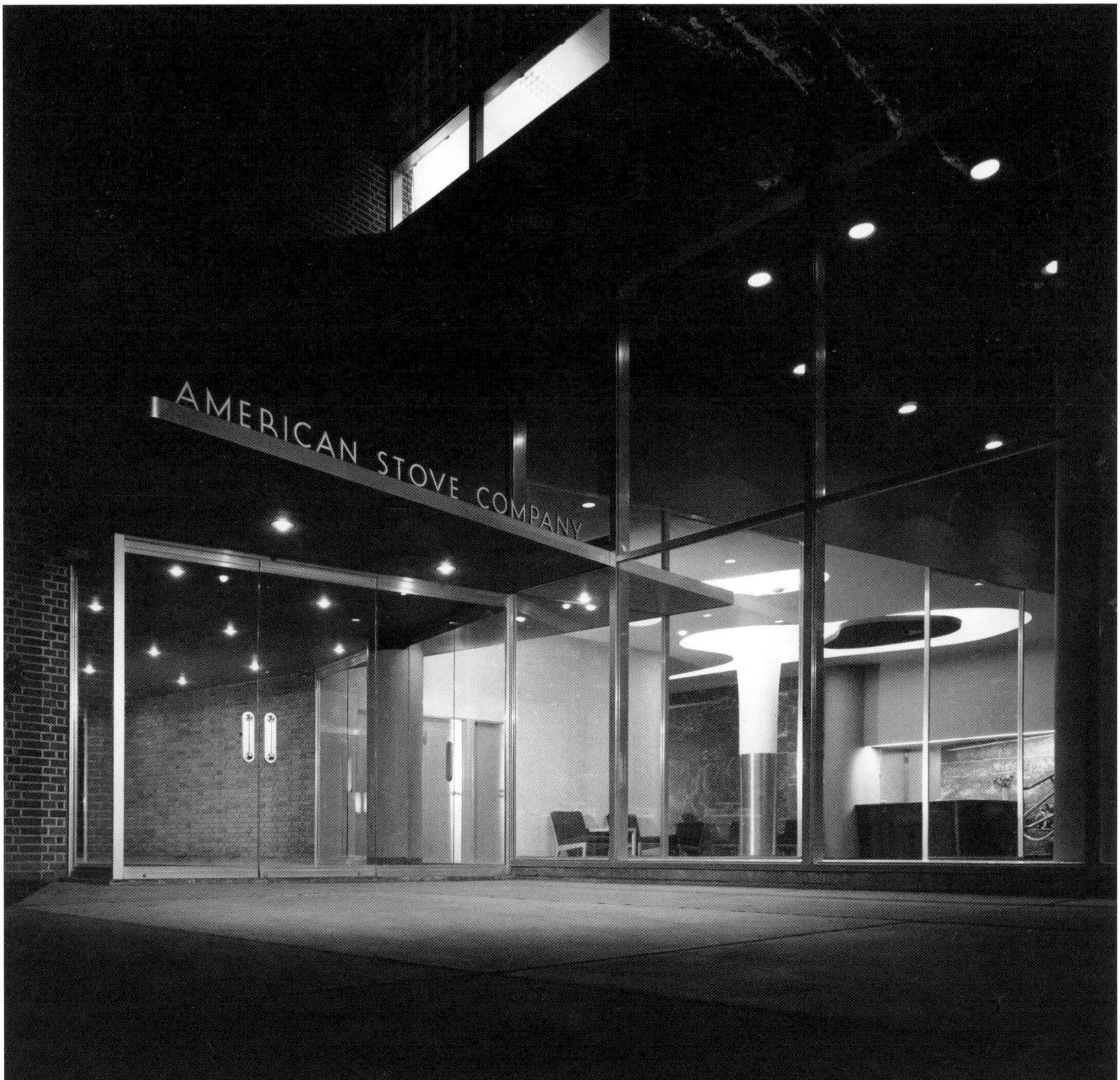

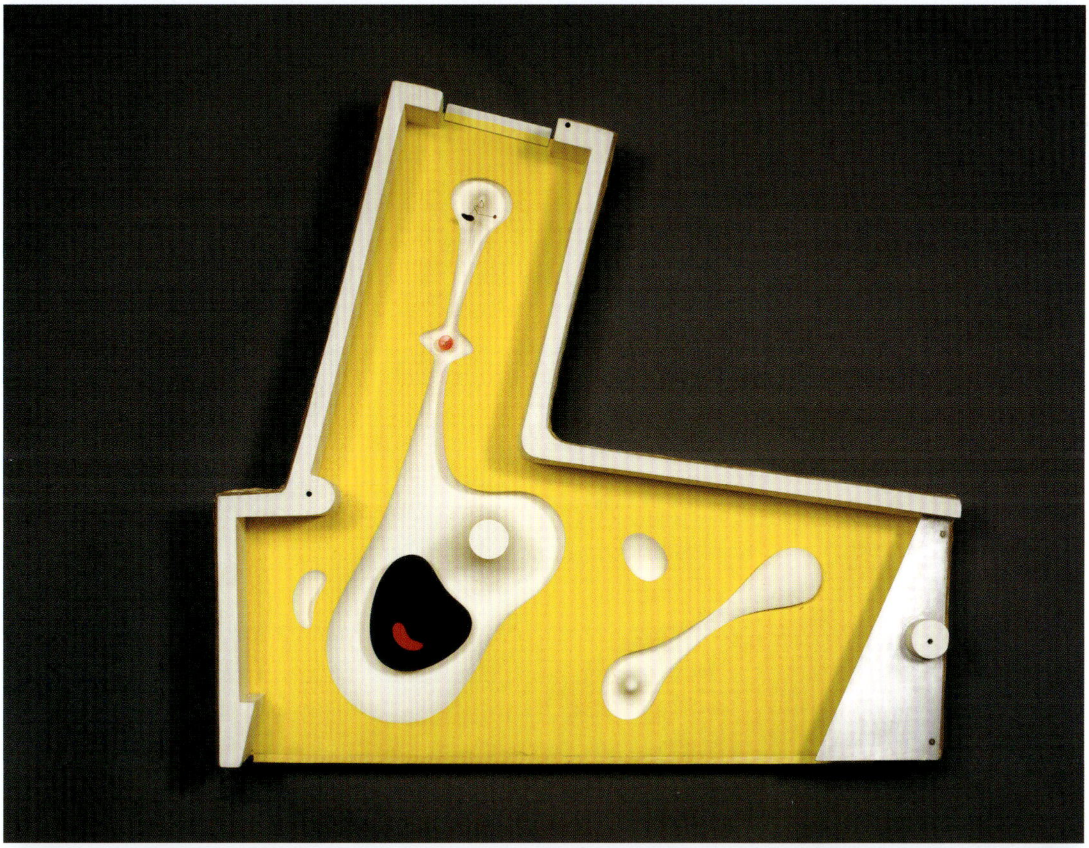

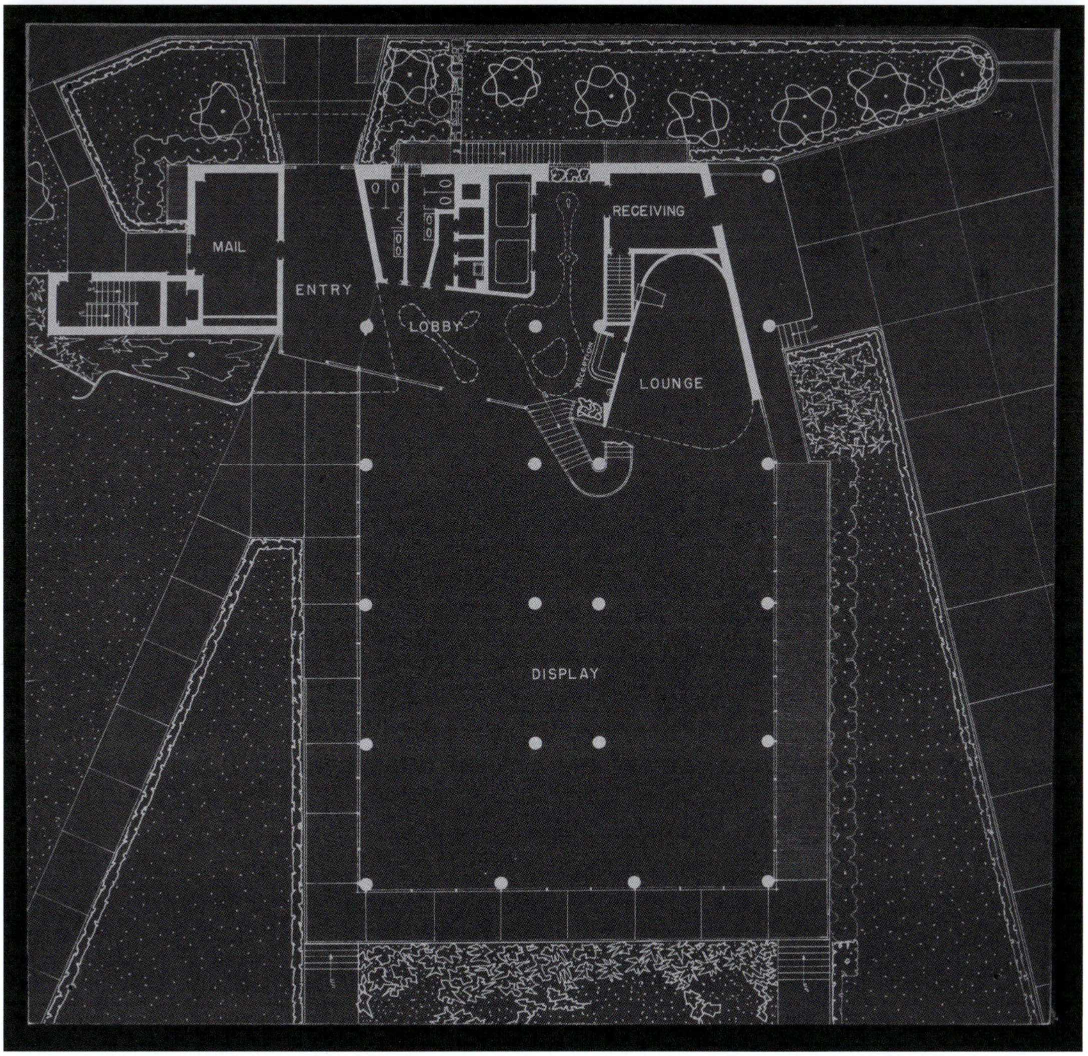

1.11
Isamu Noguchi, *Model for Lobby Ceiling, American Stove Company Building*, 1946–47. Plaster, wire, plexiglass, and aluminum, 40 3/8 in. × 43 in. × 7 1/2 in. Saint Louis Art Museum, Missouri. Gift of Mr. and Mrs. Harris Armstrong, 86: 1970.

1.12
Plot Plan (detail) for the American Stove Company Building, 1946. Architect: Harris Armstrong. Harris Armstrong Collection, 1924–1972. University Archives, Department of Special Collections, Washington University Libraries, St. Louis, Missouri.

job site. They used Noguchi's model, but there seems to have been some consternation during the process. Armstrong wrote to the sculptor that there had been "quite a bit of conversation about the method of executing the ceiling," but that it was decided to "direct it in metal lath and plaster on the job, with full size templates." He expressed hope that Noguchi would not mind how they fabricated the work as "long as we get the final results you contemplate." In this regard Noguchi's sculpture did not only mirror the surrounding architecture through materials, but also was executed in a similar manner, with design plans realized by a team of skilled construction laborers.[19]

Both the design and final result of Noguchi's commission consisted of three, sinuous sculptural incisions into the ceiling over the lobby, just past the main entrance of the building (figure 1.13). All three cavities incorporated recessed lighting. The form closest to the front doors was a relatively slender, oblong shape, its center portion narrower than its two curved ends. A protruding nodule emerged from cutout ceiling on the end closest to the showroom. There was also a flat, curving mass that swelled from the center point into a flattened balloon shape. Hung a few inches from the topmost section of the ceiling it obscured the light bulbs placed behind, casting the form in shadow. Just beyond was the smallest element: an imperfect circle resembling a Swiss-cheese hole lit by a single bulb that illuminated its lipped edge. The largest principal form encircled one of the columns visible on the ground floor—itself plastered white with a polished metal covering beginning halfway down. At the other end, a dark irregular globular form, made of opaque glass, seemed to hover, hanging from the scored ceiling. Standing in the lobby, this kidney shape narrowed and continued past the corner, progressing as a thinner strip that flowed around two additional distensions: a dark circular disk and another vertically extending node, with a metal arrow hanging from its end, pointing to the elevators below.

Crucial to Noguchi's design were the layered permutation of plastic form, whether cut into or built up, and electric light. The American Stove Company commission emerged from a longstanding interest the artist had in creating illuminated sculptures. While he did not design his Akari lamps until the early 1950s, he began experimenting with electric lighting early in the 1920s and 1930s in neon works such as *Power House* (1928) and his *Musical Weathervanes* (1933). The series of works from the early 1940s that Noguchi referred to as the Lunars, however, possessed the clearest affinity with the American Stove Company Building ceiling. Made from modeled magnesite, or magnesium oxychloride, these sculptures bubbled and bulged, broken up by gashes and folds that revealed their defining feature: hidden recessed light bulbs. Noguchi first used magnesite in his *Chassis Fountain* (1938) at the 1939 World's Fair in New York, after being introduced to the material by Buckminster Fuller, though this was neither the first nor the last time the artist would embrace new industrial materials to create sculpture (figure 1.14). As Noguchi wrote, "The question is whether they will be used to advantage, for new concepts born of their time, or whether they are to be degraded as handicrafts and all the abominations of commercial decoration. The answer is a matter of

1.13
Isamu Noguchi, *Ceiling for Magic Chef Building*, 1948. Interior design with plaster, colored glass, and electric components, dimensions variable. American Stove Company Building, St Louis, Missouri. Architect: Harris Armstrong.

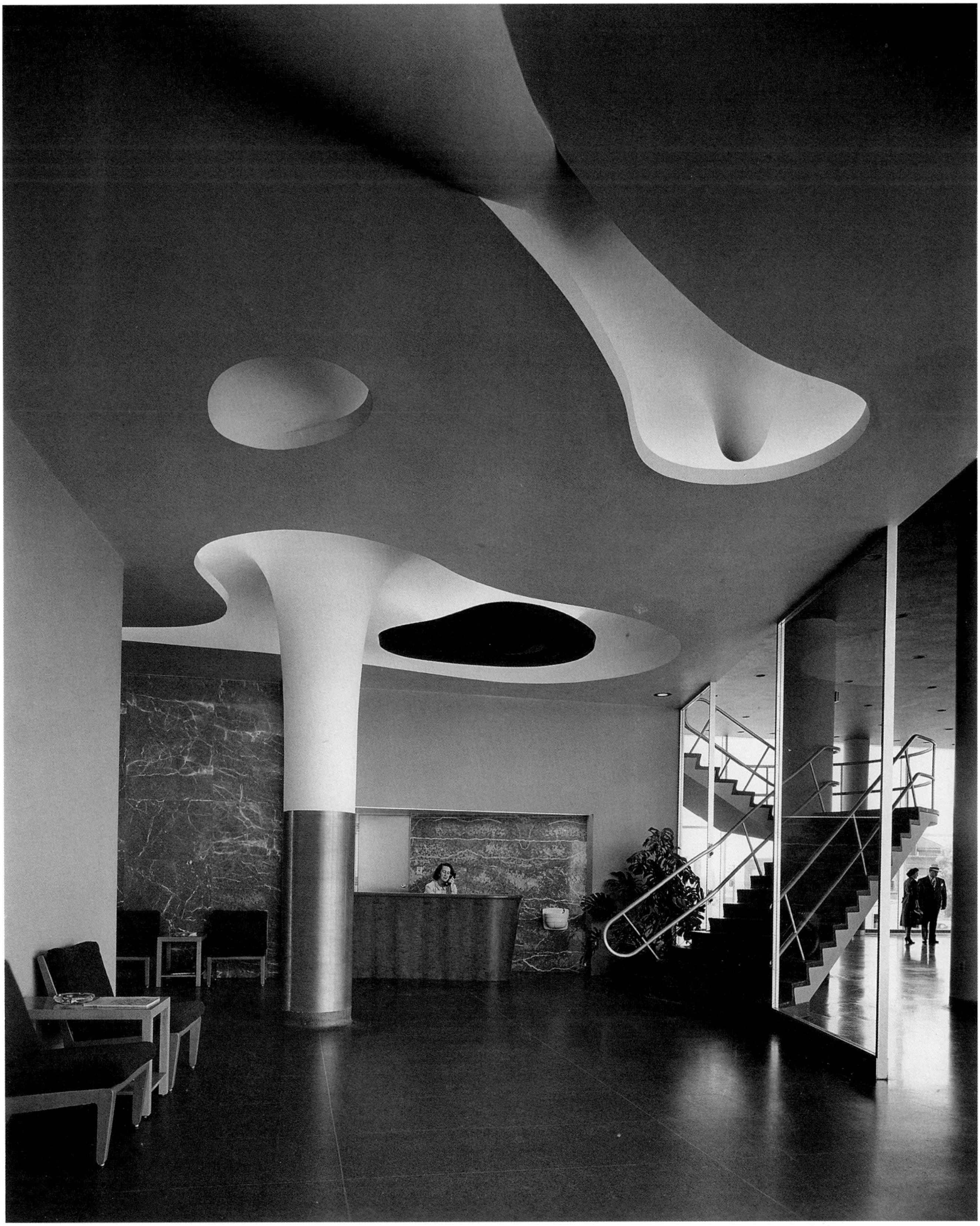

choice—it depends on our taste, our sense of materials, and finally, on our concept of what is sculpture and what is not." Noguchi's Lunars indeed represented a new conception of the medium: one that merged decorative lighting elements with biomorphic plastic innovation (figure 1.15).[20]

Some examples, like *Lunar Infant* (1944), hung from sculptural framework supports, while others, like *Red Lunar Fist* (1944), were more contained, organically shaped objects. Others were panels that became "lunar landscapes," affixed like wall reliefs or sometimes laid on a horizontal support. As art historian Bruce Altshuler writes, these works "seamlessly bridged the gap between fine and functional art." Indeed, they were described in the press at the time as "lamps" and "light plaques" meant "to be hung on [a] wall as a piece of plaster sculpture as well as a source of soft light." Arthur Drexler, curator and architectural editor for *Interiors*, noted in a substantial feature on new trends in lighting in architecture and interior design: "Since the appearance of sculpture is inextricably bound up with the light by which we see it, it is rather surprising that sculptors have done almost nothing about light." The exception, according to Drexler, was Noguchi, who "uses light as a palpable and controlled factor." *Lunar Landscape* (1943) and *Floating Lunar* (1943–44) were the only examples of artwork to be included in the

1.14
Isamu Noguchi, *Ford Fountain for the New York World's Fair (Chassis Fountain)*, 1938. Magnesite. 1939 World's Fair, Flushing Meadows, New York.

1.15
Isamu Noguchi, *Lunar Landscape*, 1943. Magnesite cement, electric lights, colored acetate sheets, cork, and string, 35 in × 25 1/4 in. × 7 in. Crystal Bridges Museum of American Art, Bentonville, Arkansas. 2006.101.

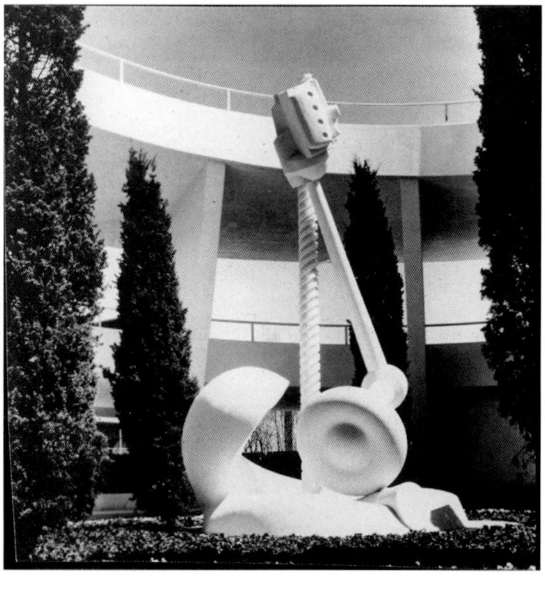

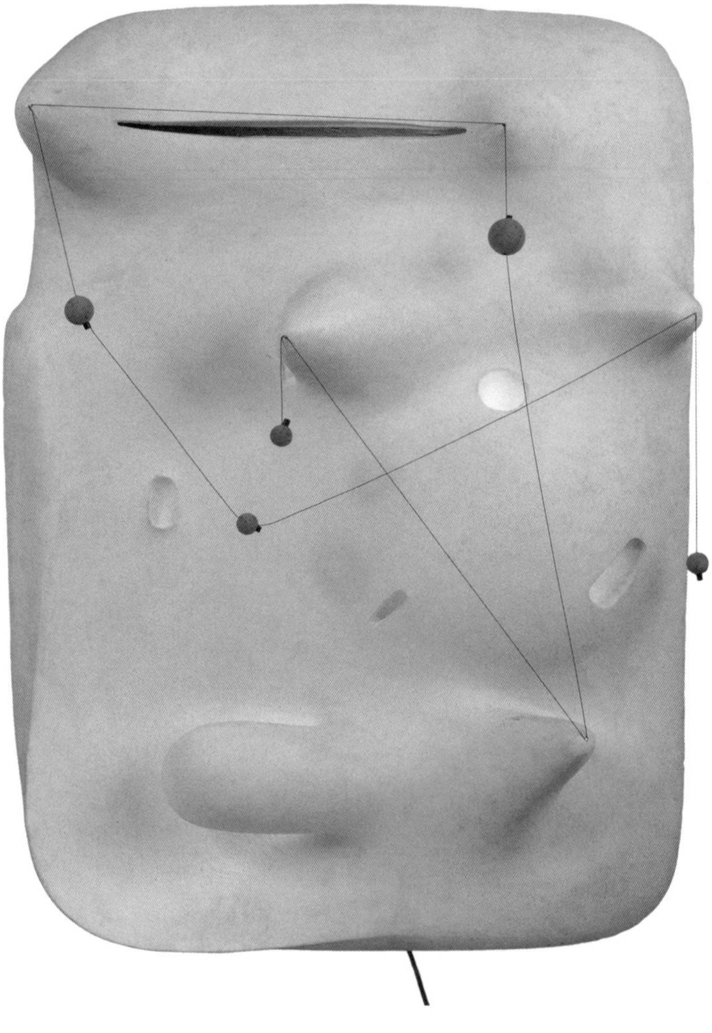

spread, illustrated alongside new goods by Sylvania Electric Products and flush ceiling fixtures designed by Finnish architect Aarno Ervi.[21]

Noguchi himself discussed the Lunars as sculptures or "self-illuminated" and "self-contained luminous objects." Though he had begun with the smaller panels and forms, he realized that their true potential was in the creation of an environment or "entire space." He wrote, "I thought of a room of music and light, a porous room within a room—in the void of space." Noguchi had the opportunity to adapt the approach on a much larger environmental scale for a handful of commissions during the late 1940s. For example, he suspended *Floating Lunar* (1948) close to the ceiling, hovering like a cloud over a table he also designed for the Chappaqua, New York, private residence of Mr. and Mrs. Samuel Dretzin. His largest commission made from magnesite and electric light in 1947 was *Lunar Voyage* (figure 1.16). The sculpture was embedded into a hallway wall of the SS *Argentina*, a luxury liner converted from a troopship in 1946 with interiors completely redesigned by Donald Deskey and billed as a "floating art gallery." However, formally, the most similar to the American Stove Company Building commission was the ceiling of the Reception Area at the Time & Life Building at 1 Rockefeller Plaza, New York City, which Harrison, Fouilhoux & Abramovitz designed (figure 1.17). Commissioned in 1944, the ceiling design also included biomorphic cutouts, and was executed in plaster.[22]

Noguchi's American Stove Company Building project, like all of the Lunars, was a conspicuous visual element in an interior space, incorporating electric light and made from a novel application of industrial building materials, in this case plaster and metal lath. To this latter point, the Metal Lath Manufacturers Association even featured the work in a sixteen-page advertorial in the September 1956 issue of *Progressive Architecture* as an "outstanding example of the manner in which metal lath and plaster can be adapted to ornamental requirements." The sculpture was one of

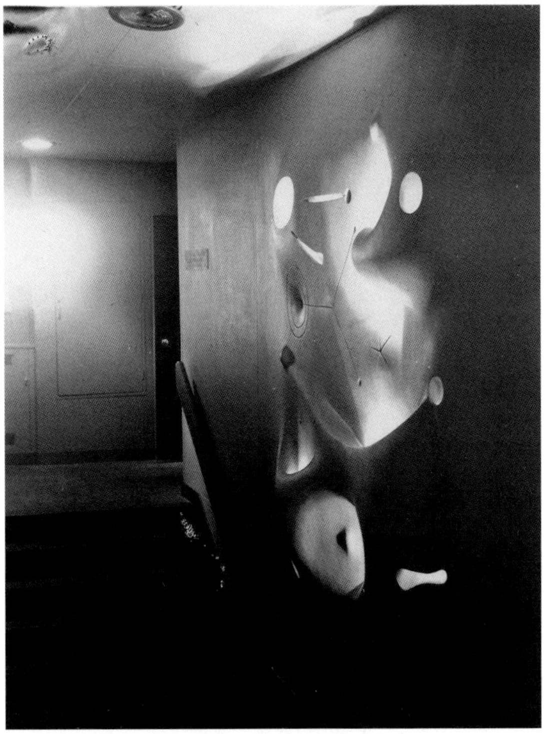

1.16
Isamu Noguchi, *Lunar Voyage*, 1947. Magnesite. Commissioned for the SS *Argentina*.

the most elaborate and largest of the "lunar landscapes" Noguchi realized, and met more than the ornamental requirements of the building.[23]

From the outset, Noguchi's commission for the American Stove Company Building was conceived as a useful architectural element. Both the contract between Armstrong and Noguchi and the subsequent press coverage described the sculpture as a "lighting recess" and "ceiling light fixture." Like the Time & Life Building ceiling, the amoeba-like and small circular incisions of the work in St. Louis created a visually arresting decorative focal point within a relatively spartan interior design. Like all of the Lunars, it possessed the ornamental functionality of a light fixture, serving as the main illuminating element in the lobby space. The American Stove Company Building ceiling, however, was more than ornamental. The sculpture conveyed a very clear directional function, literally pointing the way to the elevators, helping guide visitors and employees through the entrance space.[24]

Noguchi also attentively aligned the form of his sculptural ceiling with Armstrong's overall architectural design. As *Architectural Forum* enthusiastically noted, the American Stove Company Building achieved the difficult combination of fulfilling the physical needs of the client company while at the same time standing as "an attractive monument to their enterprise." The publication specifically highlighted Noguchi's illuminated ceiling, declaring that it was a "sculpture integral with the architecture… The highly successful work surely is unique in institutional building, together with the spirit that prompted and encouraged it." One of the most immediately apparent ways this occurred was through color. The ceilings in the display area of Magic Chef appliances were a deep blue, and

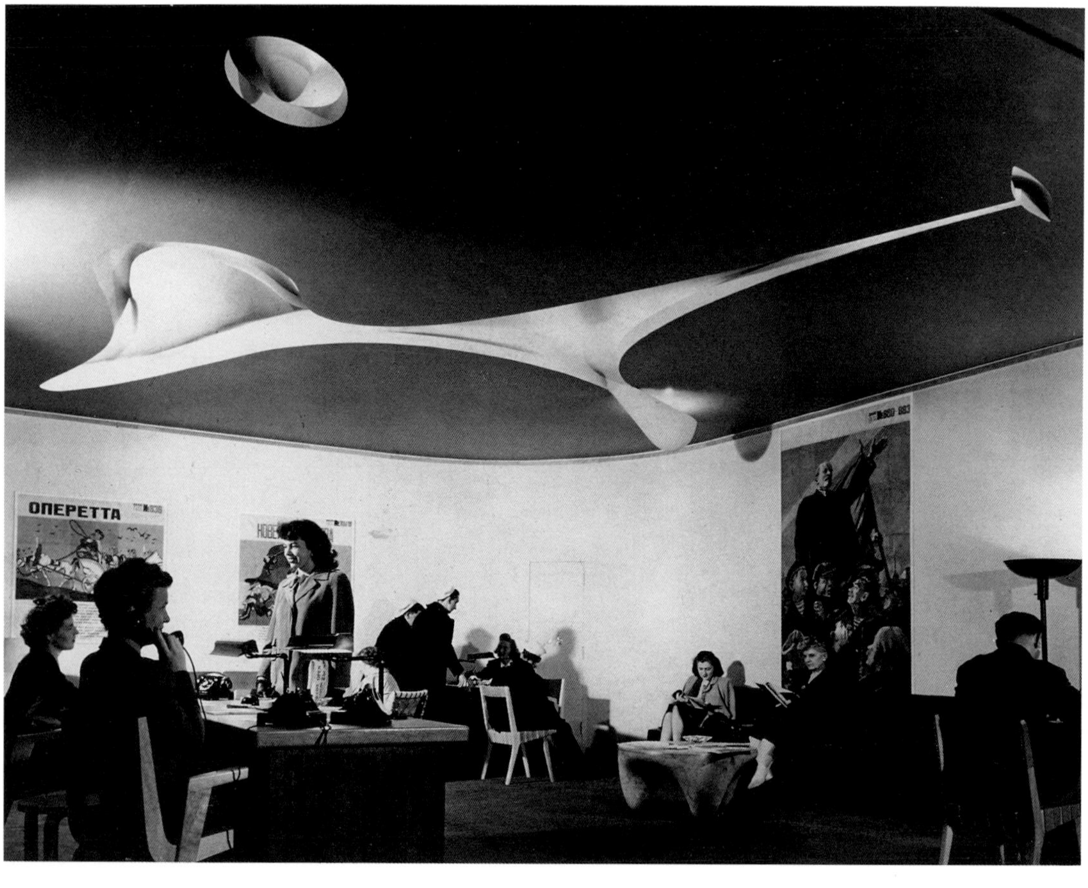

1.17
Isamu Noguchi's interior for Reception Area, Time & Life Building, 1 Rockefeller Plaza, New York City, 1944. Interior design with plaster and electric components, dimensions variable. Architect: Harrison, Fouilhoux & Abramovitz.

the drop ceiling in the lobby, a citrine yellow. Noguchi's design strategy mirrors Armstrong's, using the same color choices to highlight details of his protruding biomorphic shapes. Evident, even in the model, is Noguchi's complementary selection of saturated pops of color, including the blue opaque-glass shape that contrasts against the pure white of the recessed features.[25]

Whether because of mutual influence or simply a sympathy of forms, there are many elements of Armstrong's design throughout the rest of the building that resonate with Noguchi's ceiling feature in the lobby. Photographs of American Stove Company president Arthur Stockstrom's office, for example, showed a sculptural colored wall panel in between two doors that almost reached up to the ceiling, where a curved perpendicular panel extended outward creating the effect of a drop-ceiling (figures 1.18, 1.19). Recessed can lights spotlighted the desk and seating areas, but a backlit section that curved around the exposed concrete column cast a Noguchi-like effect over the entirety of the space. Similar backlit drop panels were used over the table in the boardroom and above the customer waiting area on the ground floor, where a flat circular disk was installed amid multiple layers of increasingly large, curved panels.[26]

Noguchi's work set a visual and spatial tone as soon as a visitor or employee entered the American Stove Company Building, which Armstrong's design continued to express on every successive floor. The commission served as a sculpture, a lighting fixture, directional signage, a decorative element, and quite simply, a designed ceiling. As Noguchi said in conjunction with the project, "The sculpture should no longer be something just stuck on architecture, but a development of the architecture itself—what you might call an emotionally functional

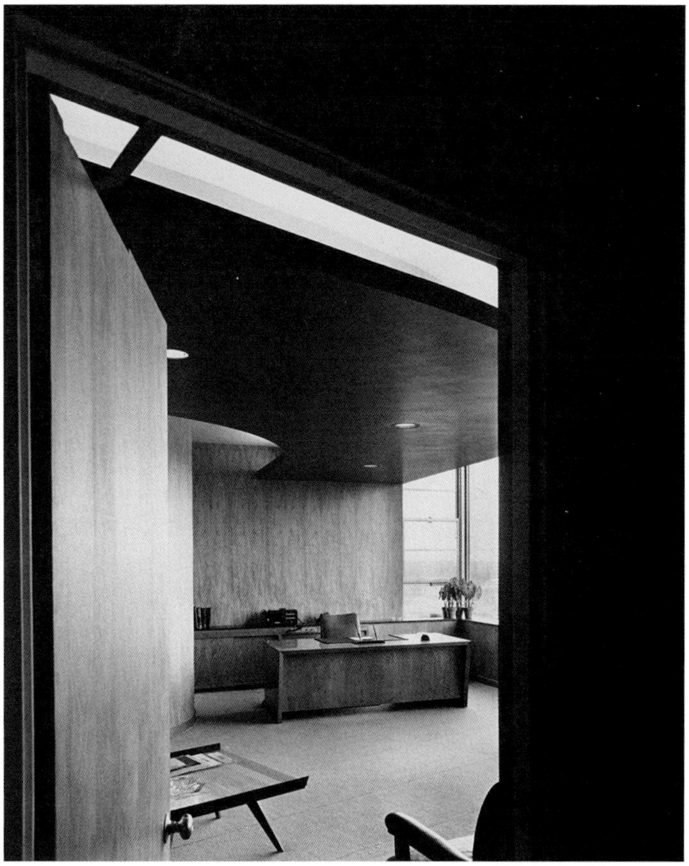

1.18 Office of president Arthur Stockstrom, American Stove Company Building, St. Louis, Missouri, 1948. Architect: Harris Armstrong. Harris Armstrong Collection, 1924–1972, University Archives, Department of Special Collections, Washington University Libraries, St. Louis, Missouri.

1.19
Office of president Arthur Stockstrom, American Stove Company Building, St. Louis, Missouri, 1948. Architect: Harris Armstrong. Harris Armstrong Collection, 1924–1972, Department of Special Collections, Washington University Libraries, St. Louis, Missouri.

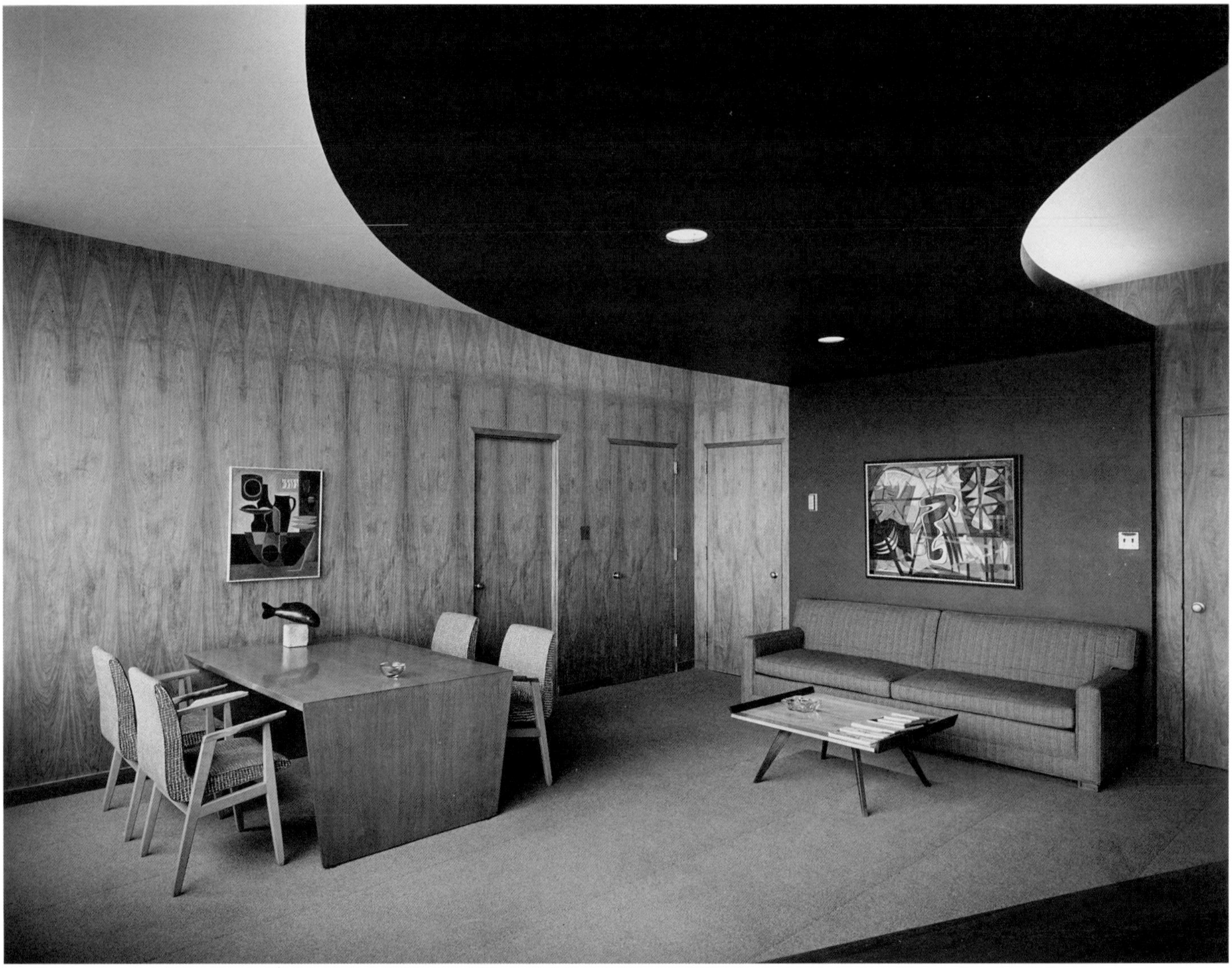

as well as just a mechanically functional thing—to accent and punctuate, giving dimensions to space." The sculpture at the American Stove Company Building activated and extended the ceiling in an innovative way, but also further intensified the connection between art, design, and architecture, collapsing the boundaries between them. The play of inverted and extruding forms, amplified by the recessed lighting elements, effectively turned sculpture into ceiling and ceiling into sculpture.[27]

Chandeliers for the Space Age

Many commissions during the immediate postwar period investigated the possibilities of sculptural ceilings or ceiling sculptures. Most artists did not do so through an upward or inward activation like Noguchi achieved for the American Stove Company Building, but rather by extending space downward by hanging objects from ceilings. A decade after the Terrace Plaza Hotel, for example, Calder and SOM collaborated again on a large-scale mobile, which hung in the center of the vaulted lobby of the International Arrivals Building (IAB) at Idlewild, then officially known as the New York International Airport (NYIA; now John F. Kennedy International Airport, figure 1.20). Opened in 1957, the IAB was part of a 660-acre core called Terminal City that had been master planned by the Port Authority of New York and New Jersey's Aviation Planning Division and headed by Thomas M. Sullivan in consultation with Wallace K. Harrison.

The new airport comprised numerous decentralized terminals, including those devoted to single airlines. Multiple architects and architectural firms contributed structures to the project, including Eero Saarinen & Associates who were responsible for the now iconic Trans World Airlines (TWA) Terminal Center. SOM designed a number of buildings in the core, including the United Airlines

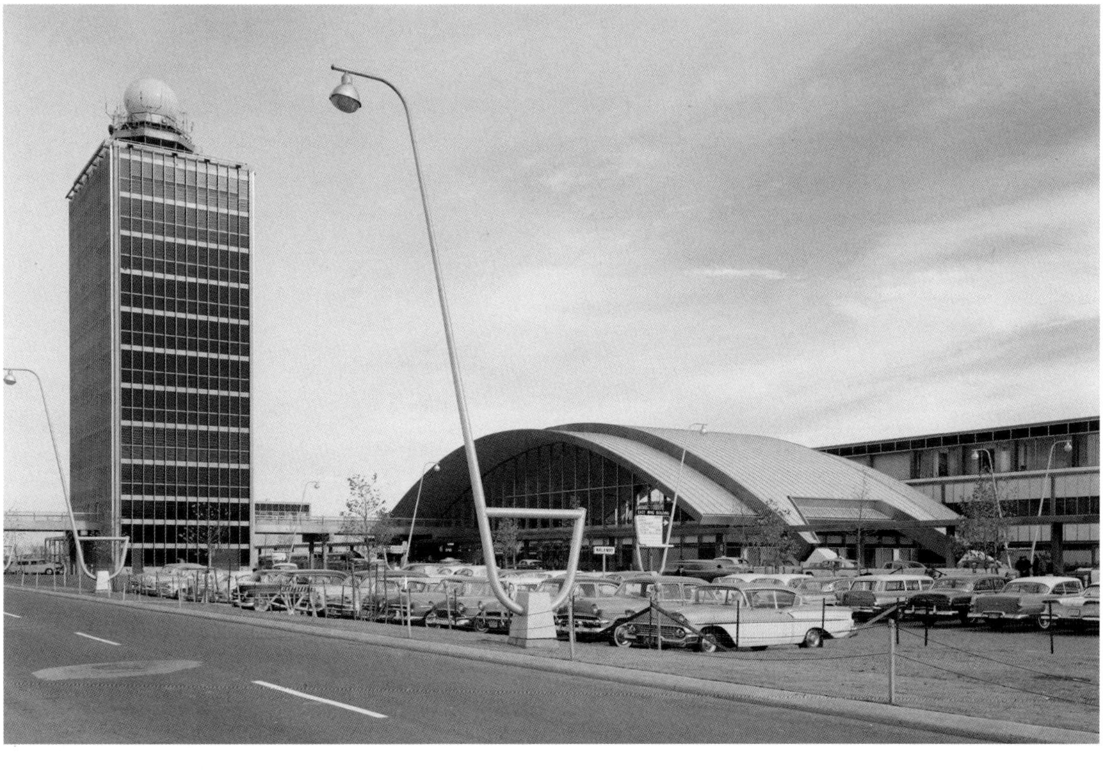

1.20 View of the International Arrivals Building (1957), Idlewild Airport, Queens, New York, 1958. Architect: Skidmore, Owings & Merrill (SOM).

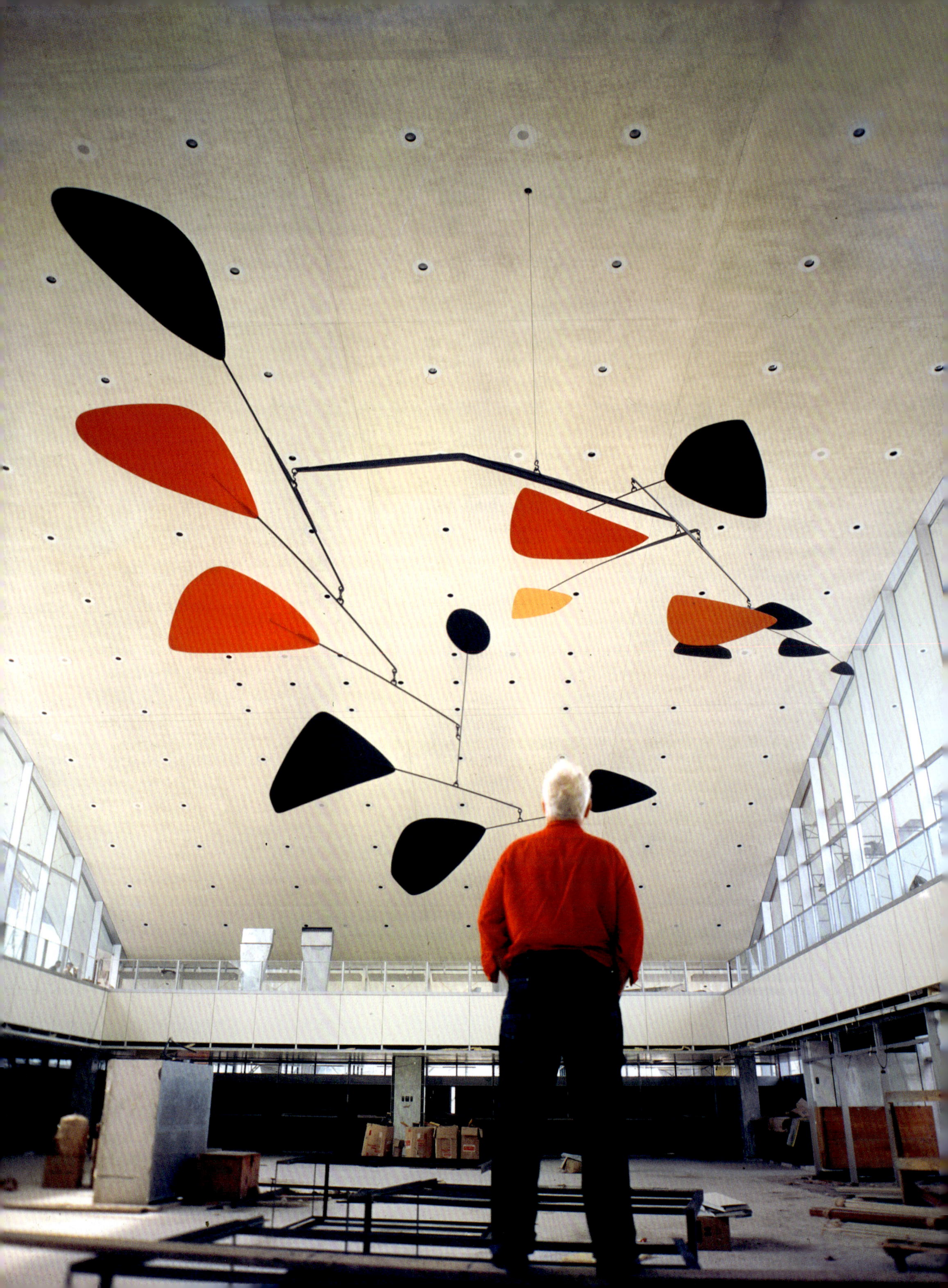

Terminal and the IAB, which served as a "gateway for overseas travelers." J. Walter Severinghaus served as the partner-in-charge, with Charles E. Hughes as project designer and Albert Kennerly as project manager. The IAB was one of the first structures to be completed at the new NYIA. The building, which included three airline wings, an eleven-story control tower, and a main terminal, stretched eleven city blocks. After clearing customs and immigration, declared *Progressive Architecture*, travelers "join their friends and exit—or enter the USA, as you will—through the great arched-roof hall, from the ceiling of which is suspended a huge (40-ft. wingspread) mobile sculpture by Alexander Calder."[28]

The sculptor titled the work *.125* (1957), in reference to the gauge of the wire he used, but it also later became known as *Flight* (figure 1.21). In terms of form, especially given its location in one of the most important airports of "jet-age America," the mobile soared in the cavernous, light-filled space, appropriately and perhaps unavoidably, evoking wings and flying. The *Saturday Evening Post* described the sculpture as "dangling from the ceiling like a run of musical notes made visible, sixteen red, black, and orange discs drift slowly through constantly changing orbits." The sculpture was meant to emphasize the theme of international air travel and a vision of a modern United States. Critic Paul J. Friedlander wrote in the *New York Times* that "if the new arrival center does nothing else, it puts this country's best foot forward toward visitors from abroad." Calder's sculpture became a prominent symbol of such efforts.[29]

While certainly fulfilling its role as a kind of sculptural welcome mat, *.125* was also structurally responsive to its architecture. As a hanging piece, it did not impede the flow of travelers or employees moving through the main terminal, but it did visually draw people to and through what was the most centralized location of the structure. The work responded to air currents, slowly moving and activating what otherwise would have been a sonorous amount of empty, unused space. The sculpture provided a dynamic yet consolidating focus by both echoing the architectural design and providing just enough visual contrast. *.125* was suspended from a single wire at the highest point of the ceiling. The subtle curve of its form was accentuated by the main cross bar, which balanced seven black and two red organically shaped metal plates on one side, and five black, one red, yellow, and orange on the other. The curvature also paralleled the two arched glass curtain walls of the hall (figure 1.22). The lowest point of the sculpture was roughly level with the mezzanine that bordered the room, meaning that it could be viewed both

< 1.21
Alexander Calder reviewing the installation of *.125* (1957), International Arrivals Building, Idlewild Airport, Queens, New York, 1957. Architect: Skidmore, Owings & Merrill (SOM).

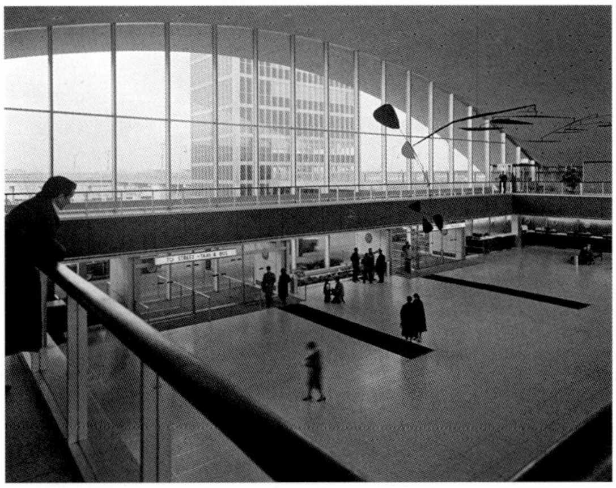

1.22
Alexander Calder, *.125*, 1957. Sheet metal, rod, and paint, 300 in. × 540 in. × 204 in. International Arrivals Building, Idlewild Airport, Queens, New York. Architect: Skidmore, Owings & Merrill (SOM).

from underneath and alongside. There was also the sheer, immense size of the mobile, which was both striking for a modern, abstract sculpture, and perfectly aligned with the ambitions of the architecture.

.125 also marked a significant increase in size from Calder's previous commissioned mobiles, even those like *Twenty Leaves and an Apple*. The commission stands as an early example of the so-called monumental work that came to define the second half of his career. In discussing the Idlewild project, Calder gave one of his most oft-quoted statements about his large-scale sculptures, "People think monuments should come out of the ground, never out of the ceiling, but mobiles can be monumental too." The decision to take on more commissions did not simply mean an opportunity to create larger and larger mobiles, but also to reorient how and where sculpture could function, especially in conjunction with architecture. Calder declared, "After the Idlewild mobile, I couldn't conceive of small things."[30]

The amplification of size, however, led to some significant changes in the engineering of his work. *.125* was too big to fabricate in Calder's own studio; and as was the case for so many of his later large-scale sculptures, he turned to Waterbury Ironworks, located near his home in Roxbury, Connecticut. There, he worked closely with Liberato "Chippy" Ieronimo. As Calder elaborated of his shift toward a more monumental scale in his mobiles:

> There's been an *agrandissement* in my work. As time goes on, I've developed new mechanical devices, such as a bearing that makes a swivel and fulcrum all in one, to cause the object to rotate *and* oscillate. It's true that I've more or less retired from the smaller mobiles. I regard them as sort of fiddling. The engineering on the big objects is important; they're mostly designed for a particular spot, and they have to fit properly or hang from the ceiling properly. Lots of times companies or government agencies have a big vacuum in their projects that they feel ought to be filled—that's where I come in.[31]

This statement reveals two crucial, if often overlooked, aspects of how Calder approached the large-scale commissioned mobiles. First, they were deeply informed by principles of engineering and thus connected back to Calder's early education and training. Second, they were constructed with a site already in mind, meaning that part of their function was to occupy, to inhabit specific spaces of architecture.

In the case of *.125*, Calder not only considered the overall context of an international airport, but also the very specific design of the IAB. Though led by other SOM architects, it was Gordon Bunshaft who had been an important interlocutor in once again bringing Calder onto the project. The sculptor later recalled that he created to scale three, seventeen-inch maquettes for a model of the building Bunshaft had shown him early in the design process. After selecting the final version, the sculpture was enlarged to forty-five feet wide and fitted together at Waterbury before being installed at Idlewild.[32]

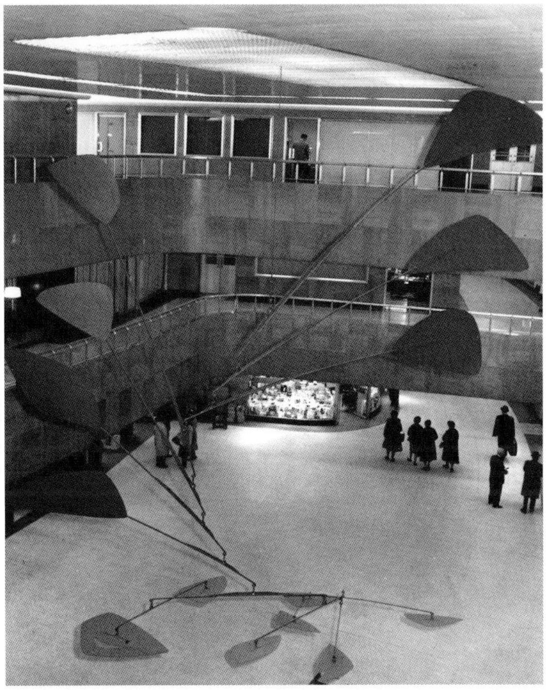

1.23
Alexander Calder, *Pittsburgh*, 1958. Sheet metal, rod, and paint, 28 ft. × 28 ft. Greater Pittsburgh International Airport, Pennsylvania.

A persistent art historical narrative over the last fifty or so years, largely shaped by the proliferation of Calder's outdoor monumental stabiles of the 1960s and 1970s, discounts the conscious, collaborative attention he gave to the large-scale mobiles. Part of the issue is that not all commissions were created equal, and not every large-scale mobile did, nor was meant to, alloy with its architecture. There are numerous examples of Calder's mobiles that are large and hang from ceilings in the interiors of buildings, but many were simply purchased, selected, or installed after the fact. A counterpoint to *.125*, for example, is Calder's 1958 *Pittsburgh* (figure 1.23). He originally created the twenty-eight-foot-wide mobile for the 1958 Carnegie International, the biennial exhibition at the Carnegie Museum of Art in Pittsburgh, where it won first prize that year. Waterbury Ironworks fabricated the work, which Calder never saw installed at the museum during the run of the exhibition, though he did later remark that it had been located in a "horrible hallway." G. David Thompson, a Pittsburgh industrialist and art collector, purchased the work and, in the wake of the NYIA opening at Idlewild and the installation of *.125*, donated it to the Alleghany County–owned Greater Pittsburgh International Airport in 1959. Calder was present for the installation of the mobile in the main terminal atrium, but perhaps the greatest direct connection of the work to its specific site—the painting of its paddles in the yellow and green of the county's colors—had occurred without Calder's permission.[33]

Both *Pittsburgh* and *.125* ended up installed in terminal halls at international airports, and made for striking sculptural installations, but the former did not respond to or engage with the architecture in the same way as its New York counterpart. For a structural, functional synergy to occur, it was vital that the artist be brought in as early as possible, or at least be made aware of the layout and design elements of the space where their work would be installed. Calder's mobiles, with their abstract forms and vibrant coloring, were easily adaptable to a variety of spaces, but became something more, something truly remarkable, when conscientiously incorporated into architectural design.

Mobiles like *.125* or *Twenty Leaves and an Apple* were not just enlarged versions of preexisting Calder mobiles, known for their dynamic and visually lively kinetic qualities. The commissions have often been judged through the same interpretive lens, however, and thus critiqued for their unwieldy and encumbered characteristics. When placed in the main hall of the IAB, *.125* still retained a graceful lightness, but it was a tremendously heavy object that was arduous to install. As Calder humorously recalled, two years after it originally went up, the airport took it down in order to feature a large paper Christmas bell for the holiday season. "When they put the mobile back up," he said, "they didn't get it up right, so I was called in to prescribe again. They've learned their lesson; no more paper bells—I hope." Sculpture in this case, after all, is not simply a decoration to be hung and swapped out depending on the season.[34]

One of the consequences of increased weight, however, was a reduction of the kineticism that had come to define the term mobile. The larger these sculptures became, the less they moved, but the more space they occupied and activated. In shifting the parameters used to examine mobiles like *Twenty Leaves and an Apple* and *.125*, what becomes apparent is how Calder imaginatively collapsed decorative tropes into sculptural reach. As early as the Terrace Plaza Hotel commission, critics were overtly referencing his mobiles as "a contemporary substitute for the pompous cut glass chandelier." In many ways, the comparison to Calder's large-scale mobiles from the immediate postwar period was apt. Chandeliers usually possess multipart or branched forms, are hung from ceilings, and viewed as ornament. Though Calder's mobiles for the Terrace Plaza Hotel, the so-called cloud or straw works Bertoia created in the 1950s and 1960s, and many of Lippold's projects including those for the Four Seasons Restaurant and Philharmonic Hall were not created to function as light fixtures per se, they could be said to possess similar characteristics (figure 1.24).[35] In the case of the latter, architect Max Abramovitz commissioned Lippold to create a sculpture for the first completed structure of the Lincoln Center complex in New York City: Philharmonic Hall, which opened in late 1962. The resulting work, *Orpheus and Apollo*, stretched the entire length of the grand foyer, measuring 190 feet in length and extending 39 feet in height (figure 1.25).

Given the long, narrow, but tall space of the lobby, Abramovitz had initially envisioned a hanging element, and even approached J. & L. Lobmeyr, the famed Viennese glassware firm responsible for most of the large crystal chandeliers in the great performance halls across Europe. Lobmeyr was enthusiastic and sent over options and a senior member of their team. As Abramovitz recalled, however, all of their designs were "modernized." He continued, "Now, the beauty of the old chandeliers was that the light came from without, from candles, and glanced off the individual facets with great delicacy. But then we got electric lights, and cords built into the chandelier, and things became clumsy and heavy. Lobmeyr's did a lot of sketches, and they were getting closer, but they just didn't quite have the

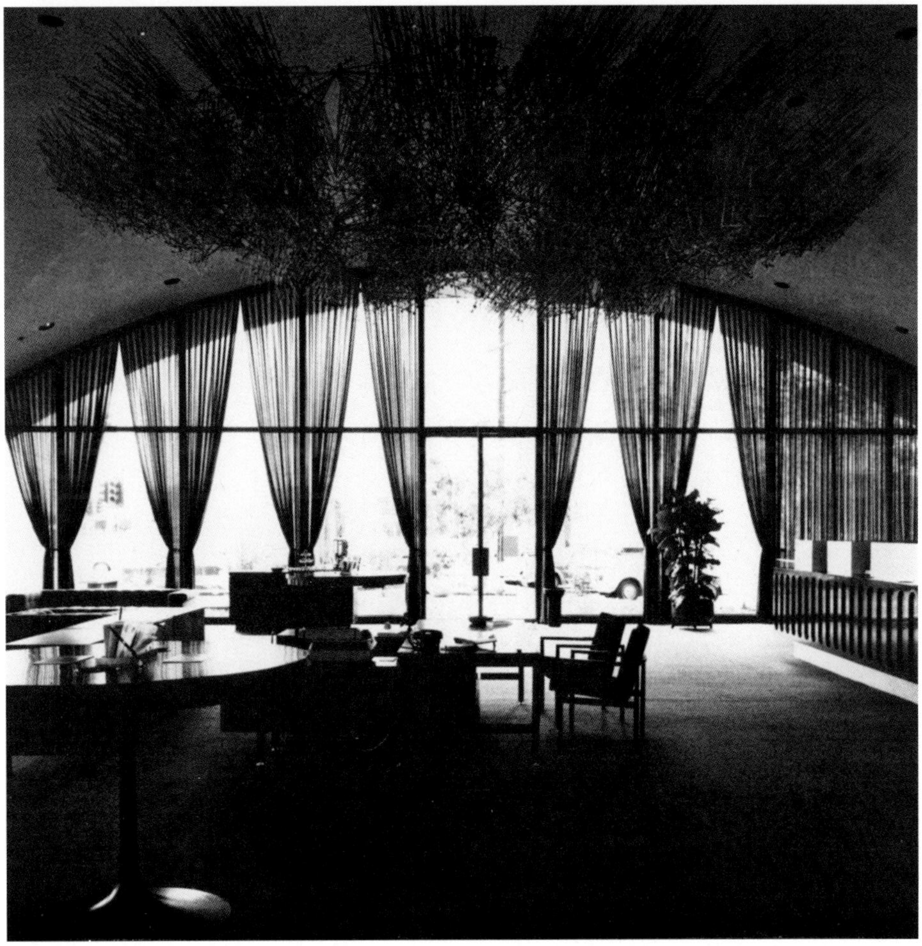

1.24
Harry Bertoia, *Untitled*, 1964. Brass-coated steel rods, 20 ft. d. Golden West Savings, Castro Valley, California. Architect: Mario Louis Gaidano.

delicacy I wanted." By 1961, he grew convinced that only a sculpture that could "float in space and relate in a contemporary manner to the interior of the foyer" would do, and that Lippold, one of the "best space-commanders around," was the only option for the job.[36]

Orpheus and Apollo weighed five tons, but like Calder's mobile for the IAB at Idlewild, its 190 sheets of highly polished metal and steel wire conveyed a surprising lightness. A number of contemporary critics, in fact, noted similarities between Lippold's and Calder's work, emphasizing their shared interest in sculptures with "presence," suspended from "taut and tempered wire," hanging from ceilings. Critic Dorothy Adlow wrote of Lippold's sculpture, "The metal strips are so placed that they tilt, turn, thrust, cluster, intersect in a tremendous variety of ways without touching. There is a sense of acceleration and deceleration, an illusion of bunching and splaying.... The Lippold construction erupts at both ends of the hall and expresses diffusion rather than containment. Furthermore, it comes closer to architectonic design than it does to the jewel-like ornamental fixture. In fact, the space sculpture vies with the architectural design and in the eyes of some may seem obtrusive to the grandeur which Mr. Abramovitz cultivated in designing this huge promenade." *Orpheus and Apollo* was not a mobile and did not possess any intended kinetic component, but it did express a "sense of motion

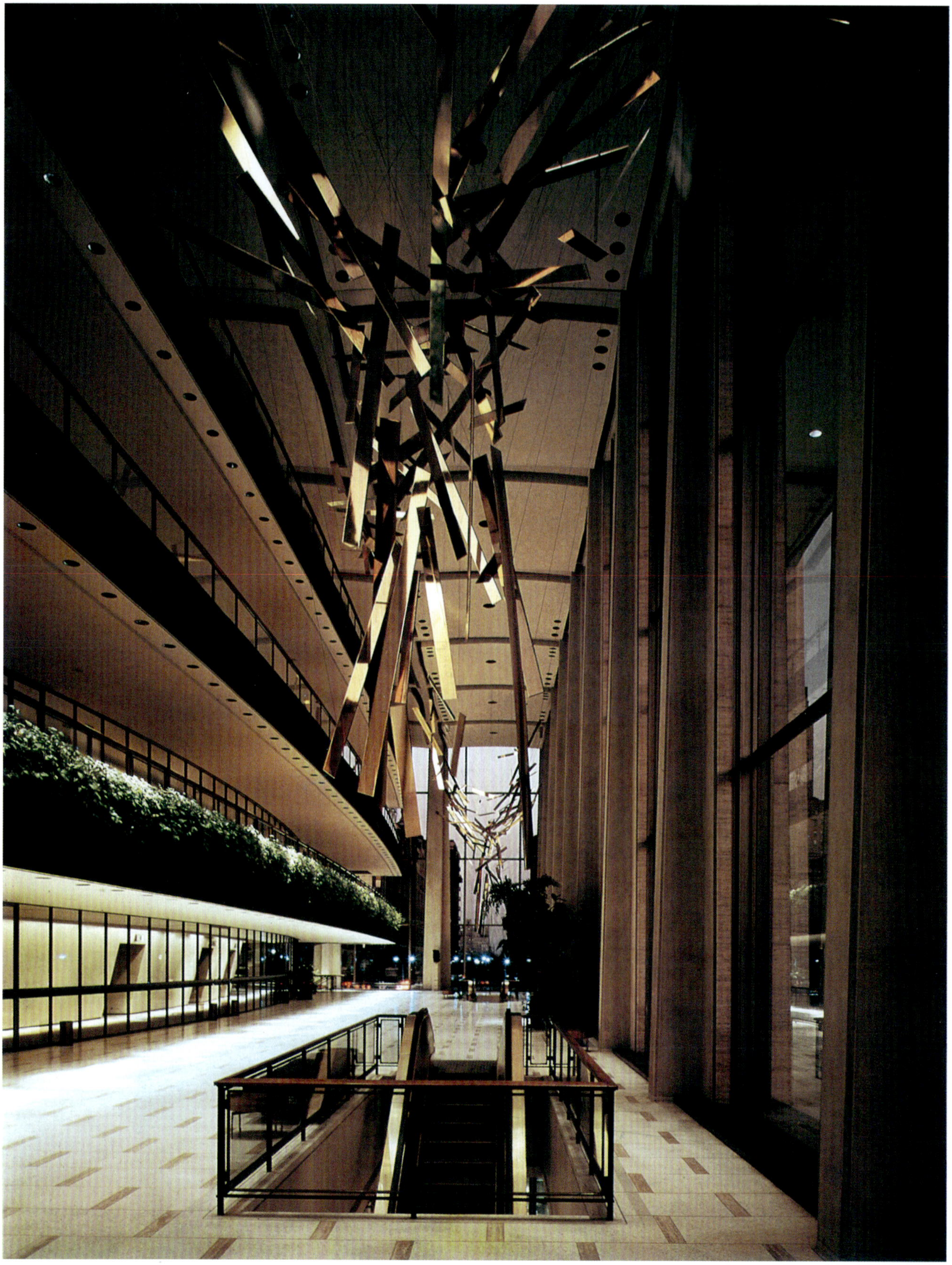

1.25
Richard Lippold, *Orpheus and Apollo*, 1962. Muntz metal and steel wire, 190 ft. × 190 ft. × 39 ft. Philharmonic Hall, Lincoln Center for the Performing Arts, New York City. Architect: Max Abramovitz.

due to the ever-changing light reflections" of the highly polished surface of the sculpture.[37]

Commissions by Lippold and Calder may have co-opted the characteristics and spatial orientation of chandeliers, but the resulting "space sculptures" were more than light fixtures' replacements or decorative baubles. For his part, Lippold described the effect he hoped to create with *Orpheus and Apollo* as akin to "one frame from a series of photographs of an explosion which might be atomic." The sculpture indeed took on the appearance of matter exploded *in medias res*: its large particles of metal catapulting outward at capricious angles, a consequence of some unknown scientific or cosmic force. The work comprised two distinct forms, each made from nearly a hundred metal sheets of varying sizes individually hung from the ceiling with wire (figure 1.26). Both forms extended vertically from what appeared as concentrated clusters at opposing ends of the foyer, while narrow limb-like bands of pieces simultaneously stretched toward each other horizontally, though without ever touching.[38]

Unabashedly abstract and precisely, asymmetrically geometric, the two masses of metal conveyed an almost organic figuration. Lippold's explanation of possible sources of inspiration, and the work's eventual title, further advanced the interpretation of the two sculptural forms as figures. Lippold personified the two masses, acknowledging their specific setting by naming the work after two figures from ancient Greek mythology: the great hero and musician, Orpheus, and the Greek god of music, Apollo. The artist even nodded to versions of the myth that claimed that Orpheus was Apollo's son, by stating that the "figure" on the east end of the foyer was the latter as it had been finished first and thus was "older."[39]

The creation, and subsequent installation, of *Orpheus and Apollo* unfolded like an ancient epic saga. Lippold started the laborious and very public process at

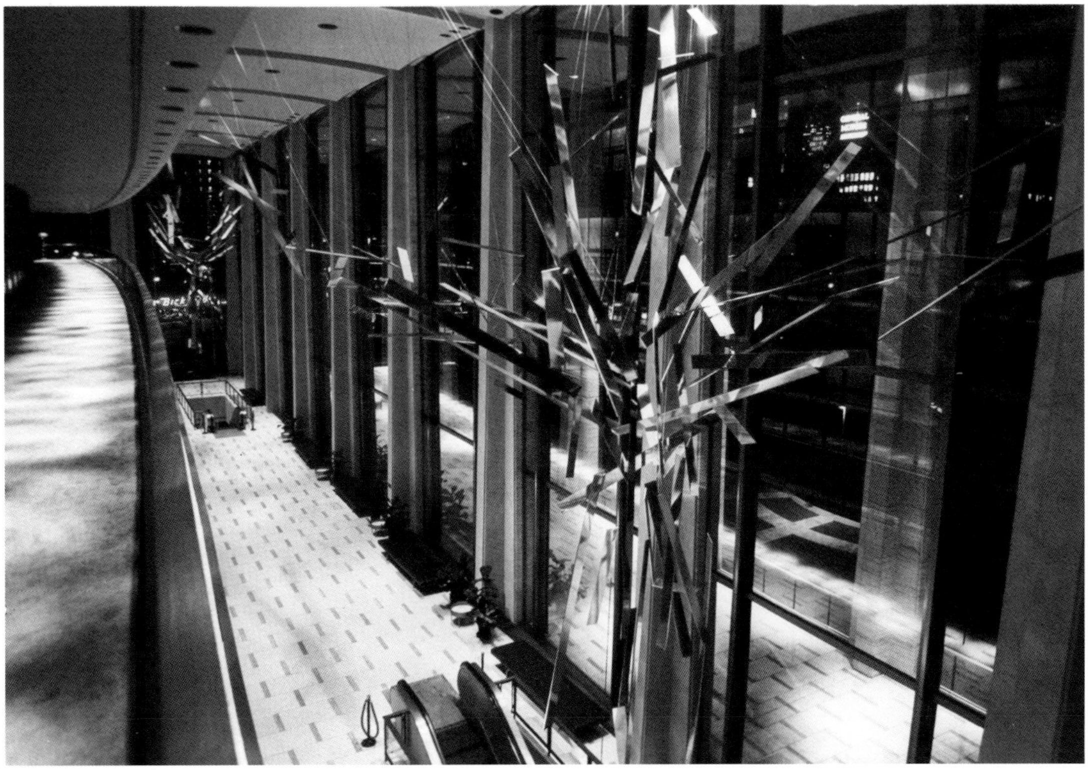

1.26
Richard Lippold, *Orpheus and Apollo*, 1962. Muntz metal and steel wire, 190 ft. × 190 ft. × 39 ft. Philharmonic Hall, Lincoln Center for the Performing Arts, New York City. Architect: Max Abramovitz.

Philharmonic Hall on July 12, 1962. The intention was to have the work completed in time for the grand opening of the venue on the evening of September 23, which was attended by approximately three thousand people—including First Lady Jacqueline Kennedy—and broadcasted as a two-hour televised special on CBS. Working alongside a small group of assistants, he painstakingly hung each wire and piece while construction of the still unfinished hall continued around him. Working on lifts, ladders, and the surrounding balconies, the installation was consistently interrupted by visitors, building bureaucracy, and an Italian work crew laying the terrazzo flooring. Lippold hung the last piece on December 5, with just enough time for the work to be cleaned of all the construction soot that had accumulated on the surface of the metallic sheets, before the official dedication of the work on December 19.[40]

The surface shine of *Orpheus and Apollo* was not simply an issue of professional presentation, but also an essential property of the sculpture. The Philharmonic Hall commission provided Lippold with an opportunity to explore the transparency, reflectivity, and what he described as the "visual definition of the age." The sculptor worked almost exclusively in metal, but unlike many contemporaries who explored the rugged, expressionistic qualities of welded iron or Cor-Ten, he preferred stainless varieties. Emphatic about not covering up surfaces with paint or obscuring the "natural qualities" of metals, he stated, "Generally my materials are polished so as to reflect light and in doing so they seem to dematerialize thus emphasizing the spatial quality of the work." The individual metal plates of *Orpheus and Apollo*, with their highly reflective surfaces, extended the spatial boundaries of the work and amplified the lighting effects, providing further illumination to one of the most public and visible spaces in the building. Richard Kelly, who had previously worked with Lippold on his commissions at the Four Seasons, was responsible for lighting the work. Kelly believed that light was crucial to understanding and experiencing the designed environment, and his lighting scheme enhanced the reflective qualities of the sculpture.[41]

The ability of sculpture to function as a modulator of light had been a preoccupation for the avant-garde since the early twentieth century, whether for artists associated with the Bauhaus like László Moholy-Nagy and György Kepes, or for modern sculptors like Constantin Brâncuși. As Jack Burnham wrote, "Reflection is a consciousness-expanding phenomenon which holds its sacred fire in the bodies of jewels, water splashes, polished metals, ice formations, and, of course, the moon. Baudelaire often seemed aware of the transcendent emotions conveyed by brilliant reflections: 'What I have always liked in the theatre, from the childhood to the present time, is the *chandelier*—a beautiful object, luminous, crystalline, complicated, circular, and symmetrical.'" Sculptors during the mid-twentieth century like Bertoia, Calder, Lippold, and Noguchi, while not interested in making chandeliers, increasingly attended to how a play between light and shadow could extend their work beyond its physical boundaries. As Burnham concluded, "Just ten years ago, writing about the 'optical properties' of sculpture would have seemed a very curious, if not oblique, approach to an art based primarily on the order of physical mass."[42]

In the case of *Orpheus and Apollo*, the work's reflectivity became particularly pronounced at night on account of Kelly's innovative lighting strategies; but even during the daytime hours, when light streamed in through the glass facade, the sculpture frequently transformed in appearance (figure 1.27). The coloration and sheen of the work's surface changed with the sun, the clouds, or the night lighting, and in turn cast shadows and bathed the surrounding architectural space in a golden glow. Lippold decided early in the commissioning process that he wanted *Orpheus and Apollo* to radiate a warm tone and explored the possibility of high-carat, gold-plated strips of aluminum. Cost issues, as well as a lack of the manufacturer's guarantee to fabricate perfectly straight pieces, led him to Muntz metal: a modern, malleable brass alloy comprised of 60 percent copper and 40 percent zinc. Similar to naval brass, the alloy originally had been used on the hulls of boats. In the twentieth century, Muntz metal became most commonly used in architectural projects because it was harder and stronger than other forms of

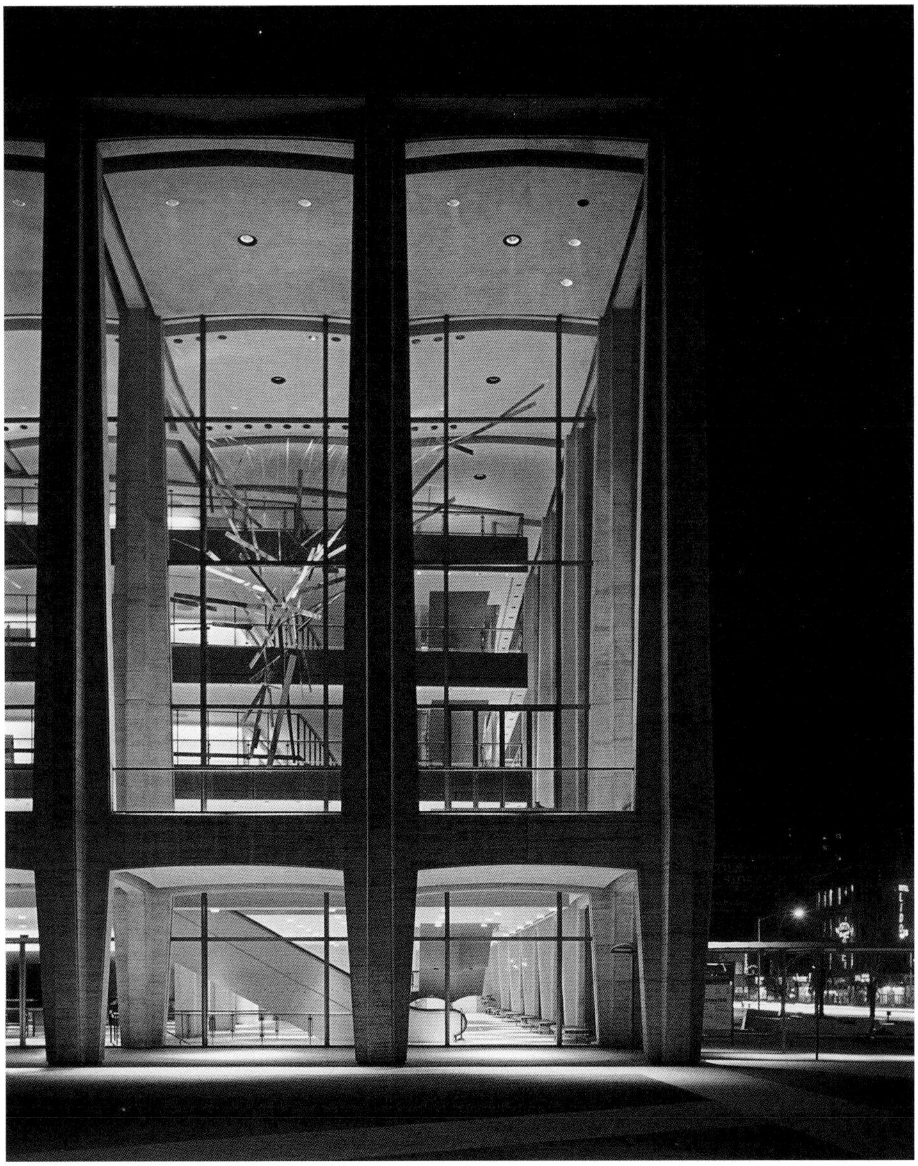

1.27
Exterior view of Philharmonic Hall, 1962. Lincoln Center for the Performing Arts, New York City. Architect: Max Abramovitz.

brass. Selecting Muntz, rather than the more malleable aluminum, meant Lippold's sculpture was heavier and harder to work with, but it was cheaper, saving tens of thousands of dollars.

Abramovitz reinforced the ceiling and Lippold carefully selected two types of steel cables, 1/16 and 1/32 inches thick, to suspend the five-ton sculpture. The wires were not simply a support system but were "as important to the design as the metal sheets," with Lippold "determined to have as many of them hanging from a single point as possible, so their diagonals and convergences would make interesting patterns." Although the wires were less visible when viewed at a distance or in daylight, they were fully evident when seen at night, for example, from the balcony. Their presence articulated the physical connection of the sculpture to the building, suturing the grand expanse of the foyer.[43]

The materials Lippold chose also directly connected the sculpture to its site and the broader historical context of postwar industry. The United States Steel Corporation highlighted this link by featuring Lippold's exaltation of industrial metals and the Lincoln Center commission in a two-page illustrated advertisement that appeared in a broad range of trade, art, and populist publications in 1965 and 1966: "Wire,"Lippold declared, "is the true linear form... it permits the use of light... it has strength and color, but is also light, and airy... It helps me to include space as part of the design." Notably, the advertisement also mentioned Lippold's desire to make art be "something more than an object to hang on a wall or stand on pedestal," to make art "a more useful part of design and architecture." The wires and plates comprising *Orpheus and Apollo* enabled Lippold to create dynamic, interconnected spatial and atmospheric effects, but also directly associated the work with industrial development not with the traditions of fine art. The material components reflected the steel frames of the glass curtain walls, and Lippold's choice of Muntz metal echoed the brass finishes and warm travertine interior of the hall. The artist aligned individual sheets with "architecturally relevant points on the ceiling," and other architectural elements such as the escalators and multiple levels of balconies. Through a shared industrial material vocabulary,

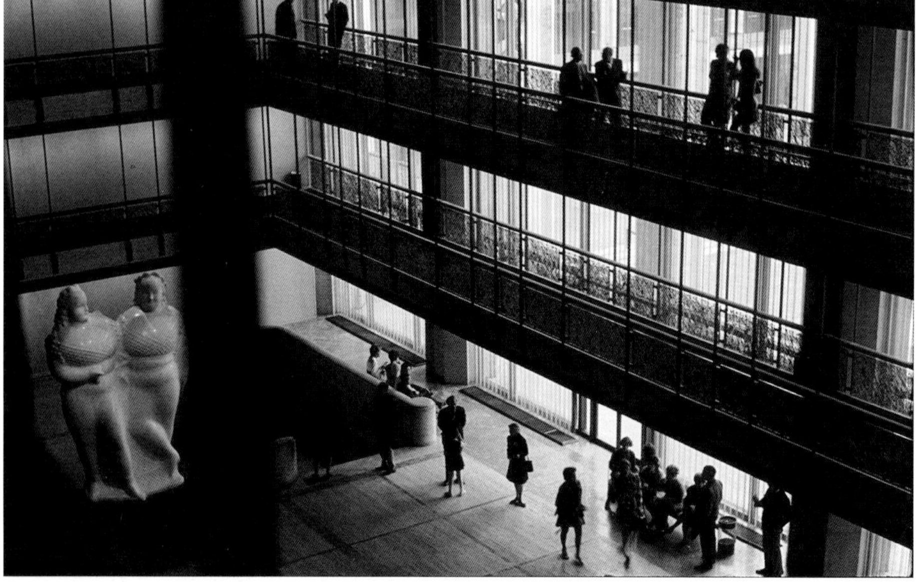

1.28
New York State Theater, 1964. Lincoln Center for the Performing Arts, New York City. Architect: Philip Johnson.

Lippold took on the functionality of chandeliers and activated the height of the space that extended downward from the ceiling in the grand foyer, alloying his sculpture with Abramovitz's architecture.[44]

Orpheus and Apollo was the first major work of art commissioned for the Lincoln Center complex and it made for "an overwhelming precedent." From the outset, Lippold knew his sculpture would have to contend with the "great open space" of the foyer and pull together its two ends in order to "relieve the feeling of extreme elongation," both horizontal and vertical. He stated, "I was very impressed by all these spatial situations and felt a great desire to provide forms which, even from the plaza outside, would invite one to move into the interior." The Philharmonic Hall commission presented "special problems" for Lippold, but he responded by creating a sculpture substantive enough to stand up to the monumental nature of Abramovitz's design as well as that of the greater Lincoln Center complex. The metal forms cut fluid arcs through the architecture and gave it a dynamic openness and, as *Time* magazine noted, did so "without removing an inch of space."[45]

Lippold's consideration of the specific architectural context, his awareness of Abramovitz's design and its limitations as he realized his sculpture, is also what sets it apart from the other artworks installed at or even commissioned for Lincoln Center. Philip Johnson included two enlargements of sculptures previously realized by Elie Nadelman in the interior of New York State Theater (figure 1.28). The architect also commissioned works for the building by painter Jasper Johns and sculptor Lee Bontecou (figure 1.29). Although the scale of all four works created dramatic focal points, none achieved the spatial transformation produced by *Orpheus and Apollo*. Like Joan Miró's mural or James Davis's reliefs at the Terrace Plaza Hotel, they added visual interest to the walls on which they were affixed without structurally assimilating with or altering the architecture.

In 1965, two notable sculptures were installed outdoors on the Lincoln Center campus following a contentious approval process by the Art Commission

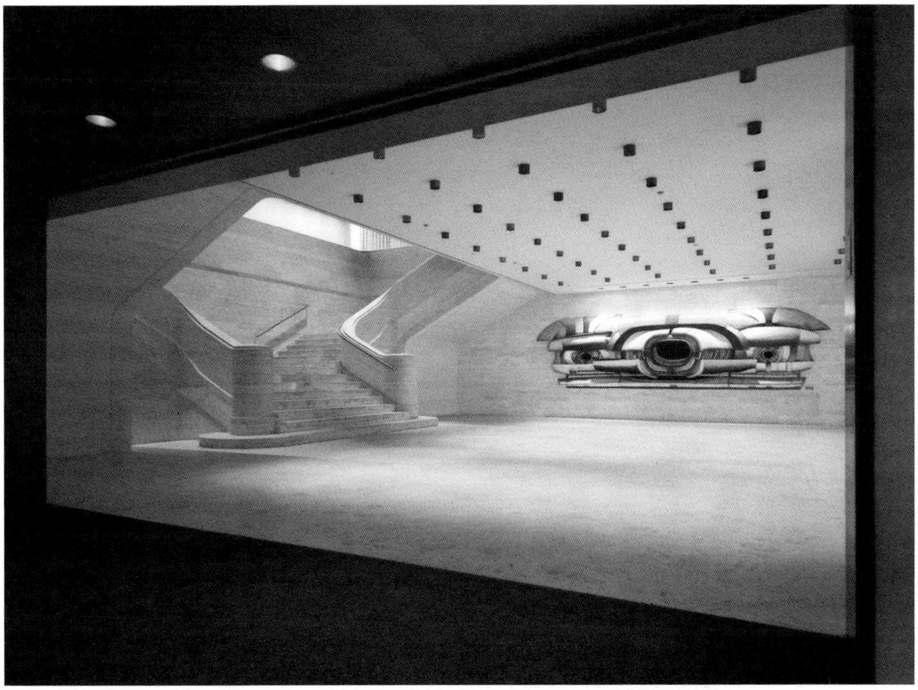

1.29
New York State Theater lower-level lobby, 1964. Lincoln Center for the Performing Arts, New York City. Architect: Philip Johnson.

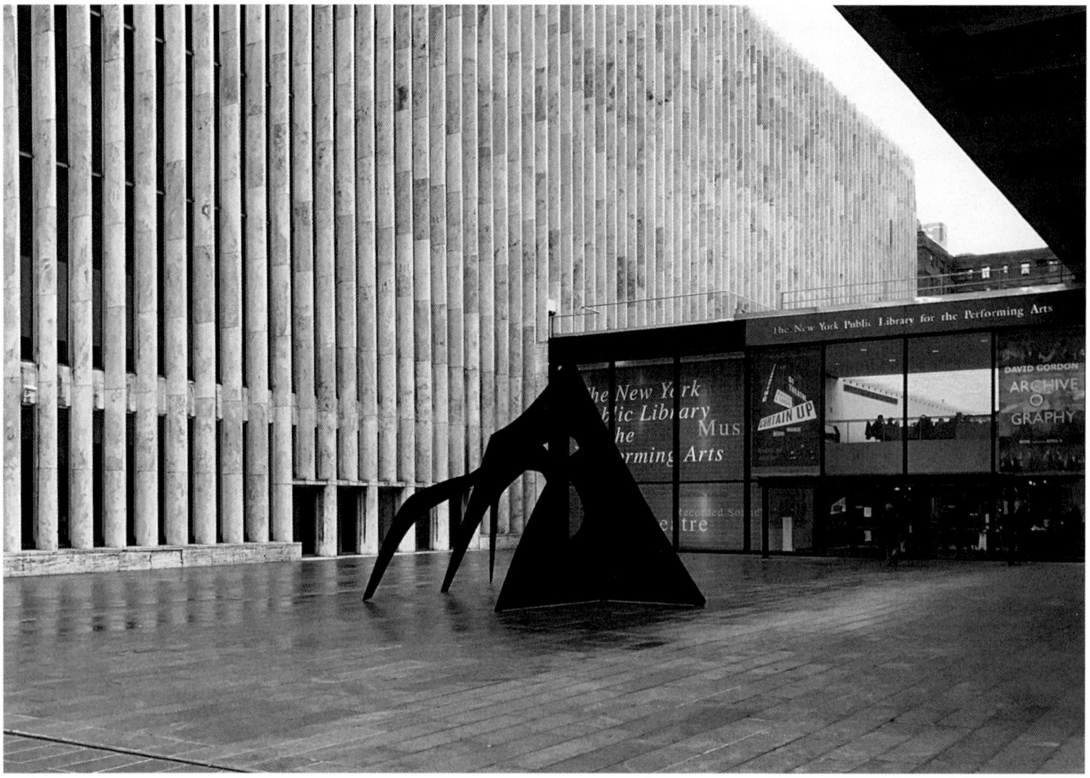

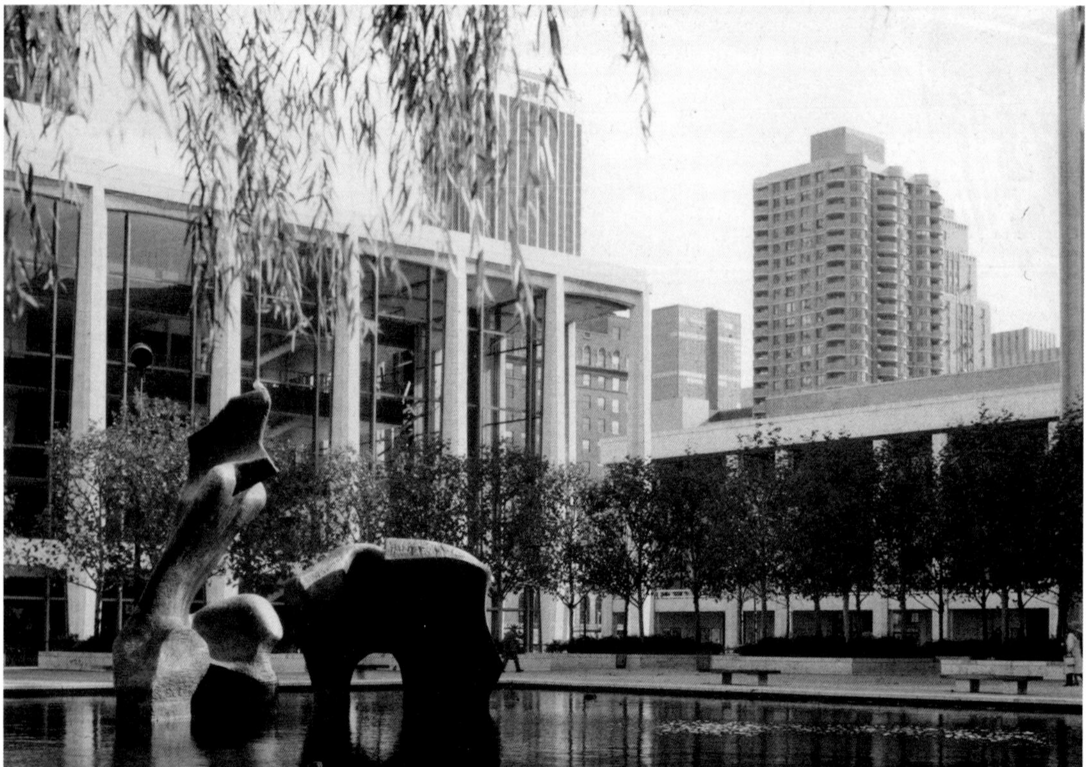

1.30
Alexander Calder, *Le Guichet*, 1963. Sheet metal, bolts, and paint, 14 ft. × 22 ft. Library and Museum of the Performing Arts, Lincoln Center for the Performing Arts, New York City. Architect: Skidmore, Owings & Merrill (SOM).

1.31
Henry Moore, *Reclining Figure*, 1963–65. Bronze, 18 ft. × 28 ft. Lincoln Center for the Performing Arts, New York City. Architect: Philip Johnson. Gift of Mr. and Mrs. Albert List.

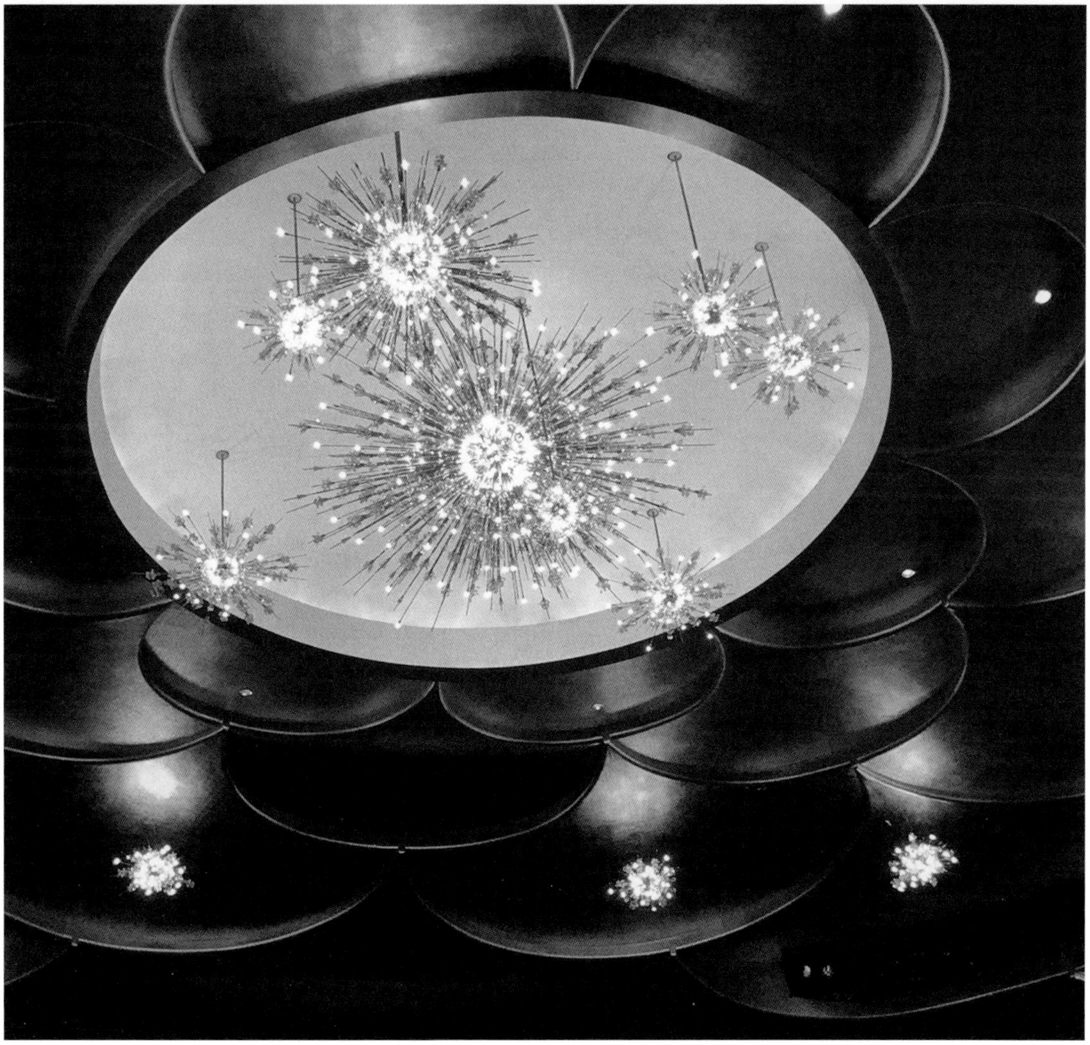

1.32
J. & L. Lobmeyr, Starburst Chandeliers, 1963–66. Brass and hand-cut Swarovski crystal, dimensions variable. Commissioned for the Metropolitan Opera House, Lincoln Center for the Performing Arts, New York City. Architect: Wallace K. Harrison.

of New York City. Calder's *Le Guichet* (1963) was installed outside the entrance to the Bunshaft-designed Library and Museum of the Performing Arts (figure 1.30) and Henry Moore's *Reclining Figure* (1963–65) was placed in the reflecting pool on the Dan Kiley–designed main plaza (figure 1.31). Calder's sculpture, however, was not made for the site, and owing to their outdoor placements, these two works possessed a different relationship with the surrounding architecture. As such, they both fall outside the scope of this study, but also speak to the challenges of realizing public art in civic spaces that emerged in earnest during the later 1960s and 1970s.[46]

Perhaps the closest comparison to Lippold's contribution at the Philharmonic Hall is not another sculpture, but the twenty-three sculptural chandeliers in the auditorium and lobby of the Metropolitan Opera House (figure 1.32). For the project, architect Wallace K. Harrison commissioned J. & L. Lobmeyr, the firm his partner Abramovitz had previously considered for the foyer of the Philharmonic Hall. Harrison also included murals by Marc Chagall, acquired sculptures by Aristide Maillol and Wilhelm Lehmbruck, and commissioned a massive high-relief sculpture by Mary Callery that extended outward from the top of the proscenium arch in the auditorium. The chandeliers, however, were the result of a much more involved

1.33
Harry Bertoia, *Untitled*, 1962. Stainless steel and 24-karat gold-plated nickel wire, 20 ft. h.,10 ft. d. Perpetual Savings & Loan Building, Los Angeles. Architect: Edward Durell Stone.

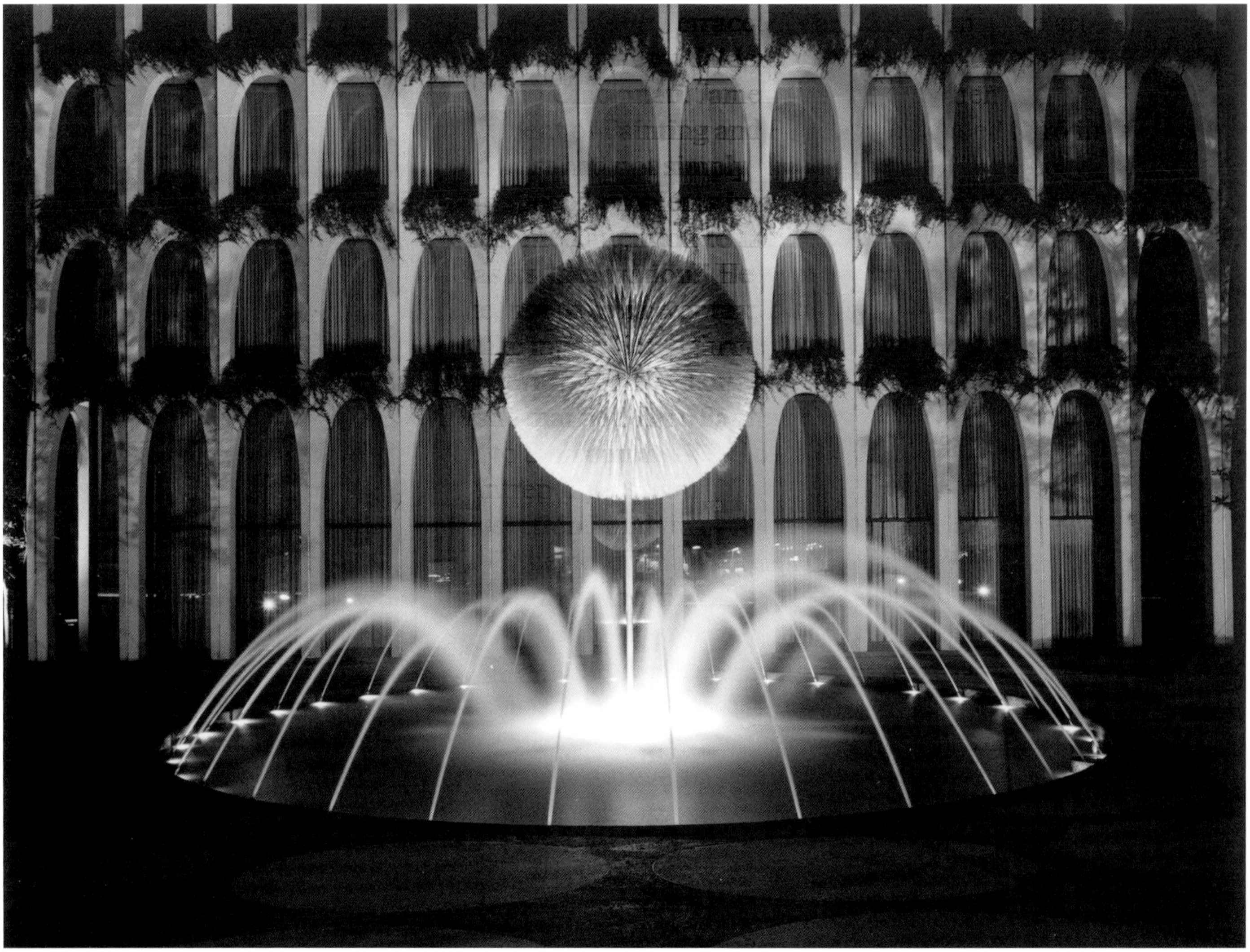

1.34
Sputnik I satellite, 1957.

1.35
Vanguard I satellite, 1958.

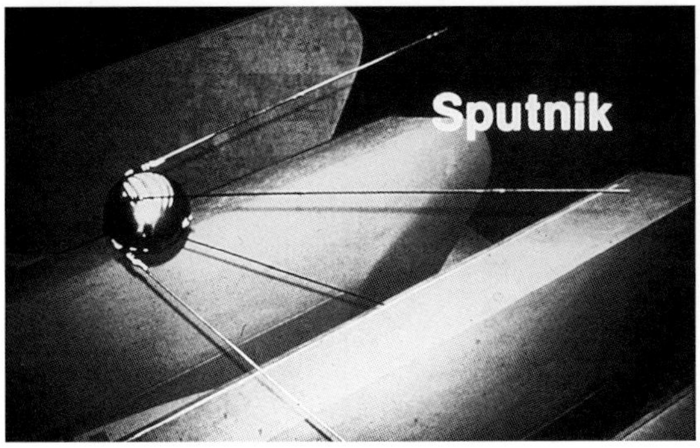

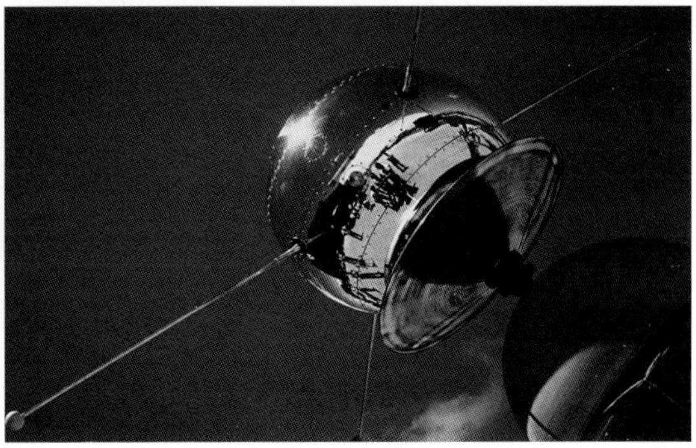

collaboration between Harrison, architect Tad Leski—who worked for Harrison & Abramovitz—and Lobmeyr designer Hans Harald Rath.[47]

The chandeliers were officially a gift of thanks from the Austrian government for the Marshall Plan, but also evoked the historical era with their resemblance to space-age satellites and galactic constellations. The group of chandeliers for the Metropolitan Opera House proved to be a modern contrast to an interior design scheme that, with its preponderance of red velvet and gold leaf, skewed far more nineteenth-century than mid-twentieth. The chandeliers' starburst form, with multiple elements radiating outward from a central core, was a common theme across midcentury modern visual culture. Similar expressions can be seen, for example, in the innovative lighting fixtures Italian designer Gino Sarfatti made for his company Arteluce in Milan, which circulated internationally in the pages of *Domus* in the 1950s; in other sculptures like Bertoia's "dandelion" commissioned by Edward Durell Stone for the plaza outside of his Perpetual Savings & Loan building in Beverley Hills, California (1962–63); and the designs of the Soviet Sputnik and American Vanguard satellites, launched in the late 1950s (figures 1.33, 1.34, 1.35).[48]

The Metropolitan Opera chandeliers were also created against the backdrop of renewed conversations and confirmations of the big bang theory that occurred during the late 1950s and early 1960s. Harrison even included a copy of *Le Ciel* by French astrophysicist Jean-Claude Pecker for inspiration when he sent a sketch and model of the proposed chandelier design to Rath in 1963. As contemporary artist Josiah McElheny states of the resulting chandeliers, "They're kind of Gilded Age/space-age objects, and they immediately looked to me like a galaxy or an explosion—a Pop image of the big bang. And just like the theater itself, they seem to have come from this weird transitional moment where modernism became infected with other influences."[49]

With the possible exception of perhaps Moore and Rath, however, none of the other practitioners who contributed art to the buildings and spaces of Lincoln Center worked as closely with the architect or intentionally fused their work to the overall architectural design more than Lippold. *Orpheus and Apollo* provided a dramatic point of convergence within the Philharmonic Hall, but the sculpture went beyond this solely aesthetic function to transmute Abramovitz's design, activating what was a grand but basic room. Part of the sculpture's task was to help resolve deficiencies in the architecture, not just adorn its surfaces. As the art critic Stuart Preston declared in his *New York Times* review of the Philharmonic Hall, "'Orpheus and Apollo' can thus be looked at in two ways. As a decorative object sparkling and reflecting rays of light, it catches and holds the eye. More importantly, its geometrical irregularity animates the whole vast interior space cradling it and relieves the severely plain and unadorned character of the architecture." The cosmic metal object functioned as both a decorative chandelier for the space age and a substantive sculptural construction that transformed and galvanized Abramovitz's architecture. In the process, *Orpheus and Apollo* became a thing among things: art among architecture, with each circulating in the other's orbit in order to make space dynamic.[50]

From Apollo to Gemini

A few years after completing *Orpheus and Apollo*, Lippold would again be asked to create sculpture for another lobby, in another postwar performing arts center. *Gemini II*, realized for the new Jesse H. Jones Hall for the Performing Arts in Houston, Texas in 1966, shared many qualities with Lippold's commission for the Philharmonic Hall (figure 1.36). Both sculptures comprised two multipart metal forms hung from the ceiling on steel wire. Each animated large, interior spaces that were open and visible to the public and evoked the spirit of the space race—a particularly appropriate characteristic for a project realized in Houston, where the Gemini Program of the National Aeronautics and Space Administration (NASA) concluded with its final space flight a month after the opening of Jesse H. Jones Hall. Both works even provoked the ire of Hilton Kramer, who directly connected them in his review of the "preposterously titled" *Gemini II*: "This overextended trinket, completely devoid of expressive interest of sculptural sensibility,

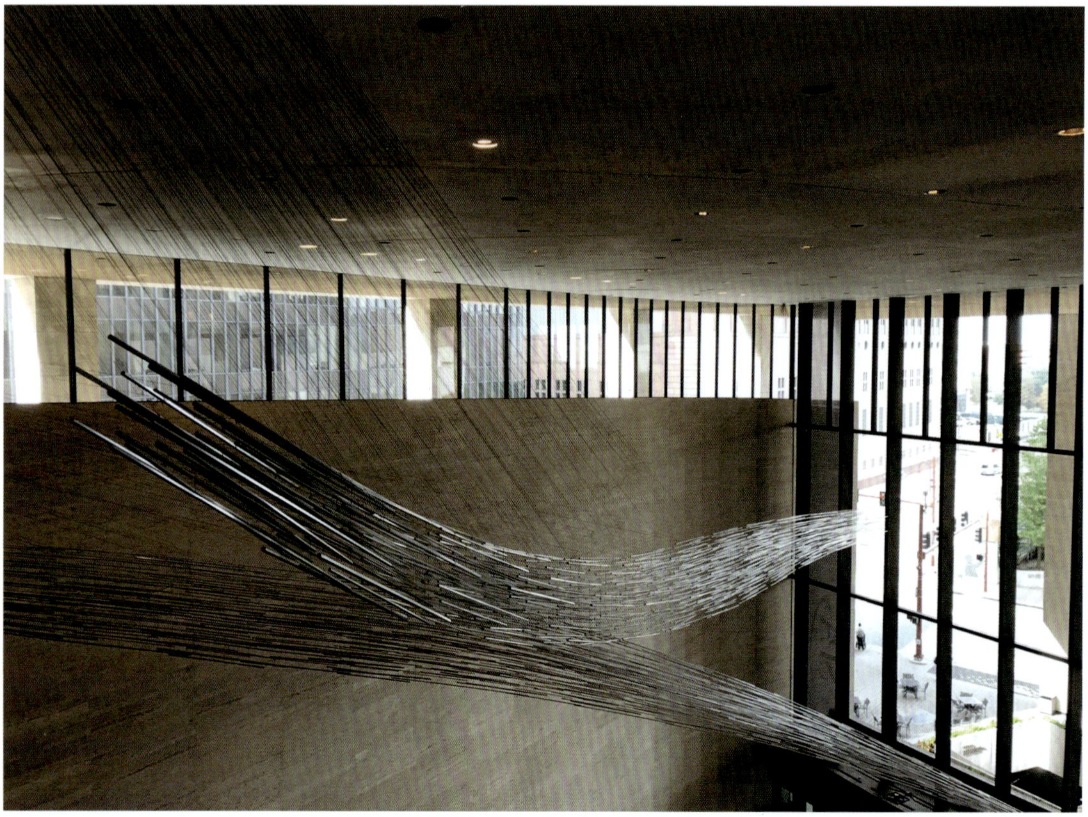

1.36
Richard Lippold, *Gemini II*, 1966. Gold-plated steel wire cable and anodized-aluminum rods, 52 ft. × 92 ft. × 80 ft. Jesse H. Jones Hall for the Performing Arts, Houston, Texas. Architect: Caudill Rowlett Scott.

is another of those decorative nullities so beloved by the sponsors of new concert halls. But at least the onus is no longer on New York for having commissioned the worst of these works."[51] For Kramer, *Gemini II* was not simply decorative but also derivative, and thus worthy of even more disdain.

The impetus behind Lippold's commission and the building it occupied was not unique to the immediate postwar period. By 1961, thirty-two American cities had built major performing arts complexes or cultural centers, with over 170 more following between 1962 and 1970. Houston became one those cities in the summer of 1962, when the Houston Endowment, a foundation established in 1937 by Jesse H. and Mary Gibbs Jones, announced the building of a new downtown performing arts center. The motivation for building the Jesse H. Jones Hall, like Lincoln Center, came in part from a desire among civic leaders to create cosmopolitan cities through significant urban redevelopment programs. As a *Newsweek* feature on the opening stated, "The cultural boom comes first. Then the city builds a magnificent sound chamber to house it. Last week it happened in Houston, as it has all across the country."[52]

Such civic ambition, however, came at a price—just as it had in New York City. Lincoln Center, architecturally, had been realized after intense disagreement about the design of the complex among the initial consulting architects (including Alvar Aalto, Pietro Belluschi, Marcel Breuer, Henry Bulfinch, and Sven Markelius) as well as the team of architects eventually hired for the project: Wallace K. Harrison (Metropolitan Opera House and overall architectural lead); Max Abramovitz (Philharmonic Hall); Philip Johnson (New York State Theater); Eero Saarinen (Vivian Beaumont Theater); SOM, with Gordon Bunshaft as lead (Library and Museum of the Performing Arts); and Pietro Belluschi (Juilliard School). The Center's architects, begrudgingly for some like Bunshaft, eventually settled on unifying design elements: exterior use of glass and travertine and classical elements, including colonnades, arches, and outdoor plazas that resembled Michelangelo's Piazza del Campidoglio (1538) in Rome. The result was a complex that, for many, expressed what architectural historian Spiro Kostof referred to as the "language of power," a style recalling antiquity preferred by fascist leaders like Adolf Hitler and Benito Mussolini before World War II (figure 1.37). Noted urbanist Jane Jacobs dismissed not only the classicism of Lincoln Center, but also critiqued what she saw as the "sacking" of New York City rather than the support of any of its real "culture." Lippold himself, speaking to a group of architecture students at Yale University in October 1964, even candidly expressed his disdain for the "neo-Nazi classicism" of Lincoln Center.[53]

Steered by postwar technocrats such as John D. Rockefeller III and Frank Stanton, the Lincoln Center project was intended, however, to serve as an example of how to bring the beauty and enrichment of high culture—the ballet, symphony, opera, and theater—to "the people" while functioning as a very public, high-profile cultural weapon of the Cold War. As a 1957 statement from the board of directors declared: "To the World, Lincoln Center will announce America's cultural maturity." Such lofty goals, even if indeed meant altruistically, were manifested through a particularly rarified, elitist definition of what culture could and should be, often excluding the very people it was meant to serve and benefit.[54]

Realized through Robert Moses's Lincoln Square Urban Renewal Project and built on land declared a "slum" under Title I of the Federal Housing Act, Lincoln Center required the razing of fourteen blocks and the displacement of largely Black and Latinx communities in the Upper West Side to accommodate what one critic referred to as New York City's "impending cultural supermarket." The individuals and institutions driving the creation of the performing arts complex also needed its architecture to be ambitious, but putting this into practice

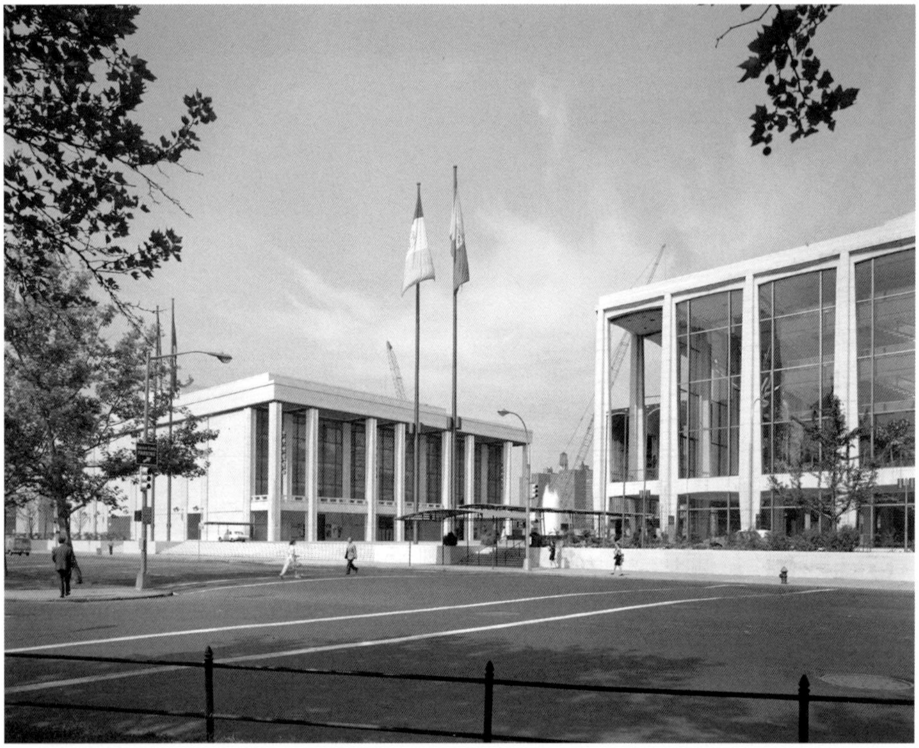

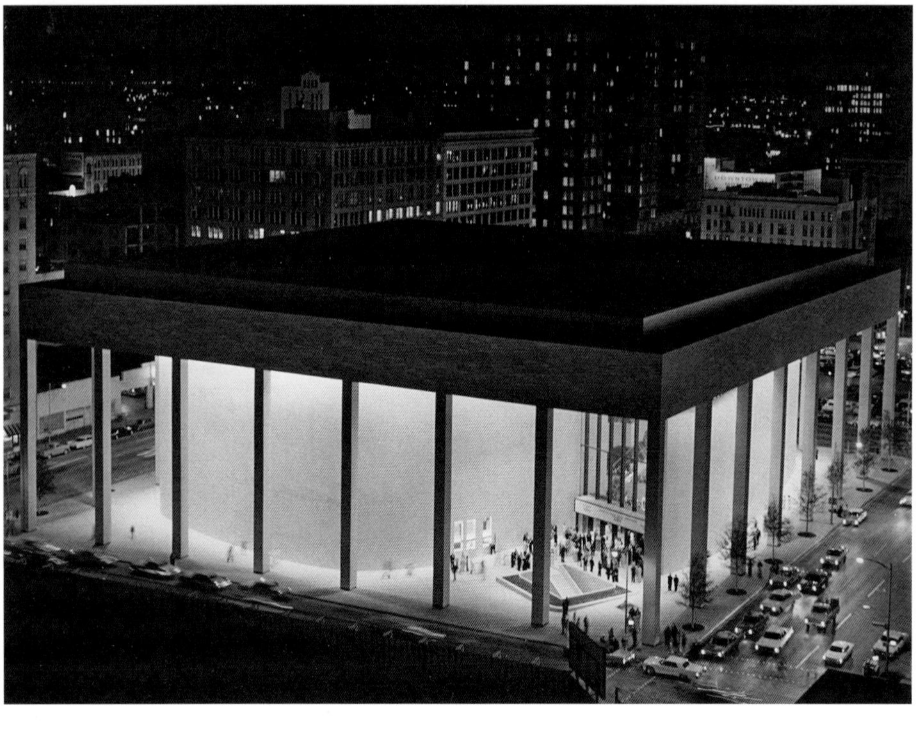

1.37
Lincoln Center for the Performing Arts, New York City, c. 1969.

1.38
Opening night of the Jesse H. Jones Hall for the Performing Arts, 615 Louisiana Street, Houston, Texas, 1966. Architect: Caudill Rowlett Scott.

proved a difficult and ultimately impossible task. In the end, Lincoln Center was an immense architectural undertaking by some of the most notable architects of a period that was instantaneously and ever since continually criticized for being too historicized in its form, not bold enough in its individual architectural innovation, and too detached from the public it was intended to serve.[55]

The project in Houston was a more modest undertaking, but both its ambitions and controversies closely mirrored those of Lincoln Center. In order to make room for the new performing arts center in Houston, the City Auditorium, which had hosted everything from wrestling and basketball games to popular musicians and the Houston Symphony between 1913 and 1954, was razed. This decision provoked larger debates around high and low culture, particularly about who was actually being served by "revitalizing" downtown Houston, with the Jesse H. Jones Hall itself illustrating "how both the physical and emotional impact of a building could signify progress and limitation at the same time." Further, while the progressive Jesse H. Jones Hall was intended to project an independent, booming, cultured city, accusations were made that the City of Houston was just "jumping on the Lincoln Center bandwagon." Despite this resistance, construction of Jesse H. Jones Hall began in January 1964 and the building opened to great fanfare and national media coverage in October 1966 (figure 1.38).[56]

Designed by the noted Texas-based firm Caudill Rowlett Scott, the building was a modernist showpiece that took up an entire city block in downtown Houston. The building's exterior was clad in travertine marble, enclosed by an eight-stories-high colonnade that ran the length of all four sides of the building, though open to, and level with, the surrounding streets. Frequently described as a "shell-like form," the interior structure of Jesse H. Jones Hall possessed sculptural characteristics that demanded to be viewed in the round, from all angles. The building shared with its New York City counterpart a nod to architecture's classical past; and such comparisons were only amplified by the selection of Lippold to create a work for the lobby. John T. Jones Jr., the chairman of the building committee and nephew of Jesse H. Jones, explained that he chose Lippold because the sculptor's "sensitivity to space in art form [was] applicable to the large grand lobby area of the hall." Like *Orpheus and Apollo* or Calder's large mobiles, *Gemini II* directly resonated with the form and spatial effects of the building for which it was designed. The miles of gold-plated steel wire cable and several-thousand hexagonal anodized-aluminum rods, ranging in length from thirty-six inches to six feet, followed the seams and lengths of the rectangular travertine wall panels as well as the row of clerestory windows (figure 1.39).[57]

Visible from both the main outdoor plaza—through the sole wall of floor-to-ceiling, steel-framed glass—and almost every position in the grand lobby, *Gemini II* swirled around the interior, changing course and appearance depending on the vantage point of the viewer. "All I did really," Lippold stated, "was to create a path through there of the way one's eyes might want to travel through that space; I was only interested in guiding people's visions through that space." Though weighing only two tons compared to *Orpheus and Apollo*'s five, *Gemini II* also appeared lithe

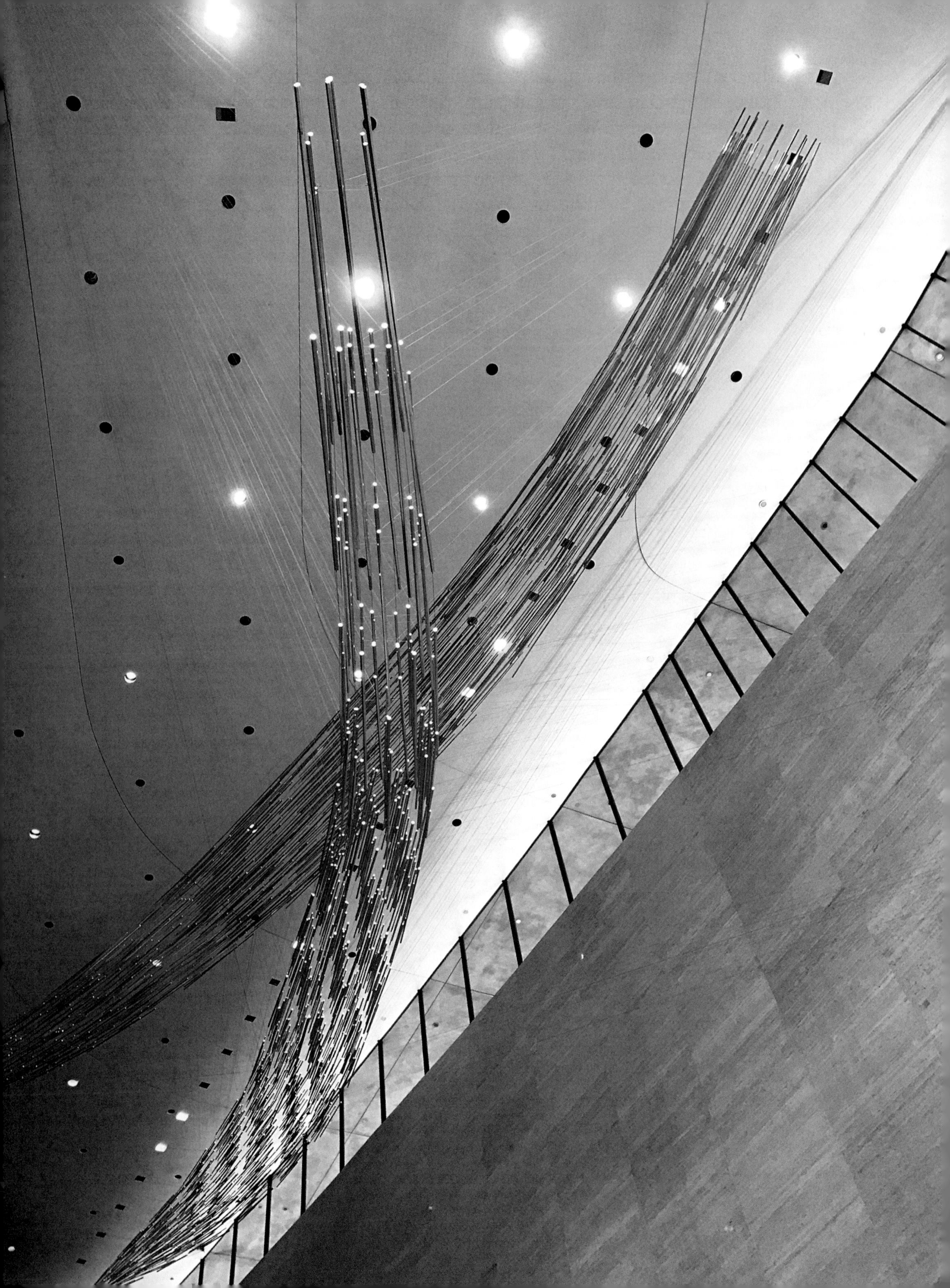

< 1.39
Richard Lippold, *Gemini II*, 1966. Gold-plated steel wire cable and anodized-aluminum rods, 52 ft. × 92 ft. × 80 ft. Jesse H. Jones Hall for the Performing Arts, Houston, Texas. Architect: Caudill Rowlett Scott.

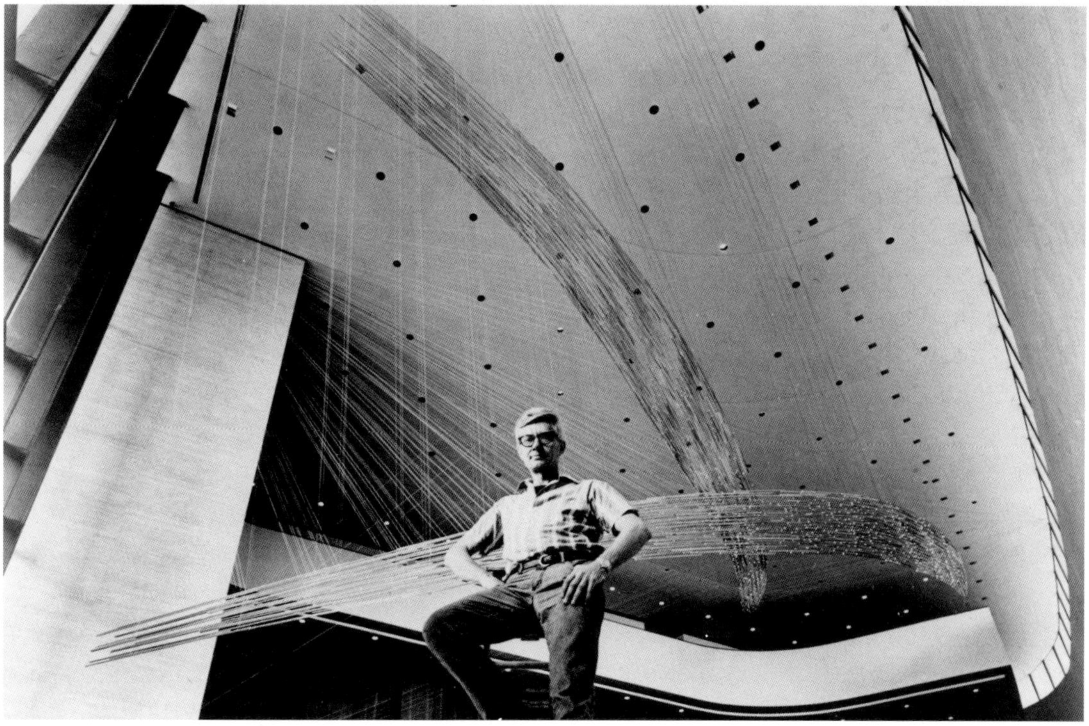

1.40
Sculptor Richard Lippold with *Gemini II*, 1966. Jesse H. Jones Hall for the Performing Arts, Houston, Texas. Architect: Caudill Rowlett Scott.

and light as it gracefully danced across the space, shimmering in the sunlight or when artificially lit in the evenings. The two masses of aluminum rods also remained distinct entities, hung midair in locations that complement and energize the architecture with maximum effect.[58]

The similarities and, perhaps more importantly, the differences, between the Philharmonic Hall and Jesse H. Jones Hall commissions, however, offer an opportunity to grasp the possibilities of a synergy of sculpture and architecture in the postwar period. In both venues, Lippold installed his sculptures into cavernous open spaces, voids that would otherwise be empty or wasted except to announce the monumental scale of the structure. From the beginning, however, Lippold positively responded to the dynamism and movement of Caudill Rowlett Scott's design, seeing more of the modern than the classical embedded in its form. The execution and installation processes also went far smoother in Houston than they did in New York City (figure 1.40). Working with only one assistant, Lippold installed the sculpture in three months, from late June through late September, and had fully completed the project in time for the opening gala on October 2, 1966.[59]

Unlike his later comments about the architecture of the Philharmonic Hall, Lippold described the architecture of the Jesse H. Jones Hall as a powerful source of inspiration for his sculpture, rather than something to react against or remedy. The function of *Gemini II* was not to rectify architectural deficiencies. *Orpheus and Apollo* was—and needed to be—a bombastic golden explosion that stitched together dead space. *Gemini II,* however, fused into the surrounding architecture, its twin forms zipping through the air like trails of a comet or metallic contrails—neither so dense that it would take away from the architecture, nor so sparse that it would disappear within the grandeur of its environment. As Lippold stated of Jesse H. Jones Hall and the resulting commission, "I've described that building as being like a Nautilus shell, and thought it really needed some kind of beautiful, scaled creature in there. I felt one would be too small or too lonely, so I made two, and two of them are prancing around in that space. In other words, I was trying to enhance, not fight the space. I don't ever want to do that. I have too much respect and love for architecture to try to kill it."[60] As a result, *Gemini II* proved a different model of collaboration between artist and architect: an alloying between sculpture and architecture.

In comparing the work with *Orpheus and Apollo*, the point is not to assert one as better than the other, but rather to address how sculpture, when thoughtfully made for specific interiors, could be woven together with architecture through a multiplicity of means. Lippold's personal reflections on the Houston project are more positive than those about the Philharmonic Hall, but the result in both cases was still a sculpture that became a natural fit with its specific architecture and site. As Lippold stated to the *Houston Post* even before he had started installing, *Gemini II* "would be meaningless outside of this hall. It needs the sympathy of this particular space, and I hope the architecture would be less without my sculpture." Even though many aspects of this sculpture produced what might be seen as a more successful day-to-day collaborative process, the sentiment of site connectedness and sympathetic synergy could just as easily apply to *Orpheus and Apollo*.[61]

The Limits of Synergy

Sculpture commissioned for architectural projects during the immediate postwar period was not always realized or attempted in ideal situations or with a full team of invested, collaborative stakeholders. The easiest or most successful examples shared not only a strong conception of how sculpture related to specific architecture, but also benefited from ardent supporters who clearly articulated the commission's function and significance to the overall project. On Friday, June 24, 1955, Bertoia completed the installation of a large, textured multiplane sculpture that hung from the ceiling in the new Dallas Public Library (figure 1.41). The work was the result of a positive, thoughtful collaboration between the artist and architect George Dahl, but became one of the messiest examples of how tenuous such undertakings could be in actual practice. Sculpture displayed in architectural interiors was experienced by a wider audience and had a more substantive presence within the built environment, but such interventions were not always understood or welcomed by the general public.

Within two weeks of Bertoia installing the commissioned piece, the ten-by-twenty-four-foot sculpture—comprised of various metal shapes made from copper, brass, and nickel alloys—was disassembled and removed from the building. Though today such a work may seem a rather benign abstract sculpture, the amputation of Bertoia's screen was the opening salvo of a public maelstrom that raged in Dallas over the entire summer of 1955. The specifics of this work—how it was realized, removed, and reinstalled—make for a compelling addition to the history of controversy in twentieth-century art, and provide fascinating insight into the cultural landscape of the United States during the postwar period—namely, how swaths of the general public received modern art. This historical context is important and should not be overlooked, but more pertinent here is why or how this work was not perceived, or received, as an integral element of the overall architectural project.

Of all the large-scale commissioned sculptures Bertoia created over the course of his career, as well as all of those created by Calder, Lippold, and Noguchi, the sculpture for the Dallas Public Library was the only one to elicit such a virulent public response or be removed under duress for nonstructural or redevelopment reasons during the artists' lifetime. The particularly fraught, admittedly anomalous, case study of Bertoia's library screen raises issues around the limitations of an artwork intended for public consumption, but also inversely catechized the parameters of what was needed for a true synergy between art and architecture to occur. Certainly, many in Dallas at the time saw its formal characteristics as too avant-garde, but the commission was also situated oddly within the library, hanging from the ceiling but in the form of a dividing screen. This functional confusion, even more than its overt modernism, made it vulnerable to a line of attack typically leveled at autonomous, or in later cases public, art.

The City of Dallas hired Dahl, a native Texan, to build a new downtown central library facility on the site of the Carnegie Library, which had fallen into disrepair in the half century since opening in 1901. Though Dahl had established

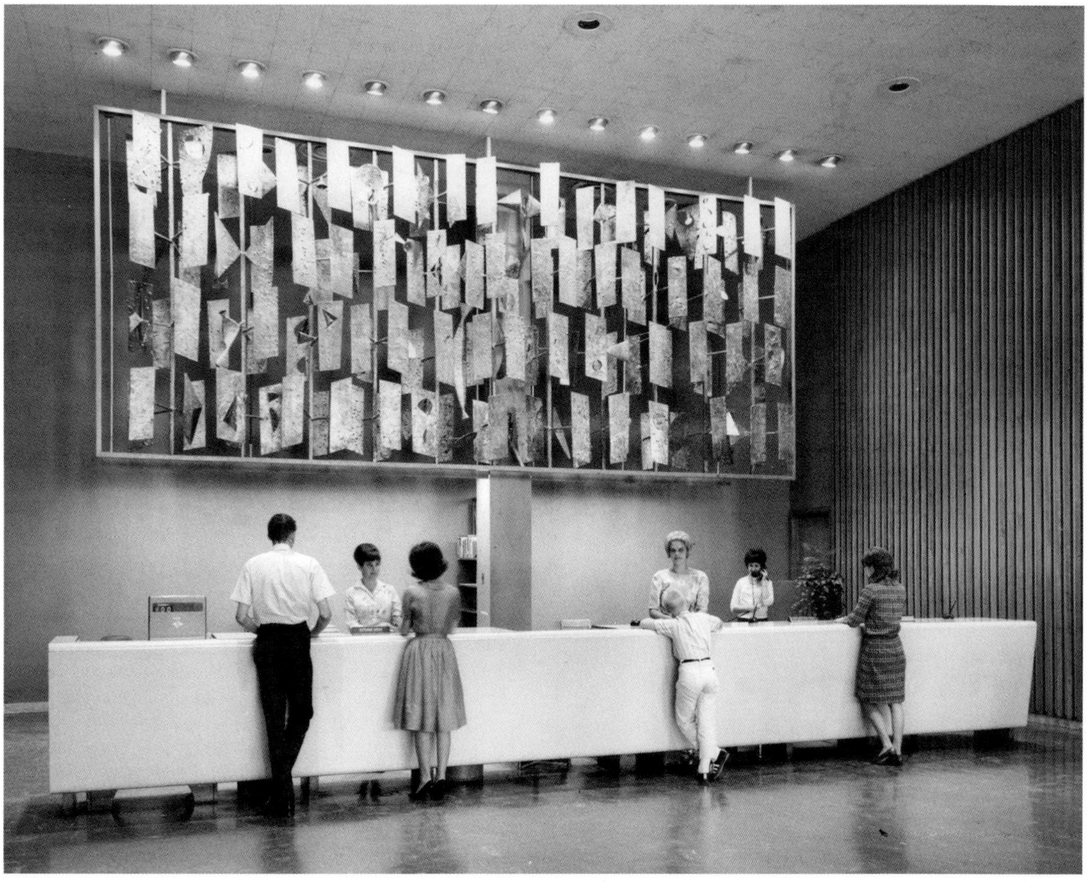

1.41
Harry Bertoia, *Untitled*, 1955. Brazed and welded copper, brass, and nickel alloys, 10 ft. × 24 ft. Dallas Public Library, Texas. Architect: George Dahl.

his prolific career in Dallas with art deco–influenced projects like the Fair Park complex, by the late 1940s he was working in a modernist style. As *Library Journal* declared in its report on the building: "The design is variously called 'contemporary' and 'ultra-modern' but it is above all functional." The new library was seen as a major cultural and social step forward for the city, which at the time was not known for its progressivism. The new building would be racially integrated, with front door access and full privileges for all of Dallas's citizens, including its then 15 percent African American population—a significant development considering other institutions in the city like the Dallas Independent School District, stores like Neiman Marcus, and more broadly the American Library Association would not fully integrate until the early 1960s. With a $2.5 million budget and exceedingly high expectations from the civic government and the citizenry of Dallas alike, the new library became one of the most significant building projects for the city during the immediate postwar period.[62]

Dahl had included an artwork in the original architectural design and corresponding budget for the building, though section 24–05 of the general contract described a mural painting, applied on a plaster screen in the main lobby. In March 1955, relatively late in the process, the architect hired Bertoia, paying him around $8,000 out of a $10,000 art allowance fund in the budget approved by the city and library board. Thus, from the very beginning, the resultant work was both associated with the concept of a mural and was inherently a very different object than intended or expected. When Bertoia arrived in Dallas to install the sculpture, it did not resemble any of the four sketches approved by the library board that he had sent to Dahl, but instead was a "combination of all of them." Bertoia told the *Dallas Morning News* that he worked on the screen, with two assistants, for ten weeks, creating as he went along and following no definite pattern. He made sure also to state that "in my workshop, we simulated the exact conditions of the Dallas Library. We re-created the library scene, keeping in mind the space, the function and the kind of architecture used."[63]

This attention to the specifics of site was and would remain a hallmark of Bertoia's commissioned work, as was the abstract form and lack of title. Never one to comment much on his sculpture, he did state at a private luncheon covered by the Dallas press that "it is very modern and contemporary of course. I have no name for it, for I do not think it should have any one name. A sculptor's art is his way of communicating." In what became a frequent quote in the ensuing controversy, Bertoia concluded, "I have been asked many times what my work means. And really what it represents is very much up to the observer. It is a mirror of the man or woman who looks at it. Those who find significance and meaning in it are those prepared to give it significance or meaning. Those who find nothing have, evidently not prepared their lives and probably are very happy about it." The people of Dallas were apparently not prepared to be reflected in such a modern, abstract sculpture.[64]

The controversy erupted when Mayor Robert Lee Thornton, along with members of the city council, previewed the sculpture shortly after its installation.

They were unimpressed. Thornton declared the work a "bunch of junk" with a cheap welding job to boot, even though Bertoia had spent about half of the total budget on materials alone and was already an accomplished master welder by 1955. Councilperson W. H. Harris bemused, "I wonder what he was thinking about when he made it. He must have had the whole family working on it, including the children." The mayor, however, did also note at this first viewing that the work was sure to "attract attention," and had "good advertising possibilities." In the following weeks, the issue of the hanging abstract screen became a massive citywide controversy, with hundreds of articles, columns, and letters sent to the editor devoted to the subject.[65]

While the city government continued to express dismay over the sum paid to Bertoia for the so-called bunch of junk, the removal of the piece came about because of Dahl. Essentially dismayed and infuriated, Dahl voluntarily offered to "purchase the mural in the Dallas Public Library and take it out, thereby relieving the taxpayers of the obligation to pay for it." In a public statement issued following the work's removal, the city declared: "We think that to buy more books and things of that character for the benefit of the most people would be a much wiser investment for the taxpayers than a mural which only a limited number would understand and enjoy, and we are deeply grateful to George Dahl for his fine contribution." In short, the City of Dallas liked the library building, just not how Dahl designed its interior.[66]

While the official reason given by the City was ostensibly about the "correct" use of taxpayer funds, their statement also revealed that the real ire was actually about the work being too modern and thus too foreign for the citizens of Dallas. Opponents of the work, including members of the local media and the countless individuals who weighed in on the matter, expressed a desire to see the work removed, and once it was, celebrated the outcome. Many were frustrated by the work's lack of a title, though one Marina Lewis of Oakland, California, aged eleven, declared to the *Dallas Morning News* that even without any, the sculpture reminded her of books. There was great confusion and consternation over what the work actually was and what to call it. Various designations included grid, screen, sculpture, curtain, frame, "maze of metal," and "metallic Christmas tree."[67]

Others critiqued Bertoia directly, decrying his artistic abilities and referring to him as "America's most expensive metal cutter." Some focused on Bertoia's outsider status, frequently identifying him specifically as a "Pennsylvania metal worker." One of the most explicitly xenophobic letters made a direct connection between the "minority who has forced the 'Bungling of Bertoia' upon us," here meant to connote the return of the sculpture to the library and the cultural elites within global Cold War / McCarthy-era politics: "The minority has done away with segregation. The minority is opposed to the Bricker Amendment and... favors One World, and to destroy our constitution. The minority wants us to stay in the United Nations, to be a tool of Russia." The majority of detractors, however, decried the fact that a more local or regional artist had not been selected. Even those who resented the "continued accusations of Communism against contemporary artists," and "ill-informed judgments" about modern art in general, were upset that talented Dallas or southwest artists were not selected for the project. Many alternatives were suggested: work by American sculptor Frederic Remington, portraits of notable Texans, and figurative paintings representing Dallas.[68]

There were supporters of the work, and they expressed concern that the response to Bertoia's screen would only further national perceptions of Dallas being culturally retrograde. Later the same year, the nascent Dallas Museum of Fine Arts (now Dallas Museum of Art) would itself become embroiled in a modern art controversy when a local women's group, the Public Affairs Luncheon Club, charged the institution with exhibiting the work of artists with Communist affiliations—including Pablo Picasso and Diego Rivera—at the expense again of local artists. While the museum, unlike the library, held firm, the Bertoia controversy was far from an isolated incident within the cultural landscape in Dallas during the postwar period.[69]

As local intellectual and *Dallas Morning News* commentator Lon Tinkle reiterated, the real issue was not the cost, but rather the resistance to modern art. He noted that, unlike so many weighing in on the issue, he had taken the trouble to go see the work—and really it cannot be overstated that the vast majority of people commenting on the screen during the summer of 1955 had not yet even seen the piece. Recounting for his readers an "exhilarating experience," Tinkle stated: "The yellows that form a color symphony simply sing forth, and the play of light and shade, of pattern echoing pattern, creates an authentic beauty. We stake our faith in public taste that the library's mural will be—once given a chance—a whopping success." He concluded by also noting that once the "gold glinting mural" was seen as intended—surrounded by greenery, books, and library staff and patrons—that the "Bertoia composition will become the rage." A handful of other commentators echoed the idea that to really grasp the work, it was important to see it in the setting it was intended for, in the finished space, rather than judging it as a work of autonomous art indifferent to its surroundings.[70]

The citizens of Dallas would eventually be given the opportunity to make up their own minds when, a month after the controversy had started, a "committee of art lovers" raised the money to buy the work back from Dahl, who had been storing the screen at his home since its removal. With the official obstacle of misuse of taxpayer funds removed, the City had little choice but to accept the gift and reinstall the work, though it did come with a firm stipulation from Dahl. The city council would have to agree by letter that the screen would be restored to its original location. By the public opening in September, Bertoia's metal screen was once again above the book-return desk, just to the right of the main entrance on the ground floor. On seeing the work reinstalled, Mayor Thornton even declared how he now liked the work because he found out it was not a "mural," but a metal screen.[71]

In the end, the new Dallas Public Library, inclusive of the Bertoia, was considered a great success. By the late 1950s, the sculptural screen had become a shorthand logo for the library, often appearing on promotional materials. The City of Dallas, however, would not establish an arts council, public art committee, or its Percent for Art program until the 1980s: policy directives that would have mitigated much of the controversy around the library commission. While the removal of a work of art had been resolved in favor of artistic freedom, it did little to fix the underlying issues that had sparked the debate. As the Dallas Chapter of the American Institute of Architects declared in their own statement issued shortly after it was agreed the work would return:

> If the object is not a worthy creative work it should not be placed in the library at all. On the other hand, if it is acceptable for use as an ornament of the building, if it is permitted to occupy the place for which it was designed, it should be paid for by the city, and neither the architect, nor one, nor a group of private citizens should be called on, or even permitted, to pay the cost of it. If the judgment of one outstanding architect cannot be accepted in a matter such as this, then the question can only be settled by a group of those who, by training and aesthetic instinct, are competent to pass judgment on the creative work of others.[72]

The city council's response to the AIA was obstinate, declaring that they had no intention of surrendering to "any architect's judgment what the city should pay for to go into a public building."[73]

For those who defended the work as well as Bertoia and Dahl, there was a belief in creative control and independence. It is understandable why the citizens of Dallas may have wanted to see the work of a local artist represented in their main public library—such an approach after all has become a bedrock in the commissioning of recent public art. It is also understandable that an ambitious modernist architect, hired in good faith by the City of Dallas, should want to express fully and freely his modern creative vision and design a building project that would attract attention beyond the region. For Dahl, commissioning an artist who had already established his reputation by completing high-profile architectural projects, like Bertoia, was a crucial element in this vision.

As Jerry Bywaters, director of the Dallas Museum of Fine Arts, stated of the library screen, "This is no wild effort seeking notoriety. It is a careful and skillful creation by an expert who knows what he is about. This decorative grid has an inventive quality that is intriguing and supplements the architecture and makes original use of the techniques for which our machine age has become famous. The price is not out of line. I have every confidence in an architect's ability to commission work in buildings they create." *Dallas Tribune Herald* columnist Rual Askew echoed Bywaters's faith in the architect's ability to embellish their commissions with the most complementary design, stating, "The basic issue is not whether the Bertoia screen was good art or bad. It was, more seriously, whether a ranking artist should suffer the indignity of a line of reasoning which [is to] say that what is unfamiliar is suspect, that what is not 'liked' by some is unacceptable to all. It smacks of that school of thought whose graduates, in a gallery of disguises, have recently prowled the land with a vengeance that hoots down reputations first and examines the facts later." Bertoia quickly moved on from the Dallas commission, spending the next twenty years of his career completing numerous other significant public and private architectural commissions—all with minimal to no controversy, even those created in cities generally considered to be less cosmopolitan or culturally sophisticated.[74]

What then was different about the screen for the Dallas Public Library? The particular cultural and social dynamics present in the city during the 1950s as well as the broader debates about modernism between so-called elites and perceived philistines certainly created a perfect storm of controversy around the library commission. More crucial, however, is the general lack of knowledge—then and now—about the ways sculpture can or should function within architecture. While the two are often conflated, architectural commissions, especially in this case, are not the same thing as "public art." The library screen was not created to represent the values of a city or community or even adorn a building or space paid for by taxpayer money, but rather commissioned as a part of Dahl's overall architectural design. When the city approved his plans and budget and then inspected the results they did not protest, for example, the expense or practicality of the polished black-granite facade.

Bertoia's sculpture, however, was not simply a costly material or high-end finishing element. The sculptor took into account the exact setting of the ground-floor lobby when creating the screen. Dahl, however, did not adapt to the specifics of the resulting work, no doubt because he was not altogether certain of what he would be getting. The work did not just contain hundreds of metal plates, but pieces welded together in an open grid that extended outward from its frame in two directions, creating a complex, textured work in high relief. Hung from the ceiling above the book-return desk, the screen was spotlighted against a green background by a row of angled, partially recessed light fixtures. Between the artificial lighting and the natural light streaming in through the front doors, the sculpture did shine and even cast some shadows, but Dahl had chosen to position the work in between two interior pillars and very close to the wall behind. There was no opportunity to see the work in the round, from multiple vantage points. Further, unlike other large-scale screens Bertoia created, the Dallas commission did not really function as a screen, but resembled something closer to a static curtain. The sculpture is a striking textural focal point in the lobby, but never became structurally or spatially entrenched within its architectural environment. In the end, the function of the work was limited to that of the mural originally included in Dahl's proposal.

As a result, the experience of Bertoia's sculpture for the Dallas Public Library was far different from walking through a lobby underneath a spinning Calder mobile, one of Lippold's large metal forms, or even looking up at Noguchi's sculpted ceiling. The success of the commission in Dallas, thus, was never bound to, nor should it have been judged on, how much people liked or disliked it, but rather on how well it spatially operated within the building and how, in turn, the building responded to the sculpture. In attempting to achieve a synergy between sculpture and architecture, willing collaboration or novel installation tactics alone were not enough. Though not articulated as such by any involved parties at the time, the ineffective or at least confused incorporation of the work with the lobby space and the overall architectural design opened the door for controversy during the summer of 1955. Such a statement is not meant to shift blame to the artist or architect from the political operatives or public largely responsible for the controversy that engulfed the work, but rather as a means to extract valuable insights about the complex matrix of material, creative, and bureaucratic conditions needed to achieve, or even attempt, a synergy between sculpture and architecture during the postwar period.

Chapter 2

Dividing Space

On June 20, 1951, the Museum of Modern Art (MoMA) in New York City opened *Modern Relief*, an exhibition comprised of "original works and photographs of reliefs in their architectural setting," stretching chronologically from ancient Egypt to early twentieth-century European modernism and American contemporary art. Jane Sabersky, the curator of the exhibition, noted in the introductory wall text that until the twentieth century, relief was an integral part of buildings and was always "conceived in relation to its background." She emphasized, however, that contemporary relief had begun to move away from the surface of the wall, becoming instead an "independent space defining element." Even when still attached to a wall in a more traditional manner, these newer expressions became "a decisive factor towards the visual destruction of that background."[1]

Isamu Noguchi's *Lunar Landscape* (1944) was one of the featured objects, as was a photograph of the artist's "ceiling decoration" for the American Stove Company Building in St. Louis (figure 2.1). The latter was installed next to an image of Jean Arp's "wall decoration," *Constellations* (1950), created for the Architects Collaborative–designed Harkness Commons dining room at Harvard University in Cambridge, Massachusetts, and two photographs of Naum Gabo's models for a "relief construction (c. 1949–50)" commissioned, but never realized, for the 51st and 52nd Street entrance halls of the Esso Building at Rockefeller Center in New York City. Painting and sculpture, as well as other photographs of works *in situ*, by twelve other artists including Mary Callery, Marcel Duchamp, and Jackson Pollock, rounded out the idiosyncratic exhibition checklist.[2]

Traditionally relief has designated a type of sculpture that projects outward, in varying degrees, from a background or support and has a long and rich history, usually associated with pictorial, narrative content, or architectural decoration.[3]

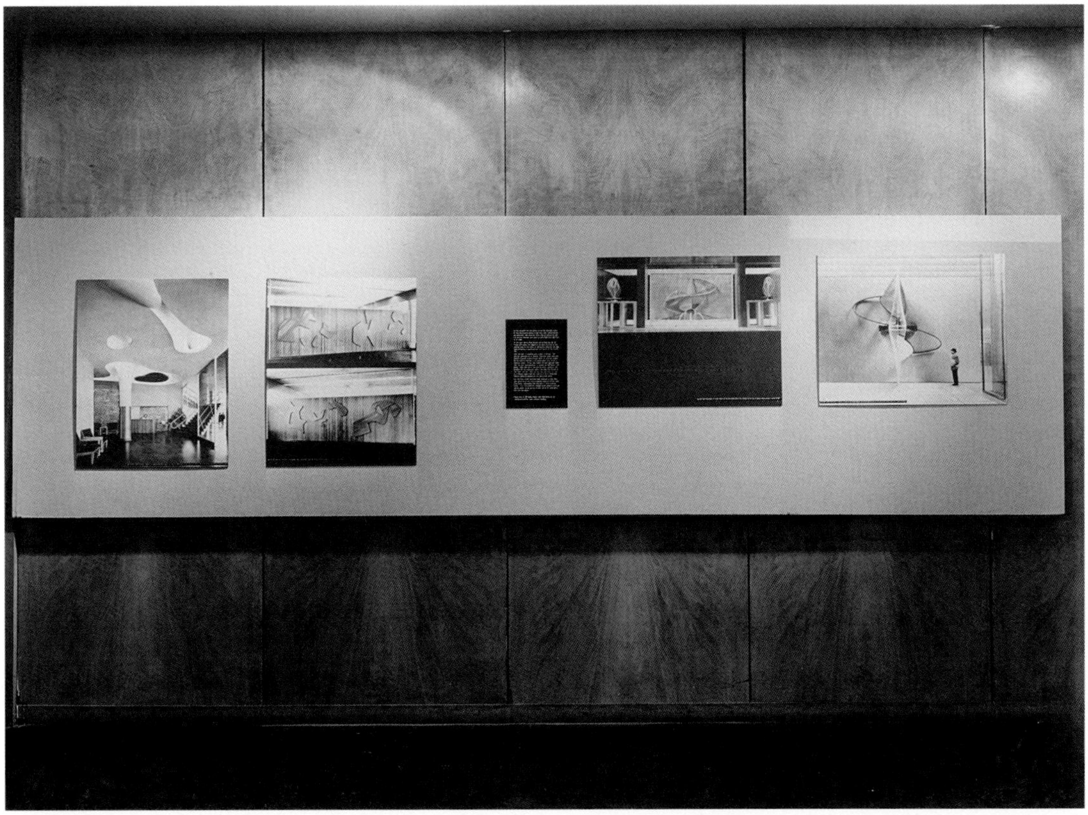

2.1
Installation view of the exhibition, *Modern Relief*, MoMA, New York City, June 20–July 15, 1951. Photographic Archive, Museum of Modern Art Archives, New York City, IN479.1.

While more portable, smaller-scale examples exist, like cameos and medals, relief is often synonymous with work that extends from, and thus belongs to, a wall. Noguchi's American Stove Company Building ceiling or *Lunar Landscape*, especially when placed next to photographs of ancient Assyrian low-relief carvings or even Pablo Picasso's wood *Relief* (1913), suggested an expansive, if at times also perplexing, definition of the exhibition's unifying theme.

In a *New York Times* review of *Modern Relief*, illustrated solely by a photograph of Noguchi's ceiling for the American Stove Company Building, art critic Stuart Preston noted that while admirable in intention, "the original works of art, shown alongside photographs of others already in place, are not numerous, nor are they all of first quality or importance." Preston continued, "This exhibition is more than just an anthology. It is tied to a theme. It is intended to instruct rather than delight. It proposes to demonstrate how artist and architect can cooperate, to their mutual benefit, on a single project.... The aim is praiseworthy and the emphasis on art's being 'practical' as well as spiritual is a familiar one in these halls. Any objections to this particular scheme can be made on its own grounds. Just how useful to builder or sculptor can this display be? To my mind it raises more questions than it answers."[4]

The diverse image and object selection of *Modern Relief* certainly led to some of the more questionable or question-raising elements of the exhibition. Noguchi's ceiling, or even his related *Lunar Voyage* (1947) realized for a hallway wall in the SS *Argentina*, may have drawn from the tradition of relief, in particular the sunken relief; but these works also suggested that a complete reevaluation of the supporting background, of the wall itself, was indeed underway. As Sabersky wrote, "Today, new building techniques and construction in steel have created a new

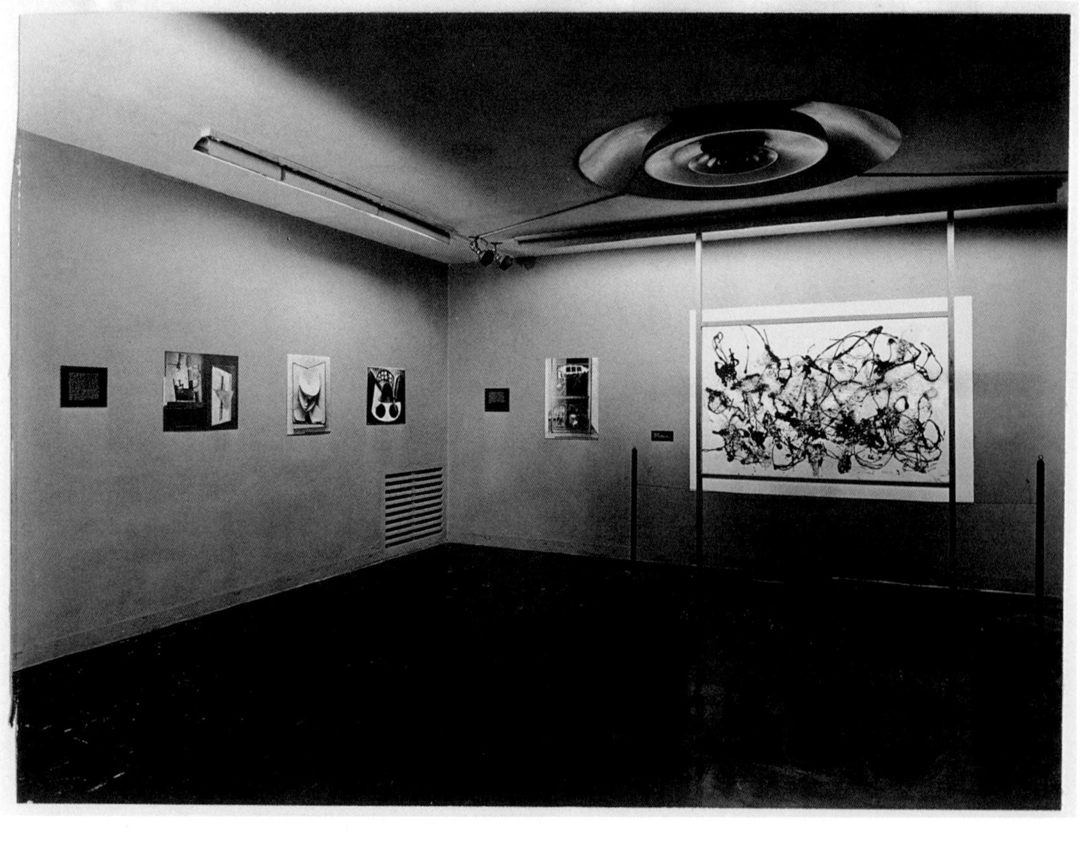

2.2
Installation view of the exhibition, *Modern Relief*, MoMA, New York City, June 20–July 15, 1951. Photographic Archive, Museum of Modern Art Archives, New York City, IN479.5.

esthetic with less emphasis on the wall, which is no longer a supporting element but an enclosing screen." By including Noguchi's works alongside a photograph of Duchamp's *The Large Glass* (1915–23) and Pollock's *No. 29, 1950* (1950), constructed from black and aluminum enamel paint, expanded steel, string, beads, colored glass and pebbles on glass, the curator was trying to articulate something new occurring within the practice of relief, even if broadly defined (figure 2.2).[5]

New materials, new techniques, and a greater emphasis on scale, texture, reflectivity, and transparency were not only transforming the relationship between art and the wall, but also the status of the wall altogether within modern architecture. By the early 1950s, artists and architects were offering new visions of how to divide and demarcate space, and increasingly incorporated murals, screens, curtains, and grilles into interior designs. The wall, broadly conceived, became a crucial site for theoretical debates around a renewal of using art in architecture during the postwar period. Many of the resulting artistic interventions or experiments, and their subsequent critical reception, focused solely on decorative function, of how art could humanize, enliven, or beautify the increasingly stark interiors of modernist architecture.

Ornamentation itself is functional, an additive process that often proves vital to an overall architectural design, but decorative expressions like sculptural screens and grilles possessed a greater structural connection with architecture, as well as a shared language of form, materials, and processes. As architectural historian Eleanor Bitterman wrote in 1952, "As sculpture is formed in the same materials as architecture, some architects consider it more appropriate than mural paintings in buildings.... There are many architectural uses for sculpture: entire walls, parts of walls, or areas in front of walls; ceilings; doorways; window frames; lintels; columns; roofs; corners; open room spaces; courtyards, gardens, and plazas." Artists like Harry Bertoia, Costantino Nivola, and Noguchi created highly sophisticated, complex examples of how sculpture could be used in architecture to a more structural effect during the immediate postwar period. Bertoia created a behemoth explosion of spill-cast, bronze wall panels for Dulles International Airport in Chantilly, Virginia. Nivola crafted a monumental sand-cast wall for the Olivetti Showroom in New York City. Noguchi created a metal sculptural wall that also functioned as a water feature, alongside another sculpted ceiling, in the lobby of a new skyscraper at 666 Fifth Avenue in New York City. Bertoia, in particular, would perhaps most extensively explore the wall as sculptural form, creating a number of large multiplane constructions secured to floors, rather than ceilings as had been in the case in Dallas, including two brazed metal pieces for the General Motors Technical Center in Warren, Michigan and the Manufacturers Trust Company Building in New York City.[6]

These sculptural projects were all decorative features in interior threshold spaces. They remained complexly connected to artistic traditions like relief while also functioning as sophisticated modern adornment. None were load bearing and they shared much with other interiors: intentionally decorative architectural elements like screens, grilles, tiling, appliqués, or fabrics that became prevalent in midcentury modern architecture. Quite simply, each was a wall. Commissions by Bertoia, Nivola, and Noguchi also never relinquished their status as sculptures. In taking on more architectural functionality and specificity, these projects blurred the boundaries between wall, relief, and sculptural object, presenting in the process another path to alloying sculpture and architecture.

Surface Decoration

Modern Relief was not the only exhibition during the late 1940s and 1950s to explore the phenomenon of modern artists creating works for architectural projects, nor the only one to offer guidance about how artists and architects could best collaborate. In 1949, the Betty Parsons Gallery in New York City presented a solo exhibition of thirty-four new paintings by Jackson Pollock. The artist regularly showed his work at the gallery during the late 1940s and 1950s, but this particular exhibition was unique as Pollock had asked Peter Blake, an architect and then head of the Department of Architecture and Design at MoMA, to help hang the exhibition. Blake met Pollock through the graphic designer Herbert Matter, during the fall of 1948 in East Hampton, New York. For the exhibition at Betty Parsons, Blake also contributed a half-inch-scale architectural model of a proposed fifty-by-one-hundred-foot building with no exterior walls and a glass roof, featuring paintings and sculptures by Pollock (figure 2.3). Blake recalled how he started thinking about the idea following his first visit to Pollock's studio in Springs, New York. The architect described the structure as a "large, somewhat abstract 'exhibit' of his work—a kind of 'Ideal Museum' in which his paintings were suspended between the earth and the sky, and set between mirrored walls so as to extend into infinity."

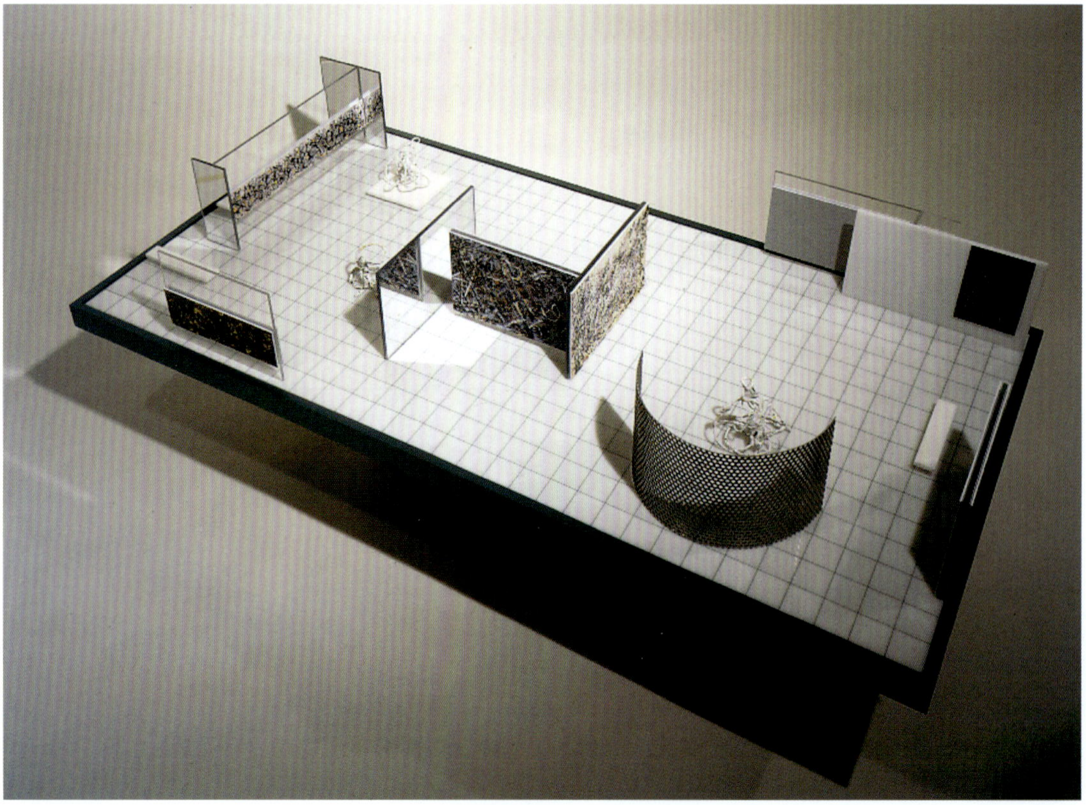

2.3
Peter Blake, *Ideal Museum*, 1949. Model of display space for Jackson Pollock's work. Recreation of the original model by Patrick Bodden 1995.

Promotional materials for the exhibition, billed as *Paintings 1949*, announced the project as: "murals in modern architecture*: A theatrical exercise using Jackson Pollock's Paintings and Sculpture. By Peter Blake.*"[7]

The project was indeed an exercise: a speculative building never realized. Blake drew inspiration from another, earlier architectural proposal: Ludwig Mies van der Rohe's Museum for a Small City project (1941–43). In Mies's drawings, sculpture and large mural-sized paintings, most predominantly Picasso's *Guernica* (1937), are presented in an open-plan structure. Most critics reviewing the exhibition at Betty Parsons made no mention of Blake's contributions or model. Arthur Drexler, the architecture editor at *Interiors* and Blake's successor at MoMA, published a feature on the model, writing that the design recalled the integration of painting and architecture found in Renaissance frescoes, but "this time without message or content. Its sole purpose is to heighten our experience."[8] While Drexler's analysis may flatten or diminish the content or achievement of the paintings at the core of the *Ideal Museum*, it did emphasize the extreme to which Blake sought to fuse Pollock's work with his architecture, offering in the process a model for a renewed, transformative exchange between art and architecture.

Blake's *Ideal Museum*, however, did not simply feature Pollock's work, but used it architecturally. Mirrors amplified the presence of the large paintings, taking on the functionality of walls. Art historian K. L. H. Wells has convincingly framed the project within the context of nineteenth-century German architect Gottfried Semper's theory of dressing. She argues that Pollock's paintings as deployed in Blake's design can also be seen as woven canvas textiles hanging "as the enclosures and creators of architectural space." Wells's analysis places the emphasis back on the expanded functionalism of art, but there is also the issue of how Blake used sculpture within the interior and thought sculpturally about the project as a whole.[9]

By fusing the paintings with walls and utilizing mirrors to divide and further expand the space, Blake's *Ideal Museum* transformed Pollock's two-dimensional work into a sculpture, reorienting the paintings' pictorial frontality and making them into something more akin to freestanding objects. Pollock also notably made three small wire and plaster sculptures, all painted in a style similar to his paintings, at Blake's specific request. The miniature objects are the only three-dimensional works Pollock made during this period of his career, and as architectural historian Eric Lum suggests, acted as "fulcrum points around which the viewer can reengage from one localized space to another." The sculptures further modulated the architecture and drew attention to the unified conception of habitable space created through the experience of art.[10]

Nearly a year after the exhibition at Betty Parsons, the *Muralist and the Modern Architect*, held at the Kootz Gallery in New York City in October 1950, would also attempt to provide a path for interdisciplinary collaboration (figure 2.4). The *Muralist and the Modern Architect* featured five collaborative projects. Gallerist Samuel Kootz matched five artists he represented with five notable modernist architects, and as the catalogue elaborated, the impetus for the exhibition was "to encourage the use of modern artists by architects and builders." The chosen architects had "planned project for the artists," and "made models showing the use of the mural in their planning." Kootz paired William Baziotes with Philip Johnson; Adolph Gottlieb with Marcel Breuer; David Hare with Frederick Kiesler; Hans Hofmann with Josep Lluís Sert and Paul Lester Wiener; and Robert Motherwell with Walter Gropius and the Architects Collaborative.[11]

Unlike Blake's vision for Pollock's paintings, or most of the architectural commissions presented in *Modern Relief*, the majority of the projects presented in the *Muralist and the Modern Architect* were essentially scaled-up easel paintings. Art historian Emily Warner has persuasively argued that this scalability, rather than simply the size of murals, is what made the form compelling to both midcentury architects and potential art collectors, as well as reflecting broader developments taking place in vanguard painting at the time. Abstract Expressionism, for example, embraced the scale of the mural, but influential critics like Clement Greenberg strove to assert and maintain the formalist autonomy of painting, its separation not only from the public sphere and social space, but also from any suggestion of functionality. This desired detachment ran counter to the inherent purpose of murals. Many theorists and practitioners touted the belief that the mural, as Warner writes, could be a "site of collective viewing and, by extension, collective social experience." Others emphasized the decorative resonance and contrast offered by the large-scale painting of the New York School, arguing that it belonged on the "pristine walls of modern architecture," as "ornamentation, conceived in an idiom of our times, to clothe these often dispirited surfaces."[12]

Kootz wrote in the catalogue of the *Muralist and the Modern Architect*, "The modern painter is in constant search of a wall," while the "creative architect demands the murals and sculpture of the modern artist." Though the dealer did not include Pollock in his exhibition, his work and its critical reception had certainly informed its framework. Kootz's statement, in fact, evokes those made by Greenberg in his review of an earlier exhibition of Pollock's work in 1948 at the Betty Parsons Gallery, where the critic heralded another "step forward" in contemporary painting. Greenberg wrote of Pollock's "concentration on surface texture and tactile qualities," as well as his "even, all-over design," while also preemptively acknowledging the critique of Pollock's work as decorative "wallpaper patterns." The critic declared, "In this day and age the art of painting increasingly rejects the easel and yearns for the wall." The scale of work by Pollock and other artists associated with Abstract Expressionism during the immediate postwar period quickly led to a new definition of mural, one synonymous with painting.[13]

There remained then an unresolved tension within the muralism of the immediate postwar period. Exhibitions like the *Muralist and the Modern Architect* encouraged the application of mural painting in architecture, while artists like Pollock and Mark Rothko, as is evidenced in his revoked commission for the Four Seasons Restaurant in New York City, were loath to have their work exploited as decoration, as mere "wallpaper." For many—both then and now—such utility was detrimental to both modern painting and modern architecture. Art historian

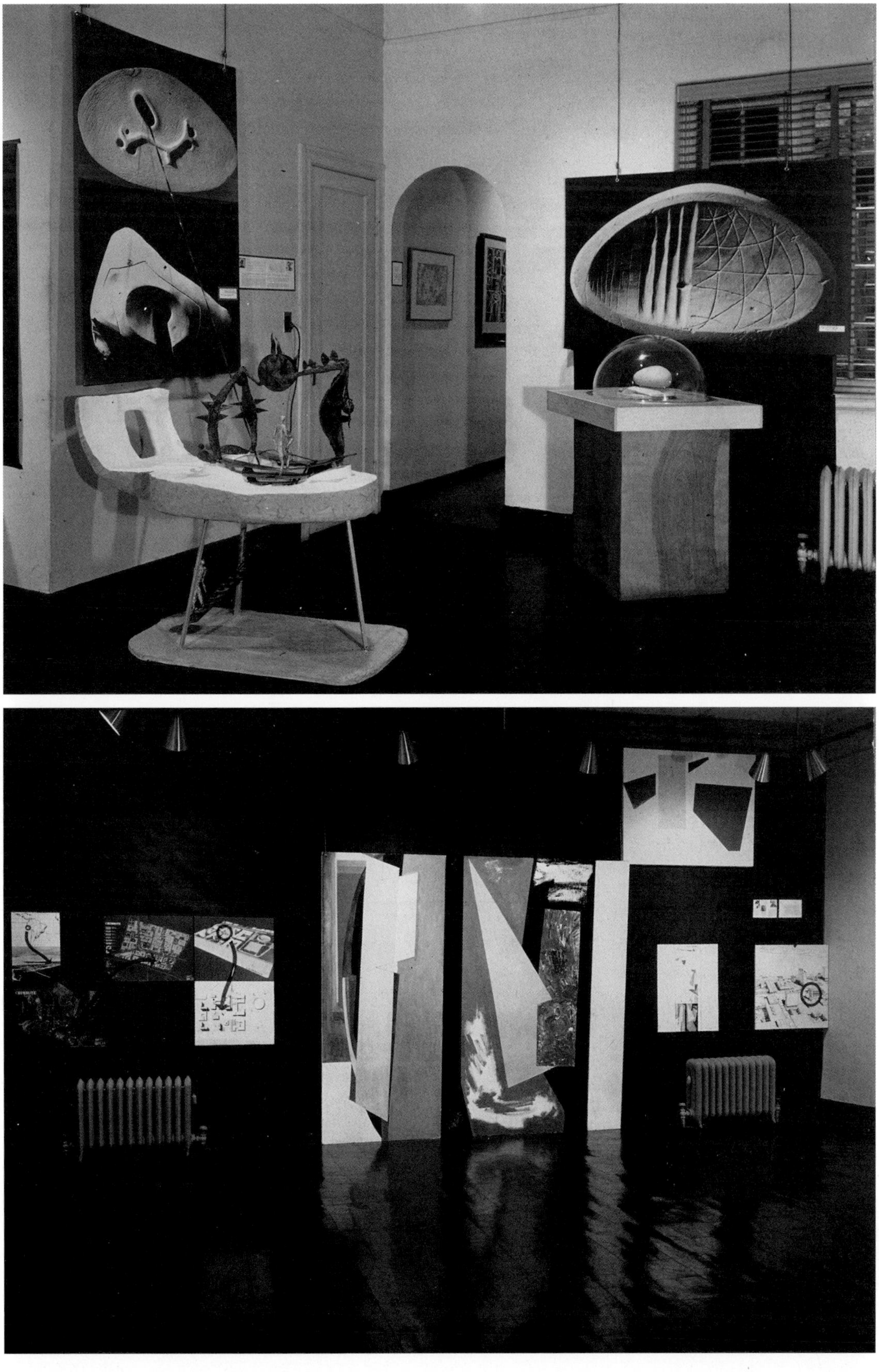

2.4
Installation view of *The Muralist and the Modern Architect*, Kootz Gallery, New York City, October 1950. Top: Frederick Kiesler's *Endless House* (1947–60) and David Hare's commissioned sculpture. Kootz Gallery scrapbook #22, Kootz Gallery Records, 1923–1966, Archives of American Art, Smithsonian Institution, Washington, DC.

William Kaizen, for example, states that when painting becomes a wall, its autonomy is lost and it approaches the status of interior decoration, while Lum succinctly summarizes this perspective writing that the "downside to this state of equilibrium would be the mutual negation of their respective effects: painting acting as a surface remedy masking the underlying formal poverty in postwar building, and architecture neutralizing abstract expressionism's heroic aspirations by delegating it the function of ornamentation." Exhibitions like the *Muralist and the Modern Architect* and *Modern Relief*, with their semantic slippage and uneven, multidisciplinary checklists, demonstrated that mural-scaled painting and wall reliefs were all too often deployed as visual embellishments, regardless of how well matched with an architect or suited for an architectural interior.[14]

The threat to painting or any vanguard art, however, was not functionality or being perceived as decorative, but rather a lack of imagination in how it could be used with the built environment, of how well art and architecture could be conceived of and realized together. While the *Muralist and the Modern Architect* may have been driven, at least in part, by a desire to facilitate collaboration between art and architecture in the public sphere, it also ended up highlighting the already well-established difficulties of such attempts. As Aline B. Louchheim noted in her review of the exhibition, "The catalogue's phraseology, saying the architects 'planned projects for the artists' is somewhat ambiguous. The buildings (all except two of them actually in work) were done before the fact and the architects then designated where in each job, they conceived a mural or where they would be willing to have one."[15]

The most well-received project featured in the *Muralist and the Modern Architect*, for example, was Hare's work with Kiesler, which was not a mural at all, but rather a sculpture. Unlike the murals or paintings featured in the exhibition, Hare's contribution was a massive sculpture presented as a bronze maquette with jagged forms accompanied by two figures entering it, made for the central core of Kiesler's speculative architectural project, *Endless House* (1947–60). As one critic wrote in praise of what ended up being a productive collaboration, "Unlike the other architects, Kiesler gave his artist a truly architectural problem—the design of a stairwell."[16]

Kiesler, like Blake before him, had the benefit of creating a model of speculative architecture, "a theatrical exercise," but both architects also shared a pronounced awareness of how sculpture was uniquely predisposed to help shape space, to achieve something greater than mere "surface remedy." They understood, as art historian Gibson Danes wrote in 1947, that "sculpture can serve as a catalyst of the space-mass-volume relations because it enriches and amplifies its spatial ambient as well as exerting its own independent existence. By its character, dynamic and lithe, or monumental and weighty, sculpture can, with its emphatic use of profile, texture, color, and movement, provide a three-dimensional counterpoint to the whole architectural ensemble."[17] Sculpture as a wall, even when deployed off a support or in a manner similar to a mural or relief, became an interloper, a physical pivot through which to navigate and shape architecture.

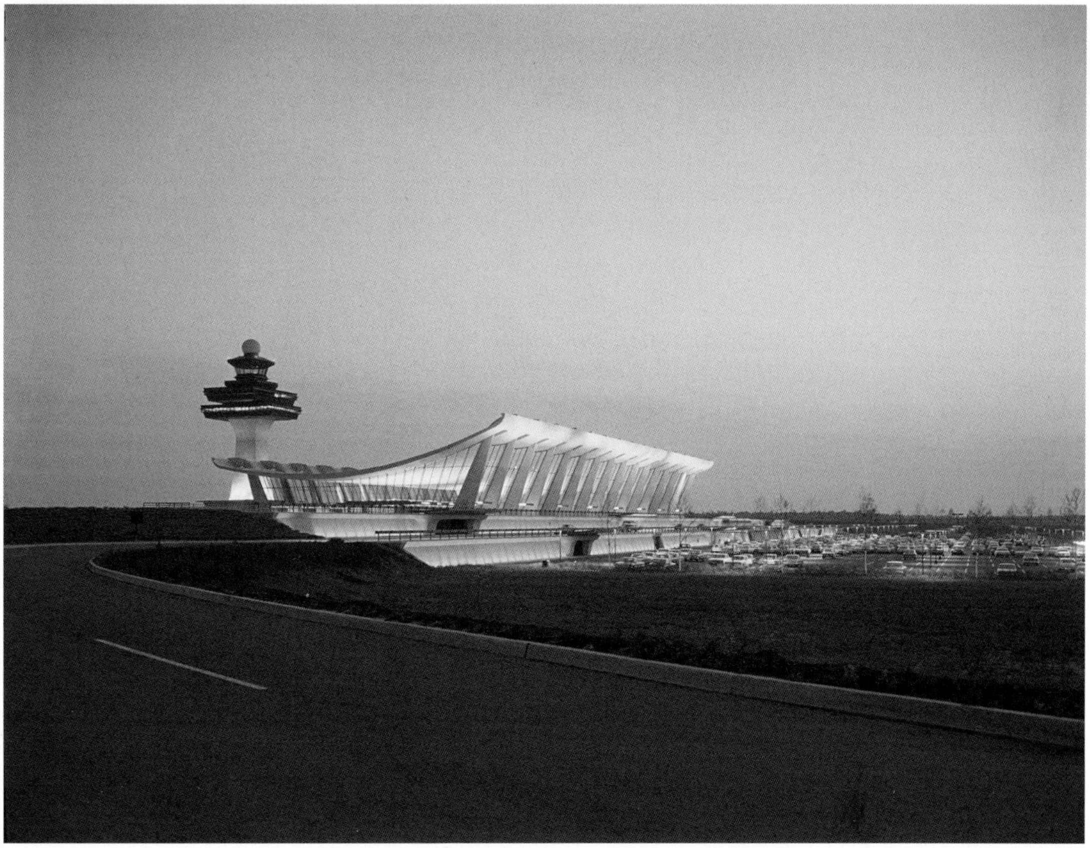

2.5
Dulles International Airport, Chantilly, Virginia, 1958–63. Architect: Eero Saarinen & Associates.

Sculpted Walls

Dulles International Airport (1958–63) opened in Chantilly, Virginia on November 17, 1962 with a dedication ceremony attended by President John F. Kennedy (figure 2.5). Heralded as an airport for the "Jet Age," Dulles was instantly lauded for its technological innovation and modern styling. Designed by Eero Saarinen, the airport boasted virtuoso use of concrete, pioneering mobile lounges, which transported passengers directly to their planes, and the largest terminal building in the United States, stretching six hundred feet in length. Critic Ada Louise Huxtable described the project as a "mature work" of architecture and a "great moment in art." In discussing the terminal building specifically, with its "soaring, sculptured, 65-foot-high concrete supports," culminating in a "striking catenary roof, to create a dominating façade," she declared, "It works esthetically, as a kind of monumental abstract sculpture. And it works symbolically, as a strong, splendid statement of the architecture of our age, our needs and our nation."[18] Dulles, like Saarinen's TWA Flight Center at Idlewild Airport that opened earlier in 1962, offered a vision of architecture as sculpture, but inside its walls, a commissioned work by Bertoia offered, in turn, a vision of sculpture as architecture.

Located in the south finger or wing of the terminal building, Bertoia's massive bronze wall comprised nine sections, each eight feet high, four feet wide, and four inches deep (figure 2.6). The south finger connected the main terminal building to the fourteen-story concrete control tower, offering two main floors of useable space for passengers and visitors to the airport (figure 2.7). Visible from

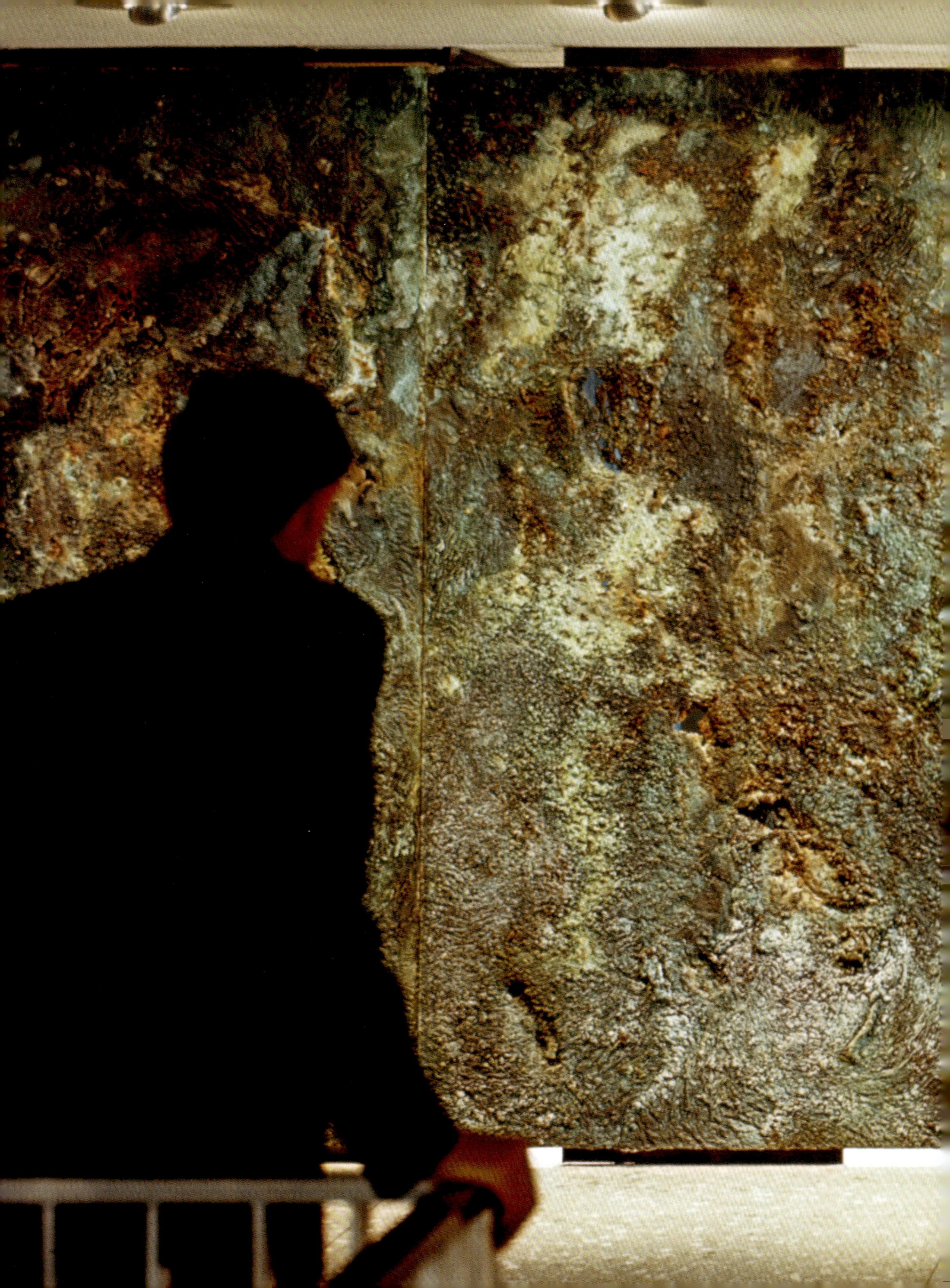

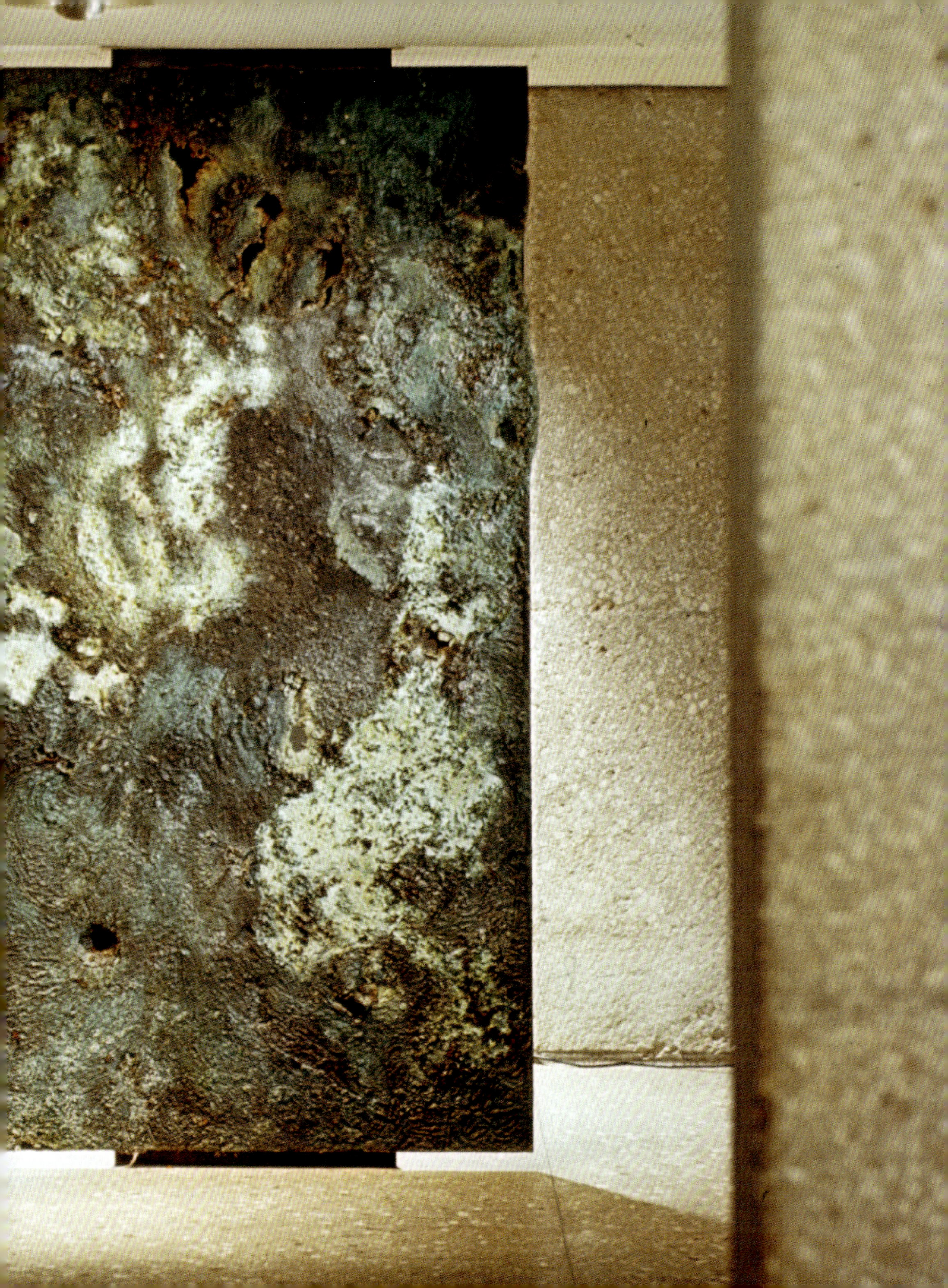

<2.6
Harry Bertoia, *Untitled* (detail), 1962. Spill-cast bronze, 8 ft. × 36 ft. × 4 in. Dulles International Airport, Chantilly, Virginia. Architect: Eero Saarinen & Associates.

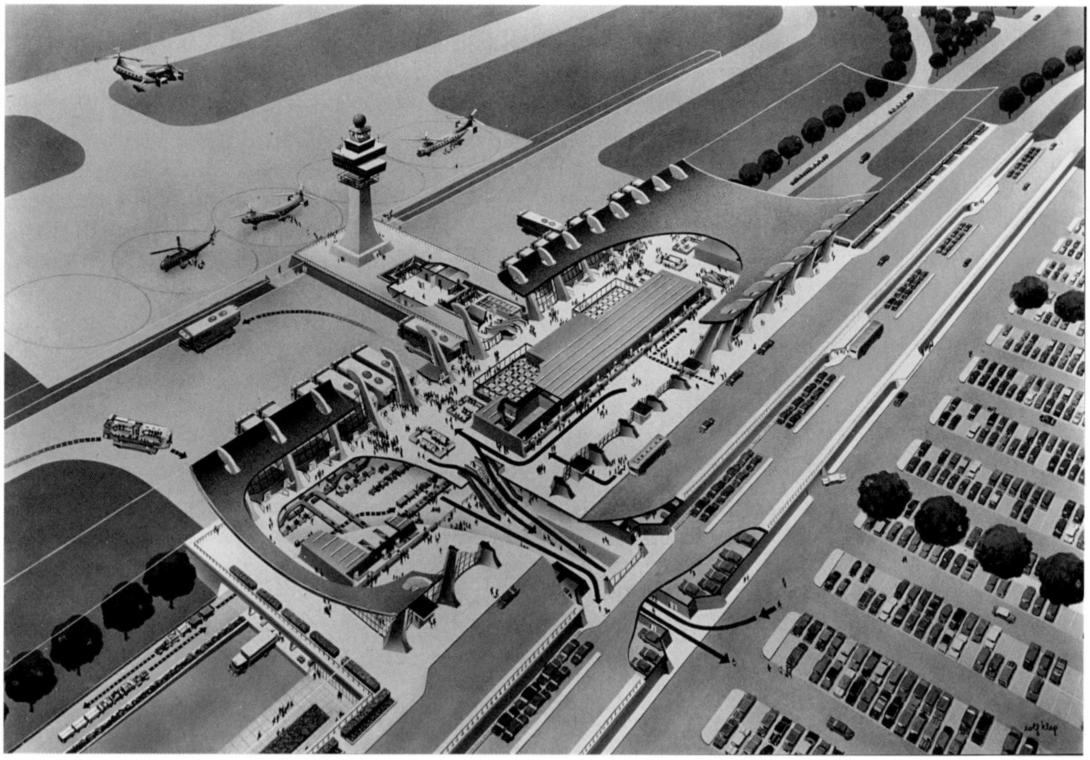

2.7
Rendering of Dulles International Airport, Chantilly, Virginia, c. 1958. Architect: Eero Saarinen & Associates. Eero Saarinen Collection MS 593, Manuscripts and Archives, Yale University Library, New Haven, Connecticut.

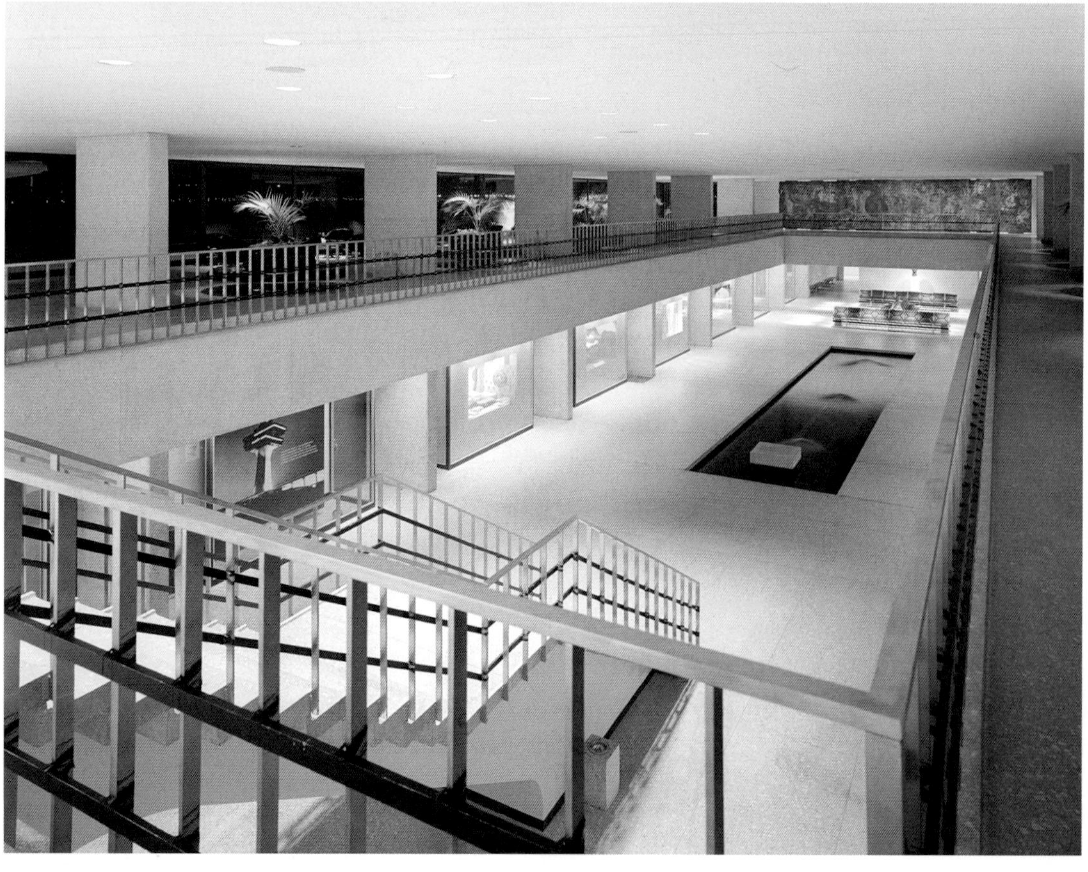

2.8
South finger, Dulles International Airport, Chantilly, Virginia, with Harry Bertoia's *Untitled* (1962) on rear wall. Architect: Eero Saarinen & Associates.

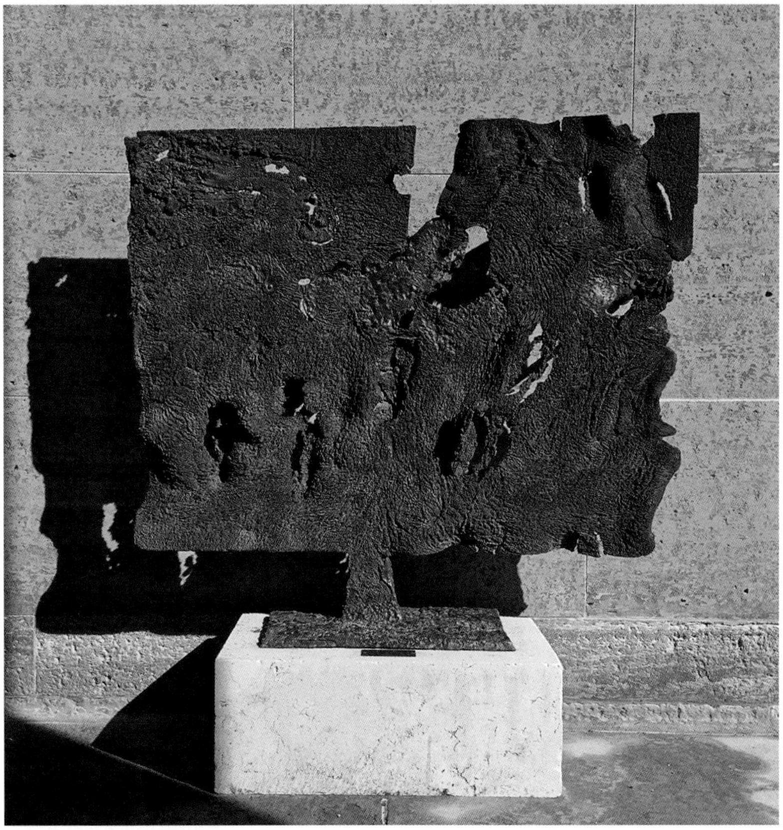

2.9
Harry Bertoia, *Ossabaw Echoes*, 1962. Spill-cast bronze, 50 in. × 53 in. Collection Cranbrook Art Museum, Bloomfield Hills, Michigan.

the main terminal, Bertoia's wall anchored the concourse space, serving as a visual and physical terminus on the mezzanine level. The sculpture separated this area from a restaurant and an observation deck behind it. Most of the space in front of the sculpture was open to the level below, accessible via a staircase at the opposite end, near the main terminal. A shallow, rectangular water feature installed on the floor below created a perpendicular echo of the sculpture's form above, as did the glass curtain walls flanking the space, punctuated by wide rectangular pillars (figure 2.8). This area of the airport was cohesive and symmetrical, both sharing the same design language as the main terminal building, while also offering a different type of functional space in the airport, at a more human scale.

Bertoia's commission was the last time he contributed a sculpture to a Saarinen-designed project. The architect unexpectedly died of a brain tumor in 1961, prior to the completion of Dulles. Kevin Roche, who had worked for Eero Saarinen & Associates since 1950, took over the project, and was actually the architect who approached Bertoia on behalf of their client, the Federal Aviation Agency (FAA; now Federal Aviation Administration), to create something for the airport. Originally, the intent had been to install a more traditional freestanding sculpture by the reflecting pool, but as Mrs. [Katherine] George Y. Wheeler, the chairman of the arts committee appointed by the FAA stated, "We decided the building was so strong and violent, a sculpture would fight with it." By late 1961, Roche officially contacted Bertoia, and soon after they met to discuss ideas for possible sculptural interventions. The artist described how at the end of a long day at the firm's project offices, pouring over the model and drawings, they seemed to be heading toward a creative impasse. “Then somehow,” he recounted, “the thought came of probably something like a map. I use the map for lack of any other, but to my mind it began to indicate the land, the earth and I said let me give some consideration to this thought of a map. All right, we left it that way.”[19]

Roche was an enthusiastic supporter of Bertoia’s subsequent proposal, though at one point, members of the arts committee rejected the plan, deciding they preferred a marble wall instead. Roche wrote to Bertoia on March 26, 1962 to inform him the commission would not be moving forward. By the summer of that year, however, the arts commission had changed course once again and finalized a contract with Bertoia. A few months later, he was installing the work in time for the official dedication of the airport in November. The official contract between the FAA and Bertoia was for a “Bronze Metal sculptured wall,” for the south finger of the terminal building of Dulles International Airport. The final work stretched thirty-six feet and was made with four tons of phosphor bronze, utilizing a proprietary technique Bertoia had recently developed known as spill casting (fig 2.9).[20]

Shortly after his initial meeting with Roche, Bertoia visited his friends Clifford B. and Eleanor T. West at their home on Ossabaw Island, off the coast of Georgia. While there, Bertoia described witnessing, “the forces of the ocean, the forces of the wind and the growth of the island, it conveyed a perpetual battle: trees were in every condition, every stage from erosion to growth, with all the changes of the elements. And this growth showed the lesson that ‘Spaceship earth’ has forever been a changing planet.” Bertoia’s evocation of a phrase popularized by Buckminster Fuller in the mid-1960s suggests an awareness of Fuller’s theories, but also underscores a shared interest in how technology and design could contribute to sustainable, interconnected life on Earth. Intentionally or not, how Bertoia described his original cartographic concept for the Dulles commission recalled Fuller’s Dymaxion Air-Ocean World Map, which had first appeared as a make-your-own cube map in *Life* in 1943 and was intended to show the whole world “fairly and all at once” as a one island in one ocean (figure 2.10).[21]

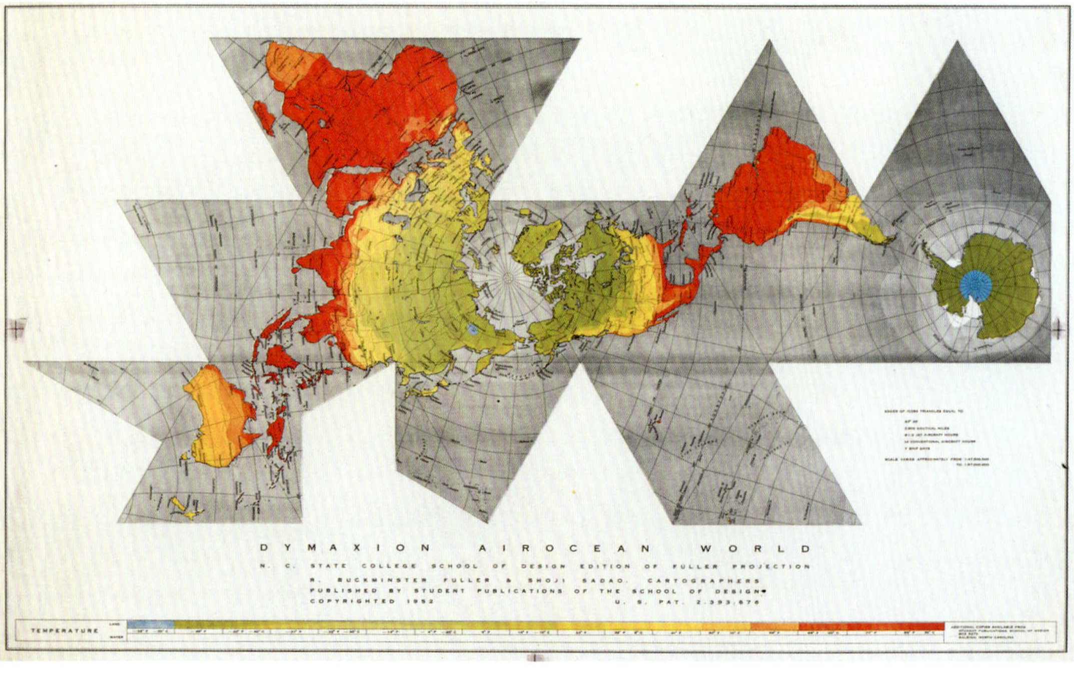

2.10
R. Buckminster Fuller and Shoji Sadao, *Dymaxion Airocean World Map*, 1954.

Natural forces and planetary awareness influenced the development of Bertoia's spill casting, but so did a deep curiosity about the technical possibilities of metal. Around the time Bertoia visited Ossabaw Island, he also made a trip to the mill at the Anaconda American Brass Company in Waterbury, Connecticut. While there, he witnessed an unattended furnace overflowing, spilling thousands of pounds of bronze. Bertoia stated of the experience:

> I saw the movements, I became aware of the forces internally, the way things happen inside this globe, great heat, movements, what we see on the surface is a volcano, eruptions, all that plus what I'd seen on [Ossabaw Island] came together and I knew then what I should be looking for. So, the casting is the result of those two visits plus then a period of experimentation on my own part to find out my limitations, but the object was for it to become something like that, whatever has to be done had to do with the earth seen from the air age.

Bertoia's experimentation with spill casting, like Fuller's Dymaxion map, was the result of the new perspectives and ways of seeing the world that emerged during the mid-twentieth century, but it also represented a new approach to creating sculpture.[22]

Echoing the statements of his painter contemporaries associated with Abstract Expressionism, Bertoia stated that spill casting prompted him, "perhaps for the first time," to use bronze in a "new way: it was not poured into a cavity, it was simply allowed to take its own shape with the least amount of personal intervention. It was cast on a bed of sand and allowed to take its own position."[23] While a highly technical process, spill casting involved relinquishing some level of artistic control in order to let the material, the bronze itself, flow and congeal on its own terms. Bertoia created several smaller-scaled, freestanding, spill-cast sculptures during the early 1960s, but the commission for Dulles International Airport was the largest and most ambitious project to utilize this technique.

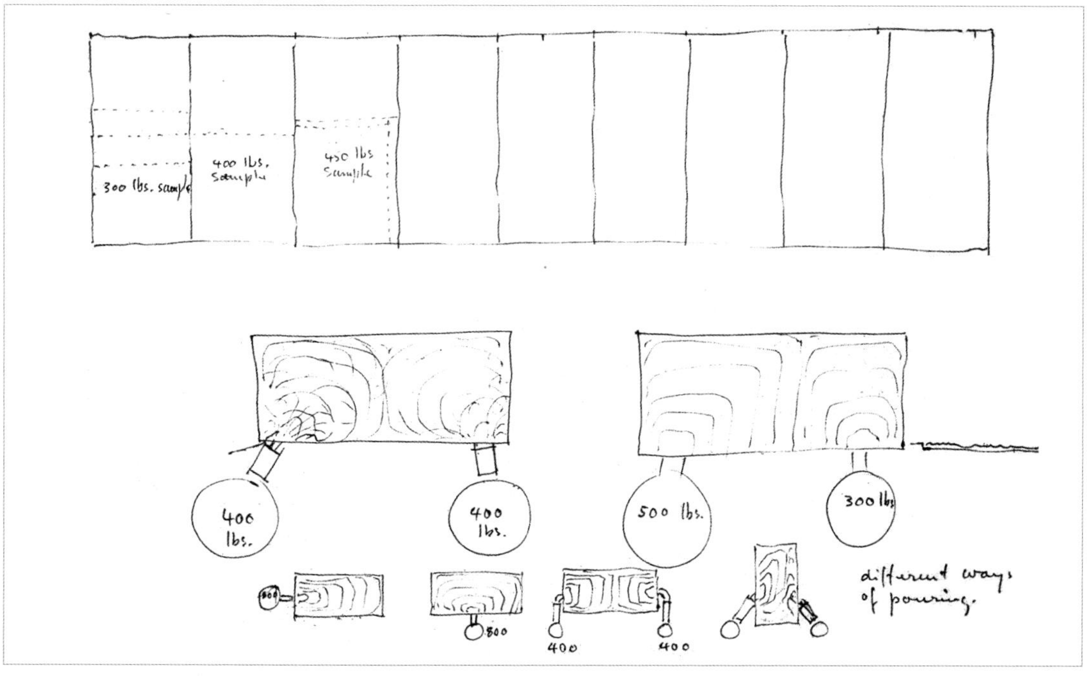

2.11
Harry Bertoia's technical drawings for Dulles International Airport commission, c. 1961. Harry Bertoia Foundation Shop Files.

To create the wall for Dulles, Bertoia fired two furnaces simultaneously and poured melt bronze onto a flatbed of sand. The panels themselves were fabricated in about twenty-four hours, though Bertoia had experimented with the technique and had predetermined the size of each panel after nearly a year of study. Though he did not always draft preparatory sketches and he rarely created exact maquettes for large-scale commissions, Bertoia did take great care to work out technical or engineering issues. Notes and drawings made in conjunction with the Dulles commission show the artist figuring out how much raw material to order, and how both different weights of molten material and "ways of pouring" might create different effects (figure 2.11). Bertoia also developed special tools specific for the project: rakes and pokers with long handles, so that he could work the bronze, even while the temperature was close to two thousand degrees Fahrenheit.[24]

After gaining confidence with his technique, Bertoia's original intention was to make one single panel for Dulles, pouring the entire piece at once. Weight, technical, and economic restrictions, however, collectively ruled out that approach. But once Bertoia determined the sculpture would have to be created in multiple panels, he remained conscious of how to keep visual continuity: of how each piece needed to "register with the next metal, the adjacent metal." His solution was to cast the "whole thing in one day." "My real reason for wanting to do it so quickly," Bertoia stated, "was that if each panel was done consecutively (without having lunch in between or a night of sleep) I would be involved in the same thought, the same action and continue, for every panel had a relation." Bertoia began early in the morning, and though he had two assistants, they ended up stopping around five in the evening owing to exhaustion, even though they only poured seven panels. The last two were completed the following day, with Bertoia asserting that while he thought "they show a difference... that last lapse is not out of character

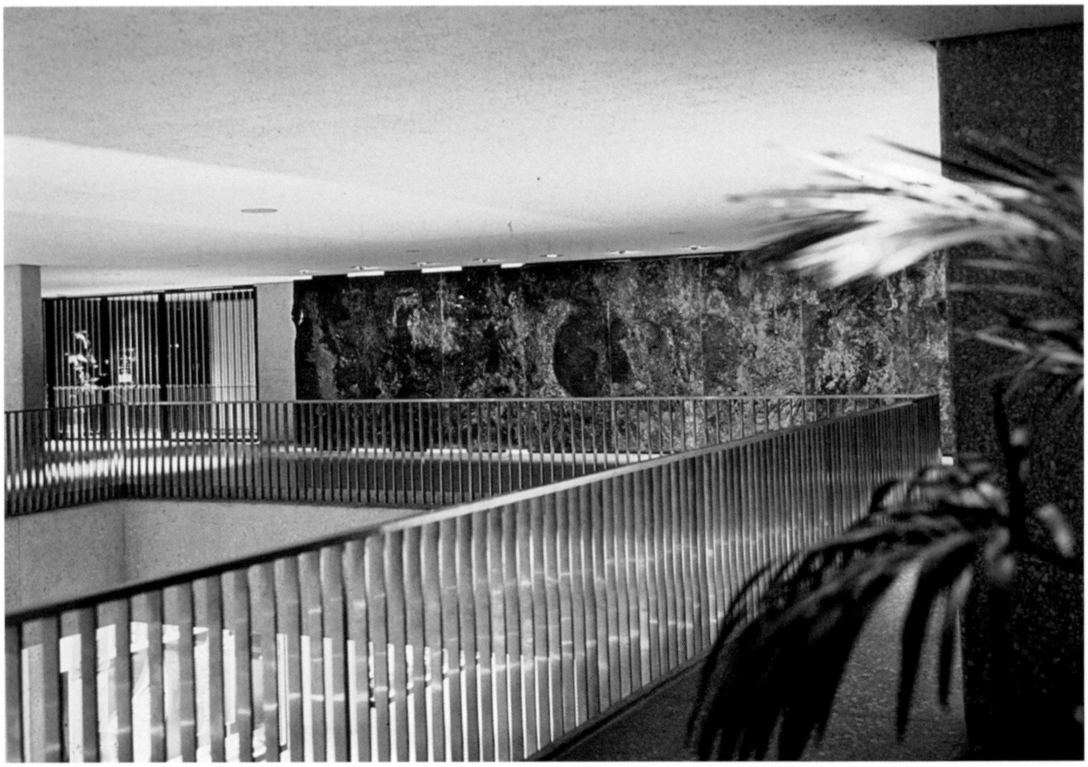

2.12
Harry Bertoia, *Untitled* (detail), 1962. Spill-cast bronze, 8 ft. × 36 ft. × 4 in. Dulles International Airport, Chantilly, Virginia. Architect: Eero Saarinen & Associates.

> 2.13
Harry Bertoia, *Untitled* (detail), 1962. Spill-cast bronze, 8 ft. × 36 ft. × 4 in. Dulles International Airport, Chantilly, Virginia. Architect: Eero Saarinen & Associates.

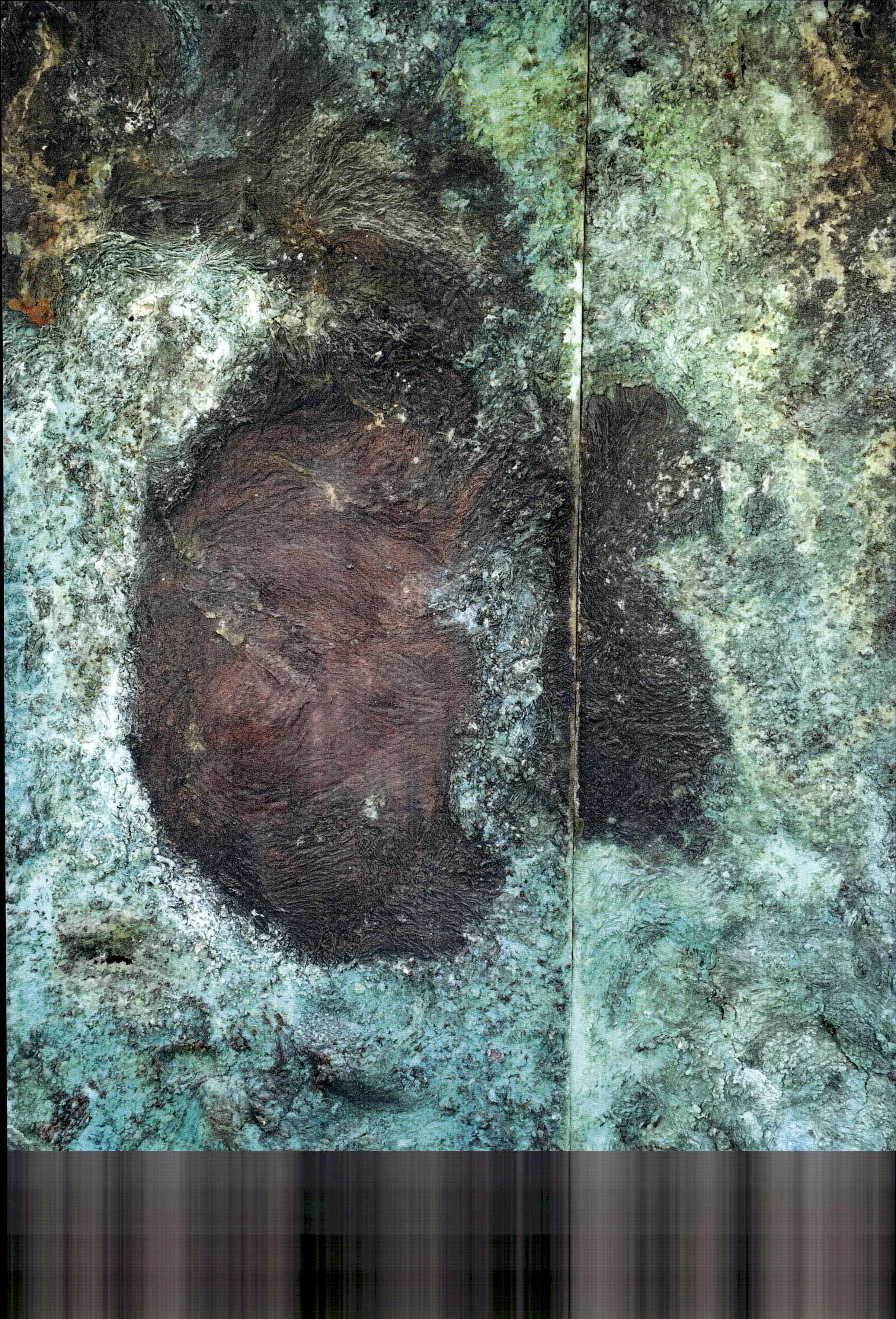

so it's still fine, it's just another combination." The fittings and anchor bolts were applied after the poured metal had fully cooled.[25]

When installed at Dulles, any variances among the panels dissolved into a single, monolithic whole. Though the seams in between each piece remained visible, when placed side by side the overall impression of the work was an imposing, solid wall (figure 2.12). Further, while complementary to the overall architectural design, the sculpture does offer an organic, irregular textural contrast within a refined, if austere, space. Even without knowledge of Bertoia's references to geological tumult and aerial perspectives, the work exudes an impression of primordial ooze and raw materiality.

Though Bertoia was hesitant to assert meaning or metaphor to his work, at least publicly, the FAA took to describing the panels as a depiction of "the awareness of the relationship of man and space and the formative process occurring within our planet through time," and "the universe the way it emerged from a cauldron." These allusions were magnified by the sculpture's surface effects (figure 2.13). The patina or coloring of the bronze was the result of changes in temperature, the addition of water, oxidation, and the combination of rocks and chemical crystal with the hot metal, which led to explosions that punctured the surface with holes. Bertoia declared, "Bronze is probably one of the most living, if I can use that word, materials, it goes with constant change and is subject to its surroundings much more so than many other things. So, color keeps coming or going, depending on what surrounds it and I [hope] these changes will continue on." The resulting colorations, then and now, were a dynamic swirl of jade greens, earthen browns, sulfuric yellows, plum blacks, and aqua blues, which infused color into the neutral palette of the surrounding architecture.[26]

The effect of Bertoia's bronze wall for Dulles Airport is almost painterly, recalling Pollock's intuitive dance of enabling paint to fall where it wanted to fall. While the sculpture possessed an architectural functionality, used to divide and define space within an interior, it also is the closest Bertoia would come to making a relief or mural in his career. The spill-cast bronze panels were always intended to be front facing and attached to a backing wall, though as a member of the architectural team remarked, it "would not need to be elaborate since the support for Bertoia's wall will be the floor itself."[27] Even with this frontal orientation and its churning, colorful surface, the Dulles commission remains a sculpture, a distinct three-dimensional thing. The work evokes qualities of relief, but collapses the boundaries between support and sculpture, fusing together sculptured work and wall.

A useful comparison can be drawn between Bertoia's wall for Dulles and a monumental sand-cast creation made by Costantino Nivola for the Olivetti Showroom at 584 Fifth Avenue in New York City (figure 2.14). Bertoia and Nivola possess many biographical and artistic similarities. Both were Italian nationals who immigrated to the United States before World War II, began their careers in design rather than fine art, and maintained strong connections with architects throughout their lives. Born in Sardinia in 1911, Nivola became an art director at

2.14
Costantino Nivola, *Untitled*, 1954. Sand-cast relief. Olivetti Showroom, New York City. Architect: Studio BBPR.

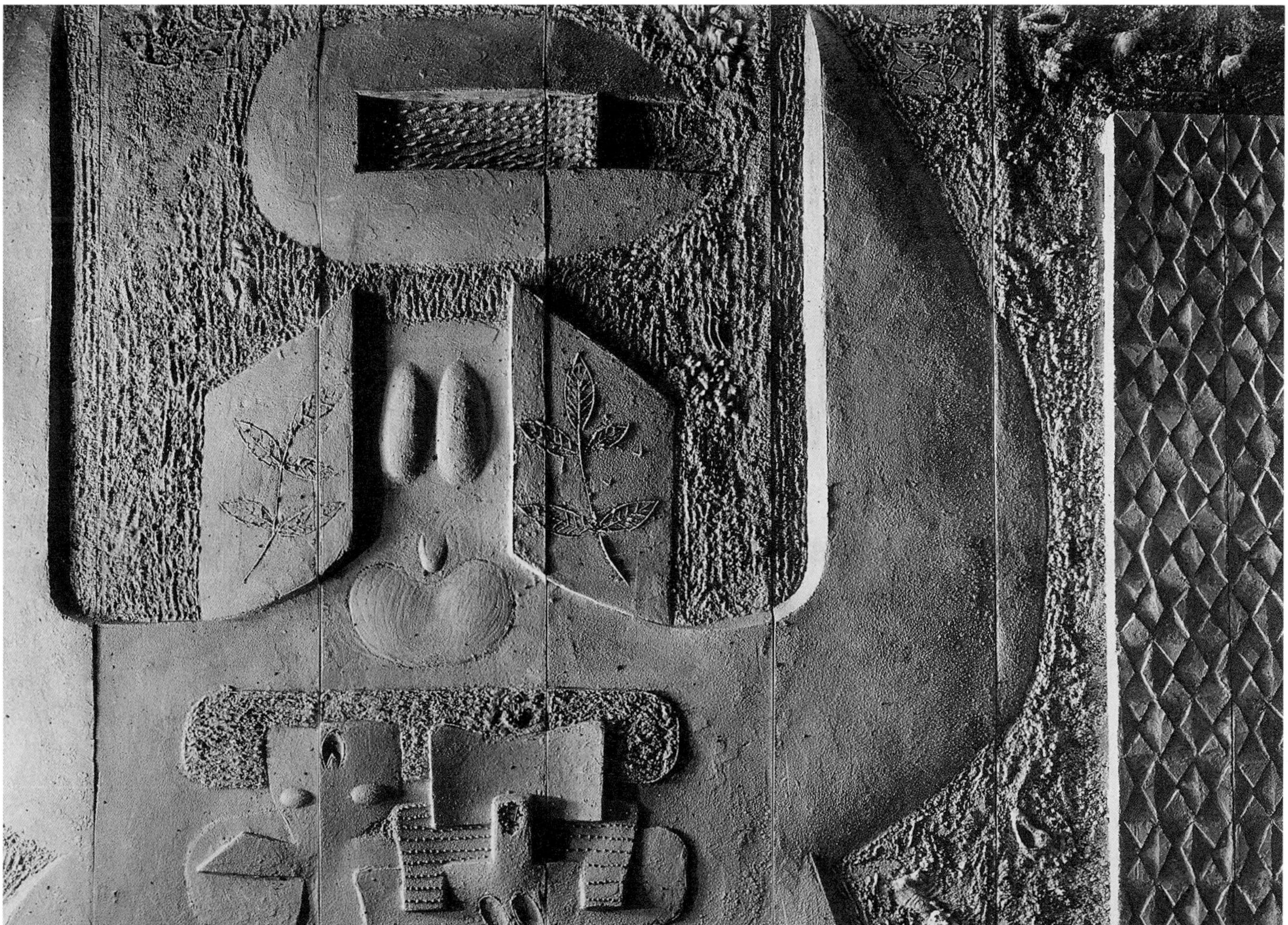

the typewriter company Olivetti in 1937, shortly after graduating from the Istituto Superiore per le Industrie Artistiche (ISIA) in Monza, just outside of Milan. He formed close relationships with architects like Josep Lluís Sert and Le Corbusier beginning in the 1940s, facilitated through his work as an art director and designer at publications like *Pencil Points* (later *Progressive Architecture*) and *Interiors*. He also became a fixture of the New York City art scene, becoming friends with contemporaries like Willem de Kooning, Saul Steinberg, Hedda Sterne, and Pollock, who also became a neighbor after Nivola and his family settled in Springs, New York in 1948.[28]

Olivetti Corporation of America, a subsidiary of Olivetti, opened its first retail space in the United States in 1954 (figure 2.15). The Italian architectural firm BBPR (Lodovico Barbiano di Belgiojoso, Enrico Peressutti, and Ernesto Nathan Rogers) were hired to design the store. Though Nivola had previously worked with BBPR on an unrealized plan for the city of Aosta in Italy, it was the progressive president of the company, Adriano Olivetti, and his brother Dino Olivetti, who were responsible for commissioning the artist for the New York City showroom. The Olivetti Showroom was unlike any other retail space in the city at the time. Every feature, every detail was luxurious, sensual, and extravagant. Marbles of different tones and veining blanketed the entirety of the interior, from the pale-pink Candoglia marble display tables to the green-malachite marble pedestals. These surfaces were topped with typewriters, made to appear as if they were emerging seamlessly from the floor below, or as one critic wrote, "a floor of beautiful marble which seems to have been pulled up like taffy to form display mounts." The blue-green marble floors had been mined from a cave in the Val d'Ossola in northern Italy, and the Murano glass company Venini made the cone-shaped glass lighting

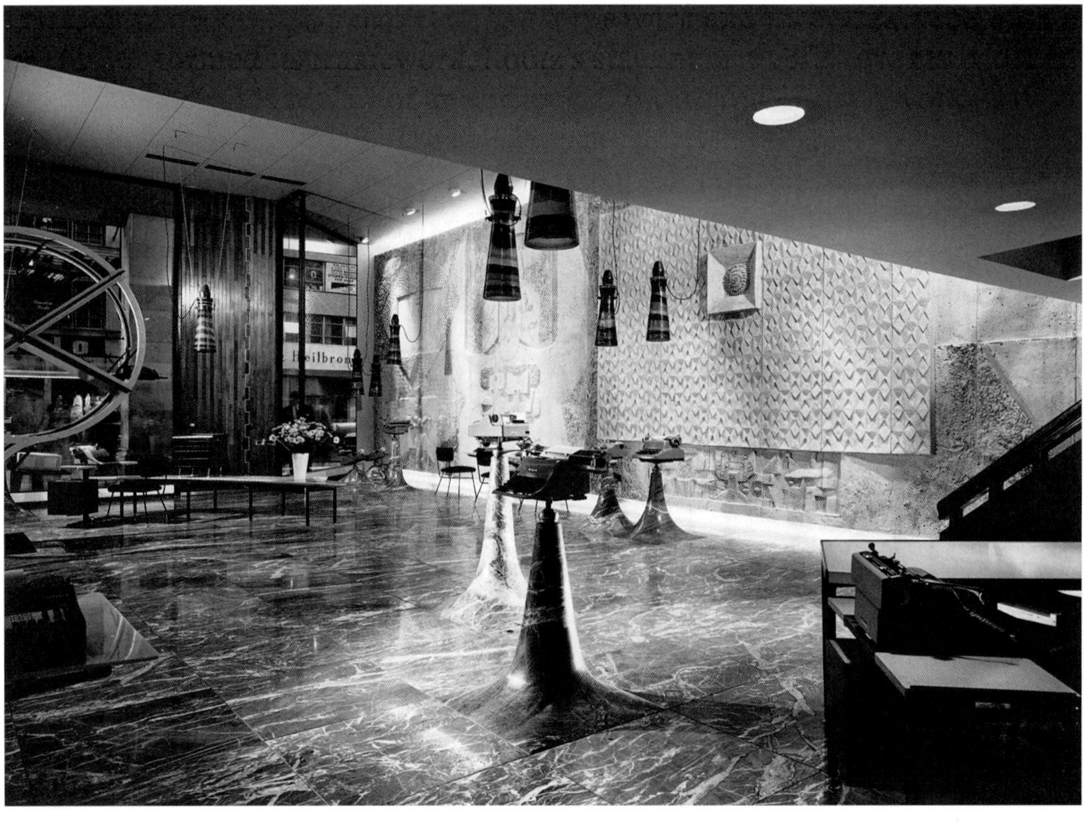

2.15
Interior of the Olivetti Showroom, 584 Fifth Avenue, New York City, 1954. Architect: Studio BBPR.

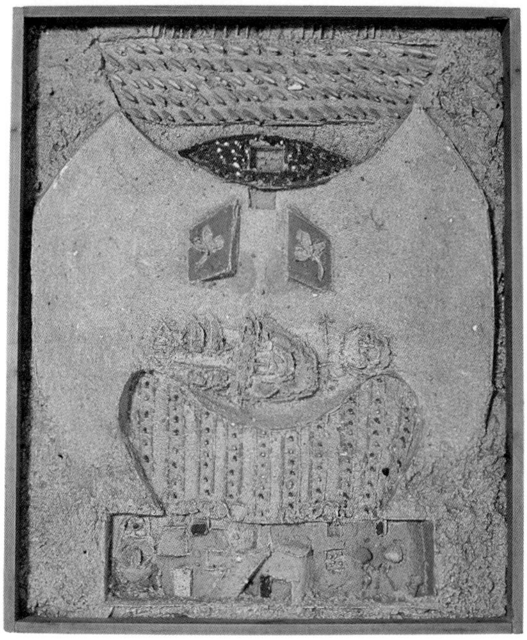

2.16
Costantino Nivola, *Bozzetto per una delle figure del relievo per lo showroom Olivetti* (*Sketch for one of the figures for the Olivetti Showroom relief*), 1952. Cast sand, gesso, sand, and tempera, 40 9/10 × 33 1/4 × 2 2/5 in. Museo Nivola, Orani, Italy.

fixtures exclusively for the shop. Rogers stated of the project, "In this long, narrow cube, we wished to give a sense of natural richness and interpenetration, like stalagmites and stalactites in some imaginable cave." Plastics, stone slabs, glass, and wood, contrasting light and dark tones, smooth and rough textures were all balanced in a dynamic, tactile interior.[29]

All of these elements sought to convey and highlight "the importance of the typewriters and business machines on display," but the drama of the space was not lost on the critics who extensively and exhaustively covered the project. Publisher and architect Gio Ponti remarked that the showroom was "full of novelty, and full of poetic values," while critic Olga Gueft described the Olivetti Showroom as a "great piece of showmanship, a stupendous display, and wonderful theater." While almost every commentator made sure to mention the curiosity of the working Lettera 22 typewriter installed outside on a stalagmite pedestal in front of the showroom's glass facade, arguably the most remarked-on feature was Nivola's commissioned sculpture, variously referred to as a "sand mural," a "sand sculpture," or "sand-sculpture wall."[30]

The sculptural relief spanned the entire length of the showroom, measuring fifteen feet high and seventy-five feet long, depicting abstract designs as well as archetypal male and female figures, as well as a variety of symbols. He fabricated the piece in sections at his home studio in Springs, where he had originally developed his sand-casting technique (figure 2.16). Nivola placed wet sand into wooden forms and then using a range of tools, including his hands, knives, and shells, to sculpt the design. He finished by pouring plaster of paris into this sand mold, noting that "when the plaster hardens, there is my sculpture, wearing a face of nice, fuzzy sand." As had been the case with Bertoia's Dulles commission, the choice of material for Nivola's wall in the Olivetti Showroom was not just a novelty or technical innovation. The abstracted sand mural added a soft organicism and rough tactility to what was otherwise a very sleek space. Indirect cove lighting was used above and below Nivola's relief adding additional drama but also accentuating the relief's presence within the space and further emphasizing its sculptural, three-dimensional quality.[31]

Nivola's wall, when installed in the showroom, formally served as something of a palette cleanser, a neutral sand-colored, soda-cracker respite from the shiny, baroque surfaces and materials that permeated the space. The opposite wall was simply painted in a similar beige-gray color, which likewise provided a bit of visual break, but also had the effect of further amplifying Nivola's contribution. His relief was a unique element that both contrasted with, and held its own against, the other design elements, its built-up, textured surface at home in a space built around so many distinctive, beautiful details. As Aline B. Saarinen wrote, "Nivola's handsome sand-mural (with its fascinating interplay of texture and shapes), the exquisite materials, the plastic forms, the concern with design of products… all these are clues to the broad program which insists on beauty in every aspect of the company's work and environment." The work was a remarkable achievement on its own terms, but also perfectly complemented the overall design and the ethos of the company, leading many critics to proclaim that a successful integration between art and architecture had been achieved. Gueft wrote that the Olivetti Showroom represented "one of the most successful collaborations between artist and architect in modern times." Huxtable pointedly highlighted Nivola's "sculptured reliefs," as one of the few projects of the period to merge truly with its architecture as it formed "actual curtain-wall panels."[32]

The success of his commission for the Olivetti Showroom propelled Nivola into many other collaborations with other architects during the postwar period. There were some additional, though smaller-scaled, interior reliefs, like the eight interlocked sand-cast figures he created for the lobby of the apartment building at 1025 Fifth Avenue in New York City in 1955. The majority of the projects he created after Olivetti, however, were sculptures for outdoor spaces and bas-reliefs for facades. Like Bertoia or Lippold, Nivola was comfortable relinquishing some level of artistic ego or individual expression in the service of a larger project. As Nivola wrote, art could "serve as a bridge between the mechanic determination of functional architecture and the organic and human element." He continued, "When given a public assignment the artist has a new and different role, a civic responsibility which demand that he subjugate his private moods and take into account considerations which are not only esthetic but also of an ethical, social and economic nature. He must make a serious attempt to achieve a harmonious relationship between his work and its architectural and social environment." With commissions like those for the Mutual Life Insurance Company of Hartford in Connecticut (1957) and the McCormick Place convention center in Chicago (1959), Nivola demonstrated how massive sand-cast, concrete bas-reliefs could add visual interest to buildings, while also truly engaging with both contemporary architecture and the urban environment.[33]

Nivola's approach and attitude made him an attractive option as a collaborator. Richard Stein, who worked with him on numerous public projects in New

York City, referred to him as the "architect's sculptor," while Eero Saarinen proclaimed himself an admirer and commissioned Nivola to create a suite of sculptures for the Samuel F. B. Morse and Ezra Stiles Colleges at Yale University in New Haven, Connecticut (1958–62) (figure 2.17). Saarinen told Nivola, "I am not looking for one piece of sculpture, nor am I looking for just wall decorations, I'm looking for a whole atmosphere created by sculpture and bas-reliefs in relation to architecture. Although Nivola's contributions to Saarinen's project were ultimately scaled back, the thirty-five sculptures he realized for Yale were a testament to the artist's overall approach to collaborating with architects.[34]

The majority of Nivola's commissions from the postwar period, by default of their outdoor locations, operated differently from those created for interiors and threshold spaces. Further, his large-scale sculptures, including the panels for the Olivetti Showroom, never fully relinquished figural qualities and thus retained a greater sense of the pictorial. Such characteristics inherently encouraged the reading of his work as a surface relief, as an image added to or placed atop rather than built from within as inextricable architectural element. Nivola's bas-relief for the Olivetti Showroom, like Bertoia's sculpture for Dulles International Airport, however, advanced the possibilities of sculpture with and within architecture, while also complicating and collapsing disciplinary categories. Their commissions are reliefs, murals, and sculptures, but most significantly, they are walls. They were made for a specific place, used to delineate architectural space and added three-dimensional tactility. Both provided texture, but their scale and function were unabashedly architectural, so large they created an environmental effect, transforming the entirety of the space.

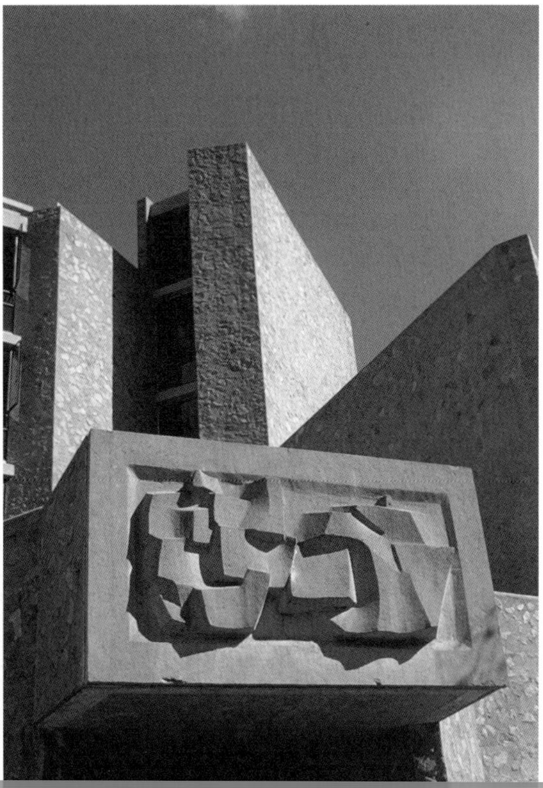

2.17
Samuel F. B. Morse and Ezra Stiles Colleges with exterior detail of courtyard relief sculpture by Costantino Nivola, Yale University, New

Bertoia and Nivola each applied newly developed techniques from their sculptural practice for these commissions, using spill and sand casting both to advance sculpture on its own terms and for use in architectural spaces. Their chosen materials directly connected their sculpture to architecture. As Nivola stated, "My sculptures are made using common materials: bricks, concrete blocks, lime and plaster, and the natural elements—sunlight, water, sand. The technique is that of a mason. My dream is to make them as big as buildings.... I learned from Le Corbusier to be conscious of the role every element must have in a plastic organization and its relation to architecture." The sculpted walls for the Dulles International Airport and the Olivetti Showroom were building blocks, experiments in sculptural scale. These projects demonstrate that a synergy with architecture did not have to mean subservience to it. Rather, by embracing sculpture's physical and categorical malleability, by exploiting its connection to the traditions of large-scale painting as well as taking on the functional and material language of architecture, the medium became something more.[35]

Sculptural Screens

Despite the sheer physical presence and the technical and material innovation of Bertoia's sculpture for Dulles International Airport, it remained something of an anomaly in his career. He would only use his spill-cast technique—no doubt owing to its difficulty—for one other large-scale commission, collaborating again with Roche in 1968 on three, four-square-foot planters for the Student Alumni Union Building on the campus of the Rochester Institute of Technology in New York (figure 2.18). He also never again created a sculptural wall that was so opaque, but he had spent much of the preceding decade producing elaborate, if far more open, multiplane constructions. These welded metal sculptures also functioned as walls, as well as screens and grilles, drawing far more on the architectural tradition of ornamental partitions and grating barriers than the artistic tradition of relief. Bertoia's screen walls also resonated with a broader trend within midcentury modern architecture: to divide space while still preserving, as the artist described, "something of openness and light." New, open floorplans required

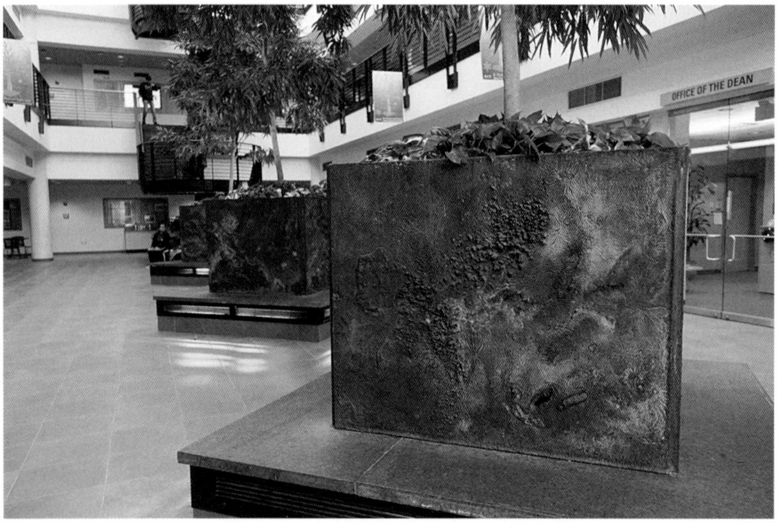

2.18
Harry Bertoia, *Three Planters*, 1968. Spill-cast bronze, 4 ft. × 4 1/2 ft. × 4 1/2 ft., each. Student Alumni Union Building, Rochester Institute of Technology, New York, 1968. Architect: Kevin Roche, John Dinkeloo & Associates. Reinstalled in the Golisano Building, Rochester Institute of Technology.

innovative solutions for how to offer privacy or separation, and architects increasingly turned to "glass and wood screens, translucent fabrics and woven tapestries, living plant arrangements, and sculptural treatments of ceramics, metal and concrete."[36]

While the equation of commissioned sculpture with interior hedgerows of ficus trees certainly did not help assuage concerns over art being utilized only as a decorative afterthought or utilitarian object, Bertoia's large-scale sculptural screens were far more multifaceted than a chainmail curtain or silk scrim, no matter how perfectly these elements were suited to the overall interior design. Bertoia's lack of an adversarial stance toward functionality, and his strong ties to the field of design that had begun at the Cranbrook Academy of Art, helped Bertoia to create work that emerged from a thoughtful consideration of architectural space. His first opportunity to connect ideas explored in both his previous design work and smaller sculptures with the demands of a large-scale commission came from Saarinen, his onetime Cranbrook colleague.

From 1945 to 1956, Saarinen oversaw the construction of the General Motors Technical Center (GMTC) in Warren, Michigan (figure 2.19). The GMTC was not a manufacturing plant but rather a development laboratory for largely white-collar workers, a center devoted to industrial, technological, and scientific research. The new suburban campus was one of several such projects realized during the immediate postwar period, including IBM's Thomas J. Watson Research Center in Yorktown Heights, New York; the Bell Telephone Laboratories in Holmdel Township, New Jersey; and the headquarters of the Connecticut General Life Insurance Company in Bloomfield, Connecticut. The 320-acre GMTC campus was organized into five groups of buildings—Research, Service Center, Process, Development, and Styling—all arranged around a rectangular, artificial lake, a third of a mile long. Modular, repeating elements created a unified scheme, but

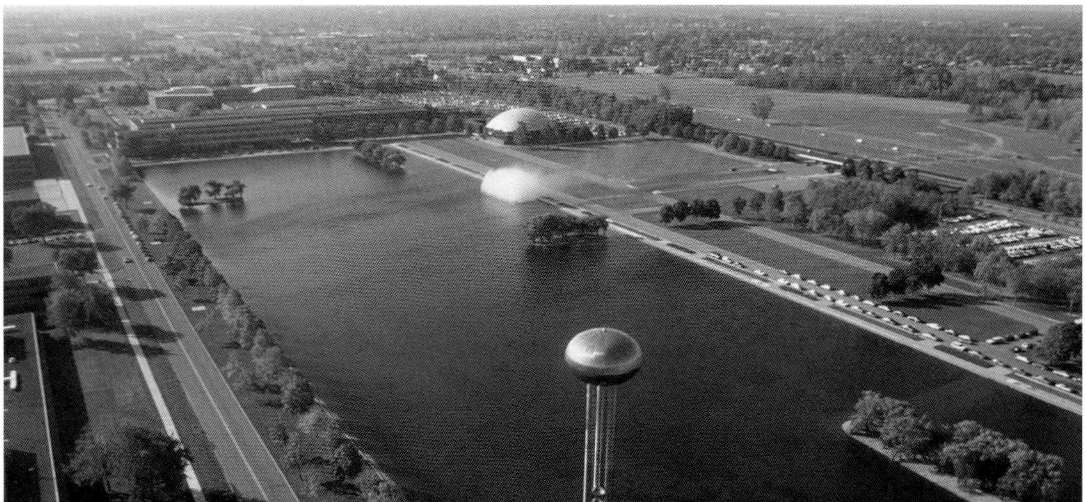

2.19
Aerial view of General Motors
Technical Center, Warren,

there were also visual “surprises as well as variety,” including the shimmering aluminum dome of the Styling Building to the colorful glazed-brick walls on the exteriors of multiple structures.[37]

Saarinen intentionally wanted the architecture of the GMTC to reflect the company it was designed for, stating, “General Motors is a metal-working industry; it is a precision industry… Thus, the design is based on steel—the metal of the automobile.” The design of the campus is notable for its sheer magnitude and technological advancements, but it also demonstrated that Saarinen, even early on in his career, was an architect open and eager to incorporate art into his projects. Prominent contributions and collaborations appeared across the GMTC, most facilitated through Saarinen’s connections from his days at Cranbrook or using Aline B. Saarinen’s contacts from when she was an active, noted critic of art and architecture. Charles Sheeler, an artist perhaps best known for his photographs and paintings of the nearby Ford Motor Company’s factory in River Rouge, Michigan, created what would be his last commissioned work, a large oil painting entitled *General Motors Research* (1956). Made for the Research Building, Sheeler’s painting also depicted the structure, including an abstracted rendering of the now-iconic staircase in the lobby, alongside other technological innovations, including the Helmholtz coil and the Dodrill-GMR mechanical heart.[38]

Saarinen collaborated with Florence Knoll on interior furnishings, while Alexander Girard served as a color consultant. Textile designer and Cranbrook faculty member Marianne Strengell worked on elements and color specifications for lobbies across the campus and the Central Restaurant Building. She also designed all the rugs for the campus, which were handwoven by her assistant, Gerda Nyberg. Another Cranbrook faculty member, Maija Grotell, contributed ceramics to many buildings, including creating the original glazes for the colorful

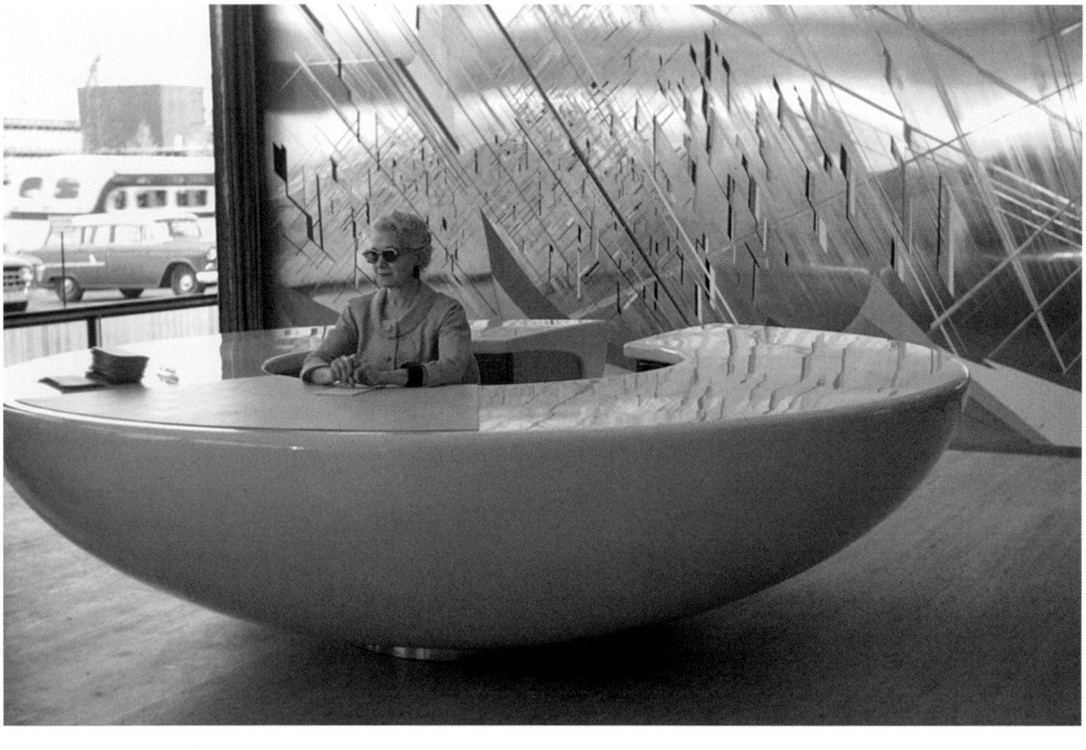

2.20
“Teacup” desk, designed by Kevin Roche, in front of Buell Mullen’s stainless-steel mural, *Lines in Motion* (c. 1956), in the lobby of the Styling Administration Building, General Motors Technical Center, Warren, Michigan, 1956. Architect: Eero Saarinen.

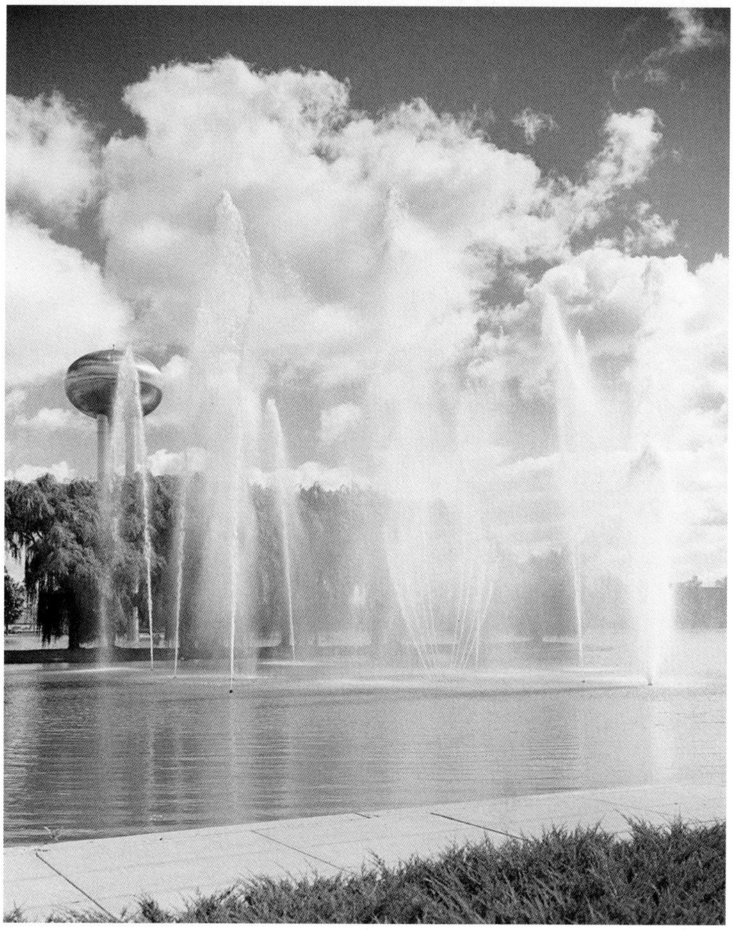

2.21
Alexander Calder, *Water Ballet*, 1956. Programmed fountain. General Motors Technical Center, Warren, Michigan. Architect: Eero Saarinen.

brick facades and the boat-shaped planters in the Styling Building color studio. These planters encircled a glass wall, behind which *Impetus*, a fiberglass and metal fountain sculpture by James McCormick, was installed in a shallow pool.[39]

Notable artworks, all designed by women and made from metals, were installed on walls throughout the Styling Building. American artist Buell Mullen, who pioneered a technique of painting on stainless steel, executed her first abstract work for the GMTC, creating a thirty-by-fourteen-foot mural, *Lines in Motion*, installed in the lobby behind a "teacup" desk designed by Roche (figure 2.20). Sculptor Gwen Lux's brushed and chromed *Power and Direction* (c. 1956) and a colorful enameled *Variation on a Theme* (c. 1954) by designer Gere Kavanaugh, then a GM Styling employee, each offered distinct visions of modern materials while still communicating what can be seen as a remarkably unified curatorial strategy.[40]

Artistic contributions were not confined to walls or interiors at GMTC, however. A twenty-foot-high sculpture by Antoine Pevsner, *Bird in Flight* (1956) was installed outside the entrance to the Styling Building. Eero and Aline B. Saarinen had first seen the sculpture in a smaller scale and under the title *La colonne développable de la victoire* (*Developable Column of Victory*, 1946) at a gallery in Paris, and Aline felt that "in heroic size it would express something of the precision and imagination represented by the automotive industry." In an interview with architectural critic and historian Sigfried Giedion, Pevsner had expressed a desire to see his work, and in particular *La colonne développable de la victoire*, in the open air, "standing amid the collective life of a great city," and by casting a larger version, the GMTC enabled the work to stand "in the sunlight for the first time."[41]

Across from Pevsner's sculpture, the central lake was further activated by a "great 115-foot water-wall fountain" as well as Alexander Calder's water sculpture or "ballet-mobile," titled *Water Ballet* (1956) (figure 2.21), though sometimes referred to as *Fantails, Seven Sisters, Plops, and Scissors*. Saarinen had approached Calder about contributing a work to the GMTC in 1951, suggesting a fountain and a sculpture. Calder offered just a fountain, a version of his *Water Ballet* the artist originally designed for the Consolidated Edison Building at the 1939 New York World's Fair. While more commonly known by the title *Water Ballet*, the work's alternate title likely originated during a preview of the work's "aquatic effects" that Calder gave the Saarinens in his backyard using a garden hose. As art critic Jed Perl writes, "By forcing the water this way and then that way, he demonstrated the varied sprays, some of which would reach forty feet high, to which he gave nicknames including 'Fantails,' 'Seven Sisters,' and 'Plops.'"[42]

All the artwork purchased or commissioned for the GMTC expressed a precision or angularity befitting an automobile research center and were thoughtfully curated across the campus. These sculptures, paintings, and ceramics enlivened and contrasted with Saarinen's architectural design, adding a further layer of aesthetic sophistication to the campus, often in unexpected ways. As critic John McAndrew declared of Calder's fountain, "How good is it for an architect and a sculptor to revive the fountain as a monumental scherzo related to severe surrounding buildings! How particularly happy here is the dramatic display of an endlessly fascinating natural material—water—in vivid contrast equilibration of machine-smooth walls of man-made rectangles of glass and enamel."[43] For the

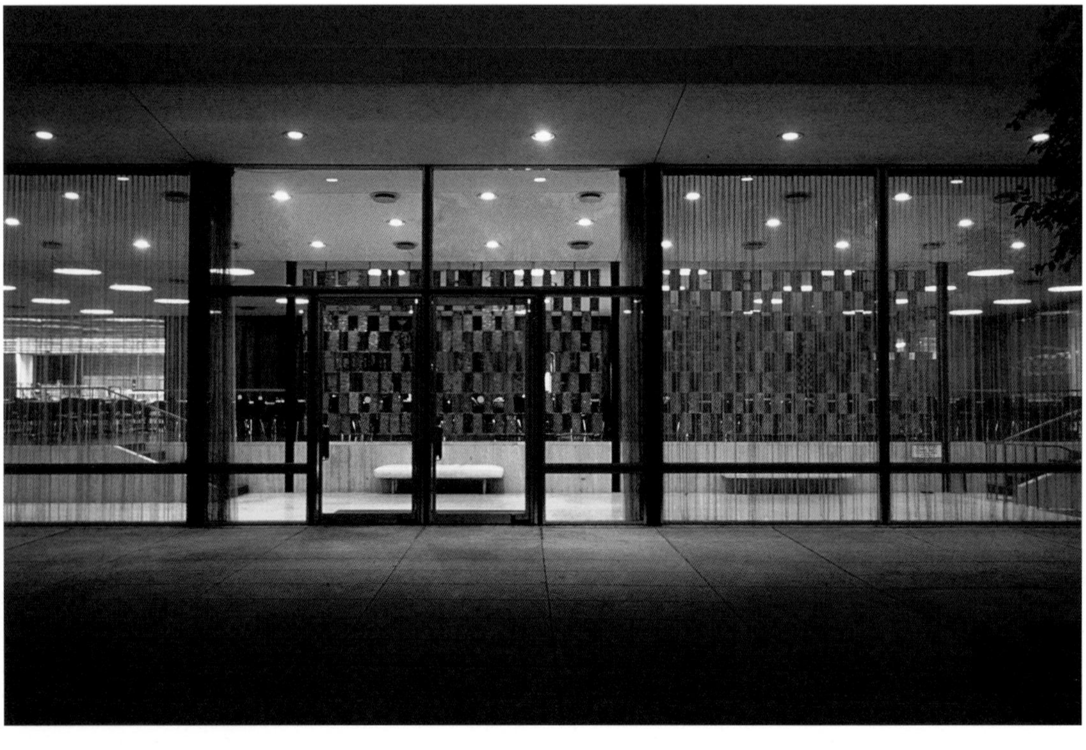

2.22
Central Restaurant Building, 1945. General Motors Technical Center, Warren, Michigan. Architect: Eero Saarinen.

> 2.23
Harry Bertoia, *Untitled*, 1953. Brazed and welded metal, 10 ft. × 36 ft. × 8 in. Central Restaurant Building, General Motors Technical Center, Warren, Michigan. Architect: Eero Saarinen.

most part, however, all of the art installed at the GMTC was approached as a finishing component rather that an architectural alloy. Any collaboration between artist or designer and architect was relegated largely to discussions of dimensions and placement. Calder's and Pevsner's sculptures, for example, while notable and well-sited, were repurposed versions of earlier works. Bertoia's contribution was the exception.

Saarinen had remained invested in Bertoia's artistic activities long after both men left Cranbrook. After seeing an exhibition of chairs and freestanding metal sculptures by Bertoia at the Knoll Showroom in New York City in 1952, Saarinen asked the artist to contribute a work to the Central Restaurant Building (figure 2.22). Though Olav Hammarstrom was the architect in charge of the design for this particular GMTC building, commissioning Bertoia was solely Saarinen's idea. The resulting sculpture, a welded metal screen approximately thirty-six feet long and ten feet high, often described as a screen or grille, separated the entrance of the Central Restaurant Building from the dining area (figure 2.23). Like the other art commissioned or purchased for the GMTC, Bertoia's sculpture was "intended to add enrichment as an ornamental element" to what was a rather stark, neutral interior, but it also took on a more structural function, acting as a wall, a threshold demarcation, and a space divider.[44]

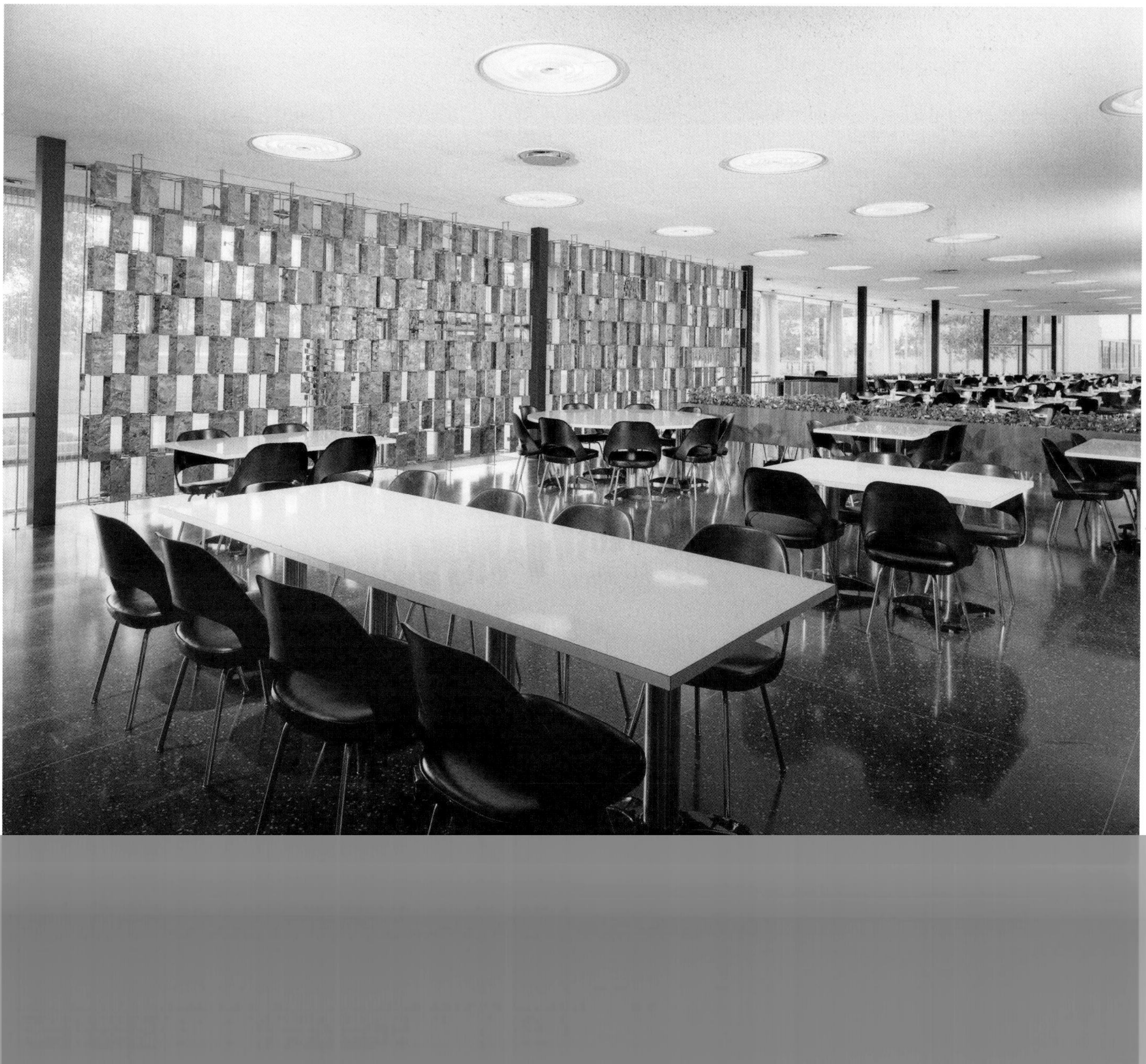

The Central Restaurant Building bounded the east end of the court in between the Engineering Staff, Process, and Development administrative buildings. As Saarinen's "Architectural Notes" for the project state, "In contrast with the 'automobile scale' of the rest of the project, this court, with its grassy lawn and large trees, has been designed especially for pedestrians. In the Restaurant, also, the effort was to achieve an especially human and relaxed environment, which would suggest a change of pace from work areas. In harmony with the other buildings at the Technical Center, the Restaurant still asserts its own individuality." The dining area was raised, affording unobstructed views of the lake save for specially designed "natural-color-fish-net curtains," which diffused the light without visual interference.[45]

The interior design scheme was carefully controlled, with a range of light and dark tones, but all expressed through a neutral color palette achieved by the careful selection of sumptuous, high-quality materials and elements including Brazilian wood panels, black terrazzo and travertine marble. Bertoia's bespoke sculpture both complemented the interior of the Central Restaurant Building, and provided a particularly rich, textured contrast. As McAndrew wrote, the sculpture was "an iridescent golden-brazen-silver grille of staccato syncopated openwork... which somehow manages, most appropriately, to be at once both gay and discreet. Such a happy association of other arts with architecture makes one greedily wish to see it oftener."[46]

Bertoia made the screen by individually welding hundreds of distinct plates of enameling steel, most around five inches wide, ten inches high, and one-eighth of an inch thick, onto a framework of horizontal and vertical rods he constructed and arranged in two planes. There are also a few additional clusters of much smaller squares of metal scattered across the composition, but he treated the surface of every element with what would become a trademark Bertoia technique of brazing, using a combination of multiple metals and metal alloys. He constructed the piece in the backyard of his Barto, Pennsylvania home in 1953, working on it for nearly a year and building scaffolding that mimicked the architectural conditions of the building (figure 2.24). Bertoia described how his approach to the commission still relied heavily on the processes he had previously been using to "work out small things," noting that it even reflected "back to the prints I had done at Cranbrook, those block prints. Even then the spatial element comes in, but still essentially, it's a flat surface, it's a light modulator, a playfulness of light and opaque surface." Understood in this context, the screen for the GMTC was clearly an extension of his previous art and design work.[47]

Bertoia's evocation of his earlier monotypes and flat surfaces suggests perhaps a greater connection of the GMTC screen to the form of a mural; in this case, a double-paned, frontally oriented object with less a recto and a verso and more simply two facing surfaces (figure 2.25). Bertoia aligned each of the discrete metal plates on an open framework. The overall effect was a unified, physically imposing structure, but also one whose form still allowed for some amount transparency. As official GM press materials describe, "The screen makes a decorative, abstract checker-board pattern in depth, allowing the diners to see the view through it. Both in its materials and in the syncopated rhythm of its design, it is wholly of the twentieth century." The open spaces in between, punctuated occasionally by configurations of small, welded squares or triangles, however, did more than just lend the screen a checkerboard appearance or allow for greater transparency. The various elements of Bertoia's work, further enhanced by the shimmering, layered combination of metals on the surface of each plate, changed as the viewer walks through the space. The internal contrast between open and closed, luminosity and opacity, and even the fundamental presence of two planes, across such a large surface, infused the work with a distinctly dynamic, sculptural volume. The screen stretched thirty-six feet across in length, and extended eight inches deep. Because Bertoia did not make the exterior metal frame to be perfectly flush with the ceiling, floor, or surrounding pillars, but rather attached it with thin metal brackets, the screen appeared to almost float in place, becoming a complex amalgamation of wall, mural, relief, and freestanding sculpture.[48]

The GMTC screen marked a significant moment in Bertoia's career: his first opportunity to create sculpture with specific architecture in mind and the first time he ever worked on such a large scale. The project, in many ways, was a grand experiment, requiring new approaches and creative solutions, not all of which proved successful. While the critical response was resoundingly positive and Saarinen was quite pleased with the outcome, Bertoia himself was less enthusiastic, remarking how dramatically the work changed after he installed it. Owing to its large dimensions, Bertoia created the work outdoors, where the lighting conditions were quite different. When installed indoors, with far less light reflecting across its various panels from the windows of the Central Restaurant Building, the work lost some of its shimmering reflectivity and often became silhouetted.[49]

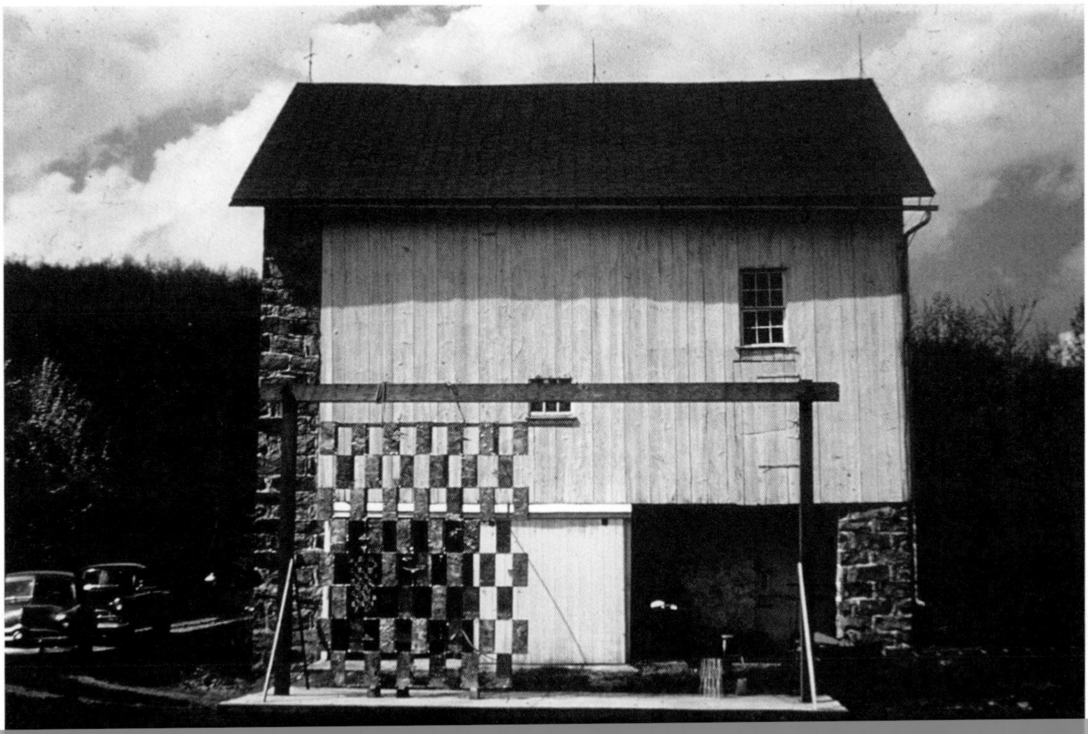

2.24
Harry Bertoia's screen for the Central Restaurant Building, General Motors Technical Center, in process, at his barn home studio in Barto, Pennsylvania, c. 1953.

> 2.25
Harry Bertoia, *Untitled*, 1953. Brazed and welded metal, 10 ft. × 36 ft. × 8 in. Central Restaurant Building, General Motors Technical Center, Warren, Michigan. Architect:

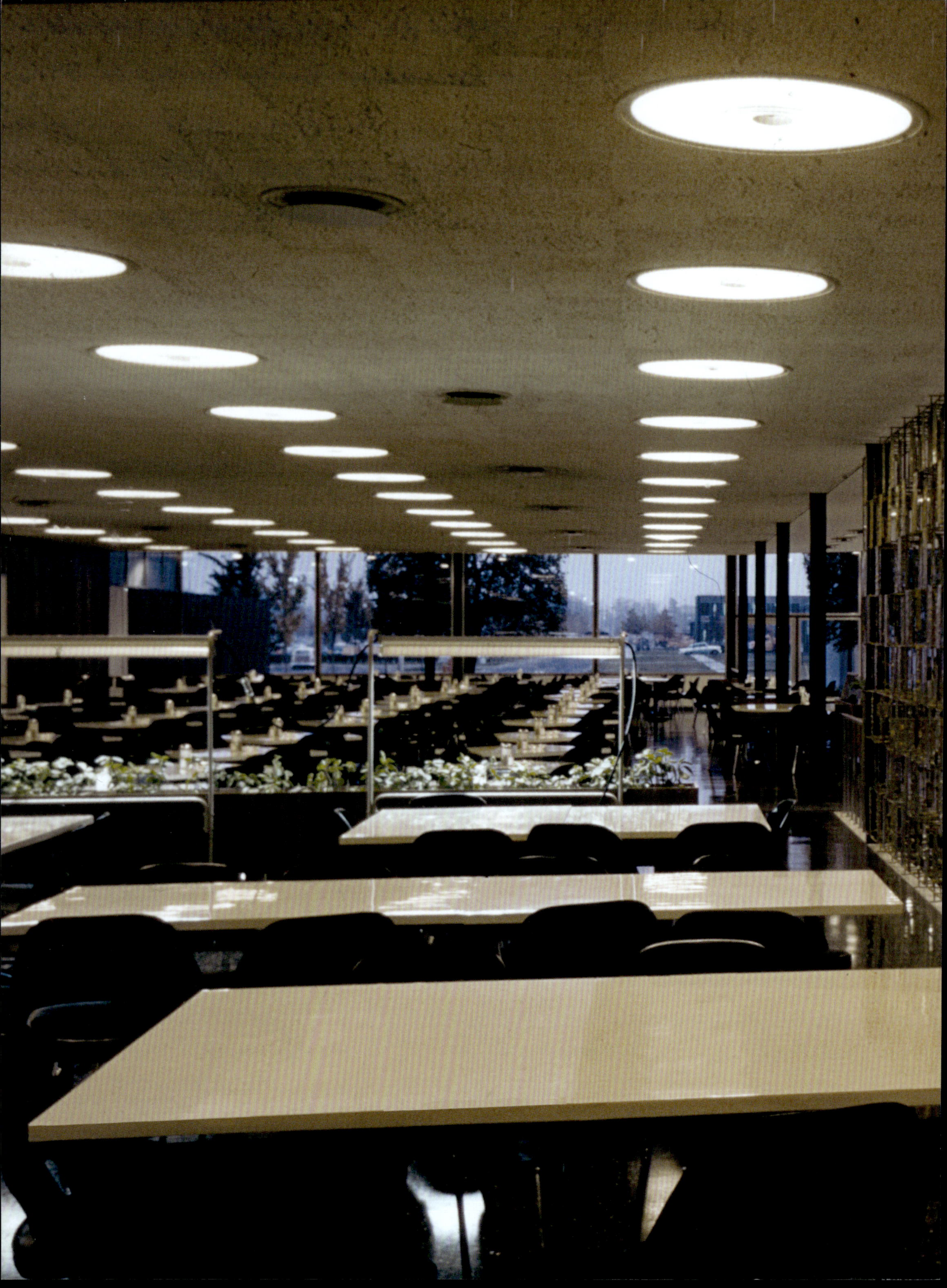

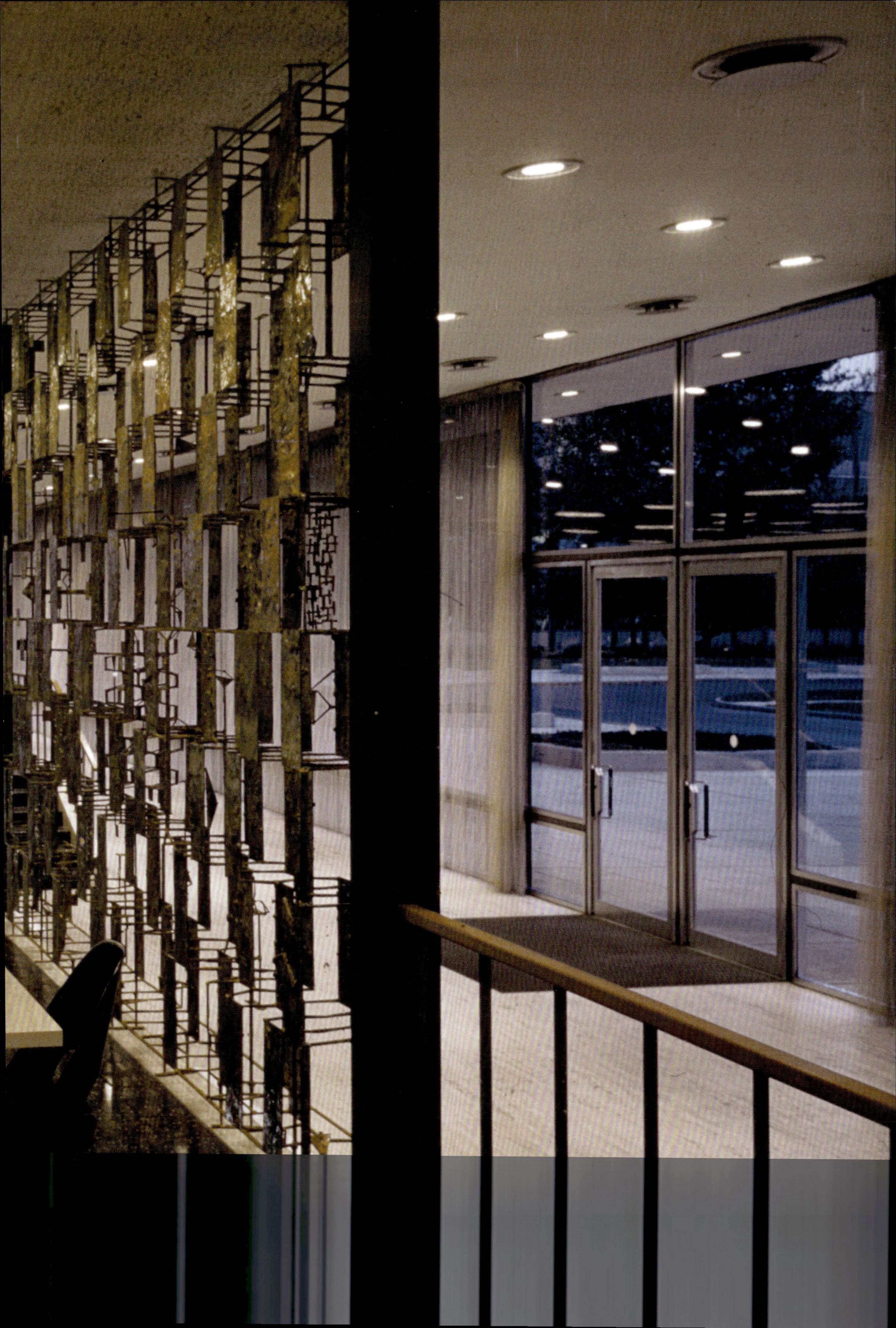

By 1956, when the GMTC was officially dedicated, Bertoia had been able to put the lessons learned from his first project into practice, completing several other large-scale commissions, including those for the Dallas Public Library, the Cincinnati Public Library, and Lambert–St. Louis Airport. Shortly after completing the GMTC sculpture, Bertoia began work on another, even larger, sculpture for the new Manufacturers Trust Company Building (MTCB, 1951–54) at 510 Fifth Avenue in New York City (figure 2.26). Many reviews of the GMTC even included references to a "similar" sculptural screen "copied" for the "ultra-modern bank," designed by Skidmore, Owings & Merrill (SOM). The February 1955 issue of *Progressive Architecture*, for example, included a multipage spread on the GMTC, including images of Bertoia's sculpture in the Central Restaurant Building, and just a few pages later, dedicated a feature solely to Bertoia's Fifth Avenue "abstractions in metal." In the latter piece, critic Eugene Clute noted the short passage of time between the creation of both screens, but erroneously stated that the sculpture for MTCB was simply a "larger version" of the GMTC screen.[50]

The confusion in comparing the MTCB and GMTC screens is understandable. Both sculptures were brazed-metal multiplane screens, comprised of a similar formal structure of welded rectangular metal plates, and made with comparable materials and techniques. Further, both commissions came about because of Bertoia's professional connections. Gordon Bunshaft, the supervising architect on the project for SOM and a friend of Saarinen, also personally selected Bertoia for the project after seeing the artist's work at the Knoll showroom. Bunshaft, like Saarinen, was also quite pleased with the resulting sculpture, remarking years after the completion of the MTCB that Bertoia "did a good job," which for a man of notoriously few words but many strong opinions, was high praise indeed.[51]

While the two commissions had much in common, their differences are not simply one of scale and size, even though the MTCB screen was almost double the size of the GMTC commission. For the bank project, Bertoia created a sculpture made with the needs of a specific site in mind and in close dialogue with the architect of that space. As handwritten, hand-drawn diagrams in the artist's papers show, what Bertoia "came up with" for the MTCB was far more ambitious, on every level, that his prior commission for the GMTC (figure 2.27). From the very beginning, Bertoia's sculpture was intended to be both a dominant, functional object—a screen separating the public and private areas of the main banking floor on the second story—and a modern sculpture lending decorative interest. The commission for 510 Fifth Avenue, also included a wire "cloud" sculpture that hung from the ceiling just across from the screen in the main banking area (figure 2.28). The second floor of the MTCB, however, was dominated by the seventy-foot-long, sixteen-foot-high rectangular sculpture object, comprised of seven, fifteen-hundred-pound sections, with six horizontal bands arranged in five distinct planes. An interior web of three, eight-inch rods connected these planes and provided additional structural support. The screen was twenty-two inches deep, packed with more organic, semiabstract elements—irregularly hewn triangular, semicircular,

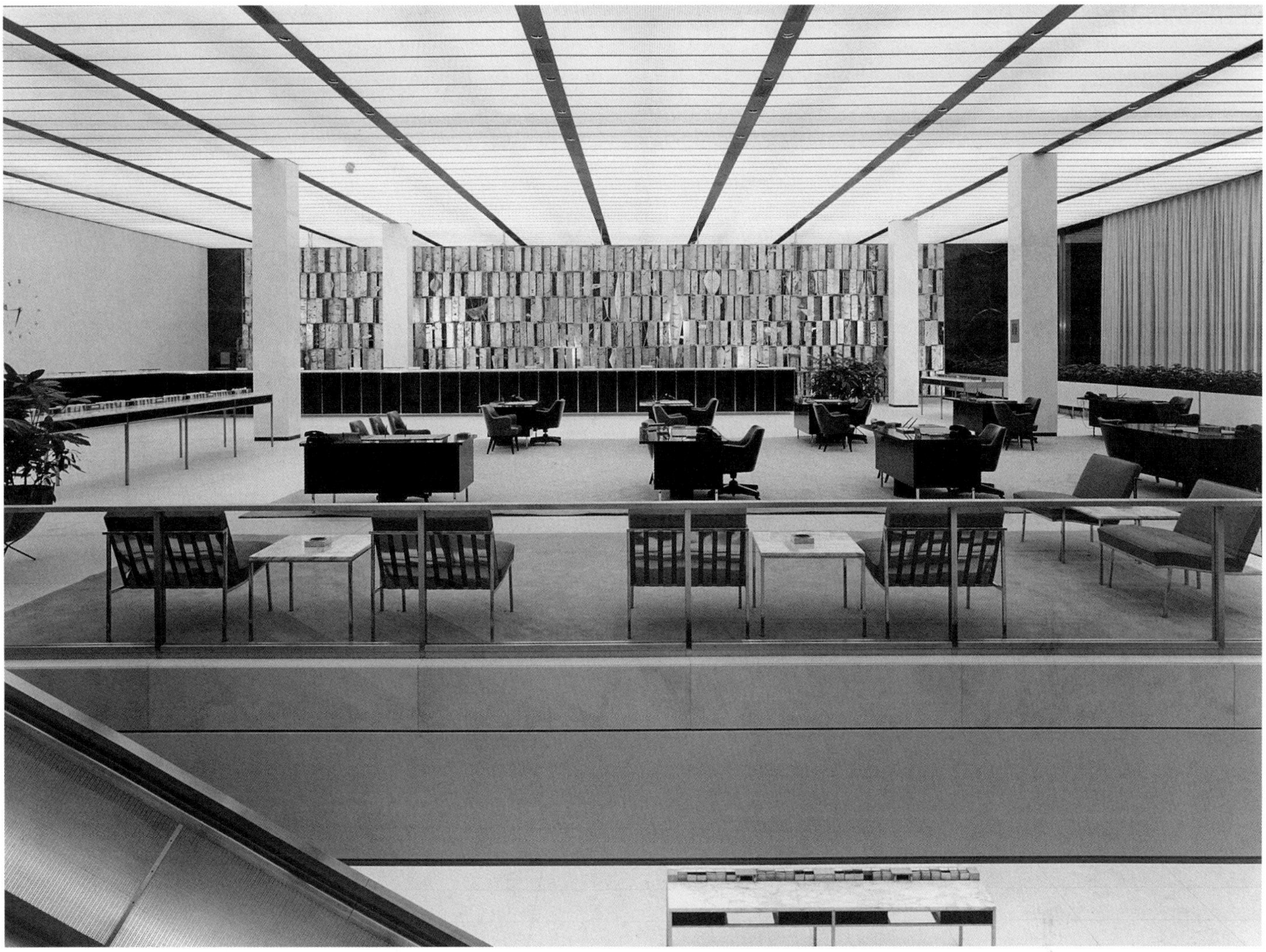

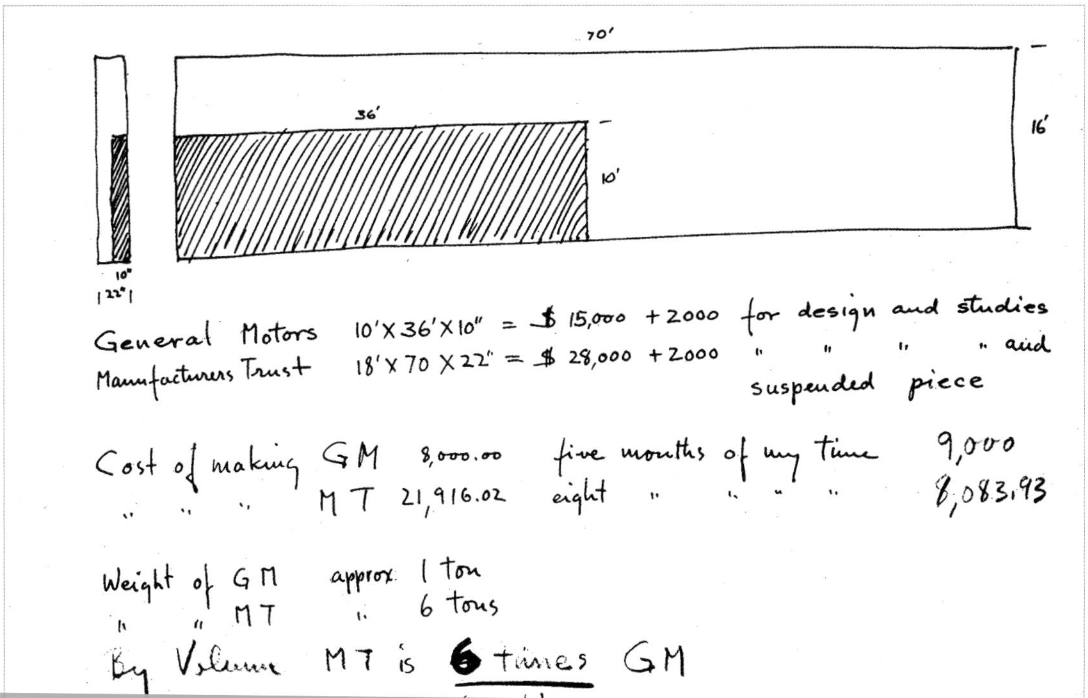

2.26
Harry Bertoia, *Untitled*, 1954. Brazed and welded metal, 16 ft. × 70 ft. × 2 ft. Manufacturers Trust Building, 510 Fifth Avenue, New York City. Architect: Skidmore, Owings & Merrill (SOM).

2.27 Harry Bertoia's technical drawings for the General Motors Technical Center (1956) and Manufacturers Trust Building (1951–54), n.d.

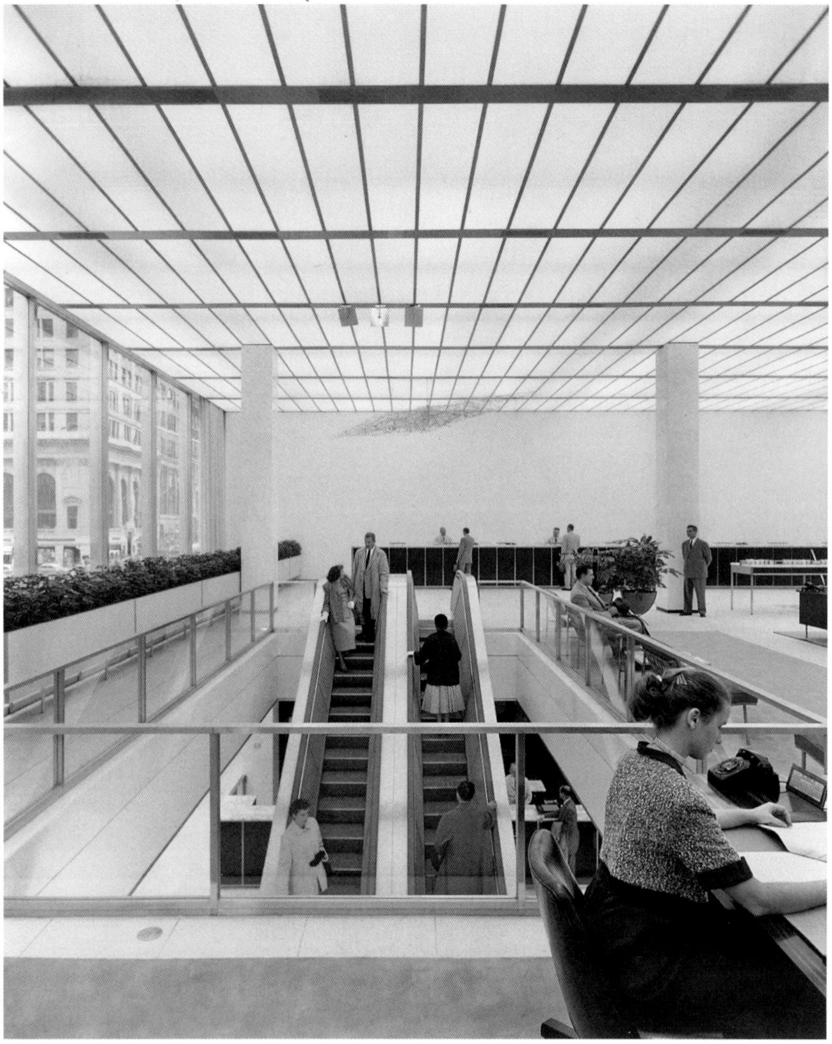

2.28
Harry Bertoia, *Untitled*, 1954. Steel wire, 18 ft. × 12 ft. × 3 ft. Manufacturers Trust Building, 510 Fifth Avenue, New York City. Architect: Skidmore, Owings & Merrill (SOM).

> 2.29
Harry Bertoia, *Untitled* (detail), 1954. Brazed and welded metal, 16 ft. × 70 ft. × 2 ft. Manufacturers Trust Building, 510 Fifth Avenue, New York City. Architect: Skidmore, Owings & Merrill (SOM).

and trapezoidal shapes—that gave the work a rich texture and immense formal complexity (figure 2.29).[52]

Bertoia anchored the screen to the floor as well as to the aluminum plates running the length of the glowing ceiling, originally fabricated in vinyl plastic by the Marlux Corporation. Welded enameling steel was the work's core material, but Bertoia treated the surface of the eight hundred plates and connecting elements with an innovative combination of liquid brass, copper, and nickel. Taken as a whole, from the front or back, the sculpture reads as a golden monolithic grid. From the ends, peering through its thin, wire-like armature, the work takes on a far more airy, transparent feeling (figure 2.30). From this vantage point, the three-dimensionality of the screen also becomes fully apparent as the additional pieces, some welded perpendicularly in between the front-facing plates, come into view. Looking even closer, the seemingly even, glistening surface of the screen explodes in areas where the mixture of melted, oozing metals have hardened into built-up pools or conversely eroded away into pockmarks, exposing a multiplicity of layers below. Silver, gold, copper, blackened, and rust tones come together, and, depending on the lighting, the individual plates cast shadows on one another, creating further color variation and effects, as well as surface diversity. As Bertoia

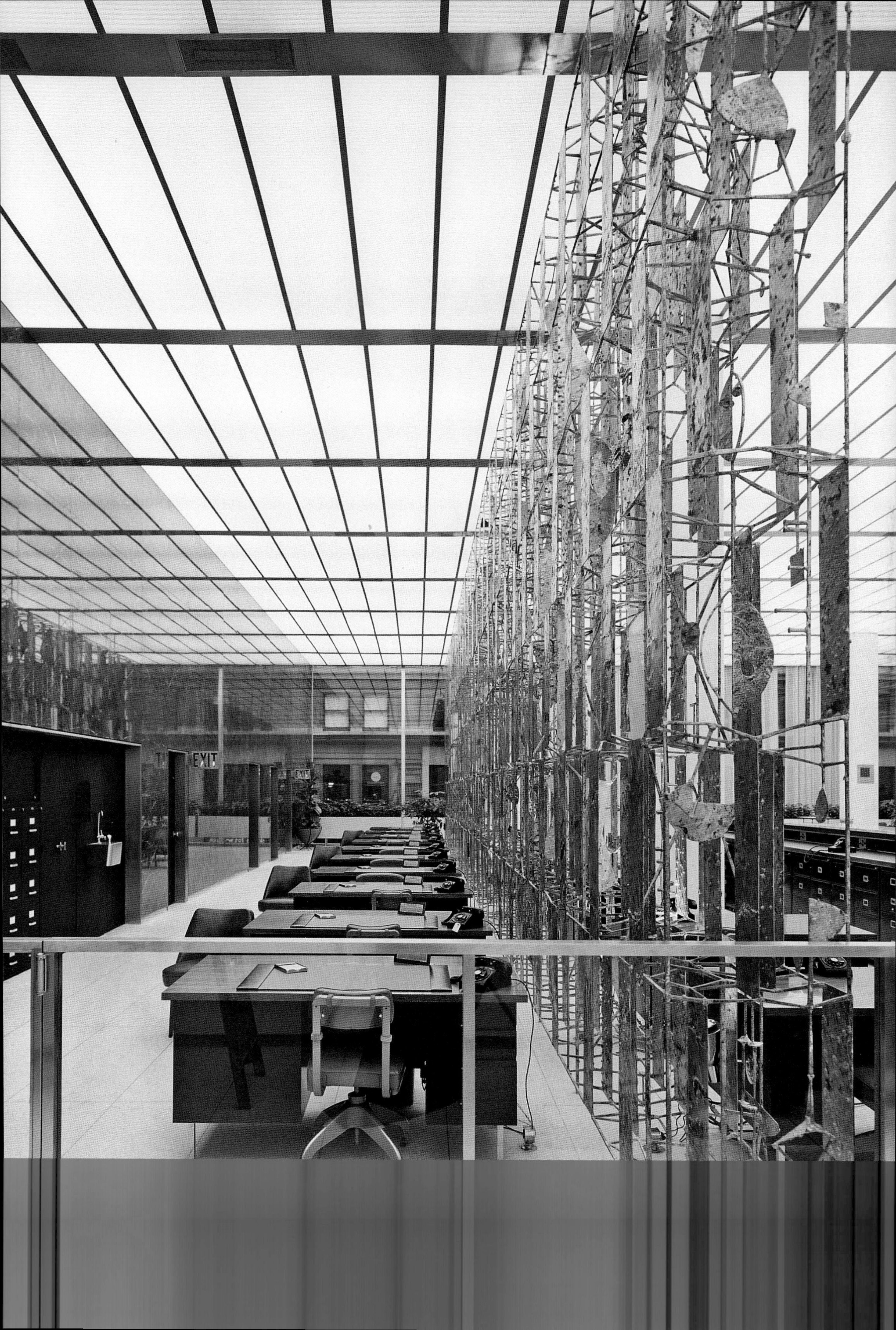
EXIT

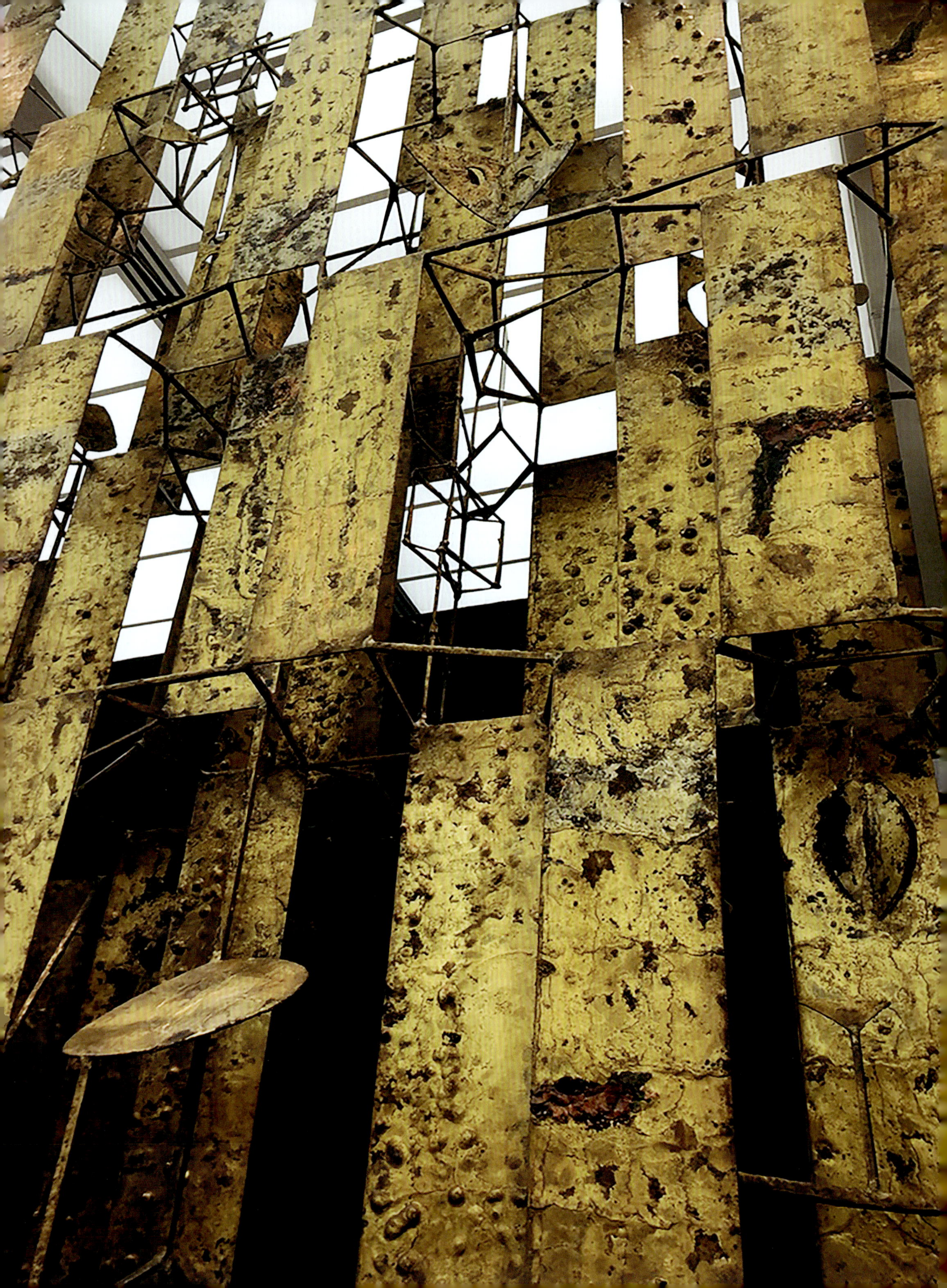

wrote, "The entire job was unusual as well as interesting. We arrived at controlled oxidation without equipment to attain color of surface by immersing the hot-coated plates into water. Initially, we had a great deal of warpage. We improved as we went along. . . . All I have to say is that I didn't have a book to find the answers as to what was going to happen for every move made. Each answer came slowly and the hard way."[53] The result of this new, experimental technique gave the entire work a rough, visually opulent quality, but it also reinforced the overall innovation of the building it occupied.

The MTCB opened to the public with great fanfare on October 4, 1954, drawing fifteen thousand visitors and receiving ample coverage in the popular and architecture press. The *Saturday Evening Post* declared that the bank's three-million-dollar "public relations gamble" had paid off, with the building giving Manufacturers Trust Company a competitive edge in banking as well as inspiring newspaper cartoons, serving as a "perennial topic of luncheon and dinner conversations," becoming a favored location for advertising and fashion shoots, and attracting tens of thousands of nonbanking visitors every year. The MTCB exemplified the clean lines and material innovation of the International Style of architecture materializing across Manhattan during the postwar period, but the four-story project was always envisioned as a distinctive banking and architectural showcase (figure 2.31). It was the first bank to be constructed with floor-to-ceiling glass that offered unobstructed views of the public banking areas, including the large vault visible from street level. As one critic remarked, the design of the MTCB was "based on the concept that banking today is selling service and is to a great extent comparable with department stores and specialty shops where the

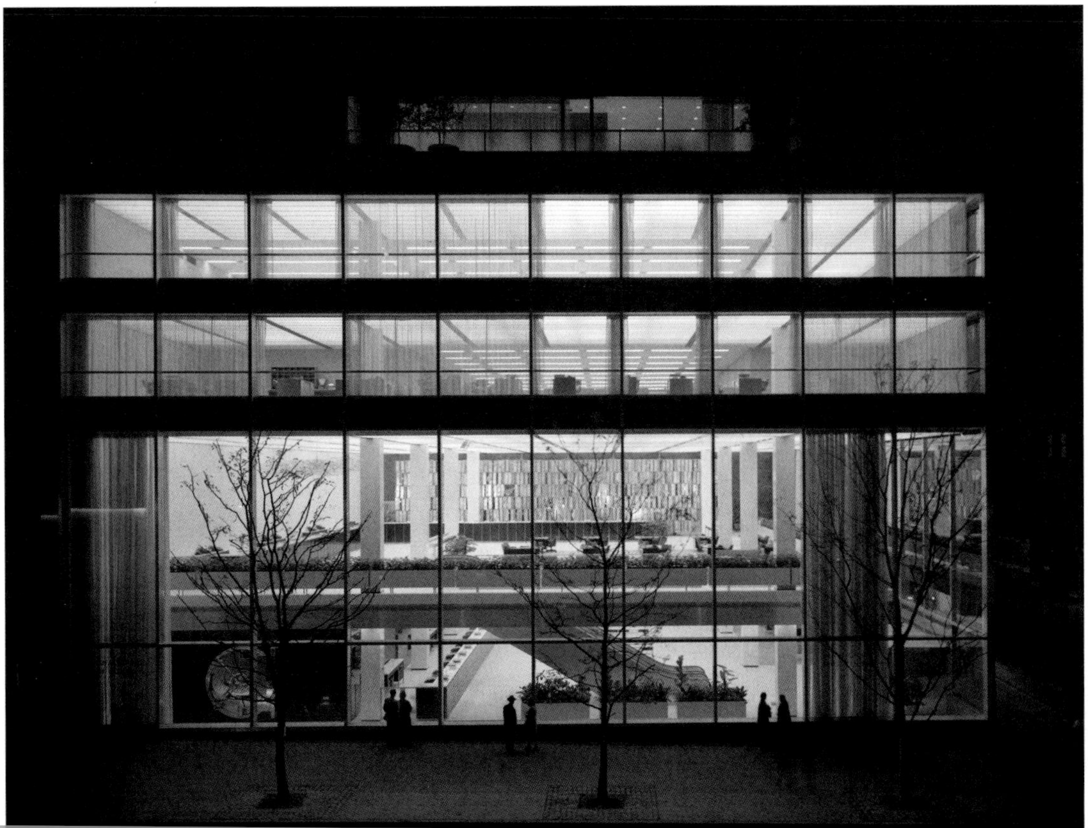

< 2.30 Harry Bertoia, *Untitled*, 1954. Brazed and welded metal, 16 ft. × 70 ft. × 2 ft. Manufacturers Trust Building, 510 Fifth Avenue, New York City. Architect: Skidmore, Owings & Merrill (SOM).

2.31 Manufacturers Trust Building, 510 Fifth Avenue, New York City, 1951–54.

aim is to provide inviting quarters and an attractive atmosphere." The inclusion of art, or more specifically the commissioning of two sculptures by Bertoia, proved crucial to making the MTCB "inviting."[54]

Like the building for which it was made, Bertoia's screen garnered extensive interest from the public and the press. The *New York Times* reported that the sculpture proved to be one of the major, if also more controversial, points of interest within the building, eliciting a broad range of comments from the public about its modern, abstract form: from "breath-taking" to "it looks like a flying bedspring" or "a pile of broken egg crates." Clute remarked in *Progressive Architecture* that the "golden glints" of Bertoia's screen mimicked "the treasure that is the banker's stock-in-trade," while also describing the work through language that emphasized its inherent, alloyed interconnectivity, of "rods welded together," and "placed at intervals, integrated with the horizontal webs." Clute continued, "The design is abstract—a composition based on space relations, reflections from planes at different angles, play of light on metal surfaces of rich textures and subtly varied coloring."[55]

The noted social and architectural critic Lewis Mumford, writing in the *New Yorker*, admitted that Bertoia's screen was "a feature that I gravely doubted when I saw the preliminary illustrations, but the truth is that it lifts the whole composition to a higher plane." Mumford continued, "Though it is purely abstract, making no effort at symbolic significance, it humanizes these quarters even more effectively than the living plants, mainly because it suggests something frail, incomplete, yet unexpected and defiant of rational statement, and thus lovable, a note that is not audible in most of the representative architectural expressions of our time."[56] Mumford acknowledged that Bertoia's massive screen managed to avoid being visually incongruous with the space or the overall decorative scheme, while also expressing enough formal gravitas to further shape and even unify the space.

Ada Louise Huxtable, for her part, noted both the contrasting and complementary qualities of the "screen wall," describing it as "a note of Byzantine splendor in an otherwise austerely elegant interior. Brilliant gold in color, primitive in texture and pattern, it is the perfect accent for the polished surroundings." She concluded her assessment of both Bertoia's sculpture and Bunshaft's building by declaring it nothing less than a "successful integration of two of the major arts." Much of the contemporary criticism came to similar conclusions, with many noting that the screen fit into the whole of the building so well that "one could not exist successfully without the other." *Arts & Architecture* declared that the MTCB "represents not only a fresh point of view in banking architecture but is an excellent example of what happens when the architect works intelligently and cooperatively with the artist." Bertoia was even given the Gold Medal of Honor in Design and Craftsmanship from the Architectural League for the project in 1955, with the award making particular note of how Bertoia incorporated the screen with the building.[57]

For a true cross-disciplinary synergy to occur, for art to function as more than simply the "intellectual application of decoration to the surface of a building," as critic Herbert Hannum stated, architects and artists needed to work together. Throughout his career, Bertoia was fortunate enough to find counterparts who were at least willing to try, including Bunshaft. Bertoia spoke highly of the architect's open-mindedness, recalling how with the MTCB commission there was a commitment to incorporate sculpture from the beginning, and a steady trust that allowed him to dictate the final form of the commission and how it would operate with and within the building. As Bertoia stated, "Gordon Bunshaft called me up, he said we're going to do a bank but before we start, I'd like you to come up with something, you know a really big sculpture. Well I said how big? Oh, it's about twenty feet high, seventy feet long... good heavens, I dropped the phone.... He was very diplomatic. He said once you come up with something, then we'll build a building around it." Bunshaft took the sculpture into consideration when designing the building, and Bertoia in return mirrored the form of the building. The rectangularity and openness of the sculpture's metal structure reflected the lines of the ceiling and other interior features, as well as the geometry of the building's steel and glass framework.[58]

Synergy between art and architecture in the MTCB, however, did not simply mean formal mimicry. As art historian Eduard Trier wrote of Bertoia's screen, "The function of the wall is to divide the interior. But while it separates one part for a special purpose, it implies the whole.... Bertoia's screening wall is an essential component of the architectural ordinance of the interior and, at the same time, a piece of sculpture in its own right." Bertoia alloyed the best elements of Bunshaft's design with the distinctly sculptural elements of his screen to create an aesthetic and structural resonance between the two, which made them each better for it. The overall effect of the screen was a precise combination of visual lightness and tangible, metallic materiality; its roughly sculpted radiant-gold surface, caught and reflected light, revealing the diversity of objects punctuating its gridded wall structure while becoming a functional part of the architecture.[59]

The Sensuous Plasticity of Surface

The artist Robert Sowers, writing in his series "Arts in Architecture" for *Craft Horizons* in the early 1960s, noted that "city streets are really interiors of a special kind—urban interiors; and it is not unusual for one of them to have, like Fifth Avenue in New York City, an overall character quite as definite as any of the elements that comprise it." The "vista on Fifth Avenue," by the end of the 1950s was certainly filled with notable examples of art in architecture. Sowers cited, for example, a frieze of bronze and walnut figures by sculptor William King in the lobby of the Bankers Trust Company at 44th Street and György Kepes's *Programmed Light Mural* (1959–60) created for the KLM Royal Dutch Airlines Ticket Office at 49th Street (figure 2.32). The latter was actually an aluminum screen stretching over fifty feet long and eighteen feet high, with some sixty-thousand random perforations and large cutouts, behind which were incandescent, fluorescent, and spotlight bulbs controlled by timing and switching devices. Sowers

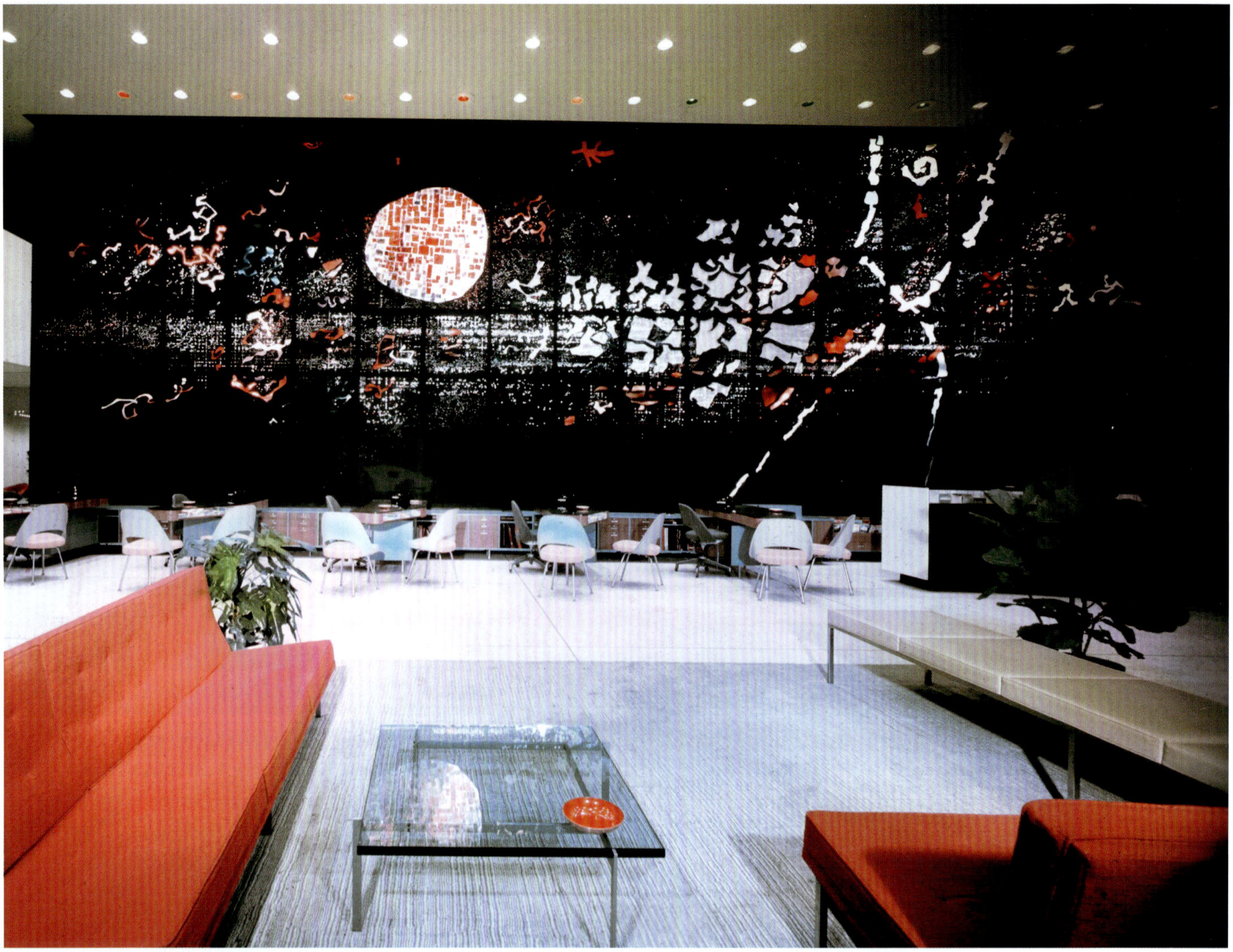

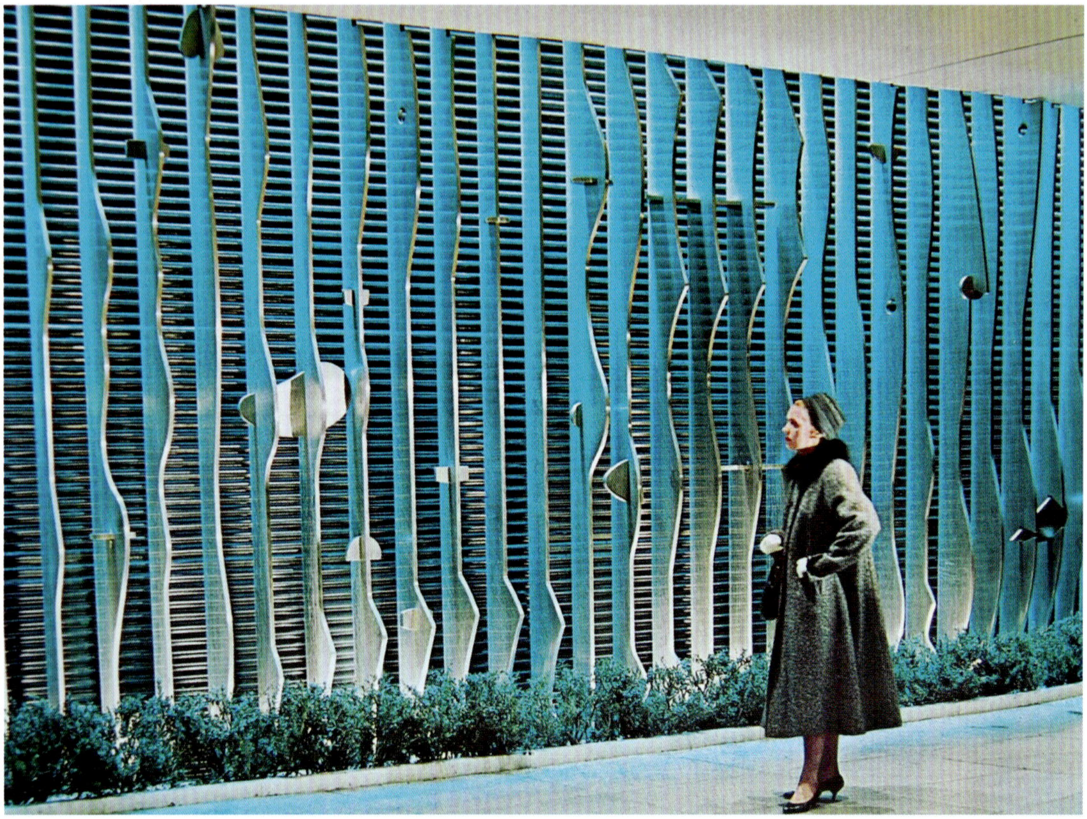

2.32
György Kepes, *Programmed Light Mural*, 1959–60. KLM Royal Dutch Airlines Ticket Office, New York City. György Kepes Papers M1796, Department of Special Collections and University Archives, Stanford University Libraries, California.

2.33
Isamu Noguchi's *666 Fifth Avenue Waterfall* (1956–57) featured in an advertisement for Bethlehem Steel in *Progressive Architecture* (July 1958).

also highlighted Bertoia's MTCB commission at 43rd Street and Nivola's Olivetti relief at 47th Street, noting that both added large-scale or even "overscale" texture to their respective interiors. He could have just as well discussed yet another example of an architecturally scaled frieze, bas-relief, and light-reflecting wall, located a few more blocks north, between 52nd and 53rd Streets: Noguchi's sculptural transformation of the lobby at 666 Fifth Avenue in 1956 (figure 2.33).[60]

On November 25, 1957, a new skyscraper designed by Carson & Lundin and constructed by the Tishman Realty & Construction opened to the public at 666 Fifth Avenue. The *New York Times* lauded the building's one-million-square-foot office space and its status as the world's largest aluminum-faced structure. The newspaper also made special mention, however, of an unusual feature in the "imposing main-floor arcade": "a waterfall pouring over a sculptured-glass background" with "stainless-steel free form fins" installed near a ceiling comprised of similar fins that ran horizontally across the lobby ceiling. Almost as an afterthought, the *New York Times* stated, "Isamu Noguchi, noted Japanese sculptor, assisted in the design of the waterfall and the lobby ceiling."[61]

A year prior, while 666 Fifth Avenue was still under construction, however, the *New York Times* had devoted an entire article to Noguchi's unusual design, noting then that Tishman Realty & Construction was responsible for commissioning the sculptor. Norman Tishman, president of the company, declared his commitment to "esthetic considerations," and highlighted Noguchi's experiments with "sculpture, light and water... for public spaces in institutional and business buildings." Tishman elaborated, "Since businesspeople generally spend most of their waking hours in office buildings, there is no reason why such structures cannot offer an environment that is as pleasant and refreshing as possible." Tishman's rationale for Noguchi's involvement with the project concerned the artist's ability to infuse a heavily trafficked lobby with a visually enjoyable decorative scheme.[62]

Very little in the way of archival material related to Noguchi's ceiling and wall components for 666 Fifth Avenue survives, but the artist recounted that the project had actually come about because of a previously established relationship with the architectural firm. In 1952, Robert Carson contacted Noguchi to create a sculpture for a bank Carson & Lundin was working on in Texas. The artist had submitted a design consisting of contoured louvers meant to indicate the "geological place of minerals." Though never realized, Carson held on to the model Noguchi made, and when the architect began working on 666 Fifth Avenue, he returned to the idea (figure 2.34).[63]

Noguchi later recounted that Carson told him he was going to adapt the design for the ceiling of the elevator lobby and asked if he might be interested in making a "waterfall wall" to complement it. The artist wrote, "I was horrified at the idea of such arbitrary use, and wishing to save my reputation, offered also to redesign the ceiling for the cost of the waterfall alone. A precise model permitted templates to be taken and executed directly in aluminum and stainless steel. The ceiling became a landscape of the clouds." Carson notified Noguchi on October 21, 1955 that his firm had submitted to their clients his "proposal to design a sculptured wall at the entrance to the new building proposed for 666 Fifth Avenue and to revise our sketches for the ceiling of the lobby so that it will be in harmony with the wall which you will design." Carson, however, also made clear that it would be the architectural firm, not the artist, who would be responsible for the "actual construction of the ceiling or the wall sculpture." Noguchi submitted the new preliminary models and invoiced Carson & Lundin in January 1956.[64]

While something of an antagonistic collaboration from the beginning, the lobby project for 666 Fifth Avenue did afford Noguchi another opportunity to think through the possibilities of sculpture within architectural spaces and continue exploring motifs developed in earlier projects. While both the ceiling and wall components for 666 Fifth Avenue remain unique in Noguchi's oeuvre of commissioned works, he had previously used louvers, not only for the unrealized bank project design, but also for an exhibition of his Akari at the Chuo Koron Gallery

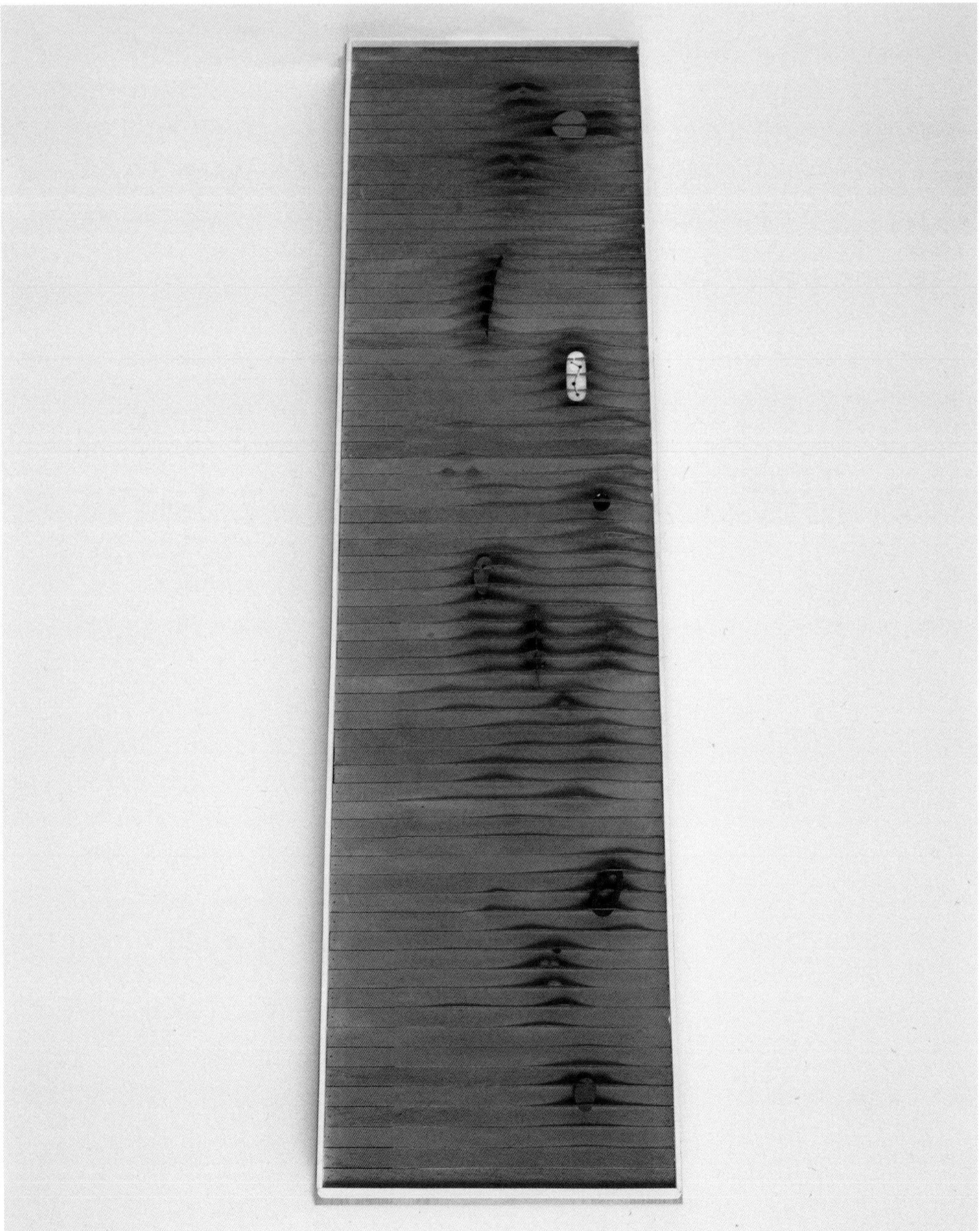

2.34
Isamu Noguchi, *Model for 666 Fifth Avenue Ceiling and Waterfall*, 1956–57. Wood, aluminum, paint, dimensions variable. 666 Fifth Avenue, New York City. Architect: Carson & Lundin.

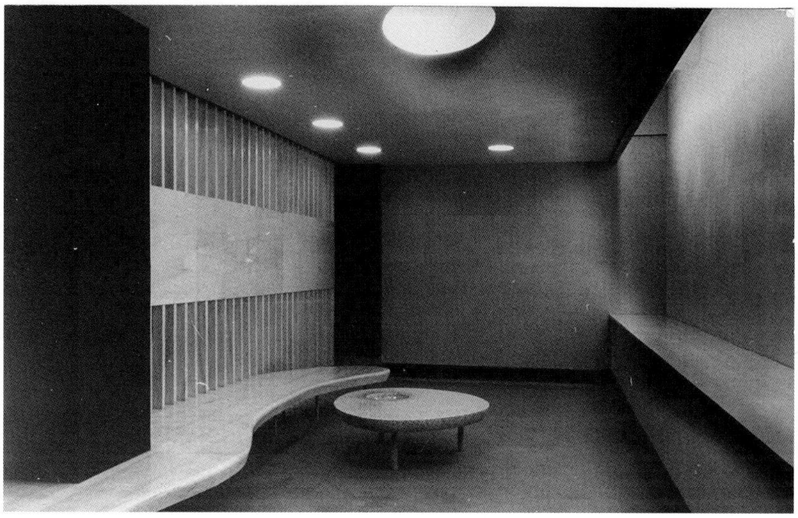

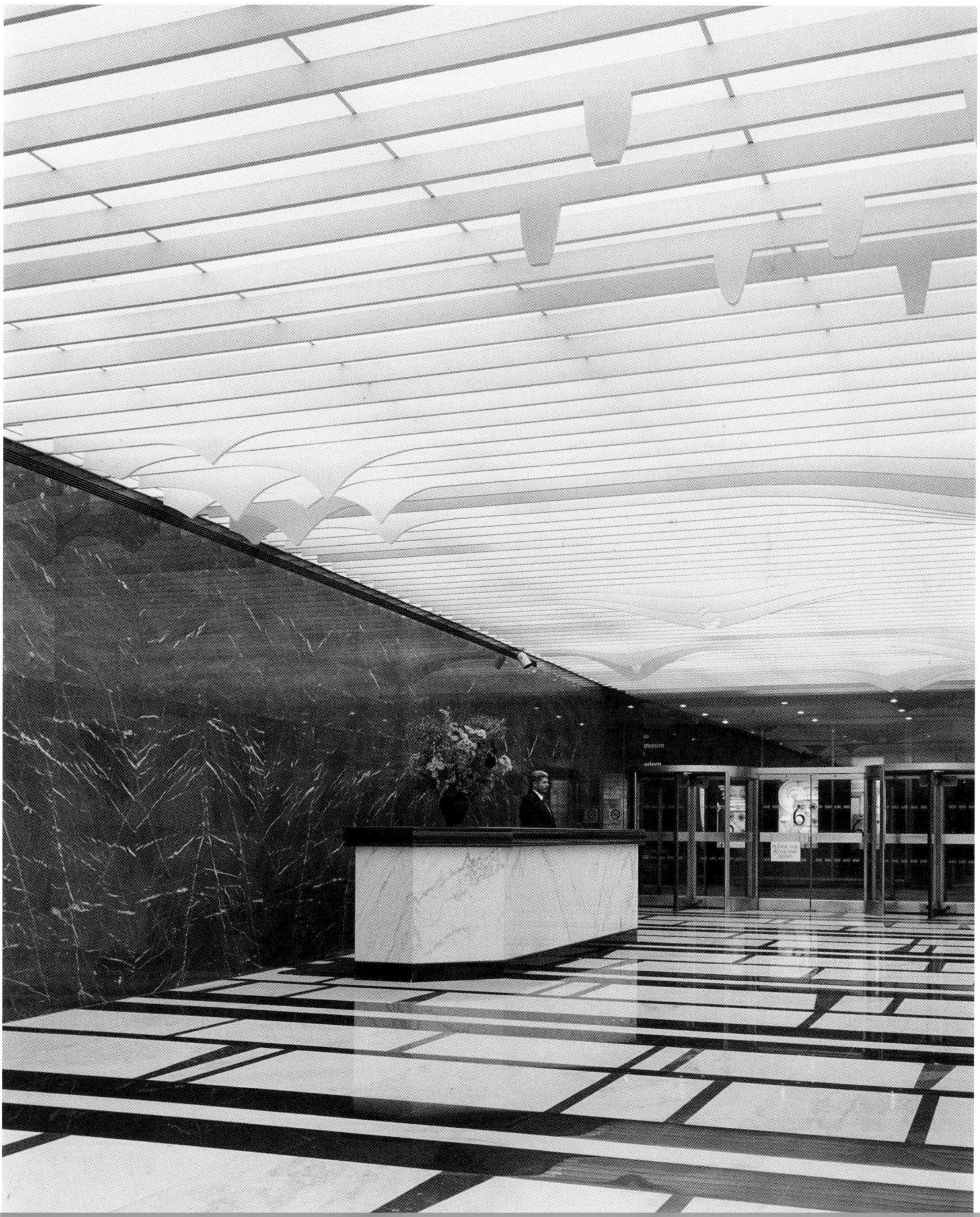

2.35
Isamu Noguchi interior and furniture design, Chuo Koron Gallery, Tokyo, Japan, 1954.

2.36
Isamu Noguchi, *666 Fifth Avenue Ceiling and Waterfall* (detail), 1956–57. Interior design with stainless steel, wood, and water. 666 Fifth Avenue, New York City.

in Tokyo in Japan in August 1954. Alongside examples of his light sculptures, Noguchi also modified the gallery space, installing at the center of the exhibition a low, ovoid granite coffee table and a long, sinuous wood bench extending from a bank of rectilinear wood louvers, all of which he designed (figure 2.35).

The louvered ceiling at 666 Fifth Avenue, in particular, can be seen as an extension of these projects, but also the American Stove Company commission—another elevator bank transformed as sculpture extended downward and inward from above (figure 2.36). For 666 Fifth Avenue, Noguchi similarly combined sinuous, sculpted elements with protruding forms and more straightforward sections, in this case, regular rectangular slats. Cold-cathode fluorescent light sources were placed above translucent panels, and, like Noguchi's earlier magnesite sculptures, the dramatic artificial lighting also played a crucial role in this "landscape of the clouds." As Huxtable wrote in her review of the project, "Workers or visitors entering the aluminum-faced Tishman Tower at 666 Fifth Avenue pass through an unusual elevator lobby of strange, milky luminosity, under the thin, white sculptured baffles of the ceiling lighting shaped in stalactite undulations." Lighting, as it had in previous projects by Noguchi, added dynamism to the white louvers and the spaces in between them, further highlighting the object quality of the ceiling's design.[65]

The 666 Fifth Avenue commission is distinct, however, for how Noguchi combined both wall and ceiling features. The design of the two sculptural components were, formally and conceptually, entwined. The glow of the ceiling, as well as its alternating curvilinear and linear forms mimicked those of the stainless-steel wall, also dramatically lit and further activated by flowing water. Together, the sculpted ceiling and wall transformed the interior, pushing out into the space of the lobby and adding vibrant, three-dimensional texture to what was a rather nondescript architectural design. Though notable for its exterior, especially regarding its expertly designed night lighting conceived by Abe Feder, Carson & Lundin's building overall was not received as an innovative example of modernist architecture—though almost every piece of press and critical coverage did make note of Noguchi's contribution. *Architectural Record*, for example, announced the building's construction alongside two other structures, New York City's 575 Lexington Avenue and the Borg-Warner Building in Chicago as "variations on a theme," but one of the two total sentences dedicated to 666 Fifth Avenue was devoted to Noguchi's novel sculptural designs.[66]

The wall and ceiling components, however, also worked as distinct entities. The metal wall ran parallel to the horizontal bands of the ceiling within the lobby, but was located in another area, in front of the elevator bank, further separated and framed around two substantial, shiny pillars (figure 2.37). Parts of the wall were just barely visible when entering the lobby from Fifth Avenue. The forty-foot-long wall separated the arcade from the elevator bank. The individual pieces of the wall were altogether more sculptural, with each one pointed, curved, or shaped in some way and extending in high relief. The shimmering steel fins were vertically oriented and extended outward in the round, though secured to the ceiling and

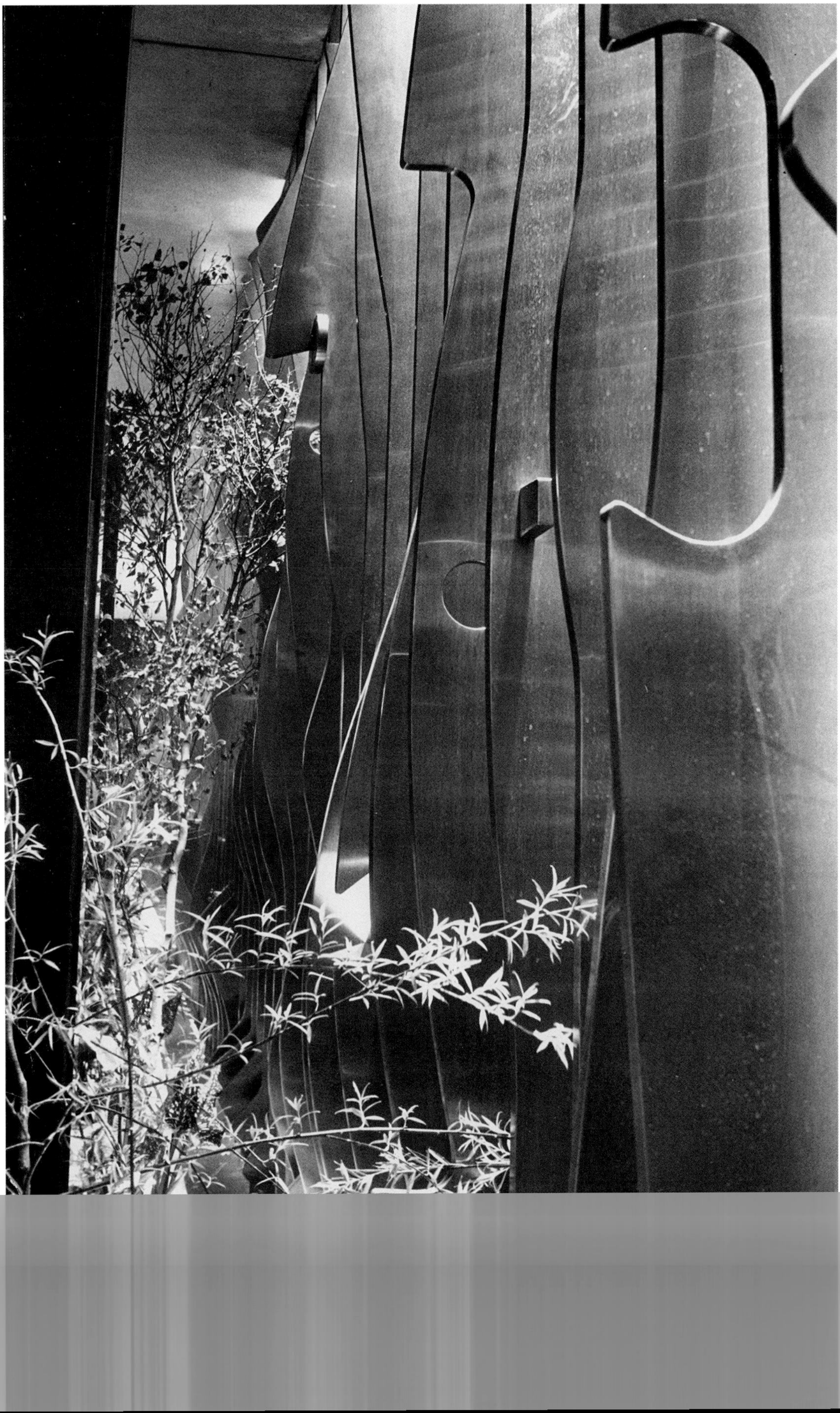

2.37
Isamu Noguchi, *666 Fifth Avenue Ceiling and Waterfall* (detail), 1956–57. Interior design with stainless steel, wood, and water. 666 Fifth Avenue, New York City. Architect: Carson & Lundin.

floor, with a grid of evenly spaced, thin horizontal silver slats visible behind. The formal push-pull of curving and straight forms was further emphasized in the waterfall as Noguchi interspersed circular cutouts and smaller irregular shapes wedged in between the vertical pieces (figure 2.38).

Like Bertoia's and Nivola's sculpted walls from the immediate postwar period, Noguchi's defied easy classification: both a functional entity used to divide space and a sculptural object created to advance an artistic vision—though one that would not circulate within the art market. A relief, a screen, a wall, and now also a waterfall fountain, Noguchi's steel structure for the lobby of 666 Fifth Avenue deftly collapsed categorical boundaries, to create a new, hybrid sculptural form that was alloyed with architecture. As Noguchi stated, "At some point architecture becomes sculpture, and sculpture becomes architecture; at some point they meet. We have to discover what that point is. For instance, a wall is an element of architecture. The dimensions of that wall are also an element of sculpture.... The sculpture should no longer be just something stuck on the architecture, but a development of the architecture itself—what you might call an emotionally functional as well as just a mechanically functional thing—to accent and punctuate, giving dimensions to space. When you put a sculpture within a given space, it allocates the space and gives it a dimension." Noguchi's evocation of allocation offers another way to understand how sculpture could operate with and within architecture, functioning as both a means to set apart and locate, connect, or fix a particular place.[67]

Like other significant sculptural commissions realized for new Fifth Avenue buildings or interiors during the immediate postwar period, Noguchi's ceiling and wall at 666 Fifth Avenue suggested that the renewed interest in using sculpture in architecture was not simply motivated by a desire for cross-disciplinary collaboration, but also a tangible exchange of form, material, and process. Sculptors like Noguchi or Bertoia, while willing to relinquish more of their own ego for the greater good of a unified design, were not interested in creating something superficially "stuck on" architecture. For their sculpture to be a "development of the architecture itself," they increasingly concentrated on its scale and functionality—a shift that would become a defining feature of the medium of sculpture during the later twentieth century.

The point of encounter between sculpture and architecture during the immediate postwar period, however, did not occur in a single direction. Architects, while commissioning sculptors to create work, also became increasingly interested in creating buildings, as Noguchi described, that resembled sculpture. Though never explicitly articulated in this way, and certainly never framed through the primacy of sculptural practice, architectural critics at the time did identify and intently debate this emergent phenomenon. While many saw the move away from "the rectilinear, modular, flat-surfaced expressions" of the Mies van der Rohe-like International Style as a detriment to modernist architecture, others sought to categorize, and even celebrate, a move toward a more diverse, organic—and sculptural—plasticity.[68]

2.38
Isamu Noguchi, *666 Fifth Avenue Ceiling and Waterfall* (detail), 1956–57. Interior design with stainless steel, wood, and water. 666 Fifth Avenue, New York City. Architect: Carson & Lundin.

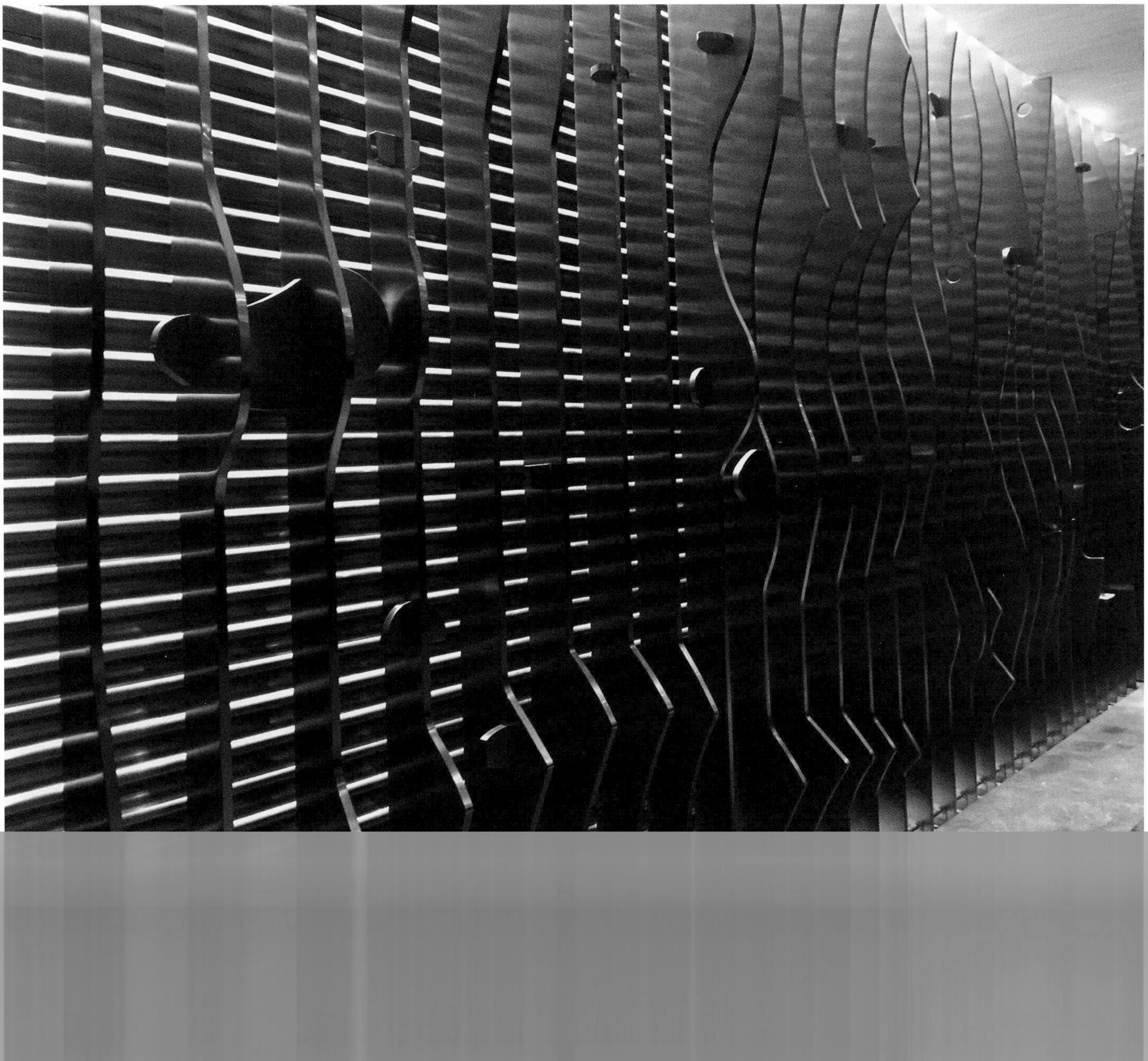

Thomas H. Creighton, for example, settled on the broad label "New Sensualism," acknowledging a multiplicity of approaches and attributes occurring across the spectrum of modernist architecture by the late 1950s. Creighton argued that sensualism or a "stress of the imagery addressing the senses as the chief element of beauty," could function as a synthesizing framework within architectural practice. He identified the loose tendencies evident in this nascent "movement" as: sensuous plasticity, sensuous delight, sculptural concept, stereo-structural sensualism, and romantic expression. Creighton conceded that a sculptural sensibility or architectural influence was hardly a new phenomenon, but his renewed focus on surface and plasticity remained a useful framework to trace how a synergy between architecture and sculpture occurred, or could occur, during the immediate postwar period, especially as it was applied in practice not just in theoretical debate.[69]

Examining the accompanying illustrations of Creighton's "The New Sensualism" and "The New Sensualism II," published in the pages of *Progressive Architecture* in 1959—which included illustrations of Le Corbusier's chapel at Ronchamp, France (1950–54), Eero Saarinen's TWA Terminal Center at Idlewild Airport, New York (1956–62), Edward Durell Stone's US Embassy in New Delhi (1954–59), and Minoru Yamasaki's College of Education at Wayne State University in Detroit (1955–59)—reveals just how much such a disciplinary transference had already manifested itself in contemporary architectural practice. Not only did such architects create exterior forms that resembled monumental sculptures, but they also frequently utilized grilles, screens, and other ornamental forms on both exterior facades and interior spaces to great effect.

Saarinen's striking birdlike concrete terminal for TWA or even Frederick Kiesler's speculative *Endless House*, which did not appear in Creighton's analysis and had a very different scale and motivation, drew heavily from the language of modern sculpture, using it to articulate new forms in modern architecture. As Kiesler stated, "Why not, after all those glass houses, let the family crawl up into a cave and pull the cave in after them?... Why not build the house all in one piece like a piece of sculpture, instead of making careful joints between a wood roof and brick walls?" With their sculptural, serpentine forms, especially pronounced in their interior spaces, structures like Saarinen's terminal and Kiesler's house were technological, vanguard visions of a future present, but they also suggested an embryonic organicism of a primordial past (figures 2.39, 2.40). Both of these strands, when executed successfully, conveyed powerful, physical sensations, beckoning and enveloping inhabitants through radically shaped space—attributes that have direct connections to vanguard midcentury sculpture.[70]

In concluding his treatise on the "sensualist" approach in modernist architecture, Creighton acknowledged that none of the resulting buildings or projects could function as feasible prototypes or roadmaps for modern architecture moving forward. Further, he wrote that "the technology of *New Sensualism*... demands an actual facility, *as a professional*, in sculpture, and very few of our architects are good sculptors. Architecture, we have said for long, is an art (the mother of the arts); yet

2.39
Interior view of Trans World Airlines Terminal Center, 1956–62. Idlewild Airport, Queens, New York. Architect: Eero Saarinen.

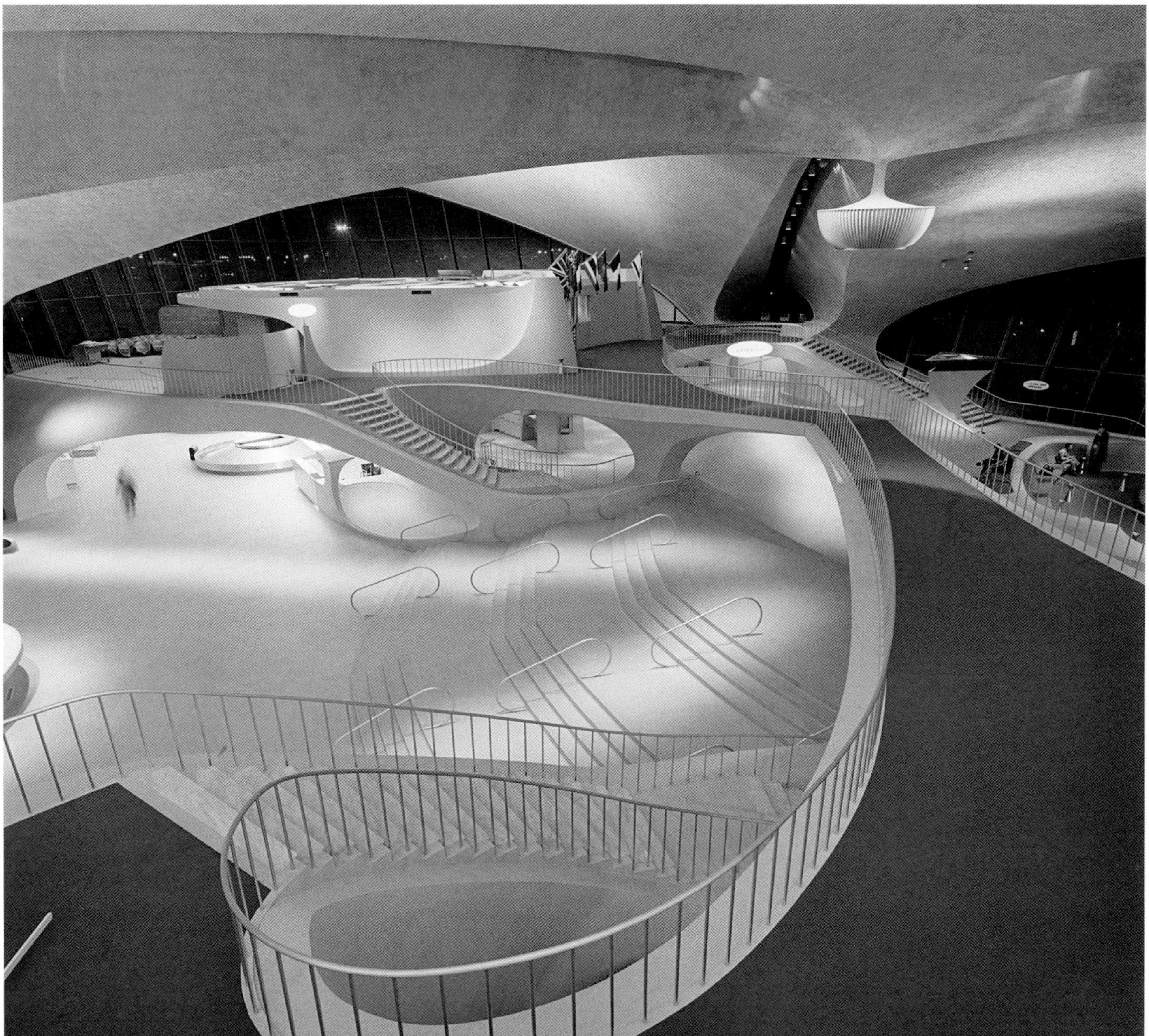

2.40
Interior view of Frederick Kiesler's *Endless House* model, 1958. Gelatin silver print, 8 in. × 10 in. MoMA Architecture & Design Study Center, New York.

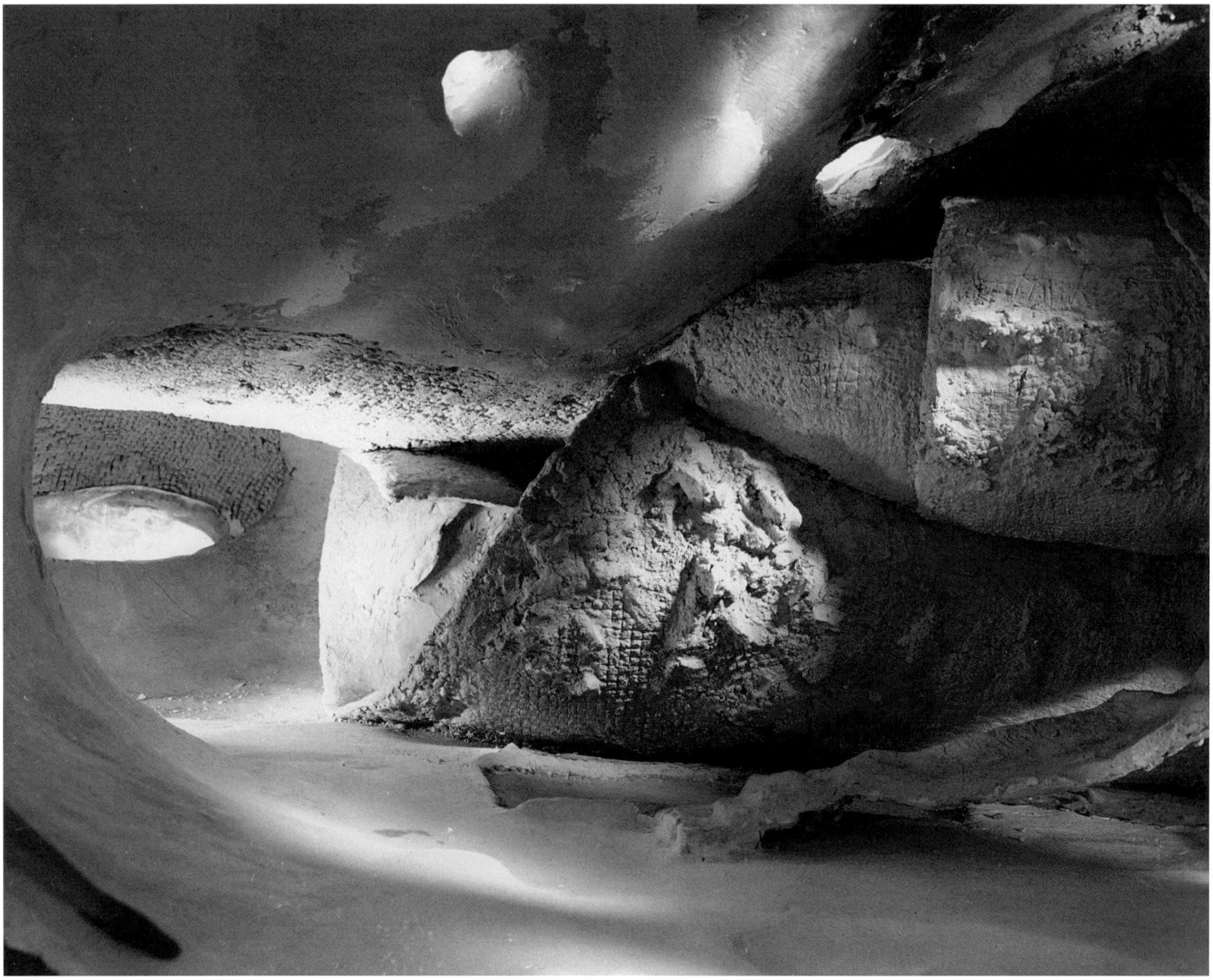

the other arts have developed their own professional attitude and modern competencies independent of architecture."[71] Certainly, during the period, many architects lodged the same criticism back at sculptors .

The buildings of architects like Saarinen are not sculpture; neither are the sculptures of Bertoia and Noguchi architecture, at least not in the strictest sense. Such projects, however, did demonstrate the disciplinary slippage and borrowing that was quickly occurring between architecture and sculpture during the immediate postwar period. Creighton asked, "Can a Bertoia, a Nivola, a Lux, a [Robert] Cronbach, a [Bernard] Rosenthal do more than a wall or a screen; could they work with the architects in basic sculptural-form molding?" Noguchi's project at 666 Fifth Avenue or Bertoia's screen for the Manufacturers Trust Company Building offer possible answers, though they need to be seen from beyond an architecture-centric perspective. These sculptures were never just screens or walls, nor were they just sculpture. Rather, they stand as space dividers, material manifestations of midcentury cross-disciplinary synergy.

Chapter 3

The Space Between

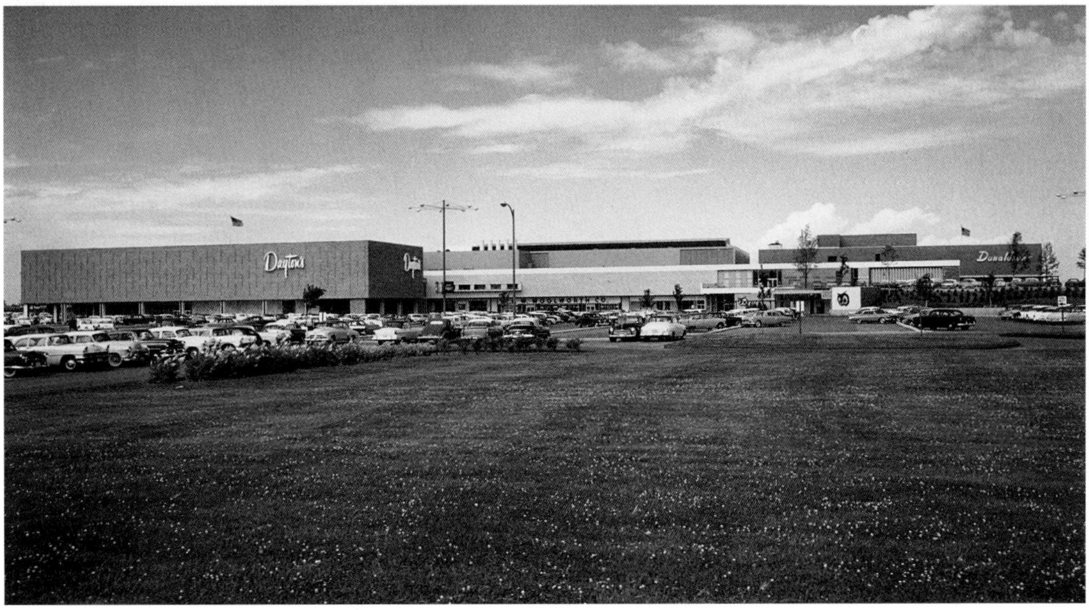

3.1
Southdale Center, Edina, Minnesota, 1956. Architect: Victor Gruen Associates. Northwest Architectural Archives, University of Minnesota Libraries, Minneapolis.

On October 4, 1956, Southdale Center, the first fully enclosed shopping center in the United States, opened to the public in Edina, Minnesota. Designed by architect Victor Gruen and developed by the Minneapolis-based retailer Dayton's, Southdale boasted over eight-hundred-thousand square feet of retail space comprising seventy-two stores on two floors and two anchor department stores, as well as a car park with five-thousand-two-hundred parking spaces (figure 3.1). The local and national press extolled the ingenuity of the project's form and function, lauding its parking, floorplan, and year-round climate control as a "break-through for two-level shopping centers." *Life* declared Southdale "the splashiest shopping center in the U.S.," while *Architectural Forum* remarked that Gruen had achieved nothing less than building a new kind of environment, "quite unlike that of any other shopping center. There is nothing suburban about it except its location. For Southdale uncannily conveys the feeling of a metropolitan downtown: the magical, intangible assurance that here is the big time, this is where things happen, here is the middle of things."[1]

Given the connotations of conformity that would come to be associated with the suburban shopping mall, Gruen's aim to inject urban planning with "diversity and variety into a meaningful organic pattern," may seem ironic or incongruous. He wrote in 1962, however, that the mission of architecture "in these times of mass production, mass consumption, population explosion and urban growth," needed to "widen its horizons; it must switch its attention from the individual structure to the entire man-made environment." Crucial to creating such a space at Southdale was the attempt to transfer the idea of the "public square" into a fully enclosed central atrium, which stretched a block long and soared five-stories high. Citing the shopping arcades of Milan and the dense city center of his native Vienna as influences, Gruen wrote, "Our concept of a mercantile is an attempt to restore some of the Old World (and Old American) market-place atmosphere in modern surroundings."[2] Southdale's Garden Court of Perpetual Spring, was a sensual spectacle of visual diversions and pleasurable details, though one devoid of signage or conspicuous advertising (figure 3.2).

Replica sidewalk cafés, twenty-five-foot magnolia trees, forty-two-foot eucalyptus trees, an elaborate lily-pond fountain filled with fish, and a twenty-one-foot-high metal birdcage filled with fifty live birds all breathed outdoor life into the space, the green sumptuousness enhanced further by hanging plants that poured from the clerestory and over the railings. A second-floor walkway horizontally bisected the space, connecting to the level below through two crisscrossing escalators. The Garden Court was lit by northern-facing skylights visible through wood louvers, a clerestory, and a variety of electric-lighting fixtures including three tall custom modern, sculptural chandeliers, which gave the "illusion of a balmy outdoor evening," and soft globe lights that hovered over the fountain, suspended on individual strands.[3]

Dominating one corner of the Garden Court, between an open staircase and the café near the Dayton's entrance, were two forty-five-foot-high, three-thousand-pound metal sculptures by Harry Bertoia (figure 3.3). Golden brazed and welded metal pieces, in various shapes and sizes, extended outward from metal posts that reached from the floor to the ceiling above. Press coverage described the sculptures as screens; and they do share some formal similarities with Bertoia's recently realized commissions for the General Motors Technical Center in Michigan and the Manufacturers Trust Company Building (MTCB) in New York City, which had been Gruen's original intention. The architect had attempted to commission Bertoia for his Northland Regional Shopping Center near Detroit three years earlier, and when the two men met in New York City in late 1954 to talk about collaborating on a project for Southdale, they went together to see the screen installed at the MTCB.[4]

Early proposals show a single, if still more vertically oriented screen, about three-quarters the size of the sculpture at the MTCB, but over the next two years a number of economic, technical, and architectural issues radically altered the form of Bertoia's commissioned sculpture for Southdale. As the artist himself stated of the final version of the sculpture, "They aren't really screens. They don't divide anything. We decided on 'trees' as a better word. That's a good word. It fits with the architectural idea of the court." What is clear from the copious statements by, and correspondence between, Gruen, other architects at his firm, and Bertoia, was that the project was truly collaborative, driven by a desire to produce the best sculpture for the space as it developed, with mutual respect among its participants. Gruen referred to Bertoia as "one of the few leading personalities in contemporary art," remarking that "too much art stays in the gallery. Bertoia's work gets in touch with people." The architect emphasized that the sculptor "can visualize how his work will fit into an architectural scheme." Bertoia confirmed the sentiment stating, "I just wanted to make something to fit in with the architect's plans." Certainly, such an assertion could be read as a deferential articulation of the fear that the only way to combine art and architecture was through a complete sublimation of the artist's autonomy and individual expression.[5]

3.2 Garden Court, Southdale Center, Edina, Minnesota, 1956. Architect: Victor Gruen Associates. Northwest Architectural Archives, University of Minnesota Libraries, Minneapolis.

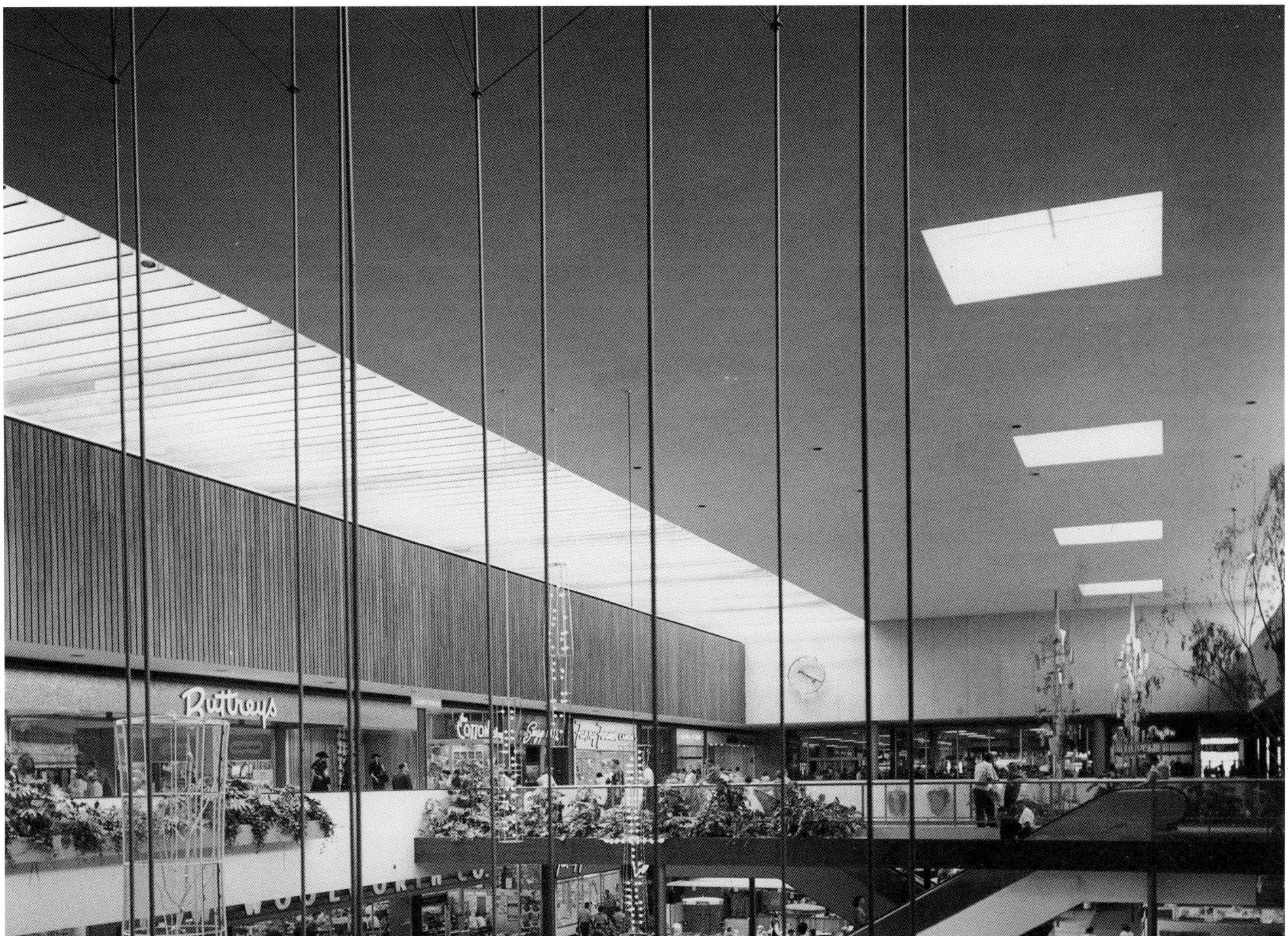

3.3
Harry Bertoia, *Untitled*, 1956. Bronze-coated steel, h. 45 ft. each. Southdale Center, Edina, Minnesota. Architect: Victor Gruen Associates.

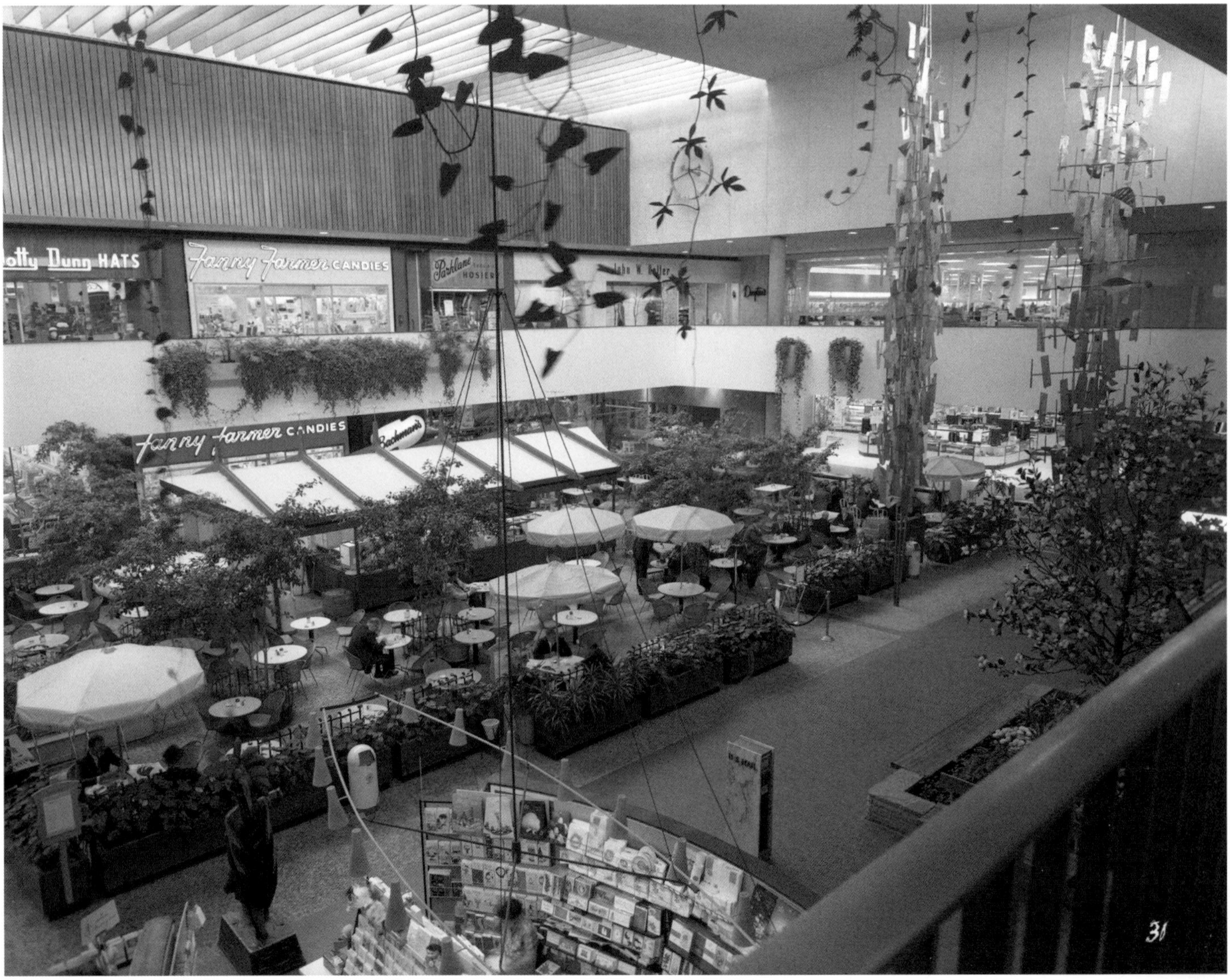

Gruen's letters, however, reveal an architect who was open to suggestion, who strove to make sure the artist never felt forced into any decisions, and who was intent on providing crucial, up-to-date information of the development of the project at hand. For example, when it was determined that the floor would not actually support a freestanding sculpture as Bertoia originally proposed, Gruen sent a drawing of the newly designated area of the Garden Court to the artist writing, "A possibility which might or might not appeal to you. Instead of one screen, there are a number of screen units placed at different distances and covering in height the space of the opening. Freestanding railings are installed between the screens. Let me know how you feel about this idea." In another letter, Gruen recounted to Bertoia his recent experience of seeing Southdale in person:

> Where, for the first time, I could have a very good idea of the spacial quality of the mall because the steel trusses have now been erected. I feel that I should convey to you my impressions for whatever bearing they might have on your work. The space appears much higher (and pleasantly so) than I anticipated. There is a very positive spaciousness about the two-story mall, and the roof seems to be quite a way up. Thus, I feel that in the sculpture the emphasis should perhaps be greater in the lower half than in the upper half, which is sen only when a definite effort to look up is made.[6]

Bertoia responded by adapting his design to accommodate the changing parameters of the space as it developed, shifting toward a more vertical and multipart construction.

When the client and architectural team requested Bertoia shift away from the original screen form to a more overtly "treelike" sculpture, he set to work and sent multiple options, including four distinct models with varying widths of central posts and configurations of "foliage." In March 1956, Rudy Baumfield, another architect based in Gruen's Los Angeles office, informed Bertoia that the final version of the work should consist of two "trees," though his reply again demonstrated the collaborative tone established by Gruen. "As you will notice," Baumfield wrote, "both trees will receive light from the immediately adjacent skylight. We also think that it would be desirable not to keep all 'leaves' in one direction but turn a smaller or larger number of them in the way which I have indicated in green pencil on the plan. Thus, without increasing the width of the structure, we will avoid a predominantly two-dimensional impression. If you don't agree, of course you are at liberty to disregard our suggestion." Final models and drawings were sent to the client, who enthusiastically received them, and by the end of the summer of 1956, Bertoia was in Minneapolis to install the sculpture.[7]

Bertoia's metal trees were not the only large-scale vertical element, nor the only sculpture in the central court, but they were the largest feature and certainly the most cohesively constructed with the specifics of place in mind. In an environment made to feel like a lush, verdant ecosystem the sculpture stood as both another species of tree, at home in Gruen's garden utopia, and a glistening, industrial metallic counterpoint. As *Architectural Forum* noted, the "magic" of Southdale owed much to the general presence of the Garden Court, but more specifically, "the way the court is sized and what goes into it are vital.... Its height is dramatized by sculpture and trees that lift the eyes up, by shafts of sunlight or dimness of dusk. All this is indispensable to the illusion of being in the midst of something that is more than a building and more than the sum of its parts." Unlike the magnolias and eucalyptus, however, Bertoia's metal trees were the only element to cut across and connect the entirety of the vertical space. The large, lofty, lanky sculptures did not just activate or aesthetically complement the tremendous height of the atrium, but also literally connected ceiling to floor. In realizing the commission in this fashion, Bertoia pushed sculpture further into the space of architecture.[8]

Bertoia's Southdale commission took on both the scale and materials of architecture in order to explore new conceptions of sculptural space. The work proved emblematic and even predictive of multiple trends that would come to dominate sculptural practice during the postwar period. Bertoia's trees, while one of his more literal large-scale commissions, exemplified the push into greater scale enabled through direct metal construction and the use of welding. In the Southdale project, Bertoia engaged with the widespread multilayered material and conceptual expressions of space occurring during the period. The work, crucially, also used sculpture to create an inhabitable environment.

Bertoia, as well as Richard Lippold, explored similar concerns in several commissions from the period, including those realized for the campus of the Massachusetts Institute of Technology in Cambridge, the Inland Steel Building in Chicago, and the Pan Am Building in New York City. These projects shared similar materials and complex engineering processes with architecture, as well as postwar science and industry. Bertoia's and Lippold's sculptural practices, like many of their contemporaries, were grounded in a profound curiosity about metal, the material's diverse materiality, and its seemingly endless ability to transform and alloy. They pushed the formal possibilities of metal and its conceptual ability to express principles of synergy. Bertoia and Lippold drew on a wealth of intellectual influences and contemporary associations to shape new forms and new spaces. These four commissioned works by Bertoia and Lippold, however, also shared a particularly distinctive feature: each was anchored to both the floor and the ceiling of their respective threshold spaces, literally tying together and activating the space in between the key structural features of architecture. The sculptures engaged with walls, ceilings, and floors simultaneously, transmuting these architectural elements, and using transparency or openness to alter space without walling it off. In the process, sculpture became an alloyed experience of space that was greater than the sum of its parts.

Seen in this context, the twenty years following the end of World War II can no longer be only understood as the story the New York School of painting or as the zenith of Greenberg's dogma of modernist formalism. Vanguard three-dimensional work of the immediate postwar period, particularly large-scale commissions realized by artists like Bertoia, Lippold, Alexander Calder, and Isamu Noguchi, suggest instead a crucial transitional moment wrought through synergy, through an artistic engagement with, and embrace of, the built environment. These artists utilized new fabrication techniques, like welding, and a wide range of industrial metals, forging even strong alliances with architecture, the sciences, and industry. The common thread across all these developments was a radical reorientation of space, something sculpture was uniquely positioned to explore and mediate. A tremendous amount of work still needs to be done in order to trace a full history of sculptural production during the mid-twentieth century in the United States through a spatially focused framework. By undertaking such a reframing, however, the sculptural production of the immediate postwar period can be seen not as deficient or a terminus, but a crucial step in sculpture's push into the scale of the architectural and the environmental, which have come to define the medium over the past five decades.

The Reciprocity of Metal

When the Inland Steel Company opened its new building in Chicago in 1958, the company's vice president Leigh Block declared that the structure "spelled steel." By the early 1950s, Chicago outranked Pittsburgh as the steel hub of the United States, and the decision to build a new headquarters in the city's downtown Loop was a testament to the rise of the industry there during the immediate postwar period. From the lobby to the executive floors, everything about the new nineteen-story skyscraper served as an advertisement for Inland Steel (figure 3.4). Clad in its namesake product, the shimmering modernist structure made a significant and immediate impression. The Inland Steel Building was the first major structure, the first skyscraper, constructed in the city's downtown core in twenty years.

Designed by Skidmore, Owings & Merrill (SOM), the building had no interior support columns, reinforced instead by steel ribs outside of the double-paned, solar-tinted glass curtain wall facade. Attached to the main building was a twenty-five-story windowless service tower, also fully clad in stainless steel, which housed the elevators, restrooms, and the HVAC system, and a two-story annex building, which handled shipping and receiving. The structure did not occupy the entirety of its land site, and the first two floors were set back twenty feet from Monroe Street, creating a small plaza with unobstructed views into its glass and steel-clad lobby, with the upper floors cantilevered to the lot line. Prominently featured in the lobby was Lippold's metallic abstract sculpture, *Radiant I* (1958) (figure 3.5). Visible through the glass curtain walls, the sculpture anchored the space from the center of a shallow pool of water and was set against a highly polished black Belgian marble wall. Radiating outward from the stainless-steel rods of its asterisk core were interlaced wires of gold, stainless steel, and fire-red enamel that diagonally stretched from floor to ceiling, knitting together the surrounding space.[9]

Radiant I was the result of a collaboration between artist and architect, or in this case a team of architects, but it was also spurred by a very involved client.

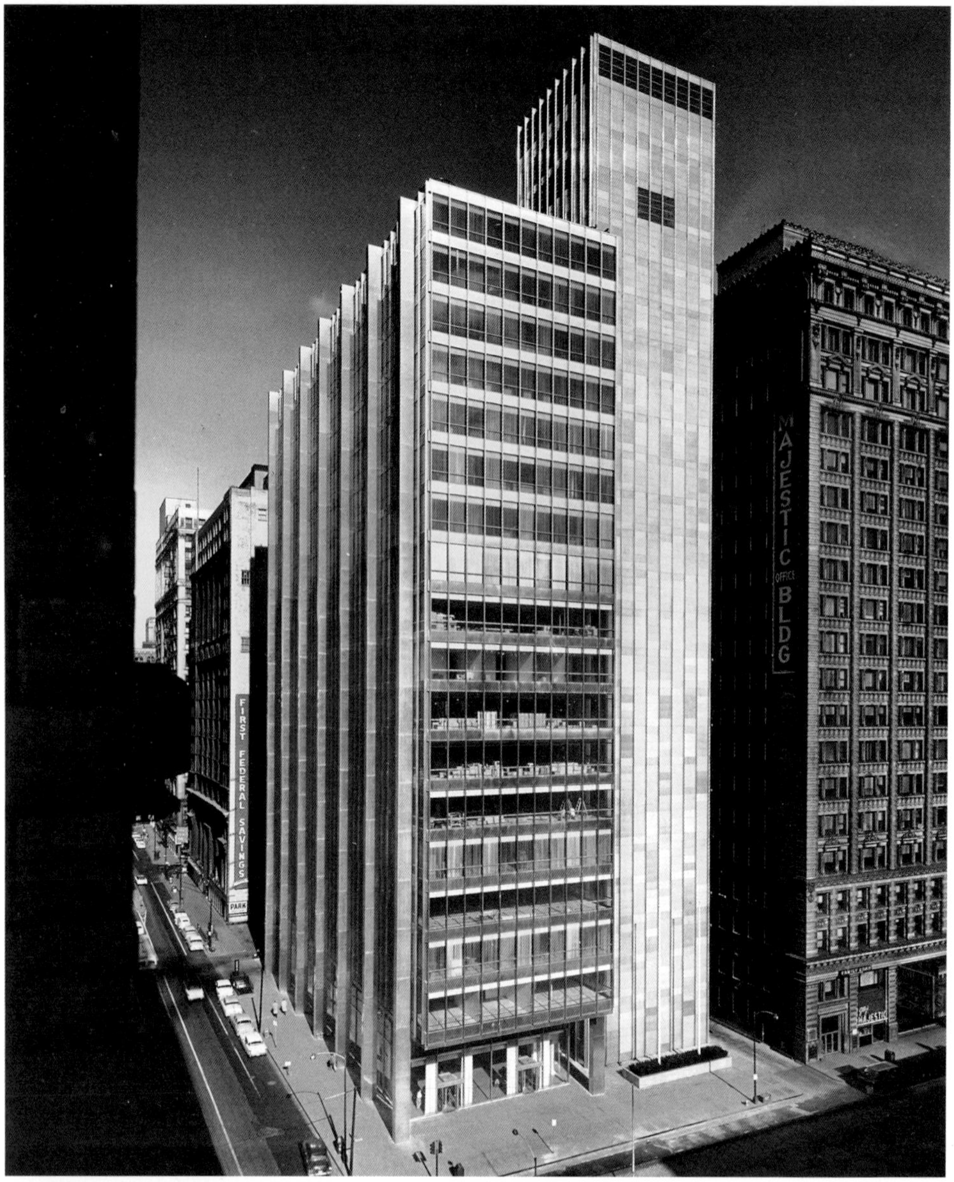

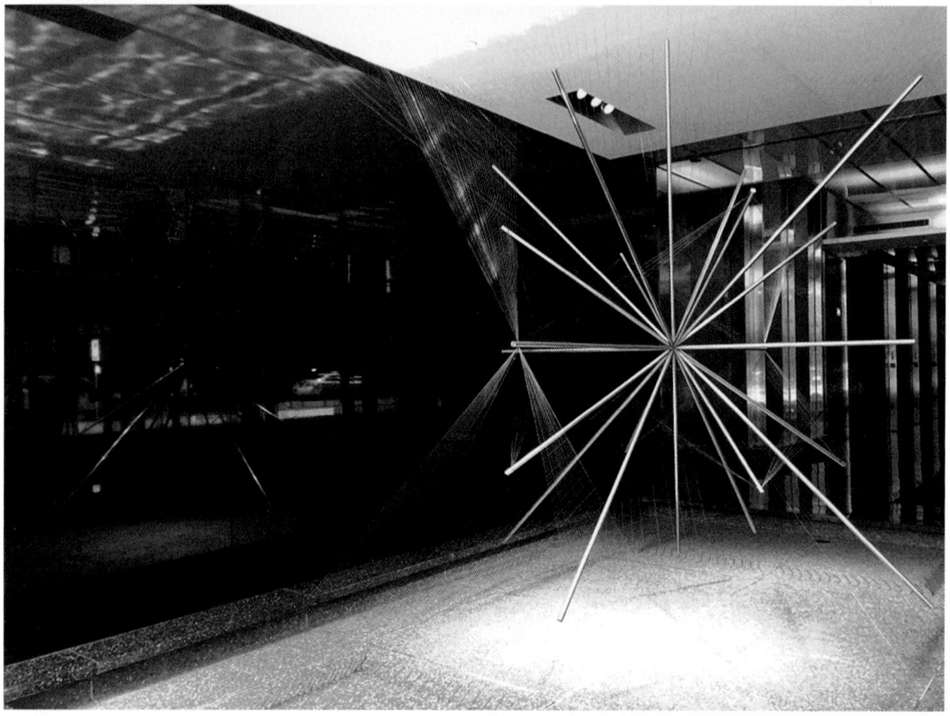

3.4
Inland Steel Building, 30 West Monroe Street, Chicago, 1956–58. Architect: Skidmore, Owings & Merrill (SOM).

3.5
Richard Lippold, *Radiant I*, 1958. Stainless steel, gold, and enameled copper, 13 ft. × 24 ft. × 15 ft. Inland Steel Building, Chicago. Architect: Skidmore, Owings & Merrill (SOM).

As William Hartmann, one of the SOM architects involved in the project, remarked, "Leigh Block was a leader of Inland and also of the project. Tremendous recognition and credit should go to him and his participation in it all the way through. Leigh and his wife, Mary, were very important. They had a great interest in art and interiors. Great, great interest in art." Inland Steel occupied the top eight floors, but the company developed and oversaw the entire building project, which featured an extensive arts program. Leigh and Mary Block were both avid art collectors, and with the permission of the board of directors, bought and installed fifty paintings and seven sculptures for the Inland Steel Building between 1956 and 1958. As Leigh remarked, "Of course, the most important thing is the sale of steel, but on the other hand, we believe that painting and sculpture belong in a modern office building to enhance its beauty." From the ground floor lobby to the north end of the top floor, the Blocks made sure art appeared everywhere in the Inland Steel Building.[10]

A carefully curated selection of painting and sculpture by American artists, many commissioned specifically for the building, appeared across executive offices, hallways, elevator banks, and the lobby. All of these works expressed "various aspects of American industry," and were selected with the building's "modern exterior design and interior décor" in mind. The nineteenth-floor executive-suite corridor, for example, featured *Hero* (1958), a seven-foot steel sculpture by Seymour Lipton. Bertoia's *Small Tree* (1956), an open-form welded construction that resembled a simpler, cooler-toned version of the Southdale sculptures, was installed in the elevator bank of the thirteenth floor of the service tower.

More than thirty paintings, including Willem de Kooning's *Bolton Landing* (1957) and Georgia O'Keeffe's *Shelton with Sunspots* (1926) also dotted the walls (figure 3.6). Hartmann recalled the strategy behind the arts program in relation to the building's architecture:

> There is very little opportunity for hand craftsmanship in a piece of flat stainless steel. You cut that with a machine, so there are little or no decorative materials in Inland. There's one marble wall. Maybe that could be called decorative. Everything else is quite machinelike—the metal acoustic ceiling and everything. There was an opportunity for Leigh to get involved in modern art to a degree that his collection didn't... He wanted this art to be in this building because he thought art was appropriate. There was no grandiose attempt to introduce art. It wasn't for show purposes.

Hartmann served as an advisor, traveling with Leigh and Mary Block to numerous galleries and artists' studios during the selection process. No additional works were purchased or installed by the company after the building opened, and the original group of paintings and sculptures were not considered to be a "collection" but rather "part of the décor of the building."[11]

Inland Steel's art program was a masterful example of how art writ large could be thoughtfully used to enhance an architectural project and infuse into it a

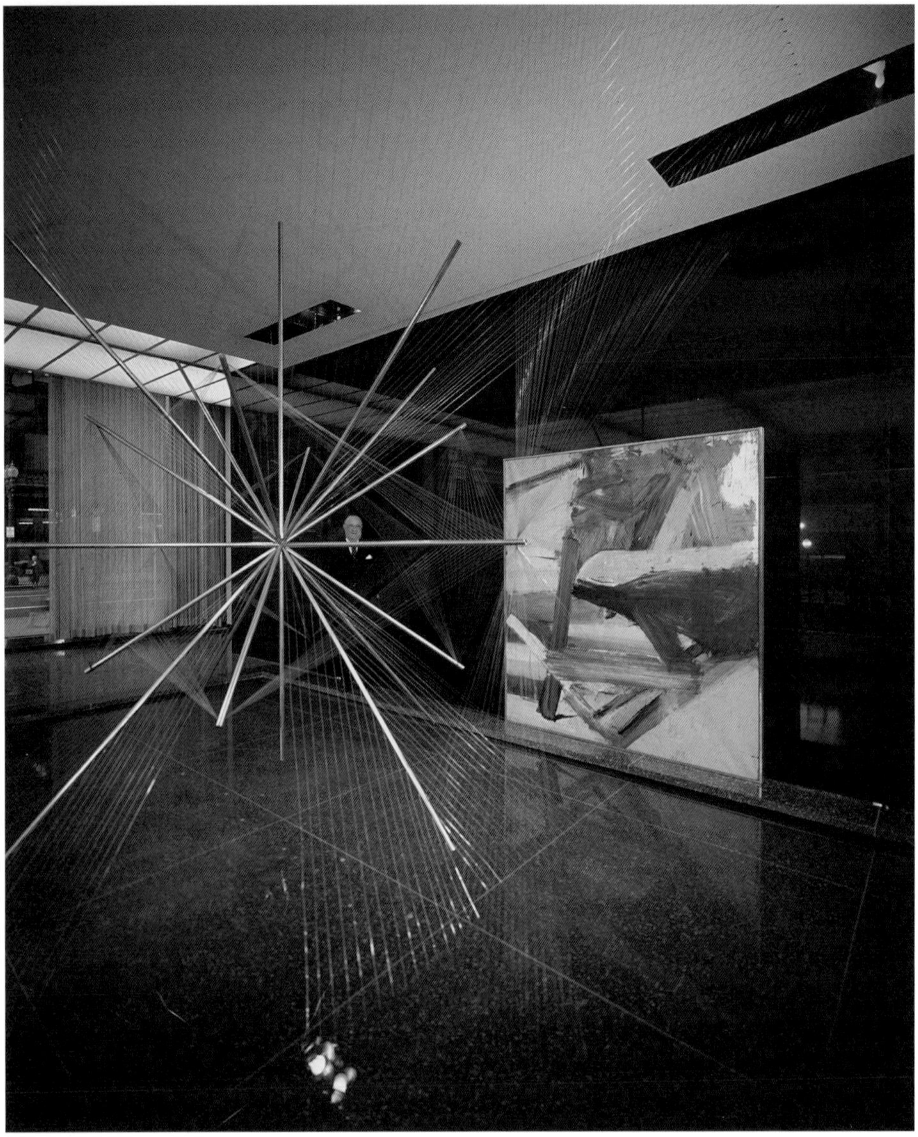

3.6
Lobby of the Inland Steel Building, Chicago with Leigh Block, company vice president in the background, 1965.

further layer of symbolism and cultural sophistication. As the architectural historian and curator Edgar J. Kaufmann, Jr. wrote in his review of the project, "the Inland Steel Building soon will become famous as a pace setter in the art of using fine arts in proud, meaningful relation to architecture.... Important art commissions and ample art budgets are not unfamiliar concomitants to new, large buildings; the interest of Inland's program lied in its unaccustomed degree of success. This can be credited to unusual cooperation and sympathy between clients and architects, referred to in the plural since each is in fact a large organization composed of many responsible individuals."[12] The most public and arresting artistic symbol of steel on Inland Steel Building was Lippold's *Radiant I*.

The architects and the company's art-advisory board commissioned Lippold to create a work specifically for the lobby. The artist was selected personally by the Blocks, who arranged an initial interview with him after seeing examples of his work in New York City. In 1950, the Museum of Modern Art acquired Lippold's *Variation Number 7: Full Moon* (1949–50), a delicate ten-foot-tall construction

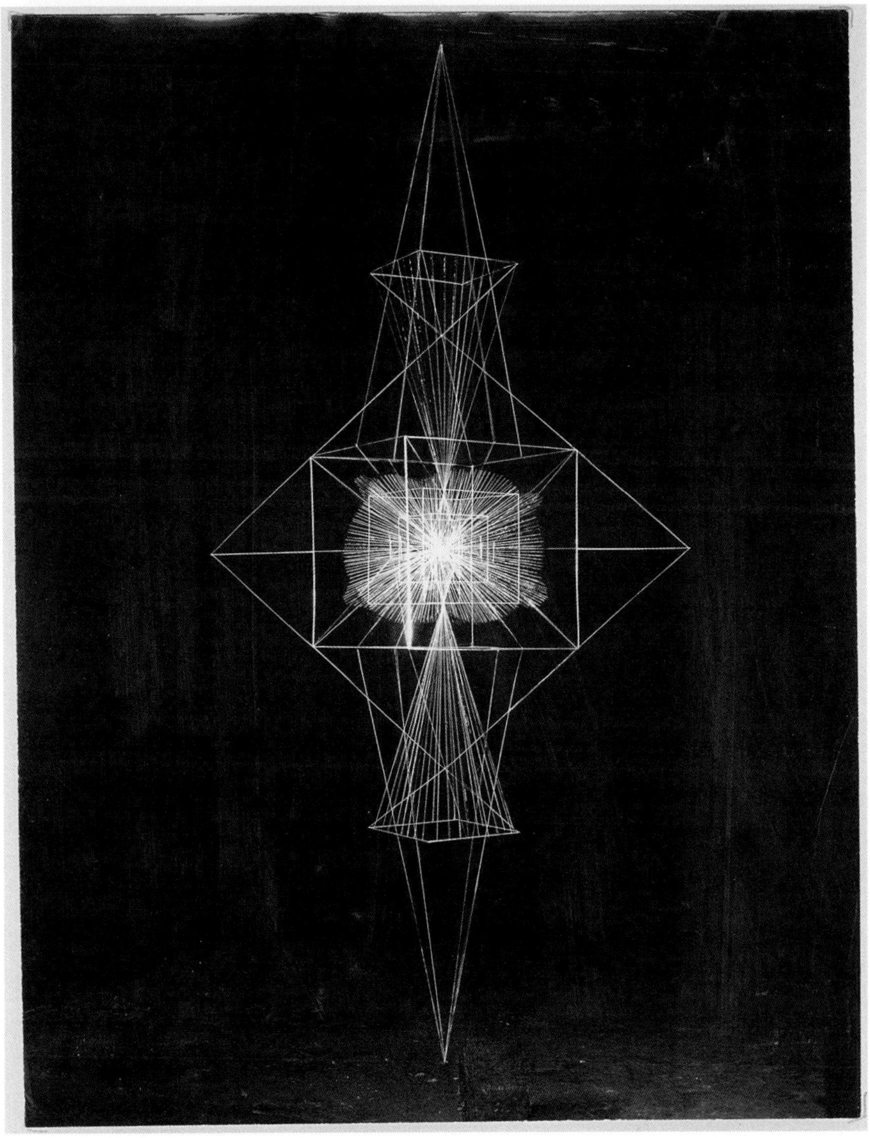

3.7
Richard Lippold, *Variation Number 7: Full Moon*, 1949–50. Brass rods, nickel-chromium and stainless-steel wire, 10 × 6 × 6 ft. Shown as installed at the exhibition *15 Americans*, MoMA, New York City, April 9–July 27, 1952. Mrs. Simon Guggenheim Fund. Photographic Archive, Museum of Modern Art Archives, New York City, IN507.25.

made from nickel-chromium and stainless-steel wire and thin brass rods, which proved so popular that it remained on view in a black-velvet, spotlighted alcove for twenty-five years straight (figure 3.7). The Metropolitan Museum of Art, at the suggestion of the artist, commissioned Lippold to create the similar, if much larger and more complex construction, *Variation within a Sphere, Number 10: The Sun* (1953–56), which was made from two miles of thin, twenty-two-carat gold wire. Art historian Jack Burnham wrote of this sculpture, "*The Sun* remained a fixture at the Metropolitan for many years, serving as a virtual magnet for architects, who, after contemplating its possibilities for their own work, descended with a raft of potential commissions."[13]

Full Moon and *The Sun* proved successful harbingers and advertisements for Lippold's large-scale commissions; though in the case Inland Steel, their impact seemed to have a greater effect on the client than the architects. Bruce Graham, who became the SOM's lead architect on the project, later stated that he had actually wanted Bertoia to do the main lobby sculpture. Both Leigh Block and

Hartmann even went as far as sending letters to Bertoia in March 1956, formally engaging him to create studies for the project and meeting with the sculptor a few months later at SOM's offices in New York City. Graham later expressed his dissatisfaction with the decision to go with Lippold, stating that he thought the wires of *Radiant I* disappeared too much when sunlight streamed into the building. Mary Block in particular, however, was insistent. While Hartmann confirmed that he had likewise worried that it would prove a challenge to recreate the drama achieved with the artificially lit installation of *Full Moon* in the open, daylit space of the Inland Steel lobby, he confirmed that Lippold had been a "deliberate choice" and had done "quite well."[14]

Though the result of a contested selection process, Lippold produced a sculpture realized through a concerted, collaborative group effort. SOM devoted time and resources to making sure the architecture and *Radiant I* served each other well. SOM hired Richard Kelly to act as a consultant on the project, realizing earlier on that lighting would prove crucial to the success of the overall lobby design and the ability of Lippold's sculpture to function within it. Graham and Lippold worked closely with Kelly, who brought in Edison Price Lighting to help design and manufacture special lighting fixtures for the space. SOM also significantly modified the design of the lobby after receiving Lippold's final proposal, adding, for example, the water feature, which was intended to amplify the reflective qualities of the sculpture. They also reconfigured the ceiling so that the custom lighting and the weight of Lippold's work would be better supported. To accommodate and better frame the sculpture, because of its large size and the wide reach of the steel wires, the black stone wall was pushed back several feet, to the detriment of the total square footage of the ground-level retail space behind it. As Kaufmann wrote of the results, "Steel embodies modern man's structural mastery of tension, one of his unique achievements; Lippold has stirringly celebrated this, stringing a web of praise with bold delicacy. He has found in architects and clients the appreciation, the patience, and the adaptability that are requisite for such commissions.... Personal confidence and encouragement, rare aids, have kept this ambitious work safe from the risk of mere rhetorical flourish to which architectural sculpture too often descends." *Radiant I* became a "key point in the building," as Leigh Block had hoped it would be.[15]

Lippold and the SOM team of designers and architects produced an eye-catching, public-facing display made to draw people in and serve as a sculptural icon of corporate identity, projected outward to the world. The sculpture can and should be seen as a strategy of what architectural historian Alice T. Friedman has referred to as the cultured corporation. Functioning as what art historian Amanda Douberley describes as a corporate trademark, it is a legible, memorable sign meant to read as synonymous with Inland Steel. If, as Kaufmann suggests, the company's commissioning intent was to create a "commanding symbol of Steel within the steel cage of its building," then Lippold was happy to oblige with a "concentrated statement big enough to register as the evident core of a great structure housing a great enterprise."[16]

Lippold was conscious of the need for his work both to function as the physical focal point of the building and as a conceptual embodiment of steel's importance within contemporary life. Lippold stated that he drew inspiration for his sculpture from both the corporation's name and its symbolic architecture, "rising like a luminous shaft of brilliant light in the heart of the Loop, the new building radiates the strength and vertical self-confidence of the personal pronoun which forms the initial letter of 'Inland.'" The sculptor settled on the title, after toying with several other options including "The Inland Eye," "The Steel Eye/ I," and "Steel Radiant," because he liked the transference suggested between the evocation of the personal pronoun and the vertical metal tube at the center of the work. The red-coated, gold-plaited, and silver wire surrounding the center rods were intended to reference further the processes of forming steel by melting, pouring, and refining.[17]

Radiant I was a striking sculptural object. It functioned as literal symbolism for a corporation, and refined decoration in a significant modernist building. The commission, however, also stands as an achievement of the synergy between sculpture and architecture. For Lippold, this type of successful collaboration required that the artist must "attach his work so tightly to the building, in similarity of proportion, material, and technique, that try as he might, the use cannot pry it loose (visually) and thus is forced to move through the sculpture or the painting to the building, and, of course, back down through it again to himself.... The architect's responsibility in this is simply to allow the artist to achieve this double rapport." *Radiant I* did not only meet the specific demands placed on the commission by SOM and its clients, but also became indivisibly attached to the Inland Steel Building itself. The value and function of the commission was more than just the sculptural embodiment of steel or savvy corporate public relations. Lippold's use of metal carried with it the associations of industry, but he deployed the material, in a variety of forms, as a means to shape space sculpturally, traversing the volume of the lobby and connecting the space between "thus giving and taking meaning from the architecture," as Lippold stated.[18]

The material reciprocity of *Radiant I* exemplified how and why the shared formal or physical vocabulary of sculpture and architecture provided a path to greater, more substantive synergy (figure 3.8). Developments occurring in contemporary vanguard sculpture, especially the adoption of industrial materials and techniques, made the medium particularly well positioned to respond to and be in dialogue with architecture. Art historian Gibson Danes remarked as early as 1947 that "just as the architect has been concerned with exploiting certain qualities natural to his materials, the sculptor has been discovering the esthetic potential of different metals and alloys as well as re-discovering the fresh beauty of traditional materials. Examples of this may be seen in the work of Calder, Noguchi, Alexander Archipenko, David Smith, and others." Dore Ashton similarly noted, over a decade later, that artists like Costantino Nivola were adamant that in order for sculpture to be truly related to architecture, there had to be a "consistency in techniques" and a similarity in "building materials." For Nivola, his sand-casting technique,

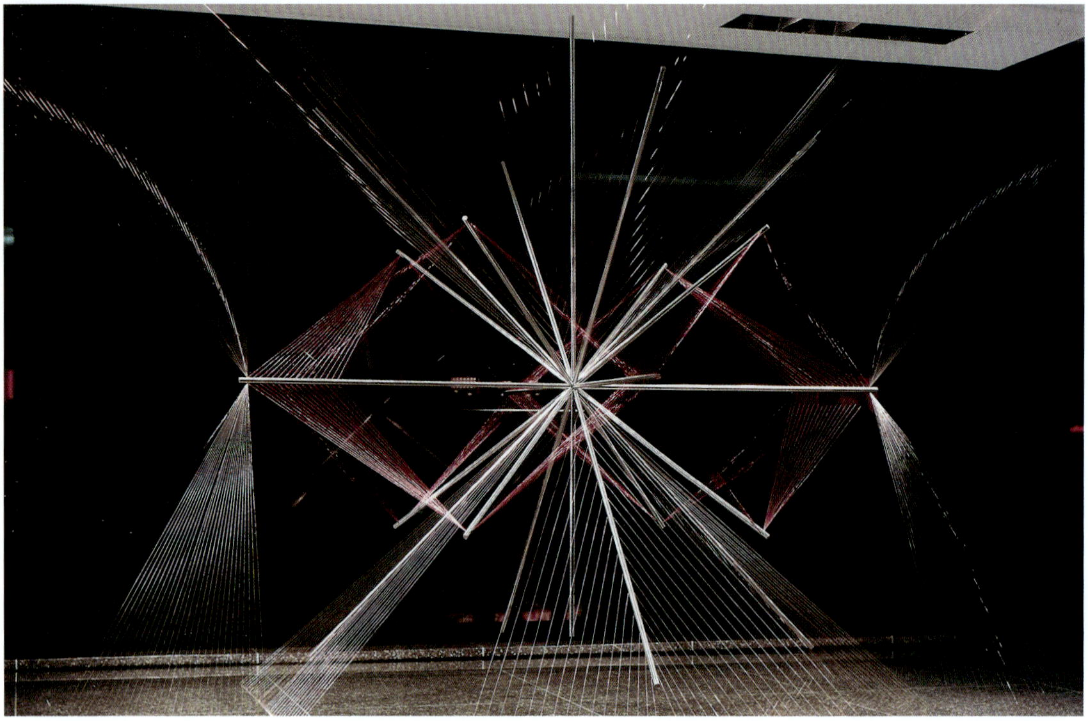

3.8
Richard Lippold, *Radiant I*, 1958. Stainless steel, gold, and enameled copper, 13 ft. × 24 ft. × 15 ft. Inland Steel Building, Chicago. Architect: Skidmore, Owings & Merrill (SOM).

with its use of plaster and concrete, created a synthesized echo of the sculpturally shaped forms of modernist architecture. Louise Bourgeois and Louise Nevelson both used wood to great architectonic effects during the period, while Noguchi likewise experimented with organic matter like wood, stone, and magnesite in his architectural commissions.[19]

The most pronounced material resonance between architecture and sculptural practice during immediate postwar period, however, was found in the application of industrial metals. Bertoia, Calder, Lippold, and Noguchi all turned to metal in order to realize increased sizes and forms in their architectural commissions. The built-up, painted, patinated, and highly polished surfaces of their resulting sculptures functioned in a decorative mode meant to complement or contrast with modernist architectural spaces, but their metallic properties inherently and inextricably linked them not only to modern architecture but also to the broader scientific and industrial developments occurring during the period. As curator Sam Hunter wrote, "The very use of metals, with their industrial associations, puts the artist in a direct relationship with his actual environment." By choosing to accept commissions to make sculpture for public, commercial, and corporate settings, however, artists like Bertoia, Calder, Lippold, and Noguchi further amplified these associations, signaling not just a formal resonance, but a profound engagement with the modern industrial age and the ability of art to function within it.[20]

As Bertoia declared, "The sculptor of today is living in an age of industry and should take advantage of it. In my work this starts with the steel mill. I take this raw material, heat treat it with bronze and other alloys, and provide a texture and a lasting surface. These metal parts are then so placed in relation to each other as to make the most of any given space." Working in metal, but more specifically experimenting with new metal alloys, enabled a formal fluidity and organicism across these artists' work, but also more closely aligned it with architecture, design, and sculpture during the mid-twentieth century. Lippold's sculpture for Inland Steel or Bertoia's for Southdale, like all of the commissions examined in this book, were neither anomalies in the artists' oeuvres nor disconnected from broader trends developing in American vanguard sculptural practice during the immediate postwar period. By the mid-twentieth century, there was an explosion of what became known as direct metal sculpture, with artists on both sides of the Atlantic increasingly employing welding techniques and new industrial materials.[21]

Calder, Julio González, and Pablo Picasso pioneered the use of welding and industrial materials in fine art sculpture prior to World War II in Europe, but it became ubiquitous during late 1940s and 1950s, especially in the United States. Metal was more affordable after the war, and oxygen-acetylene welding torches became more readily available. Although techniques like welding, burnishing, brazing, and riveting allowed sculptors to create new forms, of equal importance was the utilization of materials like sheet metal, I-beams, different forms of steel, welding rods, and new composite alloys. Even sculptures made of bronze, like Bertoia's spill-cast walls or Lippold's Four Seasons commission, were not fabricated by using traditional casting methods.[22]

Sculptors of the late 1940s and 1950s took new artistic processes and combined them with the literal substances driving science, industry, and technology. Iron and steel may have possessed, as David Smith claimed, "little art history," but in the context of postwar America, these materials carried with them the associations of "this century: power, structure, movement, progress, suspension, destruction, brutality." Metals like Monel, Cor-Ten steel, naval brass, and stainless steel originated for industrial applications, but many sculptors themselves became apt alchemists, mixing and creating their own combinations of molten matter. Ibram Lassaw and Bertoia, for example, became particularly capable at layering alloys to create highly textured and colorful sculptures, and some, like Calvin Albert, even developed and marketed their own alloys, in his case Modalloy, which sculptor Herbert Ferber briefly incorporated into his work along with lead, copper, and brass.[23]

The direct use of metal became, in many ways, the defining characteristic of American sculpture during the immediate postwar period. Critics and curators alike fixated on the new image of the modern sculptor, "forging, welding, hammering, cutting, or riveting [metal] into the desired shape," rather than creating through a multistage process of molding clay or plaster and sending their work to be produced in a foundry. Sculptors like Bertoia, David Hare, Ferber, Lassaw, Lipton, Theodore Roszak, and Smith seized on the possibilities these new materials and techniques offered, creating works just as directly and intuitively as their painter contemporaries, with built-up surfaces, moody patinas, and fluid flourishes. Made without a preformed plan, preparatory sketches, or the traditional use

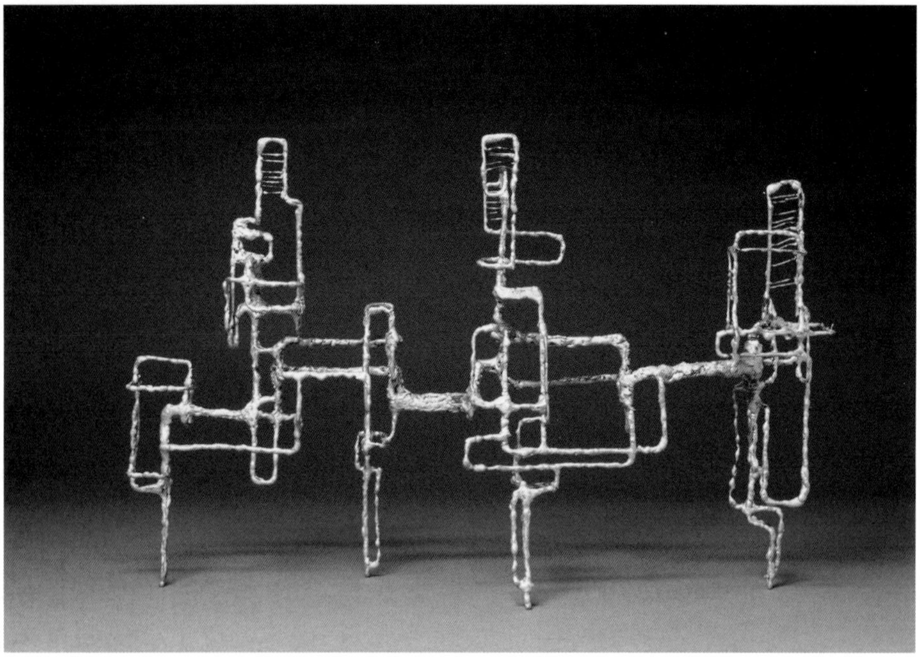

3.9
Ibram Lassaw, *The Hyades*, 1951. Bronze, 13 3/4 × 21 1/2 × 6 1/2 in. Smithsonian American Art Museum, Washington, DC. Gift of Patricia and Phillip Frost, 1986.92.64.

of maquettes, the resulting sculptures looked nothing like the bronze-cast figures of the past, but were often gestural, open constructions.[24]

Unlike the fabrication practices of the later postwar period, sculptors were more often than not directly responsible for the construction of their work. Bertoia and Lippold constructed by hand almost every work they ever realized. Lassaw, for example, described how welding offered more immediate contact than traditional bronze casting (figure 3.9). "My conceptions forced me to use direct metal techniques. The welding medium has its limitations, but the freedom it gives me to makes it the most suitable for the kind of structures I plan.... One must think and dream directly with the material. The experience of manipulating material teaches the imagination. The discoveries, the accidents, the experiments one makes lead to an expansion of the areas of exploration."[25] For most sculptors, however, direct metal materials and techniques were appealing not simply for their contemporaneous associations but also for the formal possibilities they offered.

The art historian and critic Herbert Read wrote, "Metals in general have certain unique qualities—they are *ductile*, which means that they can be drawn out into wires, and they are *malleable*, which means they can be shaped into form by hammering; and they can be melted and cast, molded into predetermined shapes or pressed. The modern sculptor takes advantage of all these possibilities.... In general, metal is so docile that it will submit to any formal conception the sculptor may have, and it is this adaptability that explains its present general use." Modern sculptors in the immediate postwar years explored and exploited the malleability of metal as well as its ability to engender both optical and tactile effects that extended beyond its physical form.[26]

Burnham noted how this was especially pronounced with work that highlighted or utilized the sheen and reflectivity of metal. He wrote, referencing Herbert Read, his English counterpart, "Some postwar American sculpture (beginning in the late 1940s and moving through the 1950s) has used what Herbert Read has termed the 'glitter principle.' Instead of deriving reflection from a continuous, coherent mass of metal, the sculptor conceived of a fragmented sculpture through semi-random, reflective surfaces position in spatial configurations. Lippold, Lassaw, and Bertoia have used this idea in open wire and sheet-metal constructions. Bertoia's altar construction for the Massachusetts Institute of Technology's Interdenominational chapel consists of many small steel squares covered with brazing brass, pitched at off angles and attached to taut wires suspended from ceiling to floor." Bertoia's commission for the MIT Chapel (Kresge Chapel) provides a particularly apt example to discuss how metal, sculpture, architecture, and industry coalesced during the immediate postwar period.[27]

The MIT Chapel (Kresge Chapel) was one of two buildings Eero Saarinen completed for a large plaza complex on the campus of the Massachusetts Institute of Technology in Cambridge in 1955. The circular MIT Chapel (1950–55) stands across from the Kresge Auditorium (1953–55), the first large-scale concrete shell building in the United States (figure 3.10). They were both made possible through a $1.5 million-dollar grant from the Kresge Foundation and were officially dedicated on May 8, 1955. The impetus behind Saarinen's MIT complex itself came out of broader conversations around synthesis, both across the arts, humanities, and sciences, as well as between the social, cultural, and even spiritual spaces needed for the science-and-technology focused MIT community to gather on campus.[28]

The MIT Chapel was notable for its distinctive round shape clad in a rough-surfaced brick and surrounded by a twelve-foot-wide, water-filled moat (figure 3.11). Saarinen stated of the building, "A circular chapel seemed preferable because it permitted a more direct relationship between the person meditating and the altar." Everything about the interior further amplified this intimacy, while simultaneously lending the space an ample amount of drama. As curator

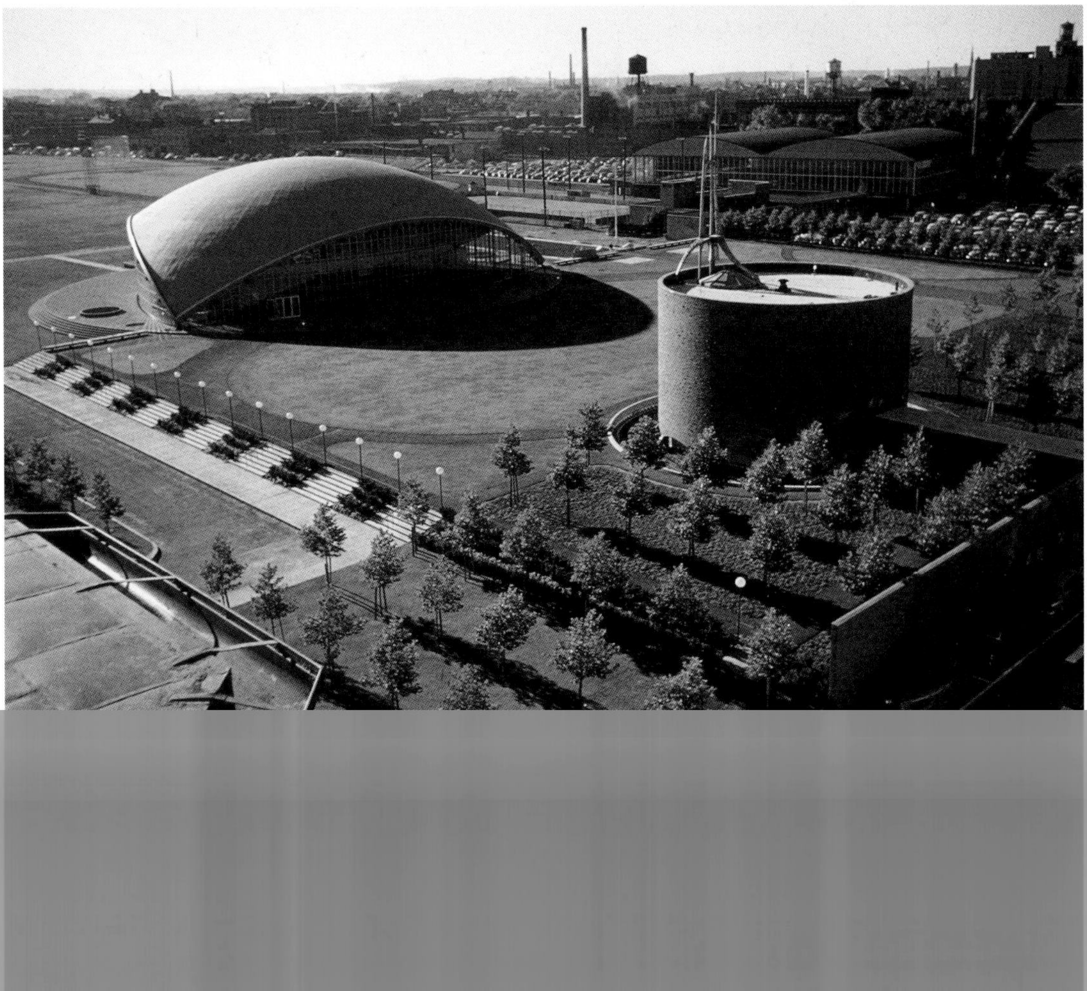

3.10
Aerial view of the Kresge Auditorium (1953–55) and MIT Chapel (Krege Chapel) (1950–55), Massachusetts Institute of Technology,

and design scholar Jennifer Komar Olivarez writes, the project was one of several nondenominational sanctuaries in Saarinen's body of ecclesiastical architecture. "Not tied to any particular religion," Komar Olivarez states, "their open programs allowed Eero room for experimentation, resulting in some resonating structures." For the MIT Chapel, for example, did not include any windows in the 128-seat nondenominational chapel, its interior enlivened by undulating redbrick walls, broken only by unobtrusive brick grilles, installed to cover four-inch, sound-insulation panels embedded behind. Natural light enters through a baffled lantern covered by a honeycombed grille directly above the dramatic white-marble altar. This oculus provided the primary light source for the interior, while a ribbon of double-glazed wainscot glass between the floor and the base of the brick wall, allowed additional light to reflect upward from the water of the moat below.[29]

An early sketch by Saarinen from 1952 reveals that he always intended there to be some sort of sculptural element separating the altar from the staircase behind it, which lead down to the robing room. At this stage, the sculptural elements were envisioned by the architect as two open, abstract metal constructions with lighting elements and what appear to be simple thin metal bars extending downward from the oculus to the floor in an open semicircle around the altar (figure 3.12). Already working together on the commission for the General Motors Technical Center, Saarinen met with Bertoia at the Knoll showroom in New York City in June 1953 to discuss also collaborating on the MIT Chapel. Hans Knoll facilitated the meeting, to which Saarinen brought a working model of the structure, so that he and Bertoia could go over the specifics of the space. The design Bertoia came up with played off the verticality evident in Saarinen's sketch,

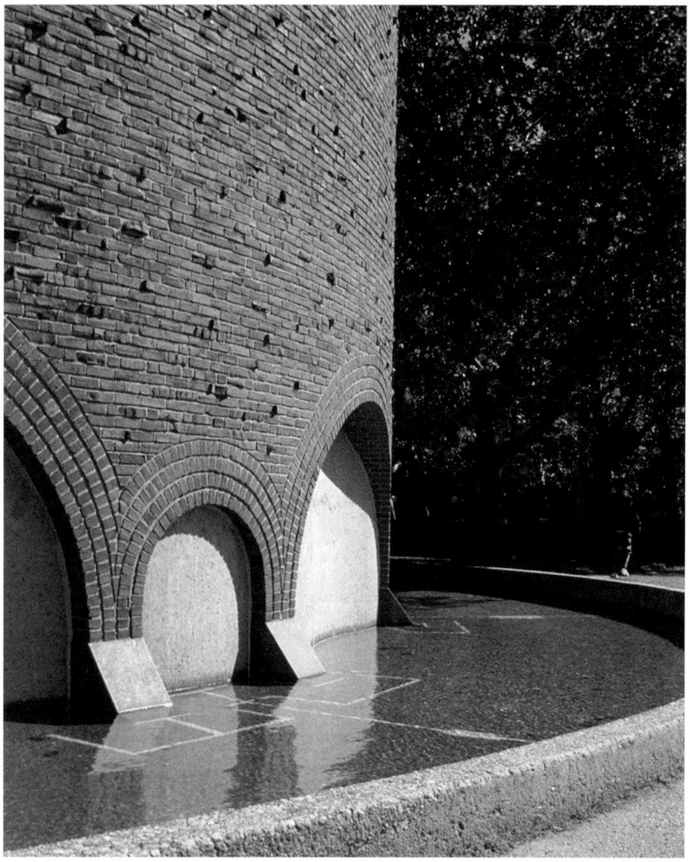

3.11
Exterior view of the MIT Chapel (Kresge Chapel), Massachusetts Institute of Technology, Cambridge, 1950–55. Architect: Eero Saarinen.

but also in essence, collapsed the three elements from the preliminary drawing into a single sculpture. In its final form, Bertoia's commission created a more unified composition that both perfectly complemented the architecture and transformed the entire chapel interior (figure 3.13).[30]

Bertoia's sculptural screen, or more accurately reredos, became a defining, central element in Saarinen's interior design. Constructed from twenty-five metal rods attached at both the ceiling and the floor, the sculpture functioned as an altar screen, but unlike the sculptures he made for the General Motors Technical Center or Manufacturers Trust Company Building, there is a greater play of negative space, allowing more dialogue between the sculpture and the wall around it. Overall, the effect is not the looming material presence of a rectangular multiplane screen, but rather a graceful cascading of almost confetti-like metal pieces that seem to float untethered, casting an ethereal silver and gold glow. One screen was not formally or conceptually superior to the other, but rather both resulted from innovative experimentation with the possibilities of metal and careful consideration of the specific aesthetics and purposes of their respective surrounding architecture.

For the MIT Chapel, Bertoia also considered the function of the building as a place of worship, further responding to Saarinen's design. Bertoia affixed hundreds of solid brazed-steel rectangles, each about one-and-a-half-by-three inches, to the vertical rods, mimicking the rectangular bricks that emerged at varying depths across the walls of the space (figure 3.14). He also attached the small metal pieces at a variety of angles, which, along with the addition of other small open-form wire shapes placed in between the plates, gave the screen a dynamic surface

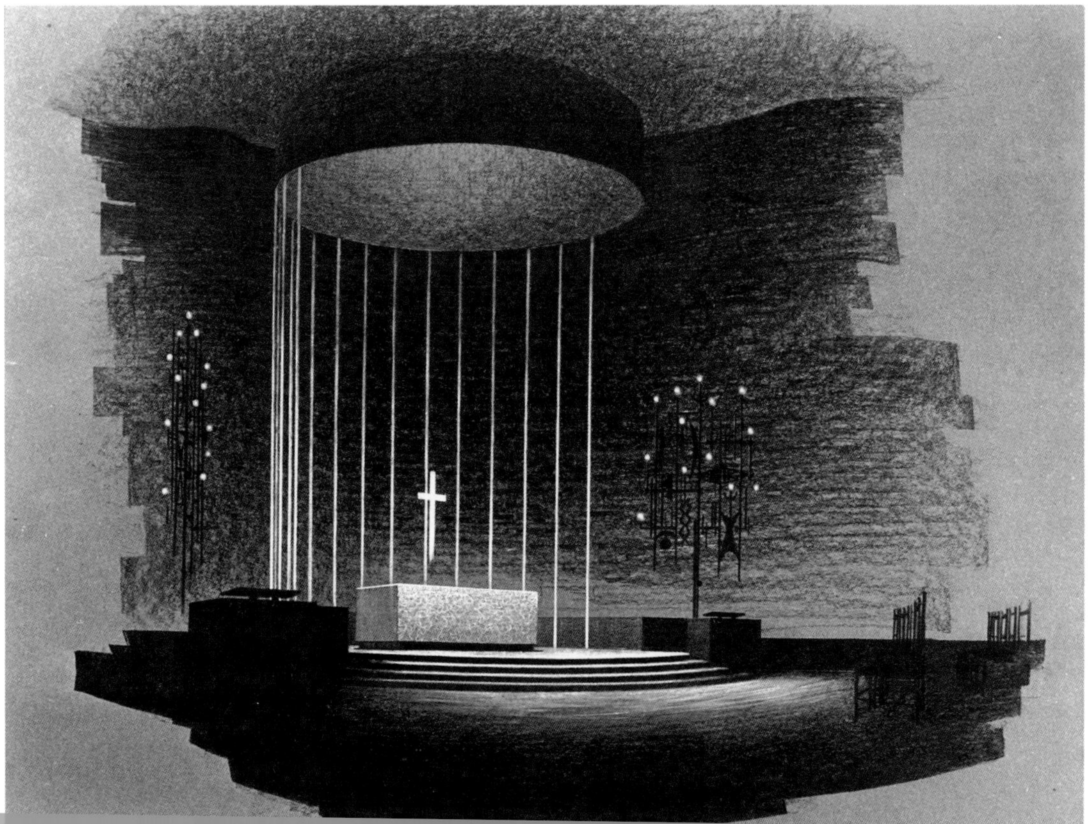

3.12
Eero Saarinen's preparatory sketch for the MIT Chapel (Kresge Chapel), 1952. Eero Saarinen Collection: MS 593, Manuscripts and Archives, Yale University Library, New Haven, Connecticut.

> 3.13
Harry Bertoia, *Altarpiece for MIT Chapel*, 1955. Brazed steel, 240 in. high. MIT Chapel (Kresge Chapel), Massachusetts Institute of Technology, Cambridge. Architect: Eero Saarinen. MIT List Visual Arts Center, Cambridge, Massachusetts, MIT: 1955.001.

>> 3.14
Harry Bertoia, *Altarpiece for MIT Chapel* (detail), 1955. Brazed steel, 240 in. high. MIT Chapel (Kresge Chapel), Massachusetts Institute of Technology, Cambridge. Architect: Eero Saarinen. MIT List Visual Arts Center,

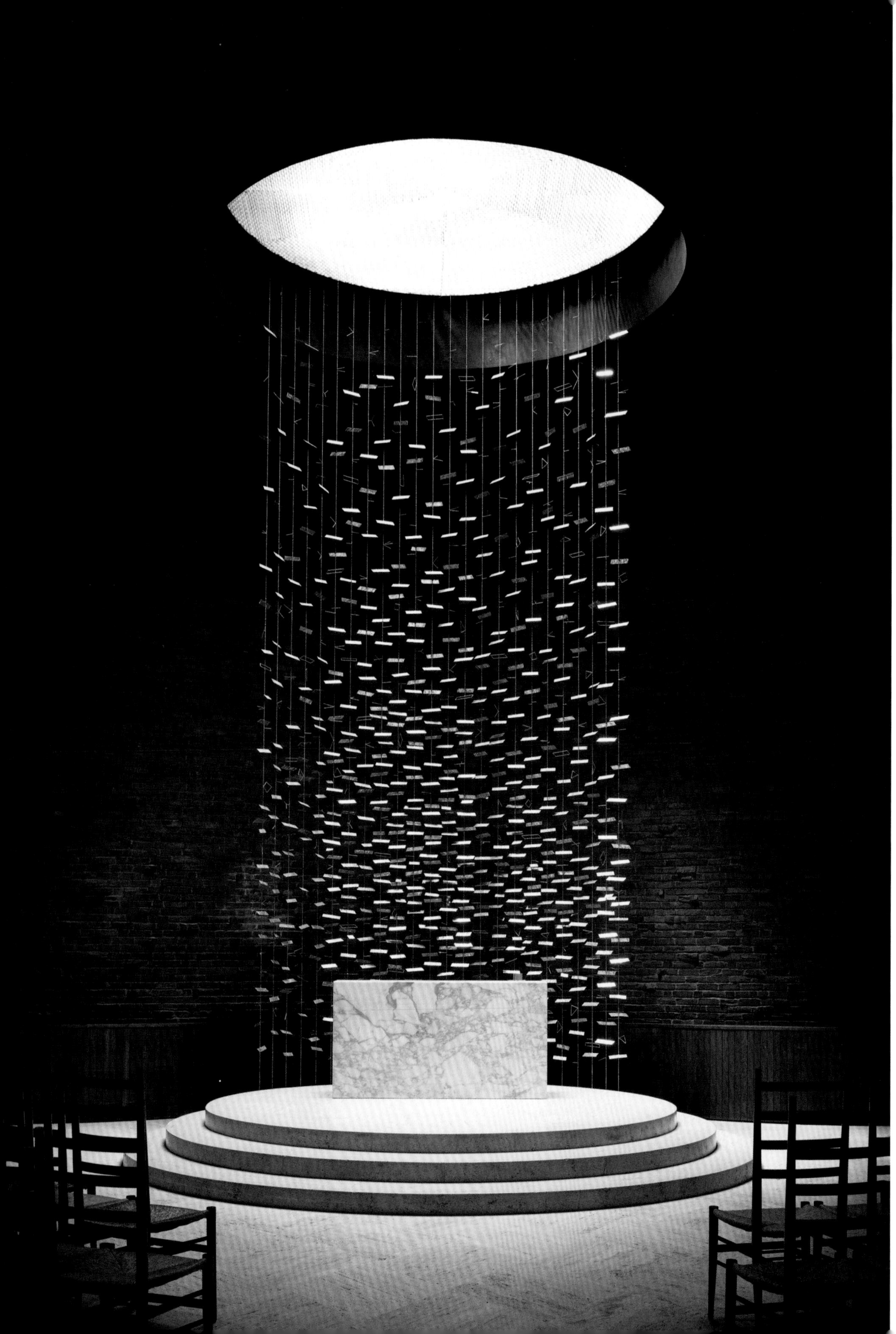

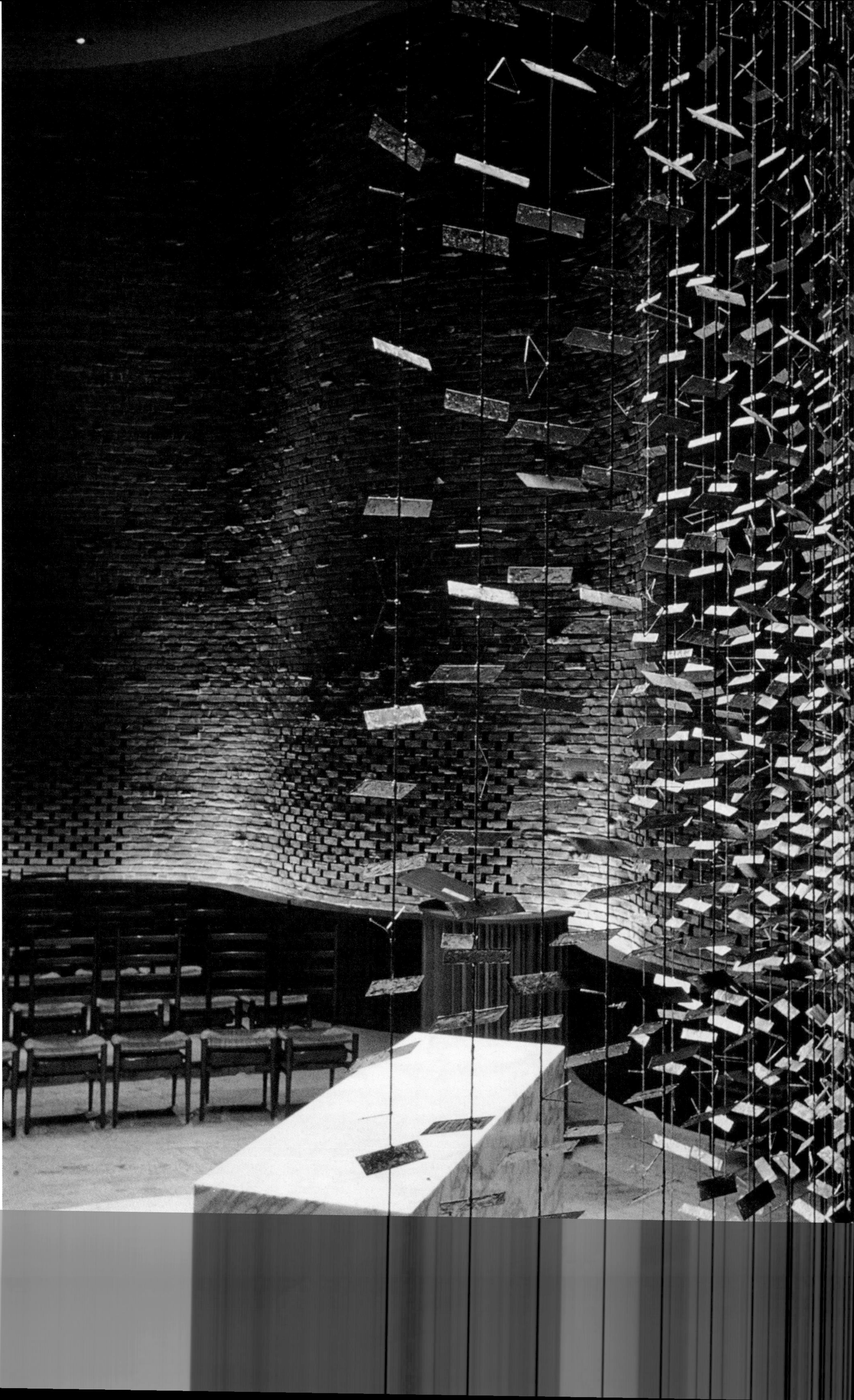

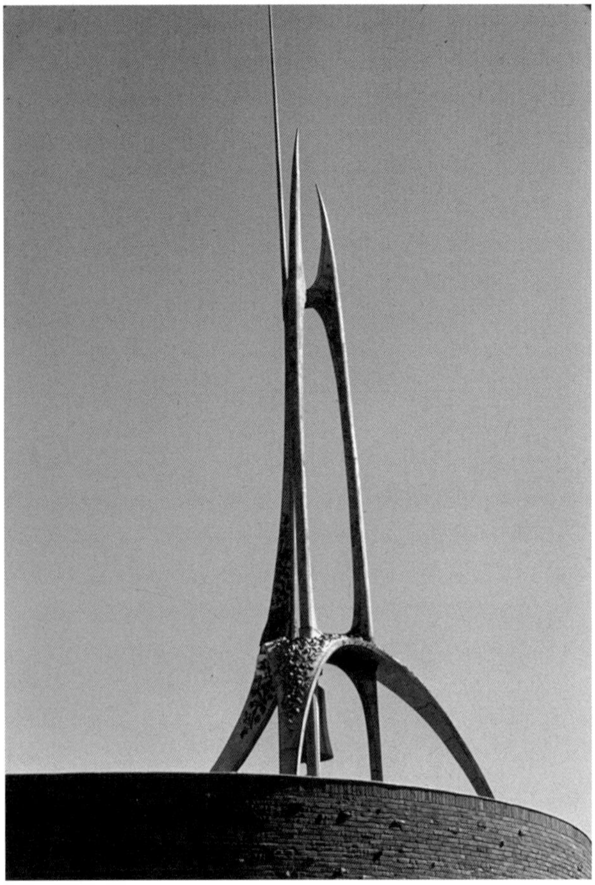

3.15
Theodore Roszak, *Bell Tower for MIT Chapel*, 1953–55. Aluminum. MIT Chapel (Kresge Chapel), Massachusetts Institute of Technology, Cambridge. Architect: Eero Saarinen. MIT. MIT List Visual Arts Center, Cambridge, Massachusetts, MIT: 1955.001.

texture, enabling it to catch and reflect the daylight coming in through the oculus. The MIT Chapel commission also incorporated a new experimental fabrication technique that involved the artist coating all of the ferrous metal (or mild steel) elements of the work with nickel-alloy welding rods, melting and fusing them to the surface with the use of a welding torch. The result was a further amplification of the reflective quality of the screen.

With its height and vertical orientation, Bertoia's screen for the MIT Chapel gave the appearance of golden rays either descending from, or ascending to, the heavens, serving as a striking contrast to Saarinen's earthen, brick edifice. The building overall possessed a strong vertical axis, anchored by Bertoia's sculpture, which extended from the floor up through the lantern. This line was extended even further toward the sky by the addition in 1955 of a forty-five-foot bell tower created by Roszak (figure 3.15). The spire was Roszak's first large-scale architectural commission, and he discussed the project as related to the architectural tradition of Gothic gargoyles and their function of warding off "evil spirits." Roszak notably altered the position of his sculpture to be vertically, rather than horizontally, oriented, pointing up toward the sky since, as the sculptor stated, "it is from the sky now that danger threatens."[31]

Though made under different circumstances and placed outdoors, Roszak, as had been the case with Bertoia, strove to make his sculpture resonate with Saarinen's design. While some saw the sculpture's resemblance to a rocket ship as a nod to Saarinen's space-age chapel, others referred to the sculpture as "a cross between an attenuated lobster claw and a fragile bottle opener." The overall effect from a distance was sleek, shiny, and sharp, yet Roszak did build up the surface of the sculpture by puddling "ingots of aluminum into 'contemporary amorphic baroque' blobs." Roszak created numerous sketches and models for the project before settling on its final form, which he made onsite at the foundry on MIT's campus.

The sculpture, which also served as a functional bell tower, comprised three abstract, vertical elements that rose from its base. The curving forms of the sculpture echoed the semicircular cutouts at the base of Saarinen's chapel, while the sculpture's built-up texture recalled that of the uneven brick exterior. Both Roszak's and Bertoia's commissions for the MIT Chapel involved inventive uses of industrial metals and complex welding processes that enabled each sculptor to create multipart sculptures that took on architectural functionality in the space for which each was made. Like the chapel itself, each work presented a vision of the modern world of the postwar period, but with its location inside an interior threshold space, Bertoia's dual anchored reredos, like Lippold's *Radiant I*, offered still something more: sculpture as a medium of total spatial transformation.[32]

Space Sculpture

The embrace of new industrial metals and techniques like welding during the immediate postwar period enabled American sculptors to create new modern forms in order to advance the medium. The critical attention given to how they made their work, however, quickly began to overshadow the why. Direct metal became a device for easy categorization, a means to group or label diverse practices—something not dissimilar to the classification of painters who became grouped together under the label of Abstract Expressionism or the New York School—but many artists who embraced the technique did so as a way to explore new conceptions of space in sculpture. The sculptors who became most closely associated with direct metal were only just beginning to hit their mature artistic strides in the early to mid-1950s through public commissions, solo exhibitions, and group exhibitions at major galleries and arts institutions across the United States. Their work, however, quickly became assessed through the combined lens of direct metal welding and the question of how well their sculpture resonated with the parallel painterly qualities coalescing around Abstract Expressionism.

The results would prove disastrous to the long-term reception and reputation of their sculpture. Quickly pigeonholed as "Direct Metal," it became easy to dismiss this work *en masse* as derivative and deficient. Art historian Wayne Andersen summarized this mode of dismissal, writing that by 1956, "the proliferation of direct-metal sculpture in this country had so thoroughly confused the issue of what the early fifties work of Ferber, Lassaw, and Lipton, for example, was all about, that it was difficult for most critics to sustain a supporting interest in their production. By about 1952, the radical developments of Roszak, Grippe, Ferber,

Lassaw, De Rivera, Hare, Lipton, and Lippold had begun to settle into a steady production with little innovation, as if the energy that they had expended in the assimilation of the old and the creation of the new had become dissipated in their solutions."[33] If new materials and processes are seen as the only innovation of note in the sculpture of the immediate postwar period, then it indeed becomes a closed circuit; an insignificant technical or material blip on the way to the revelations of the truly vanguard sculpture of the later 1960s, when the easily labeled phenomena of assemblage, pop, and minimalism appeared.

Speaking at a symposium on the New Sculpture held at the Museum of Modern Art in 1952, Ferber, Lippold, Roszak, and Smith all echoed the critical exhaustion of the fetishistic focus on welded metal. Smith, for example, expressed his high regard of iron and steel, but stated that "the need to observe the virtue of the material, its natural planes, its hard lines, its natural oxides, its need for paint or its unifying method is only valid when within concept." Ferber furthered the sentiment declaring, "When the new techniques are mistaken for new plastic ideas and when the materials are held in reverence; when one hears a voice pitched in awesome eulogy on high melting points... art goes out the window." That same year in the accompanying catalogue for the *15 Americans* exhibition at MoMA, Ferber pointed to an alternative framework, one that might allow for a holistic reevaluation of vanguard American sculpture of the postwar period without flattening its complexity (figure 3.16). Ferber wrote, "Contemporary sculpture, to my mind, achieves a good deal of its excitement from the way in which it extends in space. Its principal sign is that of extension and often it is not extension from a central mass but rather extension in and about space in such a way that the space becomes a part of the sculpture; it is displaced by the work as water is when a ship is launched. The sculpture moves in space, it pierces and holds space in tension."[34] Ferber's words offer a path for reorientation, one not centered exclusively on materials or an adherence to more painterly modes expression, but rather on how objects shape and are shaped by space.

What is all too easily overlooked in discussions around metal sculpture, but what was present all along, was a significant and sustained exploration of space being undertaken by sculptors. The term space appears, in multivalent ways, with prodigious frequency in the contemporaneous critical and scholarly literature during the postwar period. From Hare's surrealist-tinged "spaces of the mind" to Lassaw's "improvisations in space," a spatial, rather than simply material, framework for making and assessing postwar sculpture was already being articulated—it just became obscured in the face of firing welding torches and complex metal constructions. *Time* magazine, for example, described how "a flood of wire and metal shapes" were turning "many a sculptor's studios into something resembling a blacksmith's shop, where the oxyacetylene torch has replaced the hammer and chisel, a welder's mask the smock," but also noted that "the trademark of the whole metal sculpture school, its practitioners agree, is 'openness.' Unlike the built-up masses of modeled sculpture or the chiseled-down solids of stone and wood, metal sculpture uses materials that give

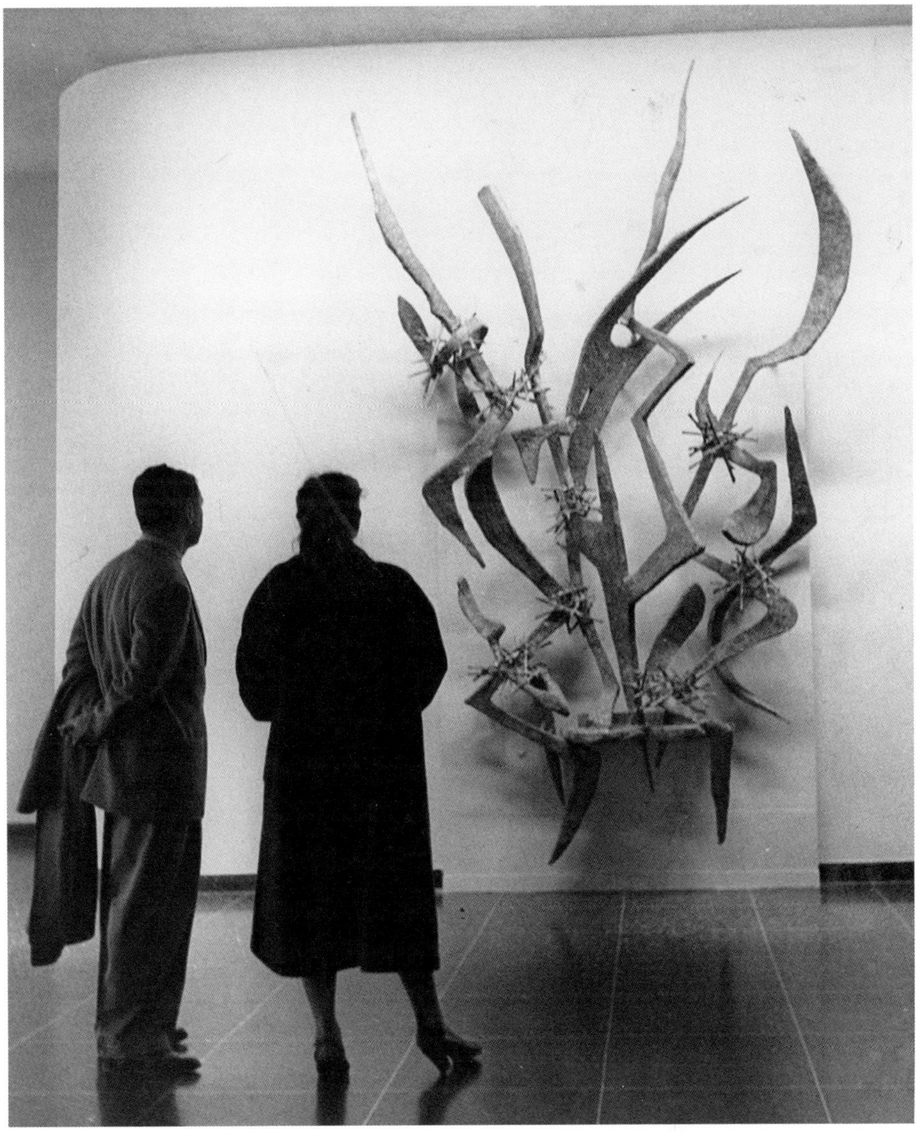

3.16
Installation view of the exhibition *15 Americans*, MoMA, New York City, April 9–July 27, 1952, showing Herbert Ferber's . . . *And the bush was not consumed* (1951). Photographic Archive, Museum of Modern Art Archives, New York City, IN507.1.

maximum strength with a maximum sense of space." Or as Noguchi declared, "I may be accused of over-extending the definition of sculpture in claiming for it the art of spaces. But it is the very root and branch of sculpture today without which it would have no relevance. Beyond architecture are those energy concentrations, irrational but meaningful, which constitute the aesthetic of sculpture. Sculpture becomes for me a preoccupation with impalpable voids and pressures, the punctuations of spaces. If sculpture is the rock, it is also the space between rocks and between rocks and man, and the communication and contemplation between them." The space of sculpture was not understood simply as three-dimensionality or an object of containment, no matter how large the size. Rather, the space of sculpture was the material itself, the interconnections between the various parts of its form, and everything around and beyond these physical boundaries.[35]

Metal and other industrial or found materials became prominent because they allowed sculptors to explore this conception of space, on multiple registers, often in a single work. As one critic stated of Lippold:

In an age when the pursuit of space and time is of the most immediate interest to men, Richard Lippold loves space most of all materials. He delights in describing his feelings for space by the slenderest means possible, generally by delicate wires—traveling into space, as he expresses it, through the seduction of the pleasantest materials he can find: polished metals, silver solders, intriguingly shaped wires—square, hexagonal, ovoid. Traveling along these good-feeling materials to the interior spaces of his work into that void, which he believes is the artist's domain, he finds revealed statements of the relationships in life of things to each other, made by certain particular relationships of space and metal.

Lippold more succinctly declared in his own essay from the *15 Americans* catalogue, accompanied by illustrations of his *Variation Number 7: Full Moon*, "My preference in materials is Space, captured by the most seductive other materials I can arrange."[36]

The focus on space in all its complicated tangible and conceptual facets—even when conveyed through the creation of supposedly autonomous fine art objects—was hardly confined to artistic practice or disconnected from the broader sociopolitical context of the United States during the postwar period. Sculptors embraced the same sense of new monumental scale simultaneously occurring in vanguard painting, but notions of space extended far beyond dimensional or art historical boundaries. A sculptural interest in space spoke to, and was the result of, the larger ethos of the era, of a developing age of technological innovation, space travel, and scientific exploration—something made apparent by the preponderance of titles of sculptures with intergalactic, planetary overtones alone. As art historian Robert Slifkin writes, "Sculpture thus becomes a means of spatial awareness, if not of literal space exploration, inviting viewers to perceive realms of space far beyond the work itself and recognize its crucial role within a technological society." For artists like Lippold, who believed that the conquest of

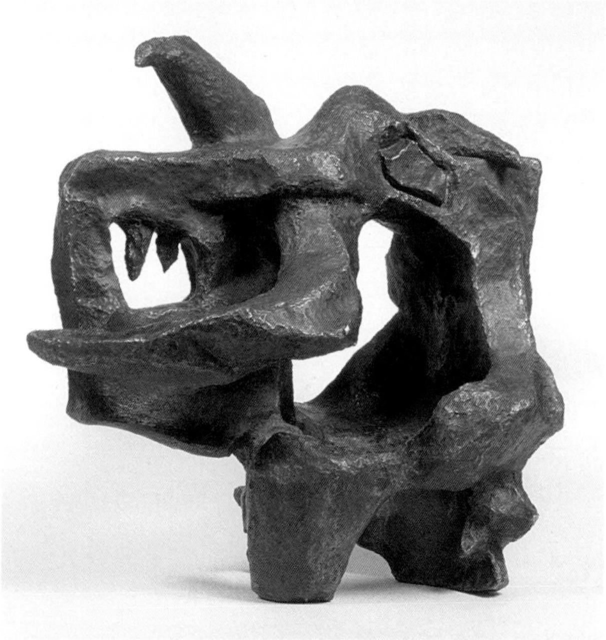

3.17
Seymour Lipton, *Moloch #3*, 1946. Lead, 23 1/2 × 23 × 19 in. Collection of the McNay Art Museum, San Antonio, Texas. Gift of Barbara Palmer.

space was the “chief twentieth century investigation,” who were intrigued, “both macrocosmically and microcosmically,” by the exploration of space, the postwar, postatomic period offered a multitude of a new ways of seeing and understanding the world — and transferring those ideas into sculptural form.[37]

Some more recent scholarly analyses, including one by Slifkin, have explored the more destructive, residual impact of this newfound spatial awareness. These studies focus on the violence rooted in so much direct metal work of the period, seeing in it, unavoidable evocations of war, violence, and atomic anxiety. Roszak’s *Spectre of Kitty Hawk* (1946–47) or Lipton’s *Moloch #3* (1946) (figure 3.17) are emblematic of this type of sculpture and its vision of “apocalyptic birds” and monstrous masses of metal. Brazed steel and molded lead swirl into serrated forms resembling prehistoric beings and skeletal remnants.[38] Even in more simplified and precise sculptures, like Lippold’s *Primordial Figure* (1947–48) (figure 3.18) it is hard not to see. As Andersen suggested, work “infused with the Surrealist concept of the undifferentiated and the undefinable — the power of the unconscious and the dream — the totemic personage idea proliferated among American sculptors, incorporating the sense of loneliness and alienation that had been conditioned by post-Second

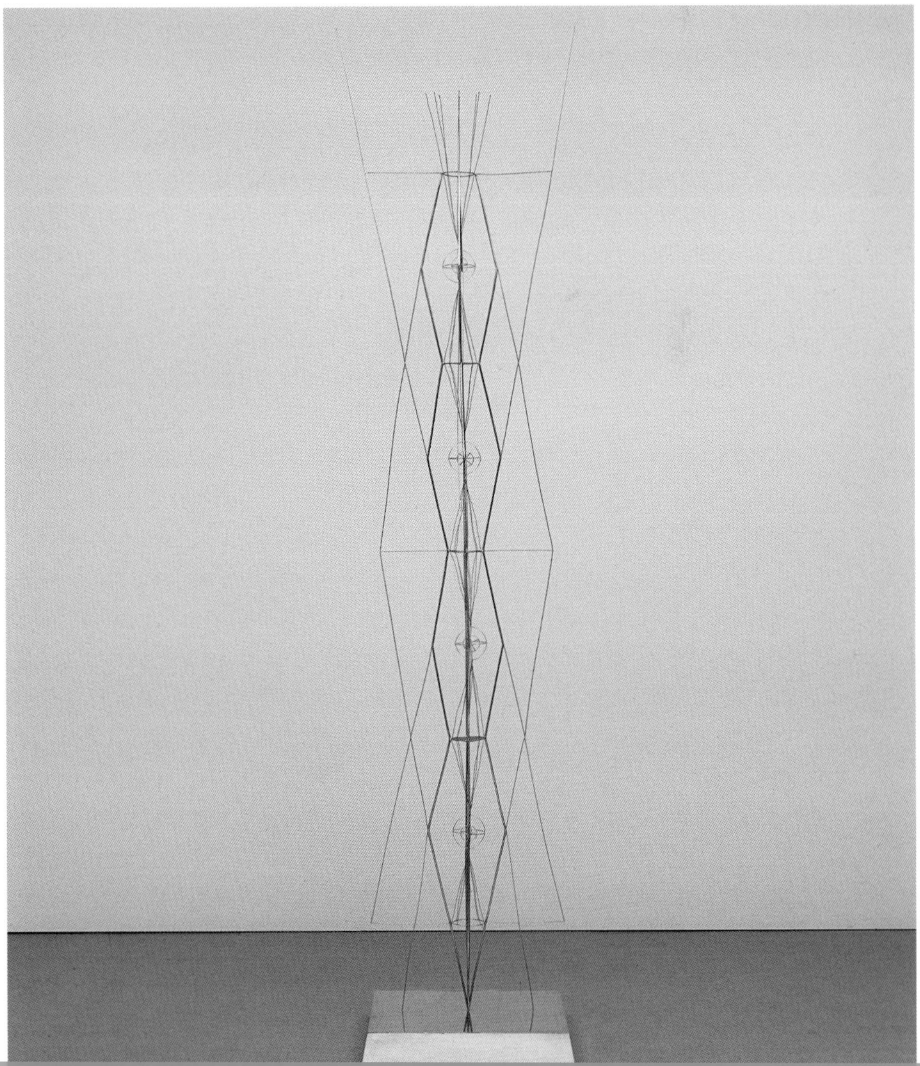

3.18
Richard Lippold, *Primordial Figure*, 1947–48. Brass and copper wire, 95 × 19 × 17 in. Whitney Museum of American Art, New York. Purchased, with funds from the Whitney Museum of American Art and

World War psychology." Lippold made such connections even more explicit in 1947: "We seem to have forgotten, or at least we have been made to forget by the diverting carnival of politics, that a new world came into being on an early morning over Hiroshima. Then, of one terribly bright moment that illuminated every corner of the earth, we knew about ourselves, we knew about the future, and we knew that ours was to be an age of final decisions.... In 1945 man at last came upon the final secrets of the atomic structure of this world and universe."[39] Many sculptors of the period, especially during the late 1940s and early '50s, did express antinuclear sentiment or traumatic pathos through their work, but many were just as likely to convey a sense of wonder regarding the possibilities wrought by new technologies and world orders.

Lippold, for example, told *Time* in 1963 that faith no longer resided in pyramids or cathedrals, but in "space, energy, [and] communications.... In the twentieth century we do not look at things; we look through them." In this new age, as the populist magazine declared, the "great preoccupation" was space, "not only the getting of things off the ground, but also the many ways of opening things up, from atomic fusion to psychoanalysis." The discussions of space and sculpture often included evocations of vitalism, radiating forces, cellular structures, and atomic explosions. Irving Sandler wrote in 1959 that Lassaw "became, and still is, convinced that the images pertinent to our technological age are most clearly expressed through space constructions." Or as Lassaw himself wrote, "My interest in a 'sculpture of relativity' reflects for me what I consider as the universe of organic relativity. The reality I see before me is [a] living organism and, I believe, all its parts are ultimately ecological interdependence. I, as a man and an artist, participate in it according to my nature, just as a carbon atom in one of my body cells participates in my being. The universe performs its divine work of art with both galactic clusters and sub-atomic particles. Life is enacted moment by moment, an illimitable network of energy transactions."[40]

Bertoia, who was far less interested than Lippold or Lassaw in ascribing larger meaning to his work, even remarked in 1959,

> You might put it this way, we are living in an atomic age... We are right in the middle of it. Everybody thinks about it, talks about it. We use the atom for power—for many things. We can measure it, weigh it—I *think* we can—we have a very good idea of its makeup. But who has ever seen an atom? It is unseen, yet we live in a time dominated by this invisible force. It is, in a sense, this force, these elements of the atomic age, that I am trying to give sculptural shape and form. I say, 'in a sense' because they are only as *I* imagine them to be.[41]

Whether or not Bertoia wanted to explicitly dwell on it, there was a "cellular structure," running throughout his work in the 1950s and '60s, including his large commissions, smaller abstract sculptures, and furniture, all of which drew from the realms of science and technology (figure 3.19).

3.19
Herbert Matter, *Abstract Overlay of Harry Bertoia Chairs*, n.d. Herbert Matter papers, c. 1937–1984. Department of Special Collections, Stanford University Libraries, California.

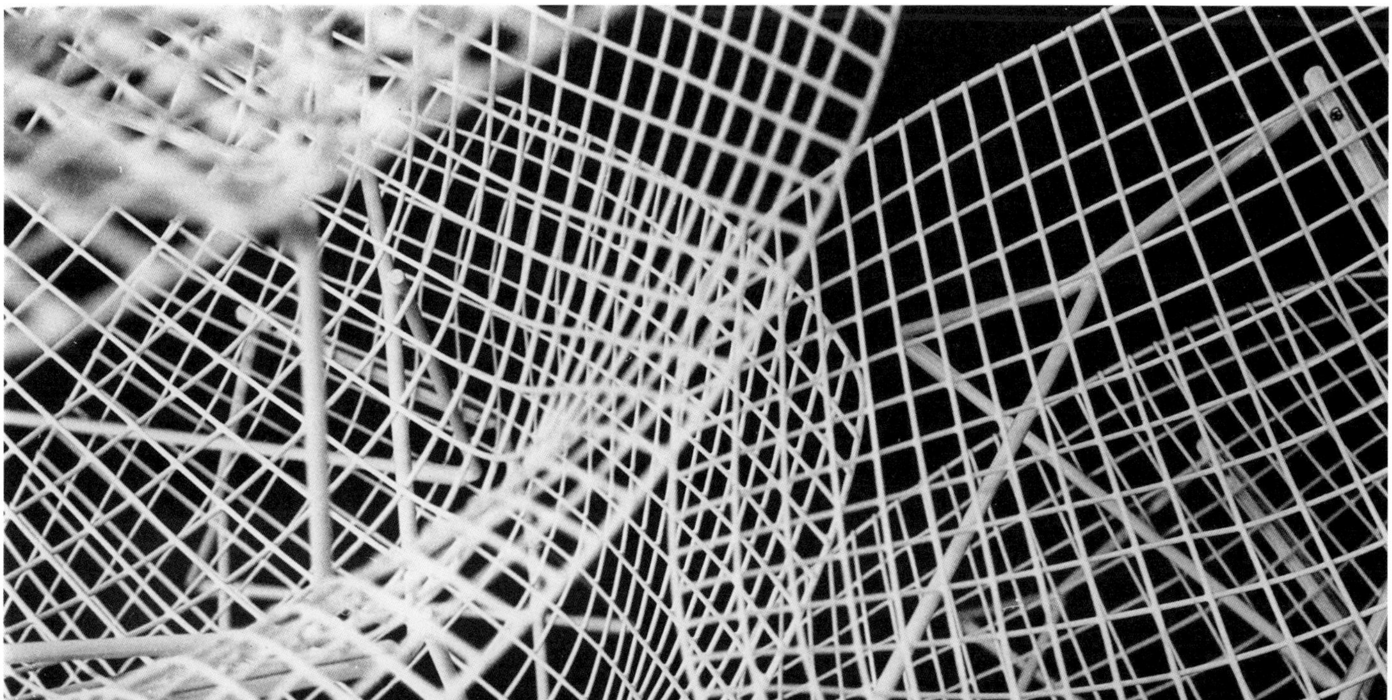

Bertoia's chairs and sculptures alike were "studies in space, form and metal," and as Olga Gueft noted in her review of the sculptor's 1952 exhibition of both at the Knoll Showroom in New York:

> Bertoia's new sculptures clarify the esthetic concept of the chairs. Bushes on tiny, firm feet, they consist of brilliant copper, silver, or gilt 'leaves'—geometric leaves—all turned the same way as if blown by the wind, on stiff twigs of metal. The structures have a cellular regularity, organic like honeycombs, chemical like crystals. With neither a beginning nor an end, they lace through space without enclosing it, are jagged, unfinished, with a magical suggestion of continued movement. The bees might at any moment add new cells to these frozen mobiles, the wind could blow the leaves another way, or a little more solution might be poured from the test tube and more of the mysterious snowflakes instantaneously appear, or recede without warning, as chemical fairylands do when the air dries or the temperature rises.[42]

In Bertoia's large-scale commissions, this oscillation between microscopic and macroscopic space, the organic and inorganic, the scientific and the aesthetic were often even more pronounced when placed alongside the shared language of modernist architecture. As Lewis Mumford concluded his review of the Manufacturers Trust Company Building, for example:

> This architecture is a formal expression of the culture that has explored the innermost recesses of the atom, that knows that visible boundaries and solid object are only figments of the intellect, that looks with the aid of X-rays and radioactive isotopes at the innerness of any sort of object, from armor plate to human bodies. The architects and sculptors should seek to express this world of transparent forms and dynamic processes, that they should actually revel in this exposure, is natural, since it is the eternal business of the artist to express in new forms what would otherwise remain at the commonplace levels of daily perception.[43]

While a testament to the technological, industrial, and aesthetic applications of metal during the immediate postwar period, large-scale commissions like Bertoia's screens for the Manufacturers Trust Company Building and the MIT Chapel or Lippold's sculpture for the Inland Steel Building suggested that space, as understood in and of the contemporary world, was the true medium specificity of sculpture and its most compelling, boundless material. The embrace of metal by Bertoia, Lippold, and many of their contemporaries was not about truth to materials or the material as such, but rather an excitement about what it could offer, about its sculptural possibilities—an approached mirrored by architects using metal to open up the space of buildings. Sculptors who established their careers in late 1940s and early 1950s did not continue to construct welded atomic monsters well into the next decade, nor did they cease their space explorations.

Instead, they increasingly embraced and created larger and larger spaces. If painting was becoming "an arena in which to act," to quote the art critic Harold Rosenberg, then sculpture was becoming the whole of the arena itself. Seen within this spatially oriented framework, it is no coincidence that so many of these same artists enthusiastically embraced the opportunity to realize commissioned work for architectural projects during the postwar period.[44]

Sculpture as Environment

When the Pan Am Building (1958–63) opened to the public on March 7, 1963, visitors entering the structure through the lobby off the adjacent Vanderbilt Avenue were greeted by a massive sculpture, 3 stories high, extending 80 feet across the space and 40 feet deep (figure 3.20). Created by Lippold and titled *Flight* (1963), the sculpture consisted of an open-form metal sphere surrounded by seven conical forms, each made from 113 strands of wire stretching 31 feet. The wire, totaling over 24,000 feet in length, all hand-placed and stretched by the artist, was 17/1000th of an inch in diameter and comprised of 22-carat gold, filled with a bronze core, custom-made at Lippold's request for the project. *Newsweek* recounted how "using rigs, motorized lifts, stepladders, pliers and miles of hand-stretched wires, Lippold articulated the space of 'Flight' into a giant spiderweb, a series of colossal cat's cradles that abandon terrestrial gravity and soar like extraterrestrial jets into infinity." Lippold had selected gold, bronze, and stainless steel as his materials to create a dramatic, modern effect, but also because of how they related to the lobby's interior, in particular its gray granite and warm travertine. The shape of the sculpture's form, Lippold wrote had likewise been chosen "and placed with regard to the space and proportions of the lobby, in an effort to continue the unity of form of the architecture and also to echo the unique angularity of the exterior of the building."[45]

The entire Pan Am Building project, like the sculpture in its lobby, was indeed a unique, ambitious undertaking. Erwin S. Wolfson, in partnership with London-based property developer Jack Cotton, developed the fifty-nine-story skyscraper at 200 Park Avenue, located over the Grand Central Station (figure 3.21). Pan American World Airways became the largest tenant, renting sixteen floors, and securing the building's namesake. The Pan Am Building was designed by committee, with Emery Roth & Sons selected by the developers as the lead architects with Walter Gropius and Pietro Belluschi serving as consultants. Gropius, however, was largely responsible for engaging Lippold for the project, writing to the sculptor in October 1960, "My client has recently given me the go ahead to engage artists for artwork in question in that building. At the main entrance from Vanderbilt Avenue opposite Forty-Fourth Street, I had in mind a large metal screen as a prominent feature when you enter the building. As a recent addition it has been suggested to put in front of this screen a large globe designed as an abstract, but incorporating the idea of the world activities of Pan Am. I would highly appreciate it if you would be willing to tackle this problem."[46]

3.20
Richard Lippold, *Flight*, 1963. Gold and stainless steel, 30 ft. x 80 ft. x 40 ft. Vanderbilt Avenue Lobby, Pan American Building, New York City. Architects: Emery Roth & Sons, Pietro Belluschi, and Walter Gropius.

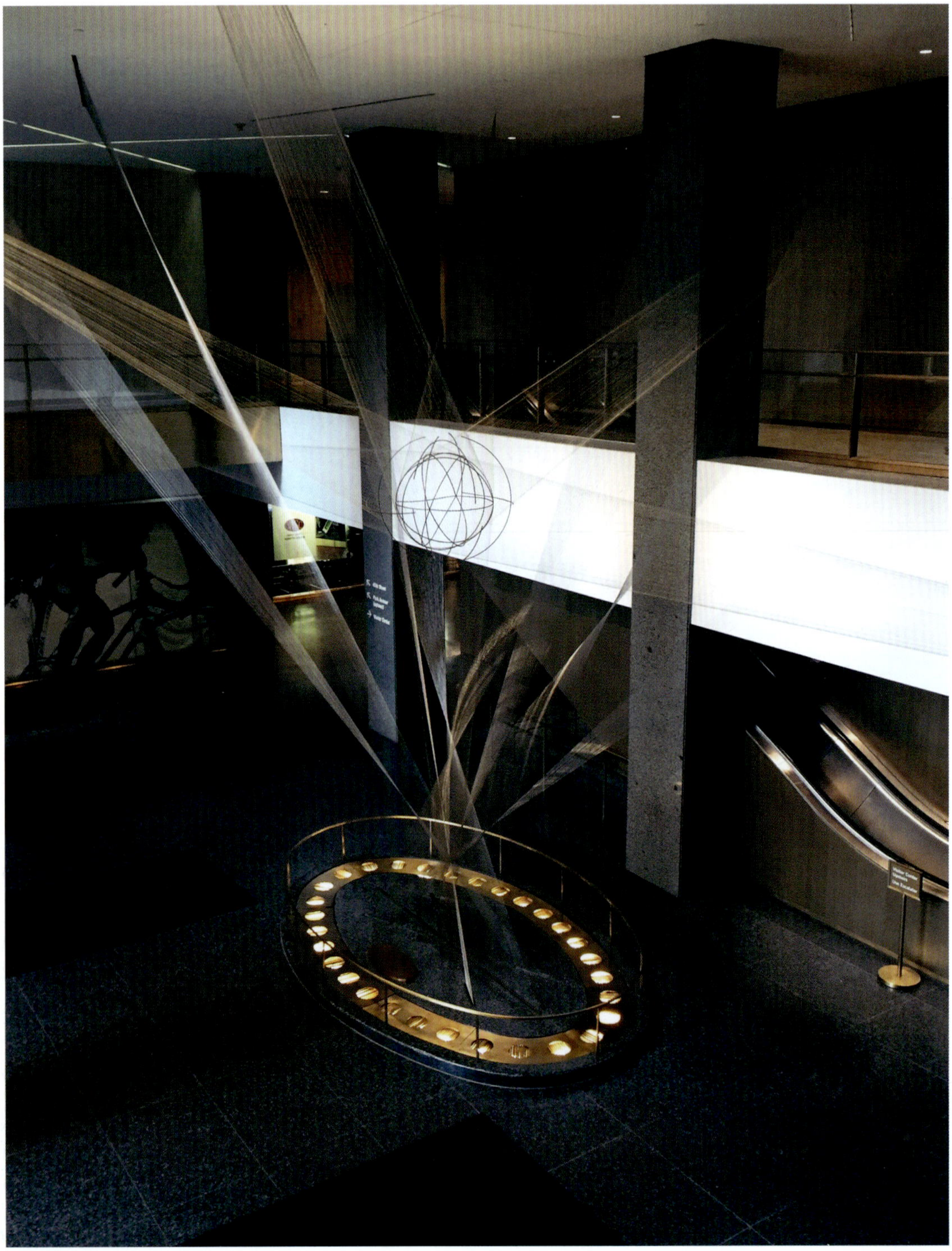

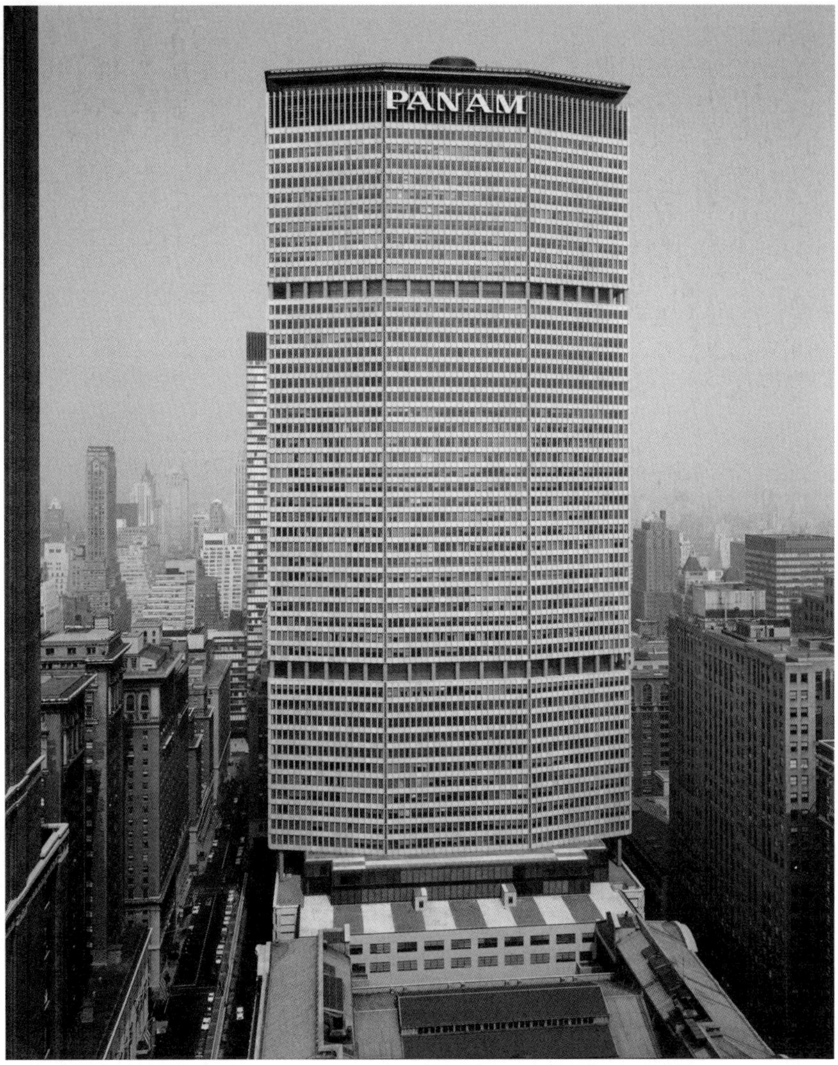

3.21
Pan American Building, 200 Park Avenue, New York City, 1959–63. Architects: Emery Roth & Sons, Pietro Belluschi, and Walter Gropius.

Given that the lobby was wide but not very deep, Lippold felt that a screen would only further compress the narrowness of the space and "make no gesture toward the very interesting spatial possibilities in the lobby." In creating a proposal, Lippold focused on the spatial specificity of the lobby. He considered how the center of the space formed a square between the walkways of the upper level and the main supporting columns. He thought about how people circumnavigated the space, moving on several levels, crossing small "bridges" and balconies, and moving diagonally on the escalators. Lippold wrote, "To provide a two-dimensional panel or even a free-standing sculpture for this space—no matter how exciting its personal meaning—seemed unnatural to me and a violation of the 'law' of this space."[47]

The design Lippold came up with for the lobby of the Pan Am Building was fixed to both the floor and ceiling, but also dynamically crossed the entirety of the space, connecting at multiple anchor points on the front and rear walls (figure 3.22). This extended the physical footprint of *Flight*, while also enabling an individual to literally walk through, to be in, the sculpture. How people would use the architectural space and encounter the sculpture within it was of tantamount

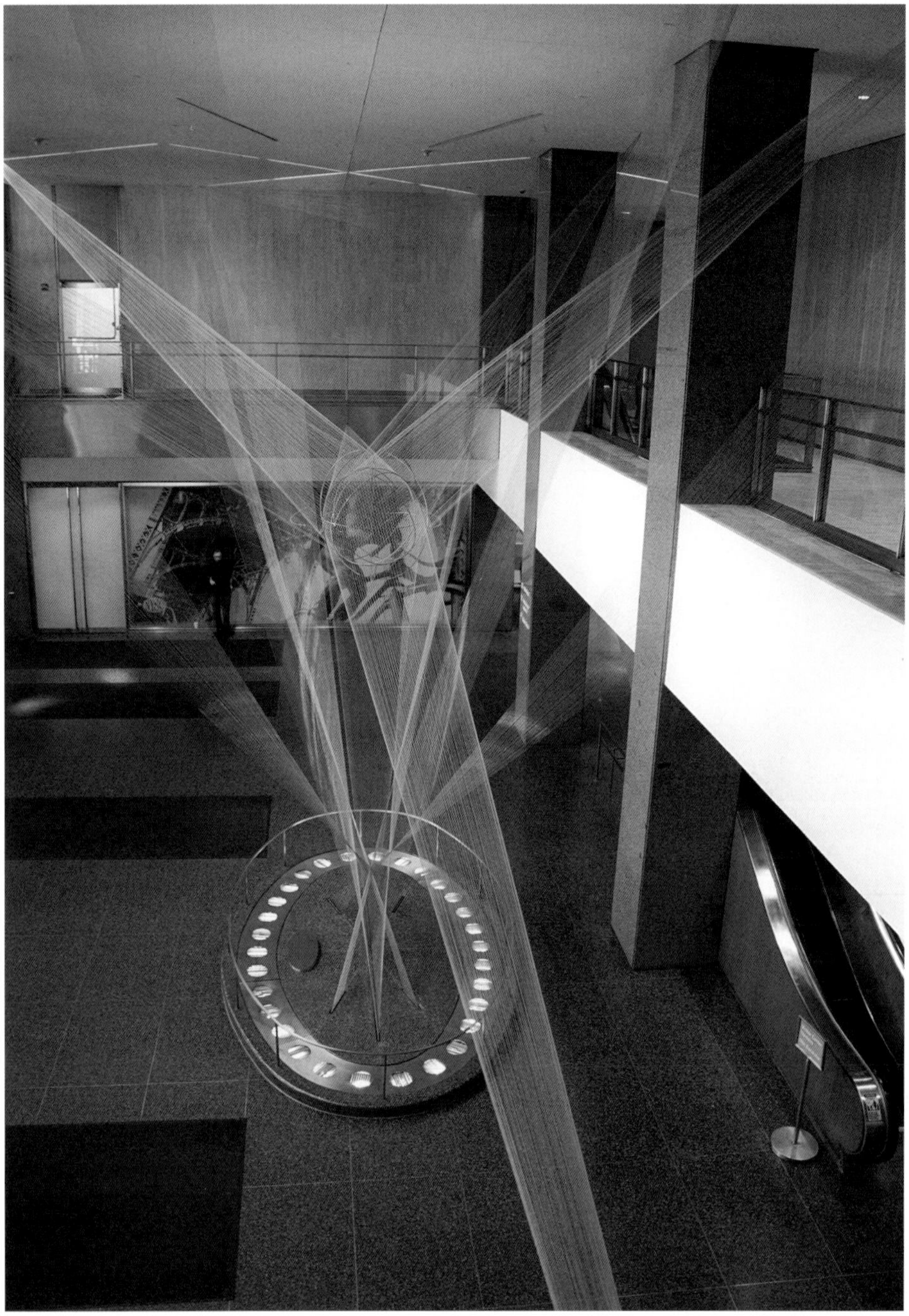

3.22
Richard Lippold, *Flight*, 1963. Gold and stainless steel, 30 ft. × 80 ft. × 40 ft. Vanderbilt Avenue Lobby, Pan American Building, New York City. Architects: Emery Roth & Sons, Pietro Belluschi, and Walter Gropius.

importance to Lippold. He included figures moving through the space in his preparatory sketches for the project. There was also the allure that with two-hundred-and-fifty-thousand people moving through Grand Central Station every day, "maybe ten percent of them" would look at the sculpture, and perhaps experience the architecture differently because of it. Lippold described how his goal of squaring the rectangular space of the lobby was to provide "visual excitement for all levels of movement into and out of the building." He continued, "Psychologically, it may effect a liaison between the scale of the building and the scale of man, holding hands with each, so to speak, quite literally touching the floors and the walkways in delicate contact with these surfaces on which men will walk." Space in this context then did not simply represent jet-age transport or even the distance in between its various wires and forms, but also took into account the entire physical environment of the lobby, collapsing the boundaries separating sculpture and architecture. As art historian Edward Lucie-Smith wrote of *Flight*, "While the sphere itself is clearly visible from every part of the space, the whole design shifts mysteriously with the slightest change in the spectator's position.... Yet the design is also reticent, in the sense that there is no one position from which every aspect of it can be seen. The spectator is always *within* the space which the sculpture occupies, never fully outside it." To achieve such complex environmental effects, however, Lippold had to endure and work through a complex approval process.[48]

Flight was one of several artworks commissioned for the Pan Am Building. György Kepes contributed two untitled aluminum screens with concentric squares placed near the information desk in the lobby on 45th Street, while Josef Albers added a bold mural of Formica panels, titled *Manhattan (1963)*, installed above the escalators that led down to Grand Central Station. Both Belluschi and Gropius were proponents of commissioning artworks for their architectural projects, and had already established relationships with all three artists. Lippold's original connection to Gropius had been facilitated by Josef and Anni Albers, who had met the sculptor at Black Mountain College. Moreover, Josef Albers, Kepes, and Lippold had all contributed artworks to Gropius's Harvard Graduate Center. Josef and Gropius's connection stretched all the way back to the Bauhaus in Germany, while Kepes and Belluschi were colleagues at MIT. Kepes also designed large stained-glass pieces for Belluschi's Church of the Redeemer in Baltimore, Maryland (1954–58) and the Trinity Episcopal Church in Concord, Massachusetts (1955–65). Lippold, working with Belluschi, realized *Trinity* (1960) (figure 3.23), a large, suspended wire sculpture hanging over the main altar of the Portsmouth Abbey Church in Rhode Island, and the massive *Baldacchino* (1967) in St. Mary's Cathedral in San Francisco.[49]

The scope and stakes of Lippold's commissioned sculpture for the Pan Am Building, however, were larger and more complex than either Albers's or Kepes's contributions. Lippold had come up with a design for the lobby by February 1961, which had the support of Gropius, Belluschi, and the rest of architectural team, as well as Wolfson. Their Pan Am clients, however, proved more indecisive, and a pivotal meeting was held in April. Staff from the *New Yorker* breathlessly reported the proceedings extensively in the magazine's Talk of Town section, noting that the developer was "intent on joining his business monument to the arts. To this heroic end, Wolfson last week invited us to march with him as he marched Drs. Gropius and Belluschi, and a young sculptor named Richard Lippold... over to the office of Pan Am President Juan Trippe, in the Chrysler Building, for a conference on the possible purchase of a Lippold creation." Also present at the meeting were Pan Am vice president, Willis Lipscomb; René d'Harnoncourt, director of MoMA; graphic designer Ivan Chermayeff; and architects Alex Cvijanovic and Edward Larrabee Barnes.[50]

Gropius, as the *New Yorker* recounted, opened by stating his emphatic support of Lippold's proposed sculpture. The architect proclaimed to the group, "I want to

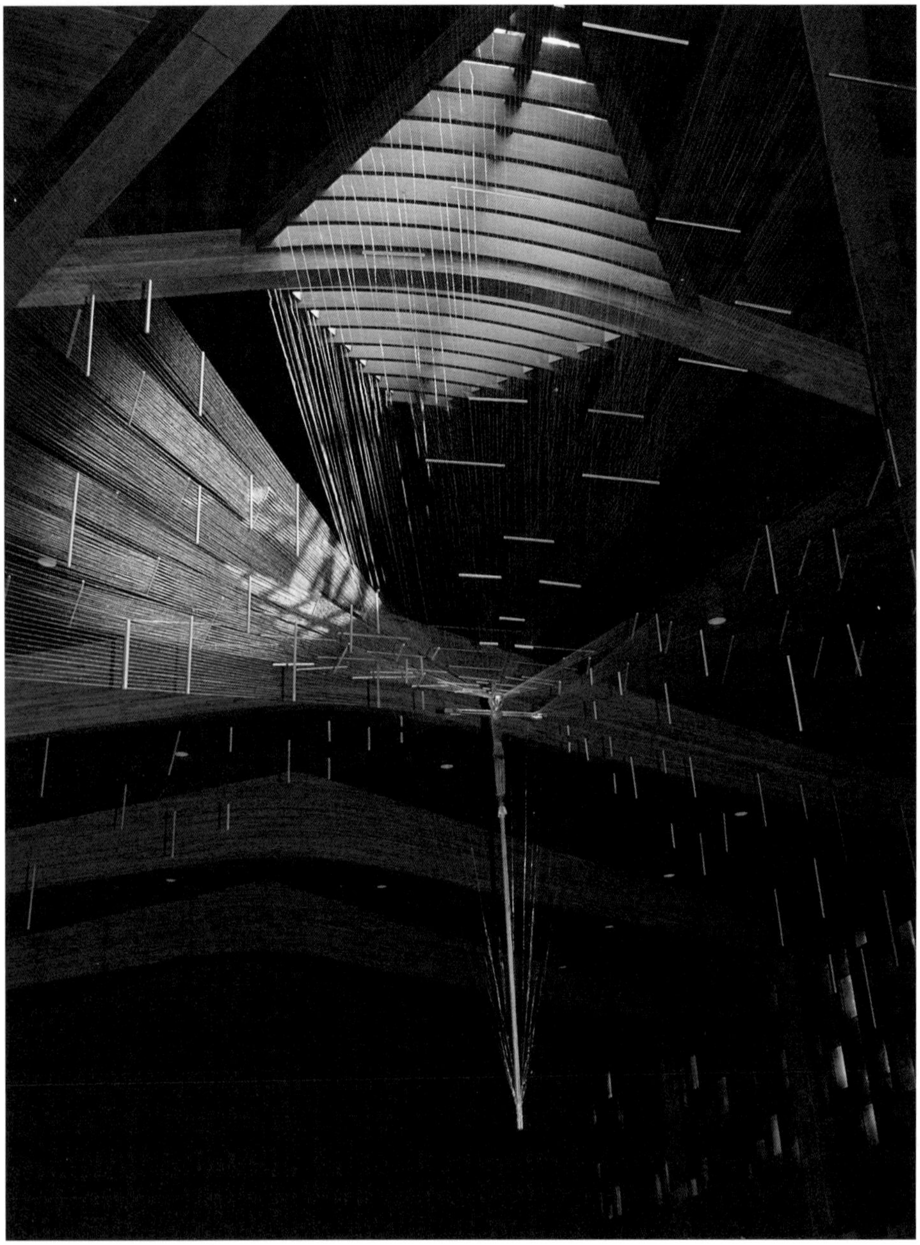

3.23
Richard Lippold, *Trinity*, 1960. Aluminum, gold, and stainless steel, 52 ft. × 68 ft. × 48 ft. Portsmouth Abbey Church, Rhode Island. Architect: Pietro Belluschi.

tell you, all my life I have tried to cooperate with painters and sculptors to create work for buildings that would be at one with the buildings, and this is the first time it has happened. Lippold's sculpture comes to one with our building." Lippold then read from a statement he prepared to accompany the proposal and preparatory sketches for the project being presented, which read in part: "*A Sculptural Symbol for Pan American World Airways*. The forms of this work are derived from the performances and shapes of modern aircraft, except for a sphere of the world in the center. From this sphere, a seven-pointed star radiates as if toward the seven continents and seven seas, its long conical arms originating in Great Circles of the globe, like the routes followed in inter-continental travel.... The sphere is thus made very spatial in character and less material, as one experiences it in the air age." The explanation of the work, while no doubt sincerely articulated, was clearly intended to offer an easily digestible vision of its meaning and one that clearly resonated with the business of the building's primary tenant.[51]

Lipscomb and the rest of the present Pan Am executives explained that they had conducted internal surveys to determine what might "linger longer in the minds [of] people who see it," and the general consensus was that a "more literal approach to a globe might capture the interest of the public on a more continuing basis." D'Harnoncourt spoke in support of the project, echoing Gropius's own proclamations. Referencing *Variation Number 7: Full Moon*, he stated, "We [MoMA] were the first people lucky enough to have one of Lippold's space designs in our lobby. I would say that *this* one would be one of the most important pieces of indoor sculpture of the twentieth century. If you want the impact of a great symbol, giving the feeling of speed through space, of expansion and lightness, you have it in this sculpture. No one who sees it is ever going to forget it." Gropius quickly followed up with one last unique aspect of Lippold's proposal, noting, "You feel as though you're in this sculpture. You stand in the lobby and you're right in the sculpture."[52]

Two months after the meeting with Pan Am, the commitment to Lippold's commission had still not been finalized. The sculptor anxiously wrote to Gropius suggesting that perhaps soliciting additional support from previous clients, including Leigh Block at Inland Steel, the Father Prior of Portsmouth Abbey, and Joseph Baum of the Four Seasons, could help their cause. He also noted that Juan Trippe and Pan Am had not been happy with how they or the meeting had been depicted by the *New Yorker*. By July 1961, all had somehow been resolved and an official contract was sent to Lippold through Marian Willard Johnson, the owner of the eponymous gallery who represented him.[53]

As the project progressed over the next two years, Lippold was busy also realizing *Orpheus and Apollo* for the Philharmonic Hall at Lincoln Center for the Performing Arts, but made sure to be as involved as possible with the architectural team during the final stages of designing the lobby space (figure 3.24). He was present during meetings to discuss finishes, including one at which it was collectively decided that a railing would need to be added to protect the sculpture "from abuse." Lippold also worked closely with Abe Feder, the lighting designer on the project, to "target and adjust all the lighting" in the space. They decided, for example, to light *Flight* with special fluorescent reflector lamps, enabling the sculpture to be viewed in greater depth (figure 3.25).[54]

The formal origins of Lippold's sculpture can be found both in Gropius's initial ideas for the project and the wishes of the client. Initially referred to as *A Sculptural Symbol for Pan American World Airways*, the title shifted to *The Globe* before ending up as *Flight*. The overall result was perhaps more literal and representational than Lippold's other commissions. Aspects of the sculpture were meant to correspond metaphorically with the forms and feelings of air travel and the arcs of flight in the jet age. Some of the most overt of these elements included the central "globe" and the combination base and plaque (figure 3.26). Lippold's statement and the process of realizing the work created an inextricable framework for the

3.24
Richard Lippold installing *Flight* (1963). Contact sheet by John D. Schiff, 1963. John (Hans) and Trudy Schiff Collection, Leo Baeck Institute, New York City.

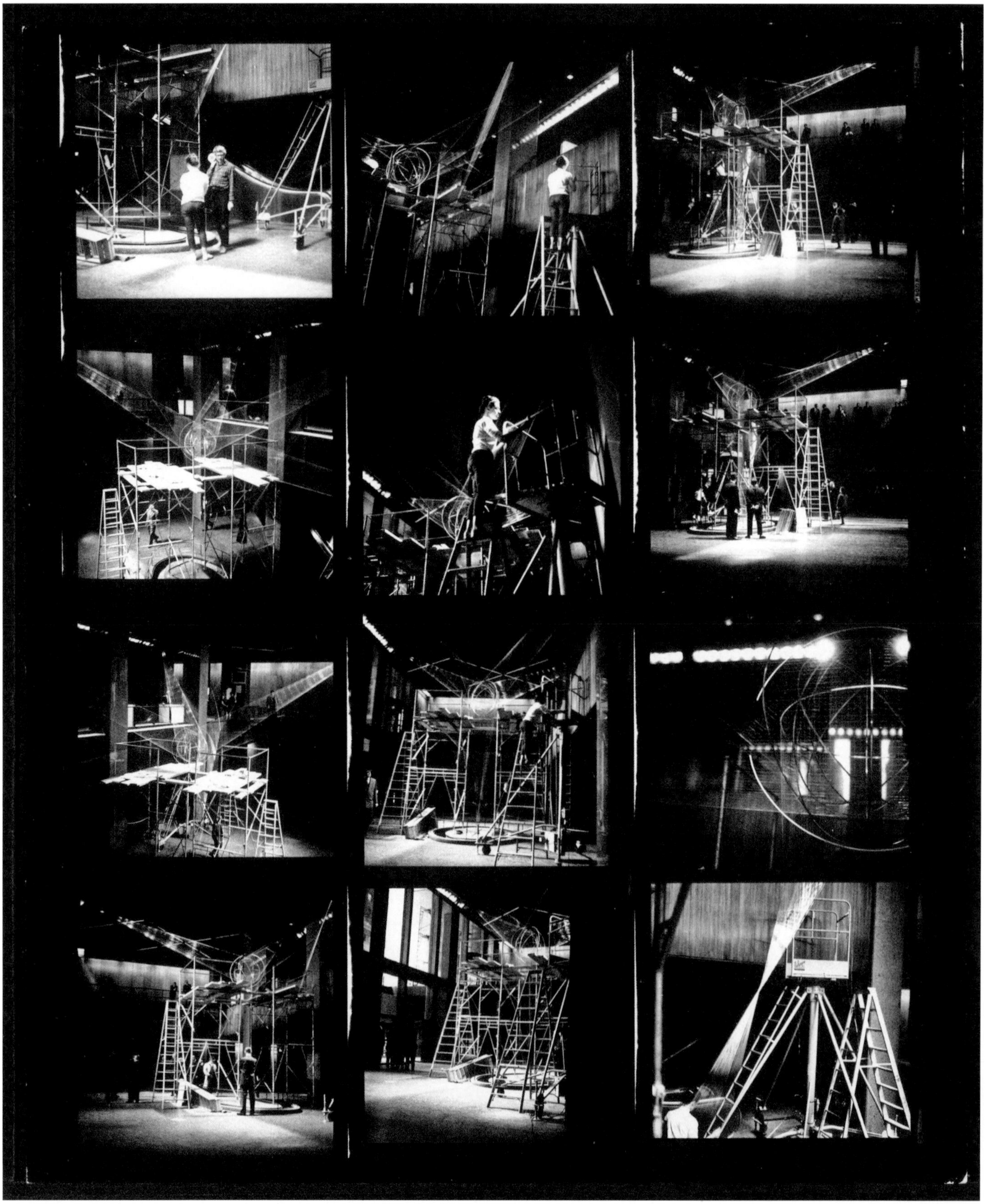

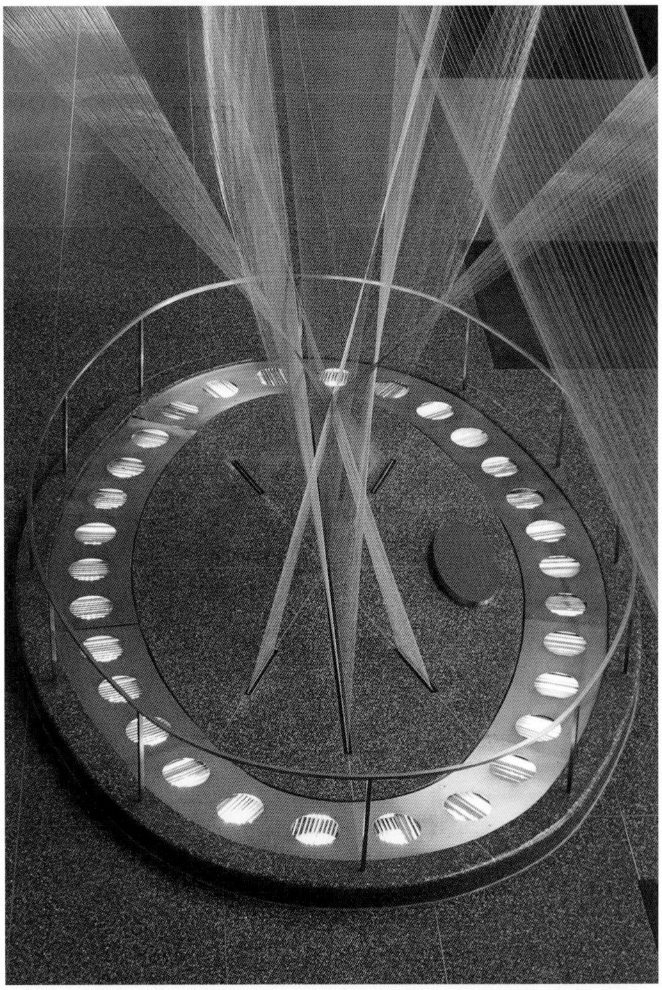

3.25, 3.26
Richard Lippold, *Flight* (detail), 1963. Gold and stainless steel, 30 ft. × 80 ft. × 40 ft. Vanderbilt Avenue Lobby, Pan American Building, New York City. Architects: Emery Roth & Sons, Pietro Belluschi, and Walter Gropius.

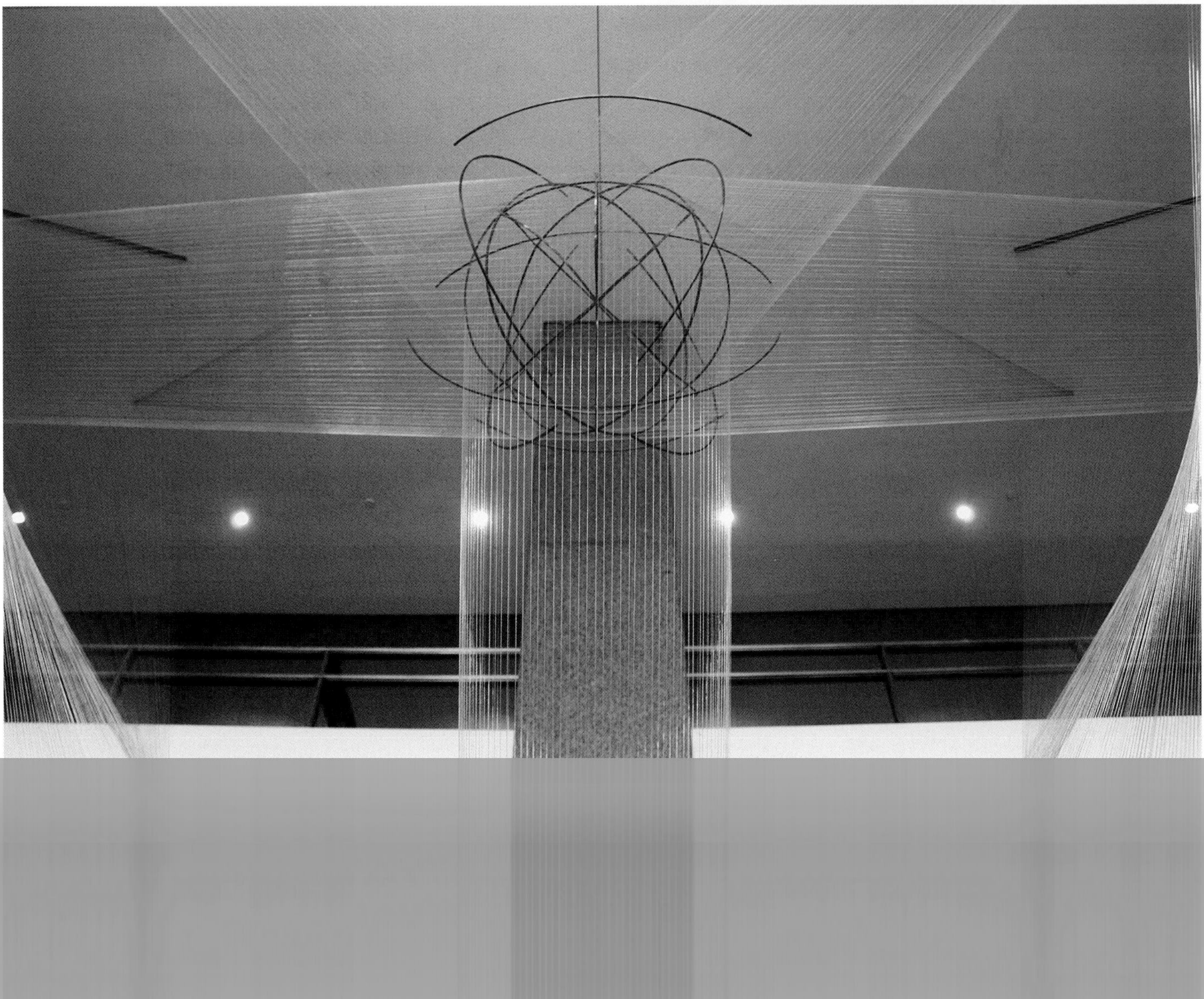

sculpture and certainly colored how it was eventually received and interpreted. Lippold himself acknowledged, "I honestly cannot say how much of it was in my subconscious awareness while I worked on the piece. I imagine, however, that, knowing the patron, the uses of the space, etc., the form was in part as predetermined by this as is a painting once the subject is seen or the first stroke made." All of the parties involved in the realization of *Flight* seemed happy with the outcome.[55]

Gropius in particular felt the commission conveyed how, "unlike most sculptors, Lippold understands and respects architecture, space, and architects." He even wrote to Lippold directly to tell him that he thought the sculpture "came out beautifully. Here is the rare case that the architecture of the space and your sculpture have become an entity." Unfortunately, the majority of the critical reception of Lippold's work and Gropius's building was not as complementary, largely overlooking how well the sculpture worked with the architecture and focusing instead on the perceived deficiencies of the project overall. The Pan Am Building was largely derided at the time for "its ugliness and arrogant disregard of its surroundings," and seen by many since as the end of the modernist experiment in architecture.[56]

Perhaps given the resounding censure of the building, the reaction to Lippold's contribution, then and now, was unenthusiastic if not outright negligent. Writing in the *New York Times*, Huxtable scathingly stated at length:

> Criticism, which has been plentiful since the building's inception five years ago, is directed largely at its physical and sociological implications.... But now that the building is virtually finished and functioning, something else becomes distressingly apparent. Bigness is blinding. A $100,000,000 building cannot really be called cheap. But Pan Am is a colossal collection of minimums. Its exterior and public spaces, in particular, use minimum good materials of minimum acceptable quality executed with a minimum of imagination... Pan Am is gigantically second-rate. This is no Michelangelesque masterwork from the late and latter-day Medici, promoter Erwin Wolfson, but a super economy package with the usual face-saving gimmick: painting and sculpture in the lobby. In this new role as an architectural cover-up, the builders of New York are turning good art into a bad joke.[57]

Architectural Forum declared Lippold's sculpture "almost crippled by the space which surrounds it (a cramped side-lobby), but lighted to good effect by Abe Feder," and noted that the work was "an exciting and beautiful construction of golden, gossamer-thin wire," shooting "a myriad of fantastic, dazzling rays of light." Another review of the building and its commissioned art in the *New York Herald Tribune* saw the whole enterprise, and in particular Lippold's and Albers's contributions as abject failures: "That the inhuman, if not actually misanthropic, character of much of our new architecture must balefully and inevitably affect the lives and spirits of the human beings who function in and around it, is by now a truism. That it can also shackle and stifle the ebullient creativity of most imaginative, independent and talented artists engaged for the decoration of such architecture—and presumably given complete freedom in tackling their assignments—is a shocking surprise." The newspaper, unlike Gropius's and Lippold's interpretations of the project, echoed the review in *Architectural Forum*, suggesting that there was a complete disconnect between the art and architecture and pointing to the space of the lobby being too small for what the artist had wanted to achieve with *Flight*. The publication declared, "His latest sculpture, immaterial as it is, and too tenuous to have real impact, is still cramped. It lacks any sense of soaring freedom or of monumentality. But that, of course, would be his own fault. The sculptor works within a fixed architectural space has the responsibility of working scale with it."[58]

The *Herald Tribune*, like many critical interpretations of Lippold's contribution to Pan Am, offered a number of possible explanations for why Lippold had created what they saw as such a cliché. They pointed to the more literal aspect of *Flight* and the sculptor's apparent "need to find an affinity between the technological advances of our time and his own ideas and forms." Perhaps "he spread himself as thin as his wires, that he's been taking on too many architectural assignments." The *Herald Tribune* concluded by declaring that Pan Am's new supersonic Concorde jet was "incredibly more beautiful as an esthetic form symbolizing speed and space than Lippold's gimmicky construction of taut wires.... Perhaps the time has come for artists to stop taking their cue from technicians. Perhaps they should try to concentrate, intensify, and truly to abstract the essence of poetic idea and human experience, rather than imitatively to reach out into space. Brancusi's shining 'Bird in Space,' done more than 40 years ago, would esthetically and symbolically have worked better in the Pan Am lobby than Lippold's 'Flight.'"[59]

Such assessments, beyond the usual aesthetic gatekeeping of criticism, faulted the sculptor both for trying to create a relevant symbol of space in the jet age and for failing to achieve such symbolism through an "appropriate" degree of abstract, essential poeticism. Evocations of the Concorde jet or even Brâncuși's *Bird in Space* (1932–40) suggest that Lippold's work should be seen through an established framework of aesthetic, if not outright economic elitism. In this view, modernist sculpture is to be assessed only by its success, or in this case failure, as an autonomous object, a masterpiece of individualism, and vehicle for supposed universal, symbolic expression. What such assertions overlooked, however, was how the impact of *Flight* was not limited to its physical boundaries. Much like Brâncuși himself had begun to explore with his use of reflective surfaces and sculptural groupings earlier in the twentieth century, Lippold sought to transform space through sculpture and sculpture through space. *Flight* may have compensated for uninspired architecture, which after all was not a new position for Lippold to find himself in, but the achievement of his sculpture for the Pan Am Building, its synergy, came from the exact thing Gropius had initially highlighted to the company's executives that to see Lippold's sculpture, to be in the lobby, was to be *in* Lippold's sculpture.

The artist himself had always thought of and approached the commission for the Pan Am Building as more than just a sculpture to be placed within the site, a dynamic decorative object, or symbol reflecting the business interests of the main tenant. In realizing *Flight,* Lippold worked within the collaborative confines established by the architecture and corporate client, while also creating a total environment facilitated through the sculpture (figure 3.27). This expansive spatial conception of the project was supported by the final form of the work, by its activation of every corner and level of the lobby, as well as Lippold's original intention to also incorporate into the project a sonic component by his friend the avant-garde composer John Cage. Early on, the sculptor learned Muzak was going to be piped into the lobbies and elevators of the Pan Am building, and he was unhappy about the prospect of such a manufactured product "seeping sweetly out of the surrounding walls and flowing around his work." Lippold believed the use of Muzak would be incompatible with his sculpture, and suggested that the architects, developers, and clients should approach Cage about creating "a suitable aural framework" for the sculpture and the lobby. The idea to bring Cage onto the project, while eventually taken seriously, had apparently begun as a flippant remark made by Lippold at a cocktail party hosted by Wolfson. Critic Calvin Tomkins reported that the developer surprised the sculptor by responding, "Go ahead." Lippold told a friend at the time, "Wolfson belongs to the new breed of industrialists who respects artists. He trusts them, he's willing to let them do what they want without interference. But, my God! Think of it! Cage is still too avant-garde for the concert halls, and here's a chance for his music to be played to an audience of thousands and thousands a day!"Cage set to work, creating plans that became a fully-fledged part of the overall artistic intervention in the Vanderbilt lobby.[60]

Cage proposed using the infrastructure installed for the Muzak and a series of photoelectric cells meant for surveillance of the space. In his repurposed system, people moving through the lobby would activate the Muzak, which would then be

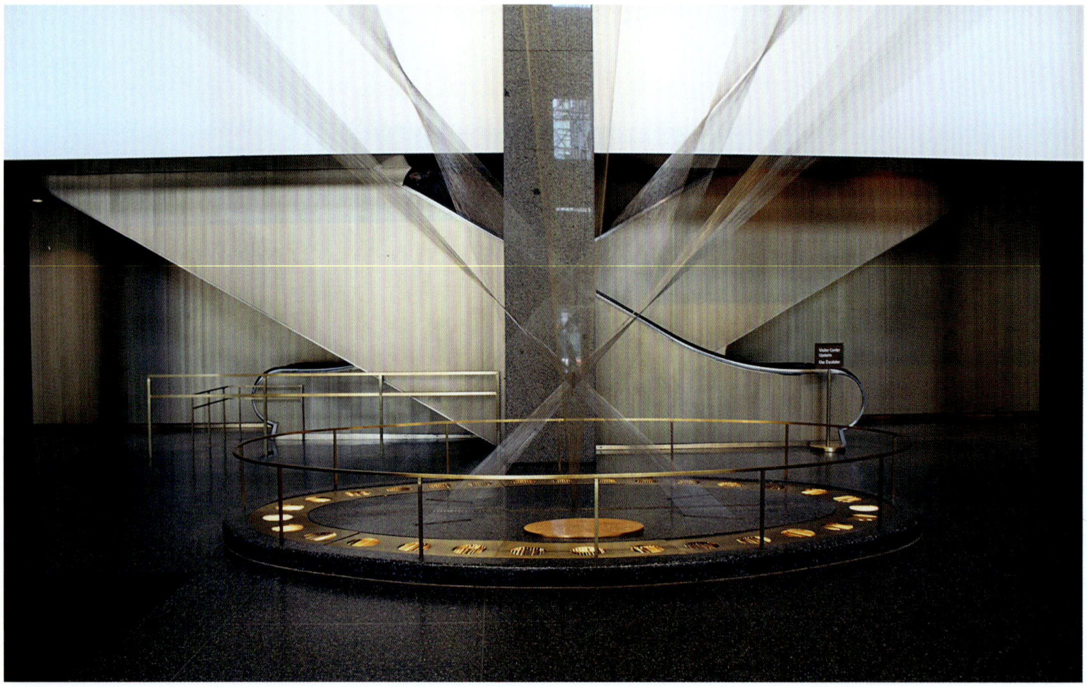

3.27
Richard Lippold, *Flight* (detail), 1963. Gold and stainless steel, 30 ft. × 80 ft. × 40 ft. Vanderbilt Avenue Lobby, Pan American Building, New York City. Architects: Emery Roth & Sons, Pietro Belluschi, and Walter Gropius.

filtered and pulverized, producing sound in the space that would be constantly varied. Lippold even consulted with Bell Laboratories on the technical components required to make it feasible. Cage's involvement in the project essentially ended, however, with Wolfson's untimely death in 1962. Wolfson's successor took the idea to Pan Am's board of directors, who after months of mulling over the composer's proposal, decided in the end there would be no music at all in the lobby.[61]

Lippold had befriended John Cage through his wife Louise Lippold, who had danced with Martha Graham and Merce Cunningham. Along with Anni and Josef Albers, the Lippolds also participated in the 1948 summer session at Black Mountain College and continued to develop their friendship through common artistic interests and a shared social circle in New York City. Lippold noted that Cage was "always talking about the spaces in music and I was always talking about the silence of art, of sculpture. So, we almost interchanged language." Both Lippold and Cage drew from music, architecture, and sculpture to create work that plumbed new conceptions of spatial openness. The latter, in describing how his music sought to account for "sounds that happen to be in the environment," made such connections explicit.[62]

Cage wrote for example, "The glass houses of Mies van der Rohe reflect their environment, presenting to the eye images of clouds, trees, or grass, according to the situation. And while looking at the constructions in wire of the sculptor Richard Lippold, it is inevitable that one will see other things, and people too, if they happen to be there at the same time, through the network of wires. There is no such thing as empty space or an empty time. There is always something to see, something to hear."[63] For Lippold, Cage's sonic contribution to the lobby of the Pan Am building would have added a dynamic, ever-changing component to the space, but he also saw it as becoming a part of his work, combining with the architecture to create a total, all-encompassing environment.

Even without Cage's involvement, however, commissions like *Flight*, especially those that literally sutured a space from floor to ceiling, suggested that spatial sculpture was more than just references to intergalactic exploration or increased physical dimensions. The story of a synergy between sculpture and architecture during the immediate postwar period is, at its core, a shared search for new conceptions of space and how to shape it through plastic form. The evocations of space as a central concept that began in the 1940s, increasingly transformed into those of environment by the late 1950s. "Art," as art historian Wayne Craven declared in 1962, "is becoming environmental and the importance of the viewer has been reaffirmed." This shift reflected the use and creation of greater and greater scales of space, enabled by new techniques and materials, but it also sought to emphasize a bodily experience within the artwork or object itself—or as Lippold was prone to state in conjunction with his large-scale commissions, the point was to create a palpable experience between the spectator, building, and sculpture.[64]

During this period, artists like Allan Kaprow, Yayoi Kusama, and Claes Oldenburg, became crucial proponents of the term environment, using it to describe artworks made to be walked into and physically inhabited. While Kaprow most certainly did not have the commissions of Bertoia, Calder, Lippold, and Noguchi in mind when he wrote the following, his words certainly offer a fitting, if perhaps unexpected, context in which to consider their significance and impact:

> With the emergence of the picture shop and museum in the last two centuries as a direct consequence of art's separation from society, art came to mean a dream world, cut off from real life and capable of only indirect reference to the existence more people knew.... Traditionally, it is supposed that art is born entirely from the heart or the head and is then brought, all shiny and finished, to the showplace. Now, however, it is less and less conceived that way and is instead drawing its substance, appearances, and enthusiasms from the common world as we know it.[65]

To return to a conception of art as environmental, was to return art to the spaces of everyday life.

Kaprow, however, was hardly the only practitioner during the 1950s or early 1960s to begin advocating for the environmental as it related to vanguard sculptural practice. A particularly early example of the phenomenon was Frederick Kiesler's *Galaxy* (1947–48) (figure 3.28), which was featured alongside Lippold's *Variation Number 7: Full Moon* in MoMA's exhibition *15 Americans*. *Galaxy*, like his speculative *Endless House*, was both a sculpture and an architectural structure, an object meant to be entered. As Kiesler wrote in the exhibition's catalogue,

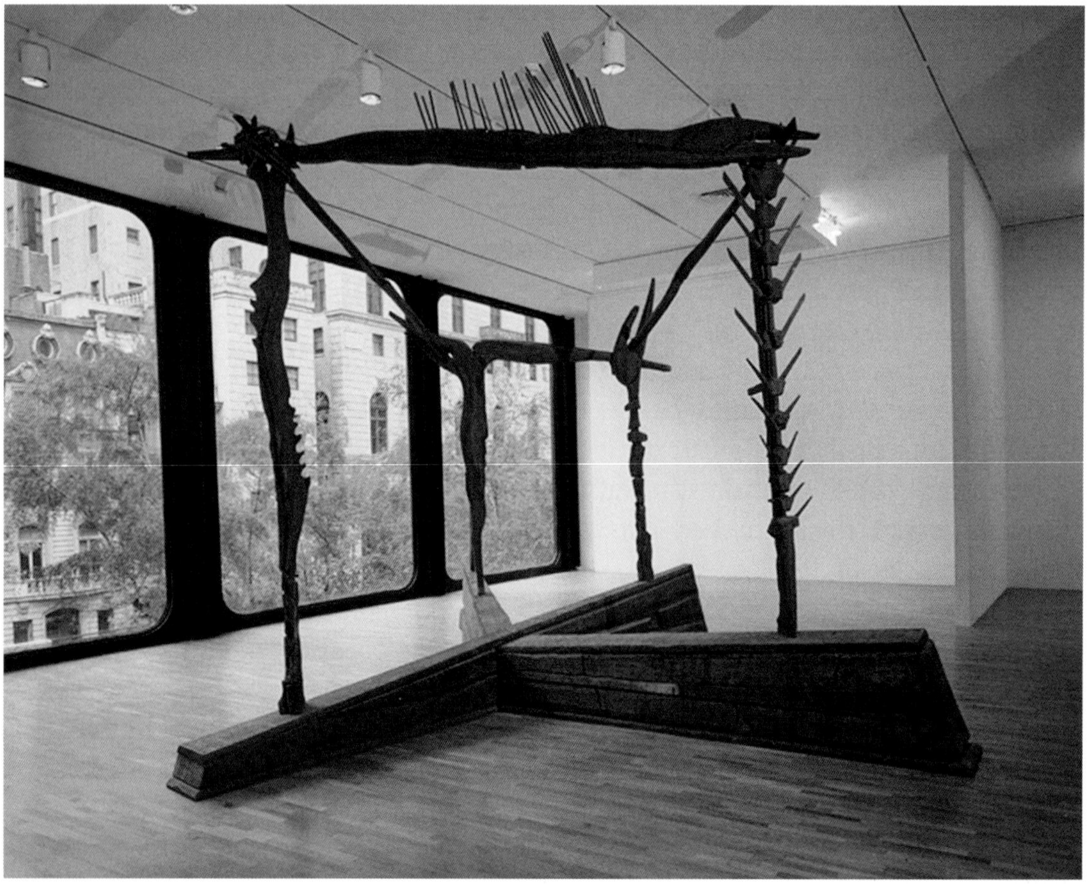

3.28
Frederick Kiesler, *Galaxy*, 1947–48 (base remade in 1951). Wood and rope, 11 ft. 11 in. × 13 ft. 10 in. × 14 ft. 3 in. Museum of Modern Art, New York City. Gift of Mrs. Nelson Rockefeller.

"My sculpture is a practical sculpture. It is both to be lived with and within.... Sculpture, painting, architecture should not be used as wedges to split our experience of art and life; they are here to link, to correlate, to bind dream and reality. To separate sculpture and painting from the flow of our daily environment is to put them on pedestals, to shut them up in frames, thus destroying their integrative potentialities and arresting their continuity with our total mode of life."[66] Kiesler's conception of space, sculpture, and lived environments would prove highly influential.

Ferber, who produced numerous sculptures during the period of smaller-scaled roofed structures, credited *Galaxy* as well as the recent "environments" created by Nevelson as precursors for a work he created for the Whitney Museum of American Art in 1961. Constructed from polyvinyl resin, his *A Sculpture by Herbert Ferber: To Create an Environment*, transformed the entirety of one of the museum's interior galleries, with multiple components attached to the ceiling, floor, and various points in the walls in between (figure 3.29). In the catalogue pamphlet produced in conjunction with the project, Whitney curator John I. H. Baur wrote, "Sculpture has gone through more radical changes in the 20th century than any traditional branch of art. The destruction of its solidity by the Constructivists, released energies as astonishing as those of the atoms." Baur described, however, how in recent years a new concept had emerged, that of "sculpture as an environment, an ambience, a surrounding and engulfing experience. The relation between the viewer and this sculpture is no longer that of spectator and object; it is the relation of man to esthetic force which embraces him totally. The experience, as Ferber has written, is akin to that of entering a chapel where one is immersed in an atmosphere that cannot be altered or dispelled except by leaving. In this respect, the new sculpture is closer to architecture than to painting." Ferber's sculpture "defined spaces activated by the drama of forms in tension," or the power of simultaneous sculptural and human presence in an interior.[67]

This mutual sharing and shaping of space by both sculptural object and spectator were, as Ferber noted, also evident in Nevelson's sculptural presentations of the period, including *Moon Garden Plus One*, held at Grand Central Moderns in 1958 and *Sky Columns Presence* at the Martha Jackson Gallery in 1959 (figure 3.30). In both cases, the sculptor installed numerous individual pieces of her black painted wood constructions. Art historian Elyse Speaks notes that Nevelson's "organic environments... jarring in the context of the architectural scale the work conveyed" can be understood as dramatic theatrical "conceptions of outer space," created in the wake of the launch of the Sputnik satellites launched by the Soviet Union and the beginnings of the space race. Critics at the time, however, were most struck by the novel way Nevelson chose to install and light her sculptures, describing *Moon Garden*, for example, as a "spectral sculptured landscape," and a "theatrical atmosphere."[68]

Dore Ashton, in her reviews of both exhibitions, noted the precedents of sculptors, including Alberto Giacometti, who "populated spaces" with multiple

3.29
Installation view of *A Sculpture by Herbert Ferber: To Create an Environment*, Whitney Museum of American Art, New York City, March 10–April 21, 1961. Frances Mulhall Achilles Library and Archives, Whitney Museum of American Art, New York City.

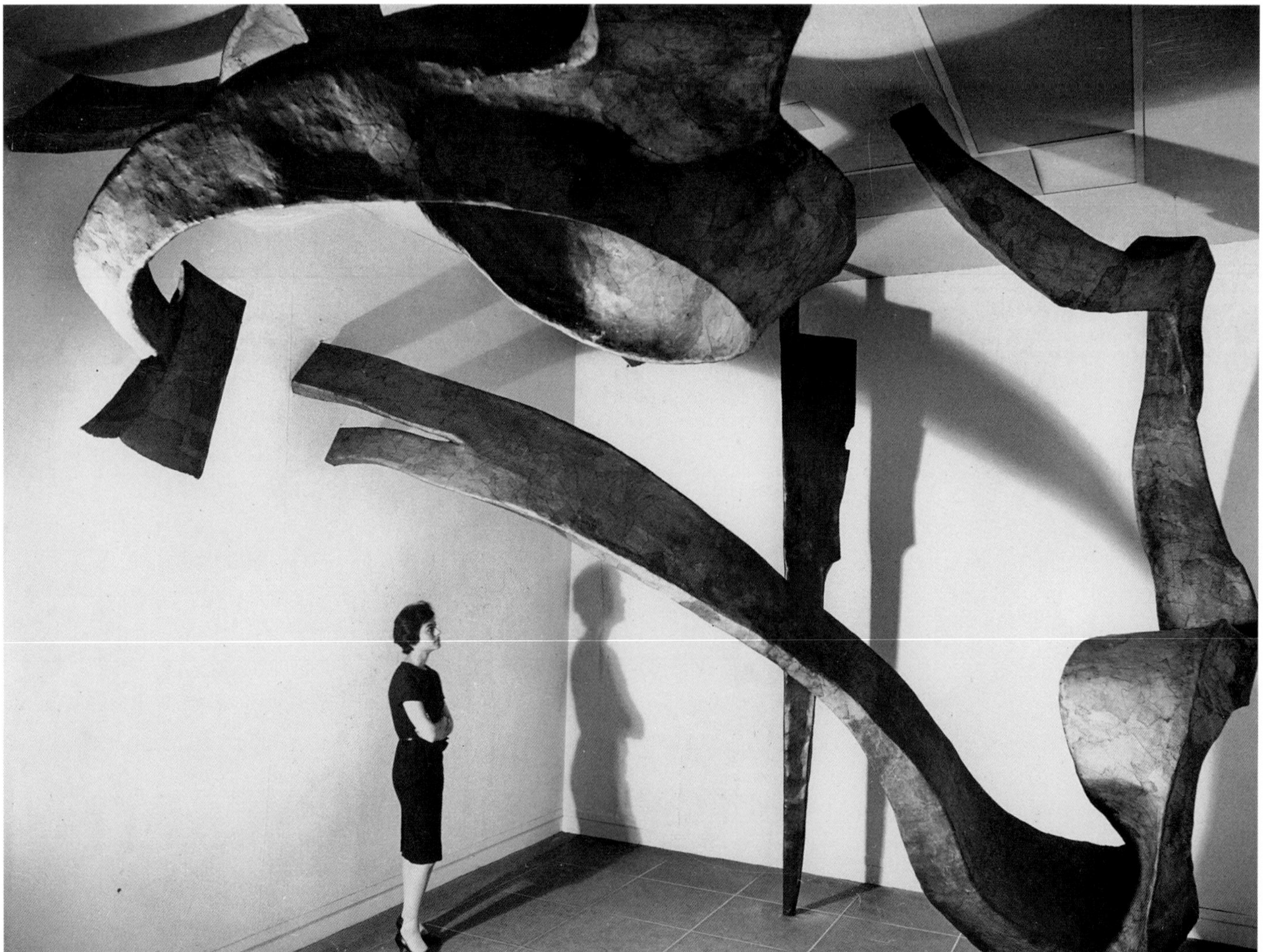

sculptures so as to create "an order in which the unit is multiplied until a totally new configuration occurs," but declared that Nevelson had presented sculpture as a "total ambience." Ashton wrote more specifically of *Sky Columns Presence,* echoing later interpretations of Lippold's *Flight,* "There is no single way of seeing the show. It may be seen as an ensemble, an intimate theatre housing what architects call an 'articulated wall'... There are circular comparisons with elegant plays of half-moon and angular shapes; long plaques with flutters of small elements sighting into 'in between places' of melting; pegs, lattices, dividers, dominoes, wheels and chevrons." Installation photos also notably show that *Sky Columns Presence* fully exploited the total architectural space of the gallery. Sculptures were not only positioned as walls, but also suspended from ceilings, perpendicularly extended from walls, and affixed to poles that ran from floor to ceiling.[69]

The sculptural environments by Kiesler, Ferber, and Nevelson were realized under far different circumstances than Lippold's *Flight* or Bertoia's reredos for the MIT Chapel. While these artists similarly explored new spatial possibilities and realized new kinds of sculptural environments, the works they created were still essentially autonomous artworks, able to be relocated with each subsequent exhibition or gallery display. No clients or architects weighed in on their form, and while imbued with the ambitions of more fully fusing the spaces of art and life, such sculptures still existed in and for the market, as well as the rarefied spaces of galleries and museums. However, to consider Lippold's *Radiant I* in the lobby of the Inland Steel Building together with Ferber's environment at the Whitney, Bertoia's metal trees at Southdale, and Nevelson's vertical wood columns in the Martha Jackson Gallery, suggests a collective force created by a sum of its parts: a spatial creation only achieved through a combination of sculpture, architecture, and all the visible and invisible spaces between. When viewed in the context of broader postwar sculptural trends—whether the move toward environmental scale or industrial materials—these projects that for so long were presumed to be little more than functional commissions for corporate public relations reveal nothing short of a crucial missing link within the established history of American art.

In May 1965, *Architectural Record* published a longform essay by Kepes entitled, "The Visual Arts and the Sciences: A Proposal for Collaboration." Illustrated by a selection of his paintings, experiments in light, and the massive kinetic mural for the KLM Ticket Office in New York City, Kepes essentially wrote a manifesto on synergy, calling for new modes of interdisciplinary collaboration and the increased relevance of sculpture and other artforms in the contemporary world. He referred to this confluence as the "new aspects of environmental art—the gearing of sculptural and pictorial tasks to the dynamic scale of the urban environment and to the new wealth of technical tools and implements." According to Kepes, there was a cultural evolution underway that demanded "broad scale interthinking," but he expressed concerns that too many artists had concentrated only on "personal comments, communicating their feelings and thoughts through the channels of galleries, museums, or private collections." Artists instead needed to

3.30
Installation view of Louise Nevelson's *Sky Columns Presence*, Martha Jackson Gallery, New York City, October–November 1959. Louise Nevelson papers, c. 1903–1982, Archives of American Art, Smithsonian Institution, Washington, D.C.

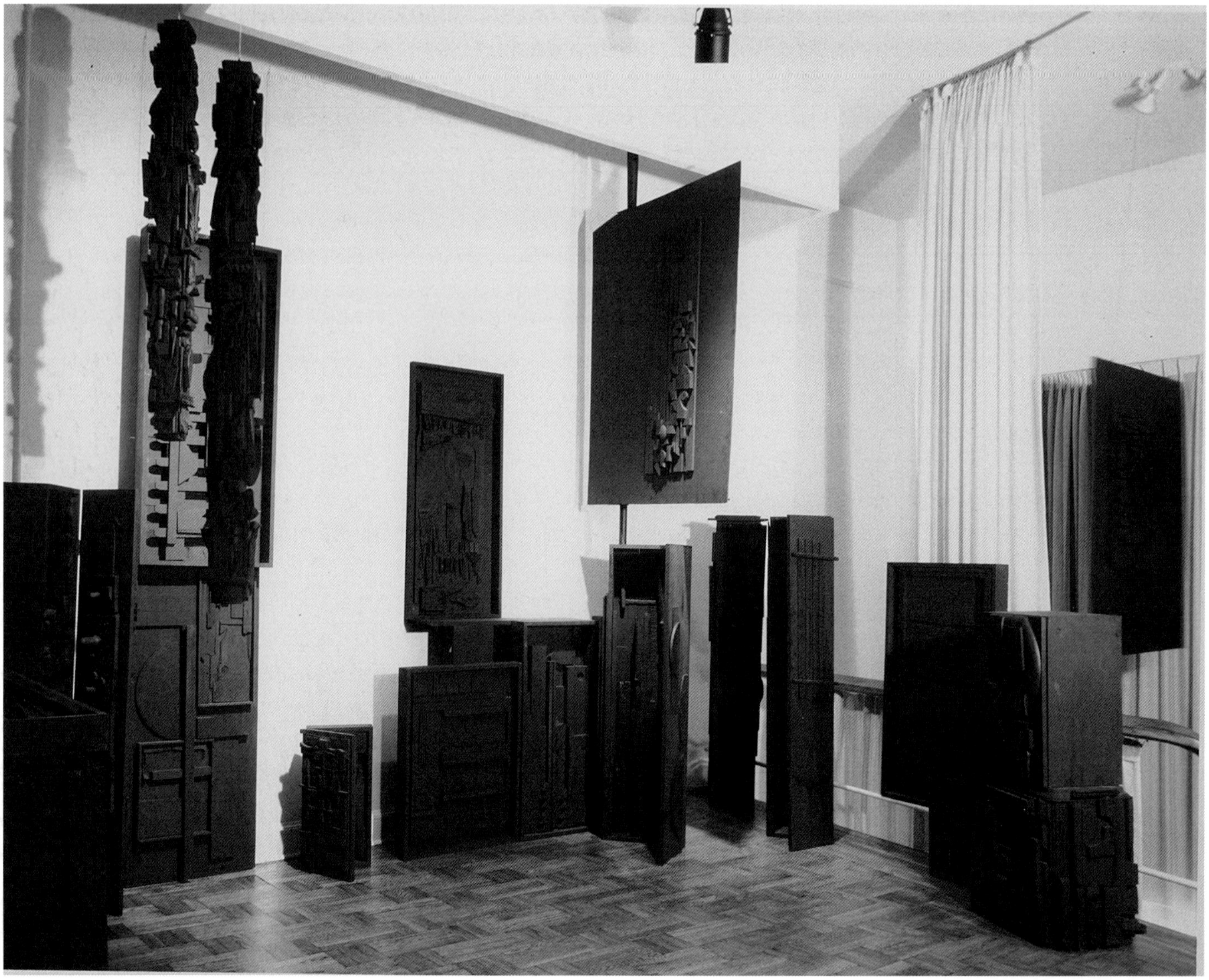

respond to urban scale in more imaginative ways, to "adjust to and communicate with architects, engineers, city planners, and many others who are working at reshaping the environment and learn to use new tools, implements of media production." Kepes continued, "The sculptural possibilities of reinforced concrete, prestressed concrete forms, plastic, stainless steel, aluminum; new techniques of welding; and the potentials of prefabricated units, pictorial use of baked enamel on steel, luminescent walls, photosensitive glass, spraying techniques ranging from metal spraying to color spraying, and new adhesives are only a few suggestions of the technology waiting to be explored."[70]

Kepes's suggested roadmap for how artists could enlarge their vision and embrace the techniques of collaboration, was the same path being forged by Bertoia, Calder, Lippold, Noguchi, and many of their sculpting colleagues during the immediate postwar period. By exploring the potential of new materials, forms, and conceptions of space, their experiments in sculpture opened the door to a public art that would spill out of lobbies onto plazas, civic spaces, and urban parks from the later 1960s. Though not directly referenced by subsequent practitioners, the sculpture of the immediate postwar period also pushed the medium further into the phenomenological realms of the environmental and experiential, which would become hallmarks within minimalist, postminimalist, and even postmodernist installation practices of the later twentieth century.

The architectural commissions of Bertoia, Calder, Lippold, and Noguchi—the ones created for the threshold spaces of modernist buildings, in close consultation with architects and clients that took on architectural functionalism—continue to serve as powerful testaments to the cooperation and the value of public good, to the ability of art to enliven, challenge, and thrive within the fabric of everyday life. While maintaining their own agency as sophisticated sculptural things, these projects also fully embodied the spirit of synergy. In embracing rather than resisting the parameters imposed by being commissioned works for inhabited architectural spaces, these large-scale sculptures, to return to the words of Buckminster Fuller, became a physical incarnation of the "cooperative action of discrete agencies such that the total effect is greater than the sum of two or more effects taken independently." This brief moment of transdisciplinary dialogue during the immediate postwar period produced fortified alloys, new composites of space, form, and function that would forever change the course of architecture and sculpture alike.

Epilogue

Preserving Space(s)

On October 25, 1974, a seventy-six-year-old Alexander Calder stood in the back of a forty-horse-drawn Schlitz Beer wagon as it rolled down State Street in Chicago's Loop past thousands of onlookers as part of a parade, which also included circus wagons, clowns, calliopes, elephants, musicians, and the festivity's ringmaster, architect Carter Manny Jr. Declared "Alexander Calder Day" by Mayor Richard J. Daley, the event celebrated the dedication of two new sculptures by the artist in Chicago. The first stop of the parade was in front of *Flamingo* (1973), a fifty-three-foot steel stabile painted bright red and installed in the plaza of Ludwig Mies van der Rohe's Federal Center (1958–74), which became one of the most important examples of postwar public art, not only in Chicago but across the United States (figure E.1). The large, outdoor public sculpture was the first work of art commissioned by the General Services Administration (GSA) under a new federal program that mandated 0.5 percent of the budget of any new construction project should go to art.

After using five-foot cardboard scissors to release hundreds of multicolored balloons at the Federal Center Plaza, Calder and the rest of the parade ventured four blocks west to the lobby of the newly completed Sears Tower (1970–74), designed by Skidmore, Owings & Merrill (SOM), where he threw "a switch setting in motion a seven-part, 33-foot-high wall mural." Calder delivered his only public address of the day at this second location, simply stating, "Mr. Arthur Wood [then board chairman of Sears] wanted me to give it a name. So, I thought of a name. I call it Mr. Wood's Universe." *Universe (1974),* as the sculpture became known, is more accurately described as a multipart, motorized kinetic sculpture, which extended from the floor to the top of the space, simultaneously resting on the ground and hanging from the ceiling, while extending outward from the east wall of the Wacker Drive lobby (figure E.2).[1]

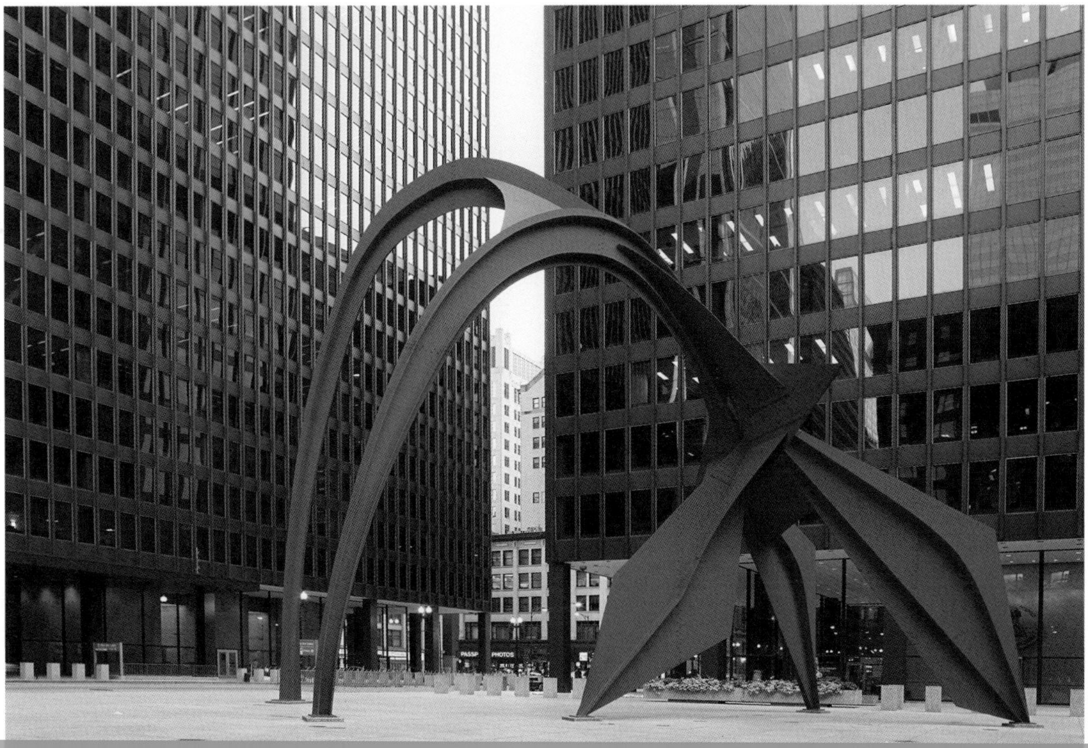

E.1
Alexander Calder, *Flamingo*, 1973. Sheet metal and paint, 53 ft. × 60 ft. × 24 ft. Federal Center Plaza, John C. Kluczynski Federal Building, Chicago. General Services

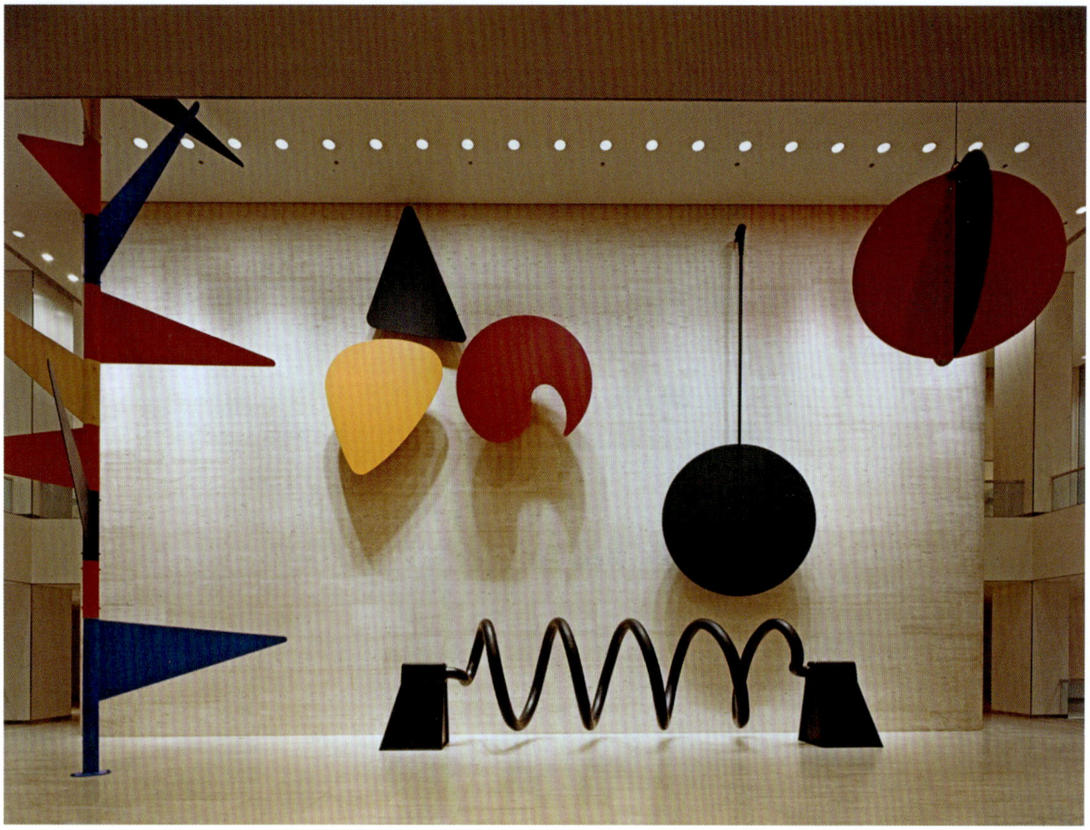

E.2
Alexander Calder, *Universe*, 1974. Sheet metal, paint, motor, 33 ft × 55 ft. Sears Tower, Chicago. Architect: Skidmore, Owings & Merrill (SOM). Collection of Sears Holding Corporation, Illinois.

Universe was engineered by the Biémont Foundry in Tours, France, near Calder's home in Saché. The work included three slowly rotating forms hanging in front of the wall, as well as a pendulum piece that moved in a thirty-degree arc. On the ground, between these elements, was a horizontally oriented rotating aluminum helix, and toward the north side, a vertically oriented, thirty-eight-foot-tall rotating "flagpole with colored pennants from tip to base."[2] *Universe* reflects many of the same themes and characteristics of the architectural commissions from the immediate postwar period. By 1974, Calder had become a well-established collaborator with architects, particularly with SOM. The sculpture activated the ceiling, defined a wall, and connected the space between. It expressed new conceptions of and references to space, used industrial materials and techniques, and though rarely discussed in these terms, created an environment predicated by sculpture.

Calder created *Universe*, however, at a moment of profound historical and art historical rupture. Realized as midcentury became late century, the work resulted from thirty years of radical upheaval in American sculpture, shaped equally by radical changes in American architecture. Yet, even at the time the work was seen as something of a relic and anomaly. By the late postwar period, the focus had shifted to new conceptions of public art and monumental commissions—freestanding sculptures installed in plazas, fountains, and green spaces for both civic and corporate clients—while more vanguard sculptural practice moved into even more radical and expansive conceptions of the environment both inside and beyond gallery spaces. Calder, along with Harry Bertoia, Richard Lippold, and Isamu Noguchi, continued to make large-scale commissioned sculpture during this period, often in conjunction with the same architects they had worked with over the preceding decades, but increasingly for outdoor sites. Lippold, for example, realized *Ad Astra* (1976) for the entrance of the National Air and Space Museum in Washington, DC. Bertoia created numerous sculptures and sculptural fountains, many with Edward Durell Stone and Minoru Yamasaki, until his death in 1978. Noguchi realized some of his best-known outdoor sculpture, playgrounds, parks, and garden spaces well into the 1980s.

Public art, especially as it relates to sculpture, is a complex term, and, as art historian Nicholas Hartigan suggests, the history of its transformation into "a veritable industry" during the last third of the twentieth century in the United States is in dire need of new scholarly analysis, yet it lies outside the scope of the current study. Germane to this study's discussion, however, is how by the 1970s, the widescale efforts to bring together art and architecture seemed to have largely dissipated—or at least the parameters and motivations of such cross-disciplinary exchanges had significantly changed. There may have been a continued emphasis on increasing public access to art and a desire to fortify corporate or civic identity through art, but as art historian Joan Marter notes, commissioned sculpture in this latter context "no longer served as ornamentation for architecture. The stark and simplified geometry of modern architectural design was best complemented by large-scale works which were separate from the surrounding buildings."[3] Artwork was still created in conjunction with the construction of new architectural projects, often mandated by new percent-for-art programs, but the purpose and function of sculpture in the public sphere had again shifted.

Calder's later-commissioned works—like *Universe* (1974) at Sears Tower, Chicago; *Eléments démontables* (1975), created for the Fourth Financial Bank and Trust Company Building in Wichita, Kansas; and *Mountains and Clouds* (1976/86) installed posthumously at the Philip A. Hart Senate Office Building in Washington, DC—offer a particularly useful framework through which to consider how the relationship between art and architecture changed at the end of the postwar period. They also illuminate the shared contemporary challenges and significant threats currently faced by the majority of the large-scale commissioned sculptures created during the three decades post World War II. In 2017, after nearly fifty years in Chicago and in the midst of a designated Year of Public Art, *Universe* was removed from the location for which it was created—the lobby of what was Sears Tower and is now, at least officially, referred to as Willis Tower—as part of a $500 million renovation of the building by its new owners. The sculpture had not been included in the building's sale and remains in limbo due to a legal dispute between the previous owners of the building and Sears Holdings Corporation. The new lobby redesign did not include the sculpture, and there are no current plans to reinstall *Universe*. For now, the sculpture is being stored at an undisclosed "fine arts handling company," and its future remains uncertain.[4]

In 2017, the advocacy group Preservation Chicago identified "20th Century Public Art" as one of the city's seven most threatened sites and included *Universe* in its group of vulnerable artworks. Even in well-meaning examples like this, however, the association with a catchall category like public art also speaks to a deeply engrained misunderstanding of how sculpture did and can function with and in architecture, a misperception that had already started to take root by the mid-1970s. By the end of the postwar period, there was a concerted move away from a collaborative, structural approach to commissioning sculpture for architectural projects. What replaced such practices was a more conventional and arguably easier method: commissioning or selecting large-scale sculptures from artists who contributed or offered works that were neither particularly concerned with responding to a specific architectural context nor to the sociopolitics of the site. The long-term result has been a change in attitude that broadly sees art in public spaces as temporary, far more attentive to site and community, and in the case of private projects, secondary to the demands of commercial developments.

The profusion and confusion of public art, in both theory and practice, has led to an overall lack of understanding or appreciation of how commissioned interior, building-specific sculptures—in which form and structure become inextricable from the surrounding architecture—function and why their presence still matters. Large-scale sculptures from the immediate postwar period have, in recent years, been subjected to significant alterations, unfortunate relocations, and outright amputations—circumstances that will no doubt continue to occur. As commissions by Bertoia, Calder, Lippold, and Noguchi were so structurally and conceptually tied to their architectural contexts, they are particularly susceptible to the changing tastes of both art and architecture, especially at a moment when many midcentury modernist buildings are eligible for landmark designation but are being increasingly modified or destroyed. Such modifications produce more than just nostalgic loss or even physical evictions. These actions also sever connective threads and reshape the built environment, past and present. Both sculpture and architecture suffer as a result.

Calder at the End of Midcentury

In 1976, the year Calder died, the Whitney Museum of American Art designated him their bicentennial artist. The museum mounted a massive retrospective exhibition, *Calder's Universe*, which included two hundred works of art, divided into seventeen categories. Accompanied by an even more comprehensive catalogue, the exhibition eventually traveled to fifteen venues across the United States and Japan through 1980. The last decade of Calder's life had seen the realization of his most notable large-scale sculptures created for public or semipublic sites—as well as some of his most disparaged or overlooked projects. While Calder's late commissions share a similar formal vocabulary with his earlier mobiles and stabiles, they also required the artist to experiment and deploy new materials and engineering solutions as the size of his projects increased. The resulting monumental sculptures engaged the surrounding space in very different ways.

Almost all of Calder's large-scale commissions from the mid-1960s onward came from corporate or civic patrons. His biomorphic but wholly abstract constructions were sufficiently modern without being controversial and came with the attention befitting an artist of Calder's well-established reputation. Though many of these later sculptures were painted black, he also drew on his early interest in bold colors to create further visual impact, often selecting a vibrant red as a contrast to imposing black and dark-brown architectural exteriors. Regardless of the color palette, however, his arching monumental works dynamically complemented the hard-edged constancy of modernist buildings. Calder's *La Grande Vitesse* (1969), a large, bright-red stabile sculpture commissioned for the Vandenberg Center Plaza in Grand Rapids, Michigan, is one of the earliest and most important examples of public art to emerge from this period and is a perfect demonstration of his approach to such projects (figure E.3).

La Grande Vitesse became part of the official logo of the City of Grand Rapids. The sculpture graces the city's stationary, and continues to appear in numerous signage, advertisements, and tourist campaigns for the area. It was the first sculpture to be funded by the National Endowment for the Arts (NEA)'s Art in Public Places program and was commissioned in 1967 as part of a broader urban renewal project for downtown Grand Rapids. Initially, *La Grande Vitesse* was met with resistance. The sculpture would replace a previously straightforward plan that called for the installation of a fountain and reflecting pool. There was also the issue of the work's modern, abstract form, as well as the unease felt at the time by some in the community over Calder living and working predominantly in France, not the United States. The city, however, raised $83,000 and along with the grant from the NEA the commanding sculpture was formally dedicated to much fanfare in June 1969.

Large-scale stabiles like *La Grande Vitesse*, as Joan Marter argues, became something of a "status symbol," serving as a kind of prestige shorthand for a cultured, committed public patronage for the commissioning municipal governments or corporations. She asserts that Calder's works were both visually appealing abstractions but were not so avant-garde or radical that they would either ruffle too many feathers or look outmoded within a couple of decades. This is certainly the case with both *La Grande Vitesse* and *Flamingo*, the work many critics and historians view as Calder's most effective and aesthetically successful public projects.

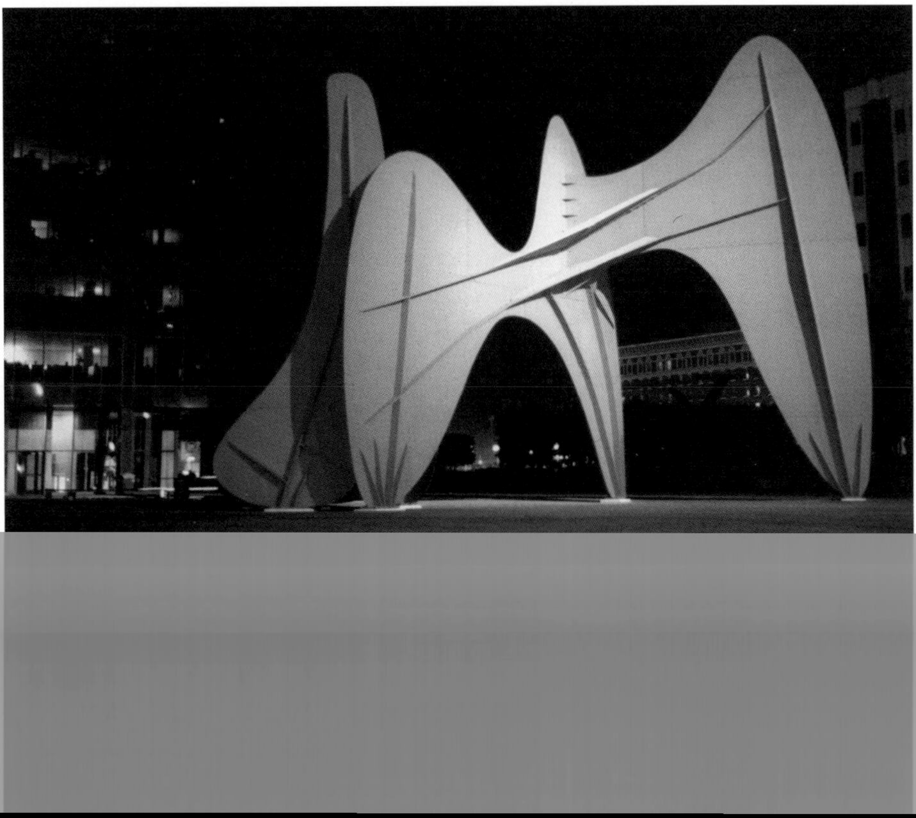

E.3
Alexander Calder, *La Grande Vitesse*, 1969. Sheet metal, bolts, and paint, 516 in. × 660 in. × 300 in. Vandenberg Center Plaza, Grand Rapids,

In the years since their installation, however, the standard art historical narrative that emerged around Calder's late stabiles has been one of disdain or dismissal.[5]

None of Calder's commissioned work adheres to the definition of site specificity as it came to be defined later in the twentieth century, and many of these pieces formally read as enlarged versions of his more autonomous, smaller-scaled sculptures. By the mid-1960s, there was also the issue of Calder's public persona. As art historian Wayne Andersen wrote, "[Calder] tends to be uncritical of his work; by personal behavior he supports an image of himself as an easygoing, overgrown child, something of a circus clown himself, with a fascination for clever stunts and, more recently, for great big sculptures to be held in awe." As Calder's work increased, so did the scrutiny around his more hands-on approach to fabrication, and what the American sculptor Richard Serra referred to as their status as "plop" sculpture.[6]

Coined by architect James Wines, who is also responsible for the phrase "turds on the plaza," "plop art," or "plop sculpture" referred to works in the public sphere that seemingly lacked site specificity or were simply preconceived, scaled-up versions of pieces found in museums or galleries that artists like Calder simply adapted and placed in civic spaces. As art historian Miwon Kwon notes, Calder often did not visit sites before creating a commissioned work, and as a "good modernist" believed in the artwork's autonomy. Kwon, like Marter, argues that Calder approached these commissions through the "logic of a logo," imparting a civic identity through the installation of a sculptural symbol. Calder's late work thus became emblematic of a ubiquitous, abstract modern sculpture that was in the best case, an aesthetically pleasing contrast to the regularity of International Style architecture and, at worst, a very public symbol of the rich and powerful that took nothing of the specific site or social context into consideration. In short, the critique of work like Calder's was that public sculpture had become too corporate, too aesthetically conservative, too establishment.[7]

Such criticisms became pronounced enough that by the early 1970s the NEA, for example, changed its guidelines for public art commissions. Whereas its original 1965 program was intended to support the work of noted individual artists and provide the opportunity for more people to see the best of American contemporary art, by 1974, the emphasis shifted to the proposed work's public engagement, to its appropriateness in relation to the site. Today, the success of a public work of art is largely determined by how well it attends to the specifics of site and engages the various constituencies, communities, and layers of history connected to it. Within this understanding of public sculpture's purpose, Calder's large-scale sculpture is indeed deficient, but this perspective also oversimplifies and misinterprets his intentions and the conditions in which he made these works.[8]

While the criticisms lodged at Calder and postwar public sculpture more broadly are valid and understandable, they overlook the positive, collaborative relationships many artists still cultivated with both architects and fabricators. They also minimize the careful consideration artists like Calder brought to each commission. Calder made models and maquettes for almost all of his large-scale commissions, and as a trained engineer, was very capable of dealing with structural issues or solving technical problems. While most of his large-scale sculptures are not reliant on the specifics of their particular site to function aesthetically or conceptually, he used photographs and architectural plans in order to understand where and how they would be sited, and took the location of the work into consideration when determining its form. While Calder may have advanced a different, less site-specific notion of public art than the one practiced today, his work from the later postwar period remained deeply informed by the approach he had helped pioneer during the 1940s and '50s.

In addition to his large-scale commissions for outdoor sites, Calder also created a handful of monumental mobiles during the last decade of his life, and these works, even more than the stabiles, suggest a strong link between his works of the immediate and later postwar periods. Their floating forms intrinsically deny a "plopped down" reading. Although the large mobiles have been even more critically dismissed or overlooked than the plaza sculptures, they similarly offered a well-suited, dynamic contrast to the often-severe, metal and glass sites of modernist architecture. Even larger than the mobiles he realized for the Terrace Plaza Hotel in Cincinnati or Idlewild Airport in New York the late 1940s and '50s, Calder's late mobiles continued to advance ideas of how sculpture could function in the built environment and question what constituted public art. These works, like his earlier projects, did not impede pedestrian traffic or access, but activated what normally might be dead space in the upper areas of building atriums. Calder's large-scale mobiles reached beyond their physical dimensions, implicating and altering the sites for which they were commissioned; and it is how well they accomplish this extension, how well they do or do not work in conversation with architecture, that should determine their perceived success.

Calder's later large-scale mobiles may not have been the result of the same close collaboration or alloyed mindset as earlier commissions, but this does not mean they were abject failures or insignificant objects. Rather, they were multifaceted experiments, realized as sculptural objects and architectural interventions with varying degrees of success. Calder's largest mobile, *White Cascade* (1976)—over one hundred feet from top to bottom and sixty feet across at its widest point—illustrates the complexities of these later projects. Calder created the sculpture for the East Court of the Federal Reserve Bank of Philadelphia in conjunction with the Philadelphia Redevelopment Authority Percent for Art Program (figure E.4). The sculpture was dedicated in October 1976, just a few weeks before the artist's death. Its fourteen white-aluminum discs, ranging in diameter from three-and-a half to nearly thirteen feet, along with stainless-steel rods and an electric motor, weigh close to ten tons, and spin clockwise in the center of the vast atrium—almost imperceptibly despite its significant weight. The mobile is massive both in size and scale, an unavoidable object extending vertically throughout the space, and yet, in large part owing to the architecture

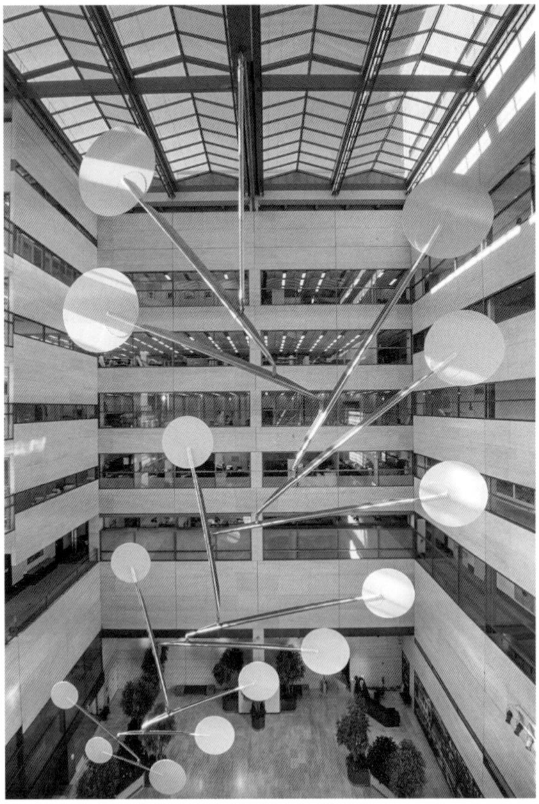

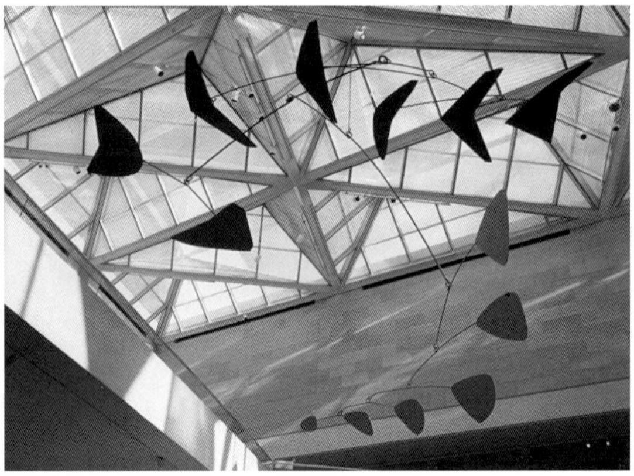

E.4
Alexander Calder, *White Cascade*, 1975. Sheet metal, rod, and paint, 110 ft. high. East Court, Federal Reserve Bank of Philadelphia, Pennsylvania.

E.5
Alexander Calder, *Untitled*, 1976. Aluminum, steel, and paint, 358 in. × 911 in. East Building, National Gallery of Art, Washington, DC. Architect: I. M. Pei. Gift of the Collectors Committee, 1977.76.1.

itself, the work feels heavy and trapped. Not helped by the choice to make the aluminum disks white, which absorb rather than contrast the muted tones of the building, the mobile is enclosed on all four sides, leaving no visual counterpoint to the work except the horizontal bands of windows. Extending downward from a reinforced beam spanning the length of the overhead glass ceiling, *White Cascade*, however, is visible from the ground level of the atrium and from the offices on the ascending floors, using its extensive physical reach to positive effect as it activates a large volume of space.

Similar issues can be seen in two large mobiles commissioned for buildings in Washington, DC that Calder did not live to see completed: *Untitled* (1976) at the National Gallery of Art (NGA), installed in 1977; and *Mountain and Clouds*, in the Philip A. Hart Senate Office Building, installed in 1986. Like *White Cascade*, Calder intended the NGA commission to include a motor, but owing to the use of more advanced, lighter-weight, hollowed aluminum components, the work instead moves slowly from the air currents alone (figure E.5). As he had done with previous projects, Calder drew inspiration from organic forms to develop the overall composition of the piece, and studied scale models of the site, in this case the NGA's new East Building designed by architect I. M. Pei. Like *White Cascade*, the NGA mobile is visible from multiple vantage points within the museum's tiered atrium. *Untitled*, however, operates more freely and was given more space to breathe, and the ways in which it complements and contrasts with its surrounding architecture are far more evident. The alternation of vertical and horizontal

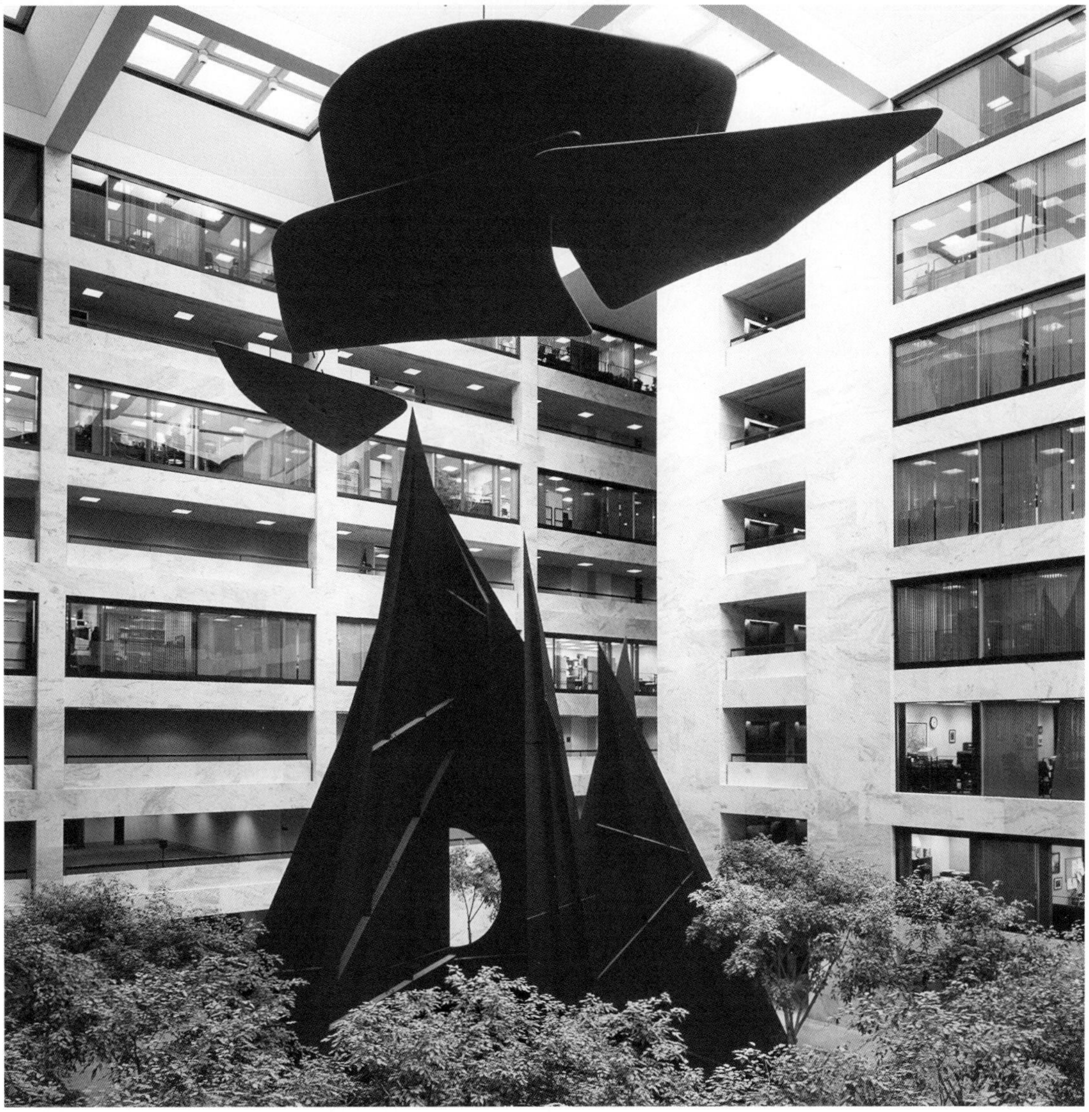

E.6
Alexander Calder, *Mountains and Clouds*, 1976/86. Sheet metal and paint, approx. 51 ft. × 42 ft. 6 in. Philip A. Hart Senate Building, Washington, DC. Architect: John Carl Warnecke and Associates. United States Senate. Gift of the Capitol Art Foundation, Inc.

orientations, the predominance of black and red, and the repetition of triangular and rounder wedge forms playfully echo Pei's design.[9]

Mountain and Clouds also activates multiple floors of an atrium space. However, it is one of the most unique large-scale Calder sculptures as it is his only monumental work to include both stabile and mobile elements (figure E.6). Commissioned for the Philip A. Hart Senate Building in 1975, the work comprises fifty-one-feet-tall "mountains" that rise up from the floor, and four aluminum "clouds" that span a total of seventy-five feet across and weigh thirty-nine tons. Calder specified both components be painted black as it "juxtaposes the sculpture with the rich shimmering qualities of the light marble architecture."[10] The mobile components originally rotated at a very slow speed as per Calder's design, but for years after their installation they were in a permanent state of stasis after a bearing broke.

Early in the design process for the Philip A. Hart Senate Building, the architects determined that the atrium would need to include a "sculptured work of art," and curators from the NGA and the Smithsonian Institution were tasked with identifying prospective artists for the project. While Calder eventually won out, the final shortlist also included Alexander Liberman, Lippold, Louise Nevelson, and George Rickey. These artists were selected because of their past work, their reputations, and the "contemporary nature of their designs," but also because of "their amenability to working with an architect in order to relate the artwork to the architecture, as well as having it stand on its own as separate work of art." As Calder had done numerous times over the past three decades, he created maquettes and plans for the sculpture, and met with the architects on the project, in this case the Architect of the Capitol and John Carl Warnecke and Associates, to discuss how his sculpture would relate to the specific space. The artist completed the design only days before his death in 1976, but the work itself was not fully installed until 1986 owing to budget cuts implemented during the construction of the building. The project was only completed due to the efforts of former senator Nicholas F. Brady, who believed the "proposed sculpture to be an integral part of the Hart Building design." He established the Capitol Art Foundation and raised the $650,000 needed to pay for the fabrication and installation of the piece.[11]

Though the "mountains" remain in the atrium, frequently appearing as a backdrop in televised interviews with senators on cable-news programs, *Mountains and Clouds* has suffered from unfortunate circumstances and continued bureaucratic issues. The mobile component was deinstalled in 2014, leading to, as Senator Chris Murphy stated, a work that is "not really a Calder in that it's not really doing what Calder wanted it to do." Calder was fearless when it came to creating work for architectural spaces that were themselves monumental, but responses from those who work in the building reveal a tension between sculpture and architecture. The senators described it as that "huge thing," which makes them "dizzy and crazy" and takes "up space." One of the more supportive responses to the current condition of the work, recognized the inherent difficulty of the atrium as a site for art: Senator Richard Blumenthal remarked, "I don't know how you could go down to the local art gallery and buy something to fit in there." Politicians are not necessarily the best arbiters of art or aesthetic considerations, but they, or at least their staff, are the individuals who use the space most often. Embedded in their comments is a tacit acknowledgement that for all of the ingenuity and drama of *Mountains and Clouds*, the sculpture itself might also be disproportioned, occupying or filling up rather than shaping the space of the Phillip A. Hart Building's atrium.[12]

Eléments démontables, one of Calder's last realized large mobiles and one of the least critically analyzed in his body of work, avoided some of the frictions of scale evident in his other late works (figure E.7). The sculpture combines many of the best aspects of Calder's previous projects, but in a manner unique to the circumstances of its commission—something perhaps fitting given that its title translates to removable or dismantled elements. Like *Mountains and Clouds*, it commands presence in a cavernous space. Like *White Cascade* in Philadelphia, Calder created a composition of circular discs of various scales attached to a series of connection beams. Like the *Untitled* mobile for the NGA, Calder utilized new materials and techniques to create a work that was not dependent on a motor to rotate, but rather slowly responded to the variable air currents of the space. Similar to *.125* (1957) at Idlewild Airport and so many of Calder's other sculptures, *Eléments démontables* exploited the effect of unflinching, sinuous curves and bold, primary colors.

The nearly fifty-feet-high mobile was, and remains, the focal point of the nine-story glass atrium at the heart of the Fourth Financial Bank and Trust Company Building, now known as the Bank of America Financial Center, in Wichita, Kansas. The project saw Calder again collaborate with SOM, and *Eléments démontables* certainly continued the tradition established by earlier postwar sculpture of contending with the hard edges of its surrounding architecture. The circular discs of the mobile provide a formal contrast to both the monolithic interior concrete pillars and the rigid horizontal and vertical steel beams. They evoke lollipops, tree branches, and the cycle of the sun—a chromatic correlation further emphasized when the setting sun streams in through the west-facing glass wall that encloses the atrium, casting its light on the red-and-yellow discs that transform into a radiating spectrum of warm colors. The diagonals of the beams are in dialogue with the angular, regular skylight panels and the work's gradated planes, each part connected to the next, mimicking the building's various levels—the

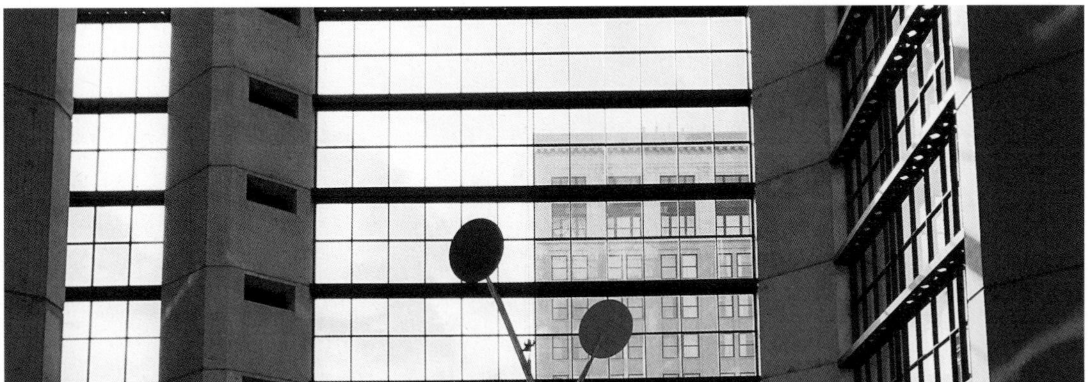

E.7
Alexander Calder, *Eléments démontables*, 1975. Sheet metal and paint, 47 ft. 5 1/5 in. × 26 ft. 8 3/4 in. Fourth Financial Bank and Trust Company Building (now Bank of America Financial Center), Wichita, Kansas. Architect:

E.8
Alexander Calder, *Eléments démontables*, 1975. Sheet metal and paint, 47 ft. 5 1/5 in. × 26 ft. 8 3/4 in. Fourth Financial Bank and Trust Company Building (now Bank of America Financial Center), Wichita, Kansas. Architect: Skidmore, Owings & Merrill (SOM).

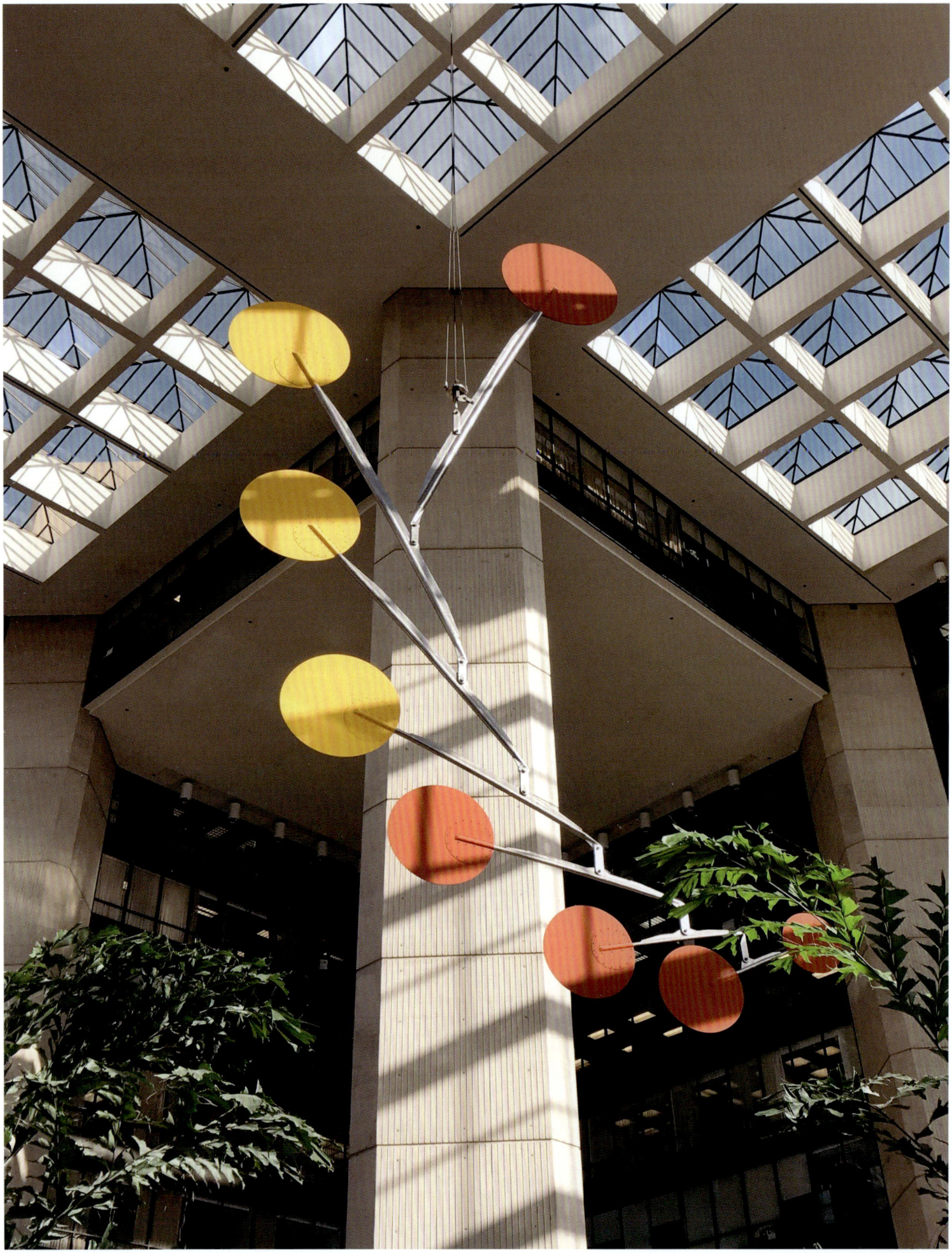

stairs to subterranean areas below, the escalators moving people to floors above, and the nine stories of offices that partially enclose the space around it.[13]

The upward curve of *Eléments démontables*, demarcated by the largest, reddest circular disc appear as a kind of visual crescendo at the topmost point of the mobile, punctuating the enormous open space (figure E.8). The work is an utmost example of architectural ornamentation, but it also pushes this notion further, suggesting that through its decorative function, sculpture can alter and draw attention to the architecture itself. Calder's mobile provides an aesthetically pleasing focal point or sense of joy and wonder to people who may happen to look up as they move through the interior space or pass by outside and see the sculpture through the facade. Through its very presence in that specific space, however, the sculpture also completes the architecture. *Eléments démontables* demonstrates how the absence of a thoughtful large-scale commissioned sculpture would fundamentally change the functionality and cohesiveness of the architectural design.

Calder's large-scale mobiles were not impervious to the criticism since lodged at his comparable stabile projects from the late postwar period, and in fact have been roundly dismissed as deficient in comparison to his smaller-scaled mobiles created earlier in the twentieth century. Monumental mobiles like *Eléments démontables*—with or without a motorized element—move far less than their earlier, more diminutive counterparts, their considerable weight and imposing size rendering the liveliness and dynamism of the kinetic, sculptural form, largely mute. Critic Jed Perl, for example, has described them as "a shift back to the clunkier, more ponderous forms of some of the earliest mobiles of the 1930s." Other criticisms have been succinctly summarized by Joan Marter who writes, "The late, oversized mobiles fabricated by ironworkers can only parody the graceful movements and compositional harmony of the earlier examples he constructed in the studio." Judging Calder's late mobiles through the same framework as his earlier works, however, misses the point. Though they share the same basic formal principles, *Eléments démontables* is not the mobile Marcel Duchamp first saw in Calder's studio in 1931, nor was it intended to be. It was created with a different purpose, meant to engage space and environment on a large-scale, in conjunction with architecture.[14]

Eléments démontables is also not just another big, unwieldy, or plopped-down sculpture. Calder never plagiarized himself or simply enlarged previous works. He created unique designs for each commission, making new models and maquettes, and was acutely aware of the unique spatial, engineering, and contextual features of each project. He might not have welded all of his commissioned works like Bertoia did or installed them by hand, piece by piece, as Lippold did, but they were still realized to his specifications. Colleagues like Noguchi often utilized a similar manner of outsourced fabrication during the postwar period, and this mode of making quickly became *de rigueur* in contemporary artistic practice more broadly. Further, Calder's large-scale works were created to live, to possess a presence and power within everyday space, not to gracefully move in a museum gallery.

Calder's late mobiles may not express an overt political message or engage with the very real social conditions present in the communities in which they were placed. There remains, however, something refreshingly radical about the seemingly simple but infinitely complex act of making something beautiful, of making something that changes, even if for a second, as one moves through the built environment. Jean-Paul Sartre wrote of Calder's sculpture, "Valéry said the sea is always beginning over again. One of Calder's objects is like the sea and equally spellbinding: always beginning over again, always new. A passing glance is not enough; you must live with it, be bewitched by it. Then the imagination revels in these pure, interchanging forms, at once free and rule-governed." This effect—not through energetic movement but through a similar shaping of space—is evident in both Calder's late mobiles and in his 1950s mobiles commissioned for lobbies and threshold spaces. Each large-scale mobile, on its own terms, invites those who temporarily share its atmosphere to revel in the "pure, interchanging forms," and its almost magical constancy in the face of an ever-changing world. [15]

Eviction and Preservation

The current status of projects like *Mountains and Clouds* or *Universe* are a reminder that both the art and architecture of the postwar period have reached a particular vulnerable moment. As sculptural objects commissioned for specific architectural spaces, the projects discussed in this book may have been created with an inherent sense of permanence, but such constancy and immovability has proved to be an illusion over the passage of more than half a century. Not only was the phenomenon of synergy between sculpture and architecture short-lived, but the resulting examples of such collaborations have become increasingly vulnerable to the changing tastes and rampant real-estate development of the twenty-first century. Whether at the moment of their creation or throughout their afterlives, large-scale sculpture commissions created by Bertoia, Calder, Lippold, and Noguchi have proven inextricably connected to the fates of the structures they inhabit, for better or worse. Synergy, after all, was predicated on the shared presence of both sculpture and architecture.

Modernist architecture, particularly that of the postwar period, finds itself at a crucial juncture and moment of critical reevaluation. In recent years, numerous regional, national, and international organizations have turned their attention to the preservation of modernist and midcentury modern architecture. The mission of Docomomo, which presently operates seventy-one chapters in Europe, North and South America, Australia, Asia, and Africa, for example, is "dedicated to the documentation and conservation of buildings, sites, and neighborhoods of the Modern Movement." Preservation advocacy groups in the United States alone, including Docomomo US, the National Trust for Historic Preservation, and Landmarks Illinois, to cite just three examples, produce annual lists of threatened sites that increasingly feature examples of architecture from the postwar period. The Cultural Landscape Foundation through its Landslide program maintains a list of at-risk landscape heritage sites, which includes urban gardens, plazas, and parks as well as works of art. In 2006, the World Monuments Fund, with founding sponsorship provided by Knoll, launched the Modernism at Risk initiative to draw attention to vulnerable modernist sites, support community engagement, and develop contemporary design solutions for preservation. [16]

While most buildings and sites created during the postwar period are now eligible to receive landmark status, having met the standard fifty-year mark, many remain unprotected or have only received partial landmark status, meaning that only parts of their structures—most commonly exteriors and facades rather than interiors—are protected. The Pan Am (now MetLife) Building and the entirety of Lincoln Center for the Performing Arts, in just New York City alone, are two examples of sites that perhaps surprisingly, given their status and impact, currently have no city, state, or National Register of Historic Places protection. As architectural historian Joan Ockman writes, "In the United States, the fact that modernism itself was responsible for the wholesale destruction of large swaths of the nation's earlier built heritage—a situation that produced such a sense of crisis by the early 1960s that the preservation movement was finally galvanized—has undoubtedly made the recent efforts to save modernist architecture paradoxical. Indeed, it is doubly difficult to mobilize citizens to save a patrimony they still regard with oedipal mistrust. The collapse of the World Trade Center in 2001 brought this love-hate relationship vividly to light, amid all the other feelings it elicited." News of potential demolitions or significant remodels of modernist structures, however, are now regular occurrences, and with the advent of social media and web platforms, are often met with swift and amplified outcry from practitioners, critics, preservationists, and historians, as well as the general public.[17]

The results of the ensuing public relations campaigns, however, have been mixed. For example, in early 2018, the current owners of 140 Broadway the skyscraper designed by Gordon Bunshaft for SOM and originally known as the Marine Midland Building (1964–67), announced plans to redesign the building's plaza in lower Manhattan. The plan, if enacted, would have significantly altered not only the outdoor space, but also Noguchi's large, askew *Red Cube* (1968), which had been created for the site in collaboration with the architect (figure E.9). The official rationale behind the changes was a desire to add more seating and plantings to "better activate the space," but as numerous news outlets reported, the changes had more to do with an attempt to deter food and other street vendors from the plaza. Because the site had been designated a New York City landmark in 2013, the plans had to be approved by the Landmarks Preservation Commission. Following the public's vocally unsupportive response to the proposed change, the group declined to grant permission. Three of the more recent high-profile preservationist failures—none of which involved significant works of commissioned sculpture—resulted in monumental change: the total redesign of Edward Durell Stone's 1964 building at 2 Columbus Circle, New York City in 2006; and the demolition of both Bertrand Goldberg's 1975 Prentice Women's Hospital Building in

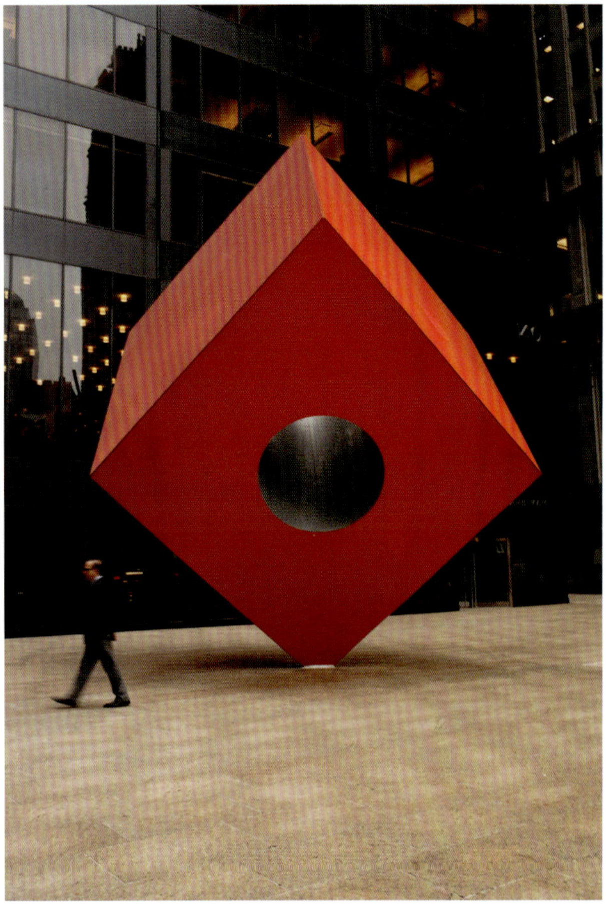

E.9
Isamu Noguchi, *Red Cube*, 1968. Steel and paint, 140 Broadway (formerly Marine Midland Building), New York City, 2010. Architect: Skidmore, Owings & Merrill (SOM).

Chicago in 2013 (figure E.10), and the 1960 Bunshaft and Natalie de Blois–designed SOM skyscraper at 270 Park Avenue, New York City, formerly known as the Union Carbide Building, in 2020.[18]

Art commissioned for modernist architecture, even sculptural projects conceived in close collaboration with the architect and/or clients, have suffered a similarly mixed fate. Only four of the projects from the immediate postwar period discussed, at length, in this book have undergone little to no changes, beyond cleaning or minor conservation, to either the sculpture or its surrounding architecture: Bertoia's 1953 screen for Eero Saarinen's GM Technical Center; Bertoia's reredos for Saarinen's MIT Chapel (Kresge Chapel) (1955); Lippold's *Flight* (1963) for the Gropius and Pietro Belluschi-helmed Pan Am Building; and Lippold's *Gemini II* (1965) for Jesse H. Jones Hall in Houston. All four sculptures remain *in situ*, properly preserved, maintained, and structurally functioning as they were originally intended. *Gemini II* continues to greet visitors on their way to a performance or moving through the lobby in Houston (figure 1.39). The General Motors Technical Center (GMTC) was named a National Historic Landmark by the US Department of the Interior and the National Park Service in 2014, and while still an active workplace, General Motors continues to renovate and maintain the entirety of the campus, including Bertoia's 1953 sculpture (figure 2.23).

The Massachusetts Institute of Technology has similarly put great effort into maintaining Saarinen's architectural contributions to its campus, which

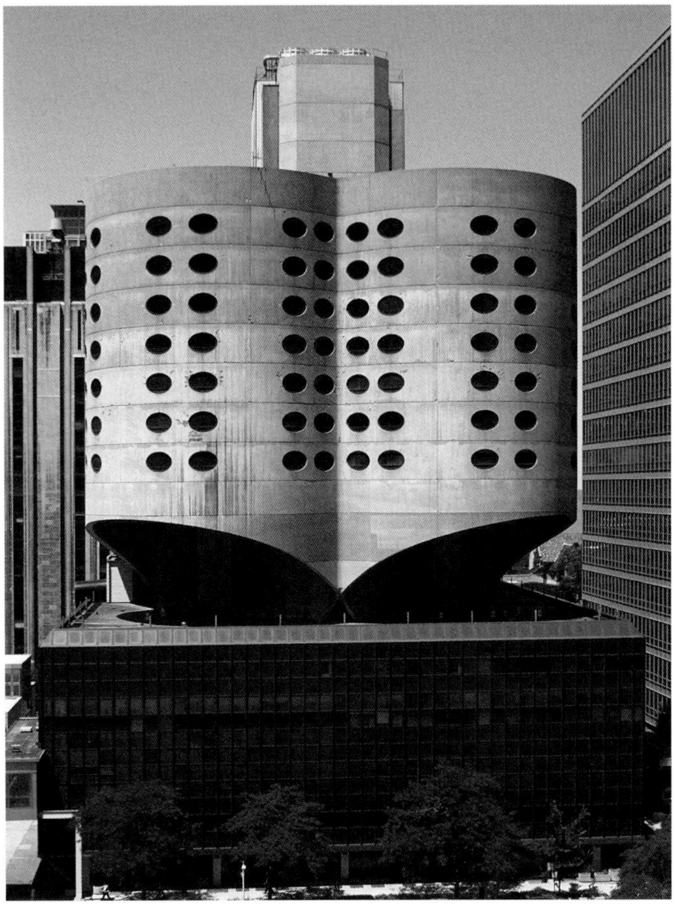

E.10
Prentice Women's Hospital, Chicago, 1975 (now destroyed, photo 2012). Architect: Bertrand Goldberg.

includes caring for Bertoia's 1955 MIT Chapel sculpture (figure 3.13). In 2015, the MIT Chapel was renovated and renewed as part of MIT's capital projects campaign. Led by the Boston-based architectural firm EYP, the project involved rebuilding the moat to prevent water leakage, restoring the stained-glass walls in the vestibule leading into the chapel, repairs to the roof, replacing the HVAC system, and upgrading or renewing various features and fixtures. The renovation received the Cambridge Historical Commission Preservation Award the following year. Bertoia's sculpture is now managed by the MIT List Visual Art Center as part of its public art collection. A condition report from 2003, done at the time of the piece's first substantive cleaning since its completion, noted that grime and dirt, as well as rust and yellowing of the nickel alloy, covered much of the piece. This was a result of both the climatic conditions of a frequently used chapel and the "electrolytic corrosion" caused by the plating and "juxtaposition of dissimilar metals." The artist's son, Val Bertoia, noted that Bertoia abandoned the technique of applying nickel welding rods over steel soon after this project because of the subsequent tendency of the steel to rust. The material complications of the piece were not limited to metallurgical issues, but also to the formal structure of the work—essentially a dust and dirt magnet that is tremendously difficult to clean.[19]

Less than ten years after Bertoia installed the work, Herbert L. Beckwith, an architect and MIT professor who had worked on the Saarinen complex, wrote a memo to the manager of the Kresge Auditorium noting that the "sculptural screen in the Chapel has lost its luminous luster and we believe because it has accumulated several years of Cambridge dust." Following the 2003 cleaning, there was actually some concern—understandable in light of recent botched art restorations—over how altered the work appeared as its surface looked far more brilliant than people had become accustomed to seeing it over the past fifty years. Conservation and continued care are issues for any work, whether sculptural or architectural, but the material and formal specificities of Bertoia's large-scale projects like the screen for the MIT Chapel speak to the synergy between sculpture and architecture in ways that continue to reverberate today. The screen was made for that specific site, to hang behind that altar, and as long as the chapel stands, MIT will not allow the work to travel or be moved from that space, not even for cleaning or restoration.[20]

The architecture of the Pan Am Building perhaps does not elicit the same reverence as Saarinen's structures now do, but, while not landmarked, the skyscraper does continue to stand close to its original form—just with a different name on its facade: MetLife. In 2000, Josef Albers's mural over the gateway to Grand Central Station was removed and placed in storage. Though the new owners of the building decided to return the mural to its original site in 2005, asbestos was discovered behind the original panels. However, using Albers's original drawings in consultation with the Albers Foundation, the mural was recreated and reinstalled in 2019. Lippold's sculpture and the Vanderbilt Avenue Lobby, however, have essentially remained untouched—save for new retailers periodically coming into the space (figure 3.20). *Flight* (1963) is still in excellent condition and while its wires, like Bertoia's metal screens, unavoidably catch copious amounts of dust, the sculpture has been regularly maintained and cleaned.[21]

A testament no doubt to his thoughtful, committed consideration of how his sculptures would synergize with architecture, the majority of Lippold's commissioned pieces have fared well and are still *in situ*, though many have undergone at least some level of modification to either sculpture or site. The Inland Steel Building was designated a Chicago landmark in 1998, and though ownership of the property has changed hands multiple times, often bringing enhancements or minor renovations to the structure, the lobby and *Radiant I* (1958) have remained largely unchanged (figure 3.5). At some point, however, the red enamel on some of the wires was removed. There is no record of why this occurred, likely unintentionally caused during a cleaning. Beyond this modification, the only other change to significantly affect the status of the sculpture in the lobby has been more recent additions of other sculptural elements—neither of which are necessarily permanent nor structurally a part of the space.

Anish Kapoor's *Blood Mirror* (2010) was installed on the wall in between the elevator banks, and while within eyesight of *Radiant I*, it reflects the sculpture in a manner that creates a dynamic, complementary dialogue between the two works. The bigger alteration to the lobby has come in the form of a massive, jagged, green-tinted glass desk, used by building security and designed by Frank Gehry,

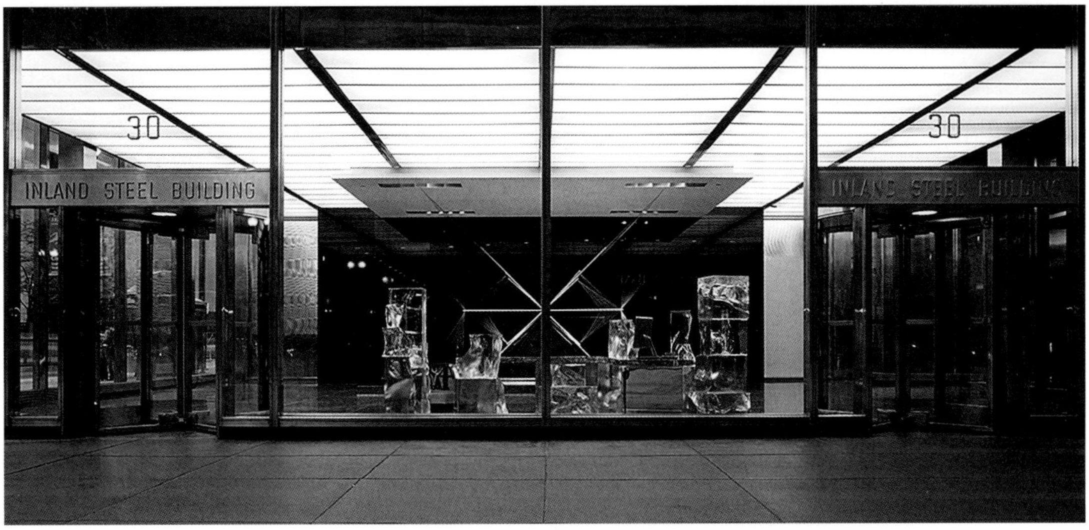

E.11
Lobby, Inland Steel Building, 30 West Monroe Street, Chicago. Architect: Skidmore, Owings & Merrill (SOM).

who was part of an investment group that purchased the Inland Steel Building in 2005. Informally called "Icehenge," the desk sits directly across from *Radiant I*, in between the two main revolving doors (figure E.11). Architecture critic Blair Kamin writes that the U-shaped desk is "best described as a piece of furniture that's been elevated to art, or is simply an emblem of excess." While acknowledging the visual excitement and expression of "Gehry's trademark sculptural brio," Kamin continued, "there's something disturbing about its lack of refinement, a series of careless details that give the impression that it was arranged with too little regard for the distinctive character of the lobby in which it sits." Additions to the architectural space of the Inland Steel lobby have altered the sightlines and spatial relations of *Radiant I*, but its environment has not been changed nearly as much as that of Lippold's hanging sculptures in the Seagram Building.[22]

On July 16, 2016, the celebrated Four Seasons Restaurant permanently closed. Ten days later, thousands of items from its elegant midcentury modern interior were auctioned off by Wright, from mundane ashtrays and ice buckets to tableware and furniture designed by Ada Louise and Garth Huxtable, Florence Knoll, Eero Saarinen, Philip Johnson, and Mies van der Rohe. The overall building, including the interior spaces of the restaurant had been landmarked after an arduous and contentious process during the 1990s, and because of this status, Lippold's 1959 sculpture along with the anodized-aluminum curtains by Marie Nichols, the walnut-paneled walls, and bronze-railed staircases, were saved from the sale (figure P.1). Almost everything else around the sculpture, however, has changed. In 2017, the restaurant spaces reopened, christened THE GRILL and THE POOL and while Lippold's sculpture still hangs over a bar and dining seating, the interior design around it has been radically altered. Some efforts were made to honor the midcentury history of the space, including the choices of new artworks like Calder's *3 Segments* (1973), which was purchased for THE POOL, the main dining space. The large black mobile, however, looks overscaled hanging above the iconic pool, and was installed only after the equally iconic surrounding ficus trees and planters had been permanently removed.[23]

Just three blocks west, similar real-estate upheavals and uncertainties have drastically altered Noguchi's 1956–57 ceiling and wall at 666 Fifth Avenue (figures 2.36, 2.37). The lobby and arcade were transformed during significant renovations to the building in the late 1990s, when the corridor to Fifth Avenue was closed to make space for more retail. The marble walls and floors were removed, and the midblock passage enclosed and reconfigured. The Isamu Noguchi Foundation offered to assist in the conservation of the ceiling, stating that rather than destroying the component, they believed that it could be "modernized with more efficient lamps, electronic ballasts, vinyl ceiling panels, and wider spacing of the lamps." The status of the commission, however, has remained precarious ever since. Largely neglected through the 2018 sale of the building by Kushner Companies to Brookfield Properties, and still not under any landmark protection, the work was finally removed in late 2020. The new owners donated the components of Noguchi's commission to the Isamu Noguchi Foundation and Garden Museum, and perhaps it will one day be reinstalled or find a new home, but the work has effectively been destroyed.[24]

Noguchi's earlier ceiling commission, for the American Stove Company Building in St. Louis, Missouri, has been subjected to a similarly tumultuous afterlife, though one with a far more heartening outcome—at least for supporters of midcentury modern art and architecture (figure 1.13). Like the commission at 666 Fifth Avenue, Noguchi's ceiling for the American Stove Company Building has contended with significant architectural changes. For years, the work was largely forgotten and hidden from public view on account of a drop ceiling and partitions installed by the current owner, U-Haul, during a significant renovation in the early 1990s. The shipping and storage company acquired the building in 1977, after sitting vacant for well over a decade having been used by the Teamsters Union as a healthcare facility. Though U-Haul had previously been involved in a protracted preservationist lawsuit with the City of St. Louis and the Heritage and Urban Design Commission Agency, by the early twenty-first century the company became committed to adaptive reuse projects. In 2015, U-Haul executive Steve Langford helped to uncover the ceiling. The company now encourages the public to come and again view the sculpture in the showroom—now filled with signage, packing tape, boxes, and cash registers rather than stoves (figure E.12).[25]

Many of Bertoia's projects have fared better than Noguchi's, even in the midst of substantive architectural changes. His 1962 spill-cast bronze wall at Dulles International Airport in Chantilly, Virginia, was temporarily removed during a large-scale renovation of the airport between 1997 and 2014 (figure 2.6). The sculpture, however, was reinstalled in 2012, only inches from its original location. New advertisements are now visible below the sculpture, and the café originally on the other side of Bertoia's wall is no longer there. The most significant change, however, has been the general flow of passengers through the concourse. The commission structurally functions the same as it always has, but few people now have reason or occasion to walk by it.

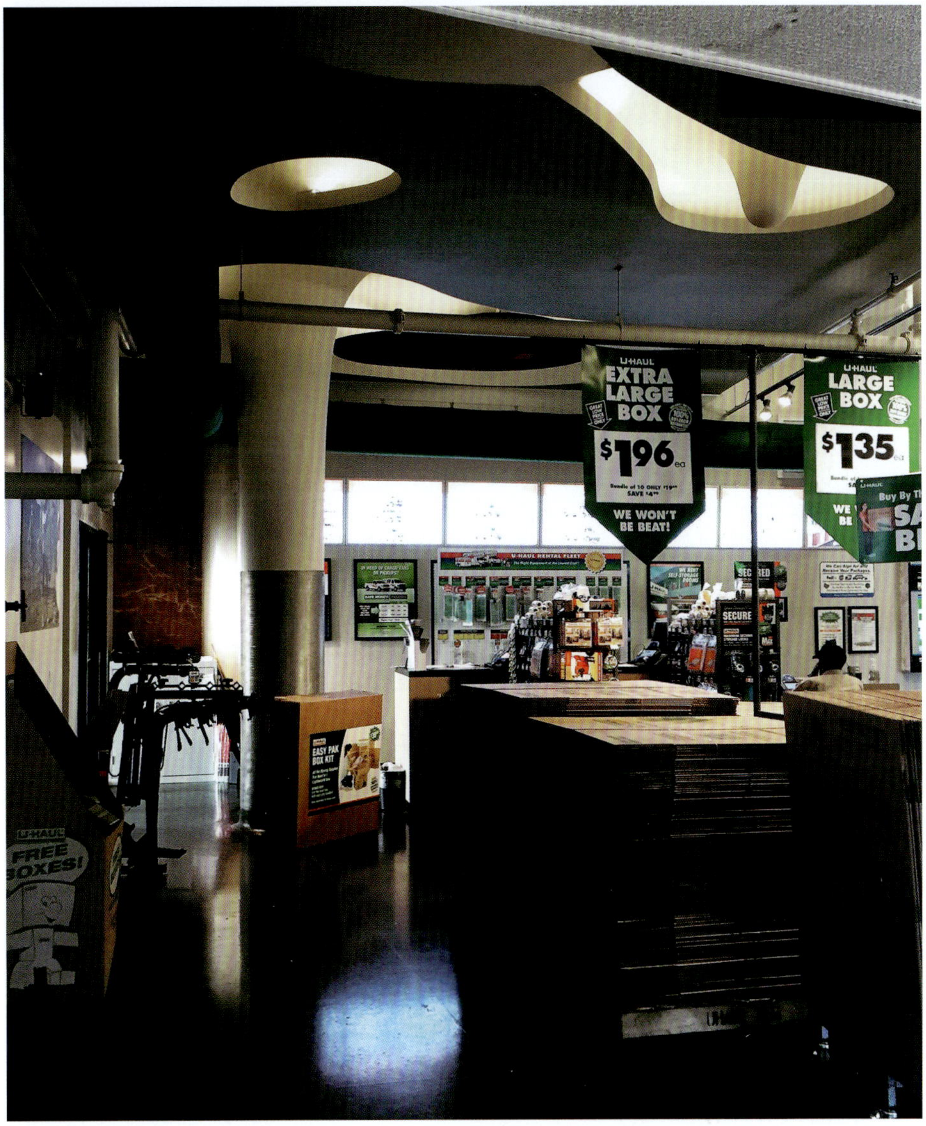

E.12
Isamu Noguchi, *Ceiling for Magic Chef Building*, 1948. Interior design with plaster, colored glass, and electric components, dimensions variable. U-Haul Storage (formerly American Stove Company Building), 1641 South Kingshighway Boulevard, St. Louis, Missouri, 2016.

Bertoia's 1956 "Golden Trees" also still grow at Southdale Center in Edina, Minnesota, underscoring the fact that all of the projects anchored to ceilings and floors discussed in this book remain *in situ* at their original sites (figure 3.3). At the mall in Edina, however, Dayton's is long gone as is almost every trace of Victor Gruen's 1956 verdant Garden Court, with its open-air cafés, fountains, live plants, and bespoke lighting (figure E.13). The overall architecture of Southdale has also seen multiple modifications at the hands of various management companies over the past five decades. In the 1980s, for example, new management reduced the size of the court and narrowed the aisles surrounding it. Now Bertoia's sculptures are surrounded by chain-food kiosks, vending machines, garbage cans, free-standing advertisements, and loud, gaudy signage: lone trees in a now desolate landscape. The work remains a striking feature and this is certainly not the only example of a commission existing in an overtly commercial space, even one modernized over the subsequent decades. In the case of Southdale, however, so much of what and how that space was intended to be experienced has been diminished

E.13
Harry Bertoia, *Untitled*, 1956. Bronze-coated steel, h. 45 ft. each. Southdale Center, Edina, Minnesota, 2016. Architect: Victor Gruen Associates.

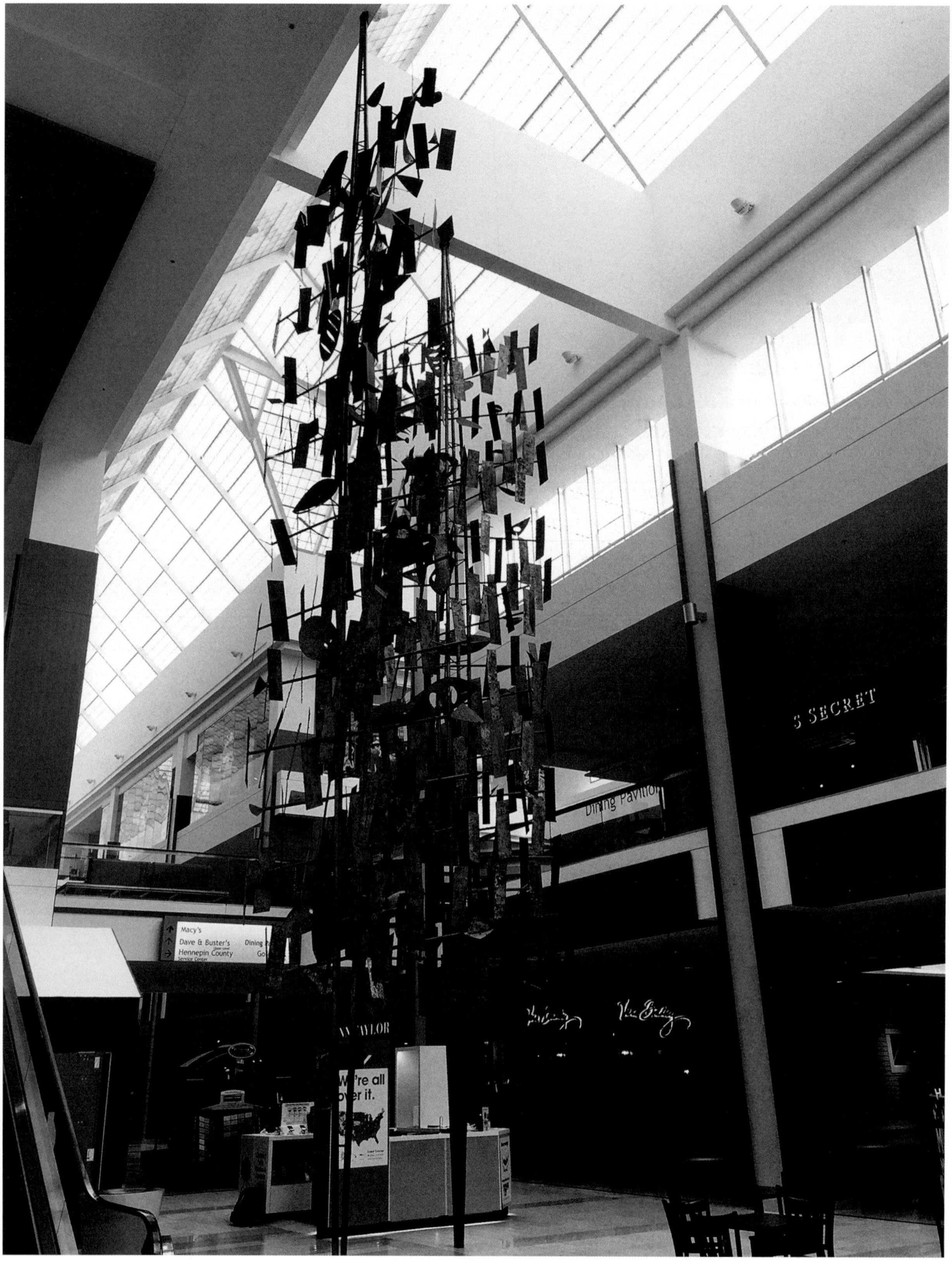

and dulled, much like the surface of the sculpture, which now possess a semimatte dark-bronze patina.[26]

Bertoia's 1954 screen and hanging sculpture for the Manufacturers Trust Company Building at 510 Fifth Avenue, New York City is one of the more turbulent examples of a commissioned sculpture that rather miraculously is still *in situ* (figures 2.26, 2.28). The exterior of the building received landmark status in 1997 but not the interior. By 2000, after various mergers and sales, Manufacturers Hanover Trust, the building at 510 Fifth Avenue, and its contents ended up in the possession of JPMorgan Chase. JPMorgan Chase sold the building in 2010 and when they closed its branch at the location, the bank decided to remove Bertoia's sculptures from the site since the interior of the building did not hold the same protection. The decision proved prescient as the new owners of the property, Vornado Realty Trust, decided to modify the two ground floors of the building to add more space for retail—a goal that came under scrutiny when the interior finally became landmarked in 2011. Vornado hired SOM to complete an "adaptive reuse" renovation, receiving permission to cut new doorways into the facade on Fifth Avenue; and, in what proved the most controversial alteration, repositioned the escalators leading up to what used to be the main banking floor. In 2012, after years of legal wrangling, real-estate transactions, and preservationist debates, Vornado and Chase reached an agreement to reinstall Bertoia's sculpture, with the former shouldering all of the conservation and reinstallation costs, and the latter agreeing to a permanent loan from the Chase collection as long as the interior remains a landmark-protected space.[27]

Even with SOM's structural changes to 510 Fifth Avenue, which resulted in the reinstallation of Bertoia's screen in a slightly different position on the second floor, both sculptures remain at home within the surrounding architecture, drawing from and adding to it. The first tenant following the renovation, Canadian low-cost clothing retailer Joe Fresh, committed a tremendous number of resources—and received a good deal of publicity in return—for making the screen a feature of their store. The company even produced a short film of the process, which played beside the work in the store on a small video monitor and remains accessible online.[28]

No longer dividing a banking floor, Bertoia's multiplane screen now separates a row of cash registers and dressing rooms, even though the lease has since changed over to the North Face (figure E.14). As David W. Dunlap wrote in the *New York Times*, "Purists might complain—not without reason—that the sculpture was reinstalled as a wall rather than as a screen, and that its subtleties can be overwhelmed by the profusion of vibrant merchandise and the incessant shopping soundtrack music.... A case can be made, however, that the retail trappings have liberated a sense of playful abandon from deep within the sculpture."[29] Bertoia's commission indeed looks different today than it did when initially installed, both concealing old qualities and bringing out unexpected ones.

New trappings can breathe new life into old architecture and sculpture or stifle or suffocate them. Calder's *.125* at Idlewild Airport, Queens, New York is another example of a work that has remained, essentially in the same location, though in its case, any relationship, any synergy it had with the original architecture has been destroyed (figure 1.21). The mobile still hangs in a terminal at an international airport in Queens; however, the airport is now the John F. Kennedy International Airport and the building is now Terminal 4. By the mid-1990s, the original International Arrivals Building was deemed outdated and was demolished to make way for a new three-level facility designed again by SOM, the original building's designers. The firm decided to install Calder's *.125* on the upper departures level of the new structure. Hung from a ribbon of skylights on the curved ceiling, the sculpture is now squeezed-in between two banks of ticketing counters above stanchions where passengers wait in line.

Calder's mobile may have stayed in roughly the same geographic place, but for all intents and purposes, it had been evicted, severed from the architecture for which it was made. The work physically still exists, can still be seen and appreciated, but it no longer functions, at least not in the manner it was envisioned by the artist in collaboration with the architect. A similar turn of events has befallen Calder's mobile for the Terrace Plaza Hotel in Cincinnati (figure 1.7). When Conrad Hilton purchased the hotel in the late 1950s, *Twenty Leaves and an Apple* (1946), along with the Miró and Steinberg murals, were not included in the sale. After the hotel was subsequently and substantially remodeled in 1965, John J. Emery, on behalf of Thomas Emery's Sons, donated all three commissioned pieces to the Cincinnati Art Museum, where they still reside today.[30]

Bertoia's 1955 sculpture for the Dallas Public Library (DPL) and Costantino Nivola's 1954 sand relief for the New York City–Olivetti Showroom have likewise found new homes in different spaces (figures 1.41, 2.14). The latter was relocated

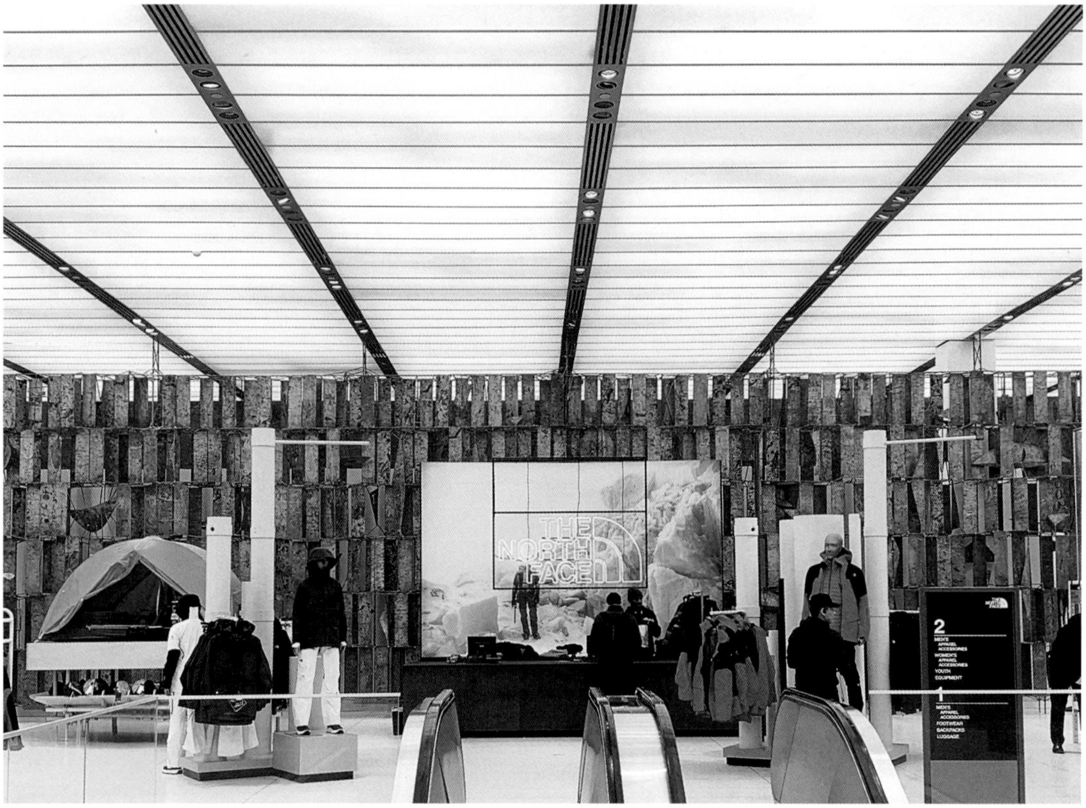

E.14
Harry Bertoia, *Untitled*, 1954. Brazed and welded metal, 16 ft. × 70 ft. × 2 ft. North Face Store, 510 Fifth Avenue (formerly Manufacturers Trust Building), New York City, 2019. Architect: Skidmore, Owings & Merrill (SOM).

in 1970 to the Josep Lluís Sert–designed Harvard University Science Center, in Cambridge, Massachusetts following the permanent closure of the Olivetti Showroom in New York. Nivola, with the assistance of Claire Nivola, his daughter, added color to the work and helped install it at Harvard in 1972. She and her son Anther Kiley further restored the relief in 2005. The move of Bertoia's DPL sculpture was similarly prompted by the closure of the original building. The old DPL building design by George Dahl shuttered in 1983, and shortly after the new J. Erik Jonsson Central Library opened. Fisher & Spillman Architects designed the new building to complement the inverted structure of the nearby I. M. Pei–designed Dallas City Hall, which had opened in late 1977 and prominently featured in its plaza Henry Moore's *Three Piece Sculpture: Vertebrae* (1978). Moore's sculpture, though installed twenty years after Bertoia's screen was first set up, it should be noted, still garnered public derision in Dallas for being too modern.[31]

At the time of its move to the new J. Erik Jonsson Central Library building, however, Bertoia's once defamed sculpture for the DPL had achieved an almost iconic status. The sculpture was reinstalled in a place of prominence in the main atrium, above an interior walkway visible from both directions. Bertoia's screen is near another midcentury bronze sculpture by Barbara Hepworth and other works of art (figure E.15). The sculpture continues to feature prominently in the promotional materials of the DPL and appears in guides to the "public art" of Dallas. This is, after all, how it was and continues to be seen—a fraught, public, cultural symbol of the city. Though poorly lit and not perfectly situated, the work now has the benefit of at least being seen as both a sculpture and a screen. Stretching out across the expanse of one of the entryways, the open design can be fully appreciated and operates closer to a screen, separating space as opposed to a sculpture hung against a wall. Bertoia, when told shortly before his death that the sculpture would be moving to the new J. Erik Jonsson Central Library building, was reportedly "delighted" to hear it would finally be installed in the manner closer to how he conceived it.[32]

Arguably the most egregious eviction of postwar sculpture commissioned for specific architectural projects, however, has been the disappearance of Lippold's *Orpheus and Apollo* (1962) from the Philharmonic Hall at Lincoln Center for the Performing Arts, New York City (figure 1.25). In 2014, the soaring sculpture, which had stretched across the expanse of the building's lobby, virtually unchanged since its installation in 1962, was quietly removed from the grand foyer of what is now called David Geffen Hall at Lincoln Center. The interior of the Philharmonic Hall, including Lippold's sculpture—as well as the entire Lincoln Center complex—does not possess landmark status, making it highly vulnerable to such alterations. In 2009, the architectural firm Diller Scofidio + Renfro completed a significant redesign of Lincoln Center's public spaces and the adjacent the Juilliard School, originally designed by Pietro Belluschi. The Philharmonic Hall alone has undergone numerous modifications and renovations since its opening, and with the transfer of naming rights to Avery Fisher Hall in 1973 and then to David Geffen

E.15
Harry Bertoia, *Untitled*, 1955. Brazed and welded copper, brass, and nickel alloys, 10 ft. × 24 ft. J. Erik Jonsson Central Library, Dallas, Texas, 2018. Architect: Fisher & Spillman Architects.

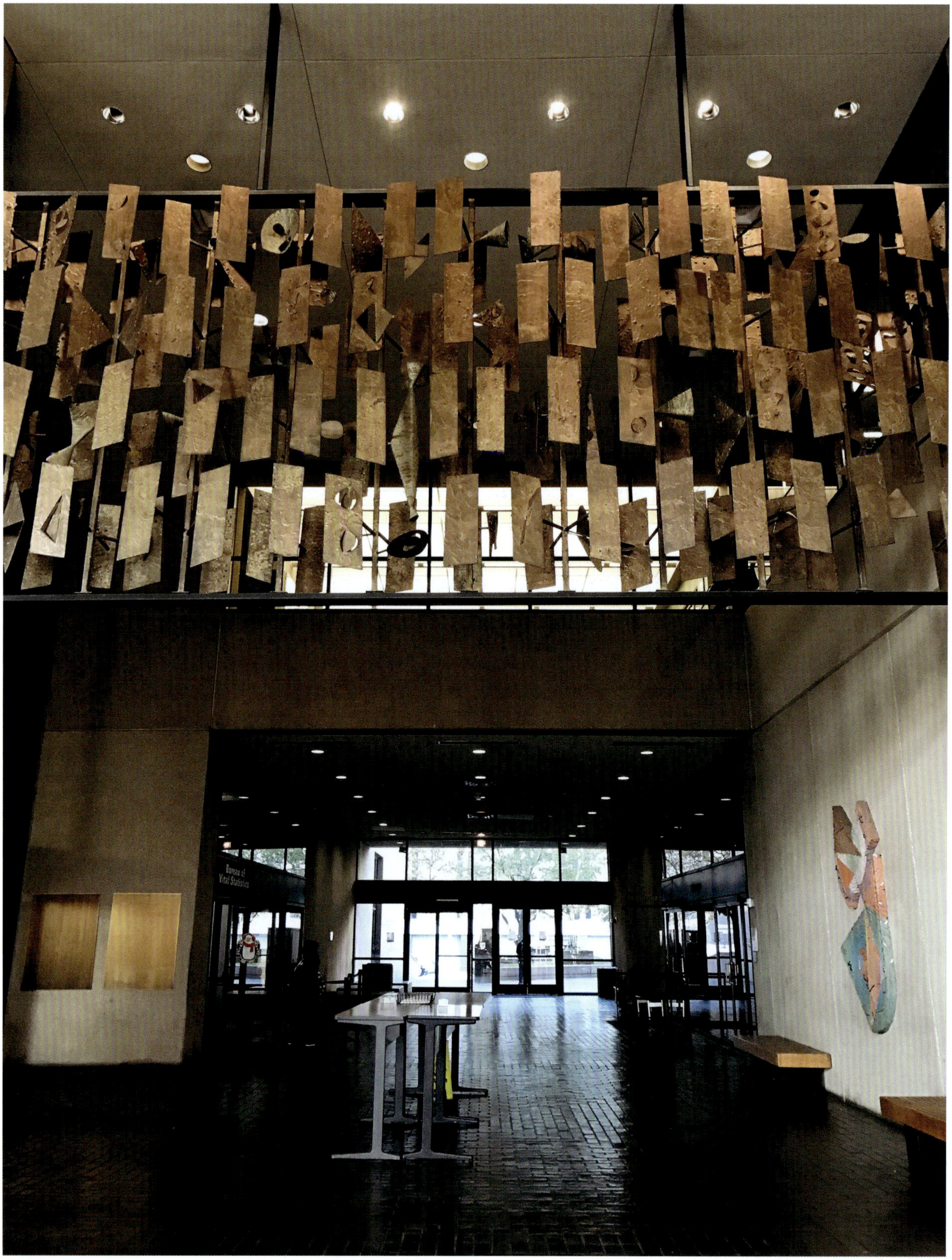

Hall in 2015, further calls for significant changes to the building have been slowed only by a lack of funds.[33]

There was little to no press attention given to the removal of *Orpheus and Apollo* until almost a year after the fact, and calls to Lincoln Center representatives suggested there were no immediate plans for reinstallation owing to uncertainty regarding a possible renovation of Max Abramovitz's building. In December 2019, the New York Philharmonic and Lincoln Center, however, announced plans for a $550 million renovation project that would focus on fixing the hall's acoustic issues. The plan noticeably made no mention of reinstalling Lippold's sculpture. The rationale for the 2014 removal had been that the work needed conservation and maintenance. Five years later, the reason changed to apparent safety concerns over how the sculpture was wired. In 2021, plans were announced for the reinstallation of *Orpheus and Apollo*—a sculpture that Abramovitz and Lippold both considered integral to the Philharmonic Hall's grand foyer—in the new Central Hall at La Guardia Airport in New York.[34]

The modification, transfer, removal, and outright destruction of commissioned large-scale sculptures from the structures for which they were made, bear tangible consequences beyond those related to historic preservation or simply the alteration of the built environment, past, present, or future. Such acts are more than just examples of clever adaptive reuse or straightforward physical evictions. They have had the long-term effect of obscuring the lessons and impact of a significant, if overlooked, moment in American art and architectural history. Further, these changes, whether minor or major, have severed connective threads—certainly, between sculpture and architecture but also, and perhaps more significantly, between art and the environment, between art and the public.

Writing in 1966, at the cusp of another cultural and political change within the American landscape, the noted art critic John Canaday took the enterprise of Lincoln Center to task, stating that it was a retrograde arts center where the elite went to experience "moribund art." While acknowledging the assured achievement of Lippold's "constellation of flying bronze slabs in the foyer of Philharmonic Hall" and declaring it would be a great loss if it was ever removed, Canaday asserted that Lincoln Center, and the overall inclusion of artworks across its campus, had come to serve as reminders that "art is not a natural part of our lives (else it would be more frequently a natural part of our architecture) but that, by gum, we can graft it on if we try." By 1996, the attempts to bridge sculpture and architecture that had flourished during the prior twenty years had proved fleeting and unsustainable. Examples of collaboration, of cross-disciplinary synergy did continue, though far less frequently and not as a concerted phenomenon. To examine this brief moment of alloying, however, is to realize its full and lasting impact on the developments of both sculpture and architecture. It altered the trajectories of both disciplines, even if this significant history has been obscured and continues to slowly be chipped away by scholarly omission, changing public tastes, and aggressive real-estate developers.[35]

In considering why large-scale sculpture commissioned for architectural projects during the postwar period was and remains important, the inclination is often to assert that such works are disadvantaged when they are removed from their original architectural environments or altered in any way. Indeed, this study is underpinned by the unequivocal contention that through such an approach, both sculpture and architecture were made better—stronger—through their material combination: a quality inherently invalidated by physical extrication. As Lippold warned in reference to *Orpheus and Apollo* and *Flight*, "I hope both these projects will find themselves at home with the architecture and that it will find them natural to it. If they are detachable in spirit from their places, from their lives, they have failed and so have I!" There are, however, different levels of detachment, different kinds of failures and salvation.[36]

An absolutist approach to the preservation of commissioned sculpture, a fetishization of its original state and conditions, misconstrues what was actually the underlying point of these projects: that art could have a function, a purpose, in the contemporary world. As Noguchi wrote at length in 1949:

> In the creation and existence of a piece of sculpture, individual possession has less significance than public enjoyment. Without this purpose, the very meaning of sculpture is in question. By sculpture we mean those plastic and spatial relationships which define a moment of personal existence and illumine the environment of our aspirations… It is apparent, therefore, that the function of sculpture, as here defined, is more than merely the decoration of architecture, or the treasure of museums. Both of these outlets, worthy though they may be, are an extension in kind of private ownership… In the technological order alive today, another channel must be opened for sculpture, if that art is to fulfill its larger purpose.[37]

The motivation to create with a more public consumption in mind came with an implicit understanding that such work would not remain the same once it was out in the world, neither should it be embalmed by the controlled climates and sterile environments of museum galleries or art storages.

Most of the sculptures realized for architectural projects during the immediate postwar period, a half-century later, look very different than when they were initially installed. Changes to their form and environment have both illuminated new qualities and masked old ones. These works were never intended to be isolated, precious objects, cordoned off or placed on a pedestal. The evocation of space—of an atomic modern world, however idealistically perceived—inherent to postwar American sculpture, was not a gimmick but rather a statement of purpose, an expression of what Noguchi referred to as the "expanded inclusiveness of sculpture." Even with works like Noguchi's ceiling for the American Stove Company Building or Bertoia's screen at 510 Fifth Avenue, which are now surrounded by sale signs, mass-produced goods, and other assorted detritus of today's consumer culture, the sculptures remain authentic, formally significant, and capable of fulfilling a "larger purpose." People shopping for moving supplies or a fleece pullover may be unaware of the importance of the sculpture in their midst, but the same could be said of a customer buying a new stove in 1948 or making a deposit in 1954. These sculptures, while aesthetic achievements and spectacular decorative objects in their own right, were not made to be seen or experienced solely as art, but rather as facilitators for "plastic and spatial relationships." If anything, it is remarkable how well these projects continue to dialogue with and enliven the surrounding architecture, even if that architecture itself has been altered or diminished.[38]

Large-scale commissioned sculpture of the immediate postwar period, work that approximated the structural functionality of ceilings and walls or activated the spaces between them in a way only sculpture could, were made to inhabit space and be inhabited in turn, to be lived with and in over time. Their adaptive resilience and their sustained existence is not dependent on the original architecture staying the same. As sculpture, they can still be seen and appreciated even if relocated, but they do lose the complexity and intended functionality enabled by their synergy with architecture. This is the reality of alloys. Their distinct parts fuse together to create new, stronger entities, while still maintaining individual, material agency. The commissions of Bertoia, Calder, Lippold, and Noguchi and the modernist architecture for which they were made became alloys. Sculpture and structure, art and architecture, remain distinct, whether physically separated or not, but it is a testament to collaboration and synergy that when cleaved and disentangled from one another, the power of their onetime combination, languishes, weakening the effect of both. Ensuring these elements remain conjoined, then, is not simply an act of historic preservation, of keeping things how they were, but a reminder of how things can be, of what can be achieved through collaboration and amalgamation.

Acknowledgments

Scribbled in the margins of notes taken at the Historical Archives of Contemporary Arts (ASAC) in Venice, Italy while conducting research for my doctoral dissertation and eventual first monograph was a name: Harry Bertoia. The artist never showed at the Venice Biennale and to this day I cannot remember why I wrote down his name, but the fact that I did, and in a location approximately one hundred kilometers from his birthplace, now seems like an act of fate. This book, in many ways, begins and ends with Bertoia. Though he died before I was even born, Bertoia has become a constant presence in my professional life over the past decade and has changed its course in ways I could have never imagined, including co-organizing a major retrospective exhibition, *Harry Bertoia: Sculpting Mid-Century Modern Life* and embarking on a multiyear project as the director of the Harry Bertoia Catalogue Raisonné. Through these activities, I have had the distinct pleasure and honor of getting to know his youngest daughter Celia Bertoia, who established and runs the Harry Bertoia Foundation. She has become a most esteemed director, colleague, and friend as well as an ardent supporter of my work on Bertoia, including this book.

Beyond these welcomed, if unexpected, professional opportunities, Bertoia also changed so much of how I think about, look at, and understand art. In 1972, he stated: “It is my meaning that art should belong to everyday life. It should be incorporated in the society where it can be seen by everyone, where it can encourage a more open attitude toward art. By this, one could reduce the distance between today’s art and the public. I am interested in my fellow being, in what they say about me and what I can tell them. The moment of sharing is equal to the moment of creation.”[1] I have returned to these words frequently over the process of writing this book, which was completed in the midst of a catastrophic global pandemic. In Bertoia’s work, like that of the other artists examined in this book, I have found solace, hope, and a reaffirmed belief in the power of art and its continued importance within the public sphere.

While Bertoia has proven a touchstone for the development of this project, many others have helped facilitate its completion. The first concrete steps of the process began while I was a Henry Moore postdoctoral fellow at the University of Leeds and then an assistant professor of art history at Keene State College (KSC) in New Hampshire. Various faculty grants from the latter enabled me to complete foundational research and supported opportunities to present material in draft stages. At KSC, I would also like to thank Jonathan Gitelson, and the absolutely fierce group of women—Amber Davisson, Jo Dery, Lisa DiGiovanni, Jamie Landau, and Emily Robins Sharpe—whose friendship, support, and guidance made my time there and early work on this project sustainable.

This book would also not have been possible without the support of two postdoctoral fellowships from the Smithsonian American Art Museum (SAAM) in Washington, DC and the Crystal Bridges Museum of American Art in Bentonville, Arkansas. My time as the George Gurney Fellow at SAAM proved absolutely vital to the project and was one of the best experiences of my professional life. Without access to the tremendous resources available through the Archives of American

Art and the Smithsonian American Art and Portrait Gallery Library, this book simply could not have been completed. I am so grateful to Karen Lemmey, who served as my fellowship supervisor but became a most appreciated mentor and colleague; and to the entire staff at the Research and Scholars Center at SAAM, especially Amelia Goerlitz and Stacy Weiland. I also want to thank the entire cohort of fellows who helped refine my thinking on the project and created such a vibrant, stimulating environment in which to work. In particular, I want to recognize Danielle O'Steen, in whom I found a kindred sculpture obsessive, brilliant scholar and curator, and great friend. While at SAAM, I was also fortunate enough to meet Robin Veder. She was an early advocate of the project, and I am most grateful to her and her entire team at *American Art*, who provided some of the most incredible, collaborative editorial guidance I have ever received on a publication, as a I prepared an article for the journal on Richard Lippold's *Orpheus and Apollo* (1962), published in 2019. I would also like to extend sincere thanks to everyone at Crystal Bridges who made my time there as a Tyson Scholar so productive, in particular: Mindy Besaw, Allison Glenn, Lauren Haynes, Jennifer Padgett, Dylan Turk, and Emily Voelker.

Numerous archives, arts institutions, foundations, libraries, and special collections have also proved invaluable to the realization of this project, including: the Avery Architectural & Fine Arts Library at Columbia University, the Calder Foundation, the Cranbrook Center for Collections and Research, the Harry Bertoia Foundation (especially the aforementioned Celia Bertoia and Wilbur Springer), the Isamu Noguchi Foundation and Garden Museum, Northwestern University's Art Library, the Ryerson and Burnham Library and Archives at the Art Institute of Chicago, and the Yale University Library. I would like to extend deep and most sincere thanks to all of the archivists and librarians who so graciously helped me track down and access key information, objects, and images. Special thanks go to Janine Biunno at the Isamu Noguchi Foundation and Garden Museum; Elizabeth Clemens at the Walter P. Reuther Library at Wayne State University; Leslie Edwards at the Cranbrook Center for Collections and Research; Miranda Rectenwald, curator of local history, Special Collections, Washington University Libraries; Becky Simmons at the Rochester Institute of Technology; and Catherine Wallack at the University Libraries of the University of Arkansas. I also wish to thank the Department of History of Art and Architecture at DePaul University, in particular Joanna Gardner-Huggett, for providing me with an academic affiliation, and the DePaul University Libraries for enabling access to key research materials during the last stages of writing the book.

Publishing in art history comes with the added challenges of reproducing high-quality images, often at great cost and effort—especially for independent scholars. I am tremendously grateful to all of the artists and artist estates, archives, individuals, public libraries, photographers, and museums who not only helped me track down wonderful image options, but who also kindly worked with me to make them feasible to include in this book. Particular thanks go to Erica Stoller, Caroline Hirsch, and the entire team at Esto who made it possible to include so many of Ezra Stoller's magnificent architectural photographs as well as: Colleen Alles and Jordan Cloud, Grand Rapids Public Library; John Blakinger; the BMW Group; Antonella Camarda, Museo Nivola; Lisa DeLong, MIT List Visual Arts Center; Julie Choma, Cheekwood Estate & Gardens (my absolute favorite registrar); Diana Edkins, Art Resource; Michael Frost, Sterling Memorial Library, Yale University Library; John Ferry and the Estate of R. Buckminster Fuller; Corey Gross, Cranbrook Art Museum; Helen Harrison, Pollock-Krasner House and Study Center; Houston Public Library; Joe Kitchen and the Henry Moore Foundation; Jeremy Lange; Leo Baeck Institute; Anahi Macauley, Federal Reserve Bank of Philadelphia; Jill Meißner-Wolfbeisser and the Frederick Kiesler Foundation; Tim Noakes, Stanford University Special Collections & University Archives; the Northwest Architectural Archives, University of Minnesota; US Senate Office of the Senate Curator; Portsmouth Abbey; Matthew Neistein, Allegheny County Airport Authority; Grace Pamperien, Crystal Bridges Museum of American Art; Liz N. Paris, McNay Art Museum; Lesley Schoenfeld, Harvard Law School Library; Richard Sorenson, Smithsonian American Art Museum; Juliet Kepes Stone; Erin John Sullivan; Daniel Trujillo, Artists Rights Society; Paulina Villanueva and Cecilia Castrillo, Fundación Villanueva; Karen Widi, Skidmore, Owings & Merrill; and the UNESCO Archives.

I also wish to extend deepest thanks to Princeton University Press (PUP). The whole team has been an absolutely joy to work with and I have felt enthusiastically supported from day one. I have been smoothly guided through the whole process by Kenneth Guay, and particular thanks are owed to Michelle Komie for believing in this book and understanding what I wanted to accomplish in writing it. I also want to acknowledge how proud I am to be publishing with PUP, not only because of its stellar reputation as a publisher of books on art and architecture, but also because of its recognition of the challenges, exclusivity, and inequities endemic to publishing—and its tangible action plan to combat these issues, which includes, among other things, newly launched grant and fellowship programs. I was fortunate to receive a Global Equity Grant from PUP to help offset some of the costs associated with image rights and reproduction. Without this grant, I simply would not have been able to publish this book, and I am tremendously grateful such support was available. I would also like to thank Alice T. Sullivan, a fellow University of Michigan–history of art PhD alumna, who proofread the manuscript, and offered meticulous edits as well as kind words of support when they were most needed.

I am most grateful to my friends and colleagues who provided invaluable support, feedback, and guidance at various stages during the course of this project. I have had the pleasure of cocurating *Harry Bertoia: Sculpting Mid-Century Modern Life* with Jed Morse, chief curator at the Nasher Sculpture Center, but he is due my deepest gratitude for the mentorship he has provided over the past fifteen-plus years. While I feel fortunate for his gracious, ever-present career counsel, I am even luckier to call him a dear friend. The scholarship and guidance of Glenn Adamson, Amanda Douberley, Alice T. Friedman, Nick Hartigan, Jeffrey Lieber,

Monica Obniski, Robert Slifkin, Shelley Selim, Sydney Skelton Simon, and Kay Wells has proved formative in how I approached the material covered in this book. I am deeply indebted to Bridget Gilman, Danielle O'Steen, and Andrew Wasserman, each of whom read and gave insightful, astute criticism of various chapters along the way. I also want to thank Andrew for being a much-trusted sounding board and all around wonderful human being. Bridget, as well as Melanie Garcia Sympson, have been the most steadfast and supportive friends since we were in the trenches together as graduate students at the University of Michigan, and while the focus of our "writing group" has certainly changed over the years, I am grateful it has remained intact. Thanks also to Lara Eggleton and Sharon Hecker for being two of my most consistent and favorite collaborators (and much-loved friends), even though an ocean now separates us.

Though not directly involved in the writing of this book, I want to particularly acknowledge Lisa Le Feuvre, executive director of the Holt/Smithson Foundation, Jane O. MacLeod, president and CEO of Cheekwood Estate & Gardens, and Michal Raz-Russo, programs director at the Gordon Parks Foundation, who in their own unique ways, are models of how to be strong, fearless, innovative leaders in the arts, and have proven to be significant mentors and guiding forces in my professional life. Additional thanks to Michal for the countless neighborhood walks, drinks on the stoop, and artworld adventures over the past few years. I also wish to extend profound, evergreen thanks to Alex Potts who continues to shape how I think about art, remains a most trusted voice in my professional life, and who I always look forward to seeing, whether to talk about sculpture or just to have a catch up over tea.

Writing a book is an all-encompassing endeavor, but an act that does not take place in a vacuum. Thanks to Patrick and Marta Coleman for the all the Friday pizza nights and other wonderful excuses to get away from my desk. Most sincere thanks to Leslie Wolowitz for helping keep things in perspective and reminding me that sometimes things can indeed just be, good enough. My family has compassionately supported me throughout the entire process, and I am most grateful to my brother, sister-in-law, and my beloved nephews — Erin, Rebekah, Jackson, and Jameson Sullivan — and to my parents — Kathleen and Patrick Sullivan. Particular thanks go to my mother, who has read every page of this manuscript — as she has done with every significant piece of writing I have ever produced. As she does with most things in life, she offered astute insights and honest feedback, though conveyed in manner infused with encouragement and kindness. Last but certainly not least, I want to extend the sincerest, if inevitably inadequate, thanks to my husband, Rob Foster. While I am pretty certain he may be the kindest and most patient person in the world, there is absolutely no doubt that he is my favorite.

Notes

In citations below, the following works or archival repositories have been identified by the following abbreviations:

AAA	Archives of American Art, Smithsonian Institution, Washington, DC.
CAOHP	Chicago Architects Oral History Project, Ernest R. Graham Study Center fwor Architectural Drawings, Department of Architecture, Art Institute of Chicago.
HAC	Harris Armstrong Collection, 1924–1972, WUA00372, Washington University Archives, St. Louis, Missouri.
HBF	Archival Shop Files, Harry Bertoia Foundation, St George, Utah.
HBP	Harry Bertoia Papers, 1917–1979, Archives of American Art, Smithsonian Institution, Washington, DC.
INF	Museum Archives, Isamu Noguchi Foundation and Garden Museum, Long Island City, New York.
RLP	Richard Lippold Papers, 1944–1977, Archives of American Art, Smithsonian Institution, Washington, DC.
Tomkins	Calvin Tomkins, "A Thing among Things," Profiles, *New Yorker*, March 3, 1963, 47–107.

Prologue: The Architectural Requirements of Space

1. The installation of Lippold's Four Seasons project was postponed two weeks until April 15, 1959, because of delays in the overall progress on the restaurant, Richard Foster of Philip Johnson Associates to Richard Lippold, March 19, 1959, RLP.
2. Seagram Corporation, "A Special Report on 375 Park Avenue: An International Address of Distinction," *New York Times*, April 18, 1957, sec. 13; Herbert Muschamp, "Best Building: Opposites Attract," *New York Times*, April 18, 1999, 92; and Phyllis Lambert, *Building Seagram* (New Haven, CT: Yale University Press, 2013), 1.
3. Thomas W. Ennis, "Building is Designer's Testament; Seagram Building Marks Apex of Mies van der Rohe's Career," *New York Times*, November 10, 1957, 313; and Lambert, *Building Seagram*, 122, 136. Ennis, writing in the *New York Times*, for example, declared that the Seagram building "culminates the architectural career of Ludwig Mies van der Rohe," and along with the United Nations Building and Lever House "is one of the most notable of Manhattan's postwar buildings."
4. Craig Claiborne, "$4.5 Million Restaurant to Open Here; Four Seasons, Nearing Completion, Said to Be World's Costliest Seagram Building Unit Is Lavishly Decorated and Landscaped," *New York Times*, July 16, 1959, 33; John F. Mariani and Alex von Bidder, *The Four Seasons: A History of America's Premier Restaurant* (New York: Crown, 1994), 27; and Karl Linn quoted in "The Four Seasons: A Collaboration for Elegance," *Progressive Architecture* 40, no. 12 (December 1959): 142. For an extensive history of Johnson and Kelly's collaboration on the Four Seasons see, Phyllis Lambert, "Light Changes: Philip Johnson, Richard Kelly, and *Stimmung* at Seagram," in *The Structure of Light: Richard Kelly and the Illumination of Modern Architecture*, ed. Dietrich Neumann (New Haven, CT: Yale University Press, 2010), 80–95.
5. Mark Rothko, "Notes on the Seagram Mural Commission," in *Rothko: The Late Series,* ed. Achim-Borchardt-Hume (London: Tate Publishing, 2008), 95. For a more thorough history of these works and the controversy surrounding Mark Rothko's contract with Seagram see, *Mark Rothko: The Seagram Mural Project* (Liverpool: Tate Gallery, 1988); and Borchardt-Hume, *Rothko: The Late Series*. Though the Four Seasons could have only accommodated seven paintings, Rothko actually executed thirty canvases.
6. Lambert, *Building Seagram*, 148.
7. Richard Lippold, "An Artist's Point of View," *Architectural Record* (December 1978): 69–70; and Richard Lippold quoted in "The Four Seasons: A Collaboration for Elegance," 144.
8. Olga Gueft, "The Four Seasons," *Interiors*, 199, no. 5 (December 1959): 86; and Philip Johnson quoted in "More Elegance at the House of Seagram," *Architectural Record* 126, no. 5 (November 1959): 202. Much contemporary criticism and even the official 1989 Landmarks Preservation Commission report stated that the rods were a "gold dipped brass," but Richard Lippold and Phyllis Lambert both explicitly stated the material was bronze. See Landmarks Preservation Commission, *Designation List 221 LP-1666* (New York: October 3, 1989), http://s-media.nyc.gov/agencies/lpc/lp/1666.pdf. This is further confirmed in a document entitled "Cleaning Instructions for Lippold Construction, 'Four Seasons Grill,'" in RLP.
9. Lambert, *Building Seagram*, 143; Gueft, "Four Seasons," 166; and "More Elegance at the House of Seagram," 202.
10. Richard Lippold at the New York City Board of Estimate hearing on the Seagram Building, Plaza, Interiors and the Four Seasons Restaurant, Calendar Nos. 40 and 41, January 25, 1990, transcript p. 42–44, box 134-OF-004, Records of the Office of Facilitates and Office Services, FSB, cited in Lambert, *Building Seagram*, 154.
11. Richard Lippold quoted in "Four Seasons: A Collaboration for Elegance," 144; and Philip Johnson quoted in David L. Shirey, "Space Man," *Newsweek*, January 29, 1968, 82.
12. Philip Johnson quoted in Tomkins, 47.
13. Ada Louise Huxtable, "Art with Architecture: New Terms of an Old Alliance," *New York Times*, September 13, 1959, 20.

Introduction: Alloying Space

1. See K.L.H. Wells, *Weaving Modernism: Postwar Tapestry between Paris and New York* (New Haven, CT: Yale University Press, 2019); Romy Golan, *Muralnomad: The Paradox of Wall Painting, Europe 1927–1957* (New Haven, CT: Yale University Press, 2009); and Louis G. Redstone, *Art in Architecture* (New York: McGraw Hill, 1968).
2. Ada Louise Huxtable, "Art in Architecture 1959," *Craft Horizons* 19, no. 1 (January/February 1959): 10–11.
3. Huxtable, 11.
4. Huxtable, 11.
5. R. Buckminster Fuller, "The Comprehensive Designer (June 1949)," *Arts & Architecture* 68, no. 2 (February 1951): 22. Fuller cited *Merriam-Webster* for his definition of synergy.
6. Fuller, 22.
7. "The Americans" exhibitions at MoMA included: *Americans 1942: 18 Artists from 9 States*, January 21–March 9, 1942; *Fourteen Americans*, September 10–December 8, 1946; *15 Americans*, April 9–July 27, 1952; *Twelve Americans*, May 30–September 8, 1956; *16 Americans*, December 16, 1959–February 17, 1960; *Americans 1963*, May 22–August 18, 1963. Noguchi voluntarily spent seven months at the beginning of WWII in an internment camp and encountered lingering anti-Japanese sentiment in postwar United States. See Amy Lyford, *Isamu Noguchi's Modernism: Negotiating Race, Labor, and Nation, 1930–1950* (Berkeley: University of California Press, 2013).

   The author wishes to acknowledge present-day debates around the colonial implications of using "American" or

"America" in reference to only the United States at the exclusion of South and Central America as well as Canada. These descriptors, however, will be used throughout this book to specify art and architecture made in the United States and by nationals of the United States for consistency and because it reflects period-specific usage.

8. Isamu Noguchi, "Artist Statement," in *Fourteen Americans*, ed. Dorothy C. Miller (New York: Museum of Modern Art, 1946), 39.
9. Cover for *Arts & Architecture* (December 1946) in Herbert Matter papers, c. 1937–1984, M1446, series 9, box 407, folder 2, Department of Special Collections & University Archives, Stanford University Libraries.
10. "Isamu Noguchi Defines the Nature and Enormous Potential of Sculpture," *Interiors* 108 (March 1949): 118; and Lippold quoted in "Orpheus and Apollo," *Time* 81, no.1 (January 4, 1963): 36. See also Brooke Kamin Rapaport, "The Greater Mystery of Things: Aspects of Vital Forms in American Art," in *Vital Forms: American Art and Design in the Atomic Age, 1940–1960*, ed. Brooke Kamin Rapaport and Kevin L. Stayton (New York: Brooklyn Museum of Art, 2001), 78–119; Paul Schimmel, *Destroy the Picture: Painting the Void, 1949–1962* (Los Angeles: Museum of Contemporary Art, 2012); Robert Slifkin, *The New Monuments and the End of Man: U.S. Sculpture between War and Peace, 1945–1975* (Princeton, NJ: Princeton University Press, 2019); and Robin Schuldenfrei, *Atomic Dwelling: Anxiety, Domesticity, and Postwar Architecture* (New York: Routledge, 2012).
11. Jack Burnham, *Beyond Modern Sculpture: The Effects of Science and Technology on the Sculpture of This Century* (New York: George Braziller, 1968), 50, 67.

    The histories of the art of the immediate postwar period and its relationship to science and industry are increasingly being reexamined. See, for example, Pamela M. Lee, *Think Tank Aesthetics: Midcentury Modernism, the Cold War, and the Neoliberal Present* (Cambridge, MA: MIT Press, 2020); and John Beck and Ryan Bishop, *Technocrats of the Imagination: Art, Technology, and the Military-Industrial Avant-Garde* (Durham, NC: Duke University Press, 2020).

    For a broader analysis on the history of science and technology during the postwar period, see, for example, Burnham, *Beyond Modern Sculpture*; Carroll Pursell, *Technology in Postwar America: A History* (New York: Columbia University Press, 2007); and Audra J. Wolfe, *Freedom's Laboratory: The Cold War Struggle for the Soul of Science* (Baltimore: Johns Hopkins University Press, 2018).

    For more on the influence of vitalism and the appearance during the postwar period of organic, biomorphic forms across the arts, design, architecture, and popular culture see, Rapaport and Stayton, *Vital Forms*.
12. For more on such transdisciplinary theories see R. Buckminster Fuller, *Synergetics: Explorations in the Geometry of Thinking* (New York: Macmillan, 1975); György Kepes, *Structure in Art and in Science* (New York: George Braziller, 1965); and Norbert Wiener, *Cybernetics: Or Control and Communication in the Animal and the Machine* (Cambridge, MA: MIT Press, 1961).

    On synergetics: "About Fuller," Buckminster Fuller Institute, https://www.bfi.org/about-fuller/big-ideas/synergetics; Fuller, *Synergetics*, 3–4, 6 (also cited in R. Buckminster Fuller, "Isamu Noguchi," in *Isamu Noguchi: Sculptural Design*, ed. Jochen Eisenbrand, Katarina V. Posch, and Alexander Von Vegesack (Weil am Rhein: Vitra Design Museum, 2001), 250); and Eva Díaz, "R. Buckminster Fuller: *Great Circle Sphere Model*," in *Leap Before You Look: Black Mountain College, 1933–1957*, ed. Helen Molesworth and Ruth Erickson (Boston: Institute of Contemporary Art, 2015), 224.
13. John R. Blakinger, "The Aesthetics of Collaboration: Complicity and Conversion at MIT's Center for Advanced Visual Studies," *Tate Papers*, no. 25 (Spring 2016), https://tate.org.uk/research/publications/tate-papers/25/aesthetics-of-collaboration. György Kepes's papers are held at Stanford University and at the AAA. For a thorough history of Kepes and his impact, see John R. Blakinger, *Gyorgy Kepes: Undreaming the Bauhaus* (Cambridge, MA: MIT Press, 2019).
14. Walter Gropius, "The Theory and Organization of the Bauhaus (Weimer, 1923)" in *Bauhaus, 1919–1928*, ed. Herbert Bayer, Walter Gropius, and Ise Gropius (New York: Museum of Modern Art, 1938), 24–25. For more on the Bauhaus and its ideology, see Barry Bergdoll and Leah Dickerman, *Bauhaus 1919–1933: Workshops for Modernity* (New York: Museum of Modern Art, 2009).
15. See, for example, Alison J. Clarke and Elana Shapira, eds., *Émigré Cultures in Design and Architecture* (London: Bloomsbury Academic, 2017); Jacquelynn Baas and Mary Jane Jacob, eds., *Chicago Makes Modern: How Creative Minds Changed Society* (Chicago: University of Chicago Press, 2012); Elizabeth Siegel, "Recollections and Reflections on László Moholy-Nagy," *Leonardo* 50, no. 3 (June 2017): 325–29; and Achim Borchardt-Hume, ed., *Albers and Moholy-Nagy: From the Bauhaus to the New World* (New Haven, CT: Yale University Press, 2006).
16. Arthur Drexler, *Buildings for Business and Government* (New York: Museum of Modern Art, 1957), 5.
17. Russell Lynes, *The Taste Makers* (New York: Harper & Brothers, 1954), 288, 299. For more on the relationship between the arts, architecture, and Cold War diplomacy see for example, Greg Castillo, *Cold War on the Home Front: The Soft Power of Midcentury Design* (Minneapolis: University of Minnesota Press, 2010); Jane C. Loeffler, *The Architecture of Diplomacy: Building America's Embassies* (New York: Princeton Architectural Press, 1990), and Frances Stonor Saunders, *The Cultural Cold War: The CIA and the World of Arts and Letters* (New York: New Press, 1999). On Calder specifically, see Alex J. Taylor, "Unstable Motives: Propaganda, Politics, and the Late Work of Alexander Calder," *American Art* 26, no. 1 (Spring 2012): 24–47.
18. Lynes, *Taste-Makers*, 299–300. Walter Paepcke's support of art and design had begun before WWII, when he financially backed the efforts of his friend and Bauhaus émigré László Moholy-Nagy to reopen the German school as the New Bauhaus (later the Institute of Design) in Chicago in the late 1930s. Paepcke would also go on to found the Aspen Institute. For a thorough history of his cultural patronage and impact see James Sloan Allen, *The Romance of Commerce and Culture: Capitalism, Modernism, and the Chicago-Aspen Crusade for Cultural Reform* (Boulder: University of Colorado Press, 2002). On the creation of the Chase Manhattan Art Collection specifically, see Marshall Lee, ed., *Art at Work: The Chase Manhattan Collection* (New York: E. P. Dutton, 1984); and Suzanne Loebl, *America's Medicis: The Rockefellers and Their Astonishing Cultural Legacy* (New York: HarperCollins, 2010). For a more general assessment of corporate patronage of the arts and architecture, see Joan Ockman, "Art, Soul of the Corporation: Patronage, Public Relations, and the Interrelations of Architecture and Art after World War II," *SOM Journal* 5 (2008): 170–86.
19. David A. Prager, "Foreword," *Business Buys American Art* (New York: Whitney Museum of American Art, 1960), 3; and Ockman, "Art, Soul of the Corporation," 171.
20. See Reinhold Martin, *The Organizational Complex: Architecture, Media, and Corporate Space* (Cambridge, MA: MIT Press, 2003). For more on the confluence of postwar corporations, design, and architecture see, for example: Amanda Ann Douberley, "The Corporate Model: Sculpture, Architecture, and the American City, 1946–1975" (PhD diss., University of Texas at Austin, 2015); John Harwood, *The Interface: IBM and the Transformation

of Corporate Design, 1945–1976 (Minneapolis: University of Minnesota Press, 2016); and Alexandrea Lange, "Tower, Typewriter, and Trademark: Architects, Designers, and the Corporate Utopia, 1956–1964" (PhD diss., New York University, 2005).

21. On the limited scholarship on Harry Bertoia see Celia Bertoia, *The Life and Work of Harry Bertoia: The Man, the Artist, the Visionary* (Atglen, PA: Schiffer Publishing, 2015); June Kompass Nelson, *Harry Bertoia: Sculptor* (Detroit: Wayne State University Press, 1970); Sydney Skelton Simon, "Harry Bertoia and Postwar American Design," (PhD diss., Stanford University, 2018); and Beverly Twitchell, *Bertoia: The Metalworker* (London: Phaidon, 2019).

    There have also been catalogues published in conjunction with significant exhibitions on the artist's work including *Harry Bertoia*, 1975–76, Allentown Art Museum, PA; *In Nature's Embrace*: *The World of Harry Bertoia*, 2006, Reading Public Museum and Art Gallery, PA; *Decisi che una sedia non poteva bastare*, Museo Civico d'Arte, 2009, Pordenone, Italy; and *Bent, Cast & Forged: The Jewelry of Harry Bertoia*, 2015, Cranbrook Art Museum, Bloomfield Hills, MI . Along with Jed Morse, the author curated a major large-scale retrospective on the artist, *Harry Bertoia: Sculpting Mid-Century Modern Life*, which is scheduled to open at the Nasher Sculpture Center in Dallas, TX in 2022, and is accompanied by a catalogue with the same title, published by Scheidegger & Spiess.

    There has only been one major museum exhibition of Richard Lippold's work, *Richard Lippold Sculpture: A Retrospective 1950–1988*, November 30, 1990–February 17, 1991, Patrick and Beatrice Haggerty Museum of Art, Marquette University, Milwaukee, WI. The exhibition catalogue is the only substantive scholarly source about Lippold: Curtis L. Carter, ed., *Richard Lippold: Sculpture* (Milwaukee, WI: Haggerty Museum of Art, Marquette University, 1990).

22. Lowery Stokes Sims, "Rothko and the Four Seasons Commission: A Parable of Art and Design at the Mid-Twentieth Century," in *Crafting Modernism: Midcentury American Art and Design*, ed. Jeannine Falino and Jennifer Scanlan (New York: Museum of Arts and Design, 2011), 56. Most of the existing scholarship has looked at the decorative in the context of modern art of the late nineteenth and early twentieth centuries. See, Jenny Anger, *Paul Klee and the Decorative in Modern Art* (Cambridge: Cambridge University Press, 2004); Elissa Auther, "The Decorative, Abstraction, and the Hierarchy of Art and Craft in the Art Criticism of Clement Greenberg," *Oxford Art Journal* 27, no. 3 (2004): 339–64; Adolf Loos, *Ornament and Crime: Selected Essays*, trans. Michael Mitchell (1962; repr., Riverside, CA: Ariadne Press, 1997); Alina Payne, *From Ornament to Object: Genealogies of Architectural Modernism* (New Haven, CT: Yale University Press, 2012); Christopher Reed, ed. and trans., *Not at Home: The Suppression of Domesticity in Modern Art and Architecture* (London: Thames & Hudson, 1996); James Trilling, *Ornament: A Modern Perspective* (Seattle: University of Washington Press, 2003); and Nancy J. Troy, *Modernism and the Decorative Arts in France: Art Nouveau to Le Corbusier* (New Haven, CT: Yale University Press, 1991).

23. Clement Greenberg, "Sculpture in Our Time (1958)," in *Modernism with a Vengeance, 1957–1969, The Collected Essays and Criticism, vol. 4*, ed. John O'Brian (Chicago: University of Chicago Press, 1993), 58, 50; Clement Greenberg, "Review of the Water-Color, Drawing, and Sculpture Sections of the Whitney Annual (1946)," in *Arrogant Purpose, 1945–1949*, The Collected Writings, vol. 2, ed. John O'Brian (Chicago: University of Chicago Press, 1986), 59.

24. Terence Riley and Edward Eigen, "Between the Museum and the Marketplace: Selling Good Design," in *The Museum of Modern Art at Midcentury: At Home and Abroad*, ed. John Elderfield (New York: Museum of Modern Art, 1994), 152; and Clement Greenberg, "Recentness of Sculpture," in *American Sculpture of the Sixties*, ed. Maurice Tuchman (Los Angeles: Los Angeles County Museum of Art, 1967), 26.

25. Hilton Kramer, "The Phenomenon of Lippold, Our Foremost Public Decorator," *New York Times*, January 14, 1968, 23. See also, Mark Wigley, *White Walls, Designer Dresses: The Fashioning of Modern Architecture* (Cambridge, MA: MIT Press, 2002).

26. Richard Meyer, "Big, Middle-Class Modernism," *October* 131 (Winter 2010): 69–70. Meyer also addresses the period association of decoration and elegance with women's femininity, men's effeminacy, and homosexuality. See also, John Canaday, "An Impossible Exhibition: Lippold's Sculptures Can't Be Shown but a Gallery Tries Happy Union around Town Science and Mysticism," *New York Times*, February 11, 1962, 123; "The Four Seasons: A Collaboration for Elegance," *Progressive Architecture* 40, no. 12 (December 1959): 142–47; Kramer, "The Phenomenon of Lippold," 23; and Tomkins, 47–107. On Lippold in this context, see Alice T. Friedman, "The Cultured Corporation: Art, Architecture, and the Postwar Office Building," in *Architectures of Display: Department Stores and Modern Retail*, ed. Patricia Lara-Betancourt, Margaret Maile Petty, and Anna I. Lasc (New York: Routledge, 2018), 233–48. See also Tom Folland, "Robert Rauschenberg's Queer Modernism: The Early Combines and Decoration," *Art Bulletin* 92, no. 4 (December 2010): 348–65. "Elegance," was frequently used as an adjective to discuss Lippold's work.

27. Isamu Noguchi quoted in, "From an Interview with Isamu Noguchi," *League Quarterly* 20 (Spring 1949): 9.

28. Isamu Noguchi, *Isamu Noguchi: A Sculptor's World* (New York: Steidl, 2015), 18; Lippold quoted in, Jack Burnham, "Richard Lippold: Shaping Space with Reflected Light," in Carter, *Richard Lippold: Sculpture*, 28.

29. "The American Pavilion, Brussels World's Fair," *Architectural Record* (July 1957); and "5 U.S. Sculptors for Fair Chosen: Modern Works, Some Done in Steel, Will Adorn Pavilion at Belgian Exposition," *New York Times*, October 27, 1957, 83. The other two sculptors selected were Mary Callery and José de Rivera. Pauline M. Anglim to Perry B. Johanson, November 9, 1967, HBP.

    Correspondence in the Bertoia Papers shows that both Bertoia and Lippold submitted and were paid for proposals, but I have been able to confirm only that Bertoia's project was actually realized. The commission consisted of twenty hanging stainless steel "willow" sculptures of varying sizes with lighting fixtures inside that hung from the ceiling of the main consumer banking area. Another notable work selected for the outdoor plaza of the First National Bank Building was Henry Moore's *Three Piece Sculpture: Vertebrae* (1968, cast 1969).

30. See Jed Perl, *Calder: The Conquest of Time; The Early Years, 1898–1940* (New York: Alfred A. Knopf, 2017).

31. Piri Halasz, "America's Own Version of Matisse and/or Picasso—'Sandy' Calder," *Smithsonian* 7, no. 9 (December 1976), 77.

32. Clement Greenberg, "Review of Exhibitions of De la Fresnaye and Stuart Davis (1945)," "Review of the Water-Color, Drawing, and Sculpture Sections of the Whitney Annual (1946)," and "Review of Exhibitions of David Smith, David Hare, and Mirko (1947)," in Greenberg, *Arrogant Purpose, 1945–1949*, 41, 59, 142.

33. See Alex J. Taylor, "The Calder Problem: Mobiles, Modern Taste, and Mass Culture," *Oxford Art Journal* 37, no. 1 (March 2014): 27–45. See also, "Alexander Calder, Inventor of Mobile, Will Paint a Jet for Braniff," *New York*

Times, June 10, 1973, 242; Jean Lipman, *Calder's Universe* (London: Thames & Hudson, 1977); Alexander S. C. Rower and Holton Rower, eds., *Calder Jewelry* (New York: Calder Foundation, 2007); Martin Eidelberg, ed., *Messengers of Modernism: American Studio Jewelry 1940–1960* (New York: Montreal Museum of Decorative Arts, 1996); Achim Borchardt-Hume, ed., *Alexander Calder: Performing Sculpture* (London: Tate Publishing, 2015); and "BMW Art Car: Alexander Calder BMW 3.0 CSL, 1975," BMW Group, http://www.artcar.bmwgroup.com/en/art-car/text/Alexander-Calder-BMW-3-0-CSL-1975-1385.html.

34. Lippold quoted in, David L. Shirey, "Space Man," *Newsweek*, January 29, 1968, 82; and Andrea Oppenheimer Dean, "Richard Lippold's Wired Universe of Gold and Silver," *Smithsonian* 13, no. 11 (February 1983): 110.
35. Hilton Kramer, "Month in Review," *Arts* 31 (October 1956), 50–51.
36. Richard Lippold quoted in Ruth Erickson, "The 1950s: Ways of Life," in Molesworth and Erickson, *Leap Before You Look*, 280. For more on Lippold's friendship and work with John Cage see Alice T. Friedman, "Through the Network of Wires: Portsmouth Abbey, Richard Lippold, and Postwar Syncretism," *Interiors* 6, no. 3 (2016): 235–58; Branden Joseph, *Experimentations: John Cage in Music, Art, and Architecture* (New York: Bloomsbury Academic, 2016); and Kenneth Silverman, *Begin Again: A Biography of John Cage* (Evanston, IL: Northwestern University Press, 2012). For more on the history of Black Mountain College see Molesworth and Erickson, *Leap Before You Look*.
37. Katherine and Michael McCoy, "Academy Designers Influence the Look of Twentieth-Century America," *Cranbrook Quarterly* 7, no. 2 (November 1981): 4; and Wolf Von Eckardt, "Our Bauhaus," *Time* 123, no. 19 (May 7, 1984): 92.
38. See Shelley Selim, ed., *Bent, Cast & Forged: The Jewelry of Harry Bertoia* (Bloomfield Hills, MI: Cranbrook Art Museum, 2015). For more on the history of Cranbrook during the postwar period, see Mark Coir, "The Cranbrook Factor," in *Eero Saarinen: Shaping the Future*, ed. Eeva-Liisa Pelkonen and Donald Albrecht (New Haven, CT: Yale University Press, 2006, 29–42; Robert Judson Clark and Andrea P. A. Belloli, eds., *Design in America: The Cranbrook Vision, 1925–1950* (New York: Metropolitan Museum of Art, 1984); and Harry Bertoia, oral history interview by Paul Cummings, June 20, 1972, transcript p. 5, AAA.
39. See Brian Lutz, *Knoll: A Modernist Universe* (New York: Rizzoli, 2010); and *The Bertoia Collection* (New York: Knoll International, 1969).
40. George O'Brienthe, "Art and Furniture Share a Showing," *New York Times*, December 13, 1963, 55.
41. Auther, "Art Criticism of Clement Greenberg," 347. For more on Florence Knoll and Knoll Associates, see Virginia Lee Warren, "Woman Who Led an Office Revolution Rules and Empire of Modern Design: Florence Knoll Gave Business 'Living' a New Look," *New York Times*, September 1, 1964, 40; Bobbye Tigerman, "'I Am Not a Decorator': Florence Knoll, the Knoll Planning Unit and the Making of the Modern Office," *Journal of Design History* 20, no. 1 (Spring 2007): 61–74; and Earl Martin et al., eds., *Knoll Textiles* (New Haven, CT: Yale University Press, 2011).
42. Isamu Noguchi, oral history interview by Paul Cummings, December 26, 1973, unpaginated transcript, AAA. Located in the Zenith Radio Corporation Display Salon at 200 N. Michigan Ave. until its closure in 1979, Bertoia's 1959 sculpture was donated soon after by the company to the Smithsonian American Art Museum in Washington, DC.
43. See Bruce Altshuler, "Isamu Noguchi Indoors: Home Furnishings and Interior Design," in Eisenbrand et al., *Isamu Noguchi: Sculptural Design*, 108–52; Isamu Noguchi, "Japanese Akari Lamps," *Craft Horizons* 14, no. 5 (October 1954): 16–18; and Isamu Noguchi, "Akari," *Arts & Architecture* 72, no. 5 (May 1955): 14, 31. Josiah McElheny, "Useful Noguchi," *Artforum* 43, no. 3 (November 2004): 177.
44. Isamu Noguchi, "The Sculptor and the Architect (1968)," in, *Isamu Noguchi: Essays and Conversations*, ed. Diane Apostolos-Cappadona and Bruce Altshuler (New York: Harry N. Abrams, 1994), 52–53, 54–55.
45. Vincent Scully, *American Architecture and Urbanism* (New York: Praeger, 1969), 121. For more on the use of sculpture in the Barcelona Pavilion and in other early twentieth-century projects, see Penelope Curtis, *Patio and Pavilion: The Place of Sculpture in Modern Architecture* (Los Angeles: Getty Publications, 2008).
46. Philip Johnson quoted in Eleanor Bitterman, *Art in Modern Architecture* (New York: Reinhold Publishing, 1952), 138. See also, Paul Damaz, "Art as Architectural Element," *AIA Journal* 46, no. 5 (November 1966): 56; and Cécile Whiting, "Philip Johnson: The Whence and Whither of Art in Architecture," *Journal of the Society of Architectural Historians* 75, no. 3 (September 2016): 318–38.
47. William Hartmann, oral history interview by Betty J. Blum, October 30, 1989–November 2, 1989, transcript 2003 p. 78, CAOHP, http://digital-libraries.saic.edu/cdm/ref/collection/caohp/id/23045.
48. Alice T. Friedman, *American Glamour and the Evolution of Modern Architecture* (New Haven, CT: Yale University Press, 2010), 9. See Thomas H. Creighton, "The New Sensualism," *Progressive Architecture* 40, no. 9 (September 1959): 141–47; Thomas H. Creighton, "The New Sensualism II," *Progressive Architecture* 40, no. 10 (October 1959): 180–90; and "Views: 'New Sensualists' Respond," *Progressive Architecture* 40, no. 11 (November 1959): 51, 53, 61, 64, 68, 236–37, 241.
49. Robin Boyd, "The Counter Revolution in Architecture," *Harper's* 219 (September 1959): 40; and Scully, *American Architecture and Urbanism*, 193. For more on the Mies-inspired "second generation" architects, see for example, Friedman, *American Glamour*; Dale Allen Gyure, *Minoru Yamasaki: Humanist Architecture for a Modernist World* (New Haven, CT: Yale University Press, 2017); Jeffrey Lieber, *Flintstone Modernism: Or the Cultural Crisis in Postwar American Culture* (Cambridge, MA: MIT Press, 2018); and Joan Ockman, *Architecture Culture, 1943–1968: A Documentary Anthology* (New York: Rizzoli, 2007).
50. Aline B. Saarinen, "Art as Architectural Decoration," *Architectural Forum* 100, no. 6 (June 1954): 133.
51. John E. Burchard, "Alienated Affectations in the Arts," in "The Visual Arts Today," ed. György Kepes, special issue, *Daedalus* 89, no. 1, (Winter 1960): 52.
52. Le Corbusier, "Architecture and the Arts," 48–49; Le Corbusier quoted in Henry-Russell Hitchcock and Philip Johnson, *The International Style* (New York: Museum of Modern Art, 1932), 73–74. See also, Troy, *Modernism and the Decorative Arts in France*.
53. For more on CIAM, see Ockman, *Architecture Culture 1943–1968*; Barry Bergdoll, "The Synthesis of the Arts and MoMA," *Docomomo Journal*, no. 42 (Summer 2010): 110–13; and Golan, *Muralnomad*.
54. For a thorough history of these commissions and the building of the UNESCO Headquarters see, Christopher E. M. Pearson, *Designing UNESCO: Art, Architecture and International Politics at Mid-Century* (Farnham, Surrey, UK: Ashgate, 2010).
55. Carlos Raúl Villanueva quoted in, Carlos Brillembourg, "Architecture and Sculpture: Villanueva and Calder's Aula Magna," in *Latin American Architecture 1929–1960: Contemporary Reflections*, ed. Carlos Brillembourg (New York: Monacelli Press, 2004), 71. See also Jorge Francisco Liernur, "Abstraction, Architecture, and the 'Synthesis of

the Arts' Debates in the Rio de la Plata, 1936–1956," in Brillembourg, *Latin American Architecture 1929–1960*, 74–98; Luis E. Carranza and Fernando Luiz Lara, *Modern Architecture in Latin America: Art, Technology, and Utopia* (Austin: University of Texas Press, 2014); and Jennifer Josten, *Mathias Goeritz: Modernist Art and Architecture in Cold War Mexico* (New Haven, CT: Yale University Press, 2018).

56. Open letter by Jean Gorin, "La Synthèse des arts majeurs, est-elle possible?," September 26, 1956, translated and paraphrased by Walter Gropius in Pietro Belluschi et al., "Views on Art and Architecture: A Conversation," 72; and Josep Lluís Sert quoted in, "A Symposium on How to Combine Architecture, Painting, and Sculpture," *Interiors* 110 (May 1951): 103.
57. Theodore J. Roszak, "Some Problems of Modern Sculpture," *Magazine of Art* 42 (February 1949): 55; and Roszak quoted in Irving Titel, "Architectural Sculpture Today," *Arts & Architecture* 69, no. 11 (November 1952): 24.
58. David Smith, "The Artist and the Architect (1957)," in *David Smith*, ed. Garnett McCoy (New York: Praeger, 1973), 145–46.
59. Peter Blake, "Architecture: Plain or Fancy?" *Design Quarterly*, no. 30 (1954): 25–26; and Harris Armstrong quoted in Bitterman, *Art in Modern Architecture*, 134–35.
60. Wallace K. Harrison, *Architecture Needs Sculpture* (New York: Architectural League, 1946), n.p.
61. Josep Lluís Sert and Walter Gropius quoted in Belluschi et al., "Views on Art and Architecture: A Conversation," 69, 73; and Ada Louise Huxtable, "Art with Architecture: New Terms of an Old Alliance," *New York Times*, September 13, 1959, 20.
62. Saarinen, "Art as Architectural Decoration," 133.
63. Eduard Trier, *Form and Space: The Sculpture of the Twentieth Century* (London: Thames & Hudson, 1961), 253.
64. Marcel Breuer quoted in Lipman, *Calder's Universe*, 25. For a comprehensive discussion of Bertoia's large-scale commissions and relationships with architects see, Marin R. Sullivan, "'The Moment of Sharing': Harry Bertoia's Large-Scale Commissions," in *Harry Bertoia: Sculpting Mid-Century Modern Life*, ed. Jed Morse and Marin R. Sullivan (Zurich: Scheidegger & Spiess, forthcoming).
65. Henry-Russell Hitchcock, *Architecture of Skidmore, Owings & Merrill, 1950–1962* (New York: Praeger, 1963), 13; Nicholas Adams, *Skidmore, Owings & Merrill: SOM Since 1936* (Milan: Electa Architecture, 2007), 11. Both Bruce Graham and William Hartmann served as trustees of the Art Institute of Chicago and helped facilitate the realization of major public artworks later in the 1960s and 1970s. For example, Hartmann was instrumental in the realization of Calder's *La Grande Vitesse* (1967) in Grand Rapids, Michigan. Bruce John Graham, oral history interview by Betty J. Blum, May 25–28, 1997, transcript c. 1998, p. 206, CAOHP, http://digital-libraries.saic.edu/cdm/ref/collection/caohp/id/20388; and William Hartmann, CAOHP, 159–160. See also, "Art + SOM: Working with Alexander Calder," Skidmore, Owings & Merrill, https://www.som.com/ideas/slideshows/art_som_working_with_alexander_calder.
66. Gordon Bunshaft, oral history interview by Betty J. Blum, April 4–7, 1989, transcript c. 1990, p. 178, CAOHP, http://digital-libraries.saic.edu/cdm/ref/collection/caohp/id/18407. Bunshaft designed the 1962 expansion of the Albright-Knox Art Gallery in Buffalo, New York, and in the 1960s and '70s he and his wife, Nina Wayler, donated several works from their private collection to the museum. For more on Bunshaft's interests in fine art, see Nicholas Adams, *Gordon Bunshaft and SOM: Building Corporate Modernism* (New Haven, CT: Yale University Press, 2019).
67. Andrea O. Dean, "Bunshaft and Noguchi: An Uneasy but Highly Productive Architect-Artist Collaboration," *AIA Journal* 65 (October 1976): 52; and Gordon Bunshaft quoted in Martin Friedman, "Noguchi's Imaginary Landscapes," *Design Quarterly*, nos. 106/107 (1978): 47. For more on the Connecticut General Life Insurance Company project, see Leaster Beall, *Building for Tomorrow* (Hartford: Connecticut General Life Insurance Company, 1957).
68. On "plop art" see James Wines, "Public Art—Private Art," *Art in America* (January 1970): 4; James Wines, *De-Architecture* (New York: Rizzoli, 1987), 60; and Richard Serra and Clara Weyergraf-Serra, *Richard Serra, Interviews, Etc. 1970–1980* (New York: Hudson River Museum, 1980), 166.
69. Serge Chermayeff quoted in "A Look at Lobbies," *Architectural Forum* 104, no. 1 (January 1956): 122.
70. Douberley, "The Corporate Model," 21; Friedman, "Cultured Corporation," 233–48.
71. Alex Potts, "Introduction: The Idea of Modern Sculpture," in *Modern Sculpture Reader*, ed. Jon Wood, David Hulks, and Alex Potts (Leeds: Henry Moore Institute, 2007), xiv.

Chapter 1: The Space Above

1. Nicholas Adams, *Skidmore, Owings & Merrill: SOM Since 1936* (Milan: Electa Architecture, 2007), 59; Russell McCormick, "Custom Built Terrace Hotel Opens," *Cincinnati Post*, July 19, 1948, 14; "Terrace Plaza Hotel Nomination", *National Register of Historic Places Registration Form*, United States Department of the Interior, uploaded by Cincinnati Preservation, 1, 2018, http://cincinnatipreservation.org/wp-content/uploads/2018/01/Terrace-Plaza-NR-Nomination-June-2017.pdf; and William Hartmann, oral history interview by Betty J. Blum, October 30–November 2, 1989, transcript c. 2003, p. 77, CAOHP, http://digital-libraries.saic.edu/cdm/ref/collection/caohp/id/23045. Morris Lapidus was the architect to the Bond clothing store, one of the two anchors in the retail space on the seven floors below the hotel.
2. "Modern Art for Cincinnati," *Art Digest* 21, no. 16 (May 15, 1947): 16.
3. Shawn Patrick Tubb, *Cincinnati's Terrace Plaza Hotel: An Icon of American Modernism* (Cincinnati, OH: Cincinnati Book Publishing, 2013), 44. Saul Steinberg came to Cincinnati to install his mural in March 1948. Costantino Nivola came with him to help.
4. "Chronology," in *Calder/Miró*, ed. Elizabeth Hutton Turner and Oliver Wick (London: Philip Wilson Publishers, 2004), 292; and Oliver Wick, " 'Je vais t'emporter en Amérique: Prépare-toi': A Long Road to Monumental Dimensions—Beyond Painting," in Turner and Wick, *Calder/Miró*, 68.
5. Wick, 79–80; *Mobiles and Stabiles by Alexander Calder* (Cincinnati, OH: Cincinnati Art Museum, 1942); and Geoffrey T. Hellman, "Onward and Upward with the Arts: Calder Revisited," *New Yorker*, October 22, 1960, 176. The exhibition at CAM ran from April 7 to May 3, 1942, predating Adams's tenure, who was not hired at CAM until 1945, so the exhibition had more to do with Matisse's advocacy of the artists he represented.
6. Alexander Calder to Keith Warner, July 1946, Keith Warner Papers, 1935–1975, AAA; Wick, "Je vais t'emporter en Amérique," 80, 86.
7. Joan Miró to Pierre Matisse, January 26, 1947 quoted in, Wick, 73.
8. Natalie de Blois, oral history interview by Betty J. Blum, March 12–15, 2002, transcript c. 2004, p. 28, CAOHP, http://digital-libraries.saic.edu/cdm/ref/collection/caohp/id/15893. De Blois recounted in the interview that Gordon Bunshaft, who came on to the project at a later stage, was more involved with the commissioned artists, "because he

was interested in that [the art]." She had lunch once with Calder and Bunshaft and met Miró, but never encountered Steinberg or any of the other artists working on pieces for the hotel.

9. Museum of Modern Art, "Museum of Modern Art Shows Newly Commissioned Mural by Joan Miro," press release no. 48302–12, March 3, 1948, https://www.moma.org/documents/moma_press-release_325592.pdf.
10. Aline B. Louchheim, "New Miro Mural Placed on Display: Work on View Here Example of Extreme Abstract Art Used in Modern Decor," *New York Times*, March 3, 1948, 26.
11. Mary Mix, "Reviews: Barroom Art in the Modern Manner," *Architectural Forum* 88, no. 4 (April 1948): 150; and Louchheim, "New Miro Mural Placed on Display," 26.
12. Adams, *SOM Since 1936*, 13; "New Landmark," *Time* 52, no.3 (July 19, 1948): 94; "When They Build Cincinnati's New Terrace Plaza Hotel. . . . They Dared to Be Different," *Hotel Monthly* (August 1948): 22–39, 72–80; and "Cincinnati's Terrace Plaza," *Architectural Forum* 88, no. 12 (December 1948): 81–96.
13. Mix, "Barroom Art in the Modern Manner," 148; "Storetop Hotel," *Life*, September 20, 1948, 83; "Arrival in Cincinnati," *Fortune* 38 (October 1948): 113, 115; and "Cincinnati's Terrace Plaza," 84.
14. James Davis quoted in, Eleanor Bitterman, *Art in Modern Architecture* (New York: Reinhold Publishing, 1952), 168. Davis would soon after abandon sculpture altogether and turn his artistic focus to avant-garde filmmaking. Little substantive scholarly attention has been given to Davis, see Robert A. Haller, ed., *Jim Davis: The Flow of Energy* (New York: Anthology Film Archives, 1992).
15. Bitterman, *Art in Modern Architecture,* 78; "Everything's up to date in Cincinnati," *Harper's* 196, no. 1177 (June 1948): 576; and "Cincinnati's Terrace Plaza," 84.
16. Bitterman, 118; and Hellman, "Calder Revisited," 176. Calder recounted in 1960, "I understand that people there [in Cincinnati / at the Terrace Hotel] now say, 'I'll meet you under that thing.'"
17. See Eric Mumford, "Triumph and Eclipse: Modern Architecture in St. Louis and the School of Architecture," in *Modern Architecture in St. Louis: Washington University and Postwar American Architecture, 1948–1973* (St. Louis, MO: Washington University, 2004), 44; and "Current Buildings: Offices," *Architects' Journal* 112, no. 2900 (September 7 and 14, 1950): 235–36. The project is also sometimes referred to as the Magic Chef Building, but on Harris Armstrong's blueprints the project is listed as the Administration Building of the American Stove Company. It will be referred to here as the American Stove Company Building.
18. Harris Armstrong quoted in Bitterman, *Art in Modern Architecture,* 134–35.
19. American Stove Building Blueprint 46–5 (3), series 5, box DR 13.11, folder 1, HAC; Genevieve Cortinovis, "Sculpting St. Louis's Modern Landscape," in *St. Louis Modern*, ed. David Conradson, Genevieve Cortinovis, and Mary Reid Brunstom (St. Louis, MO: Saint Louis Art Museum, 2015), 56; Robert Campbell Plastering Company is named as the lathing and plastering contractor on the job in "Metal Lath News," advertising feature, *Progressive Architecture* 37, no. 9 (September 1956), n.p. "Progress in St. Louis—The American Stove Company," *Architectural Forum* (October 1948): 77; and Harris Armstrong to Isamu Noguchi, August 8, 1946, INF. The model remained in the possession of Armstrong until he gifted it to the Saint Louis Art Museum in 1970.
20. See "The Isamu Noguchi Catalogue Raisonné," Isamu Noguchi Foundation and Garden Museum, https://www.noguchi.org/research/catalogue; Shoji Sadao, *Buckminster Fuller and Isamu Noguchi: Best of Friends* (Milan: 5 Continents, 2011), 115, 145; and Isamu Noguchi, "Meanings in Modern Sculpture (1949)," in *Isamu Noguchi: Essays and Conversations*, ed. Diane Apostolos-Cappadona and Bruce Altshuler (New York: Harry N. Abrams, 1994), 35.

    There were two *Musical Weathervane* works, both made in 1933 and incorporating light bulbs. One is made from plaster, while the other is magnesite. There are other works in Noguchi's oeuvre that have "lunar" in the title, some of which bear formal resemblance to Lunar light sculptures. In addition to the related ceilings for American Stove Company and Time & Life Buildings, there are thirteen works made of magnesite that also incorporate electric components. Fuller's first geodesic dome used in a commercial design project, covered the interior courtyard of the Ford Pavilion from the 1939 World's Fair, that had been moved by the company to Dearborn Michigan in 1953.
21. Bruce Altshuler, "Isamu Noguchi Indoors: Home Furnishings and Interior Design," in *Isamu Noguchi: Sculptural Design*, ed. Jochen Eisenbrand, Katarina V. Posch, and Alexander Von Vegesack (Weil am Rhein: Vitra Design Museum, 2001), 131; "New Shapes for Lighting," *Life*, March 10, 1952, 114–15, 117; and Arthur Drexler, "Lighting Restudied," *Interiors* 110, no. 4 (November 1950): 119.
22. Isamu Noguchi, *Isamu Noguchi: A Sculptor's World* (New York: Steidl, 2015), 27; Altshuler, "Isamu Noguchi Indoors," 132; and Janine Biunno, Noguchi Museum archivist, email to the author, May 24, 2019.

    Very little primary or secondary information exists on the commissions for both the SS *Argentina* and the Time & Life Building. *Lunar Voyage* (1947) was destroyed when the ship was scuttled during the 1960s and the Time & Life ceiling was also lost following the corporation's move in 1959 to the new Time & Life Building at 1271 Avenue of the Americas. Harrison was involved at Rockefeller Center between 1932 and 1935, and with the Time & Life Building in 1937, and the Associated Press Building in 1938, over one of the main exterior doors of which Noguchi created the stainless-steel, high-relief sculpture *News* (1938–40). Harrison was responsible for the overall space in the Time & Life Building where the ceiling and "sloping walls" were installed but does not seem to have worked directly with Noguchi on the project. There were multiple partners at Harrison's firm during these years, and the *New Yorker* article—Philip Hamburger and Brendan Gill, "No More Shirts," *New Yorker*, December 2, 1944, 23—cited a Mr. Yamasaki and Ann Hatfield as in charge of the project, though it is unclear what contributions either of them made.
23. "Metal Lath News," n.p.
24. Undated handwritten contract from Harris Armstrong to Isamu Noguchi, INF; and "Progress in St. Louis," 71.
25. "Progress in St. Louis," 71. Few color photos of the building at the time of its construction exist, but color choices in the lobby are noted in "Current Buildings: Offices," 238.
26. "Offices Influence Results," *American Business* 19, no. 5 (May 1949): 53–54.
27. Isamu Noguchi quoted in "Progress in St. Louis," 76.
28. "NYIA," *Progressive Architecture* 38, no. 12 (December 1957): 86.
29. "Fine New Front Door for Jet-Age America," *Life*, December 16, 1957, 102–4; Richard Lemon, "Mobiles: The Soaring Art of Alexander Calder," *Saturday Evening Post*, February 27, 1965, 31; and Paul J. Friedlander, "Idlewild Transformed," *New York Times*, December 8, 1957, 3. See also, "Chronology," Calder Foundation, http://calder.org/life/chronology. The work is usually cited as being forty-five not forty feet wide. Additionally, while Calder finished the work on schedule in April 1957, the completion of the building fell behind. It was kept in a storeroom near

the IAB, and Calder was present for the installation in September 1957.

30. Calder quoted in, Robert Osborn, "Calder's International Monuments," *Art in America* 57 (March/April 1969): 37; and Calder quoted in, "Design in Motion," *Time*, May 26, 1958, 84.
31. Calder quoted in Hellman, "Calder Revisited," 169.
32. Osborn, "Calder's International Monuments," 37; and Hellman, 168.
33. Osborn, 35. For the Carnegie International, the mobile's paddles were white and the corresponding bars black. Calder later convinced the Pittsburgh Airport to repaint the whole work red and sent them four cans of paint to use. However, the airport diluted the paint and the work ended up a salmon pink.
34. Osborn, 37.
35. Mix, "Reviews: Barroom Art in the Modern Manner," 150.
36. Max Abramovitz quoted in, Tomkins, 48.
37. Harriet Janis, "Mobiles," *Arts & Architecture* (February 1948), 58; and Dorothy Adlow, "Lippold's Latest," *Christian Science Monitor* (December 24, 1962), accessed in Richard Lippold Scrapbooks, 1935–1968, reel N69-117, Willard Gallery Records, c. 1940–1956, AAA; Stuart Preston, "Art: 'Orpheus and Apollo': Lippold's Copper Alloy-Steel Sculpture Is Hung in Philharmonic Hall," *New York Times*, December 21, 1962, 5.
38. Richard Lippold quoted in, Nelson Lansdale, "Lippold and His Sculpture," in *Philharmonic Hall: Lincoln Center for the Performing Arts, 1962–1963*, 29, accessed in Philharmonic: Clippings, box 20, folder 3, Max Abramovitz Architectural Records and Papers Collection, Drawings and Archives, Avery Architectural and Fine Arts Library, Columbia University, New York City.
39. Tomkins, 49, 102.
40. John P. Shanley, "TV at Lincoln Center: C.B.S. to Cover First Program Tonight From New Philharmonic Hall," *New York Times*, September 23, 1962, 145; "Fanfare and Flourishes for a Temple of Music," *Life*, October 5, 1962, sec. A, 100–103, sec. B, 100, 102; and Tomkins, 79, 93, 105.
41. Richard Lippold quoted in Jack Burnham, "Richard Lippold: Shaping Space with Reflected Light," in *Richard Lippold: Sculpture*, ed. Curtis L. Carter (Milwaukee, WI: Haggerty Museum of Art, Marquette University, 1990), 26, 28. On Richard Kelly see Margaret Maile Petty, "Illuminating the Glass Box: The Lighting Designs of Richard Kelly," *Journal of the Society of Architectural Historians* 66, no. 2 (June 2007): 194–219.
42. Jack Burnham, *Beyond Modern Sculpture: The Effects of Science and Technology on the Sculpture of This Century* (New York: George Braziller, 1968), 159.
43. Lippold quoted in Tomkins, 52, 54, 80; and George S. Brady, *Materials Handbook: An Encyclopedia for Purchasing Agents, Engineers, Executives, and Foremen* (New York: McGraw-Hill, 1963), 497. Also known as "yellow metal," the alloy was named after George Frederick Muntz, who patented it in Birmingham, England in 1832.
44. Ellipses appear in the original manuscript for the advertisement, C. James Price to Richard Lippold, June 16, 1965, Proofs and layouts from Richard Lippold, Art and Artist Files, Smithsonian American Art and Portrait Gallery Library, Smithsonian Libraries, Washington, DC; and Richard Lippold, "Projects for Pan Am and Philharmonic," *Art in America* 50, no. 2 (Summer 1962): 55.
45. Adlow, "Lippold's Latest"; Lippold, "Projects for Pan Am and Philharmonic," 55; Lippold quoted in, Tomkins, 49; and "Orpheus and Apollo," *Time* 81, no. 1 (January 4, 1963): 36.
46. John Canaday, "Lincoln Center Pool Gets Huge Sculpture: Henry Moore to Supervise Installation," *New York Times*, August 25, 1965, 41; Grace Glueck, "Ticket Window (Nonfunctional) Is Installed at Lincoln Center," *New York Times*, November 12, 1965, 45; Pauline Rose, "Henry Moore's American Patrons and Public Commissions," in *Henry Moore: Sculptural Process and Public Identity*, ed. Jennifer Mundy and Christopher Griffin (Tate Research Publication, 2015), https://www.tate.org.uk/art/research-publications/henry-moore/pauline-rose-henry-moores-american-patrons-and-public-commissions-r1145958; and Harriet F. Senie, *Contemporary Public Sculpture: Tradition, Transformation, and Controversy* (Oxford: Oxford University Press, 1992), 93–139.
47. John Canaday, "The List of Art: Of the 8 Works Decorating the Met, Dufy's May Prove the Most Successful," *New York Times*, September 17, 1966, 17. Canaday described Callery's sculpture as "nominally the most modern work in the place, but its weaknesses are such that only its placement, pinned up like a piece of junk jewelry atop a proscenium arch that seems to have been built of gilded Nabisco Wafers, could lend it any illusion of weight and strength." Little to no scholarship has been devoted to Callery or her work, but she did create a number of commissioned sculptures for architectural projects during the mid-twentieth century. She was also an important interlocutor, especially between artists and architects during the period. For example, Callery and Harrison were close friends, she introduced him to Calder in Paris before WWII. See also, Victoria Newhouse, *Wallace K. Harrison: Architect* (New York: Rizzoli, 1989). The main auditorium of the Metropolitan Opera House features twelve chandeliers; the lobby, eleven.
48. See Charles A. Riley, *Art at Lincoln Center: The Public Art and List Print and Poster Collections* (Hoboken, NJ: John Wiley & Sons, 2008); Alexandria Symonds, "The Space-Age Story Behind the Metropolitan Opera's Chandeliers," *T: The New York Times Style Magazine*, May 13, 2016, https://www.nytimes.com/slideshow/2016/05/13/t-magazine/metropolitan-opera-chandeliers/s/Lobmeyr-slide-B0YW.html; Cécile Whiting, "Philip Johnson: The Whence and Whither of Art in Architecture," *Journal of the Society of Architectural Historians* 75, no. 3 (September 2016): 318–38; Wallace K. Harrison to Hans Harald Rath, September 25, 1963, cited in Symonds, "The Space-Age Story"; and Kyna Leski, "Metropolitan Opera Chandelier Concept Sketch," Medium, September 24, 2017, https://medium.com/@kynaleski/metropolitan-opera-chandelier-concept-sketch-35fab9d520c2.
49. Josiah McElheny and Scott Rothkopf, "1000 Words," *Artforum* 44 (November 2005): 237. McElheny has explored the form of the "sputnik" chandeliers from the Metropolitan Opera in a number of recent sculptural works, including his *An End to Modernity* (2005). For more on these projects and their relationship to the J. & L. Lobmeyr chandeliers, see Helen Molesworth, *Some Pictures of the Infinite* (Boston: Institute of Contemporary Art, 2012); and Lynne Cooke and Josiah McElheny, eds., *A Space for an Island Universe* (Madrid: Museo Nacional Centro de Arte Reina Sofia, 2009).
50. Preston, "Orpheus and Apollo," 5.
51. Hilton Kramer, "Sculpture: Eduardo Chillida in Houston; Full Survey Points Up Artist's Development," *New York Times*, October 15, 1966, 25. Lippold did in fact create a previous *Gemini* (1947) leading to the inclusion of "II" for the Houston piece. *Gemini* is a smaller (15 ¾ x 11 ½ x 8 in.), two-part autonomous sculpture made of brass, steel, and copper, currently held in the collection of the Munson-Williams-Proctor Arts Institute in Utica, NY. For more on NASA's Gemini Program, see "Gemini: Bridge to the Moon," NASA, https://www.nasa.gov/mission_pages/gemini/index.html.
52. Wesley Janz, "Theaters of Power: Architectural and Cultural Productions," *Journal of Architectural Education*

50, no. 4 (May 1997): 230; Howard Brick, *Age of Contradiction: American Thought and Culture in the 1960s* (New York: Twayne Publishers, 1998), 11–12; and Martin Mayer, *Bricks, Mortar and the Performing Arts: Report on the Twentieth Century Fund Task Force on Performing Arts Centers* (New York: Twentieth Century Fund, 1970); Ann Holmes, "Jesse H. Jones Hall for the Performing Arts Opening Night Program," pp. 18–20, RLP; and "Debut in Houston," *Newsweek*, October 17, 1966, 108.

53. See Newhouse, *Wallace K. Harrison*; Spiro Kostof, *A History of Architecture* (New York: Oxford University Press, 1985), 719; Jane Jacobs, *The Death and Life of Great American Cities* (New York: Vintage Books, 2016), 168; and Richard Lippold, "Architecture 45a Class Session on the Integration of Art and Architecture," (lecture, Department of Architecture, Yale University, New Haven, CT, October 29, 1964), transcript, p. 2, RLP.

    John Harwood adds that, "nearly from its beginning, [Lincoln Center] bore an unfortunate epithet: 'Monumental Modernism.' It is unfortunate because this derogatory stylistic term, often linked with degenerate or fascist architecture, has discouraged many an architectural historian or preservationist from studying Lincoln Center's complicated history," "More Lincoln Center than Lincoln Center: Max Abramovitz versus the Fortress," *Docomomo*, no. 31 (September 2004): 96.

54. Julia L. Foulkes, "The Other West Side Story: Urbanization and the Arts Meet at Lincoln Center," *Amerikastudien / American Studies* 52, no. 2 (2007): 232; Edgar B. Young, *Lincoln Center: The Building of an Institution* (New York: New York University Press, 1980); and "Text of Statement by Lincoln Center for the Arts," *New York Times*, September 12, 1957, 28.

55. Foulkes, "Other West Side Story," 242; Sidney Tillim, "In the Galleries: Richard Lippold," *Arts Magazine* 36, no. 7 (April 1962): 55, cited in Richard Lippold Scrapbooks, 1935–1968, reel N69–117, Willard Gallery Records, c. 1940–1956, AAA.

    For more thorough analyses of the sociopolitical dynamics involved in the realization of Lincoln Center, see, for example, Robert A. Caro, *The Power Broker: Robert Moses and the Fall of New York* (New York: Alfred A. Knopf, 1974); Hilary Ballon and Kenneth T. Jackson, eds., *Robert Moses and the Modern City: The Transformation of New York* (New York: W. W. Norton, 2007); and Samuel Zipp, *Manhattan Projects: The Rise and Fall of Urban Renewal in Cold War New York* (New York: Oxford University Press, 2010).

56. "Debut in Houston," 108; and Kyle Shelton, "Culture War in Downtown Houston: Jones Hall and the Postwar Battle over Exclusive Space," *Southwestern Historical Quarterly* 116, no. 1 (July 2012): 4.

57. John T. Jones Jr. quoted in "Lippold Sculpture Commissioned," *Houston Post*, February 13, 1966. See also pamphlet produced by the Jesse H. Jones Hall for the Performing Arts in conjunction with the Grand Opening Commemorative Week (October 2–9, 1966), RLP.

58. Lippold quoted in Eleanor Kempner Freed, "Mr. Lippold Explains," *Houston Post*, February 16, 1966, 32; and Richard Lippold, "An Artist's Point of View," *Architectural Record* (December 1978): 71. Originally the work was to extend outdoors, through the glass entrance wall, but due to irresolvable engineering issues regarding how to maintain climate control inside, this was not realized. The intended supports are still visible in the travertine-marble portico near the ceiling of the outdoor plaza area.

59. Pamphlet produced by the Jesse H. Jones Hall, 1966, RLP.

60. Lippold, "An Artist's Point of View," 71, 73.

61. Richard Lippold quoted in Eleanor Kempner Freed, "A Human Dimension," *Houston Post*, September 18, 1966, 14.

62. Vernon Porterfield, "New Dallas Library," *Library Journal* 80, no. 21 (December 1, 1955): 2669; and David McComb, *Spare Time in Texas: Recreation and History in the Lone Star State* (Austin: University of Texas Press, 2008), 113.

63. Bertoia quoted in "3,000 Pounds: New Mural Now Hangs in Library," *Dallas Morning News*, June 25, 1955.

64. Bertoia quoted in "3,000 Pounds"; and "Art for Art's Sake: Library's Abstract Mural Sparks Query: What Is It?," *Dallas Times Herald*, June 26, 1955.

65. R. L. Thornton and W. H. Harris quoted in Allen Quinn, "'A Bunch of Junk' Mayor Comments on Gilded Mural," *Dallas Morning News*, June 28, 1955.

66. Allen Quinn, "Library Architect Purchases Mural," *Dallas Morning News*, July 9, 1955; and Bob Stanley, "Mural's 'Demise' Arouses Artist," *Dallas Times Herald*, July 9, 1955.

67. Allen Quinn, "Controversial Mural to Hang in Library," *Dallas Morning News*, July 23, 1955.

68. H. Branch, "Powerful Minority," *Dallas Morning News*, August 7, 1955; and Jack Hughes, "Future Mural (Letters)," *Dallas Morning News*, July 19, 1955.

69. On Dallas controversies see, Jerry Bywaters, *Seventy-Five Years of Art in Dallas: The History of the Dallas Art Association and the Dallas Museum of Fine Arts* (Dallas, TX: Dallas Museum of Fine Arts, 1978); Alfred Frankfurter, "Shame in Dallas," *ARTnews*, Summer 1955; and George Lee, "The Foundation for the Arts," in *Dallas Museum of Art 100 Years*, ed. Dorothy Kosinski et al. (Dallas, TX: Dallas Museum of Art, 2003), 22.

70. Lon Tinkle, "Notes from the World: We Find Library's Mural Grand," *Dallas Morning News*, July 3, 1955; and "Art for Art's Sake: Library's Abstract Mural Sparks Query: What is it?," *Dallas Times Herald*, June 26, 1955.

71. Quinn, "Controversial Mural to Hang in Library"; and Mayor Thornton quoted in "Art Screen up Again at Library," *Dallas Times Herald*, September 1955.

72. Dorothea McGrath, "AIA Urges City to Pay for Mural," *Dallas Morning News*, July 24, 1955.

73. Allen Quinn, "Councilmen Accept Mural for Library," *Dallas Morning News*, July 26, 1955.

74. Jerry Bywaters quoted in "Comment of Library Mural Ranges from Castigation to Approval," *Dallas Times Herald*, June 27, 1955; and Rual Askew, "Art & Artists: That Bertoia 'Affair' Just Won't Go Away," *Dallas Times Herald*, July 10, 1963.

Chapter 2: Dividing Space

1. Museum of Modern Art, "Modern Relief Exhibition to Be Shown at Museum of Modern Art," press release no. 510614–33, June 19, 1951, 2, https://www.moma.org/documents/moma_press-release_325781.pdf. *Modern Relief* was on view at MoMA from June 20 to July 15, 1951.

2. "MoMA Exh 0479 (*Modern Relief*) Master Checklist, Museum of Modern Art," 1951–1952, 1–2, https://assets.moma.org/documents/moma_master-checklist_325780.pdf.

3. See for example, Oxford Art Online: Grove Art Online, s.v. "Relief Sculpture," by Charles Avery, 2003, https://doi.org/10.1093/gao/9781884446054.article.T071316.

4. Stuart Preston, "Museum Shows Architectural Art," *New York Times*, June 24, 1951, 82.

5. MoMA, "Modern Relief Exhibition."

6. Eleanor Bitterman, *Art in Modern Architecture* (New York: Reinhold Publishing, 1952), 77.

7. Peter Blake, *No Place like Utopia: Modern Architecture and the Company We Kept* (New York: Alfred A. Knopf, 1993), 111; and Announcment card for Jackson Pollock, November 21–December 10, 1949, Betty Parsons Gallery, New York City, Series 1: Artist Files, Pollock, Jackson: Announcements, 1948–1983, box 13, folder 12, Betty Parsons Gallery Records and Personal Papers, 1916–1991, AAA. This phrase appeared on one of the announcement cards for the exhibition, which took place from November

21–December 19, 1949, and featured paintings numbered consecutively *1–5, 7–37.*

8. Arthur Drexler, "Unframed Space: A Museum for Jackson Pollock's Painting," *Interiors* (January 1950): 90.
9. K. L. H. Wells, *Weaving Modernism: Postwar Tapestry between Paris and New York* (New Haven, CT: Yale University Press, 2019, 205–6.
10. Eric Lum, "Pollock's Promise: Toward an Abstract Expressionist Architecture," *Assemblage* no. 39 (August 1999): 66.
11. See *The Muralist and the Modern Architect* (New York: Kootz Gallery, 1950). William Baziotes worked with Philip Johnson on a mural for the Wiley House, New Canaan, CT (completed 1952). Adolph Gottlieb worked with Marcel Breuer on a mural for the Ferry Jr. Cooperative house, Vassar College, NY (completed 1951). David Hare worked with Frederick Kiesler on a staircase sculpture for *Endless House* (1947–60; never realized). Hans Hofmann worked with Josep Lluís Sert and Paul Lester Wiener on a mosaic mural for the bell tower of a civic center in Chimbote, Peru. Robert Motherwell worked with Walter Gropius and the Architects Collaborative on a mural for the Peter Thacher Junior High School in Attleboro, MA (completed in 1948).
12. Emily S. Warner, "Marketing the Monumental: Wall Painting at Midcentury," *Archives of American Art Journal* 56, no. 2 (Fall 2017): 37; and Jules Langsner, "More about the School of New York," *Arts & Architecture* (May 1951): 20.
13. Samuel M. Kootz, quoted in "The Muralist and the Modern Architect," *Arts & Architecture* 68, no. 4 (April 1951): 18–19; and Clement Greenberg, "Review of Exhibitions of Worden Day, Carl Holty, and Jackson Pollock (1948)," in *Arrogant Purpose, 1945–1949*, The Collected Essays and Criticism, vol. 2, ed. John O'Brian (Chicago: University of Chicago Press, 1986), 201–2.
14. William Kaizen, "Framed Space: Allan Kaprow and the Spread of Painting," *Grey Room*, no. 13 (Autumn 2003): 87–88; and Lum, "Pollock's Promise," 82.
15. Aline B. Louchheim, "Architect, Painter, and the Mural: Five Modernists Present Their Solutions for Projects," *New York Times*, October 1, 1950, 117.
16. "Exhibitions. Between Painters and Architects," *Interiors* 110, no. 4 (November 1950): 12. For more on Kiesler's *Endless House* see, "Frederick J. Kiesler's Endless House and Its Psychological Lighting," *Interiors* 110, no. 4 (November 1950): 122–29.
17. Gibson Danes, "Architectural Sculpture Today," *Magazine of Art* 40 (May 1947): 175.
18. Ada Louise Huxtable, "Jet Age Triumph: Saarinen's New Airport for Washington Is a Superb Monument to Our Time," *New York Times*, April 8, 1963, 363.
19. Rasa Gustaitis, "FAA Helps Put Government Structures on a New Plane," *Washington Post*, December 2, 1962, sec. E, 2; and Harry Bertoia, oral history interview by Paul Cummings, June 20, 1972, transcript p. 5, AAA.
20. Kevin Roche to Harry Bertoia, March 26, 1962, HBP; and Telegram from A. P. Meyers, Federal Aviation Agency to Harry Bertoia, 1962, HBP. The official contract was countersigned by the FAA on September 1, 1962.
21. Bertoia quoted in Beverly Twitchell, *Harry Bertoia* (Allentown, PA: Allentown Art Museum, 1976), 36; and "*Life* Presents R. Buckminster Fuller's Dymaxion World," *Life*, March 1, 1943, 41–55. Fuller requested a patent for the map in 1944 and was granted one, the first cartographic projection process ever to receive a US Patent in 1946. He published a version, made with Shoji Sadao in 1954, under the name "Dymaxion Airocean World," while at Black Mountain College in North Carolina.
22. Harry Bertoia, oral history interview by Paul Cummings, June 20, 1972, transcript p. 21, AAA.
23. Bertoia quoted in Twitchell, *Harry Bertoia*, 36.
24. Two undated sketches showing wall for Dulles International Airport, Commissions for Architects, Corporations, Institutions and Individuals, Eero Saarinen & Associates: Dulles International Airport (1962–63), HBF.
25. Harry Bertoia, oral history interview by Paul Cummings, June 20, 1972, transcript p. 22, AAA.
26. Undated document describing artwork at Dulles International Airport, HS500 IAD.02, Records of the Federal Aviation Agency, National Archives, Washington DC; this phrase is also attributed to FAA Administrator Najeeb E. Halaby, quoted in Gustaitis "FAA Helps Put Government Structures on New Plane," *Washington Post*, December 2, 1962; and Harry Bertoia, oral history interview by Paul Cummings, June 20, 1972, transcript p. 22, AAA.
27. Richard M. Huber to Mr. Richard F. Bates, Federal Aviation Agency, August 13, 1962, Commissions for Architects, Corporations, Institutions and Individuals, Eero Saarinen & Associates: Dulles International Airport (1962–63), HBF.
28. Micaela Martegani, "Costantino Nivola in Springs," in *Costantino Nivola in Springs*, ed. Micaela Martegani (Southampton, NY: Parrish Art Museum, 2003), 17. Nivola left Italy in the summer of 1939 with his wife Ruth Guggenheim, who was Jewish, amid the rise of Fascism in Italy and the rest of Europe. Nivola also served as the director of the Design Workshop of the Harvard Graduate School of Design between 1954 and 1957.
29. Ernesto N. Rogers quoted in "Typewriter Palazzo in New York," *Architectural Forum* 101, no. 2 (August 1954): 99; and "Natural," Talk of the Town, *New Yorker*, June 5, 1954, 21.
30. Page Beauchamp, "Showrooms," *Progressive Architecture* 35, no. 11 (February 1954), 126; Gio Ponti, "Italia a New York," *Domus*, no. 298 (September 1954): 3; Olga Gueft, "Olivetti New York," *Interiors* 114, no. 4 (November 1954): 124; Dore Ashton, "Art, Artists and Architecture: Sand Sculpture by Costantino Nivola," *Architectural Record* 120, no. 4 (October 1956), 202; Ada Louise Huxtable, "Art with Architecture: New Terms of an Old Alliance," *New York Times*, September 13, 1959, 20; and "Typewriter Palazzo in New York," 99. The poet Frank O'Hara famously composed many poems on the outdoor Olivetti typewriter, many of which would be published in his *Lunch Poems* (San Francisco: City Light Books, 1964). For more on the Olivetti Showroom and the company's exhibition and promotion activities in New York City during the 1950s, see Jim Carter, "Italy on Fifth Ave: From the Museum of Modern Art to the Olivetti Showroom," *Modern Italy: Journal of the Association for the Study of Modern Italy* 23, no. 1 (February 2018): 103–22.
31. Alessandro Nivola quoted in "Natural," 21.
32. Aline B. Saarinen, "Business and Art: New and Encouraging Developments Looking Toward the Future," *New York Times*, June 6, 1954, 6; Gueft, "Olivetti New York," 124; and Huxtable, "Art with Architecture," 20.
33. Costantino Nivola, "Nivola between Sculpture and Architecture," *Zodiac* 4 (1959): 180.
34. Martegani, "Costantino Nivola in Springs," 28–30; and Eero Saarinen and Costantino Nivola, "Sculpture for Yale," *Art in America* 51, no. 1 (February 1963): 88.
35. Untitled statement by Costantino Nivola promoting his exhibition at the Peridot Gallery, New York City, December 13, 1955 to January 7, 1956, Artist Pamphlets, Ryerson Library Pamphlet File P-17190, Ryerson and Burnham Libraries at the Art Institute of Chicago; also, "The Work of Costantino Nivola," *Progressive Architecture* 37, no. 4 (April 1956): 116.
36. Harry Bertoia quoted in "For Architecture and Ornament: Ways of Diving the Cube," *Interiors* 125, no. 2 (September 1965): 134–37. Those still *in situ* on the campus of RIT, the planters were moved to the atrium of the Golisano Building. In August 1964, Bertoia had also proposed a pair

of freestanding poured bronzes for the entrance of the new Neiman Marcus store for the NorthPark Center mall in Dallas, TX that was being designed by Kevin Roche; but Stanley Marcus unexpectedly decided he no longer wanted to proceed with the commission.

37. John McAndrew, "First Look at the General Motors Technical Center," *Art in America* 44, (Spring 1956): 26–27. For more on this topic see, Louise A. Mozingo, *Pastoral Capitalism: A History of Suburban Corporate Landscapes* (Cambridge, MA: MIT Press, 2011). Eero Saarinen designed IBM's Thomas J. Watson Research Center and the Bell Telephone Laboratories in Holmdel, NJ. Gordon Bunshaft and SOM designed the headquarters of the Connecticut General Life Insurance Company in Bloomfield, CT.
38. Eero Saarinen, *Eero Saarinen on His Work: A Selection of Buildings Dating from 1947 to 1964 with Statements by the Architect*, ed. Aline B. Saarinen (New Haven, CT: Yale University Press, 1962), 30; Memorandum by Aline B. Saarinen to Eero Saarinen, August 9, 1954, folder 264, box 137, Series IV, Eero Saarinen Collection, MS 593, Manuscripts and Archives, Yale University Library, New Haven, CT; and Susan Skarsgard, *Where Today Meets Tomorrow: Eero Saarinen and the General Motors Technical Center* (New York: Princeton Architectural Press, 2019), 176. Sheeler visited the GMTC, while still under construction, in 1955.
39. Skarsgard, 115. The date for *Impetus* is unknown.
40. John Brunini and Geoffrey T. Hellman, "Metal Painter," Talk of the Town, *New Yorker*, August 25, 1956, 25.
41. Aline B. Saarinen quoted in Joy Hakanson, "A Walk in the Shadow of a Genius: The Widow of Eero Saarinen Casts an Eye on the Tech Center 10 Year Later," *Detroit News Pictorial Magazine*, June 26, 1966, 17; and Pevsner quoted in Sigfried Giedion and Antoine Pevsner, "On the Space-Emanating Power of Contemporary Sculpture (A Radio Dialogue) (1949)" and "Postscript (1957)," in *Architecture You and Me: The Diary of a Development* (Cambridge, MA: Harvard University Press, 1958), 57, 60. The gallery in Paris was likely the Galerie René Drouin as *La Colonne Développable de la Victoire* (1946) was shown there and also included in the MoMA exhibition *Naum Gabo and Antoine Pevsner*, February 10–April 25, 1948.
42. Eero Saarinen to Calder, 15 August 1951, "Chronology," Calder Foundation, http://www.calder.org/life/chronology; and Jed Perl, *Calder: The Conquest of Time; The Early Years, 1898–1940* (New York: Alfred A. Knopf, 2017) 263.
43. McAndrew, "First Look," 30; and Rosamond Fletcher, "The General Motors Technical Center: A Collaborative Enterprise," in *Eero Saarinen: Shaping the Future*, ed. Eeva-Lisa Pelkonen and Donald Albrecht (New Haven, CT: Yale University Press, 2011), 231.
44. Mark Coir, "The Cranbrook Factor," in *Eero Saarinen: Shaping the Future*, 41; Marianne Strengell and Olav Hammarstrom, oral history interview by Mark Coir, December 17, 1990, transcript p. 47, Oral History Collection, Cranbrook Archives, Bloomfield Hills, MI; and "Restaurant for an Industrial Complex," box 137, folder 263, Eero Saarinen Collection, Yale.
45. Eero Saarinen quoted in "Architectural Notes on the Central Restaurant Building of General Motors Technical Center," box 137, folder 257, Eero Saarinen Collection, Yale.
46. McAndrew, "First Look," 28.
47. Harry Bertoia, oral history interview by Paul Cummings, June 20, 1972, transcript p. 18, AAA.
48. "Architectural Notes on the Central Restaurant Building of General Motors Technical Center," Eero Saarinen Collection, Yale.
49. Harry Bertoia, oral history interview by Paul Cummings, June 20, 1972, transcript p. 19, AAA. Eero Saarinen and Aline B. Louchheim stopped by Bertoia's property in Pennsylvania toward the end of the construction of the GMTC screen, and the architect was reportedly thrilled and quite satisfied by the result. Saarinen was still married to Lily Swann Saarinen at this point, though he would marry Louchheim in 1954.
50. "General Motors Technical Center: Restaurant Building," *Progressive Architecture* 36, no. 2 (February 1955), 97; and Eugene Clute, "Abstractions in Metal," *Progressive Architecture* 36, no. 2 (February 1955): 104. For more information and a comprehensive list see, Marin R. Sullivan, "Appendix: Harry Bertoia's Large-Scale Commissions," in *Harry Bertoia: Sculpting Mid-Century Modern Life* (Zurich: Scheidegger & Spiess, forthcoming).
51. Nicholas Adams, "What Convinces Is Conviction," December 15, 2014, Medium, https://som.medium.com/gordon-bunshaft-4a52e5b2852d; and Gordon Bunshaft, oral history interview by Betty J. Blum, April 4–7, 1989, transcript c. 1990 p. 257, CAOHP, http://digital-libraries.saic.edu/cdm/ref/collection/caohp/id/18407.
52. Commissions for Architects, Corporations, Institutions and Individuals, Skidmore, Owens [sic], Merrill/ Gordon Bunshaft (1952–63), HBP.
53. Harry Bertoia to William M. Simpich, October 11, 1954; and Commissions for Architects, Corporations, Institutions and Individuals, HBP.
54. "15,000 Ooh and Ah at Opening of Dazzling, 'Newfangled' Bank," *New York Times*, October 5, 1954, 29; Jack Alexander, "The Bank That Has No Secrets," *Saturday Evening Post*, November 30, 1957, 37; "Showcase Bank Holds a Preview," *New York Times*, September 23, 1954, 51; "15,000 Ooh and Ah," 29; and "Manufacturers Trust Builds New Quarters," *Women's Wear Daily*, August 17, 1953, 8.

    The Manufacturers Trust Company Building is also sometimes referred to as the Manufacturers Hanover Trust Building, the original name of the bank that commissioned the structure. In 1961, the Manufacturers Trust Company merged with Central Hanover Bank & Trust Company, resulting in the Manufacturers Hanover Trust Company. The building is referred to here as the Manufacturers Trust Company Building and 510 Fifth Avenue, since both names are used by the architectural firm SOM. For additional information on the architectural design of the Manufacturers Hanover Trust Building and Skidmore, Owings & Merrill in general, see, for example, Nicholas Adams, *Skidmore, Owings & Merrill: SOM Since 1936* (Milan: Electa Architecture, 2007); Ernst-Joachim Danz, *SOM 1: Architecture of Skidmore, Owings & Merrill, 1950–1962* (New York, Monacelli, 2009); and Gordon Bunshaft, oral history, CAOHP, p. 257.

    Based on the few photographs published in the press, the fourth-floor offices were also decorated with a selection of modern paintings and sculptures, including a work by Marino Marini, but the Bertoia sculptures seem to be the only artworks commissioned specifically for the building.
55. "15,000 Ooh and Ah," 29; and Clute, "Abstractions in Metal," 104.
56. Lewis Mumford, "Crystal Lantern (1954)," in *From the Ground Up: Observations on Contemporary Architecture, Housing, Highway Building, and Civic Design* (New York: Harcourt, Brace, 1956), 173–74.
57. Ada Louise Huxtable, "Banker's Showcase," *Arts* 29 (December 1, 1954): 13; and "Metal Sculpture—Harry Bertoia," *Arts & Architecture* 72, no. 1 (January 1955): 18.
58. Herbert Hannum, "Collaboration," *Craft Horizons* 16, no. 3 (May/June 1956): 11; and Harry Bertoia, oral history interview by Paul Cummings, June 20, 1972, transcript p. 20, AAA.

59. Eduard Trier, *Form and Space: The Sculpture of the Twentieth Century* (London: Thames & Hudson, 1961), 264.
60. Robert Sowers, "Arts in Architecture: The Vista on Fifth Avenue," *Craft Horizons* 21, no. 1 (January/February 1961): 38–39. For more on the Kepes mural, see György Kepes, "The Visual Arts and the Sciences: A Proposal for Collaboration," *Architectural Record* 137, no. 5 (May 1965): 145–56.
61. "666 Fifth Avenue Opens Tomorrow; $40,000,000 Building Has Aluminum Face, Million Square Feet of Space Building Has Arcade," *New York Times*, November 24, 1957, 303.
62. Norman Tishman quoted in "Unusual Design for Office Lobby: Sculptor to Do Layout for Entrance to Skyscraper at 666 Fifth Avenue," *New York Times*, January 15, 1956, 4.
63. Robert Carson to Isamu Noguchi, October 21, 1955, INF.
64. Isamu Noguchi, *Isamu Noguchi: A Sculptor's World* (New York: Steidl, 2015), 18; Bruce Altshuler, "Isamu Noguchi Indoors: Home Furnishings and Interior Design," in *Isamu Noguchi: Sculptural Design*, ed. Jochen Eisenbrand, Katarina V. Posch, and Alexander Von Vegesack (Weil am Rhein: Vitra Design Museum, 2001), 132; and Letter from Robert Carson to Isamu Noguchi, October 21, 1955, INF.
65. Huxtable, "Art with Architecture," 20.
66. "Lighting is Architecture: Assertion," *Progressive Architecture* 39, no. 9 (September 1958): 145; "The Record Reports: Buildings in the News," *Architectural Record* 120, no. 3 (September 1956), 11.
67. Noguchi quoted in, "Progress in St. Louis—The American Stove Company," *Architectural Forum* (October 1948): 76.
68. Thomas H. Creighton, "The New Sensualism," *Progressive Architecture* 40, no. 9 (September 1959): 141–47.
69. Creighton, 141–47; Thomas H. Creighton, "The New Sensualism II," *Progressive Architecture* 40, no. 10 (October 1959): 180–90; and "Views: 'New Sensualists' Respond," *Progressive Architecture* 40, no. 11 (November 1959): 51, 53, 61, 64, 68, 236–37, 241.
70. Frederick Kiesler quoted in "The Endless House," *Architectural Forum* 93, no. 5 (November 1950): 124–26.
71. Creighton, "The New Sensualism II," 186–87.

Chapter 3: The Space Between

1. "The Splashiest Shopping Center in the U.S.," *Life* December 10, 1956, 61; "Two-level shopping centers," *Architectural Forum* 105, no. 6 (December 1956): 117. For a thorough history of Southdale and Gruen's other shopping center projects during the immediate postwar period see M. Jeffrey Hardwick, *Mall Maker: Victor Gruen, Architect of an American Dream* (Philadelphia: University of Pennsylvania Press, 2004).
2. Victor Gruen quoted in Ester McCoy, "West Coast Architects III: Victor Gruen," *Arts & Architecture* 81, no 10 (October 1964): 27; Victor Gruen, "Environmental Architecture," in "The Architect and the City: The 1962 AIA-ACSA Seminar Papers Presented at the Cranbrook Academy of Art, Part II," special issue, *Journal of Architectural Education* 17, no. 3, (December 1962): 97; Victor Gruen, *The Heart of Our Cities: The Urban Crisis, Diagnosis and Cure* (New York: Simon & Schuster, 1964); and Victor Gruen, quoted in G. H. Stedman, "The Rise of Shopping Centers," *Journal of Retailing* 31 (Spring 1955): 13.
3. Timothy Mennel, "Victor Gruen and the Construction of Cold War Utopias," *Journal of Planning History* 3, no. 2 (May 2005): 133. Dayton's was the one exception to Gruen's ban of signage outside of any store.
4. Victor Gruen to Harry Bertoia, August 13, 1953; Harry Bertoia to Victor Gruen, August 19, 1953; and Victor Gruen to Harry Bertoia, November 26, 1954, reel 14118, HBF.
5. Scott Donaldson, "You Can 'Rest in Wonderment'—A (Metal) Tree Grows in Southdale," *Minneapolis Star*, August 27, 1956, sec. A, 11.
6. Victor Gruen to Harry Bertoia, August 2, 1955 and February 1, 1956, reel 14118, HBF.
7. Edgardo Contini to Harry Bertoia, February 6, 1956; R. L. Baumfield to Harry Bertoia, March 9, 1956, reel 14118, HBF. While there had been talk of Bertoia creating three tree forms, they decided that the space could only feasibly accommodate two. The two sculptures were shipped to Minneapolis in late July 1956. Bertoia installed the work during the last two weeks of August 1956.
8. "Two-Level Shopping Centers," *Architectural Forum* 105, no. 6 (December 1956): 117; and "Buildings in Brief: Stores," *Architectural Forum* 106, no. 4 (April 1957): 132. A budget of $50,000 was allocated for art at Southdale, though the majority of this budget and certainly the majority of the focus went to the Bertoia commission. A twelve-foot sculpture of abstracted unicycle performers made of brazed copper and bronze sheet by Minneapolis-based sculptor Dorothy Berge adorned an outdoor upper-level terrace, a small-scaled sculpture of abstracted boys on stilts made from laminated walnut by Louise Kruger was placed near the eucalyptus tree in the central court, and a glass mosaic by Joseph Young adored the exterior walls of the newsstand, also in the garden court.
9. Inland Steel Pamphlet, Inland Steel Company Collection, Pamphlet File P-25969, Ryerson and Burnham Libraries at the Art Institute Chicago. A pamphlet produced for the building's open house states that the building took only 55 percent of the land site, while "Inland Steel Building Fact Sheets," February 3, 1958 states this number as 66 percent.
10. William Hartmann, oral history interview by Betty J. Blum, October 30–November 2, 1989, transcript c. 2003, pp. 116–119, CAOHP, http://digital-libraries.saic.edu/cdm/ref/collection/caohp/id/23045; and Leigh Block quoted in, "How to Spell Steel," *Time* 71, no. 6 (February 10, 1958): 82.
11. Open House pamphlet produced by the Inland Steel Company, 1957, "Inland Steel Building: Fact Sheets," 3 February 1958, 5; J. N. Macomb, Jr. to Mrs. Sylvia Leonard Wolf, 24 January 1967; and "Furnishings and Art: Inland Steel Building," pamphlet, all from Pamphlet File P-25969, Ryerson and Burnham Libraries at the Art Institute Chicago; and William Hartmann, oral history, CAOHP, 117.

    The letter from Macomb included a typed addendum stating that its contents are "nearly verbatim from Leigh B. Block." Leigh Block would also serve as the president of the Board of Trustees of the Art Institute of Chicago and would donate funds to establish an art exhibition venue at Northwestern University in 1980, today known as the Block Museum.
12. Edgar J. Kaufmann, Jr., "Inland Steel and Its Art," *Art in America* 45, no. 4 (Winter 1957): 23.
13. Jack Burnham, "Richard Lippold: Shaping Space with Reflected Light," in *Richard Lippold: Sculpture*, ed. Curtis L. Carter (Milwaukee, WI: Haggerty Museum of Art, Marquette University, 1990), 24. There is some discrepancy about whether the Blocks saw Lippold's *The Moon* (1949–50) or *The Sun* (1953–56), and at which museum they saw his work at all, prior to commissioning Lippold for the Inland Steel Building, but it is likely they would have seen both. *The Sun* was lent to the National Air and Space Museum in Washington, DC in 1976, where it was exhibited until 1984. It was briefly reinstalled at the met in New York in the late 1980s, but went into storage and is now too fragile to be shown. For more information see, "Richard Lippold: Variation within a Sphere, Number 10: The Sun

1953–56," MET Collection, https://www.metmuseum.org/art/collection/search/632931.

14. Commissions for Architects, Corporations, Institutions and Individuals, Inland Steel Company (1956), HBP; Leigh Block to Harry Bertoia, March 14, 1956, reel 14121, HBP; Bruce John Graham, oral history interview by Betty J. Blum, May 25–28, 1997, transcript c. 1998, p. 101, CAOHP, http://digital-libraries.saic.edu/cdm/ref/collection/caohp/id/20388; William Hartmann, oral history, CAOHP, 116–119; and Walter Netsch, oral history interview by Betty J. Blum, May 8 and June 5–28, 1995, transcript c. 1997, pp. 104–9, 114, CAOHP, https://digital-libraries.artic.edu/digital/collection/caohp/id/19289/..

    Walter Netsch did the first model for Inland Steel, but Bruce Graham took over the project when Netsch moved on to the Air Force Academy. Graham stated, "I'm not satisfied with the Lippold in Inland Steel. I should have been more aggressive. Bunshaft would have been more aggressive," Bruce John Graham, oral history, CAOHP, 101.
15. Richard Kelly to Mr. Clarence Weinberg, vice president of Inland Steel, October 31, 1957, reel D-342, RPL; and Kaufmann, "Inland Steel and Its Art," 26.
16. Alice T. Friedman, "The Cultured Corporation: Art, Architecture, and the Postwar Office Building," in *Architectures of Display: Department Stores and Modern Retail*, ed. Patricia Lara-Betancourt, Margaret Maile Petty, and Anna I. Lasc (New York: Routledge, 2018), 233–48; Amanda Ann Douberley, "The Corporate Model: Sculpture, Architecture, and the American City, 1946–1975" (PhD diss., University of Texas at Austin, 2015); and Kaufmann, "Inland Steel and Its Art," 26.
17. Richard Lippold, Untitled Statement on *Radiant I*, 1958, reel D-342, RPL.
18. Statement by Lippold originally published in 1957 in *Balance*, reel D-342, RPL; reprinted in Tomkins, 75.
19. Gibson Danes, "Architectural Sculpture Today," *Magazine of Art* 40 (May 1947): 174–75; and Dore Ashton, "Costantino Nivola," *Craft Horizons* 19, no. 1 (January/February 1959): 39.
20. Sam Hunter, *Irons in the Fire: An Exhibition of Metal Sculpture* (Houston, TX: Contemporary Arts Museum, 1957), n.p.
21. Harry Bertoia quoted in "Metal Sculpture—Harry Bertoia," *Arts & Architecture* 72, no. 1 (January 1955): 18.
22. Beverly Twitchell, *Harry Bertoia* (Allentown, PA: Allentown Art Museum, 1976), 6.
23. David Smith quoted in "The New Sculpture" (symposium, Museum of Modern Art, New York City, February 12, 1952), transcript p. 4, 30 N47n.7, Museum of Modern Art Library Archives, New York.
24. A. L. Chanin, "Machine Age in Sculpture," *New York Times*, May 3, 1959, 24. For the history of Modalloy, see Dorothy Seckler, "Revolution for Sculptors," *ARTnews* 49 (April 1950): 40–41, 64–65. Also see, Lisa Phillips, *The Third Dimension: Sculpture of the New York School* (New York: Whitney Museum of American Art, 1984), 20.
25. Nancy G. Heller, "Drawing in Space Ibram Lassaw (1913–2003)," *American Art* 18, no. 2 (Summer 2004): 108; and Ibram Lassaw, "Perspectives and Reflections of a Sculptor: A Memoir," *Leonardo* 1, no. 4 (October 1968): 352.
26. Herbert Read, *A Concise History of Modern Sculpture* (New York: Praeger, 1964), 245.
27. Jack Burnham, *Beyond Modern Sculpture: The Effects of Science and Technology on the Sculpture of This Century* (New York: George Braziller, 1968), 161. Burnham incorrectly cites the date of Bertoia's MIT commission as 1954. The work was completed and installed in 1955.
28. "M.I.T. Gets Cylindrical Chapel," *New York Times*, May 1, 1955, 84; and "M.I.T. Dedicates Its New Center: Cylindrical Chapel, Domed Auditorium Built by Grant From Kresge Foundation," *New York Times*, May 9, 1955, 48. For more on the Kresge Complex project see, Jayne Merkel, *Eero Saarinen* (London: Phaidon, 2005); and Eeva-Liisa Pelkonen and Donald Albrecht, eds., *Eero Saarinen: Shaping the Future* (New Haven, CT: Yale University Press, 2011). The project was originally to include a student union, and a plaza to connect the three buildings.
29. Eero Saarien quoted in "Buildings in the Round," *Architectural Forum* 104, no. 1 (January 1956): 116–21; Jennifer Komar Olivarez, "Churches and Chapels: A New Kind of Worship Space," in Pelkonen and Albrecht, *Eero Saarinen: Shaping the Future*, 269; and "M.I.T. Chapel," *Architectural Record* 119, no. 1 (January 1956): 156.
30. Hans Knoll to Harry Bertoia, June 16, 1953, reel 14032, HBF.
31. Theodore Roszak quoted in Howard Griffin, "Totems in Steel," *ARTnews* 55 (October 1956): 65.
32. "Puddled Spire," *Time* 66, no. 23 (December 5, 1955): 88.
33. Wayne Andersen, *American Sculpture in Process: 1930/1970* (Boston: New York Graphic Society, 1975), 90.
34. David Smith quoted in *New Sculpture*, 7; Herbert Ferber quoted in, *New Sculpture*, 24; and Herbert Ferber quoted in *15 Americans*, ed. Dorothy C. Miller (New York: Museum of Modern Art, 1952), 10.
35. Robert Goldwater, "David Hare," in *Three American Sculptors*, ed. George Fall (New York: Grove Press, 1959), 27; David Hare, "The Spaces of the Mind," *Magazine of Art* (February 1950); "Metal Sculpture: Machine-Age Art," *Time* 66, no. 7 (August 15, 1955): 52; and Chanin, "Machine Age in Sculpture," 24; and Isamu Noguchi, "Meanings in Modern Sculpture (1949)," in *Isamu Noguchi: Essays and Conversations*, ed. Diane Apostolos Cappadona and Bruce Altshuler (New York: Harry N. Abrams, 1994), 35.
36. "Designing in Space," *Craft Horizons* (June 1952): 34; and Richard Lippold in Miller, *15 Americans*, 24.
37. Robert Slifkin, *The New Monuments and the End of Man: U.S. Sculpture between War and Peace, 1945–1975* (Princeton, NJ: Princeton University Press, 2019),104; and Lippold quoted in Burnham, "Richard Lippold: Shaping Space with Reflective Light," 26.
38. See Slifkin; and Phillips, *Third Dimension*, 24.
39. Wayne Andersen, "Calder at the Guggenheim: Why Calder Should Be Taken Seriously," *Artforum* 3, no. 6 (March 1965), 37; and Richard Lippold, "Wire Sculpture and Accompanying Article," *Arts & Architecture* (August 1947): 22.
40. Lippold quoted in Stuart Preston, "Art: 'Orpheus and Apollo': Lippold's Copper Alloy-Steel Sculpture Is Hung in Philharmonic Hall," *New York Times*, December 21, 1962, 5; Irving Sandler, "Ibram Lassaw," in Fall, *Three American Sculptors*, 48; and Lassaw, "Perspectives and Reflections of a Sculptor," 354–55. On vitalism see, Brooke Kamin Rapaport, "The Greater Mystery of Things: Aspects of Vital Forms in American Art," in *Vital Forms: American Art and Design in the Atomic Age, 1940–1960*, ed. Brooke Kamin Rapaport and Kevin L. Stayton (New York: Brooklyn Museum of Art, 2001), 78–119; Joan Marter, "Abstract Sculpture of the Atomic Age," in *Art of Another Kind: International Abstraction and the Guggenheim, 1949–1960*, ed. Tracey R. Bashkoff (New York: Solomon R. Guggenheim Museum, 2012), 61; Paul Schimmel, *Destroy the Picture: Painting the Void, 1949–1962* (Los Angeles: Museum of Contemporary Art, 2012); and Slifkin, *The New Monuments and the End of Man*.
41. Harry Bertoia quoted in Edward F. Pierce, "He Creates with a Blowtorch," *Think* (May 1959): 33.
42. "Pure Design Research," *Architectural Forum* 97, no. 3 (September 1952): 142–43; and Olga Gueft, "Bertoia: His Sculpture, His kind of Wire Chair," *Interiors*, 112 (October 1952): 119.
43. Lewis Mumford, "Crystal Lantern (1954)," in *From the Ground Up: Observations on Contemporary Architecture,*

Housing, Highway Building, and Civic Design (New York: Harcourt, Brace, 1956), 175.

44. Douglas Dreishpoon, "Sculptors and Critics, Arenas and Complaints," in *Action/Abstraction: Pollock, De Kooning, and American Art 1940–1976*, ed. Norman L. Kleeblatt (New York: Jewish Museum, 2008), 227–28.
45. David L. Shirey, "Space Man," *Newsweek,* January 29, 1968, 82; Richard Lippold, "Projects for Pan Am and Philharmonic," *Art in America* 50, no. 2 (Summer 1962): 54.
46. Walter Gropius to Richard Lippold, October 13, 1960, reel D-342, RLP.
47. Lippold, "Projects for Pan Am and Philharmonic," 54.
48. Lippold, 54; and Edward Lucie-Smith, "Richard Lippold: Poet of Space," in Carter, *Richard Lippold: Sculpture*, 34.
49. Meredith L. Clausen, *The Pan Am Building and the Shattering of the Modernist Dream* (Cambridge, MA: MIT Press, 2005), 143. Kepes and Lippold would also go on after the Pan Am Building to collaborate again with Belluschi on Saint Mary's Cathedral in San Francisco, Lippold creating *Baldacchino* (1967–70), which hangs above the central altar. In addition to these large commissions, at some point a bronze bust of Erwin S. Wolfson, who had died in 1962 before the Pan Am Building was complete, was installed across the lobby from Lippold's sculpture, in between the revolving doors. Robert Berks sculpted the bust.
50. Lillian Ross, "Symbol," Talk of the Town, *New Yorker,* April 8, 1961, 48.
51. Gropius quoted in Ross, 48; and Richard Lippold, Untitled Statement for Pan Am Project, reel D-342, RPL
52. Ross, "Symbol," 49.
53. Richard Lippold to Walter Gropius, 4 May 1961, reel D-342, RPL.
54. Irving Gershon of Emery Roth & Sons to William Zimmerman of Grand Central Buildings, Inc., October 1, 1963, reel D-342, RPL; Lippold quoted in Harry Gilroy, "Sculptor Becomes a High-Wire Artist in Pan Am Lobby," *New York Times*, April 25, 1963, 35; and "Pan Am Lobby Gets Look of Art Gallery: Art Adorns Pan Am Building Lobby," *New York Times*, July 7, 1963, 1. The quoted number of 250,000 daily visitors to Grand Central is from 1963.
55. "Pan Am Building to Have Sculpture," *New York Times*, September 3, 1961; and Lippold, "Projects for Pan Am and Philharmonic," 54.
56. Walter Gropius quoted in, Shirey, "Space Man," 82; Walter Gropius to Richard Lippold, August 27, 1963, reel D-342, RPL.
57. Wolf Von Eckardt, "Pan Am's Glass House," *New Republic* (August 13, 1962): 24; and Ada Louise Huxtable, "Architecture Stumbles On," *New York Times* April 14, 1963, 119. MetLife acquired the building in 1981, and replaced the Pan Am logo with its own in 1992. For an exhaustive recounting of the Pan Am project overall and the subsequent reception and criticism see, Clausen, *Pan Am Building*, 143.
58. "New York Sculpture," *Architectural Forum* 119, no. 2 (August 1963): 17; "The Decorations Reflect the Building, Alas," *New York Herald Tribune*, June 9, 1963, cited in Richard Lippold Scrapbooks, 1935–1968, reel N69-117, Willard Gallery Records, c. 1940–1956, AAA.
59. "The Decorations Reflect the Building."
60. Lippold quoted in, Tomkins, 79.
61. Tomkins, 82; Clausen, *Pan Am Building,* 151; M. V. Mathews, Head of Human Information Processing Research Department, Bell Laboratories to Richard Lippold, February 9, 1962, reel D-342, RPL; and Raymond Ericson, "Music World: No Sound at All," *New York Times*, August 12, 1962, 9. For more on Cage's unrealized contribution at Pan Am, see also Hannah Pivo, "Selling Silence, Controlling Chaos: John Cage's Interventions into Muzak," *Public Art Dialogue* 9, no. 1 (2019): 95–118; Branden Joseph, *Experimentations: John Cage in Music, Art, and Architecture* (New York: Bloomsbury Academic, 2016); and Alice T. Friedman, "Through the Network of Wires: Portsmouth Abbey, Richard Lippold, and Postwar Syncretism," *Interiors* 6, no. 3 (2016): 235–58.
62. Richard Lippold, oral history interview by Paul Cummings, December 1, 1970, transcript pp. 93–94, AAA.
63. John Cage, "Experimental Music," in *Silence: Lectures and Writings* (Middletown, OH: Wesleyan University Press, 1961), 6–7.
64. Wayne Craven, *The Sculpture of Herbert Ferber* (Minneapolis, MN: Walker Art Center, 1962), 7; and Lippold, "Projects for Pan Am and Philharmonic," 55.
65. Allan Kaprow, *Assemblages, Environments, and Happenings* (New York: Harry N. Abrams, 1965), 183. For further discussion of connections between Kaprow and Yayoi Kusama see Marin R. Sullivan, *Sculptural Materiality in the Age of Conceptualism: International Experiments in Italy* (London: Routledge, 2017).
66. Frederick Kiesler in Miller, *15 Americans* (New York: Museum of Modern Art, 1952), 8.
67. John I. H. Baur, *A Sculpture by Herbert Ferber: To Create and Environment* (New York: Whitney Museum of Art, 1961), n.p.
68. Elyse Speaks, "Experiencing Louise Nevelson's Moon Garden," *American Art* 21, no. 2 (Summer 2007): 99; and author "Weird Woodwork of Lunar World," *Life* March 24, 1958, 77.
69. Dore Ashton, "Art: Worlds of Fantasy," *New York Times*, October 29, 1959, 44; and Dore Ashton, "Art," *Arts & Architecture* 75, no. 3 (March 1958): 33–34.
70. György Kepes, "The Visual Arts and the Sciences: A Proposal for Collaboration," *Architectural Record* 137, no. 5 (May 1965): 146–47.

Epilogue: Preserving Space(s)

1. Alexander Calder quoted in Carol Oppenheim, "A Whatchama-Calder Sculpture Conquers the City," *Chicago Tribune*, October 26, 1974, sec. B, 1. For a comprehensive analysis of Calder's *Flamingo* (1973–74) and public sculpture more broadly, see Nicholas Evan Hartigan, "The Purpose of Public Sculpture: Artistic, Institutional, and Cultural Motivations Since 1965" (PhD diss., University of Michigan, 2016).
2. Gwen Morgan, "Calder Wall Takes Shape," *Chicago Tribune*, July 31, 1974, sec. C, 16.
3. Hartigan, "The Purpose of Public Sculpture," xvi; and Joan Marter, "Alexander Calder's Stabiles: Monumental Public Sculpture in America," *American Art Journal* 11, no. 3 (July 1979): 82.
4. Blair Kamin, "Willis Tower Calder Mobile Coming Down," *Chicago Tribune*, March 28, 2017, https://www.chicagotribune.com/news/ct-calder-mobile-willis-tower-met-0328-20170327-story.html; Erica Gunderson, "Preservation Chicago Sounds the Alarm Over 'Flamingo' Sculpture," *WTTW News*, March 30, 2017, https://news.wttw.com/2017/03/30/preservation-chicago-sounds-alarm-over-flamingo-sculpture; "Calder's The Universe Sculpture at Willis Tower Disassembled with Future Unknown," Preservation Chicago, n.d., https://preservationchicago.org/newsletter_posts/calders-the-universe-sculpture-at-willis-tower-disassembled-with-future-unknown/. Willis Tower is currently owned by Blackstone, a private equity firm based in New York City.
5. Joan Marter, *Alexander Calder* (Cambridge: Cambridge University Press, 1991), 232; Harriet Senie, "Calder's Public Art as Civic Sculpture: The Realization of a Modernist Ideal," in *Calder and Abstraction: From Avant-Garde to Iconic*, ed., Stephanie Barron and Lisa Gabrielle Mark (Los Angeles: Los Angeles County Museum of Art, 2013),

136–50; and Nancy Mulnix Tweddale Papers, Grand Rapids History and Special Collections Archive, Grand Rapids Public Library, Michigan.

6. Wayne Andersen, "Calder at the Guggenheim: Why Calder Should Be Taken Seriously," *Artforum* 3, no. 6 (March 1965), 38.
7. James Wines, "Public Art—Private Art," *Art in America* (January 1970): 4; and Miwon Kwon, *One Place after Another: Site-Specific Art and Locational Identity* (Cambridge, MA: MIT Press, 2002), 60–61.
8. For more on public art see John Beardsley, *Art in Public Places: A Survey of Community Sponsored Projects Supported by the NEA* (Washington, DC: Partners for Livable Places, 1981); Hartigan, "The Purpose of Public Sculpture"; and John Wetenhall, "Camelot's Legacy to Public Art: Aesthetic Ideology in the New Frontier," in "Critical Issues in Public Art," ed. Harriet Senie and Sally Webster, special issue *Art Journal* 4, no. 4 (December 1989): 303–8.
9. "Mr. Pei Goes to Washington," *Architectural Record* (August 1978): 79–92. This article reports the weight of the sculpture as 700 lbs., but the National Gallery of Art, Washington, DC, states it is 920 lbs., "Alexander Calder: Untitled, 1976," National Gallery of Art Collection, https://www.nga.gov/collection/art-object-page.56517.html.
10. Architect of the Capitol, "Mountains and Clouds," press release, April 29, 1987, Alexander Calder, Art and Artist Files, Smithsonian American Art and Portrait Gallery Library, Smithsonian Libraries, Washington, DC. The mobile elements of *Mountains and Clouds* were fabricated by Nelson Young of Crystallizations Systems, Inc. in Long Island, New York, who had also worked on the NGA mobile, while the stabile components were the work of Carmen Segre of Segre Iron Works in Waterbury, Connecticut.
11. "Mountains and Clouds." Calder met with the architectural team to discuss the maquette for *Mountain and Clouds* on November 10, 1976 and returned to New York City that evening. He passed away in the early hours of November 11.
12. Kristina Peterson, "Calder Sculpture Triggers Heavenly Debate in Washington," *Wall Street Journal*, December 25, 2014, https://www.wsj.com/articles/alexander-calder-sculpture-triggers-heavenly-debate-in-washington-1419546333.
13. See James H. Thomas, *"The Fourth, The Financial Center of Kansas": A History of the Fourth National Bank and Trust Company* (Oklahoma City: Western Heritage Books for the Center for Entrepreneurship and Small Business Administration, Wichita State University, 1980).
14. Jed Perl, *Calder: The Conquest of Time; The Early Years, 1898–1940* (New York: Alfred A. Knopf, 2017), 529; and Marter, *Alexander Calder,* 227, 232.
15. Jean-Paul Sartre, "The Mobiles of Calder (1946/47)," in *Calder: Gravity and Grace* (London: Phaidon, 2004), 70.
16. "Take Action: Threatened Sties," Docomomo_US, https://docomomo-us.org/take-action/threatened-sites; National Trust for Historic Preservation; "Most Endangered Historic Places in Illinois," Landmarks Illinois, http://www.landmarks.org/preservation-programs/most-endangered-historic-places-in-illinois/; "About Landslide," Cultural Landscape Foundation, https://tclf.org/stewardship/about-landslide; "Modernism at Risk," World Monuments Fund, https://www.wmf.org/project/modernism-risk.
17. Joan Ockman, "Introduction," *Docomomo*, no. 31 (September 2004): 44. See also, Jeffrey Lieber, *Flintstone Modernism: Or the Cultural Crisis in Postwar American Culture* (Cambridge, MA: MIT Press, 2018).
18. See Amy Plitt, "Lower Manhattan's Celebrated 140 Broadway May Get Unwelcome Ornament," *Curbed New York*, January 30, 2018, https://ny.curbed.com/2018/1/30/16950098/financial-district-modern-architecture-140-broadway-landmarks; "Lower Manhattan's 140 Broadway Under Threat," Cultural Landscape Foundation, January 29, 2018, https://tclf.org/lower-manhattan-140-broadway-under-threat#.Wm_S-9ozvN0.twitter; "2 Columbus Circle," New York Preservation Archive Project, http://www.nypap.org/preservation-history/2-columbus-circle/; "The Campaign to Preserve 2 Columbus Circle," Landmark West!, https://www.landmarkwest.org/project/2-columbus-circle/; Michael R. Allen, "Prentice Hospital Could Become Modernism's 'Penn Station Moment,' " *Next City,* October 15, 2013, https://nextcity.org/daily/entry/prentice-hospital-could-become-modern-architectures-penn-station-moment; Alexandra Lange, "Demolition of Prentice Womens Hospital by Bertrand Goldberg and Penn Station," *Architect Magazine,* October 31, 2013, https://www.architectmagazine.com/design/demolition-of-prentice-womens-hospital-by-bertrand-goldberg-and-penn-station_o; Alexandra Lange, "Why SOM's Modernist Union Carbide Building Is Worth Saving," *Curbed New York*, February 22, 2018, https://ny.curbed.com/2018/2/22/17038040/nyc-architecture-midtown-east-skidmore-owings-merrill-union-carbide; and Elizabeth Kim, "270 Park Avenue, A Quintessential Modernist Skyscraper, Is Being Slowly Destroyed by Chase Bank," *Gothamist*, January 8, 2020, https://gothamist.com/news/270-park-avenue-quintessential-modernist-skyscraper-being-slowly-destroyed-chase-bank.
19. Treatment Report by Daedalus, Inc., September 2003, Object File, MIT List Visual Art Center , Cambridge, MA.
20. Herbert L. Beckwith to James Murphy, October 31, 1963, MIT List Visual Art Center.
21. Nancy Coleman, "Once Removed and Destroyed, a Modernist Mural Makes Its Return," *New York Times*, September 24, 2019, 2.
22. Fred A. Bernstein, "Frank Gehry (a Part Owner) Helps Develop a Landmark," *New York Times*, November 16, 2010, https://www.nytimes.com/2010/11/17/realestate/commercial/17steel.html#:~:text=Frank%20Gehry%20(a%20Part%20Owner)%20Helps%20Develop%20a%20Landmark,By%20Fred%20A&text=It's%20not%20every%20day%20that,owns%20a%20part%20of%20it; and Blair Kamin, "Gehry Provokes with 'Icehenge,' " *Chicago Tribune*, July 28, 2013, https://www.chicagotribune.com/news/ct-xpm-2013-07-28-ct-met-gehry-desk-0728-20130728-story.html.
23. For a thorough history of the landmarking of the Four Seasons Restaurant see, Phyllis Lambert, *Building Seagram* (New Haven, CT: Yale University Press, 2013). The Four Seasons Restaurant signed a new lease a few blocks south at 280 Park Avenue and opened in 2018, before shuttering for good a year later. The Pool and The Grill, two new restaurants managed by the Major Food Group opened at the Seagram Building in 2017. There was a copious amount of press coverage on both the closure of the restaurant as well as the subsequent auction and restaurant redesign. See for example, Suzanne Stephens, "Goodbye to All That," *Architecture Record* (June 24, 2016), https://www.architecturalrecord.com/articles/11752-goodbye-to-all-that-the-four-seasons-restaurant-leaves-the-seagram-building; Tejal Rao, "The Last Dinner at the Four Seasons," *New York Times*, July 17, 2016, https://www.nytimes.com/2016/07/18/dining/the-last-dinner-at-the-four-seasons.html; Guy Trebay, "Four Seasons Restaurant Auction Tops $4.1 Million," *New York Times*, July 27, 2016, https://www.nytimes.com/2016/07/28/fashion/four-seasons-restaurant-auction-total.html; and Pete Wells, "The Pool Strives to Deal With Its Famous Dining Room," *New York Times,* October 17, 2017, https://www.nytimes.com/2017/10/17/dining/the-pool-review.html. For a full list of the lots in the auction see, "The Four Seasons / 26 July 2016 10:00 am et," Wright, https://www.wright20.com/auctions/2016/07/the-four-seasons/info.

24. Bruce Altshuler, "Isamu Noguchi Indoors: Home Furnishings and Interior Design," in *Isamu Noguchi: Sculptural Design*, ed. Jochen Eisenbrand, Katarina V. Posch, and Alexander Von Vegesack (Weil am Rhein: Vitra Design Museum, 2001), 132; Shoji Sadao, executive director of the Isamu Noguchi Foundation to Nobutaka Ishihara, October 1, 1997, INF; Joseph Giovannini, "Isamu Noguchi Artwork in Midtown Building Is in Peril," *New York Times*, February 25, 2020, https://www.nytimes.com/2020/02/25/arts/design/isamu-noguchi-midtown-installation.html; and Alex Greenberger, "Iconic Isamu Noguchi Sculpture Removed from New York Building Amid Renovation," *ARTnews*, December 11, 2020, https://www.artnews.com/art-news/news/isamu-noguchi-sculpture-666-fifth-avenue-removed-1234579083/.
25. Allison Meier, "A Noguchi Ceiling in a U-Haul Showroom is Restored to Its Former Glory, *Hyperallergic*, May 5, 2016, https://hyperallergic.com/296383/a-noguchi-ceiling-in-a-u-haul-showroom-is-restored-to-its-former-glory/; and Robert W. Duffy and Kelly Moffitt, "Modernist Treasure Hidden for Decades in U-Haul Building Set to Reappear in the Spring," St. Louis Public Radio, December 8, 2015, https://news.stlpublicradio.org/arts/2015-12-08/modernist-treasure-hidden-for-decades-in-u-haul-building-set-to-reappear-in-the-spring.
26. M. Jeffrey Hardwick, "Creative Destruction: Victor Gruen and the Shopping Mall's Past and Future," *Docomomo*, no. 31 (September 2004): 56.
27. David W. Dunlap, "Behind the Low-Priced Clothing, a Priceless Midcentury Sculpture," *City Room* (blog), *New York Times*, May 31, 2012, https://cityroom.blogs.nytimes.com/2012/05/31/behind-the-low-priced-clothing-a-priceless-midcentury-sculpture/. For more information on the more recent history of the Manufacturers Hanover Trust Building see, "510 Fifth Avenue," *Architectural Record* 201, no. 6 (June 1, 2013): 125; C. J. Hughes, "The Tricky Task of Renovating a Building Without Altering Its Landmark Insides," *New York Times*, November 23, 2011; and Robin Pogrebin, "Modernist Landmark behind a Court Battle," *New York Times*, September 28, 2011, https://www.nytimes.com/2011/09/29/arts/design/manufacturers-hanover-trust-landmark-battle.html; and "510 Fifth Avenue Renovation and Adaptive Reuse," Projects, SOM, http://www.som.com/projects/510_fifth_avenue_renovation_and_adaptive_reuse.
28. Joe Fresh commissioned Steven Sebring to create a film on the reinstallation of Bertoia's Screen for 510 Fifth Avenue, see Steven Sebring, *Harry Bertoia's Golden Arbor* (2012), short film, 9:54 min., https://vimeo.com/41582988.
29. Dunlap, "Behind the Low-Priced Clothing."
30. Oliver Wick, "'Je vais t'emporter en Amérique: Prépare-toi': A Long Road to Monumental Dimensions—Beyond Painting," in *Calder/Miró*, ed. Elizabeth Hutton Turner and Oliver Wick (London: Philip Wilson Publishers, 2004), 80.
31. George Dahl's building, or the Old Library as it is known today, permanently closed in 1983, and remained empty until the *Dallas Morning News* renovated and moved into in it in 2017. For more on the Henry Moore commission see, Pauline Rose, "Henry Moore in Dallas 1965–1984," *Sculpture Journal* 17, no. 1 (2008): 52–69.
32. Henry Tatum, "'Junk' Sculpture finds a Home in New City Library," *Dallas Morning News*, November 17, 1981.
33. See Robin Pogrebin, "When Renovations Meets Redo," *New York Times*, June 1, 2009, https://www.nytimes.com/2009/06/02/arts/design/02land.html; Anthony Tommasini, "Lincoln Center: Mixed Reviews," *New York Times*, May 10, 2009, 26; and Michael Cooper and David Masello, "Orpheus' Descended; Now What?" *New York Times*, November 26, 2015, 1. Substantial renovations to Philharmonic Hall were completed in 1963, 1964, 1969, 1976, and 1992, though none included any changes beyond cleaning to the installation of Lippold's *Orpheus and Apollo*. The lack of a reinstallation plan was reiterated to the author in phone communications with Lincoln Center representatives in October 2016.
34. See Monica Castillo, "Lincoln Center Scraps Richard Lippold's Chandelier Sculpture in $550M Renovation Plans," *Hyperallergic*, December 6, 2019, https://hyperallergic.com/532025/lincoln-center-scraps-richard-lippolds-chandelier-sculpture-in-550m-renovation-plans/; and Elizabeth Kim, "Lincoln Center's Renovation Reignites a Battle to Save a Dismantled Sculpture," *Gothamist*, February 6, 2020, https://gothamist.com/arts-entertainment/lincoln-center-richard-lippold-sculpture; and Hilarie M. Sheets, "Lippold's Soaring Lincoln Center Sculpture Lands at La Guardia," *New York Times*, April 7, 2021, https://www.nytimes.com/2021/04/07/arts/design/richard-lippold-orpheus-and-apollo-la-guardia-airport.html. Preservationist groups in New York, like Landmarks West! have mounted substantive efforts to bring public awareness to the removal of Lippold's sculpture and to put pressure on Lincoln Center to reinstall it though such efforts proved unsuccessful. See for example, "Richard Lippold & Orpheus and Apollo," Landmark West!, https://landmarkwest.org/lippold.
35. John Canaday, "Curtain Call," New York Times, September 25, 1966, 135.
36. Richard Lippold, "Projects for Pan Am and Philharmonic," Art in America 50, no. 2 (Summer 1962): 55.
37. Isamu Noguchi, "Towards a Reintegration of the Arts," College Art Journal 9, no.1 (Autumn 1949): 59.
38. "Isamu Noguchi Defines the Nature and Enormous Potential of Sculpture," Interiors + Industrial Design 108 (March 1949): 118.

Acknowledgments

1. Harry Bertoia quoted in Ingebjørg Nesheim, "The World of Bertoia," Frisprog (November 18, 1972), unpaginated transcript sent to Harry Bertoia by the Galleri KB (Kaare Berntsten), February 16, 1973, HBF.

Index

Page numbers in italics indicate figures.

Photography and Copyright Credits

All Bertoia works © Harry Bertoia / Harry Bertoia Foundation / Artists Rights Society (ARS), New York

All Calder works © 2021 Calder Foundation, New York / Artists Rights Society (ARS), New York

All Lippold works © Estate of Richard Lippold / Artists Rights Society (ARS), New York

All Noguchi works © Isamu Noguchi Foundation / Garden Museum, New York / Artists Rights Society (ARS), New York

Photo: Allegheny County Airport Authority (figure 1.23)

Photo: © Author (figures 1.30, 2.13, 2.29, 2.30, 2.38, E.7, E.8, E.12, E.13, E.14, E.15)

Courtesy of *Architectural Record* (figure I.7)

© Estate of Harry Bertoia / Harry Bertoia Foundation (figures I.8, I.17, I.20, I.22, 1.24, 2.9, 2.11, 2.24 2.27)

Photo: BMW AG (figure I.9)

Photo: Rudolph Burckhardt. © 2021 Estate of Rudy Burckhardt / Artists Rights Society (ARS), New York (figure 1.16)

Photo: Calder Foundation, New York / Art Resource, NY (figures 1.21, E.2)

Photo: Tom Harris, Hedrich Blessing Photographers. Courtesy of Capital Properties and MB Real Estate (figure E.11)

© 2021 Center for Creative Photography, Arizona Board of Regents / Artists Rights Society (ARS), New York (figure I.18)

Courtesy of Cranbrook Archives, Cranbrook Center for Collections and Research, Bloomfield Hills, Michigan (figure I.11)

Photo: Dallas Public Library Archives (figure 1.41)

Photo: Courtesy of the Federal Reserve Bank of Philadelphia (figure E.4)

Photo: Ezra Stoller. © Ezra Stoller / Esto, esto.com (figures P.1, P.3, P.4, P.6, 1.2, 1.3, 1.4, 1.6, 1.7, 1.22, 1.27, 1.29, 1.37, 2.8, 2.23, 2.26, 2.28, 2.31)

Photo: C. Fiorentini, 2017. Licensed under CC BY-SA 4.0: (figure 1.32)

Courtesy of the Estate of R. Buckminster Fuller (figures I.3, 2.10)

Photo: Gottscho-Schleisner, Inc. Library of Congress, Prints & Photographs Division, Gottscho-Schleisner Collection LC-G612-71723 (figure P.2)

Photo: Nancy Mulnix Tweddale Papers, Grand Rapids History & Special Collections, Archives, Grand Rapids Public Library, Grand Rapids, Michigan (figure E.3)

Photo: Peter Harris Studio (figure 3.13)

Photo: Carol M. Highsmith. Library of Congress, Prints & Photographs Division, photograph by LC-DIG-highsm-02582, (figure E.1)

Photo: Dixon Photo Collection (MSS0089-001), Houston Public Library (figure 1.38)

Photo: Morris Huberland; Photo: Erik Johnson (00885) (figure I.15)

© Estate of György Kepes (figure 2.32)

© 2021 Austrian Frederick and Lillian Kiesler Private Foundation, Vienna (figure 2.4)

Photo: Balthazar Korab, Library of Congress, Prints & Photographs Division, Balthazar Korab Collection: LC-DIG-krb-00713, LC-DIG-krb-00706, LC-DIG-krb-00049, LC-DIG-krb-00136, LC-DIG-krb-00130, LC-DIG-krb-0074, DIG-krb-00794, LC-DIG-krb-00131, LC-DIG-krb-00261 LC-DIG-krb-00609, LC-DIG-krb-00238, LC-DIG-krb-00258, LC-KRB00-54 (figures 2.5, 2.6, 2.12, 2.17, 2.19, 2.20, 2.21, 2.22, 2.25, 2.40, 3.10, 3.11, 3.14)

Photo: Jeremy M. Lange (figure E.9)

Photo: Library of Congress, Prints and Photographs Division, LC-USZ62-105611 (figure 1.40)

© 2021 Estate of Richard Lippold / Artist Rights Society (ARS), New York. Photo: Author (figures P.5, 1.36, 1.39, 3.5, 3.22, 3.26, 3.27)

LOOK Magazine Photograph Collection, Library of Congress, Prints & Photographs Division, [LC-L904A-65-2251, no. 20] (figure 3.6)

Photo: Norton & Peel 290883F, Minnesota Historical Society, St Paul, Minnesota (figure 3.3)

© Successió Miró / Artists Rights Society (ARS), New York / ADAGP, Paris 2021; Photo: Missouri Historical Society, MHS Photographs and Prints Collection, St. Louis, Missouri (figure 1.8)

© Henry Moore Foundation. All Rights Reserved, DACS / henry-moore.org. Photo: Jenny Hicks. Reproduced by permission of the Henry Moore Foundation (figure 1.31)

Photo: George Barrows, © Museum of Modern Art, Licensed by SCALA / Art Resource, NY (figure 2.40)

Photo: Eliot Elisofon. © Museum of Modern Art, Licensed by SCALA / Art Resource, NY (figure I.1)

Photo: © Museum of Modern Art, Licensed by SCALA / Art Resource, NY (figure 3.28)

Photo: William Leftwich. © Museum of Modern Art, Licensed by SCALA / Art Resource, NY (figure I.6)

Photo: Soichi Sunami. © Museum of Modern Art, Licensed by SCALA / Art Resource, NY (figures I.4, 2.1, 2.2, 3.7)

© Museum of Modern Art, Licensed by SCALA / Art Resource, NY (figures P.7, 3.16)

Photo: National Aeronautics and Space Administration (NASA) (figures 1.34, 1.35)

© 2021 Estate of Louise Nevelson / Artists Rights Society (ARS), New York. © Photography Collection, New York Public Library (figure 1.28)

Photo: Oliver Baker (figure 3.30)

Photo: Courtesy of Fondazione Nivola, Orani, Italy (figures 2.14, 2.15, 2.16)

Photo: Henry Elkan; Isamu Noguchi Foundation and Garden Museum, New York / Artists Rights Society (ARS), New York: 12435, 01637, 01528, 01644, 00413, 01778, 00417 (figures 1.16, 1.11, 1.13, 1.14, 1.17, 2.33, 2.34, 2.35, 2.36, 2.37)

Photo: Jeff Heatley. Courtesy of Pollock-Krasner House and Study Center, East Hampton, New York (figure 2.3)

Photo: Courtesy of Portsmouth Abbey (figure 3.23)

Photo: Dwight Primiano (figure 1.15)

© 2021 Estate of Theodore Roszak, Licensed by VAGA at Artists Rights Society (ARS), New York. Photo: Balthazar Korab. Library of Congress, Prints & Photographs Division, Balthazar Korab Collection, LC-DIG-krb-00253 (figure 3.15)
Photo: A. Sue Weisler, Rochester Institute of Technology (figure 2.18)

Photo: John Schiff. Courtesy of the Leo Baeck Institute, New York (figures 1.25, 1.26, 3.8)

Photo: © Longley Photography. Courtesy of SOM (figure 1.1)

Photo: © Hedrich Blessing, Courtesy of SOM (figure 3.4)
© Saul Steinberg Foundation / Artists Rights Society (ARS), New York. Photo: Ezra Stoller; Photo: Erin John Sullivan (figures 3.20, 3.25)

Photo: Umbugbene, 2012. Licensed under CC BY-SA 3.0 (figure E.10)

Photo: UNESCO / Michel Claude. Collection of UNESCO Archives (figure I.19)

Photo: Edward Durell Stone Papers, Special Collections, University of Arkansas Libraries, Fayetteville, Arkansas (figure 1.33)

Photo: U.S. Senate Collection (figure E.6)

Photo: Paolo Gasparini. Courtesy of Archivio Fundación Villanueva (figure I.21)

Photo: Travis Fullerton. © Virginia Museum of Fine Arts (figure I.14)

© Whitney Museum of American Art, Licensed by SCALA / Art Resource, NY (figures 3.18, 3.29)

Photo: Wurts Bros. (New York, NY). Museum of the City of New York. X2010.7.1.10129 (figures 1.20, 3.21)

Published by Princeton University Press,
41 William Street, Princeton, New Jersey 08540

In the United Kingdom: Princeton University Press,
99 Banbury Road, Oxford OX2 6JX

press.princeton.edu

Cover art: Harry Bertoia, *Untitled*, 1954. Brazed and welded metal, 16 ft. × 70 ft. × 2 ft. Manufacturers Trust Building, 510 Fifth Avenue, New York City. Architect: Skidmore, Owings & Merrill (SOM). Photo: Author. © Estate of Harry Bertoia.

Library of Congress Cataloging-in-Publication Data
Names: Sullivan, Marin R., author.
Title: Alloys : American sculpture and architecture at midcentury / Marin R. Sullivan.
Description: Princeton : Princeton University Press, [2022] | Includes bibliographical references and index.
Identifiers: LCCN 2021035090 (print) | LCCN 2021035091 (ebook) | ISBN 9780691215778 (hardcover) | ISBN 9780691232461 (ebook)
Subjects: LCSH: Site-specific sculpture—United States—20th century. | Modernism (Art)—United States. | Sculpture, American—20th century. | Sculpture and architecture—United States—History—20th century.
Classification: LCC NB212.5.M63 S85 2022 (print) | LCC NB212.5.M63 (ebook) | DDC 731.0973/0904—dc23
LC record available at https://lccn.loc.gov/2021035090
LC ebook record available at https://lccn.loc.gov/2021035091
British Library Cataloging-in-Publication Data is available

Design: Office of Luke Bulman

This book has been composed in Stanley and Untitled Sans

Printed on acid-free paper. ∞

Printed in Italy

10 9 8 7 6 5 4 3 2 1